Computing with Words
in Information/Intelligent Systems 2

Studies in Fuzziness and Soft Computing

Editor-in-chief

Prof. Janusz Kacprzyk
Systems Research Institute
Polish Academy of Sciences
ul. Newelska 6
01-447 Warsaw, Poland
E-mail: kacprzyk@ibspan.waw.pl

Vol. 3. A. Geyer-Schulz
Fuzzy Rule-Based Expert Systems and Genetic Machine Learning, 2nd ed. 1996
ISBN 3-7908-0964-0

Vol. 4. T. Onisawa and J. Kacprzyk (Eds.)
Reliability and Safety Analyses under Fuzziness, 1995
ISBN 3-7908-0837-7

Vol. 5. P. Bosc and J. Kacprzyk (Eds.)
Fuzziness in Database Management Systems, 1995
ISBN 3-7908-0858-X

Vol. 6. E. S. Lee and Q. Zhu
Fuzzy and Evidence Reasoning, 1995
ISBN 3-7908-0880-6

Vol. 7. B. A. Juliano and W. Bandler
Tracing Chains-of-Thought, 1996
ISBN 3-7908-0922-5

Vol. 8. F. Herrera and J. L. Verdegay (Eds.)
Genetic Algorithms and Soft Computing, 1996,
ISBN 3-7908-0956-X

Vol. 9. M. Sato et al.
Fuzzy Clustering Models and Applications, 1997,
ISBN 3-7908-1026-6

Vol. 10. L. C. Jain (Ed.)
Soft Computing Techniques in Knowledge-based Intelligent Engineering Systems, 1997,
ISBN 3-7908-1035-5

Vol. 11. W. Mielczarski (Ed.)
Fuzzy Logic Techniques in Power Systems, 1998,
ISBN 3-7908-1044-4

Vol. 12. B. Bouchon-Meunier (Ed.)
Aggregation and Fusion of Imperfect Information, 1998
ISBN 3-7908-1048-7

Vol. 13. E. Orłowska (Ed.)
Incomplete Information: Rough Set Analysis, 1998
ISBN 3-7908-1049-5

Vol. 14. E. Hisdal
Logical Structures for Representation of Knowledge and Uncertainty, 1998
ISBN 3-7908-1056-8

Vol. 15. G.J. Klir and M.J. Wierman
Uncertainty-Based Information, 1998
ISBN 3-7908-1073-8

Vol. 16. D. Driankov and R. Palm (Eds.)
Advances in Fuzzy Control, 1998
ISBN 3-7908-1090-8

Vol. 17. L. Reznik, V. Dimitrov and J. Kacprzyk (Eds.)
Fuzzy Systems Design, 1998
ISBN 3-7908-1118-1

Vol. 18. L. Polkowski and A. Skowron (Eds.)
Rough Sets in Knowledge Discovery 1, 1998,
ISBN 3-7908-1119-X

Vol. 19. L. Polkowski and A. Skowron (Eds.)
Rough Sets in Knowledge Discovery 2, 1998,
ISBN 3-7908-1120-3

Vol. 20. J. N. Mordeson and P. S. Nair
Fuzzy Mathematics, 1998
ISBN 3-7908-1121-1

Vol. 21. L. C. Jain and T. Fukuda (Eds.)
Soft Computing for Intelligent Robotic Systems, 1998
ISBN 3-7908-1147-5

Vol. 22. J. Cardoso and H. Camargo (Eds.)
Fuzziness in Petri Nets, 1999
ISBN 3-7908-1158-0

Vol. 23. P. S. Szczepaniak (Ed.)
Computational Intelligence and Applications, 1999
ISBN 3-7908-1161-0

Vol. 24. E. Orłowska (Ed.)
Logic at Work, 1999
ISBN 3-7908-1164-5

continued on page 610

Lotfi A. Zadeh
Janusz Kacprzyk (Eds.)

Computing with Words in Information/Intelligent Systems 2

Applications

With 154 Figures
and 54 Tables

Physica-Verlag

A Springer-Verlag Company

Prof. Lotfi A. Zadeh
Berkeley Initiative in Soft Computing (BISC)
Computer Science Division and
Electronics Research Laboratory
Department of Electrical and Electronics
Engineering and Computer Science
University of California
Berkeley, CA 94720-1776
USA
E-mail: zadeh@cs.berkeley.edu

Prof. Janusz Kacprzyk
Systems Research Institute
Polish Academy of Sciences
ul. Newelska 6
01-447 Warsaw
Poland
E-mail: kacprzyk@ibspan.waw.pl

ISBN 978-3-7908-2461-2   e-ISBN 978-3-7908-1872-7

Cataloging-in-Publication Data applied for
Die Deutsche Bibliothek – CIP-Einheitsaufnahme
Computing with words in information/intelligent systems: with 54 tables / Lotfi A. Zadeh;
Janusz Kacprzyk (ed.). – Heidelberg; New York: Physica-Verl.
  2. Applications. – 1999
  (Studies in fuzziness and soft computing; Vol. 34)

Hardcover Design: Erich Kirchner, Heidelberg
88/2202-5 4 3 2 1 0 – Printed on acid-free paper

Foreword

These two volumes consisting of *Foundations* and *Applications* provide the current status of theoretical and empirical developments in „computing with words".

In philosophy, the twentieth century is said to be the century of language. This is mainly due to Wittgenstein who said:

„The meaning of a word is its use in the language game".
„The concept *game* is a concept with blurred edges".

In the first phrase, „the language game" implies the everyday human activity with language, and in the latter, „game" simply implies an ordinary word. Thus, Wittgenstein precisely stated that a word is fuzzy in real life.

Unfortunately this idea about a word was not accepted in the conventional science. We had to wait for Zadeh's fuzzy sets theory. Remembering Wittgenstein's statement, we should consider, on the one hand, the concept of „computing with words" from a philosophical point of view. It deeply relates to the everyday use of a word in which the meaning of a word is fuzzy in its nature.

On the other hand, „computing with words" can be considered in the perspective of history of computing with language in computer science and also in artificial intelligence. We can go back to the 1950s when an attempt to machine translation started. As we know, this computer scientific adventure to computing with language terminated in 1965 when the US Air Force pronounced machine translation a failure. Researchers continued their activities in computing with language under different titles such as parsing, question-answering or expert systems and the like in the setting of artificial intelligence. There was, however, a strict line between natural language processing and computing, as pointed out by Halliday. Computing was not intelligent in any sense. It was considered just as a tool to realize an intelligent system.

A breakthrough was made in the 1990s by Zadeh's idea of „computing with words". The history of computing with language has now made a revolutionary turn. We have entered the true age af computing with language. Computing itself is now viewed from a perspective of human intelligence. Human cogitation is nothing but „computing with words" as Zadeh points out. Cogitation is essentially connected with recognition. In human recognition, we see the world with words. We articulate the physical world with Wittgenstein's blurred words. According to Zadeh, this articulation is a „fuzzy granulation".

As such, fuzzy logic is a promising tool to play a very important role in intelligent computing. From now on, we will be able to view any computing as „computing with words". This idea would become a main stream to create „an artificial brain".

This volume, Part 2: *Applications*, includes neuro-fuzzy and genetic systems approaches to "computing with words" and linguistic models in information/intelligent systems, and covers numerous areas of applications.

I wish to congratulate the editors, Professors Zadeh and Kacprzyk for these volumes for their great success. In particular, I wish to acknowledge Professor Janusz Kacprzyk who has been mainly the driving force behind this project.

Tokyo, March 1999   Michio Sugeno
                                                President
                                                International Fuzzy Systems
                                                Association (IFSA)

Contents

Foreword   v
  M. Sugeno

1. NEURO-FUZZY AND GENETIC SYSTEMS FOR COMPUTING
    WITH WORDS

Neural Fuzzy Intelligent Agents   3
  S. Mitaim and B. Kosko

Neuro Fuzzy Systems for Data Analysis   35
  S. Siekmann, R. Neuneier, H.G. Zimmermann and R. Kruse

*A New Fuzzy Inference System Based on Artificial Neural Network
and Its Applications*   75
  J. Łęski and E. Czogała

*Encouraging Cooperation in the Genetic Iterative Rule Learning
Approach for Qualitative Modeling*   95
  O. Cordón, A. Gonzales, F. Herrera and R. Pérez

2. TOOLS FOR LINGUISTIC DATA MODELING AND ANALYSIS

*Fuzzy Graphs with Linguistic Input-Outputs by Fuzzy Approximation
Models*   121
  H. Lee and H. Tanaka

Fuzzy Random Variables: Modeling Linguistic Statistical Data   137
  M.A. Gil, P.A. Gil and D.A. Ralescu

3. LINGUISTIC MODELS IN SYSTEM RELIABILITY, QUALITY
    CONTROL AND RISK ANALYSES

Linguistic Model of System Reliability Analysis   161
  T. Onisawa and A. Ohmori

Lifetime Tests for Vague Data   176
  P. Grzegorzewski and O. Hryniewicz

Systems Analytic Models for Fuzzy Risk Estimation   195
  Ch. Huang and D. Ruan

4. LINGUISTIC MODELS IN DECISION MAKING, OPTIMIZATION AND
    CONTROL

Decision Analysis by Advanced Fuzzy Systems   223
  H. Kiendl

Group Decision Making and a Measure of Consensus under Fuzzy
Preferences and a Fuzzy Linguistic Majority   243
  J. Kacprzyk, H. Nurmi and M. Fedrizzi

Linear Programming with Words   270
  S. Chanas and D. Kuchta

Computing with Words in Control   289
  J.J. Buckley and Th. Feuring

On Linguistic Fuzzy Constraint Satisfaction Problems   305
  R. Kowalczyk

5. LINGUISTIC AND IMPRECISE INFORMATION IN DATABASES AND
    INFORMATION SYSTEMS

Data Models for Dealing with Linguistic and Imprecise Information   325
  G. Chen

Fuzzy Set Approaches to Model Uncertainty in Spatial Data and
Geographic Information Systems   345
  F.E. Petry, M. Cobb and A. Morris

Computing Fuzzy Dependencies with Linguistic Labels   368
  J.C. Cubero, J.M. Medina, O. Pons and M.A. Vila

The Paradigm of Computing with Words in Intelligent
Database Querying   383
  J. Kacprzyk and S. Zadrożny

Linguistic Data Mining   399
  W. Pedrycz

Evaluation of Connectionist Information Retrieval in a Legal
Documemt Collection   421
  R.A. Bustos and T.D. Gedeon

6. APPLICATIONS

Using Linguistic Models in Medical Decison Making   437
  M.E. Cohen and D.L. Hudson

The Fuzzy Logic Advisor for Social Judgements: A First Attempt 459
  J.M. Mendel, S. Murphy, L.C. Miller, M. Martin and N. Karnik

Conceptualisation with GABEK: Ideas on Social Change in South Africa 484
  J. Zelger, A.G. de Wet, A.-M. Pothas and D. Petkov

A Linguistic Decision Model to Suppliers Selection in International
Purchasing   500
  F. Herrera, E. López, C. Mandaña and M. Rodríguez

Fuzzy System for Air Traffic Flow Management   525
  L. Zerrouki, B. Bouchon-Meunier and R. Fondacci

A Fuzzy Approach to Contracting Electrical Energy in Competitive
Electricity Markets   548
  G. Michalik and W. Mielczarski

Fuzzy Logic and Intelligent Computing in Nuclear Engineering   567
  D. Ruan

Computational Intelligence Techniques in Landmine Detection   586
  A. Filippidis, L.C. Jain and N.M. Martin

1

NEURO-FUZZY
AND GENETIC SYSTEMS
FOR COMPUTING WITH WORDS

Neural Fuzzy Intelligent Agents

Sanya Mitaim and Bart Kosko
Signal and Image Processing Institute
Department of Electrical Engineering—Systems
University of Southern California
Los Angeles, California 90089-2564

Abstract

An intelligent agent must both learn what a user likes or dislikes and search databases on behalf of the user. A neural fuzzy system can learn an agent profile of a user when it samples user question-answer data. A fuzzy system uses if-then rules to store and compress the agent's knowledge of the user's likes and dislikes. A neural system uses training data to form and tune the rules. The profile is a preference map or a bumpy utility surface defined over the space of search objects. Rules define fuzzy patches that cover the surface bumps as learning unfolds and as the fuzzy agent system gives a finer approximation of the profile. The agent system searches for preferred objects with the learned profile and with a new fuzzy measure of similarity. The appendix derives the supervised learning law that tunes this matching measure with fresh sample data. We test the fuzzy agent profile system on object spaces of flowers and sunsets and test the fuzzy agent matching system on an object space of sunset images. Rule explosion and data acquisition impose fundamental limits on the system designs as they do for all fuzzy systems.

1 Intelligent Agents: Profile Learning and Object Matching

The design of intelligent agent depends on the answer to at least the questions: How can we teach an agent what we like and dislike? How can an agent search new databases on our behalf? These are core questions for both human agents and intelligent software agents. We explore these questions with the joint tools of fuzzy rule-based systems and neural learning. These tools exploit the filter and set-theoretic structure of agent search.

An intelligent agent can act as a smart database filter [13, 30]. The agent can search a database or search a space of objects on behalf of its user. The agent can find and retrieve objects that the user likes. Or the agent can find and then ignore or delete objects that the user does not like. Or it can perform some mix of both. The agent acts as a filter because it maps a set of objects to one or more of its subsets. The agent is "smart" [3, 31, 57] to the degree that it can quickly and accurately learn the user's tastes or object profile and to the degree that it can use that profile map to search for and to rank preferred objects. Figure 1 shows how a neural-fuzzy agent can learn and store user tastes as a bumpy preference surface defined over search objects [27].

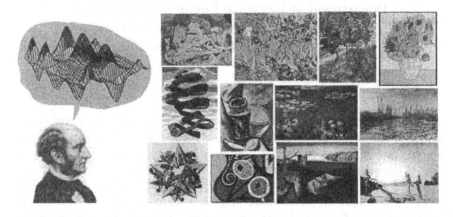

Figure 1: Profile learning. A neural fuzzy agent learns a user's utility surface as the user samples a database of classic paintings. The 12 bumps or extrema on the preference map show how much the user (or the agent who acts on the user's behalf) likes or dislikes the 12 paintings. Here the evolving utility surface forms in the "mind's eye" of a neural fuzzy agent based on nineteenth-century English philosopher John Stuart Mill as in the novel *Nanotime* [27].

Agent search depends on set structure in a still deeper way. The search system itself may have many parts to its design and may perform many functions in many digital venues [7, 62]. But at some abstract level the agent partitions the object space into two fuzzy or multivalued sets with blurred borders. The agent partitions the space into the fuzzy set of objects that it assumes the users likes and into the complement fuzzy set of objects that it assumes the user does not like. All search objects belong to both of these fuzzy sets to some degree. Then the agent can rank some or all of the objects in the preferred set and can pick some of the extremal objects as its output set.

The agent needs a profile of its user so that it can group objects and rank them. The agent must somehow learn what patterns of objects the user likes or dislikes and to what degree he likes or dislikes them [32, 49]. This profile is some form of the user's implicit preference map. The user may state part of this map in ordinal terms: "I like these red flowers more than I like those blue flowers. I like the large purple flowers about the same as I like the small red-white flowers." The objects may be fuzzy patterns or fuzzy clusters in some feature space [28, 43, 44].

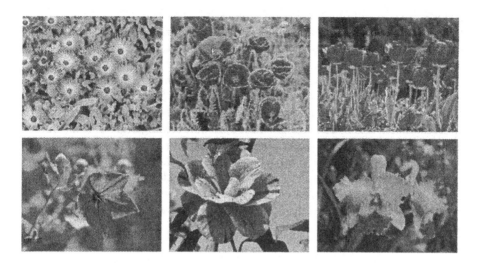

Figure 2: Search Objects. Samples of flower images in the test database. (With permission: Hitachi Viewseum, Copyright ©1995, 1996, 1997, Hitachi, America, Ltd. All rights reserved.)

Microeconomic theory ensures that under certain technical conditions these complete ordinal rankings define a numerical utility function. The utility function is unique up to a linear transformation [9, 15, 42]. So we can in theory replace the ordinal claim "I like object A at least as much as I like object B" with some cardinal relation $u(A) \geq u(B)$ and vice versa. The utility function $u : \mathcal{O} \rightarrow R$ converts the ordinal preference structure into a numerical utility surface in an object space $\mathcal{O}$ of low or high dimension [9, 15, 42]. The user likes the surface's peak objects and dislikes its valley objects.

We use neural fuzzy systems to learn the user's profile or utility surface as a set of adaptive fuzzy if-then rules [37]. The rules compress the profile into modular units. The rules grow the profile from a first set of sample data or question-answer queries and change the profile's shape as the agent samples more preference data. The modular structure of the rules lets the user add or delete knowledge chunks or heuristics or "hints" [1, 2]. We can also use such neural-fuzzy systems for other agent tasks that deal with multimedia image or motion estimation [20].

These fuzzy systems are universal approximators [23] but they suffer from exponential rule explosion in high dimension [25]. Their first set of rules give a quick but rough approximation of the user's profile. Each rule defines a fuzzy patch or subset of the object space (or product object space). Mean-square optimal rules cover the extrema or bumps of the profile surface [25]. Then other rule patches tend to quickly fill in between these bumps as learning unfolds. Figure 2 shows some of the flower test images we used to form a

4-D feature space of objects. Figure 5 shows how a neural fuzzy system with 100 rules approximates a 2-D profile surface. The utility profiles grow finer as the user states more numerical ranks for test objects or pattern clusters. Rule explosion remains the chief limit to this approach.

We also combine neural learning and fuzzy set theory to search for preferred objects. We cast this search problem as one of fuzzy similarity matching and define a new measure for the task and show how supervised learning updates this measure. The user gives the system matching degrees in the unit interval for a test space of sunset images. Supervised gradient descent tunes the measure and defines a similarity surface over the sunset object space. Similar objects have nearly the same utility but objects with the same utility need not be similar. Other systems might combine the "smart" techniques of fuzzy profile learning with fuzzy object matching to aid in the agent search process.

2 Neural Fuzzy Function Approximation: Patch the Bumps

This section reviews the basic structure of additive fuzzy systems. The appendices review and develop the more formal mathematical structure that underlies the neural fuzzy agent systems.

A fuzzy system $F : R^n \to R^p$ stores m rules of the word form "IF $X = A_j$ THEN $Y = B_j$" or the patch form $A_j \times B_j \subset X \times Y = R^n \times R^p$. The if-part fuzzy sets $A_j \subset R^n$ and then-part fuzzy sets $B_j \subset R^p$ have set functions $a_j : R^n \to [0,1]$ and $b_j : R^p \to [0,1]$. The system can use the joint set function a_j or some factored form such as $a_j(x) = a_j^1(x_1) \cdots a_j^n(x_n)$ or $a_j(x) = \min(a_j^1(x_1), \ldots, a_j^n(x_n))$ or any other conjunctive form for input vector $x = (x_1, \ldots, x_n) \in R^n$.

An additive fuzzy system [22, 23] sums the "fired" then-part sets B_j' :

$$B(x) \;=\; \sum_{j=1}^{m} w_j B_j' \;=\; \sum_{j=1}^{m} w_j a_j(x) B_j. \tag{1}$$

Figure 3a shows the parallel fire-and-sum structure of the standard additive model (SAM). These systems can uniformly approximate any continuous (or bounded measurable) function f on a compact domain [23].

Figure 3b shows how three rule patches can cover part of the graph of a scalar function $f : R \to R$. The patch cover shows that all fuzzy systems $F : R^n \to R^p$ suffer from *rule explosion* in high dimensions. A fuzzy system F needs on the order of k^{n+p-1} rules to cover the graph and thus to approximate a vector function $f : R^n \to R^p$. Optimal rules can help deal with the exponential rule explosion. Lone or local mean-squared optimal rule patches cover the extrema of the approximand f [25]. They "patch the bumps." Bet-

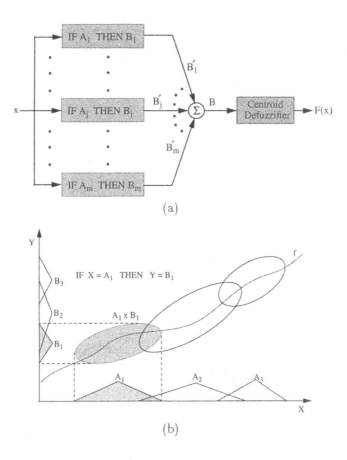

(a)

(b)

Figure 3: Feedforward fuzzy function approximator. (a) The parallel associative structure of the additive fuzzy system $F : R^n \to R^p$ with m rules. Each input $x_0 \in R^n$ enters the system F as a numerical vector. At the set level x_0 acts as a delta pulse $\delta(x - x_0)$ that combs the if-part fuzzy sets A_j and gives the m set values $a_j(x_0) = \int_{R^n} \delta(x - x_0)a_j(x)dx$. The set values "fire" or scale the then-part fuzzy sets B_j to give B_j'. A standard additive model (SAM) scales each B_j with $a_j(x)$. Then the system sums the B_j' sets to give the output "set" B. The system output $F(x_0)$ is the centroid of B. (b) Fuzzy rules define Cartesian rule patches $A_j \times B_j$ in the input-output space and cover the graph of the approximand f. This leads to exponential rule explosion in high dimensions. Optimal lone rules cover the extrema of the approximand as in Figure 4.

8

ter learning schemes move rule patches to or near extrema and then fill in between extrema with extra rule patches if the rule budget allows.

The scaling choice $B'_j = a_j(x)B_j$ gives a *standard additive model* or SAM. Appendix A shows that taking the centroid of $B(x)$ in (1) gives [22, 23, 24, 25] the SAM ratio

$$F(x) \;=\; \frac{\displaystyle\sum_{j=1}^{m} w_j a_j(x) V_j c_j}{\displaystyle\sum_{j=1}^{m} w_j a_j(x) V_j} \;=\; \sum_{j=1}^{m} p_j(x) c_j. \tag{2}$$

Here V_j is the finite positive volume or area of then-part set B_j and c_j is the centroid of B_j or its center of mass. The convex weights $p_1(x),\ldots,p_m(x)$ have the form $p_j(x) = \frac{w_j a_j(x) V_j}{\sum_{i=1}^{m} w_i a_i(x) V_i}$.

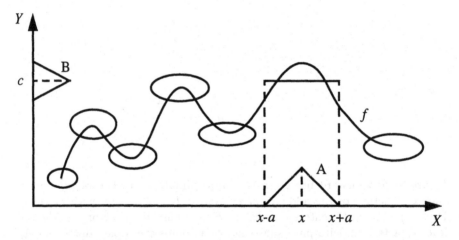

Figure 4: Lone optimal fuzzy rule patches cover the extrema of approximand f. A lone rule defines a flat line segment that cuts the graph of the local extremum in at least two places. The mean value theorem implies that the extremum lies between these points. This can reduce much of fuzzy function approximation to the search for zeroes $\hat{x}$ of the derivative map $f' : f'(\hat{x}) = 0$.

Now we give a simple *local* description of optimal lone fuzzy rules [25, 26]. We move a fuzzy rule patch so that it most reduces an error. We look (locally) at a minimal fuzzy system $F : R \to R$ of just one rule. So the fuzzy system is constant in that region: $F = c$. Suppose that $f(x) \neq c$ for $x \in [a, b]$ and define the error

$$e(x) \;=\; (f(x) - F(x))^2 \;=\; (f(x) - c)^2. \tag{3}$$

We want to find the best place $\hat{x}$. So the first-order condition gives $\nabla e = 0$ or

$$0 = \frac{\partial e(x)}{\partial x} = 2(f(x) - c)\frac{\partial f(x)}{\partial x}. \tag{4}$$

Then $f(x) \neq c$ implies that

$$\frac{\partial e(x)}{\partial x} = 0 \qquad \Longleftrightarrow \qquad \frac{\partial f(x)}{\partial x} = 0 \tag{5}$$

at $x = \hat{x}$. So the extrema of e and f coincide in this case. Figure 4 shows how fuzzy rule patches can "patch the bumps" and so help minimize the error of approximation.

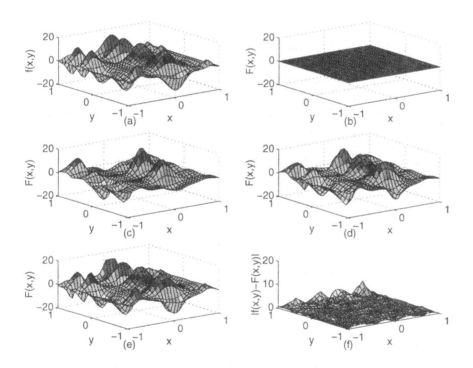

Figure 5: Fuzzy function approximation. 2-D Sinc standard additive model (SAM) function approximation with 100 fuzzy if-then rules and supervised gradient descent learning. (a) Desired function or approximand f. (b) SAM initial phase as a flat sheet or constant approximator F. (c) SAM approximator F after it initializes its centroids to the samples: $c_j = f(m_j)$. (d) SAM approximator F after 100 epochs of learning. (e) SAM approximator F after 6000 epochs of learning. (f) Absolute error of the fuzzy function approximation ($|f - F|$).

Figure 5 shows how supervised learning moves and shapes the fuzzy rule patches to give a finer approximation as the system sample more user choices. Appendix B derives the supervised SAM learning algorithms for Laplace and sinc set functions [26, 36]. Supervised gradient descent changes the SAM parameters with error data. At each time instant t the system takes an input-output pair (x_t, y_t) from a training data set or from sensor data. A user may define this input-output data pair during the Q & A session or in a feedback or evaluation processes. Then the fuzzy system computes output vector $F(x_t)$ from input vector x_t. The learning laws update each SAM parameter to minimize the squared-error $E(x_t) = \frac{1}{2}(f(x_t) - F(x_t))^2$. This process repeats as needed for a large number of sample data pairs (x_t, y_t). Learning moves and shapes the rule patches that define the SAM system F and gives a finer approximation of f. Figure 5e displays the absolute error of the fuzzy function approximation.

3   Agent Architecture

Figure 6 shows our schematic view of an intelligent agent. The agent can reside in a physical world (robot) or in a virtual world (softbot) [16, 33]. The interface/sensor module transforms the information into a bit stream. The preprocessor compresses the pattern of objects or actions. The compressed patterns might be colors or textures used in image search or filtering [41, 58], keywords used in text search or e-mail classifiers or news-filtering agents [30], or object features that agents use if they bargain or negotiate [6, 45, 50, 51, 55].

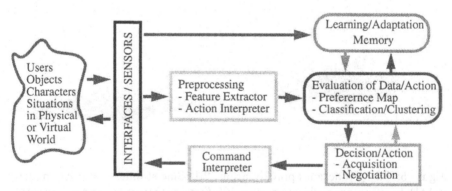

Figure 6: Agent environment. Schematic view of an autonomous agent in a physical or virtual world. The agent interacts with objects or characters in the environment and adapts itself to better execute its goals.

A learning and memory module records the compressed patterns of the utility surface. The surface changes over time as the user gives more Q & A samples. This gives a bumpy surface that tends to better and better match the user's underlying preference map.

The decision maker module receives the data from the evaluation module and then decides what to do [32]. A classifier agent sends the control signal to that class to which the object belongs [30]. Then an agent must decide which step to take next. The agent may need to bargain or negotiate with other agents [6, 50].

This paper deals largely with the block that computes the "value" or "worth" of an object or action. The preference map $u : \mathcal{O} \rightarrow R$ defines the value of each object. The user prefers object O_1 to object O_2 (or $O_1 \succeq O_2$ in preference notation) if and only if $u(O_1) \geq u(O_2)$. Information agents need some form of these preference maps to decide search issues on their user's behalfs [17, 21, 39, 60]. A fuzzy function approximator can give a good approximation of the preference map if the fuzzy system does not need too many rules and if the system can sample enough accurate user preference data. We also suggest a method to elicit consistent user preference data.

4 Profile Learning with Sunsets and Flowers

Users can define preference maps on an image space of sunsets or flowers. Each person has his own likes or dislikes that define his own fuzzy pattern of object clusters. The clusters depend on the features that define the objects. Recent work on object recognition [58] and content-based image retrieval [41] suggests that features define the "look" of the images. These features include colors, shapes, and textures. Research in machine vision seeks invariant features that can map all images into smaller clusters [4, 5, 12, 41, 46, 47, 58, 61].

Figure 7 shows a block diagram of a neural fuzzy agent that learns a user profile in a space of images. We used a multi-dimensional histogram of an image as features for our fuzzy agent prototype. Niblack [41] and Swain [58] used color histograms to recognize images and to structure their image database retrieval systems. The histogram technique itself ignores the spatial correlation of pixels in images. This has led many researchers to suggest other local features [4, 41, 46]. We use the image dispersion σ_{ij} as an extra feature [48]:

$$\sigma_{ij} = \frac{1}{W^2} \Big[\sum_{m=-w}^{w} \sum_{n=-w}^{w} [x(i+m, j+n) - \bar{x}(i+m, j+n)]^2 \Big]^{1/2} \quad (6)$$

where $W = 2w + 1$ and where

$$\bar{x}(i, j) = \frac{1}{W^2} \sum_{m=-w}^{w} \sum_{n=-w}^{w} x(i+m, j+n) \quad (7)$$

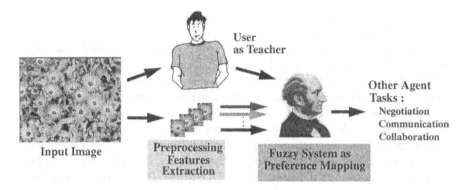

Figure 7: Data acquisition. A fuzzy agent can learn a user's unknown preference map. The user acts as a teacher or supervisor and gives the system question-answer training samples. Then supervised gradient descent tunes the fuzzy system to better approximate the user's preference map.

defines the sample mean in the $W \times W$ window centered at pixel location (i, j).

For each image we obtain its 4-D normalized histogram. The first three components are hue h, saturation s, and intensity v in the hue-saturation-intensity color space [48]. The other component is the standard deviation σ of the intensity component. We view this normalized 4-D histogram as an input discrete probability density function to the fuzzy system and write it in the form

$$T(h, s, v, \sigma) \tag{8}$$

$$= \sum_{i=1}^{N_h}\sum_{j=1}^{N_s}\sum_{k=1}^{N_v}\sum_{l=1}^{N_\sigma} t_{i,j,k,l}\, \delta(h - \bar{h}_i)\, \delta(s - \bar{s}_j)\, \delta(v - \bar{v}_k)\, \delta(\sigma - \bar{\sigma}_l). \tag{9}$$

Here N_h, N_s, N_v, and N_σ are the number of bins on axes of hue, saturation, intensity, and standard deviation. So the total number of histogram bins is $N = N_h \times N_s \times N_v \times N_\sigma$. The term $\bar{h}_i$ is the bin center of the ith hue and likewise for $\bar{s}_j$, $\bar{v}_k$, and $\bar{\sigma}_l$. The term $t_{i,j,k,l}$ is a normalized frequency of occurrence of the feature vector $(\bar{h}_i,\ \bar{s}_j,\ \bar{v}_k,\ \bar{\sigma}_l)$. We write the N-bin histogram T in the more compact form

$$T(h, s, v, \sigma) = T(x) = \sum_{n=1}^{N} t_n\, \delta(x - \bar{x}_n). \tag{10}$$

The vector $\bar{x}_n$ has the center of the histogram bin as its components: $\bar{x}_n = (\bar{h}_{i_n}, \bar{s}_{j_n}, \bar{v}_{k_n}, \bar{\sigma}_{l_n})$ as in (9). The normalized frequency of occurrence t_n replaces the corresponding t_{i_n,j_n,k_n,l_n} in (9).

This histogram T is the input to the fuzzy system. Appendix A shows that this gives a generalized SAM ratio (2) [22, 26] as a *set* SAM system:

$$F(T) = \frac{\displaystyle\sum_{j=1}^{m} a_j(T)V_j c_j}{\displaystyle\sum_{j=1}^{m} a_j(T)V_j} = \sum_{j=1}^{m} p_j(T)c_j. \tag{11}$$

The convex coefficients $p_j(T) \geq 0$ and $\sum_{j=1}^{m} p_j(T) = 1$ have the form

$$p_j(T) = \frac{a_j(T)V_j}{\displaystyle\sum_{i=1}^{m} a_i(T)V_i}. \tag{12}$$

The correlation of a fuzzy set function $a_j : X \subset R^4 \rightarrow [0,1]$ with a 4-D histogram of an image T has the form

$$a_j(T) = \int_X a_j(h, s, v, \sigma)\, T(h, s, v, \sigma)\, dh\, ds\, dv\, d\sigma \tag{13}$$

$$= \sum_{n=1}^{N} t_n\, a_j(\bar{x}_n). \tag{14}$$

The value $a_j(T)$ states the degree to which fuzzy set T belongs to fuzzy set A_j. The set correlation $a_j(T)$ need not lie in the unit interval. It can take on any finite nonnegative value: $a_j(T) \in [0, \infty)$. The set SAM ratio in (11) still gives an output as a convex sum of the then-part set centroids c_j as the point SAM in (2).

We tested the fuzzy agents with 88 flowers images and 42 sunsets images. Figure 2 shows some of the test images. We assigned subjective values to all images as numbers from 0 to 10. The value 10 stands for "It is maximally beautiful" or "I really love it." The value 0 stands for "It is minimally beautiful" or "I really hate it." The histogram bins were 8:4:4:4 for $h : s : v : \sigma$. So there were a total of 512 bins. The fuzzy system also had 512 fuzzy rules. We initialized the fuzzy agent so that it would be "indifferent" to all images (a score of 5) and trained it with supervised gradient-descent learning. The initial maximum absolute error was 5 and the mean absolute error was 2.45. The fuzzy agent converged after 40,000 epochs to our preference map and gave a score close to ours. This held for almost all test images. The maximum absolute error was 0.96 and the mean absolute error was 0.18. This error stemmed from too few features. Using more features tends to improve the system's accuracy but at the expense of greater rule complexity.

We used a histogram based on color and variance because it captured the relative amount of colors in the image that affect much of human perception

[41, 58]. We can also compute histograms easily and they are translation and rotation invariant [58]. Our systems for profile learning and searching did not depend on how we chose object features. The fuzzy agent could use other inputs from this image database or from others. These input features might include shapes [41, 46], textures [4, 41, 46, 47], wavelet transforms [5, 59], or other statistical measures [46].

5 Adaptive Fuzzy Object Matching

This section presents fuzzy equality as a measure of similarity between objects and shows how to tune it. A search or filter agent matches objects in the databases to the query object and acts on the match results. Supervised learning tunes the fuzzy equality measure to better approximate the user's perception of similar objects.

A fuzzy system can assist in database search in many ways. Fuzzy matching is perhaps the simplest way. The fuzzy equality measure [26] between two fuzzy sets can define the similarity between objects. The equality measure $\mathcal{E}(A, B)$ measures the degree to which fuzzy set A equals fuzzy set B. It measures how well A matches B and vice versa. Suppose fuzzy sets A and B are nonempty. Then $\mathcal{E}(A, B) = \mathcal{E}(B, A) \in [0, 1]$, $\mathcal{E}(A, A) = 1$, and $\mathcal{E}(A, \emptyset) = 0$ for the empty set $\emptyset$. The equality measure depends on the *counting* or *cardinality* [22] function c of a fuzzy set as

$$\mathcal{E}(A, B) \quad = \quad \text{Degree}(A = B) \quad = \quad \frac{c(A \cap B)}{c(A \cup B)} \tag{15}$$

$$= \quad \frac{\int \min(a(x), b(x)) \, dx}{\int \max(a(x), b(x)) \, dx} \tag{16}$$

where

$$c(A) \quad = \quad \sum_{i=1}^{N} a_i \quad \text{or} \quad c(A) \quad = \quad \int_{R^n} a(x) \, dx \tag{17}$$

for an integrable fuzzy set function $a : X \to [0, 1]$. The fuzzy equality measure rests on the theory of fuzzy sets as points in unit hypercubes or fuzzy cubes. Appendix C reviews this unit-cube geometry of discrete fuzzy sets [22, 26].

Consider an example. Let $a = (.8 \quad .4 \quad 0)$ and $b = (.1 \quad .5 \quad .2)$ be discrete set functions for fuzzy sets A and B in $X = \{x_1, x_2, x_3\}$. So the set function or fit vector $a = (a_1 \quad a_2 \quad a_3)$ defines the fuzzy set A as $a_1 = a(x_1) = .8$, $a_2 = a(x_2) = .4$, and $a_3 = a(x_3) = 0$. The fit vector b defines the fuzzy set B as $b_1 = b(x_1) = .1$, $b_2 = b(x_2) = .5$, and $b_3 = b(x_3) = .2$. Then fuzzy set A equals fuzzy set B to degree one-third:

$$\mathcal{E}(A, B) \quad = \quad \text{Degree}(A = B) \quad = \quad \frac{c(A \cap B)}{c(A \cup B)} \tag{18}$$

$$= \frac{\sum\limits_{i=1}^{3} \min(a_i, b_i)}{\sum\limits_{i=1}^{3} \max(a_i, b_i)} \qquad (19)$$

$$= \frac{.1 + .4 + 0}{.8 + .5 + .2} = \frac{1}{3}. \qquad (20)$$

A fuzzy system maps two objects (or their two vectors of "features") to the output fuzzy sets A and B. Then the equality measure gives a value near 1 if the two objects match well or "look alike." It gives a value near 0 if they match poorly.

We use the same histogram features as in the prior section to match images. Let T_A and T_B be the histograms of two images. Again we view these two normalized N-bin histograms as discrete probability density functions whose domain $X = \{\bar{x}_1, \ldots, \bar{x}_N\}$ is a set of vectors $\bar{x}_i$ that define the bin centers. This gives the same form as in (10). Then we compute the correlation of a set function a_j with two histograms T_A and T_B as in (14) with

$$A_j = a_j(T_A) = \sum_{n=1}^{N} T_A(\bar{x}_n) a_j(\bar{x}_n) \qquad (21)$$

$$B_j = a_j(T_B) = \sum_{n=1}^{N} T_B(\bar{x}_n) a_j(\bar{x}_n). \qquad (22)$$

This gives two m-D vectors of set values $(A_1, \ldots, A_m)$ and $(B_1, \ldots, B_m)$ from m fuzzy rules. The standard additive structure of fuzzy systems suggests that the output fuzzy set should equal the sum of the scaled then-part sets [26]. So we define the then-part sets to be the same as the if-part sets. So the output fuzzy sets A and B from the histograms T_A and T_B have the form

$$A(x) = \sum_{j=1}^{m} A_j a_j(x) \qquad (23)$$

$$B(x) = \sum_{j=1}^{m} B_j a_j(x) \qquad (24)$$

where $x = (h, s, v, \sigma) \in X$. The input to the system is an N-bin histogram on the discrete domain $X = \{\bar{x}_1, \ldots, \bar{x}_N\}$. Then we can view the output sets A and B as discrete sets and rewrite (23) - (24) as

$$A(\bar{x}_n) = \sum_{j=1}^{m} A_j a_j(\bar{x}_n) \qquad (25)$$

$$B(\bar{x}_n) = \sum_{j=1}^{m} B_j a_j(\bar{x}_n) \qquad (26)$$

for $n = 1, \ldots, N$. Then the fuzzy equality (in the discrete case) in (16) measures the degree to which fuzzy set A equals or matches fuzzy set B:

$$\mathcal{E}(A, B) = \frac{\sum_{i=1}^{N} \min(A(\bar{x}_i), B(\bar{x}_i))}{\sum_{i=1}^{N} \max(A(\bar{x}_i), B(\bar{x}_i))} \tag{27}$$

This in turns measures the "similarity" between two images.

The similarity measure depends on how we define the m fuzzy rules. Tuning or learning schemes can move or reshape the fuzzy sets to approximate desired matching values. Appendix C derives the learning laws that tune the set-function parameters in $\mathcal{E}$.

Figure 8 shows a block diagram of how a fuzzy agent matches images. The simulation used a 4-D version of the 1-D Laplace set function $a_j(x) = \exp\{-\left|\frac{x - m_j}{d_j}\right|\}$ in (114) - (115). We trained the fuzzy matching system on a space of sunset images with the histogram intersection in [58]:

$$S(H, I) = \frac{\sum_{i=1}^{N} \min(H_i, I_i)}{\sum_{i=1}^{N} H_i}. \tag{28}$$

The fuzzy system gave a rough approximation of the histogram intersection. We may not be able to find a closed-form formula for matching in the general case. Then the fuzzy matching process might learn from Q & A sessions or from other user feedback.

6   Conclusions: The Q & A Bottleneck

Neural fuzzy systems can assist agents in many ways. We have shown how these adaptive function approximators can both help learn a user's preference map and help choose preferred search objects cast as features of low dimension. The color histogram we used did not give a complete set of features. Other neural fuzzy systems can more fully combine these two fuzzy tasks to aid in agent database search. Future research may depend on advances in pattern recognition and machine vision. Neural fuzzy systems might also assist agents when agents bargain [6, 50, 51] or cooperate [10, 38] with other agents. Then an agent may try to learn a second or third user's profile as well as learn its master's profile.

Agents could also help neural fuzzy systems approximate functions from training samples. Today most neural fuzzy systems work with just one fuzzy

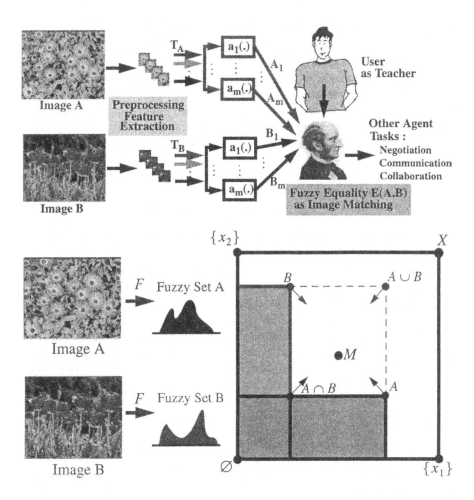

Figure 8: Adaptive fuzzy search. Fuzzy equality measures the likeness of two objects A and B. Supervised learning tunes the fuzzy equality measure $\mathcal{E}(A, B)$ inside the fuzzy-cube state space to better approximate the user's perception of similar images. The equality measure grows to unity as the A and B set points approach each other. The cube midpoint M is the maximally fuzzy set where $\mathcal{E}(M, M^c) = 1$. Binary sets V lie at the 2^n cube vertices and they alone give $\mathcal{E}(V, V^c) = 0$.

system and one supervised or unsupervised learning law. Rule explosion in high dimensions may force the user to replace the lone fuzzy system with several smaller systems. Agents can help combine these fuzzy systems [24, 26] if they pick and change the weights or rankings of each system based on sample data or domain knowledge. Agents can also pick which learning law to use or which set of parameters to use as the system tunes its rules on-line. Still more complex hybrids can use nested agents within multi-system function approximators and use the approximators to help higher-level agents learn profiles and search databases and perhaps perform other agent tasks.

The other critical problem still remains. How does an agent get numerical values for sample objects? What questions should the agent ask the user in a Q & A session? How many objects must a user rank? These questions reveal the practical weakness of any search system that depends on numbers. Cardinal data eases numerical processing but comes at the expense of a question-answer bottleneck. The neural fuzzy agent needs to improve how it acquires knowledge [19, 56]. The agent should not ask the user too many questions. The agent needs to learn the user's profile fast enough before it tires the user. Efficient agents would make the user state rankings that are at most linear in the number of search objects or search-object clusters. Our system asks the user a large number of numerical questions even though the user may not want to give and perhaps cannot give precise numerical answers to these questions. Researchers have long searched for techniques that can lessen the number of numerical questions the system must ask the user [19, 56]. The agent may use techniques in decision theory [8, 17, 18, 52, 53, 54] to rank objects from the user's ordinal answers. Additional criteria [14, 35] can help reduce number of questions the user needs to answer. The bootstrap and other statistical methods [11] may offer more efficient ways for an adaptive agent to sample its user and its environment. Ordinal or chunking techniques [29, 34, 40] may also ease the burden of preference acquisition. But all such techniques tend to increase the complexity of the neural and fuzzy systems.

7 Acknowledgement

A research grant from the Annenberg Center for Communication at the University of Southern California partly funded this research.

References

[1] Y. S. Abu-Mostafa, "Learning from Hints in Neural Networks," *Journal of Complexity*, pp. 192–198, 1990.

[2] Y. S. Abu-Mostafa, "Hints," *Neural Computation*, pp. 639–671, 1995.

[3] R. Brooks, "Intelligence Without Reason," in *The Artificial Life Route to Artificial Intelligence: Building Embodied, Situated Agents*, L. Steels and R. Brooks, Eds., chapter 2, pp. 25–81. Lawrence Erlbaum Associates, Inc., 1995.

[4] T. Caelli and D. Reye, "On the Classification of Image Regions by Colour, Texture and Shape," *Pattern Recognition*, vol. 26, no. 4, pp. 461–470, 1993.

[5] S. F. Chang and J. R. Smith, "Extracting Multi-Dimensional Signal Features for Content-Based Visual Query," in *SPIE Symposium on Visual Communications and Signal Processing*, May 1995.

[6] A. Chavez and P. Maes, "Kasbah: An Agent Marketplace for Buying and Selling Goods," in *Proceedings of the Conference on the Practical Application of Intelligent Agents and Multi-Agent Technology*, April 1996.

[7] M. Colombetti and M. Dorigo, "Training Agents to Perform Sequential Behavior," *Adaptive Behavior*, vol. 2, no. 3, pp. 247–275, 1994.

[8] W. D. Cook and M. Kress, *Ordinal Information and Preference Structures: Decision Models and Applications*, Prentice Hall, Englewood Cliffs, New Jersey, 1992.

[9] G. Debreu, "Representation of a Preference Ordering by a Numerical Function," in *Mathematical Economics: Twenty Papers of Gerard Debreu*, chapter 6, pp. 105–110. Cambridge University Press, 1983.

[10] M. Dorigo, V. Maniezzo, and A. Colorni, "Ant System: Optimization by a Colony of Cooperating Agents," *IEEE Transactions on Systems, Man, and Cybernetics–Part B: Cybernetics*, vol. 26, no. 1, pp. 29–41, February 1996.

[11] B. Efron and R. J. Tibshirani, *An Introduction to the Bootstrap*, Chapman & Hall, 1993.

[12] B. V. Funt, "Color Constant Color Indexing," *IEEE Transactions on Pattern Analysis and Machine Intelligence*, vol. 17, no. 5, pp. 522–529, May 1995.

[13] W. I. Grosky, "Multimedia Information Systems," *IEEE Multimedia*, vol. 1, no. 1, pp. 12–24, Spring 1994.

[14] P. T. Harker, "Incomplete Pairwise Comparison in the Analytic Hierarchy Process," *Mathematical Modelling*, vol. 9, no. 11, pp. 837–848, 1987.

[15] W. Hildenbrand and A. P. Kirman, *Introduction to Equilibrium Analysis*, North Holland, 1976.

[16] N. R. Jennings and M. Wooldridge, "Software Agents," *IEE Review*, vol. 42, no. 1, pp. 17–20, January 1996.

[17] R. L. Keeney and H. Raiffa, *Decision with Multiple Objectives: Preferences and Value Tradeoffs*, John Wiley & Sons, New York, 1976.

[18] M. Kendall and J. D. Gibbons, *Rank Correlation Methods*, Edward Arnold, A division of Hodder & Stoughton, London, fifth edition, 1990.

[19] F. A. Kilpatrick, G. H. Gunsch, and E. Santos Jr., "Induction and State-Space Search for an Intelligent Training System," in *Proceedings of the Midwest Artificial Intelligence and Cognitive Science Conference*, 1996.

[20] H. M. Kim and B. Kosko, "Neural Fuzzy Motion Estimation and Compensation," *IEEE Transactions on Signal Processing*, vol. 45, no. 10, pp. 2515–2532, October 1997.

[21] J. Kirman, A. Nicholson, M. Lejter, T. Dean, and E. Santos Jr., "Using Goals to Find Plans with High Expected Utility," in *Proceedings of the Second European Workshop on Planning*, 1993, pp. 158–170.

[22] B. Kosko, *Neural Networks and Fuzzy Systems: A Dynamical Systems Approach to Machine Intelligence*, Prentice Hall, Englewood Cliffs, New Jersey, 1991.

[23] B. Kosko, "Fuzzy Systems as Universal Approximators," *IEEE Transactions on Computers*, vol. 43, no. 11, pp. 1329–1333, November 1994.

[24] B. Kosko, "Combining Fuzzy Systems," in *Proceedings of the IEEE International Conference on Fuzzy Systems (IEEE FUZZ-95)*, March 1995, pp. 1855–1863.

[25] B. Kosko, "Optimal Fuzzy Rules Cover Extrema," *International Journal of Intelligent Systems*, vol. 10, no. 2, pp. 249–255, February 1995.

[26] B. Kosko, *Fuzzy Engineering*, Prentice Hall, 1996.

[27] B. Kosko, *Nanotime*, Avon Books, 1997.

[28] R. Krishnapuram and J. M. Keller, "A Possibilistic Approach to Clustering," *IEEE Transactions on Fuzzy Systems*, vol. 1, pp. 98–110, May 1993.

[29] J. E. Laird, A. Newell, and P. S. Rosenbloom, "SOAR: An Architecture for General Intelligence," *Artificial Intelligence*, vol. 33, pp. 1–64, 1987.

[30] P. Maes, "Agents that Reduce Work and Information Overload," *Communications of the ACM*, vol. 37, no. 7, pp. 31–40, July 1994.

[31] P. Maes, "Artificial Life Meets Entertainment: Lifelike Autonomous Agents," *Communications of the ACM*, vol. 38, no. 11, pp. 108–114, November 1995.

[32] P. Maes, "Modeling Adaptive Autonomous Agents," in *Artificial Life: An Overview*, C. G. Langton, Ed., pp. 135–162. MIT Press, 1995.

[33] P. Maes, T. Darrel, B. Blumberg, and A. Pentland, "The ALIVE System: Wireless, Full-body Interaction with Autonomous Agents," *Multimedia Systems*, Spring 1996.

[34] G. A. Miller, "The Magical Number Seven, Plus or Minus Two: Some Limits on Our Capacity for Processing Information," *The Psychological Review*, vol. 63, no. 2, pp. 81–97, March 1956.

[35] I. Millet and P. T. Harker, "Globally Effective Questioning in the Analytic Hierarchy Process," *European Journal of Operational Research*, vol. 48, pp. 88–97, 1990.

[36] S. Mitaim and B. Kosko, "What is the Best Shape for a Fuzzy Set in Function Approximation?," in *Proceedings of the 5th IEEE International Conference on Fuzzy Systems (FUZZ-96)*, September 1996, vol. 2, pp. 1237–1243.

[37] S. Mitaim and B. Kosko, "Neural Fuzzy Agents for Profile Learning and Adaptive Object Matching," *Presence: Special Issue on Autonomous Agents, Adaptive Behavior, and Distributed Simulations*, vol. 7, no. 5, October 1998.

[38] A. Moukas, "Amalthaea: Information Discovery and Filtering Using a Multiagent Evolving Ecosystem," in *Proceedings of the Conference on the Practical Application of Intelligent Agents and Multi-Agent Technology*, April 1996.

[39] T. Mullen and M. P. Wellman, "A Simple Computational Market for Network Information Services," in *Proceedings of the First International Conference on Multi-Agent Systems*, June 1995, pp. 283–289.

[40] A. Newell and P. S. Rosenbloom, "Mechanisms of Skill Acquisition and the Law of Practice," in *Cognitive Skills and Their Acquisition*, J. R. Anderson, Ed., chapter 1, pp. 1–55. Lawrence Erlbaum Associates, Inc., 1981.

[41] W. Niblack, R. Barber, W. Equitz, M. Flikner, E. Glassman, D. Petkovic, P. Yanker, and C. Faloutsos, "The QBIC Project: Querying Images by Content Using Color, Texture, and Shape," Research Report RJ 9203 (81511), IBM, February 1993.

[42] G. Owen, *Game Theory*, Academic Press, third edition, 1995.

[43] N. R. Pal and J. C. Bezdek, "On Cluster Validity for the Fuzzy c-Means Model," *IEEE Transactions on Fuzzy Systems*, vol. 3, no. 3, pp. 370–379, August 1995.

[44] N. R. Pal, J. C. Bezdek, and R. J. Hathaway, "Sequential Competitive Learning and the Fuzzy c-Means Clustering Algorithms," *Neural Networks*, vol. 9, pp. 787–96, July 1996.

[45] S. Parsons and N. R. Jennings, "Negotiation through Argumentation–A Preliminary Report," in *Proceedings of the International Conference on Multi-Agent Systems*, 1996.

[46] A. Penland, R. W. Picard, and S. Sclaroff, "Photobook: Tools for Content-Based Manipulation of Image Databases," in *SPIE: Storage and Retrieval for Image and Video Database II*, February 1994, vol. 2185, pp. 34–47.

[47] R. W. Picard and T. P. Minka, "Vision Texture for Annotation," *Multimedia Systems*, vol. 3, pp. 3–14, 1995.

[48] W. K. Pratt, *Digital Image Processing*, Wiley Interscience, second edition, 1991.

[49] D. W. Rasmus, "Intelligent Agents: DAI Goes to Work," *PC AI*, pp. 27–32, January/February 1995.

[50] W. S. Reilly and J. Bates, "Natural Negotiation for Believable Agents," Technical Report CMU-CS-95-164, Carnegie Mellon University, Pittsburgh, PA, June 1995.

[51] J. S. Rosenschein and G. Zlotkin, "Consenting Agents: Designing Conventions for Automated Negotiation," *AI Magazine*, vol. 15, no. 3, pp. 29–46, Fall 1994.

[52] T. L. Saaty, "A Scaling Method for Priorities in Hierarchical Structures," *Journal of Mathematical Psychology*, vol. 15, pp. 234–281, 1977.

[53] T. L. Saaty, "Axiomatic Foundation of the Analytic Hierarchy Process," *Management Science*, vol. 32, no. 7, pp. 841–855, July 1986.

[54] T. L. Saaty, "Highlights and Critical Points in the Theory and Application of the Analytic Hierarchy Process," *European Journal of Operational Research*, vol. 74, pp. 426–447, 1994.

[55] T. Sandholm and V. Lesser, "Issues in Automated Negotiation and Electronic Commerce: Extending the Contract Net Framework," in *Proceedings of the First International Conference on Multi-Agent Systems*, June 1995, pp. 328–335.

[56] E. Santos Jr. and D. O. Banks, "Acquiring Consistent Knowledge," Technical Report AFIT/EN/TR96-01, Air Force Institute of Technology, January 1996.

[57] L. Steels, "The Artificial Life Roots of Artificial Intelligence," in *Artificial Life: An Overview*, C. G. Langton, Ed., pp. 75–110. MIT Press, 1995.

[58] M. J. Swain and D. H. Ballard, "Color Indexing," *International Journal of Computer Vision*, vol. 7, no. 1, pp. 11–32, 1991.

[59] M. Vetterli and J. Kovačević, *Wavelets and Subband Coding*, Prentice Hall, 1995.

[60] M. P. Wellman and J. Doyle, "Preferential Semantics for Goals," in *Proceedings of the Ninth National Conference on Artificial Intelligence (AAAI-91)*, July 1991, pp. 698–703.

[61] J. K. Wu, A. D. Narasimhalu, B. M. Mehtre, and Y. J. Gao, "CORE: A Content-Based Retrieval Engine for Multimedia Information Systems," *Multimedia Systems*, vol. 3, pp. 25–41, 1995.

[62] B. Yamauchi and R. Beer, "Integrating Reactive, Sequential, and Learning Behavior Using Dynamical Neural Networks," in *Proceedings of the Third International Conference on Simulation of Adaptive Behavior*, D. Cliff, P. Husbands, J. A. Meyer, and S. Wilson, Eds. 1994, pp. 382–391, MIT Press.

Appendix A. The Standard Additive Model (SAM) Theorem

This appendix derives the basic ratio structure (2) of a standard additive fuzzy system.

SAM Theorem. Suppose the fuzzy system $F : R^n \rightarrow R^p$ is a standard additive model: $F(x) = \text{Centroid}(B(x)) = \text{Centroid}(\sum_{j=1}^{m} w_j a_j(x) B_j)$ for if-part joint set function $a_j : R^n \rightarrow [0,1]$, rule weights $w_j \geq 0$, and then-part fuzzy set $B_j \subset R^p$. Then $F(x)$ is a convex sum of the m then-part set centroids:

$$F(x) = \frac{\sum_{j=1}^{m} w_j a_j(x) V_j c_j}{\sum_{j=1}^{m} w_j a_j(x) V_j} = \sum_{j=1}^{m} p_j(x) c_j. \tag{29}$$

The convex coefficients or discrete probability weights $p_1(x), \ldots, p_m(x)$ depend on the input x through

$$p_j(x) = \frac{w_j a_j(x) V_j}{\sum\limits_{i=1}^{m} w_i a_i(x) V_i}. \tag{30}$$

V_j is the finite positive volume (or area if $p = 1$) and c_j is the centroid of then-part set B_j:

$$V_j = \int_{R^p} b_j(y_1, \ldots, y_p) \, dy_1 \cdots dy_p > 0, \tag{31}$$

$$c_j = \frac{\int_{R^p} y \, b_j(y_1, \ldots, y_p) \, dy_1 \cdots dy_p}{\int_{R^p} b_j(y_1, \ldots, y_p) \, dy_1 \cdots dy_p}. \tag{32}$$

Proof. There is no loss of generality to prove the theorem for the scalar-output case $p = 1$ when $F : R^n \to R^p$. This simplifies the notation. We need but replace the scalar integrals over R with the p-multiple or volume integrals over R^p in the proof to prove the general case. The scalar case $p = 1$ gives (31) and (32) as

$$V_j = \int_{-\infty}^{\infty} b_j(y) \, dy \tag{33}$$

$$c_j = \frac{\int_{-\infty}^{\infty} y \, b_j(y) \, dy}{\int_{-\infty}^{\infty} b_j(y) \, dy} \tag{34}$$

Then the theorem follows if we expand the centroid of B and invoke the SAM assumption $F(x) = \text{Centroid}(B(x)) = \text{Centroid}(\sum\limits_{j=1}^{m} w_j \, a_j(x) \, B_j)$ to rearrange terms:

$$F(x) = \text{Centroid}(B(x)) \tag{35}$$

$$= \frac{\int_{-\infty}^{\infty} y \, b(y) \, dy}{\int_{-\infty}^{\infty} b(y) \, dy} \tag{36}$$

$$= \frac{\int_{-\infty}^{\infty} y \sum\limits_{j=1}^{m} w_j \, b'_j(y) \, dy}{\int_{-\infty}^{\infty} \sum\limits_{j=1}^{m} w_j \, b'_j(y) \, dy} \tag{37}$$

$$= \frac{\int_{-\infty}^{\infty} y \sum_{j=1}^{m} w_j \, a_j(x) \, b_j(y) \, dy}{\int_{-\infty}^{\infty} \sum_{j=1}^{m} w_j \, a_j(x) \, b_j(y) \, dy} \tag{38}$$

$$= \frac{\sum_{j=1}^{m} w_j \, a_j(x) \int_{-\infty}^{\infty} y \, b_j(y) \, dy}{\sum_{j=1}^{m} w_j \, a_j(x) \int_{-\infty}^{\infty} b_j(y) \, dy} \tag{39}$$

$$= \frac{\sum_{j=1}^{m} w_j \, a_j(x) \, V_j \dfrac{\int_{-\infty}^{\infty} y \, b_j(y) \, dy}{V_j}}{\sum_{j=1}^{m} w_j \, a_j(x) \, V_j} \tag{40}$$

$$= \frac{\sum_{j=1}^{m} w_j \, a_j(x) \, V_j \, c_j}{\sum_{j=1}^{m} w_j \, a_j(x) \, V_j}. \tag{41}$$

Generalizing the SAM system leads to the *set* SAM F that maps fuzzy sets A in the input space R^n to vector points y in the output space R^p. So the set SAM $F : F(2^{R^n}) \to R^p$ has as its domain the fuzzy power set $F(2^{R^n})$ or the set of all fuzzy subsets $A \subset R^n$ with arbitrary set function $a : R^n \to [0, \infty)$. The point SAM is a special case of the set SAM for a singleton input fuzzy set $A = \{x_0\} \subset R^n$: $a(x) = \delta(x - x_0)$ where δ is a Dirac delta function in the continuous case or a unit bit vector in the discrete case. Correlation computes the "fired" fit value of the jth set $a_j(A)$ as [26]

$$a_j(A) = \int a(x) \, a_j(x) \, dx. \tag{42}$$

Then the fired fit value $a_j(x_0)$ of the singleton set $A = \{x_0\}$ follows from the sifting property of delta pulses:

$$a_j(A) = \int a(x) \, a_j(x) \, dx \tag{43}$$

$$= \int \delta(x - x_0) \, a_j(x) \, dx \tag{44}$$

$$= a_j(x_0). \tag{45}$$

The set SAM equation follows from the SAM additive combiner $B(A) =$

$$\sum_{j=1}^{m} w_j \, a_j(A) \, B_j \ [26]:$$

$$F(A) \ = \ \mathrm{Centroid}(B(A)) \tag{46}$$

$$= \ \mathrm{Centroid}\Big(\sum_{j=1}^{m} w_j \, a_j(A) \, B_j \Big) \tag{47}$$

$$= \ \frac{\displaystyle\sum_{j=1}^{m} w_j \, a_j(A) \, V_j \, c_j}{\displaystyle\sum_{j=1}^{m} w_j \, a_j(A) \, V_j} \ = \ \sum_{j=1}^{m} p_j(A) \, c_j \tag{48}$$

where the convex coefficients $p_1(A), \ldots, p_m(A)$ depend on the input fuzzy set A through

$$p_j(A) \ = \ \frac{w_j \, a_j(A) \, V_j}{\displaystyle\sum_{i=1}^{m} w_i \, a_i(A) \, V_i}. \tag{49}$$

Appendix B. Supervised SAM Learning

Supervised gradient descent can tune all the parameters in the SAM model (2) [24, 26]. A gradient descent learning law for a SAM parameter ξ has the form

$$\xi(t+1) \ = \ \xi(t) - \mu_t \, \frac{\partial E}{\partial \xi}, \tag{50}$$

where μ_t is a learning rate at iteration t. We seek to minimize the squared error

$$E(x) \ = \ \frac{1}{2} \, (f(x) - F(x))^2 \tag{51}$$

of the function approximation. Let ξ_j^k denote the kth parameter in the set function a_j. Then the chain rule gives the gradient of the error function with respect to ξ_j^k, with respect to the then-part set centroid c_j, and with respect to the then-part set volume V_j:

$$\frac{\partial E}{\partial \xi_j^k} \ = \ \frac{\partial E}{\partial F} \frac{\partial F}{\partial a_j} \frac{\partial a_j}{\partial \xi_j^k} \tag{52}$$

$$\frac{\partial E}{\partial c_j} \ = \ \frac{\partial E}{\partial F} \frac{\partial F}{\partial c_j} \tag{53}$$

$$\frac{\partial E}{\partial V_j} \ = \ \frac{\partial E}{\partial F} \frac{\partial F}{\partial V_j} \tag{54}$$

where

$$\frac{\partial E}{\partial F} \ = \ -(f(x) - F(x)) \ = \ -\varepsilon(x), \tag{55}$$

$$\frac{\partial F}{\partial a_j} = \frac{\left(\sum_{i=1}^{m} w_i\, a_i(x)\, V_i\right)(w_j\, V_j\, c_j) - w_j\, V_j \left(\sum_{i=1}^{m} w_i\, a_i(x)\, V_i\, c_i\right)}{\left(\sum_{i=1}^{m} w_i\, a_i(x)\, V_i\right)^2} \tag{56}$$

$$= \frac{[c_j - F(x)]\, w_j\, V_j}{\sum_{i=1}^{m} w_i\, a_i(x)\, V_i} = [c_j - F(x)]\frac{p_j(x)}{a_j(x)}. \tag{57}$$

The SAM ratio (2) gives [24]

$$\frac{\partial F}{\partial c_j} = \frac{w_j\, a_j(x)\, V_j}{\sum_{i=1}^{m} w_i\, a_i(x)\, V_i} = p_j(x) \tag{58}$$

and

$$\frac{\partial F}{\partial V_j} = \frac{w_j\, a_j(x)\, [c_j - F(x)]}{\sum_{i=1}^{m} w_i\, a_i(x)\, V_i} = \frac{p_j(x)}{V_j}[c_j - F(x)] \tag{59}$$

Then the learning laws for the centroid and volume have the final form

$$c_j(t+1) = c_j(t) + \mu_t\, \varepsilon(x)\, p_j(x) \tag{60}$$

and

$$V_j(t+1) = V_j(t) + \mu_t\, \varepsilon(x)\, \frac{p_j(x)}{V_j}[c_j - F(x)]. \tag{61}$$

Learning laws for set parameters depend on how we define the set functions. The scalar Laplace set function has the form: $a_j(x) = \exp\left\{-\left|\frac{x - m_j}{d_j}\right|\right\}$. The partial derivatives of the set function with respect to its two parameters m_j and d_j have the form

$$\frac{\partial a_j}{\partial m_j} = \text{sign}(x - m_j)\frac{1}{|d_j|}a_j(x) \tag{62}$$

$$\frac{\partial a_j}{\partial m_j} = \text{sign}(d_j)\frac{|x - m_j|}{|d_j^2|}a_j(x) \tag{63}$$

where we define the sign function as

$$\text{sign}(x) = \begin{cases} 1 & \text{if } x > 0 \\ -1 & \text{if } x < 0 \\ 0 & \text{if } x = 0 \end{cases} \tag{64}$$

Substitute (62)-(63) in (52) and in (50) to obtain the learning laws

$$m_j(t+1) = m_j(t) + \mu_t\varepsilon(x)\, [c_j - F(x)]\, p_j(x)\, \text{sign}(x - m_j)\frac{1}{|d_j|} \tag{65}$$

$$d_j(t+1) = d_j(t) + \mu_t\varepsilon(x)\, [c_j - F(x)]\, p_j(x)\, \text{sign}(d_j)\frac{|x - m_j|}{d_j^2}. \tag{66}$$

The partial derivatives for the scalar sinc set function

$$a_j(x) = \sin\left(\frac{x - m_j}{d_j}\right) \bigg/ \left(\frac{x - m_j}{d_j}\right) \tag{67}$$

have the form

$$\frac{\partial a_j}{\partial m_j} = \begin{cases} \left(a_j(x) - \cos\left(\frac{x - m_j}{d_j}\right)\right)\frac{1}{x - m_j} & \text{for } x \neq m_j \\ 0 & \text{for } x = m_j \end{cases} \tag{68}$$

$$\frac{\partial a_j}{\partial d_j} = \left(a_j(x) - \cos\left(\frac{x - m_j}{d_j}\right)\right)\frac{1}{d_j} \tag{69}$$

So this scalar set function has the learning laws

$$m_j(t+1) = m_j(t) \tag{70}$$

$$+ \mu_t\, \varepsilon(x)\, [c_j - F(x)]\frac{p_j(x)}{a_j(x)}\left(a_j(x) - \cos\left(\frac{x - m_j}{d_j}\right)\right)\frac{1}{x - m_j} \tag{71}$$

$$d_j(t+1) = d_j(t) \tag{72}$$

$$+ \mu_t\, \varepsilon(x)\, [c_j - F(x)]\frac{p_j(x)}{a_j(x)}\left(a_j(x) - \cos\left(\frac{x - m_j}{d_j}\right)\right)\frac{1}{d_j}. \tag{73}$$

Like results hold for the learning laws of product n-D set functions. A factored set function $a_j(x) = a_j^1(x_1)\cdots a_j^n(x_n)$ leads to a new form for the error gradient. The gradient with respect to the parameter m_j^k of the jth set function a_j has the form

$$\frac{\partial E}{\partial m_j^k} = \frac{\partial E}{\partial F}\frac{\partial F}{\partial a_j}\frac{\partial a_j}{\partial a_j^k}\frac{\partial a_j^k}{\partial m_j^k} \tag{74}$$

where

$$\frac{\partial a_j}{\partial a_j^k} = \prod_{i \neq k}^n a_j^i(x_i) = \frac{a_j(x)}{a_j^k(x_k)}. \tag{75}$$

We used product of the scalar sinc set function to define the if-part fuzzy set $A_j \subset R^n$ in the fuzzy profile approximator and we used product of the scalar Laplace set function for the fuzzy equality measure. But we used the set SAM system instead of the simple point SAM. The learning laws follow from the structure of the set SAM.

We now derive learning laws for the set SAM. The chain-rule terms in (52) become

$$\frac{\partial E}{\partial \xi_j^k}(A) = \frac{\partial E}{\partial F}(A)\frac{\partial F}{\partial a_j}(A)\frac{\partial a_j}{\partial \xi_j^k}(A) \tag{76}$$

$$\frac{\partial E}{\partial c_j}(A) = \frac{\partial E}{\partial F}(A)\frac{\partial F}{\partial c_j}(A) \tag{77}$$

$$\frac{\partial E}{\partial V_j}(A) = \frac{\partial E}{\partial F}(A)\frac{\partial F}{\partial V_j}(A). \tag{78}$$

Then (55) - (59) give

$$\frac{\partial E}{\partial F}(A) \;=\; -(f(A) - F(A)) \;=\; -\varepsilon(A) \tag{79}$$

$$\frac{\partial F}{\partial a_j}(A) \;=\; [c_j - F(A)]\frac{p_j(A)}{a_j(A)} \tag{80}$$

$$\frac{\partial F}{\partial c_j}(A) \;=\; p_j(A) \tag{81}$$

$$\frac{\partial F}{\partial V_j}(A) \;=\; \frac{p_j(A)}{V_j}[c_j - F(A)]. \tag{82}$$

The learning laws for then-part set centroids c_j and volumes V_j are

$$c_j(t+1) \;=\; c_j(t) + \mu_t\,\varepsilon(x)\,p_j(A) \tag{83}$$

$$V_j(t+1) \;=\; V_j(t) + \mu_t\,\varepsilon(x)\,\frac{p_j(A)}{V_j}[c_j - F(A)]. \tag{84}$$

But the partial derivative of the jth set function with respect to its parameters ξ_j^k has the new form

$$\frac{\partial a_j}{\partial \xi_j^k}(A) \;=\; \frac{\partial}{\partial \xi_j^k}\int a_j(x)\,a(x)\,dx \tag{85}$$

$$= \begin{cases} \displaystyle\int \frac{\partial a_j}{\partial \xi_j^k}(x)\,a(x)\,dx & \text{continuous case} \\[2ex] \displaystyle\sum \frac{\partial a_j}{\partial \xi_j^k}(x)\,a(x) & \text{discrete case} \end{cases} \tag{86}$$

Then we substitute these partial derivatives into (50) to obtain the set-SAM learning rules.

Appendix C. Sets as Points: The Geometry of Discrete Fuzzy Sets

This appendix reviews the unit-cube geometry of discrete fuzzy system and derive the new adaptive equality measure. Let X be a set of n elements: $X = \{x_1, \ldots, x_n\}$. Any subset $A \subset X$ defines a point in the n-D unit hypercube $I^n = [0,1]^n$. The set of all fuzzy subsets of X or $F(2^X)$ fill in the cube. So the ordinary power set 2^X or the set of all 2^n subsets of X equals the Boolean n-cube $B^n : 2^X = B^n$. Fuzzy subsets $A \subset X$ define the points *inside* or on the n-D unit hypercube [22, 26] as in Figure 9. A set $A \subset X$ is fuzzy when the "laws" of noncontradiction and excluded middle do not hold: $A \cap A^c \neq \emptyset$ and $A \cup A^c \neq X$.

Figure 9 shows an example when $X = \{x_1, x_2\}$. Then there are 4 binary subsets of $X : 2^X = \{\emptyset, \{x_1\}, \{x_2\}, \{x_1, x_2\}\}$. The space $X = \{x_1, x_2\}$ lies at

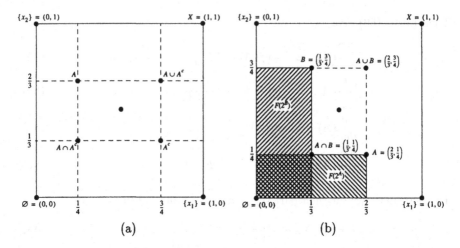

Figure 9: Geometry of discrete fuzzy sets. Sets as points in a unit hypercube or fuzzy cube. Fuzzy set $A \subset X = \{x_1, \ldots, x_n\}$ defines a point in the fuzzy cube $[0, 1]^n$. Here $X = \{x_1, x_2\}$, $A = (\frac{2}{3}, \frac{1}{4})$, and $B = (\frac{1}{3}, \frac{3}{4})$. We define fuzzy-set intersection fitwise with pairwise minimum, union with pairwise maximum, and complementation with order reversal $(a^c(x) = 1 - a(x))$. $F(2^A)$ and $F(2^B)$ define the fuzzy power sets or the sets of of all fuzzy subsets of A and B. Each set $C \subset X$ is a subset of A to some degree and so C belongs to $F(2^A)$ to some degree. C is a 100% subset of A if and only if $c(x) \leq a(x)$ for all $x \in X$. Then $C \in F(2^A)$ and so the set point C lies on or inside the hyper-rectangle $F(2^A)$. Partial subsets lie outside $F(2^A)$.

$(1, 1)$. The empty set $\emptyset$ lies at the origin $(0, 0)$ and the other two (standard) subsets $\{x_1\}$ and $\{x_2\}$ are at $(1, 0)$ and $(0, 1)$. A fuzzy subset $A \subset X$ defines the *fuzzy unit* or *fit* vectors $A = (a_1, a_2) \in I^2$ for $a_1, a_2 \in [0, 1]$. Figure 9a shows an example of a fuzzy set A. The geometrical view reveals the 2^n-fold symmetry of the set A and its set operation products with respect to the midpoint. The midpoint is the maximal fuzzy set. It alone obeys $A = A^c$. The midpoint alone has spherical symmetry and lies equidistant to all 2^n cube vertices.

Figure 9b shows the 2-D cube with the fuzzy sets $A = (\frac{2}{3}, \frac{1}{4})$ and $B = (\frac{1}{3}, \frac{3}{4})$. We can define fuzzy-set intersection fitwise with pairwise minimum, union with pairwise maximum, and complementation with order reversal:

$$a \cap b(x) \quad = \quad \min(a(x), b(x)) \qquad (87)$$
$$a \cup b(x) \quad = \quad \max(a(x), b(x)) \qquad (88)$$
$$a^c(x) \quad = \quad 1 - a(x) \qquad (89)$$

The subsethood theorem [22] measures the degree to which a set A contains in a set B and does so in a simple ratio of cardinalities:

$$S(A, B) \;=\; \text{Degree}(A \subset B) \;=\; \frac{c(A \cap B)}{c(A)} \qquad (90)$$

where c is a *counting* or *cardinality* [22] measure

$$c(A) \;=\; \sum_{x_i \in X} a(x_i) \qquad \text{or} \qquad c(A) \;=\; \int_X a(x)\, dx \qquad (91)$$

for integrable fuzzy set function $a : X \to [0, 1]$. This positive measure stems from the geometric interpretation of the fuzzy power sets $F(2^A)$ and $F(2^B)$ [22, 26]. The subsethood measure extends the histogram intersection in (28). The subsethoods need not be symmetric: $S(A, B) \neq S(B, A)$. So we use a new symmetric measure [26] of fuzzy equality as in (16) :

$$\mathcal{E}(A, B) \;=\; \text{Degree}(A = B) \;=\; \frac{c(A \cap B)}{c(A \cup B)} \qquad (92)$$

$$=\; \frac{S(A, B)\, S(B, A)}{S(A, B) + S(B, A) - S(A, B)\, S(B, A)}. \qquad (93)$$

Then we use the identities $\min(a, b) = \frac{1}{2}(a + b - |a - b|)$ and $\max(a, b) = \frac{1}{2}(a + b + |a - b|)$ to derive (97):

$$\mathcal{E}(A, B) \;=\; \frac{c(A \cap B)}{c(A \cup B)} \;=\; \frac{\displaystyle\int \min(a(x), b(x))\, dx}{\displaystyle\int \max(a(x), b(x))\, dx} \qquad (94)$$

$$=\; \frac{\displaystyle\int a(x) + b(x) - |a(x) - b(x)|\, dx}{\displaystyle\int a(x) + b(x) + |a(x) - b(x)|\, dx} \qquad (95)$$

$$=\; \frac{1 - \dfrac{\int |a(x) - b(x)|\, dx}{\int a(x) + b(x)\, dx}}{1 + \dfrac{\int |a(x) - b(x)|\, dx}{\int a(x) + b(x)\, dx}} \qquad (96)$$

$$=\; \frac{1 - \bar{d}(A, B)}{1 + \bar{d}(A, B)} \qquad (97)$$

where fuzzy set $A \subset R^n$ has set function $a : R^n \to [0, 1]$ and $B \subset R^n$ has set function $b : R^n \to [0, 1]$ and

$$\|A - B\| \;=\; \int |a(x) - b(x)|\, dx \qquad (98)$$

$$\|A + B\| \;=\; \int |a(x) + b(x)|\, dx \qquad (99)$$

$$\text{and} \qquad \bar{d}(A, B) \;=\; \frac{\|A - B\|}{\|A + B\|} \;=\; \frac{\int |a(x) - b(x)| \, dx}{\int |a(x) + b(x)| \, dx} \qquad (100)$$

Sums can replace the integrals in the discrete case.

We next derive a supervised learning law to tune the parameters of the set functions. Square error for a desired matching value D has the form $E = \frac{1}{2}(D - \mathcal{E})^2$. The chain rule gives the derivative of the squared error with respect to the kth parameter of the jth set function m_j^k as

$$\frac{\partial E}{\partial m_j^k} \;=\; \frac{\partial E}{\partial \mathcal{E}} \frac{\partial \mathcal{E}}{\partial \bar{d}} \frac{\partial \bar{d}}{\partial m_j^k} \qquad (101)$$

The derivatives have the form

$$\frac{\partial E}{\partial \mathcal{E}} \;=\; -[\, D(A, B) - \mathcal{E}(A, B) \,] \qquad (102)$$

$$\frac{\partial \mathcal{E}}{\partial \bar{d}} \;=\; -\frac{1 + \mathcal{E}(A, B)}{1 + \bar{d}(A, B)} \qquad (103)$$

$$\frac{\partial \bar{d}}{\partial m_j^k} \;=\; \frac{1}{\|A + B\|} \left(\frac{\partial}{\partial m_j^k} \|A - B\| - \bar{d}(A, B) \frac{\partial}{\partial m_j^k} \|A + B\| \right) \qquad (104)$$

We now derive the derivatives of the "norms" $\|A - B\|$ and $\|A + B\|$ for the discrete sets A and B with respect to the parameter m_j^k in our image matching problems. The result follows from equations (21)-(22) and

$$\bar{d}(A, B) \;=\; \frac{\|A - B\|}{\|A + B\|} \;=\; \frac{\displaystyle\sum_{i=1}^{N} |A(\bar{x}_i) - B(\bar{x}_i)|}{\displaystyle\sum_{i=1}^{N} |A(\bar{x}_i) + B(\bar{x}_i)|} \qquad (105)$$

and the assumption that each set has its own independent parameters (so $\dfrac{\partial a_i}{\partial m_j^k} = 0$ for $i \neq j$) :

$$\frac{\partial}{\partial m_j^k} \|A - B\| \;=\; \frac{\partial}{\partial m_j^k} \sum_{i=1}^{N} |A(\bar{x}_i) - B(\bar{x}_i)| \qquad (106)$$

$$=\; \sum_{i=1}^{N} \text{sign}(A(\bar{x}_i) - B(\bar{x}_i)) \frac{\partial}{\partial m_j^k} (A(\bar{x}_i) - B(\bar{x}_i)) \qquad (107)$$

$$=\; \sum_{i=1}^{N} \left[\text{sign}(A(\bar{x}_i) - B(\bar{x}_i)) \frac{\partial}{\partial m_j^k} \left(\sum_{l=1}^{m} A_l \, a_l(\bar{x}_i) - \sum_{l=1}^{m} B_l \, a_l(\bar{x}_i) \right) \right] \qquad (108)$$

$$=\; \sum_{i=1}^{N} \left[\text{sign}(A(\bar{x}_i) - B(\bar{x}_i)) \frac{\partial}{\partial m_j^k} \left(\sum_{l=1}^{m} a_l(\bar{x}_i) \, (a_l(T_A) - a_l(T_B)) \right) \right] \qquad (109)$$

$$= \sum_{i=1}^{N} \left[\text{sign}(A(\bar{x}_i) - B(\bar{x}_i)) \sum_{l=1}^{m} \left(\frac{\partial}{\partial m_j^k} a_l(\bar{x}_i) (a_l(T_A) - a_l(T_B)) \right) \right] \quad (110)$$

$$= \sum_{i=1}^{N} \text{sign}(A(\bar{x}_i) - B(\bar{x}_i)) \left[[a_j(T_A) - a_j(T_B)] \frac{\partial a_j(\bar{x}_i)}{\partial m_j^k} \right.$$
$$\left. + a_j(\bar{x}_i) \left(\frac{\partial a_j(T_A)}{\partial m_j^k} - \frac{\partial a_j(T_B)}{\partial m_j^k} \right) \right] \quad (111)$$

$$= [a_j(T_A) - a_j(T_B)] \sum_{i=1}^{N} \text{sign}(A(\bar{x}_i) - B(\bar{x}_i)) \frac{\partial a_j(\bar{x}_i)}{\partial m_j^k}$$
$$+ \left(\frac{\partial a_j(T_A)}{\partial m_j^k} - \frac{\partial a_j(T_B)}{\partial m_j^k} \right) \sum_{i=1}^{N} \text{sign}(A(\bar{x}_i) - B(\bar{x}_i)) a_j(\bar{x}_i) \quad (112)$$

The derivation proceeds in like manner for $\frac{\partial}{\partial m_j^k} \|A + B\|$ as

$$\frac{\partial}{\partial m_j^k} \|A + B\| = [a_j(T_A) + a_j(T_B)] \sum_{i=1}^{N} \frac{\partial a_j(\bar{x}_i)}{\partial m_j^k}$$
$$+ \left(\frac{\partial a_j(T_A)}{\partial m_j^k} + \frac{\partial a_j(T_B)}{\partial m_j^k} \right) \sum_{i=1}^{N} a_j(\bar{x}_i) \quad (113)$$

since $a(x) \geq 0$ for all $x \in X$. The condition $a_j(T_A) = \sum_{i=1}^{N} t_A^i a_j(\bar{x}_i)$ and $a_j(T_B) = \sum_{i=1}^{N} t_B^i a_j(\bar{x}_i)$ from (14) gives

$$\frac{\partial a_j}{\partial m_j^k}(T_A) = \sum_{i=1}^{N} t_A^i \frac{\partial a_j}{\partial m_j^k}(\bar{x}_i) \quad (114)$$

$$\frac{\partial a_j}{\partial m_j^k}(T_B) = \sum_{i=1}^{N} t_B^i \frac{\partial a_j}{\partial m_j^k}(\bar{x}_i) \quad (115)$$

Appendix B derives the partial derivatives of the Laplace set function a_j with respect to its two parameters in equations (62)-(63). Then substitute (114)-(115) into (112)-(113) to obtain (104) and substitute (102)-(104) to obtain (101) and the learning law for each parameter in the form of (50):

$$m_j^k(t + 1) = m_j^k(t) - \mu_t \left(D(A, B) - \mathcal{E}(A, B) \right) \frac{1 + \mathcal{E}(A, B)}{1 - \bar{d}(A, B)} \frac{1}{\|A + B\|} \times$$
$$\left[\left(a_j(T_A) - a_j(T_B) \right) \sum_{i=1}^{N} \text{sign}\left(A(\bar{x}_i) - B(\bar{x}_i) \right) \text{sign}(\bar{x}_i - m_j^k) \frac{1}{|d_j^k|} a_j(\bar{x}_i) \right.$$

$$+ \left(\sum_{i=1}^{N} (t_A^i - t_B^i) \operatorname{sign}(\bar{x}_i - m_j^k) \frac{1}{|d_j^k|} a_j(\bar{x}_i) \right) \sum_{i=1}^{N} \operatorname{sign}\left(A(\bar{x}_i) - B(\bar{x}_i) \right) a_j(\bar{x}_i)$$

$$- \bar{d}(A, B) \left((a_j(T_A) - a_j(T_B)) \sum_{i=1}^{N} \operatorname{sign}(\bar{x}_i - m_j^k) \frac{1}{|d_j^k|} a_j(\bar{x}_i) \right.$$

$$\left. + \left(\sum_{i=1}^{N} (t_A^i - t_B^i) \operatorname{sign}(\bar{x}_i - m_j^k) \frac{1}{|d_j^k|} a_j(\bar{x}_i) \right) \sum_{i=1}^{N} a_j(\bar{x}_i) \right) \right] \tag{116}$$

$$d_j^k(t+1) = d_j^k(t) - \mu_t \left(D(A, B) - \mathcal{E}(A, B) \right) \frac{1 + \mathcal{E}(A, B)}{1 - \bar{d}(A, B)} \frac{1}{\|A + B\|} \times$$

$$\left[\left(a_j(T_A) - a_j(T_B) \right) \sum_{i=1}^{N} \operatorname{sign}\left(A(\bar{x}_i) - B(\bar{x}_i) \right) \operatorname{sign}(d_j^k) \frac{|\bar{x}_i - m_j^k|}{|d_j^k|^2} a_j(\bar{x}_i) \right.$$

$$+ \left(\sum_{i=1}^{N} (t_A^i - t_B^i) \operatorname{sign}(d_j^k) \frac{|\bar{x}_i - m_j^k|}{|d_j^k|^2} a_j(\bar{x}_i) \right) \sum_{i=1}^{N} \operatorname{sign}\left(A(\bar{x}_i) - B(\bar{x}_i) \right) a_j(\bar{x}_i)$$

$$- \bar{d}(A, B) \left((a_j(T_A) - a_j(T_B)) \sum_{i=1}^{N} \operatorname{sign}(d_j^k) \frac{|\bar{x}_i - m_j^k|}{|d_j^k|^2} a_j(\bar{x}_i) \right.$$

$$\left. + \left(\sum_{i=1}^{N} (t_A^i - t_B^i) \operatorname{sign}(d_j^k) \frac{|\bar{x}_i - m_j^k|}{|d_j^k|^2} a_j(\bar{x}_i) \right) \sum_{i=1}^{N} a_j(\bar{x}_i) \right) \right]. \tag{117}$$

Neuro Fuzzy Systems for Data Analysis

Stefan Siekmann[1], Ralph Neuneier[1], Hans Georg Zimmermann[1], and
Rudolf Kruse[2]

[1] Siemens AG, Corporate Technology
 D-81730 Munich, Germany
 Stefan.Siekmann@mchp.siemens.de
 Ralph.Neuneier@mchp.siemens.de
 Georg.Zimmermann@mchp.siemens.de
 phone: +49 89-636 44495
[2] Otto-von-Guericke University Magdeburg
 Faculty of Computer Science
 D-39106 Magdeburg, Germany
 phone: +49 391-18 706

Abstract. We present, how neural networks and fuzzy-systems can be combined
to improve or create rules, which consist of linguistic expressions represented by
fuzzy-sets. Due to the fuzzy-component we are able to integrate and extract expert
knowledge. The neural component is used for optimization with historical data by
transforming the rule base into a special neural network architecture. The parameters of these neural network are optimized with gradient descent techniques, which
are combined with a semantic preserving algorithm. Therefore the optimized parameters can be transformed into an improved and still interpretable rule base.
The special architectures enables us to change the form of the fuzzy-sets **and** the
structure of the rule base. For structural optimization we use so called pruning
techniques on premises and rules. Rules can be deleted or changed by deletion
and/or insertion of single premises. Also the creation of semantically correct rules
is possible using this techniques.
 In section 1 and 2 an introduction to neuro-fuzzy-methods in financial data
analysis is given. In chapter 3 different neural network architectures are presented,
which can be applied for optimization of rule based systems. Section 4 shows, how
to optimize a neuro-fuzzy-system using the proposed architectures and the learning
algorithms of neural networks.
 To show the potential of the approach, we build neuro-fuzzy models for prediction of the daily returns of the German Stock Index DAX.
 The presented methods are implemented in the software environment for neural networks SENN of Siemens Nixdorf . A tutorial can be found at the web page
`http://www.sni-usa.com/snat/SENN/tutorial`.

Keywords: neuro-fuzzy, daily prediction of DAX, semantic-preserving
learning algorithm, pruning of rules and premises, rule generation, data
analysis

1 Computing with Words in Finance

We assume, that we have a numerical description of the state of dynamical system by time series observation (e.g. historical data). There are at least two ways to get from this state description to a prediction of the state in future. We can use numerical data to make computations like linear regressions or neural networks. Alternatively, one can use linguistic expressions to represent a state and compute with words. For the latter, the data has to be transformed into a linguistic expression, e.g. '$\Delta dax = +0.1\%$ becomes to "dax = increasing". The next processing step, called "fuzzy inference", computes verbal forecasts using "IF/THEN"-rules. A rule gives a verbal forecast ("dax will increase" or "dax will decrease", etc.) computed by the current input. These verbal forecasts have to be transformed back into a crisp output value (e.g. "$\Delta dax = +0.3\%$"). The process of moving from a numerical description to a numerical forecast by computing with words is illustrated in **figure (1)** and a detailed description of the three steps, fuzzyfication, inference and defuzzification is found in the next sections.

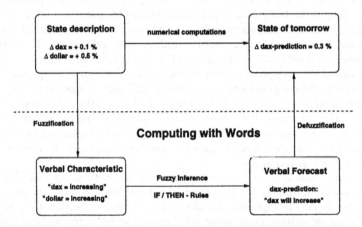

Fig. 1. Numerical Computation and Computing with Words

1.1 Fuzzification

Fuzzification is the transformation of a numerical value to a verbal description. The fuzziness does not mean that the numerical value is not necessary, but the linguistic descriptions are used in a fuzzy way. Linguistic expressions can be represented with fuzzy-sets. For example, a condition like "dax is increasing" can achieve values between 1 and 0, with large values corresponding to a high degree of fulfillness of the condition. If someone says "dax is stable", he does not expect a crisp value of zero but "more or less zero". If the crisp value is zero in fact, then the condition "dax is stable" is fulfilled with the highest degree of membership 1. The more the crisp value differs from zero the lower the degree of membership. A degree of membership of 0 means, that the condition "dax is stable" is not fulfilled.

Local semantics like "zero" can be adequately represented by a Gaussian membership function expressing the linguistic term "more or less zero". Monotonous fuzzy-sets like "increasing" or "positive" may be represented by logistic membership functions. Larger absolute input values corresponds to larger degree of membership. In **figure (2)** three fuzzy-sets are defined for an input variable, using Gaussian and logistic membership functions (see section 9). In the fuzzy literature many other membership functions are discussed, for

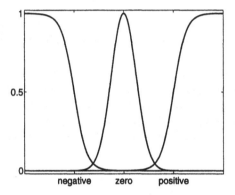

Fig. 2. Combination of logistic and Gaussian membership function.

example triangles or other local linear functions, which are non differentiable. Since we want to apply gradient descent optimization methods they can not be used by the neuro algorithms. Here we focus on differentiable membership functions.

1.2 Inference of Premises and Rules

The output of a rule is typically evaluated using the AND-operator on the degree of membership of its premises. In boolean logic the AND-operator is defined a table. Since fuzzy logic uses real values in the interval [0,1] to quantify the fulfillness of premises, the output of a rule can be determined by

$$\text{degreeOfTruth}(x \text{AND} y) = x * y. \tag{1}$$

Note, that the boolean AND-table is a special case of equation (1). A complete IF/THEN-rule has the form :

$$
\begin{aligned}
\text{IF} \quad & x_1 = eval_1 \\
\text{AND} \quad & x_2 = eval_2 \\
\text{AND} \quad & ... \\
\text{THEN} \ z \ & = eval_z
\end{aligned}
$$

where $eval_i$ may be *increasing*, *stable* or *decreasing*, etc. Evaluation of the membership function of $eval_i$ leads to the degree of fulfillness of the elementary part of the premise. The combined degree of fulfillness of the whole premise is computed by the AND-operator. There are many other possibilities to generalize from boolean logic to fuzzy logic. An example is the min-operator:

$$
\text{degreeOfTruth}(x\text{AND}y) = \min(x, y). \tag{2}
$$

We use differentiable functions to be able to apply the backpropagation algorithm. The product as a generalization of the AND-operator is a successful realization.

An practical way to construct a rule base is to ask an expert (e.g. a person in a trading room of a bank, trader) each day, why the market behaves like it does. The expert may formulate a sentence like "Since the US-dollar exchange rate was stable yesterday and the Dow Jones Index increased yesterday the DAX has increased". This opinion is added to the rule base as follows:

Rule R_i:

IF	Δdow_t	= *increasing*
AND	Δusd_t	= *stable*
THEN	Δdax_{t+1}	= *increasing*

where Δdow_t represents the change of the Dow Jones Index and Δusd_t the change of the US-\$/DM-exchange. Of course, there are many sophisticated and faster methods to generate and initial rule base. In the following, we focus on the optimization of this expert knowledge. If the expert formulates a rule using the OR-operator, this can be realized by breaking this rule into several rules, e.g.:

Rule R_i:

IF	Δdow_t	= *increasing*
OR	Δusd_t	= *increasing*
THEN	Δdax_{t+1}	= *increasing*

will become to:

Rule R_i:

IF	Δdow_t	$= increasing$
THEN	Δdax_{t+1}	$= increasing$

Rule R_{i+1}:

IF	Δusd_t	$= increasing$
THEN	Δdax_{t+1}	$= increasing$

1.3 Defuzzification

In rule systems there are as many linguistic outputs as rules are given. Defuzzification describes the transformation of linguistic outputs to a single output value. The often used "center of singleton"-defuzzifier computes this value by a weighted average of the conclusion with weightings as the normalized activation of the rules. This function is differentiable and this attribute shows the advantages of this defuzzification procedure against other fuzzy approaches. Beside this, the defuzzification procedure harmonize perfectly to the soft-max procedure, which is a well known feature used in neural networks. For details see section 3.

2 From Fuzzy to Neuro-Fuzzy

This section shows, how historical data can be used to improve the expert knowledge and to build good models, which still have the transparency of an expert system.

In recent years neural networks have been applied to the problems of financial analysis. The advantages of using neural networks in contrast to classical methods are established in the possibility to learn from data and in the property, that they approximate well in high dimensional problems. As a disadvantage it is difficult to integrate explicitly expert knowledge about the specific application. On the other hand extracting useful information from an optimized neural network is hard An interesting approach is to combine fuzzy-methods with neural network learning algorithms (e. g. [6], [7]) and to study so called neuro-fuzzy-architectures. The interdependence between neural networks and fuzzy-systems are shown in **figure (3)**.

How can we optimize rules? Two different concepts are possible: first the optimization of the position and shape of fuzzy-sets (parameter optimization) and second the improvement of the rule structure (structural optimization). After optimization the rule R_i may look like the following:

The premise $\Delta dax_t = increasing$ has been added to the rule. Also the form of the fuzzy-sets probably has changed. If the semantic of the fuzzy-sets have changed (e.g. because of noisy or inconsistence data) this can not be examined by observing the rule. **Figure (4)** shows fuzzy-sets after optimization, which semantic is destroyed. The form of the fuzzy-sets must be

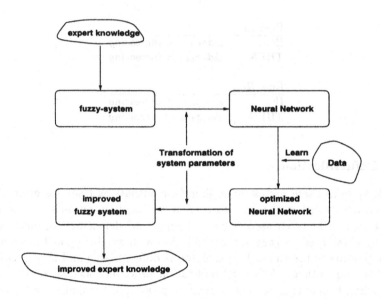

Fig. 3. Combination of fuzzy-systems with neural networks

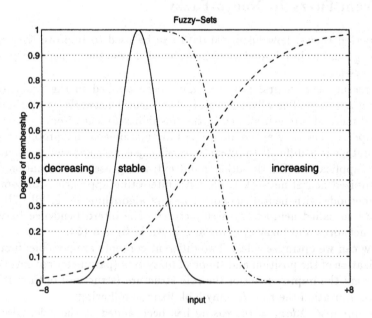

Fig. 4. Fuzzy-sets with wrong semantic

Rule R_i:

IF	Δdow_t	$= increasing$
AND	Δusd_t	$= stable$
AND	Δdax_t	$= increasing$
THEN	Δdax_{t+1}	$= increasing$

checked if the learning algorithm does **not** ensure semantically correctness. But how should the learning algorithm know something about the semantic ? (see section 5). The main problem with straight forward combinations is that typical neuro-fuzzy-systems and adaptive fuzzy-systems destroy their initial rule base during learning. The presented neuro-fuzzy-architectures are combined with a semantic-preserving learning algorithm which ensures that the rules always allow a meaningful interpretation after learning. The user can check which rules remains unchanged in the system and which rules are deleted or changed by the neural network (see above). Applying the optimized system to a specific task, one can observe, which rules are active and is able to explain why the systems predicts something. For example, experts like traders at the stocket exchange can relate their theories to the real data of the financial market by formulating a rule base and observing the rule base during learning. If some rules or premises do not fit the structure in the data, the learning algorithm will delete these elements (see section 4).

A typical problem in the field of data analysis is the overfitting effect because the data is very noisy and often not available to the necessary extent [11]. The integration of expert knowledge into a neural network can be useful to reduce the effect of overfitting and prevent bad generalization (see section 7). Since rules given by an human expert are generally low dimensional and each rule takes only a small number of input variables into account, the resulting architecture of our neuro-fuzzy-system is very sparse. The complexity of the network is further reduced by the mentioned semantic-preserving learning algorithm. The applicability of pruning techniques to delete non relevant or inconsistent premises and rules results in a even smaller number of parameters. This filtering effect is comparable to the learning with noise concept of neural networks [4].

2.1 Neuro-Fuzzy and Genetic Algorithms

In principle the optimization of rule based systems could also be realized by genetic algorithms. We believe, that the connection of neuro-fuzzy is superior to the genetic-fuzzy combination. First, the algorithm has to optimize many continuous parameters (parameters of membership functions or rule weights). The learning algorithms of neural networks (backpropagation) supports this optimization with a lot of gradient information, which is usually ignored by genetic algorithms. The problem of local minima seems to be not so important as in the pure neural modeling, because the neuro-fuzzy-network is initialized with expert rules instead of randomized weights. The optimization of premises or rules seems to be possible with genetic algorithms, but even here the gradient information from the learning algorithms of neural networks allows highly sophisticated optimization methods (see section 6).

2.2 Remarks

Most of the so called neuro-fuzzy-system only use an optimization algorithm based on backpropagation to optimize form and position of fuzzy-sets. Often the rule structure can not be changed by the systems. In most cases the backpropagation algorithm is the only method, which is transformed from neural networks to fuzzy-systems. Therefore the correct name of those systems should be "adaptive fuzzy-systems" because they are not able to apply other useful concepts of neural network like pruning algorithms.

3 Transformation of Fuzzy Systems into Different Neural Network Architectures

3.1 Introduction

The parameters of the fuzzy system (position and form of the fuzzy-sets, conclusions, rule structure) have to be transformed into a neural network. This section describes different neuro-fuzzy-architectures, which can be used to optimize all parameters of the fuzzy-system with the algorithms available for neural networks. For illustration, the rule base shown in **table (1)** will be transformed into the proposed architectures.

Table 1. Initial rule base

Premises		Conclusion
IF dax is stable	AND US-Dollar is decreasing	THEN dax will decrease
IF dax is stable	AND US-Dollar is increasing	THEN dax will increase
IF dax is stable	AND US-Dollar is stable	THEN dax will stable
IF dax is increasing	AND US-Dollar is decreasing	THEN dax will decrease
IF dax is increasing	AND US-Dollar is increasing	THEN dax will increase
IF dax is increasing	AND US-Dollar is stable	THEN dax will increase
IF dax is decreasing	AND US-Dollar is decreasing	THEN dax will decrease
IF dax is decreasing	AND US-Dollar is increasing	THEN dax will increase
IF dax is decreasing	AND US-Dollar is stable	THEN dax will decrease

A detailed description of the definition of fuzzy-sets and constraints is found in section 5.

3.2 The RBF-Architecture

A popular architecture for optimization of a given rule base is the Radial Basis
Function (RBF) network (see for example [8]). This network consists of one
input, one hidden and one output-layer, where each neuron in the hidden-
layer represents a rule of the fuzzy-system (see **figure (5)**). The weights
of the connection between input and hidden-layer contains the parameters
concerning the position and shape of the membership function (fuzzy-sets).
For each rule i the conclusion is transformed into the weight w_i between the
hidden-layer and the output-layer.

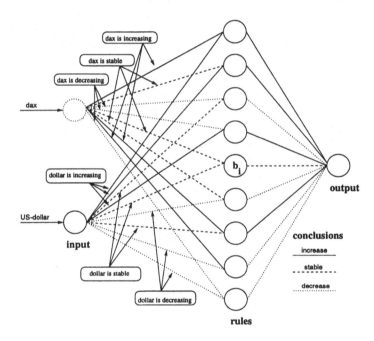

Fig. 5. RBF-architecture initialized with the fuzzy-rule base shown in table 1

Fuzzification: For each membership function m_{ij} the degree of membership
is computed for logistic functions by

$$m_{ij}(x_j) = (1 + \exp(-4s_{ij}(x_j - \mu_{ij})))^{-1}. \tag{3}$$

The parameter μ_{ij} specifies the position of the turning and s_{ij} stands for the
slope at the turning point of a membership function i for input variable j.
For Gaussian membership functions the degree of membership is computed

by

$$m_{ij}(x_j) = \exp\left(-0.5\frac{(x_j - \mu_{ij})^2}{\sigma_{ij}^2}\right). \tag{4}$$

The parameter μ_{ij} specifies the center and the parameter σ_{ij} stands for the width of a Gaussian membership function i for input variable j.

Inference: For each rule i the fulfillness of the conclusion $b_i(\underline{x})$ (rule activity) is computed by

$$b_i(\underline{x}) = \kappa_i \Pi_{j=1}^m m_{ij}(x_j), \tag{5}$$

with R number of rules, m represents the number of membership functions. The parameter κ_i is a rule weight representing a "measure of belief" into the rule i. The positive rule weights κ_i are constrained, that their sum has to be equal to a constant. The constant may be one or equal to the number of rules. The values have to be positive or zero and can be initialized by the expert (user). The weights can be optimized by a constraint learning algorithm to ensure positive values for all κ_i. Only the interrelationship of the rule weights is of interest, not their absolute value. Due to the defuzzification (see equation (7)) the multiplication by a factor has no influence on the output value. In our approach the rule weights are normalized such that its maximum value is equal to one. Neural network used the sum-operator for computation of the input of a neuron, and therefore the AND-operator (equation (1)) is transformed into a sum using natural logarithm and exponential function:

$$b_i(\underline{x}) = \kappa_i \Pi_{j=1}^m m_{ij}(x_j) = \kappa_i \exp\left(\sum_{j=1}^m \ln(m_{ij}(x_j))\right). \tag{6}$$

Defuzzification: The crisp output value of the neural network is computed by

$$y(\underline{x}) = \sum_{i=1}^R w_i \frac{b_i(\underline{x})}{\sum_{i=1}^R b_i(\underline{x})} \tag{7}$$

where $b_i(\underline{x})$ represents the fulfillness of the combined premises of rule i (basis function) on input $\underline{x}$. R is the number of rules. This defuzzification method is called "center of singleton"-method, because only the conclusion weight is needed to compute the crisp output.

Distributed Parameters: The problems within this architecture are established in transformation of the parameters of the membership functions. One can see that for example the membership function *increasing* of the input variable *dax* is stored in three different weights of the neural network (see **figure (5)**), because it is part of different rules. This is a problem during optimization, because the weights belonging to the same membership function may be driven to different values by the learning algorithm. Due to the fact, that these weights belong to the same membership function they have to be treated as an equivalence class. That means, after an adaptations step, the parameters of an equivalence class have to be equal. This can be done by averaging all values of a class. The same problem appears during the optimization of the conclusion weights and can be solved in the same way as above. The complexity of this neural network can be only reduced by deleting rules (resp. hidden neurons). This problem will be discussed in section 4.

The number of free parameters is computed by

$$size = R + 2m + c, \tag{8}$$

where R represents the number of rules, m represents the number of different membership functions (e.g. three per input variable) and c stands for the number of different conclusions (e.g. three). Assuming three fuzzy-sets per input and three different conclusions the number of free parameters is

$$size = R + 6n + 3, \tag{9}$$

with n representing the number of input variables. Equation (8) and (9) are correct only if the mentioned equivalence class concept is used.

If only Gaussian membership functions are used, this network is similar to a RBF neural network, which uses a soft-max on the rule layer ("partitioning to One"). Note, that a RBF neural network does not ensure, that the weights belonging to the same membership function are identical after optimization (equivalent classes). Logistic membership functions can be realized because these functions could be described by the same type of parameters (a mean and a width parameter) used for Gaussian membership functions.

3.3 The 4-Layer Neuro-Fuzzy-Network

This architecture consists of is an additional layer, which each neuron representing a single membership function (see **figure (6)**). The parameters of the membership functions are stored as weights of the connection between the input-layer and the first hidden-layer called "membership function" -layer. In this way the parameter of a membership function are stored only in one weight of the neural network and the problems of the RBF-architecture concerning the different weights for the same membership function parameter are obsolete. Rule weights and conclusions weights are transformed as shown in the RBF architecture. The structure of the rules, that means, which fuzzy-sets are used in a specific rule, is directly seen in the connection between the "membership function"-layer and the "rule"-layer. The weight p_{ij} connects neuron i in the "membership function"-layer and neuron j in the "rule"-layer. A weight $p_{ij} = 1$ indicates, that fuzzy-set j (e.g. "$dax = increasing$") is used in rule i (e.g. IF "$dax = increasing$" THEN "..."). If the weight $p_{ij} = 0$, then the fuzzy-set j is not used in rule i. Only values of 0 and 1 are allowed for p_{ij}. This weights are frozen during the training. The structure of the rule base could be changed by skipping the weights p_{ij} from 0 to 1 (insertion of premise) resp. from 1 to 0 (deletion of premise)

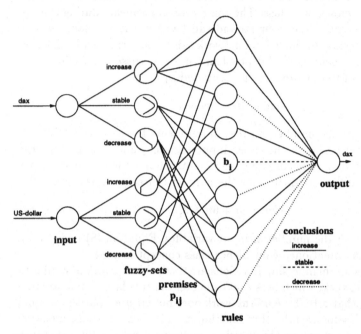

Fig. 6. 4-layer neuro-fuzzy-architecture initialized with the fuzzy-rule base shown in table 1

Fuzzification: The fuzzification is done as for the RBF-architecture (see equation (3)) and (4).

Inference: For each rule i the activity $b_i(\underline{x})$ is computed by

$$b_i(\underline{x}) = \kappa_i \Pi_{j=1}^m m_{ij}(x_j)^{p_{ij}}, \tag{10}$$

where R is the number of rules, m represents the number of membership functions, κ_i represents a rule weight. The weight p_{ij} indicates if fuzzy set j is active ($p_{ij} = 1$) in rule i or not ($p_{ij} = 0$) (see above).

As mentioned above, the AND-operator is realized by using the natural logarithm in the "membership function"-layer and the exponential function in the "rule"-layer. The output of the "membership function"-layer is not equal to the degree of membership for each premise. The AND-operator is transformed into a sum-operator similar to the RBF-architecture (see equation (6)):

$$b_i(\underline{x}) = \kappa_i \Pi_{j=1}^m m_{ij}(x_j)^{p_{ij}} = \kappa_i \exp\left(\sum_{j=1}^m p_{ij} \ln(m_{ij}(x_j))\right). \tag{11}$$

Defuzzification: The crisp output is computed as for the RBF-architecture (see equation (7)).

Another advantage of this architecture is established in the possibility to use so called pruning algorithms for optimizing of the rule structure (see section 4). The number of free parameters is computed as shown for the RBF-architecture.

3.4 The "kappaX" -Network

In this section, the architecture of section 3.3 is extended so that the rule weights depend on some input variables.

Fuzzification: The fuzzification step is done as for the RBF-architecture (see equation (3)) and (4).

Inference: For each rule i the activity $b_i(\underline{x})$ is computed

$$b_i(\underline{x}) = \kappa_i(\underline{x})\Pi_{j=1}^m m_{ij}(x_j)^{p_{ij}}, \tag{12}$$

All variables except $k_i(x)$ are defined as for the 4-layer neuro-fuzzy-architecture. The rule weights $k_i(x)$ are not longer a equal to constant but dependent on the input. The rule weights are calculated by

$$\kappa_i(\underline{x}) = \frac{\exp(f_i(\underline{x}))}{\sum_{j=1}^R \exp(f_j(\underline{x}))}, \tag{13}$$

if rule i exists and

$$\kappa_i(\underline{x}) = 0, \tag{14}$$

if rule i has been deleted (see section 6.2). Additionally

$$f_i(\underline{x}) = \text{NN}(\underline{w_i}, \underline{x}). \tag{15}$$

NN can be linear in its parameters (as shown in **figure (7)**) or a non linear neural network. If $f_i(\underline{x}) \ll f_j(\underline{x})$ then κ_i is very small. The rule weights can depend on the same inputs as the rules, but also on different inputs. The dependence on inputs may be an advantage for some applications. For

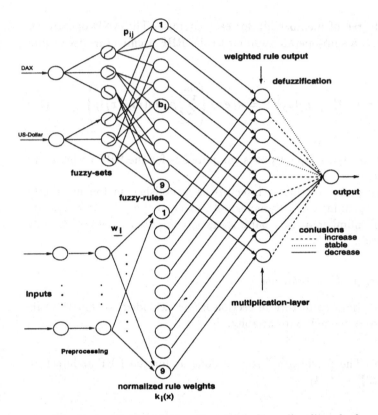

Fig. 7. Architecture with rule weights depending linearly from inputs

example at the stocket market investors sometimes only focuses on the US-market, sometimes on a European stocks. This situations can be captured by an input dependent rule weight. We should have in mind, that even the standard setting

$$b_i(\underline{x}) = \kappa_i \Pi_{j=1}^m m_{ij}(x_j)^{p_{ij}} \tag{16}$$

can be interpreted as a "kappaX" network by

$$b_i(\underline{x}) = \kappa_i \Pi_{j=1}^e m_{ij}(x_j)^{p_{ij}} \Pi_{j=e+1}^m m_{ij}(x_j)^{p_{ij}} \tag{17}$$

The first part of the formula can be understand as an input dependent κ_i'

$$\kappa_i'(\underline{x}) = \kappa_i \Pi_{j=1}^e m_{ij}(x_j)^{p_{ij}}. \tag{18}$$

Some of the membership functions can be interpreted as rule weights combined with a shorter rule description. The realization of rule weights as a separated neural network has the following advantage. In contrast to the logistic and Gaussian membership functions the input dependent rule weights $\kappa_i(\underline{x})$ can create decision lines, which are not parallel to the input dimension.

The "kappaX"-architecture allows a match of the flexibility of a neural network and ability of a neuro-fuzzy-system to integrate and extract expert knowledge. By realizing the rule weights κ as in equation (13) the normalization to a constant and $\kappa_i > 0$ is automatically assured.

Defuzzification: The fuzzification is computed as before (see equation (7)).

Remarks: The parameter vector $\underline{w_i}$, which connects the input-layer and "rule weight"-layer can be optimized by the learning algorithms. Pruning techniques can be used to reduce the overfitting effect. On the one hand, weights can be deleted from the weight vector w_i on the other hand single rules may be deleted by applying pruning techniques to the neurons of the multiplication-layer (see **figure (7)**). The "Preprocessing"-layer may be used to delete single inputs [4]. Assuming NN to be linear the number of free parameters is computed by

$$size = R(n+1) + 2m + c, \tag{19}$$

where the variables are defined as in equation (8).

4 Optimization of Rules Bases with Neural Networks

4.1 Overview

Figure (8) shows, how a neuro-fuzzy-model can be optimized using expert knowledge and historical data. The initialization with expert knowledge and

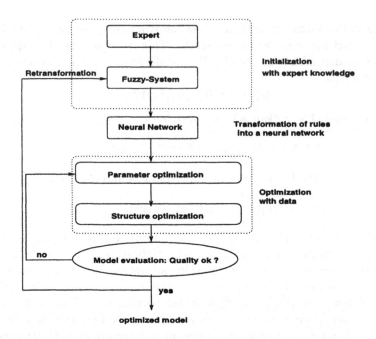

Fig. 8. Optimization of rule based system with neural networks

the transformation of rules into neural network architectures has been described before. In this section, we focus on the optimization with data. The evaluation of models is explained in section 7.6. Note, that there are two different optimization steps (parameter and structural optimization), where most neuro-fuzzy-approaches focuses only on the parameter optimization. Before optimizing parameters we have to define initial values and constraints. This is explained in the following sections.

4.2 Definition of Parameters

As shown in section 3 we use Gaussian and logistic membership functions, which are defined by

$$\text{LOGISTIC}\ (x, \mu, s) = (1 + \exp(-4s(x - \mu)))^{-1},$$

$$\text{GAUSS}\ \ \ \ (x, \mu, \sigma) = \exp\left(-0.5\frac{(x-\mu)^2}{\sigma^2}\right),$$

(20)

where μ determines the center of a Gaussian membership function resp. the position of the turning point of a logistic membership function. The parameter σ represents the width of the Gaussian membership function and s defines the slope at the turning point of a logistic membership function. For example, the fuzzy-sets *increasing, stable* and *decreasing* are usually defined by

$$increasing = \text{LOGISTIC } (x, \mu_{inc}, s_{inc})$$

$$stable \quad = \text{GAUSS} \quad (x, \mu_{sta}, \sigma_{sta}) \tag{21}$$

$$decreasing = \text{LOGISTIC } (x, \mu_{dec}, s_{dec})$$

The actual values of the parameters are determined by analyzing the distribution of the input value (see **figure 9**). Assume that mp represents the

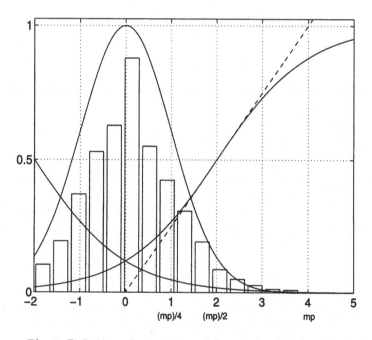

Fig. 9. Definition of parameters of the membership functions

largest possible value of the input variable in the training set and mn defines the lowest possible input value. To ensure, that the fuzzy sets *increasing* resp. *decreasing* become the highest degree of membership for these extreme values and the Gaussian membership functions is not to broad, the parameters μ and σ resp. s can be defined as following:

$$\mu_{sta} = 0,$$

$$\sigma_{sta} = \tfrac{1}{4} \max(mp, |mn|),$$

$$\mu_{inc} = \tfrac{1}{2} mp,$$

$$\mu_{dec} = \tfrac{1}{2} mn,$$
(22)

$$s_{inc} = (mp)^{-1},$$

$$s_{dec} = (mn)^{-1}.$$

The conclusion weights w_i are determined by

$$w_{sta} = 0,$$

$$w_{inc} = mp,$$
(23)

$$w_{dec} = mn,$$

to ensure, that the system can model these extreme values (see equation (7)).

4.3 Unconstraint Parameter Optimization

The set of parameters parameter μ_i and σ_i representing position and shape of the fuzzy-sets, the rule weights κ_i and the conclusion weights w_i can be optimized by a neural network described in section 3. Typical learning algorithms based on gradient descent techniques can be applied. In our experiments, we use "VarioEta" (see [4]). The adaptation step is normally done after computing the gradients using 5 to 30 pattern. Alternatively one can use "Pattern by Pattern" - learning, which adapts the weights after each pattern. The pattern can be presented in chronological order or permutated. A detailed description, how neural networks may be efficiently trained for identification of noisy time series, is found in [4]. As mentioned before, the problem of unconstraint optimization is, that the semantic of the fuzzy sets and rules will probably be changed.

5 Parameter Optimization with Semantic Preserving Learning

To avoid, that the parameters of the membership functions move too far from their original values and destroy the initial semantic (see **figure (4)**), the user can express different types of constraints: equality constraints, constraints within a membership function, order constraints, constraints on premises.

5.1 Equality Constraints

First, one may demand that the parameters of different membership functions have the same value, e. g. belonging to one equivalence class. For example, a rule describing a trend behavior looks like

$$\begin{aligned}
\text{IF} & \quad \Delta dax_{t-1} = increasing_{t-1} \\
\text{AND} & \quad \Delta dax_t \;\; = increasing_t \\
\text{THEN} & \quad \Delta dax_{t+1} = increase
\end{aligned}$$

where Δdax_t measures the relative difference between the last two days of the DAX. Since the fuzzy-sets $increasing_{t-1}$ and $increasing_t$ are used by the same time series, the user may link all parameters of these membership function:

$$increasing_t = increasing_{t-1}. \tag{24}$$

It is also possible to share only some parameters, e.g. the parameter μ:

$$\mu_{increasing_t}^{\Delta dax_t} = \mu_{increasing_{t-1}}^{\Delta dax_{t-1}} \tag{25}$$

Additionally, a parameter may be set constant, e.g.:

$$\mu_{stable}^{\Delta dax_t} = 0. \tag{26}$$

In this case, the center of the Gaussian membership function is set to zero and can not be adapted by the learning algorithm.

5.2 Constraints within a Membership Function

A further reduction of the free degrees of the neural network is possible by using special membership functions, where each membership function has only one parameter:

$$\text{NORMLOG}\,(x, s) = \text{LOGISTIC}\,(x, \tfrac{0.5}{s}, s),$$

$$\text{ZERO} \qquad (x, \sigma) = \text{GAUSS} \qquad (x, 0, \sigma). \tag{27}$$

The parameter μ can not be specified by the user and is set to $\frac{0.5}{s}$, to ensure that the tangent through the turning point cuts the x-axis at zero (see **figure (10)**). For the membership function ZERO the parameter μ is set to zero and can not be adapted by the learning algorithm, to implement the semantic of "stable" or "zero" for normalized inputs. In **figure (10)** fuzzy-sets using different values for the parameter s are displayed. The position of the turning point changes with the parameter s: if s is large (e.g. $s = 0.5$), the position of the turning point is near to zero, if s is small (e.g. $s = 0.125$), the position of the turning is far away from zero.

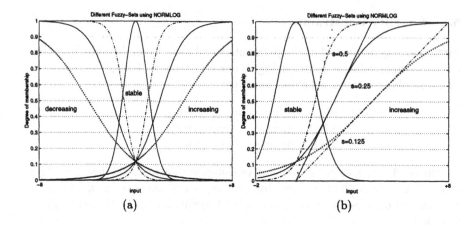

Fig. 10. Fuzzy-sets using ZERO and NORMLOG

5.3 Order Constraints

To ensure an interpretable rule base after optimization and to reduce the free degrees of the neural network, one can define constraints on the parameters of the fuzzy-system. Constraints may be defined on the form of a membership function. The free parameters of a membership function can be bounded by a minimum and a maximum value, e.g. :

$$min_{\mu_{increase}} < \mu_{increase} < max_{\mu_{increase}} \tag{28}$$

For the membership functions GAUSS and LOGISTIC, the relations may be defined by

$$
\begin{aligned}
min_{\sigma_{sta}} < \quad &\sigma_{sta} < max_{\sigma_{sta}}, \\
\mu_{sta} = \quad &0, \\
min_{\mu_{inc}} < \quad &\mu_{inc} < max_{\mu_{inc}}, \\
min_{\mu_{dec}} < \quad &\mu_{dec} < max_{\mu_{dec}}, \\
min_{s_{inc}} < \quad &s_{inc} < max_{s_{inc}}, \\
min_{s_{dec}} < \quad &s_{dec} < max_{s_{dec}},
\end{aligned}
\tag{29}
$$

where

$$max_{s_{inc}} = 2.0\, s_{inc},\ min_{s_{inc}} = 0.5\, s_{inc},$$

$$max_{\mu_{inc}} = 2.0\, \mu_{inc},\ min_{\mu_{inc}} = 0.5\, \mu_{inc},$$

$$min_{s_{dec}} = 2.0\, s_{dec},\ max_{s_{dec}} = 0.5\, s_{dec}, \tag{30}$$

$$max_{\mu_{dec}} = 2.0\, \mu_{dec},\ min_{\mu_{dec}} = 0.5\, \mu_{dec},$$

$$max_{\sigma_{sta}} = 2.0\, \sigma_{sta}.$$

These constraints can be defined independent from each other. Note, that $s_{dec} < 0$ and $s_{inc} > 0$. The parameter $min_{\sigma_{sta}}$ whose controls the minimal width of the Gaussian membership function is not yet defined. We have to define a value for this constraint to guarantee, that the membership function meets the semantic (see **figure (11)**) even if the width approaches its smallest possible value. This value has to be captured by the following two situations. First, it has to be ensured, that the degree of membership of *decreasing* is

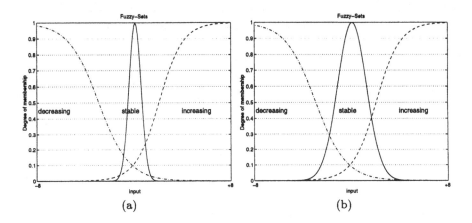

Fig. 11. Fuzzy-sets with wrong (a) and correct semantic(b)

smaller than the degree of membership of *stable* for positive input values. Second, the degree of membership of *increasing* has to be smaller than the degree of membership of *stable* for negative inputs. Assuming, that the membership functions GAUSS and LOGISTIC are defined as in **figure (11b)**, this leads to the following conditions:

$$(1 + \exp(-4max_{s_{dec}}(x - max_{\mu_{dec}})))^{-1} < \exp\left(-0.5(\frac{x - \mu_{sta}}{min_{\sigma_{sta}}})^2\right), \tag{31}$$

where $x > 0$ and

$$(1 + \exp(-4min_{s_{inc}}(x - min_{\mu_{inc}})))^{-1} < \exp\left(-0.5(\frac{x - \mu_{sta}}{min_{\sigma_{sta}}})^2\right) \qquad (32)$$

where $x < 0$. To compute a value for $min_{\sigma_{sta}}$, we set $x = 3min_{\sigma_{sta}}$ resp. $x = -3min_{\sigma_{sta}}$ because on this input the Gaussian membership function is close to zero. This leads to

$$min_{\sigma_{sta}} = \max(bound_{inc}, bound_{dec}), \qquad (33)$$

where

$$bound_{inc} = \frac{1}{3}\left(\frac{1}{4min_{s_{inc}}}\ln(\exp(4.5) - 1) + \mu_{sta} - min_{\mu_{inc}}\right), \qquad (34)$$

and

$$bound_{dec} = \frac{1}{3}\left(\frac{1}{-4max_{s_{dec}}}\ln(\exp(4.5) - 1) - \mu_{sta} + max_{\mu_{dec}}\right). \qquad (35)$$

Using NORMLOG and ZERO as membership functions, we achieve the following value for the minimal width of a Gaussian membership function:

$$min_{\sigma_{sta}} = \max(bound_{inc}, bound_{dec}) \qquad (36)$$

where

$$bound_{inc} = \frac{1}{3}\left(\frac{1}{4min_{s_{inc}}}(\ln(\exp(4.5) - 1) - 2) + \mu_{sta}\right), \qquad (37)$$

and

$$bound_{dec} = \frac{1}{3}\left(\frac{1}{-4max_{s_{dec}}}\ln(\exp(4.5) - 1) - 2) - \mu_{sta}\right). \qquad (38)$$

Note, that $max_{s_{dec}} < 0$ and $min_{s_{inc}} > 0$.

5.4 Remarks

Our experience is, that a narrow Gaussian membership function with a small width parameter as realization of the fuzzy-set *stable* achieves better results than having a Gaussian membership function with large width. Large values for the width parameter lead to a high degree of membership for *all* inputs which intern reduces the extractable information of this fuzzy-set. If constraints are to restrictive the learning algorithm is not able to change the parameters adequately, if the initial definition of the fuzzy sets does not fit to the data.

5.5 Constraints on Premises

Since the initial structure of the rule base can be changed by deletion and insertion of single premises, the user has to define constraints to ensure that the system creates only semantically correct and consistent rules. The consistency can be controlled by the algorithm automatically, while the semantic has to be defined by the user. Two possible examples describe this constraints.

Consistency constraints: Two premises of the same input variable must **not** occur in the same rule, e.g. :

$$
\begin{array}{ll}
\text{IF} & \Delta dax_t = increasing \\
\text{AND} & \Delta dax_t = decreasing \\
\text{THEN} & \Delta dax_{t+1} = increase
\end{array}
$$

The structural optimization of our approach has to take care of this.

Semantic Constraint: The user can define some constraints on the premises to assure application-dependent "correct" rules ("User Constraints"), e.g. :

$$
\begin{array}{ll}
\text{IF} & \Delta usd_t = decreasing \\
\text{THEN NOT} & \Delta dax_{t+1} = increase
\end{array}
$$

That means, that rules predicting an *increasing* DAX by a *decreasing* US-\$/DM-exchange are not allowed. This is a constraint which ensures semantically correctness from the point of view of the expert.

5.6 Constraint Optimization

We describe now, how the semantic-preserving algorithm works: After one training cycle the parameters are changed in a direction computed by the learning algorithm, using gradient information. We have to ensure that the constraints are fulfilled, before the new training cycle starts. In [9], several ways are described to ensure that the initial knowledge is preserved during training. These methods use penalties, stop-training methods or dynamical allocation of additional neurons in order to avoid that the parameters move too far from their original values. Such techniques may lead to situations where the rule base does not meet the semantic. General constraint-optimization methods have the disadvantage that they heavily enlarge the computing time. We solve the constraint by ranking the them and applying a variation of a active set technique [5]. If parameters leave their defined range, they must be corrected. As the correction can lead to a situation where other constraints are not met, the process might have to be iterated. If all constraints can not be solved within a given number of iteration the user is given a warning that the rule base is not consistent with the data. Then one can change the rules or release some constraints. In our experiments the algorithm needs rarely more than one iteration and has always converged.

The semantic-preserving learning algorithm ensures that interpretation after training is always possible and can give useful insights for an improved system understanding. As mentioned in section 2 the constraints reduce the effective number of parameters which intern can avoid overfitting. The premise constraints are used during the structural optimization (see section 6).

6 Structural Optimization

6.1 Motivation

One possibility to achieve models with high generalization performance is to eliminate neurons or parameters which are only approximating the noise in the data. Structural optimization is used to reduce the number of weights and delete rédundant or inconsistent parameters of the neural network. This concept can be applied on the proposed neuro-fuzzy-architectures to delete rules and change the structure of rules by deletion or insertion of single premises.

6.2 Pruning of Rules

We assume, that the RBF-layer or 4-layer architecture is used for optimization. In this case, the positive rule weights κ_i are constrained that their sum has to be equal to a constant (see also section 3). If the learning algorithm increases a rule weight, others have to decrease their values. Ideally, this might lead to automatical elimination of unimportant or inconsistent rules, because these rule weights will driven to zero. Alternatively, the user can prune rules with low κ_i. Thus, after optimization inconsistent rules or rules which do not fit to the data are deleted. Using the "kappaX'-architecture (see section 3.4) the rule weights are computed by the exponential function in combination with the soft-max norm to assure positive and normalized rule weights,

$$\kappa_r' = \frac{\exp(\kappa_r(\underline{x}))}{\sum_{l=1}^{R} \exp(\kappa_l(\underline{x}))}. \tag{39}$$

To delete a single rule r, the neuron r in the "multiplication"-layer has to be removed using so called node-pruning (see **figure (12)**). To test a neuron (rule) r, the difference between the error function of the neural network without neuron r ($\kappa_r' = 0$) and the error function of the neural network with neuron r ($\kappa_r' = 1$) is computed:

$$t_r = \sum_{i=1}^{P} E(NN(\underline{x_i})|\kappa_r' = 0) - \sum_{i=1}^{P} E(NN(\underline{x_i})|\kappa_r' = 1), \tag{40}$$

with P representing the number of patterns on the training set. E() is the error function (e.g. mean squared error, see section 7.6). NN($\underline{x}_i$) represents the output of the neural network NN on input $\underline{x}_i$. Negative test values indicate that these rules are not relevant or inconsistent with the data. Based on these statistics the user can delete some rules, thus reducing the complexity of the neuro-fuzzy-system.

Note, that for each neuron a forward path has to be computed.

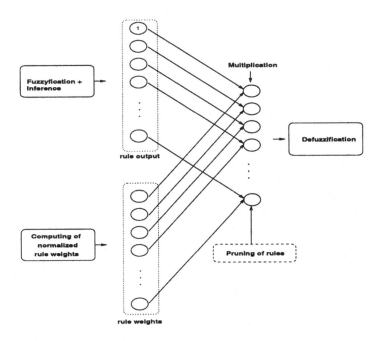

Fig. 12. Pruning rules with standard algorithms

6.3 Pruning Premises with Typical Pruning Algorithms

As mentioned in section 3.3 the advantages of the 4-layer neuro-fuzzy-architecture are established in the possibility to use typical pruning algorithms (**Early-Brain-Damage** EBD-pruning, [10], **Optimal-Brain-Damage**, OBD-pruning [2]) to change the structure of the rule base by deletion of single premises. For each existing premise a test value is computed with low values indicating that these premises are not relevant or inconsistent with the data.

Our experience is, that the EBD-pruning algorithm leads to the best results. EBD approximate the change of the error function, if a weight p_{kj} is deleted:

$$t_{kj} \approx \sum_{i=1}^{P} \mathrm{E}(\mathrm{NN}(\underline{x_i})|p_{kj} = 0) - \sum_{i=1}^{P} \mathrm{E}(\mathrm{NN}(\underline{x_i})|p_{kj} = 1), \qquad (41)$$

where the variables are defined as before. Low values indicate, that p_{kj} can be deleted. Note, that only one forward path is necessary to compute this test value.

6.4   The "WorstPerRule" Pruning Technique

For each premise a test value is computed, which answers the question: "Which premise has to be deleted from this rule, to get the most error reduction of the system?" The test values are ranked and the premises with the smallest test value can be deleted from the rule. The test value for deletion of the "worst" premise i for each rule j is computed by :

$$t_j^{del} = \min_{i=1,..,\mathrm{mfs}} \left(\sum_{t=1}^{P} \mathrm{E}(\mathrm{NN}(\underline{x_t})|p_{ij} = 0) - \sum_{t=1}^{P} \mathrm{E}(\mathrm{NN}(\underline{x_t})|p_{ij} = 1) \right), \qquad (42)$$

where $E()$ is the error function or another cost function, mfs is the number of membership functions, P represents the number of patterns. $\mathrm{NN}(\underline{x})$ is the output of the model on input vector $\underline{x}$.

If $t_j^{del} <= 0$ an error reduction is possible and premise i will be deleted ($p_{ij} = 0$). This test must be done for each rule, which has not been deleted. One can iterate deletion of premises and training with the semantic-preserving learning algorithm until a sufficient performance is achieved (see section 6.5).

Using the semantic-preserving learning algorithm for optimization of parameters and the pruning methods for reducing the complexity of the system, we implicitly assume, that the structure of the rule base defined by the expert is correct and complete, e.g. all situations, which occur in the data can be described by the rules. In practice the initial rule base may be not complete or wrong and the rule structure must be changed by insertion of premises to create new rules.

6.5   Rule Generation with Typical Pruning Algorithms

We assume, that an expert has defined the fuzzy-sets for each input variable (e. g. 3) and the singletons for the output variable. Since expert knowledge is available, an initial rule base and premise constraints may be formulated. If no expert knowledge except the fuzzy-sets is available the algorithm has to start with all possible rules or with a (randomized) subset of this, where the number of premises have to be restricted (e.g. 2 or 3 per rule) and surplus premises are deleted. Additionally, the consistency and the user constraints must be checked (see section 5.5). Now, test values for each premise using typical pruning algorithm are computed to create new rules or to change rules. Existing premises with low test values are deleted and non active premises with low test values are inserted. After pruning, the parameters of the system can be trained using the semantic-preserving learning algorithm. Pruning and training have to be iterated. The rule generation is complete, if the system error or the system performance achieved a defined value. Note, that only pruning algorithms can be applied, which allow insertion of weights, e.g. EBD-pruning.

6.6 Rule Generation with "BestPerRule"-Algorithm

The initialization of the fuzzy sets and rules and the constraint check is done as described in section 6.5.

To create new rules or change existing rules, it is necessary to compute test values to delete **and** insert premises for a each rule. The test values are ranked and the premises with the smallest test value can be inserted into the rule resp. deleted from the rule. The algorithm works by iteration of two different steps: the "deletion"-step and the "insertion"-step, which are described now.

The "deletion" - step: For the "deletion"- step the algorithm computes a test value for each existing premise ($p_{ij} = 1$) of each rule. The algorithm returns a lists of test values, with a negative value indicating an improvement of the error function. The premise which leads to the most error reduction ("worst" premise) is deleted from the rule. If all test values are positive there is no improvement possible by deletion of a premise and the rule will not be changed. The test value for deletion of the "worst" premise i for each rule j is computed by:

$$t_j^{del} = \min_{i=1,..,\mathrm{mfs}} \left(\sum_{t=1}^{P} \mathrm{E}(\mathrm{NN}(\underline{x_t})|p_{ij} = 0) - \sum_{t=1}^{P} \mathrm{E}(\mathrm{NN}(\underline{x_t})|p_{ij} = 1) \right), \quad (43)$$

where $E()$ is the error function, mfs is the number of membership functions, P represents the number of patterns. $\mathrm{NN}(\underline{x})$ is the output of the model on input vector $\underline{x}$.

The "insertion"-step: The "insertion"-step works similar to the "deletion"-step. The algorithms returns a lists of test values for all non active premises ($p_{ij} = 0$). A negative test value indicates an improvement of the error function if the premise is inserted into the rule. The premise leading to the most error reduction ("best" premise) is inserted. If all test values are positive, no improvement is possible by insertion of a premise and the rule is not changed.

The test value for insertion of the "best" premise i for each rule j is computed by:

$$t_j^{ins} = \min_{i=1,..,\text{mfs}} \left(\sum_{t=1}^{P} \text{E}(\text{NN}(\underline{x})|p_{ij} = 1) - \sum_{t=1}^{P} \text{E}(\text{NN}(\underline{x})|p_{ij} = 0) \right). \quad (44)$$

If $t_j^{ins} <= 0$ then the premise i has to be inserted($p_{ij} = 1$).

Note, that a previously deleted premises could be inserted by an "insertion" - step.

If the "deletion"-step and the "insertion"-step do not change the rule base the algorithm has converged. The algorithm achieves a local minimum, because each action reduces the error of the system. Alternatively the user can stop the algorithm, if the performance is convenient. It is also possible to train the parameters of the system between an "insertion" and a "deletion" - step using the semantic-preserving learning algorithm. If the initial rule base consists only of a small number of premises per rule, (e. g. $<= 2$), we usually starts with the "insertion" - step.

Note, that the constraints are still active. Therefore the algorithms can create only semantically correct rules. A further error reduction is possible while optimizing the parameters of the membership functions by the semantic-preserving learning algorithm.

6.7 Remarks

The rule generation using typical (inexpensive) pruning techniques like EBD works better if the dimension of the problem is extremely high or there are many patterns, because it is only one forward path necessary to compute test values for the premises. The "bestPerRule"-algorithm can be used for problems, where the number of patterns is small. To overcome this problem, one can divide the pattern set into subsets and compute test values only on this subsets. Also only a subset of the rule base can be used for computation of test values for the premises, because the expert (user) do not want to change the structure of the other rules.

7 Experiments with Real Data

7.1 Overview

In this section some simulations using real data (DAX) are presented. First some technical indicators are described, from which the inputs of the neuro-fuzzy-model are derived. Then the description of input variables and the definition of the initial rule base is given. The behavior of the semantic preserving learning algorithm is shown. The last section shows encouraging results on the task to predict the daily returns of the German Stock index DAX.

7.2 The German Stock Index DAX

The recently growing dynamics of the international stock markets has made portfolios consisting of such assets more attractive than bonds or other investments. In this article, we focus on the German stock index DAX because the 30 companies forming the index are responsible for about 70% of the turnover at the stock market in Frankfurt. Since the DAX is a weighted mixture of stocks it behaves like a real portfolio. The task is to predict the daily returns (relative differences) of the DAX using only technical indicators computed from the DAX time series and the US-$/DM-exchange rate.

7.3 Technical Indicators

In this section some technical indicators are described. The inputs are derived from this. See also [6].

The **Moving Average** over the last n days is computed by

$$\text{MA}_t(x, n) = \frac{1}{n} \sum_{k=t-n+1}^{t} x_k, t = n, ..., T \tag{45}$$

where x_k represents the time series at time step k. T represents the number of all patterns. If $x_t > \text{MA}(x, n)$ then prediction is *increase*, ($target_{t+1} > 0$), if $x_t < \text{MA}(x, n)$ then prediction is *decrease* ($target_{t+1} < 0$).

The **Momentum** is computed by

$$\text{MOM}_t(x, n) = x_t - x_{t-n}. \tag{46}$$

if $\text{MOM}_t(x, n) > 0$ (*increasing*) then prediction is increase, otherwise the prediction is *decrease*.

The **Relative Strength Index** is calculated by

$$\text{RSI}_t(x, n) = \frac{\sum profit_n(x)}{\sum loss_n(x) + \sum profit_n(x)}, \tag{47}$$

where $profit_n(x)$ represents the sum of all positive returns at the last n days and $loss_n$ stands for the sum of all negative returns at the last n days, beginning at time step t. The values lie between 0 and 1.0. If $\text{RSI}_t(x, n) > 0.7$ then market is *overbought* and the prediction is *decrease*. If $\text{RSI}_t(x, n) < 0.3$ then the market is *oversold* and the prediction is *increase*.

Additionally one can compute the **K-Stochastic** and the **D-Stochastic** by

$$\text{Stochastic}_t^{Kn}(x) = \frac{x_t - max(x_t, n)}{max(x_t, n) - min(x_t, n)} * 100 \tag{48}$$

$$\text{Stochastic}_t^{Dn}(x) = \frac{1}{n} \sum_{k=t-n+1}^{t} \text{Stochastic}_k^{Kn}(x), \tag{49}$$

where the function $max(x_t, n)$ or $min(x_t, n)$ returns the maximum or the minimum value, respectively, of the time series x beginning at time step t. If Stochastic(x) ¡ 0.7, then the market is *overbought* and the predition is *decrease*. If Stochastic(x) ¡ 0.3, then the market is *oversold* and the prediction is *increase*.

7.4 Input Time Series

In this section the 12 input variables of the model are explained.

Table 2. Inputs at time step t.

input	description
Δdax_t	$(\frac{dax_t}{dax_{t-1}} - 1)$
diffaver_t^5	$dax_t - MA_t(dax, 5)$
diffaver_t^{10}	$dax_t - MA_t(dax, 10)$
$\Delta \text{momentum}_t^5$	$MOM_t(dax, 5) - MOM_{t-1}(dax, 5)$
$\Delta \text{momentum}_t^{10}$	$MOM_t(dax, 10) - MOM_{t-1}(dax, 10)$
$RSI_t(dax, 5)$	see above
$RSI_t(dax, 10)$	see above
$\text{Stochastic}_t^{k5}(dax)$	see above
$\text{Stochastic}_t^{k10}(dax)$	see above
$\text{Stochastic}_t^{d5}(dax)$	see above
$\text{Stochastic}_t^{d10}(dax)$	see above
Δusd_t	$(\frac{usd_t}{usd_{t-1}} - 1)$

7.5 The Initial Rule Base

For each input variable of **table (2)** three fuzzy-sets are defined: *decreasing*, *stable* and *increasing* resp. *oversold*, *normal* and *overbought*. Only the fuzzy-set *stable* resp. *normal* is realized by a Gaussian membership function, the others by logistic membership functions. The parameters of the membership functions are defined by analyzing the distributions of the variables as shown in section 9. The center of the fuzzy-set *stable* is set to zero and could not be adapted. As an example the membership functions of the input variable Δdax and the distribution of input data are displayed in **figure (13)**.

$$decreasing : m_{ij}(x_j) = (1 + \exp\left(-4(-0.25)(x_j + 2.0)\right))^{-1}$$

$$stable \quad : m_{ij}(x_j) = \exp\left(-0.5x_j^2\right) \tag{50}$$

$$increasing : m_{ij}(x_j) = (1 + \exp\left(-4(0.25)(x_j - 2.0)\right))^{-1}$$

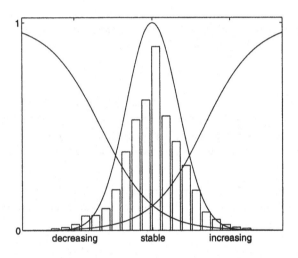

Fig. 13. Membership function with histogram of the input variable DAX

By relating the input Δdax_t to each of 10 technical indicators and the input Δusd_t using all combination of the fuzzy-sets $99 = 9 * 11$ rules are constructed. Note, that only pairwise correlations are used. The rules are constructed according assumed structural relationships (for details, see [3]). An subsection of this rule base can be found in section 3.

7.6 Performance Measurements

Some measurements are presented which are usually computed for evaluation of models for time series prediction. T represents the number of predicted patterns on test set.

The Mean Squared Error: The accuracy of models can be valuate by the mean squared error

$$mse = 0.5\frac{1}{T}\sum_{t=1}^{T}(output_t - target_t)^2, \tag{51}$$

where $output_t$ is the output of the model on pattern t and $target_t$ is the demanded value. To predict the behavior of a time series like the DAX using a neuro-fuzzy-system NF, $target_t$ and $output_t$ can be defined by

$$target_t = \frac{dax_{t+1}}{dax_t} - 1 \text{ or } target_t = \ln(\frac{dax_{t+1}}{dax_t}),$$
$$output_t = NF(\underline{x_t}). \tag{52}$$

Mean Squared Error and the Model Size: Another measurement for evaluation of models is the following criteria:

$$crit = N\log(mse) + kp, \tag{53}$$

where N represents the number of patterns and p is model size (see section 3). This measurement selects a model with low mean squared error and small model size. k controls the relation between model error and model size (e.g. $k = 2$). The lower $crit$ the better the model. For more information see [1].

Return On Invest: The performance of models can be compared by computing the return on invest (roi). This curve measures the return of a trading system by

$$roi = \sum_{t=1}^{T}(\frac{dax_{t+1}}{dax_t} - 1) * \text{sign}(NF(\underline{x_t})) \tag{54}$$

where $\text{sign}(NN(\underline{x_t}))$ is the predicted direction of the DAX. roi increases if the predicted direction is correct, otherwise it decreases. A value $roi = 1.0$ is equal to a return of invest of 100 %. The annualized return on invest ($aroi_{td}$) is computed by

$$aroi_{td} = \frac{td}{T} * roi. \tag{55}$$

where td represents the trading days per year (e.g. $td = 260$).

Hit Rate: The hit rate ($hitrate$) measures, how often the sign of the change of the DAX (*increase* or *decrease*) is correctly predicted:

$$hitrate = \frac{1}{T}\sum_{t=1}^{T}\text{sign}(\frac{dax_{t+1}}{dax_t} - 1) * \text{sign}(NF(\underline{x_t})) \tag{56}$$

7.7 Experiment 1: Semantic Preserving Learning

After initializing the neuro-fuzzy-architecture (4-layer) with the rules the network is trained with a backpropagation based learning algorithm (e.g. "VarioEta", see [4]).

The partitioning of the data in training, cross-validation, and test set is shown in **table (3)**. The cross-validation set is not used for training of the system, but gives a hint when to stop training [11]. If the error on this portion of the data starts to increase we usually stop training and try to reduce the complexity of the network by pruning. Afterwards we train again until the next increase of the error.

Table 3. Partitioning of the data.

Set	Start	End	Number of patterns
Training	1994/01/01	1995/31/95	509
Cross-Validation (CV)	1996/01/01	1996/12/31	262
Test	1997/01/01	1997/08/97	163

In **figure (14)** the behavior of the mean squared error is shown up to the 200th epoch without the semantic preserving learning algorithm. In **figure (15)** the behavior of the return on invest curve is shown. In **figure (14a)**

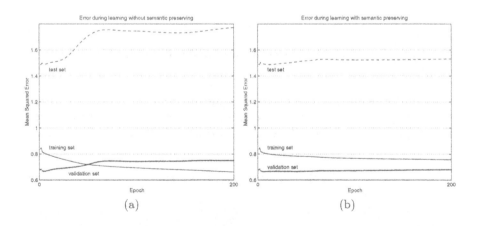

(a)   (b)

Fig. 14. Mean Squared Error without (a) and with (b) semantic preserving learning

one can observe, that the error on validation and test set starts to increase immediately if the learning algorithm do not use semantic preserving. The error on training set using normal backpropagation is lower than the error on training set using semantic-preserving (see **figure (14b)**). This is an additional hint for overlearning without semantic preserving. These effect can be also seen by observing the return On Invest curves. The model trained with normal learning algorithm achieved a higher return on invest on training set but on validation and test set the model using semantic-preserving learning is superior (see **figure (15)**).

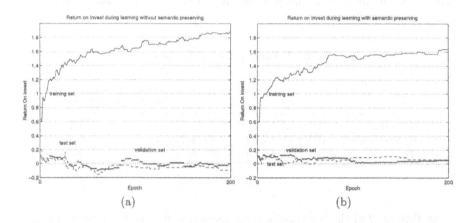

Fig. 15. Return on invest without (a) and with (b) semantic preserving learning

7.8   Experiment 2: Daily Prediction of the German Stock Index DAX

In this section the results of a neuro-fuzzy model predicting the daily returns of the German stock index DAX are presented. This model was constructed using the partitioning of the data shown in **table (4)**. The optimization was

Table 4. Partitioning of the data.

Set	Start	End	Number of patterns
Training	1986/01/16	1993/02/26	1856
Cross-Validation (CV)	1993/03/01	1994/02/26	261
Test	1994/03/01	1997/09/22	929

done by iterating training ("VarioEta") and EBD-Pruning on the premises as described in section 6.

To evaluate the resulting neuro-fuzzy-models we construct a trading strategy going long if the network prediction is positive and selling short if the prediction is negative.

Benchmarks: The benchmarks which are used to compare the performance are the following trading systems respectively models:

- **Buy&Hold:** buy the DAX at the beginning of the test set and sell it at the end. This strategy assumes an efficient capital market which does not allow excess return because the conditional expectation of the returns are zero. The Buy&Hold strategy gains only by exploiting the market trend.
- **naive prediction:** buy or hold the DAX if the last difference is positive and sell otherwise. The naive prediction assumes that the market behaves like a random walk.

Results: The presented model was constructed in October 1995, where test set and validation set had similar sizes. From time to time we added new data to the test set and since March 1997, we tested the model in reality on online prediction. The optimized model consists of 64 rules, the others has been deleted by rule pruning resp. premise pruning. In **figure (16)** the return on invest curves of the neuro-fuzzy model and the benchmarks on test set are shown. Especially at the end of the test set, where the market is decreasing with high volatility, the model performance is very encouraging, especially because the model only takes two input time series into account. In **figure (17)** the output-target curves of the neuro-fuzzy model in 1997 are shown. In **table (5)** the return on invest on test set is presented. Note, that this model is always interpretable due to the semantic preserving learning algorithm.

Table 5. Results.

Model	roi in %		$aroi_{260}$ in %	
naive prediction	+0.126	12, 6	+0.035	3, 5
Buy & Hold	+0.712	71, 2	+0.199	19, 9
Neuro-fuzzy	+1.281	128, 1	+0.358	35, 8

We divide the test set into four subsections and compute the return on invest on each subset (see **table (6)**). The variable roi_i represents the return on invest on test set i. Note that $\sum roi_i = roi$. The neuro-fuzzy model is always better than the benchmarks.

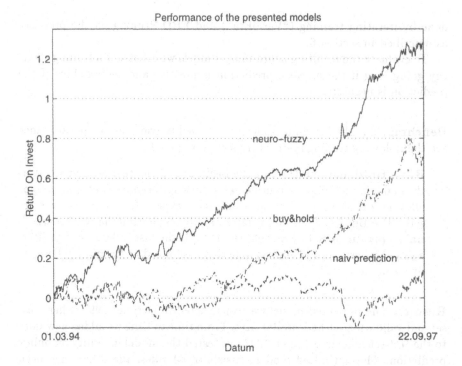

Fig. 16. The *roi*-curves of different models.

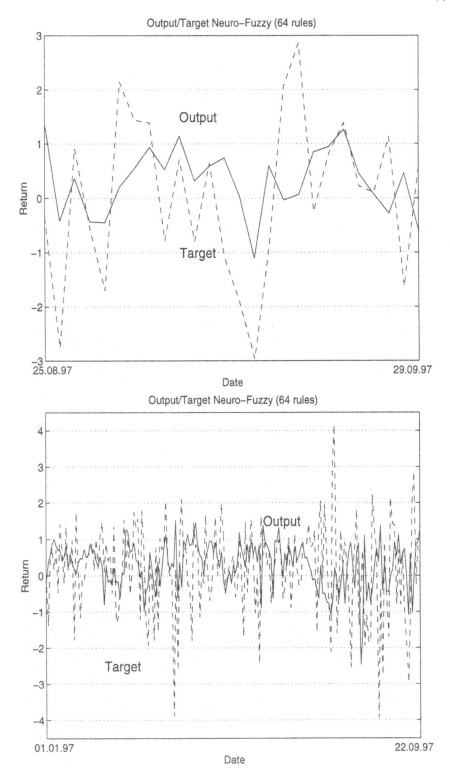

Fig. 17. Output-target curves of the neuro-fuzzy model.

Table 6. Results on divided test set.

Model	roi_1	roi_2	roi_3	roi_4
naive prediction	-0.047	+0.100	+0.016	+0.058
Buy & Hold	+0.022	+0.092	+0.170	+0.427
Neuro-fuzzy	+0.204	+0.298	+0.213	+0.566

Analysis of some optimized rules: Since we use a semantic preserving learning algorithms an interpretation of the system is possible. In **table (7)** a subset of the optimized rule base is presented. The response rate of a rule is computed by

$$response = \sum_{i=1}^{P} b_i(\underline{x}), \tag{57}$$

where P represents the number of patterns on training set and $b_i(\underline{x})$ is the rule activity. Rules with low response rate are only active on a small number of input patterns. That does not mean, that the rules must have a low rule weight (e.g. rule 43 and rule 44). Simple rules normally have a higher response rate than rules, which are complicated. Rule 52 is an example for a simple rule with large response rate. Rules with a low response may represent a situation, which rarely captured in the data ("Black Friday", etc.), but for which an expert can define rules. A neural network ignores such patterns and handle this situations as outliers, which are not be modeled.

Rule 52 can be interpreted as a rule for the inflation, because the market has an increasing trend. This rule achieved the highest weighting (1) and a high response rate. Rule 19 may be deleted from the rule base, because it has a low rule weight and relative small response rate.

8   Conclusions

It was shown in this article that neuro-fuzzy approaches are able to build interpretable models for data analysis (e.g. time series prediction). The models have used linguistic rules which can be formulated by expert and understand by persons without mathematically background, which is necessary for data analysis using regressions. It is possible to use knowledge of people, who are experts in the field of (e.g. traders) but no expert in statistics. Computing with words combined with the ability of neural networks to learn from data is an approach, with will come more and more important in time series prediction and asset management. Our experience is, that many people (e.g. banker, trader) would apply neural networks to time series prediction, but have problems with the "Black Box" behavior. The combination with fuzzy-

Table 7. Some rules of the optimized neuro-fuzzy-system.

Rule R_{19}:

IF	Δdax_t	=	*decreasing*
AND	$\Delta MOM_t(5)$	=	*stable*
THEN	Δdax_{t+1}	=	*decrease*
WEIGHTING 0.0869		RESPONSE 11.96	

Rule R_{43}:

IF	Δdax_t	=	*stable*
AND	$\Delta RSI_t(10)$	=	*overbought*
THEN	Δdax_{t+1}	=	*decrease*
WEIGHTING 0.4763		RESPONSE 0.17	

Rule R_{44}:

IF	Δdax_t	=	*stable*
AND	$\Delta RSI_t(10)$	=	*oversold*
THEN	Δdax_{t+1}	=	*increase*
WEIGHTING 0.2447		RESPONSE 508.79	

Rule R_{52}:

IF	Δdax_t	=	*increasing*
THEN	Δdax_{t+1}	=	*increase*
WEIGHTING 1.000		RESPONSE 414.01	

systems solve many problems concerning the "Black-Box" - critic and leads to more confidence.

References

1. Kevin Martin Bossley. *Neurofuzzy Approaches in System Identification.* PhD thesis, University of Southampton, may 1997. PhD thesis.
2. Y.le Cun, J.S.Denker, and S.A.Solla. Optimal brain damage. In *Advances in Neural Information Processing Systems, NIPS'89*, volume 2, pages 589–605. Morgan Kaufmann, San Mateo, CA, march 1990.
3. Hubert Dichtl. *Zur Prognose des Deutschen Aktienindex DAX mit Hilfe von Neuro-Fuzzy-Systemen.* Institut für Kapitalmarktforschung, J. W. Goethe-Universität, Frankfurt, 1995.
4. Ralph Neuneier and Hans Georg Zimmermann. How to train neural networks. In *Tricks of the Trade: How to make algorithms really to work.* Springer Verlag, Berlin, 1998.
5. P.E.Gill, W.Murray, and M.H.Wright. *Practical Optimization.* Academic Press, 1981.

6. S.Siekmann, R.Kruse, R.Neuneier, and H.G.Zimmermann. Neuro-fuzzy methods in financial engineering. In R. Ribeiro, H.-J. Zimmermann, R.R. Yager, and J. Kacprzyk, editors, *Softcomputing in Financial Engineering*. Physica-Verlag,Springer, 1998. to appear.

7. Detlef Nauck und Frank Klawonn und Rudolf Kruse. *Foundations of Neuro-Fuzzy-Systems*. Wiley & Sons, 1997. to appear.

8. R.Neuneier und V.Tresp. Radiale basisfunktionen, dichteschätzungen und neuro-fuzzy. In H. Rehkugler and H. G. Zimmermann, editors, *Neuronale Netze in der Ökonomie*. Verlag Franz Vahlen, 1994.

9. V.Tresp, J.Hollatz, and S.Ahmad. Network structuring and training using rule-based knowledge. In S.J.Hanson, J.D.Cowan, and C.L.Giles, editors, *Advances in Neural Information Processing Systems*, volume 5. 1993.

10. V.Tresp, R.Neuneier, and H.G.Zimmermann. Early brain damage. In *Advances in Neural Information*, 1996. In Proc. of NIPS'96.

11. W.Finnoff, F.Hergert, and H.G.Zimmermann. Improving generalization by non-convergent model selection methods. *Neural Networks*, 6, 1992.

A NEW FUZZY INFERENCE SYSTEM BASED ON ARTIFICIAL NEURAL NETWORK AND ITS APPLICATIONS

J. Łęski and E. Czogała
Institute of Electronics, Technical University of Silesia
Akademicka 16, 44-101 Gliwice, Poland
e-mail: jl@biomed.iele.polsl.gliwice.pl

Abstract. In this paper a new artificial neural network based fuzzy inference system (ANNBFIS) has been described. The novelty of the system consists in the moving fuzzy consequent in if-then rules. The location of this fuzzy set is determined by a linear combination of system inputs. This system also automatically generates rules from numerical data. The proposed system operates with Gaussian membership functions in premise part. Parameter estimation has been made by connection of both gradient and least squares methods. For initialization of unknown parameter values of premises, a preliminary fuzzy c-means clustering method has been employed. For cluster validity Xie-Beni, Fukujama-Sugeno and our new indexes have been applied. The applications to the design of a classifier are considered in this paper as well. The method of classifier construction for two classes and an extension for a greater number of classes has been presented. The selection method of target values for classifier outputs minimizing number of false classifications is also presented. The applications to prediction of chaotic time series, pattern recognition and system identification are considered in this paper. The tests of the ANNBFIS are carried out on the basis of the data bases known from literature: Mackey-Glass chaotic time series, Anderson's iris and MONKS classification problems, Box-Jenkins data from the gas oven.
Keywords: Fuzzy system, Automatic rule generation, Neuro-fuzzy modeling.

1. Introduction

In literature several methods of automatic fuzzy rule generation from given numerical data have been described [3,5,6,7,10]. The simplest method of rule generation is based on a clustering algorithm and estimation of proper fuzzy relations from a set of numerical data. Kosko's fuzzy associative memory (FAM) [10] can store such fuzzy relations and process fuzzy inference simultaneously. This approach, however, causes some difficulties because of conflicts appearing among the generated rules.

Wang et al. [17] proposed a method for generating fuzzy rules from numerical data without conflicting rules. However, they used too many heuristic procedures and a trial-and-error choice of membership functions.

Another type of methods which use the learning capability of neural networks and the fact that both fuzzy systems and neural nets are universal approximators, has been successfully applied to various tasks. The problem here is the difficulty in understanding the identified fuzzy rules since they are implicitly acquired into the network itself.

Mitra et al. [12] have proposed a fuzzy multilayer perceptron generating fuzzy rules from the connection weights. Several methods of extracting rules from the given data are based on a class of radial basis function networks (RBFNs). The fact that there is a functional equivalence between RBFNs and the fuzzy system has been used by Jang et al. [6] to construct Sugeno type of adaptive network based fuzzy inference system (ANFIS) which is trained by the back propagation algorithm. More general fuzzy reasoning schemes in ANFIS are employed by Horikawa et al. [5]. Such developed radial basis function based adaptive fuzzy systems have been described by Cho and Wang [3] and applied to system identification and prediction. The paper [9] presents a fuzzy C-regression model used for automatic generation of if-then rules.

The aim of this paper is the theoretical description and structure presentation of a new artificial neural network based fuzzy inference system ANNBFIS. The novelty of the system consists in the introduction of the moving fuzzy consequent in if-then rules. The described system is applied to prediction, pattern recognition and identification problems.

The paper is organized as follows: some introductory remarks and the main goal of the paper are formulated in section 1. Section 2 introduces the basics of fuzzy systems. In section 3 the structure of ANNBFIS and the adaptation of the parameters are shown. In section 4 the method of target values for classifier outputs minimizing the number of false classifications is presented. Section 5 illustrates the theoretical considerations by means of application of the system to the chaotic time series prediction, pattern recognition and system identification problems. Finally, concluding remarks are gathered in section 6.

2. Fundamentals of fuzzy systems

In approximate reasoning realized in fuzzy systems the if-then fuzzy rules or fuzzy conditional statements play an essential and up to now the most important role. Often they are also used to capture the human ability to make a decision or control in an uncertain and imprecise environment. In this section we will use such fuzzy rules to recall the important approximate reasoning methods which are basic in our further considerations.

Assume that m numbers of n-input and one-output (MISO) fuzzy implicative rules or fuzzy conditional statements are given. The i-th rule may be written in the following forms:

$$R^{(i)}: \ if \ X_1 \ is \ A_1^{(i)} \ and...and \ X_n \ is \ A_n^{(i)} \ then \ Y = f^{(i)}(X_1,...X_n) \qquad (1)$$

or in a pseudo-vector notation

$$R^{(i)}: \ if \ X \ is \ A^{(i)} \ then \ Y = f^{(i)}(X) \qquad (2)$$

where:

$$X = [X \ \ X \ \ ... \ \ X \ ]^T \tag{3}$$

$X_1,...,X_n$ and Y are linguistic variables which may be interpreted as inputs of fuzzy system ($X_1,...,X_n$) and the output of that system (Y). $A_1^{(i)},...,A_n^{(i)}$ are linguistic values of the linguistic variables $X_1,...X_n$ and $f^{(i)}$ is a function of variables $X_1, ...,X_n$.
A collection of the above written rules for i=1,2,...m, creates a rule base which may be activated (fired) under the singleton inputs:

$$X_1 \text{ is } x_{10} \text{ and...and } X_n \text{ is } x_{n0} \tag{4}$$

or

$$X \text{ is } x_0 \tag{5}$$

It can easily be noticed that such a type of reasoning, where the inferred value of i-th rule output for crisp inputs (singletons) may be written in the form:

$$R_i(x_{10},...,x_{n0}) \rightarrow f^{(i)}(x_{10},...,x_{n0}) = R_i(x_0) \rightarrow f^{(i)}(x_0) \tag{6}$$

Here the symbol $\rightarrow$ stands for fuzzy relation representing an if-then rule interpreted as product, minimum etc. It has to be pointed out that there is another interpretation of an if-then rule in the spirit of the classical logic implication as a fuzzy implication. However, under several conditions there is an equivalence between these both interpretations (e.g. product corresponds to the Reichenbach fuzzy implication and minimum corresponds to the Lukasiewicz fuzzy implication) [see another our chapter of this book].

$$R_i(x_{10},...,x_{n0}) = R_i(x_0) = A_1^{(i)}(x_{10}) \text{ and...and} A_n^{(i)}(x_{n0}) = A^{(i)}(x_0) \tag{7}$$

denotes the degree of activation (the firing strength) of the i-th rule with respect to minimum ($\wedge$) or product ($\cdot$) representing explicit connective (AND) of the predicates X_l is $A_l^{(i)}$ (l=1,...,n) in the antecedent of an if-then rule.
A crisp value of the output for Larsen's product and aggregation (sum) can be evaluated from formula [3]:

$$y_0 = \frac{\sum\limits_{i=1} R_i(x_{10},...,x_{n0}) \cdot f^{(i)}(x_{10},...,x_{n0})}{\sum\limits^{m} R(x\ ,...,x\ )} = \frac{\sum\limits_{i=1} R_i(x_0) \cdot f^{(i)}(x_0)}{\sum\limits^{m} R(x)} \tag{8}$$

Taking into account that function $f^{(i)}$ is of the form:

$$f^{(i)}(x_{10},...,x_{n0}) = f^{(i)}(x_0) = p_0^{(i)} \tag{9}$$

where $p_0^{(i)}$ is crisply defined constant in the consequent of the i-th rule. Such a model is called a zero-order Sugeno fuzzy model. The more general first-order Sugeno fuzzy model is of the form:

$$f^{(i)}(x_{10},...,x_{n0}) = p_0^{(i)} + p_1^{(i)} x_{10} + ... p_n^{(i)} x_{n0} \tag{10}$$

where $p_0^{(i)}$, $p_1^{(i)}$,...,$p_n^{(i)}$ are all constants.
In vector notation it takes the form:

$$f^{(i)}(x_0) = p^{(i)T} x_0' \tag{11}$$

where x_0' denotes an extended input vector:

$$x_0' = \begin{bmatrix} 1 \\ x_0 \end{bmatrix} \tag{12}$$

Notice that in both models the consequent is crisp. The above recalled method is called Takagi-Sugeno-Kang method of reasoning.

Now let us consider a more general form of MISO fuzzy rules, i.e. the rules in which the consequent is represented by a linguistic variable Y:

$$R^{(i)}: \text{ if } X_1 \text{ is } A_1^{(i)} \text{ and...and } X_n \text{ is } A_n^{(i)}, \text{ then } Y \text{ is } B^{(i)} \tag{13}$$

Membership functions of fuzzy sets $B^{(i)}$ can be represented by the parameterized functions in the form:

$$B^{(i)} \sim f^{(i)}(Area(B^{(i)}), y^{(i)}) \tag{14}$$

where $y^{(i)}$ is the center of gravity (COG) location of the fuzzy set $B^{(i)}$:

$$y^{(i)} = COG(B^{(i)}) = \frac{\int y \, B^{(i)}(y) \, dy}{\int B^{(i)}(y) \, dy} \tag{15}$$

Next we will consider the constructive type of systems with Larsen's product as fuzzy relation and sum as aggregation.
A general form of final output value can be put in the form:

$$y_0 = \frac{\sum\limits_{i=1} y^{(i)} \cdot \mathbf{Area}(B^{(i)/})}{\sum\limits^{m} \mathbf{Area}(B^{(i)/})} \tag{16}$$

where $B^{(i)'}$ is a resulting conclusion for i-th rule before aggregation.
For symmetric triangle (isosceles triangle) fuzzy values we can write a formula:

$$y_0 = \frac{\sum_{i=1}^{m} \frac{w^{(i)} R_i(x_0)}{2} y^{(i)}}{\sum_{=}^{m} \frac{w^{(i)} R_i(x_0)}{2}} \qquad (17)$$

when $w^{(i)}$ is the width of the triangle base. It should be noted that the $w^{(i)}/2$ factor may be interpreted as a respective weight of i-th rule or its certainty factor.

3. Moving consequent fuzzy set

In equation (17) the value describing the location of COG's consequent fuzzy set in if-then rules is constant and equals $y^{(i)}$ for i-th rule. A natural extension of the above described situation is an assumption that the location of the consequent fuzzy set is a linear combination of all inputs for i-th rule:

$$y^{(i)}(x_0) = p^{(i)T} x_0' \qquad (18)$$

Hence we get the final output value in the form:

$$y_0 = \frac{\sum_{i=1}^{m} \frac{w^{(i)} R_i(x_0)}{2} p^{(i)T} x_0'}{\sum_{=}^{m} \frac{w^{(i)} R_i(x_0)}{2}} \qquad (19)$$

Additionally, we assume that $A_1^{(i)}, ..., A_n^{(i)}$ have Gaussian membership functions:

$$A_j^{(i)}(x_{j0}) = \exp\left(-\frac{(x_{j0} - c_j^{(i)})^2}{2 s_j^{(i)^2}} \right) \qquad (20)$$

where $c_j^{(i)}, s_j^{(i)}$; $j=1,2,...,n$; $i=1,2,...,m$ are the parameters of the membership functions. On the basis of (7) and for explicit connective AND taken as product we get:

$$A^{(i)}(x_0) = \prod_{j=1}^{n} A_j^{(i)}(x_{j0}) \qquad (21)$$

Hence, on the basis of (20) we have:

$$R_i(x_0) = \exp\left(-\sum_{j=1}^{n} \frac{(x_{j0} - c_j^{(i)})^2}{2 s_j^{(i)^2}} \right) \qquad (22)$$

For n inputs and m if-then rules we have to establish the following unknown parameters:

- $c_j^{(i)}$, $s_j^{(i)}$; $j=1,2,...,n$; $i=1,2,...,m$, the parameters of membership functions of input sets,
- $p_j^{(i)}$; $j=0,1,...,n$; $i=1,2,...,m$; the parameters determining the location of output sets,
- $w^{(i)}$; $i=1,2,...,m$; the parameters of output sets.

Obviously, the number of if-then rules is unknown. Equations (19, 22) describe a radial neural network. The unknown parameters (except the number of rules m) are estimated by means of a gradient method performing the steepest descent on a surface in the parameter space. Therefore the so called learning set is necessary, i.e. a set of inputs for which the output values are known. This is the set of pair $(x_0(k), y_0(k))$; $k=1,2,...,N$. The measure of the error of output value may be defined for a single pair from the training set:

$$E = \frac{1}{2}(t_0 - y_0)^2 \qquad (23)$$

where t_0 - the desired (target) value of output.
The minimization of error E is made iteratively (for parameter α):

$$(\alpha)_{new} = (\alpha)_{old} - \eta \frac{\partial E}{\partial \alpha}\bigg|_{\alpha = (\alpha)} \qquad (24)$$

where η - learning rate.
Now we derive the negative partial derivatives of error E according to the unknown parameters:

$$-\frac{\partial E}{\partial c_j^{(i)}} = (t_0 - y_0) \frac{y^{(i)}(x_0) - y_0}{\sum\limits_{k=1}^{m} \frac{w^{(k)}}{2} R_k(x_0)} \frac{w^{(i)}}{2} R_i(x_0) \frac{x_{j0} - c_j^{(i)}}{s_j^{(i)2}} \qquad (25)$$

$$-\frac{\partial E}{\partial s_j^{(i)}} = (t_0 - y_0) \frac{y^{(i)}(x_0) - y_0}{\sum\limits_{k=1}^{m} \frac{w^{(k)}}{2} R_k(x_0)} \frac{w^{(i)}}{2} R_i(x_0) \frac{(x_{j0} - c_j^{(i)})^2}{s_j^{(i)3}} \qquad (26)$$

$$\mathop{\forall}\limits_{j \ne 0} \quad -\frac{\partial E}{\partial p_j^{(i)}} = (t_0 - y_0) \frac{\frac{w^{(i)}}{2} R_i(x_0)}{\sum\limits_{=}^{m} \frac{w^{(k)}}{2} R_k(x_0)} x_{j0} \qquad (27)$$

$$-\frac{\partial E}{\partial p_0^{(i)}} = (t_0 - y_0) \frac{\frac{w^{(i)}}{2} R_i(x_0)}{\sum\limits_{k=1}^{m} \frac{w^{(k)}}{2} R_k(x_0)} \qquad (28)$$

$$-\frac{\partial E}{\partial w^{(i)}} = (t_0 - y_0) \frac{y^{(i)}(x_0) - y_0}{\sum\limits_{k=1}^{m} \frac{w^{(k)}}{2} R_k(x_0)} \frac{R_i(x_0)}{2} \qquad (29)$$

The unknown parameters may be modified on the basis of (24) after the input of one data collection into the system or after the input of all data collections (cumulative method). Additionally, the following heuristic rules for changes of η parameter have been applied [8]. If in four sequential iterations the mean square error has diminished for the whole learning set, then the learning parameter is increased (multiplied by n_I). If in four sequential iterations the error has been increased and decreased commutatively then the learning parameter is decreased (multiplied by n_D).

Another solution accelerating the convergence of the method is the estimation of parameters $p^{(i)}$; i=1,...,m. by means of least squares method. The output value y_0 of the system in equation (19) may be considered to be a linear combination of unknown parameters $p^{(i)}$; i=1,...,m. If we introduce the following notation

$$S^{(i)}(x_0) = \frac{\dfrac{w^{(i)}}{2} R^{(i)}(x_0)}{\displaystyle\sum_{k=1}^{m} \frac{w^{(k)}}{2} R^{(k)}(x_0)} \tag{30}$$

$$D(x_0) = [S^{(1)}{x_0'}^T \vdots S^{(2)}{x_0'}^T \vdots \dots \vdots S^{(m)}{x_0'}^T]^T \tag{31}$$

$$P = [p^{(1)T} \vdots p^{(2)T} \vdots \dots \vdots p^{(m)T}]^T \tag{32}$$

equation (19) may be written in the form:

$$y_0 = D(x_0)^T P \tag{33}$$

Hence parameters P may be estimated by means of the least square method. To eliminate the matrix inverse we use the recurrent method. For (k+1)-th step ((k+1)-th element from the learning set) we get [11]:

$$\hat{P}(k+1) = \hat{P}(k) + G(k)D(x_0(k+1))[y_0(k+1) - D(x_0(k+1))^T\hat{P}(k)] \tag{34}$$

$$G(k+1) = G(k) - G(k)D(x_0(k+1)) \times$$
$$[D(x_0(k+1))^T G(k)D(x_0(k+1)) + 1]^{-1}D(x_0(k+1))^T G(k) \tag{35}$$

To initialise computation we take:

$$\hat{P}(0) = \underline{0}$$
$$G(0) = \alpha I \tag{36}$$

where I is an identity matrix, α is a large positive constant (e.g. 10^6). Finally in each iteration parameters $p^{(i)}$; i=1,...,m. are estimated on the basis of equations (34, 35), whereas the other parameters by means of a gradient method (24,25, 26, 29).

Another problem is the estimation of the number m of if-then rules and initial values of membership functions for premise part. This task is solved by means of preliminary clustering of training data, for which fuzzy c-means method has been used [1]. This method assigns each input vector $x_0(k)$; $k=1,2,...,$ N to clusters represented by prototypes v_i; $i=1,...c$ measured by grade of membership $u_{ik} \in [0, 1]$. A c x n dimensional matrix called a partition matrix fulfils the following assumptions:

$$\begin{cases} \forall k, \ \sum_{i=1}^{c} u_{ik} = 1 \\ \forall i, \ \sum_{k=1}^{N} u_{ik} \in [0, N] \end{cases} \tag{37}$$

The c-means method minimizes the scalar index for parameter $r > 1$:

$$J_m = \sum_{k=1}^{N} \sum_{i=1}^{c} u_{ik}^{r} \ \|x_0(k) - v_i\|^2 \tag{38}$$

Defining $D_{ik} = \| x_0(k) - v_i \|^2$, where $\|\circ\|$ is a vector norm (the most frequent Euclidean norm), we get an iterative method of commutative modification of partition matrix and prototypes [1]:

$$\forall i; \ v_i = \frac{\sum_{k=1}^{N} u_{ik}^{r} \ x_0(k)}{\sum_{k=1}^{N} u_{ik}^{r}} \tag{39}$$

$$\forall i,k; \ u_{ik} = \left| \sum_{j=1}^{c} \left(\frac{D_{ik}}{D_{jk}} \right)^{\frac{2}{r-1}} \right|^{-1} \tag{40}$$

According to the above written equations the obtained calculations are initialized if we take into account a random partition matrix U which fulfils conditions (37). Such a method leads to the local minimum of index (38). Therefore the most frequently used solution is multiple repeated calculations in accordance with equations (39, 40) for various random realizations of partition matrix initializations. As a termination rule we have applied the execution of the set number of iterations (in our case 500) or when in sequential iterations the change of index value J_m is less than the set value (in our case 0.001) the computation has been completed. Cluster validity is estimated by means of Xie-Beni index [13]:

$$\vartheta_{XB} = \frac{\sum_{i=1}^{c} \sum_{k=1}^{N} u_{ik}^{r} \|x_0(k) - v_i\|^2}{N \min_{i \neq j} (\|v_i - v_j\|^2)} \tag{41}$$

and Fukujama-Sugeno index:

$$\vartheta_{FS} = \sum_{i=1}^{c} \sum_{k=1}^{N} u_{ik}^{r} \|x_0(k) - v_i\|^2 - \sum_{i=1}^{c} \left| \left(\sum_{k=1}^{N} u_{ik}^{r} \right) \|v_i - v\|^2 \right| \tag{42}$$

where v is grand mean over all data $x_0(k)$.

Further on, we propose a new index which is the mean quotient of dissipation against the cluster prototype by dissipating prototypes against the prototype of a given cluster. The definition of the index takes account of the cardinality of clusters. The measure of data dissipation against the i-th prototype is as follows:

$$\sigma_i = \frac{\sum_{k=1}^{N} u_{ik}^{r} \|x_0(k) - v_i\|^2}{\sum_{k=1}^{N} u_{ik}^{r}} \tag{43}$$

whereas the measure of dissipation prototypes against other prototypes with regard to the cluster cardinality takes the following form:

$$\mu_i = \sum_{j=1}^{c} \|v_j - v_i\|^2 \frac{(n_j + n_i)}{n} \tag{44}$$

where n_i is the fuzzy cardinality of the i-th cluster defined as:

$$n_i = \sum_{k=1}^{N} u_{ik} \tag{45}$$

The cluster validity is defined as:

$$\vartheta_{VAL} = \sum_{i=1}^{c} \frac{\sigma_i \frac{n_i}{n}}{\mu_i} \tag{46}$$

Finally, we obtain:

As a result of preliminary clustering the following assumption for ANNBFIS

$$
\hat{v}_{VAL} = \sum_{i=1}^{c} \frac{n_i \sum_{k=1}^{N} u_{ik}^r \| x_0(k) - v_i \|^2}{\sum_{k=1}^{N} u_{ik}^r \sum_{j=1}^{c} \| v_j - v_i \|^2 (n_j + n_k)}
\tag{47}
$$

initialization can be made: $c^{(j)} = v_j$, j=1,2,...,m and:

$$
s^{(i)} = \frac{\sum_{k=1}^{N} u_{ik}^r [x_0(k) - v_i]^2}{\sum_{=}^{N} u_{ik}^r}
\tag{48}
$$

Clustering was carried out for 50 various random realisations of partitions matrix U. The parameters of the premises are determined on the basis of the above dependencies for a realisation for which we obtain the smallest value of the applied cluster validity index.

For calculations presented in section 5, the following parameter values: $\eta = 0.01$, $n_I = 1.1$, $n_D = 0.9$, $\alpha = 10^6$, $r = 2$ have been applied.

4. Classifier based on ANNBFIS

The fuzzy system described in the previous section can be applied to pattern recognition. If patterns from a learning set belong to classes ω_1 and ω_2 then we can build a fuzzy system whose output takes positive values for patterns from class ω_1 and negative values for class ω_2. If we denote a fuzzy system as $y_0 = FNN(x_0)$, we get:

$$
y_0(k) = FNN_{12}[x_0(k)] \begin{cases} > 0, & if \, x_0(k) \in \omega_1 \\ \leq 0, & if \, x_0(k) \in \omega_2 \end{cases}
\tag{49}
$$

During the learning process of a classifier we take $t_0(k) = 1$ for pattern $x_0(k)$ from class ω_1 and $t_0(k) = -1$ for pattern from class ω_2. For a bigger number of classes (ω_1, ω_2,...,ω_p, $p > 2$) we use an extension class-rest or class-class [4,16]. Because of existing common feature regions for which the classificator class-rest does not give the answer which class the classified pattern belongs to the method class-class has been applied. The disadvantage of such a solution is the necessity of constructing a greater number of classifiers. Let us denote a classifier making decision whether a pattern belongs to the i-th or j-th class as:

$$
y_0(k) = FNN_{ij}[x_0(k)] \begin{cases} > 0, & if \, x_0(k) \in \omega_i \\ \leq 0, & if \, x_0(k) \in \omega_j \end{cases}
\tag{50}
$$

Obviously we do not construct the classifier FNN_{ii} and the information about membership to i-th and j-th classes can be obtained on the basis of FNN_{ij} or FNN_{ji}

classifiers. Hence we construct $p(p-1)/2$ classifiers FNN_{ij} for $1 \le i < p; j > i$. The classification condition to i-th class has the form:
The learning process goes as follows: for each pair of indices ij ($1 \le i < p; j > i$) we

$$\mathop{\forall}_{j \ne i} FNN_{ij} [x_0(k)] > 0 \;\rightarrow\; x_0(k) \in \omega_i \tag{51}$$

assume $t_0(k) = 1$ for pattern $x_0(k)$ belonging to class ω_i and $t_0(k) = -1$ for pattern $x_0(k)$ belonging to class ω_j (the patterns belonging to other classes are removed from the training set) and we conduct the learning process of the classifier. The final pattern recognition is conducted on the basis of condition (51).

Table 1. An example of comparison of classification quality criteria.

t_0	y_0 (case I)	y_0 (case II)
1	0.9	0.1
-1	-1.1	-0.1
-1	0.1	-0.1
	E = 1.23	E = 2.43

Table 1 presents the example results of classifier learning for three patterns. For case one from that table we may observe the least mean square value of the error, however, for case two we see the least number of erroneus classifications. Hence we may imply that the construction of fuzzy system should fulfil the following conditions:

$$\varphi_k = \begin{cases} +1 & \textit{if } x_0(k) \in \omega_1 \\ -1 & \textit{if } x_0(k) \in \omega_2 \end{cases} \tag{52}$$

where

$$\mathop{\forall}_{1 \le k \le N} \varphi_k\, FNN(x_0(k)) > 0 \tag{53}$$

The inequality system (52) may be written as:

$$\mathop{\forall}_{1 \le k \le N} \begin{cases} \varphi_k\, FNN(x_0(k)) = t_0(k) \\ t_0(k) > 0 \end{cases} \tag{54}$$

The question arises how values $t_0(k)$ should be considered. We apply an iterative modification of their values where the following rule is employed: if the output value of the fuzzy system $\varphi_k y_0(k)$ is higher than its target value of $t_0(k)$ then we increase $t_0(k)$, otherwise no changes occur. In other words in this method we match the output values of the fuzzy system with the target value in such a way that their values should grow (it assures the fulfilling of the condition $t_0(k) > 0$). After each modification of the system outputs values the learning process is iteratively continued. Let us note:

$$e_k^{(l)} = \varphi_k \; FNN(x_0(k)) - t_0(k)^{(l)} \tag{55}$$

where: l stands for iteration index, $t_0(k)^{(l)}$ the target output value of the system for k-th pattern in l-th iteration. The iterative modification of $t_0(k)$ may be written in the form:

$$t_0(k)^{(l)} = t_0(k)^{(l-1)} + \begin{cases} c e_k^{(l)} & \text{if } e_k^{(l)} > 0 \\ 0 & \text{if } e_k^{(l)} \leq 0 \end{cases} \tag{56}$$

where c denotes the convergence coefficient. In appendix A it has been proved that the method is convergent for $0 \leq c \leq 2$. The iterations may start with arbitrarily chosen values. In further examples we apply $t_0(k)^{(1)} = 1$ for all indexes k. For c=0 we get a method described at the beggining of this section.

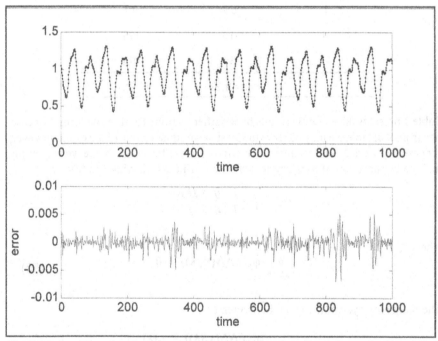

Fig. 1. Mackey-Glass chaotic time series (continous line) and predicted time series (dotted line) (upper), prediction error (lower).

5. Examples of applications
5.1. Application to chaotic time series prediction

A chaotic time series (a discrete signal) obtained on the basis of the solution of the Mackey-Glass equation was investigated:

$$\frac{dx(t)}{dt} = \frac{0.2\ x(t-\tau)}{1+x(t-\tau)^{10}} - 0.1x(t) \tag{57}$$

Prediction of the time series generated by means of equation (57) was realized by many authors [3, 7]. To make a precise comparison we applied data generated by Jang and obtained via anonymous ftp (ftp://ftp.cs.cmu.edu/users/ai/areas/fuzzy/systems/anfis). For obtaining such a time series Jang applied fourth-order Runge-Kutta method with the following parameters: time step 0.1, $x(0)=0.1$, $\tau=17$ [7, 8]. Such generated data are combined in the embedded vector $[x(n)\ x(n-6)\ x(n-12)\ x(n-18)]^T$. The goal is the prediction of value $x(n+6)$ for the embedded vector as input. The data consist of 500

Table 2. Simulation results of Mackey-Glass chaotic time series prediction.

m	$NDEI_{trn}$ Fukujama-Sugeno index	$NDEI_{trn}$ Xie-Beni index	$NDEI_{trn}$ New index	$NDEI_{chk}$ New index
2	0.0423	0.0423	0.0423	0.0420
3	0.0190	0.0190	0.0190	0.0190
4	0.0168	0.0167	0.0167	0.0173
5	0.0165	0.0130	0.0130	0.0172
6	0.0161	0.0163	0.0160	0.0170
7	0.0131	0.0116	0.0116	0.0141
8	0.0121	0.0120	0.0120	0.0123
9	0.0102	0.0078	0.0070	0.0110
10	0.0072	0.0057	0.0075	0.0091
11	0.0070	0.0085	0.0059	0.0080
12	0.0063	0.0075	0.0060	0.0077
13	0.0059	0.0057	0.0059	0.0074
14	0.0053	0.0055	0.0054	0.0065
15	0.0049	0.0049	0.0049	0.0061
16	0.0041	0.0047	0.0040	0.0056

pairs of input-output data of the learning set and 500 pairs of the testing set. By means of the system described in section 3, 500 iterations were carried out, the number of rules changing from 2 to 16. Prediction quality has been evaluated with non-dimensional error index (NDEI). This index is defined as a root mean square error divided by standard deviation of the target time series. We applied the assessment of the cluster validity by means of Xie-Beni, Fukujama-Sugeno indexes as well as the index presented in section 3. Table 2 shows the results. Taking into account the above mentioned time series and applying 16 if-then rules Jang [7] obtained the value of non-dimensional error index $NDEI_{trn} = 0.007$ for a training set and $NDEI_{chk} = 0.0066$ for a testing set. Applying 23 if-then rules Cho and Wang [3] obtained the values of root mean square error $RMSE_{trn} = 0.0096$ and $RMSE_{chk} = 0.0114$, which corresponds to $NDEI_{trn} = 0.04200$ and $NDEI_{chk} = 0.04987$. Using the system presented in section 3 the results comparable to Jang's results were obtained when 14 if-then rules were applied. However, the results comparable to Wang's results were obtained after only 2 if-then rules (cf, Table 2) have been applied. Fig. 1 shows the examined chaotic time series (a continuous line), predicted time series (a dotted line) and the prediction error for

Table 3. Simulation results for classification of the famous iris problem.

Confusion Matrix											
$c = 0.0$			$c = 0.5$			$c = 1.0$			$c = 2.0$		
50	0	0	50	0	0	50	0	0	50	0	0
0	50	0	0	49	1	0	50	0	0	49	1
0	2	48	0	1	49	0	0	50	0	1	49

examined chaotic time series for 16 if-then rules. From that Fig. we may observe the same character of error signal for learning part of data (discrete time 1-500) and testing part of data (discrete time 501-1000). On the basis of Table 2 we can see that smaller NDEI can be obtained if the cluster validity index proposed in section 3 is used.

To sum up the investigations in this sub-section, we can conclude that the system described in section 3 may be successfully applied to the prediction of time series generated by means of nonlinear differential equations.

5.2. Application to the famous iris problem

The iris database is perhaps the best known database to be found in the pattern recognition literature. The data set contains 3 classes of 50 instances each, where each class refers to a type of iris plant. The vector of features consists of: 1).sepal length in cm, 2).sepal width in cm, 3).petal length in cm, 4).petal width in cm. We consider three classes of patterns: Iris Setosa, Iris Versicolour i Iris Virginica. A confusion matrix for 50 learning iterations and two if-then rules has been shown in Table 3. The lowest error rate equalling 0% has been obtained for coefficient $c = 1$. For the rest of the values of coefficient c the error rate equals 1.33%. The results were independent of the applied index of cluster validity.

5.3. Application to MONK's problems

The MONK's problem was the basis of the first international comparison of learning algorithms. The result of this comparison is summarized in [15]. One significant characteristic of this comparison is that it was performed by a collection of researchers, each of whom was an advocate of the technique they tested (often they were the authors of various methods). In this sense, the results are less biased than in comparison with results obtained by a single person advocating a specific learning method, and more accurately reflect the generalization behavior of the learning techniques as applied by knowledgeable users. There are three MONK's problems. The domains for all MONK's problems are the same. One of the MONK's problems has noise added. For each problem, the domain has been partitioned into a training and testing set. The vector of features for each pattern consists of 7 features which take the following values: first feature - 1,2,3, second - 1,2,3, third - 1,2, fourth - 1,2,3, fifth - 1,2,3,4, sixth - 1,2. The patterns are classified into two classes. Taken from [15], the results of testing for various methods are collected in Table 4. The testing results obtained by means of the method described in this paper are presented in Table 4 as well. It should be pointed out that methods which gave the highest percentage of correct classification have been selected for coefficient $c = 0.5$.

Table 4. Simulation results for classification of MONKS problems.

Method		MONKS-1	MONKS-2	MONKS-3
AQ-15 Genetic		100 %	86.8 %	100 %
Assistant Professional		100 %	81.3 %	100 %
mFOIL		100 %	69.2 %	100 %
ID5R-hat		90.3 %	65.7 %	-
CN2		100 %	69.0 %	89.1 %
PRISM		86.3 %	72.7 %	90.3 %
ECOBWEB leaf prediction		71.8 %	67.4 %	68.2 %
Backprop. with weight decay		100 %	100 %	97.2 %
Cascade Correlation		100 %	100 %	97.2 %
ANNBFIS	$c = 0.0$	100 %	100 %	97.6 %
	$c = 0.5$	100 %	100 %	98.2 %
m = 3	$c = 1.0$	100 %	100 %	97.8 %
	$c = 2.0$	100 %	100 %	97.5 %

The number of executed iterations varied from 12 to 6000 depending on the considered problem. Like in the previous case, the results were independent of the applied index of cluster validity.

5.4. Application to system identification

The benchmark data originating from Box and Jenkins work [2] concerning the identification of a gas oven were included in our examination as well. Air and methane were delivered into the gas oven (gas flow in ft/min - an input signal x) to obtain a mixture of gases containing CO_2 (percentage content - output signal y). The data consisting of 296 pairs of input-output samples in 9sec. periods are presented in Fig. 3. To identify a model the following vectors have been applied as input: $[y(n-1) ...y(n-4) \ x(n) \ x(n-1) ... x(n-6)]^T$ and output $y(n)$. The results of examinations carried out for the numbers of if-then rules changing from 2 to 6 are shown in Table 5 after 500 iterations. The calculations were carried out by applying indexes described in section 3 in order to evaluate cluster validity. In original book [2] Box and Jenkins obtained the value of RMSE = 0.8426 for linear methods, which is a worse result than ours obtained for 2 if-then rules. Paper [9] presents the comparison of performance of the methods of fuzzy modelling known from literature for Box-Jenkins data. According to this comparison the best results were obtained for the method proposed in paper [9]. In this case RMSE equal to 0.2345 was obtained. The worst result obtained on the basis of modelling presented in section 3 amounts to RMSE = 0.2168. Fig. 4 presents an original (a continuous line) and modelled (a dotted line) output signal course and the error signal course, respectively.

6. Conclusions

In this paper a new artificial neural network based fuzzy inference system (ANNBFIS) has been described. Such a presented system can be used for the automative if-then rule generation. The novelty of that system in comparison with the one well known from literature is a whole moving fuzzy consequent. A particular case of our system is Jang's ANFIS (moving consequent considered as singleton) or Cho and Wang AFS with a constant fuzzy consequent. A connection of the gradient and least squares methods of parameter optimization for ANNBFIS has been used. For initialization of calculations (the parameters of premise part and number of if-then rules) preliminary fuzzy c-means clustering has been used. The cluster validity is estimated by means of Xie-Beni and Fukujama-Sugeno indexes and our new index. A method of optimization of the output target values of such a classifier minimizing the number of false classifications has been presented. The efficiency of the proposed classifier has been confirmed using the standard data bases: iris and MONKS. Promising applications of the presented system to chaotic time series prediction, pattern recognition and system identification have been shown.

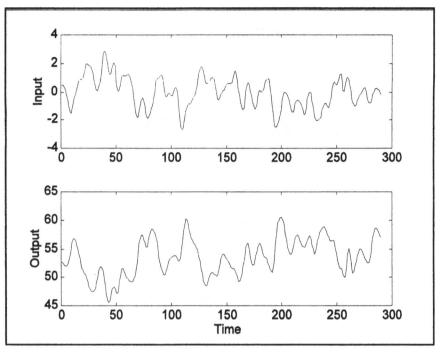

Fig 2. Box-Jenkins data for system identification.

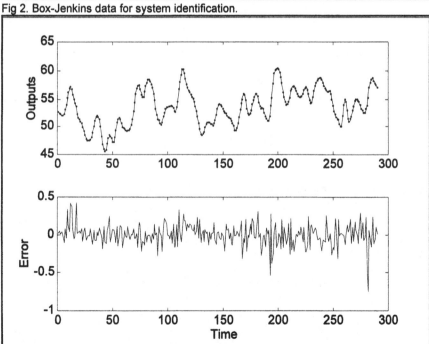

Fig. 3. Original (continous line) and modeled (dotted line) output signal for Box-Jenkins data (upper), error signal (lower) for six if-then rules.

APPENDIX A

Equation (33) may be written for all patterns as:

$$Y = F \, P \qquad (A.1)$$

where:

$$
F = \begin{vmatrix} D(x_0(1))^T \\ D(x_0(2))^T \\ \cdot \\ \cdot \\ \cdot \\ D(x\,(N))^T \end{vmatrix} \quad ; \qquad Y = \begin{vmatrix} y_0(1) \\ y_0(2) \\ \cdot \\ \cdot \\ \cdot \\ y_0(N) \end{vmatrix} \qquad (A.2)
$$

Similarly, we may present in matrix form (55):

$$E^{(l)} = F \, P^{(l)} - T^{(l)} \qquad (A.3)$$

where:

$$
T^{(l)} = \begin{vmatrix} t_0(1)^{(l)} \\ t_0(2)^{(l)} \\ \cdot \\ \cdot \\ \cdot \\ t\,(N)^{(l)} \end{vmatrix} \qquad (A.4)
$$

$P^{(l)}$ - the parameter vector in l-th iteration.
The applied for estimation of parameter p recurrent least square method may be written in non-recurrent form:

$$P^{(l)} = (F^T F)^{-1} F^T T^{(l)} = F^{\#} T^{(l)} \qquad (A.5)$$

where $F^{\#}$ is pseudoinverse matrix.
Equation (56) takes the form:

$$T^{(l+1)} = T^{(l)} + \frac{c}{2} \, [E^{(l)} + |E^{(l)}|] \qquad (A.6)$$

On the basis of (A.3) and (A.5) we get:

$$E^{(l)} = F F^{\#} T^{(l)} - T^{(l)} = (F F^{\#} - I) \, T^{(l)} \qquad (A.7)$$

Substituting equation (A.7) for (l+1) index to equation (A.6) and denoting:

$$E^{(l)} = E^{(l)} + |E^{(l)}| \qquad (A.8)$$

we get:

$$E^{(l+1)} = (FF^\# - I)(T^{(l)} + \frac{c}{2}\bar{E}^{(l)})$$
$$= E^{(l)} + \frac{c}{2}(FF^\# - I)\bar{E}^{(l)}$$
(A.9)

Next we determine the square of vector $E^{(l+1)}$ norm:

$$\|E^{(l+1)}\|^2 = \|E^{(l)}\|^2 + \|\frac{c}{2}(FF^\# - I)\bar{E}^{(l)}\|^2 + cE^{(l)T}(FF^\# - I)\bar{E}^{(l)}$$
(A.10)

On the basis of equations (A.5) and (A.7) we get:

$$E^{(l)T}FF^\# = (FP^{(l)} - T^{(l)})^T FF^\# = (FF^\# T^{(l)} - T^{(l)})FF^\# = 0$$
(A.11)

Transforming the second component of the right side of equation (A.10) with the use of equation (A.11) we have:

$$\|\frac{c}{2}(FF^\# - I)^T \bar{E}^{(l)}\|^2 = \frac{c}{4}\bar{E}^{(l)T}(FF^\# - I)^T(FF^\# - I)\bar{E}^{(l)} = \frac{c}{4}\|\bar{E}^{(l)}\|^2$$
$$- \frac{c^2}{2}\bar{E}^{(l)T}FF^\#\bar{E}^{(l)} - \frac{c^2}{4}\bar{E}^{(l)T}(FF^\#)^T FF^\#\bar{E}^{(l)}$$
(A.12)
$$= \frac{c^2}{4}\|\bar{E}^{(l)}\|^2 - \frac{c^2}{4}\bar{E}^{(l)T}(FF^\#)^T FF^\#\bar{E}^{(l)}$$

On the basis of (A.10), (A.11) and (A.12) we get:

$$\|E^{(l+1)}\|^2 = \|E^{(l)}\|^2 + \frac{c}{2}(\frac{c}{2} - 1)\|\bar{E}^{(l)}\|^2 - \frac{c^2}{4}\bar{E}^{(l)T}FF^\#\bar{E}^{(l)}$$
(A.13)

hence for $0 \leq c \leq 2$ the following condition is satisfied:

$$\underset{l}{\forall} \quad \|E^{(l+1)}\|^2 \leq \|E^{(l)}\|^2$$
(A.14)

Bibliography

1. J. C. Bezdek, Pattern recognition with fuzzy objective function algorythms (Plenum, New York, 1981).
2. G.E.P. Box, G.M. Jenkins, Time Series Analysis, Forecasting and Control (Holden Day, San Francisco, 1970).
3. K. B. Cho, B. H. Wang, Radial basis function based adaptive fuzzy systems and their applications to system identification and prediction, Fuzzy Set and Systems 83 (1996) 325-339.
4. R.O.Duda, P.E.Hart, Pattern classification and scene analysis (Wiley, New York, 1973).
5. S. Horikawa, T. Furuhashi, Y. Uchikawa, On fuzzy modeling using fuzzy neural networks with the back-propagation algorithm, IEEE Trans. Neur. Net., 4 (1992) 801-806.

6. J. R. Jang, C. Sun, Functional equivalence between radial basis function and fuzzy inference systems, IEEE Trans. Neur. Net., 4 (1993) 156-159.

7. J. R. Jang, C. Sun, Neuro-fuzzy modeling and control, Proc. IEEE, 83 (1995) 378-406.

8. J. R. Jang, C. Sun, E. Mizutani, Neuro-fuzzy and soft computing: a computational approach to learning and machine inteligence (Prentice-Hall, Upper Saddle River, 1997).

9. E.Kim, M.Park et al, A new approach to fuzzy modeling, IEEE Trans. Fuzzy Sys., 3 (1997) 328 - 337.

10. B. Kosko, Fuzzy associative memories, in: A.Kandel. Ed., Fuzzy Expert Systems (CRC Press, Boca Raton, 1987).

11. P. de Larminat, Y. Thomas, Automatique des systemes lineaires, 2. Identification, (Flammarion Sciences, Paris, 1977).

12. S. Mitra, S. K. Pal, Fuzzy multi-layer perceptron, inferencing and rule generation, IEEE Trans. Neur. Net., 6 (1995) 51-63.

13. N. R. Pal, J. C. Bezdek, On cluster validity for the fuzzy c-means model, IEEE Trans. Fuzzy Systems, 3 (1995) 370-379.

14. B. R. Ripley, Pattern Recognition and neural network, (Cambridge University Press, Cambridge, 1996).

15. S. B. Thrun et al., The MONK's promlems. A performance comparison ofdifferent learning algorithms, Scientific Report CMU-CS-91-197, Carnegie Mellon University, 1991.

16. J. T. Tou, R. C. Gonzalez, Pattern recognition principles, (Addison-Wesley London, 1974).

17. L. Wang, J. M. Mendel, Generating fuzzy rules by learning from examples, IEEE Trans. Systems Man Cyber., 22 (1992) 1414-1427.

Encouraging Cooperation in the Genetic Iterative Rule Learning Approach for Qualitative Modeling *

O. Cordón, A. González, F. Herrera, R. Pérez

Department of Computer Science and Artificial Intelligence
University of Granada
18071 - Granada, Spain
e-mail: {ocordon,A.Gonzalez,herrera,fgr}@decsai.ugr.es

Abstract. Genetic Algorithms have proven to be a powerful tool for automating the Fuzzy Rule Base definition and, therefore, they have been widely used to design descriptive Fuzzy Rule-Based Systems for Qualitative Modeling. These kinds of genetic processes, called Genetic Fuzzy Rule-Based Systems, may be based on different genetic learning approaches, with the Michigan and Pittsburgh being the most well known ones.

In this contribution, we briefly review another alternative, the Iterative Rule Learning approach, based on generating a single rule in each genetic run, and dealing with the problem of obtaining the best possible cooperation among the generated fuzzy rules. Two different ways for encouraging cooperation between rules in this genetic learning approach are presented, which are used in two different Genetic Fuzzy Rule-Based Systems based on it, SLAVE and MOGUL. Finally, the behaviour of these two processes in solving a qualitative modeling problem, the rice taste analysis, is analysed, and the results obtained are compared with two other design processes with different characteristics.

Keywords. Fuzzy Logic, Fuzzy Rules, Fuzzy Rule-Based Systems, Qualitative Modeling, Genetic Algorithms, Genetic Fuzzy Rule-Based Systems.

1 Introduction

Genetic Algorithms (GAs) are search algorithms that use operations found in natural genetics to guide the trek through a search space. GAs are theoretically and empirically proven to provide robust search capabilities in complex spaces, offering a valid approach to problems requiring efficient and effective searching [14]. Although GAs are not learning algorithms, they may offer a powerful and domain-independent search method for a variety of learning tasks. In fact, there has been a good deal of interest in using GAs for machine learning problems [21].

* This work has been supported by CICYT under Projects TIC95-0453 and TIC96-0778

Fuzzy Rule Based Systems (FRBSs), initiated by Mamdani applied to control problems, are now considered as one of the most important applications of fuzzy set theory. FRBSs are knowledge-based systems that make use of the known knowledge of the process, expressed in the form of fuzzy rules collected in the fuzzy rule base (FRB). They have been applied to a wide range of areas [2]. A *descriptive FRBS* is a model that is described or expressed using linguistic terms in the framework of fuzzy logic. A crucial reason why the descriptive fuzzy rule-based approach is worth considering is that it may remain verbally interpretable. This FRBS has been widely used and has obtained very good results in many different applications [2]. Focusing on the use of GAs in the field of fuzzy modeling, particularly in FRBS, GAs have proven to be a powerful tool for automating the definition of the FRB, since adaptive control, learning and self-organizing fuzzy systems may be considered in a lot of cases as optimization or search processes. Their advantages have extended the use of GAs in the development of a wide range of approaches for designing fuzzy systems in the last few years. These approaches receive the general name of *Genetic Fuzzy Systems* (GFSs) and *Genetic Fuzzy Rule Based Systems* (GFRBSs) [7, 23]. Among the different approaches considered in the genetic learning of FRBs there is the Iterative Rule Learning (IRL) approach [15, 20] that is based on the coding of one rule per chromosome, selecting one rule per population by including the GA in an iterative scheme based on obtaining the best current rule for the system, and incorporating this rule into the final FRB.

In this contribution we deal with genetic learning processes based on the IRL approach for designing descriptive FRBSs. In particular, we shall focus on the analysis of the cooperation in the genetic learning processes for qualitative modeling using linguistic fuzzy rules. We present two alternatives used for introducing cooperation in two different GFRBSs. The first one, used in SLAVE (Structural Learning Algorithm in Vague Environments) [15, 17, 19], modifies the iterative process in order to obtain rules that cooperate with the previously learnt rules, and the second one, used in MOGUL (Methodology to Obtain GFRBSs Under the IRL approach) [10, 11], dividing the genetic learning process into, at least, two stages, thereby achiving cooperation between the fuzzy rules generated in the second stage. In order to do this we organize the contribution as follows: Section 2 introduces some preliminaries such as descriptive FRBSs (qualitative modeling), Evolutionary and Genetic Algorithms, and GFRBSs; Section 3 studies the IRL approach and the problem of the lack of cooperation between rules; Section 4 presents two alternatives for including collaboration in the genetic learning processes based on the IRL approach; Section 5 shows some experimental results; and finally, Section 6 presents some concluding remarks.

2 Preliminaries

2.1 Qualitative modeling: descriptive FRBSs

Qualitative modeling based on fuzzy logic is considered as a system model based on linguistic descriptions [36]. The linguistic descriptions are represented by fuzzy membership functions, and they are used in an FRB composed of linguistic IF-THEN rules such as:

IF (a set of conditions are satisfied) THEN (a set of consequences may be inferred)

The contents of both IF- and THEN-parts are usually expressed in terms of linguistic variables. In an FRBS, the compositional rule of inference is used to draw conclusions from the set of known premises. Thereby the concept of linguistic variable [40] plays a central role.

There are different kinds of FRBSs in the literature, amongst which we should mention the Mamdani, TSK and DNF models.

1. The generic expression of the TSK rules is the following:

    IF X_1 is a_1 and ... and X_n is a_n THEN $Y = p_1 \cdot X_1 + \ldots + p_n \cdot X_n + p_0$

    where $X_1, ..., X_n$ and Y are the input variables and the output variable, respectively, a_i are linguistic variables with an associated fuzzy set defining their semantics, and p_i are real numbers.

2. In the Mamdani model, the FRB is composed of a collection of fuzzy rules with the following structure:

    IF X_1 is a_1 and ... and X_p is a_n THEN Y is B

3. The DNF model is an extension of the Mamdani model with the following structure:

    IF X_1 is A_1 and ... and X_n is A_n THEN Y is B

    where each variable X_i has a referential set U_i and takes values in a finite domain D_i, for $i \in \{1, \ldots, n\}$. The referential set for Y is V and its domain is F. The value of the variable y is B, where $B \in F$ and the value of the variable X_i is A_i, where $A_i \in P(D_i)$ and $P(D_i)$ denotes the set of subsets of D_i.

We can find some important differences between these kinds of fuzzy rules. While DNF-type and Mamdani-type fuzzy rules consider a linguistic variable in the consequent [15, 27, 28, 29], TSK fuzzy rules are based on representing the consequent as a polynomial function of the inputs [37]. The main difference between types 2 and 3 of rules is that type 3 allows subset of labels as values of a variable.

The Mamdani and DNF are linguistic models based on collections of $IF - THEN$ rules with fuzzy quantities associated with linguistic labels, and the fuzzy model is essentially a qualitative expression of the system. An FRBS in which the fuzzy sets giving meaning (semantic) to the linguistic labels are uniformly defined for all rules included in the FRB follows the *descriptive* approach since the linguistic labels take the same meaning for all the fuzzy rules contained in the FRB. In this case, the FRB is usually called Knowledge Base and it is composed of two components: the Rule Base (RB), constituted by the collection of fuzzy rules themselves, and the Data Base (DB), containing the membership functions defining their semantics.

2.2 Evolutionary and genetic algorithms

Evolutionary Computation (EC) uses computational models of evolutionary processes as key elements in the design and implementation of computer-based problem solving systems. There are a variety of evolutionary computational models that have been proposed and studied which are referred to as *Evolutionary Algorithms* (EAs). There have been three well-defined EAs which have served as the basis for much of the activity in the field, Genetic Algorithms, Evolution Strategies and Evolutionary Programming (EP) [1].

An EA maintains a population of trial solutions, imposes random changes to these solutions, and incorporates selection to determine which ones are going to be maintained in future generations and which will be removed from the pool of the trials. There are however important differences between them. GAs emphasize models of genetic operators as observed in nature, such as crossover (recombination) and point mutation, and apply these to abstracted chromosomes. ESs and EP emphasize mutational transformations that maintain the behavioral linkage between each parent and its offspring.

In the following, we briefly review the GAs, the most extended and most used EA.

A GA starts off with a population of randomly generated *chromosomes*, and advances toward better *chromosomes* by applying genetic operators modeled on the genetic processes occurring in nature. The population undergoes evolution in a form of natural selection. During successive iterations, called *generations*, chromosomes in the population are rated for their adaptation as solutions, and on the basis of these evaluations, a new population of chromosomes is formed using a selection mechanism and specific genetic operators such as crossover and mutation. An *evaluation* or *fitness function* (f) must be devised for each problem to be solved. Given a particular chromosome, a possible solution, the fitness function returns a single numerical fitness, which is supposed to be proportional to the utility or adaptation of the solution represented by that chromosome.

Although there are many possible variants of the basic GA, the fundamental underlying mechanism consists of three operations:

1. evaluation of individual fitness,
2. formation of a gene pool (intermediate population) through selection mechanism, and
3. recombination through crossover and mutation operators.

The next procedure shows the structure of a basic GA, where $P(t)$ denotes the population at generation t.

GAs may deal successfully with a wide range of problem areas. The main reasons for this success are: 1) GAs can solve hard problems quickly and reliably, 2) GAs are easy to interface to existing simulations and models, 3) GAs are extendible and 4) GAs are easy to hybridize. All these reasons may be summed up in only one: GAs are *robust*. GAs are more powerful in difficult environments

Procedure Genetic Algorithm
begin (1)
    $t = 0$;
    initialize $P(t)$;
    evaluate $P(t)$;
    While (**Not** *termination-condition*) **do**
    begin (2)
        $t = t + 1$;
        select $P(t)$ *from* $P(t - 1)$;
        recombine $P(t)$;
        evaluate $P(t)$;
    end (2)
end (1)

where the space is usually large, discontinuous, complex and poorly understood. They are not guaranteed to find the global optimum solution to a problem, but they are generally good at finding acceptably good solutions to problems acceptably quickly. These reasons have been behind the fact that, over the last few years, GA applications have grown enormously in many fields.

The basic principles of GAs were first laid down rigorously by Holland ([25]), and are well described in many books, such as [14, 30]. It is generally accepted that the application of a GA to solve a problem must take into account the following five components:

1. *A genetic representation of solutions to the problem,*
2. *a way to create an initial population of solutions,*
3. *an evaluation function which gives the fitness of each chromosome,*
4. *genetic operators that alter the genetic composition of offspring during reproduction, and*
5. *values for the parameters that the GA uses (population size, probabilities of applying genetic operators, etc.).*

2.3 Genetic fuzzy rule based systems

EAs are applied to modify/learn the definition of the membership function shapes (DB) and/or the composition of the fuzzy rules (RB) in the way shown in Figure 1. Therefore, it is possible to distinguish three different groups of GFRBSs depending on the FRB components included in the learning process [7, 23]:

1. *Genetic definition of the membership functions*
2. *Genetic derivation of the fuzzy rules*
3. *Genetic learning of the whole FRB*

For a wider description of each family see [7, 23] and for an extensive bibliography see [8], Section 3.13, and [9], Section 13. Different approaches may be found in [22, 33, 34].

Carse et al. [6] divide the third family into two different subgroups depending on the simultaneousness in the learning of both FRB components. Therefore, they differentiate between learning them in a single process or in different stages.

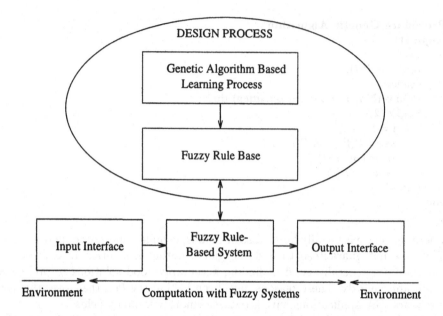

Fig. 1. Genetic Fuzzy Rule-Based Systems

3 Iterative Rule Learning Approach: Competition and Cooperation

In this Section we introduce the IRL approach and analyze the cooperation problem in the model under the cooperation versus competition versus problem.

3.1 IRL approach

The main problem that has to be solved to design a GFRBS consists of finding a suitable representation capable of gathering the problem characteristics and representing the potential solutions to it.

Classically, two genetic learning approaches, adopted from the field of genetic-based machine learning systems, have been used: the *Michigan* [5, 26] and *Pittsburgh* [35] approaches. In the Michigan approach, the chromosomes are individual fuzzy rules and the FRB is represented by the entire population. The collection of fuzzy rules is adapted over time using some genetic operators applied at the level of the individual rule. This evolution is guided by a credit assignment system that evaluates the adaption of each single fuzzy rule. On the other hand, in the Pittsburgh approach, each chromosome represents an entire FRB and the evolution is developed by means of genetic operators applied at the level of fuzzy rule sets. The fitness function evaluates the accuracy of the complete FRBS encoded in the chromosome.

In the last few years, the *IRL* approach has been used by some authors to obtain several GFRBSs following a new learning model [15, 20]. In the latter, as in the Michigan one, each chromosome in the population represents a single fuzzy rule, but only the best individual is considered to form part of the final FRB. Therefore, in this approach the EA provides a partial solution to the problem of learning, and, contrary to both previous ones, it is run several times to obtain the complete FRB. This substantially reduces the search space, because in each sequence of iterations only one rule is searched for.

In order to obtain a set of rules, which will be a true solution to the problem, the GA has to be placed within an iterative scheme similar to the following:

1. Use a GA to obtain a rule for the system.
2. Incorporate the rule into the final set of rules.
3. Penalize this rule.
4. If the set of rules obtained is adequate to represent the examples in the training set, the system ends up returning the set of rules as the solution. Otherwise return to step 1.

A very easy way to penalize the rules already obtained, and thus be able to learn new rules, consists of eliminating from the training set all those examples that are covered by the set of rules obtained previously.

The main difference with respect to the Michigan approach is that the fitness of each chromosome is computed individually, without taking into account cooperation with other ones.

In the literature we can find some genetic learning processes that use this model such as *SLAVE* [15, 17, 20], *SIA* [38] and *MOGUL* [10, 11].

¿From the description shown above, we may see that in order to implement a learning algorithm based on GAs using the IRL approach, we need, at least, the following:

1. a criterion for selecting the best rule in each iteration, and
2. a penalization criterion, and
3. a criterion for determining when there are enough rules available to represent the examples in the training set.

The first criterion is normally associated with one or several characteristics that are desirable so as to determine good rules. Usually criteria about the rule strength have been proposed (number of examples covered), criteria of consistency and completeness of the rule or criteria of simplicity (for some examples, see [10, 17, 20, 24]).

The second criterion is often associated with the elimination of the examples covered by the previous rules.

Finally, the third criterion is associated with the completeness of the set of rules [10, 17, 24] and must be taken into account when we can say that all the examples of a concept in the training set are sufficiently covered and no more rules are needed to represent them. This criterion is often associated, although it is not necessary, with the elimination of the examples in a concept covered by the previous rules.

This scheme is usually employed in GFRBSs based on inductive learning, in which the penalization of the fuzzy rules already generated is done by removing from the training data set all those examples that are still covered by the FRB obtained until that time. As has been previously said, a key characteristic of the IRL is that it substantially reduces the search space, because in each iteration only one fuzzy rule is searched. This allows us to obtain good solutions in GFRBSs for off-line learning problems.

3.2 Competition and cooperation in the IRL approach

Associated to the previous criteria needed in the development of an IRL algorithm, we include a natural way for competition and cooperation relations between the rules. So, the first criterion establishes the *competition between members of the population representing possible solutions to the problem*. In this case, this characteristic is due to the mechanisms of natural selection on which the EA is based. On the other hand, the second and third criteria include *cooperation relations between the rules that describe the same concept*, since, as was previously mentioned, normally the goal of the third criterion consists of trying to remove all the examples that are being learnt from the training set, when these are covered by some rules to a sufficient degree.

One of the most interesting features of an FRBS in qualitative modeling problems is the interpolative reasoning it develops. This characteristic plays a key role in the high performance of FRBSs and is a consequence of the *cooperation among all the fuzzy rules composing the FRB*. As is known, the output obtained from an FRBS is not usually due to a single fuzzy rule but to the cooperative action of several fuzzy rules that have been fired, because they match the input for the system to some degree. So, a very interesting way to solve the problem of designing an FRBS consists of adding both features to the learning algorithm: competition to achieve the best rules and cooperation between rules from the same or different value of the consequent variable. This is referred to as the cooperation versus competition problem (*CCP*) [4].

However, the cooperation between rules from different concepts is not included within the IRL approach. The difficulty of solving the problem of taking into account this kind of cooperation depends directly on the genetic learning approach followed by the GFRBS. GFRBSs based on the IRL approach try to solve the CCP at the same time as reducing the search space by encoding a single fuzzy rule in each chromosome. To put this into effect, these processes can use different ways:

- adding new criteria to the evaluation of the rule for including this kind of cooperation within the IRL approach,
- dividing the genetic learning process into, at least, two stages. Therefore, the CCP is solved in two steps acting on two different levels, with the competition between fuzzy rules in the first one, the genetic generation stage, and with

the cooperation between these generated fuzzy rules in the second one, a postprocessing stage.

In the following section we present these two alternatives.

4 Alternatives for Including Cooperation in the IRL Approach

In this Section, we present two alternatives used for introducing cooperation in two different GFRBSs based on the IRL approach. The first one, used in SLAVE [15, 17, 20], includes cooperation relations between rules from different values of the consequent value within the IRL approach, and the second alternative, used in MOGUL [10, 11], based on dividing the genetic learning process into, at least, two stages, managing cooperation between the generated fuzzy rules in the second one.

4.1 Cooperation within the IRL approach

In the proposal for the IRL approach the cooperation is defined between the rules from the same value in the consequent variable in a natural way, as previously has been mentioned. In many cases, this cooperation level is sufficient when the concepts are exclusive and there is no noise or inconsistency in the example set. However, with databases affected by noise and inconsistency and when the concepts are not exclusive, a higher degree of cooperation must be established that permits good collaboration between rules from different values of the consequent variable.

Normally, the degree of collaboration between rules from different concepts is measured using the inference model associated to the learning algorithm. It is not easy to establish this cooperation between rules, since the IRL approach learns the rules one by one, and the learning process does not has the whole rule set for applying the inference model.

A way for defining this cooperation level consists of applying the inference model partially on a subset of the examples and including this information in the evaluation of the rules. This subset contains the examples of the concepts that have been learnt by the learning algorithm. So, the cooperation between rules is measured by the error that produces the new rule in the outputs of the inference model, when this rule is included in the rule set.

The IRL approach, without this kind of collaboration, tries to extract the knowledge that the examples represent for each concept from the training set. The rule set obtained in this way, provides a comprehensible description of the system that we want to learn. From our point of view, the inclusion of cooperation must keep this comprehensible description of the system and furthermore it must improve the interpolative reasoning between the rules. This is important since an inappropriate use of the cooperation measure, may provoke a reduction in the quality of the rule (with respect to the interpretability of the rule set) because the goal of the learning process is to reduce the error in the output as far as possible.

SLAVE is a learning algorithm based on the IRL approach that takes into account cooperation between the rules from different concepts in the sense previously described. SLAVE was initially proposed in [15] and later developed in [17, 18]. The algorithm begins with a simple description of the problem: the consequent variable (concept variable) and the set of all the available antecedent variables for generating the rules that describe the consequent variable. The learning algorithm, using this description and a set of examples, will decide for each value of the consequent variable and each rule which variables are needed to describe the concept (feature selection), and the rest will be eliminated.

The basic element of the SLAVE learning algorithm is its model of rules that was described in Section 2.1 (type 3). The key to this rule model is that each variable may take as a value an element or a subset of elements in its domain, i.e., we let the value of a variable be interpreted more as a disjunction of elements than just one element in its domain.

Consistency and Completeness in SLAVE In the SLAVE learning process (Figure 2), finding the best rule consists of determining the best combination of values from the antecedent variables, given a fixed value of the consequent variable and a set of examples. The best rule concept uses a simple quantitative criterion; the best rule will be the rule covering the maximum number of examples. However, there are problems with this criterion, if we do not restrict the set of possible rules.

Classical learning theory proposes conditions that must be verified for the set of rules that are obtained by a learning algorithm. These conditions, which provide the logical foundation of the algorithms for concept learning from examples, are called *consistency condition* and *completeness condition* [31].

These conditions are associated on the whole set of rules. SLAVE obtains the set of rules that describes the system, extracting one rule in each iteration of the learning process. Due to this reason, we need to define these concepts on each rule. Moreover, we are not interested in proposing hard definitions on fuzzy problems, thus we propose a degree of completeness and a degree of consistency.

Definition 1. The degree of completeness of a rule $R_B(A)$ is defined as

$$\Lambda(R_B(A)) = \frac{n^+(R_B(A))}{n_B}$$

where $n_B = \sum_{i=1}^{m} U(e_i, B)$ is the number of examples of the value B of the consequent variable in the training set, m is the number of examples in the training set and $n^+(R_B(A))$ is the number of positive examples covered by the rule $R_B(A)$.

With respect to the soft consistency degree [17] it is based on the possibility of admitting some noise into the rules. Thus, in order to define the soft consistency

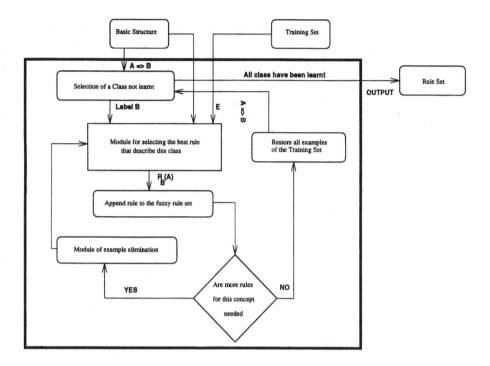

Fig. 2. SLAVE learning process

degree we use the following set:

$$\Delta^k = \{R_B(A)/n^-(R_B(A)) < k\, n^+(R_B(A))\}$$

which represents the set of rules having a number of negative examples strictly less than a percentage (depending on k) of the positive examples.

Definition 2. The degree to which a rule satisfies the soft consistency condition is

$$\Gamma_{k_1 k_2}(R) = \begin{cases} 1 & \text{if } R \in \Delta^{k_1} \\ \frac{k_2 n_E^+(R) - n_E^-(R)}{n_E^+(R)(k_2 - k_1)} & \text{if } R \notin \Delta^{k_1} \text{ y } R \in \Delta^{k_2} \\ 0 & \text{otherwise} \end{cases}$$

where $k_1, k_2 \in [0, 1]$ and $k_1 < k_2$, and $n_E^-(R)$, $n_E^+(R)$ are the number of positive and negative examples to the rule, R.

This definition uses two parameters, k_1 is a lower bound of the noisy threshold and k_2 is an upper bound of the noisy threshold.

Thus, SLAVE selects the rule that simultaneously verifies the completeness and soft consistency conditions to a high degree. Therefore, rule selection in SLAVE can be solved by the following optimization problem:

$$\max_{A \in D} \{ \Lambda(R_B(A)) \, \Gamma_{k_1 k_2}(R_B(A)) \}$$

where $D = P(D_1) \times P(D_2) \times \ldots \times P(D_n)$.

Adding Cooperation between Rules The main component of SLAVE is a genetic algorithm [18]. The goal of the genetic algorithm is to find the most consistent and complete rule at each step given the available set of examples. However, we want a rule set that includes cooperation between rules from different values of the consequent variable and with understandable rules.

For this reason, it is necessary to establish measures on the simplicity of the rule and on the degree of cooperation between rules and these measures must be taken into account for evaluating the rule. So, the evaluation function for determining the best rule is defined by a multiobjective function.

The measures for evaluating the simplicity of the rule were proposed in [19]. Now, we describe briefly the way used by SLAVE for including cooperation among rules.

SLAVE distinguishes two kinds of learning problems, when the consequent variable takes values in a discrete range (Classification Problems) and when the consequent variable takes values in a continuous range (Qualitative Modeling Problems). This difference between both problems is important since the inference method associated for each one of them is different. In the first case, the inference method can be seen as a competition between the rules for determining which of them will be the most appropriate for classifying a certain example, that is, the inference method selects only one rule each time. However, in the second case, the output of the rule set is obtained by the combination of the output of each rule that can be applied for classifying the example.

In the first case, we establish competition relations between rules from different values of the consequent variable for improving the overall behaviour of the rule set. The description of this process is to be found in [19]. In the second case, where the output is obtained by interpolative reasoning, SLAVE includes cooperation relations between rules in the following form:

a) defining in a special way the concepts of the number of positive and negative examples covered by a rule, and
b) including an error measure that determines the cooperation degree of the new rule with the rest of the rules that are members of the rule set.

The definition of the number of positive and negative examples covered by a rule is related to the results that this rule will obtain in the inference process, that is, with successes and failures. Using this idea, we built the following definitions:

Definition 3. A rule $R_B(A)$ classifies correctly an example e if

$$U(e, A) > 0 \text{ and } U(e, B) > 0$$

where $U(e, A)$ is the adaptation between the example and the antecedent of the rule and $U(e, B)$ is the adaptation between the example and the consequent of the rule. The definition of this adaptation function is to be found in [17].

Definition 4. A rule $R_B(A)$ does not correctly classify an example e if

$$U(e, A) > 0 \text{ and } U(e, B) = 0$$

¿From the previous definitions, we can establish the definitions of the number of positive and negative examples in the following way:

$$n^+(R_B(A)) = |\{e \in E \mid U(e, A) > 0 \text{ and } U(e, B) > 0\}|$$

$$n^-(R_B(A)) = |\{e \in E \mid U(e, A) > 0 \text{ and } U(e, B) = 0\}|$$

The previous definitions allow us to determine the goodness of the rule, but a difference of the sense proposed in the crisp problems [19], in fuzzy problems it is not necessary to grade the trust of the successes, since the rules work in cooperation for obtaining the output.

However, these definitions are not sufficient for maximizing the relations of cooperation between the rules. For this reason, SLAVE includes in the evaluation of the rule, a measure of the collaboration degree. This measure is based on the error that the new rule produces in the output when it is included in the rule set.

The error measure is obtained using the inference method on the subset of the examples that are members of some of the classes from the rules learnt. So, the rule evaluation function is composed by three criteria:

Criterion 1: The degree to which the rule represents the examples from the concepts that we want to learn, i.e., the verification of the completeness and soft consistency conditions to a high degree.

Criterion 2: Influence on the output from the Knowledge Base of the inclusion of the new rule, i.e., error measure.

Criterion 3: Simplicity and understanding of the rule, i.e., simplicity measures.

Therefore, the evaluation function is a multicriteria function that contains the previous criteria. For the evaluation, a lexicographical order is applied, where the main criterion is to maximize the degree for representing the examples of the concepts that we want to learn (criterion 1). In a tie situation among them the rule is selected that produces less error in the output (criterion 2). If a new tie situation is produced, then it selects the simpler rule (criterion 3) among them.

4.2 Cooperation in stages

As the generation process does not envisage any relationship between the fuzzy rules generated, it is necessary to employ any other postprocessing to simplify and/or adjust the FRB obtained, thereby forming a multi-stage GFRBS. Therefore, the CCP is solved in two steps acting on two different levels:

- *the genetic generation stage forces competition between fuzzy rules*, as the genetic learning processes based on the Michigan approach, *to obtain an FRB composed of the best possible fuzzy rules*. The cooperation between them is only smoothly addressed by means of the rule penalization criterion. This generation stage uses a covering method which is developed as an iterative process that allows us to obtain a set of fuzzy rules covering the example set. In each iteration, it runs the generating method, obtaining the best fuzzy rule according to the current state of the training set, considers the relative covering value this rule creates over it, and removes the examples from it with a covering value greater than ϵ, provided by the system designer. It ends up when the training set is left empty.

  Each time the generating method is run, it produces a set of candidate fuzzy rules by generating the fuzzy rule best covering every example from the training set. The accuracy of the candidates is measured by using a multicriteria fitness function, composed of three different criteria measuring the covering that each rule creates over the training set. Their expressions are to be found in [10]. Finally, the best fuzzy rule is selected from the set of candidates and given as the method output.

  The designer is allowed to build the generation stage by using different kinds of algorithms and not only a GA as in the previous existing processes following the IRL approach. It is possible to employ a non-evolutionary inductive algorithm or an Evolution Strategy [1] instead of the usual GA [10]. The way of working is still the same but the difference is the speed of the generation process, which is higher in the latter cases.

- *the postprocessing stage forces cooperation between the fuzzy rules generated in the previous stage* by refining or eliminating the redundant or unnecessary fuzzy rules from the previously generated fuzzy rule set *in order to obtain the best possible FRB*.

The postprocessing stage will present two important characteristics. On the one hand, it will be designed by means of a GA based on the Pittsburgh learning approach, but significatively reducing the solution space by working only over the FRB generated in the first stage, i. e., not modifying the membership function definitions. In this way, it will simplify the FRB obtained until now by removing the redundant or unnecessary fuzzy rules not cooperating adequately with the others. This operation mode will allow us to obtain the best possible FRB composed of the best combination of the fuzzy rules generated in the first stage.

On the other hand, a genotypic sharing function [13] will be considered to obtain not only a single FRB as output from the process but different ones presenting the best possible cooperation between the fuzzy rules composing them, and thereby the best possible behavior. Due to this, we will refer to this second stage as the *multisimplification process*.

The *Sequential Niche Technique* [3] is used to induce niches in this GFRBS stage, with the genetic simplification process proposed in [24] being the basic optimization technique iterated in each run of the multisimplification process. The following subsections introduce the basic simplification algorithm and the particular aspects of the multisimplification one, respectively.

The Basic Genetic Simplification Process As mentioned earlier, the basic genetic simplification process was first proposed in [24]. It is based on a binary coded GA, in which the selection of the individuals is performed using the stochastic universal sampling procedure together with an elitist selection scheme, and the generation of the offspring population is put into effect by using the classical binary multipoint crossover (performed at two points) and uniform mutation operators.

The coding scheme generates fixed-length chromosomes. Considering the rules contained in the rule set B^g derived from the previous step counted from 1 to m, an m-bit string $C = (c_1, ..., c_m)$ represents a subset of candidate rules to form the FRB finally obtained as this stage output, B^s, such that,

$$\text{If } c_i = 1 \text{ then } R_i \in B^s \text{ else } R_i \notin B^s$$

Following MOGUL assumptions, the initial population is generated by introducing a chromosome representing the complete previously obtained rule set B^g, i.e., with all $c_i = 1$. The remaining chromosomes are selected at random.

As regards the fitness function, $F(C_j)$, it is based on two different criteria:

- On the one hand, we have a global error measure that determines the accuracy of the FRBS encoded in the chromosome. We usually work with the mean square error (SE), although other measures may be used. SE over a training data set, E_{TDS}, is represented by the following expression:

$$E(C_j) = \frac{1}{2|E_p|} \sum_{e_l \in E_p} (ey^l - S(ex^l))^2$$

where $S(ex^l)$ is the output value obtained from the FRBS using the FRB coded in C_j, $R(C_j)$, when the input variable values are $ex^l = (ex_1^l, \ldots, ex_n^l)$, and ey^l is the known desired value.

- On the other hand, since there is a need to keep the τ-completeness property considered in the previous stage, we shall ensure this condition by forcing every example contained in the training set to be covered by the encoded FRB to a degree greater than or equal to τ,

$$C_{R(C_j)}(e_l) = \bigcup_{j=1..T} R_j(e_l) \geq \tau, \quad \forall e_l \in E_p \text{ and } R_j \in R(C_j)$$

where τ is the minimal training set completeness degree accepted in the simplification process. Usually, τ is less than or equal to ω, the compatibility degree used in the generation process.

Therefore, we define a *training set completeness degree* of $R(C_j)$ over the set of examples E_p as

$$TSCD(R(C_j), E_p) = \bigcap_{e_l \in E_p} C_{R(C_j)}(e_l)$$

The final expression of the fitness function is:

$$F(C_j) = \begin{cases} E(C_j), & \text{if } TSCD(R(C_j), E_p) \geq \tau, \\ \infty, & \text{otherwise} \end{cases}$$

The Genetic Multisimplification Process In order to induce niching in the sequential niche algorithm, there is a need to define some kind of *distance metric* which, given two individuals, returns a value of how close they are [3]. We use a *genotypic sharing* [13] due to the fact that the metric considered is the Hamming distance measured on the binary coding space. With $A = (a_1, ..., a_m)$ and $B = (b_1, ..., b_m)$ being two individuals, it is defined as follows:

$$H(A, B) = \sum_{i=1}^{m} a_i \cdot b_i$$

Making use of this metric, the *modified fitness function* guiding the search on the multisimplification process is based on modifying the value associated to an individual by the basic algorithm fitness function, multiplying it by a *derating function* penalizing the closeness of this individual to the previously obtained solutions. Hence, the modified fitness function used by the multisimplification process is the following:

$$F'(C_j) = F(C_j) \cdot G(C_j, S)$$

where F is the basic genetic simplification process fitness function, $S = \{s_1, ..., s_k\}$ is the set containing the k solutions already found, and G is a kind of *derating function*. We consider the following, taking into account the fact that the problem we deal with is a minimization one:

$$G(C_j, S) = \begin{cases} \infty, & \text{if } d = 0 \\ 2 - (\frac{d}{r})^\beta, & \text{if } d < r \text{ and } d \neq 0 \\ 1, & \text{if } d \geq r \end{cases}$$

where d is the minimum value of the Hamming distance between C_j and the solutions s_i included in S, i. e., $d = Min_i\{H(C_j, s_i)\}$, and the penalization is considered over the closest solution, r is the *niche radius*, and β is the *power factor* determining how concave ($\beta > 1$) or convex ($\beta < 1$) the derating curve is. Therefore, the penalization given by the derating function takes its maximum value when the individual C_j encodes one of the solutions already found. There is no penalization when the C_j is far away from S with a value greater than or equal to the niche radius r.

The algorithm of the genetic multisimplification process is shown below:

1. *Initialization: Equate the multisimplification modified fitness function to the basic simplification fitness function: $F'(C_j) \leftarrow F(C_j)$.*
2. *Run the basic genetic simplification process, using the modified fitness function, keeping a record of the best individual found in the run.*
3. *Update the modified fitness function to give a depression in the region near the best individual, producing a new modified fitness function.*
4. *If all the simplified FRBs desired have not been obtained, return to step 2.*

Hence, the number of runs for the sequential algorithm performed is the number of solutions desired to be obtained. We allow the FRBS designer to decide this number as well as the values of parameters r and β.

5 Example: Rice Taste Analysis

Subjective qualification of food taste is a very important but difficult problem. In the case of the rice taste qualification, it is usually put into effect by means of a subjective evaluation called the *sensory test*. In this test, a group of experts, usually composed of 24 persons, evaluate the rice according to a set of characteristics associated to it. These factors are: *flavor, appearance, taste, stickiness,* and *toughness* [32].

Because of the large quantity of relevant variables, the problem of rice taste analysis becomes very complex, thus leading to solve it by means of modeling techniques capable of obtaining a model representing the non-linear relationships existing in it. Moreover, the problem-solving goal is not only to obtain an accurate model, but to obtain a user-interpretable model as well, capable of putting some light on the reasoning process made by the expert for evaluating a kind of rice in a specific way. Due to all these reasons, in this Section we deal with obtaining a qualitative model to solve the said problem.

In order to do so, we are going to use the data set presented in [32]. This set is composed of 105 data arrays collecting subjective evaluations of the six variables in question (the five mentioned and the overall evaluation of the kind of rice), made up by experts on this number of kinds of rice grown in Japan (for example, Sasanishiki, Akita-Komachi, etc.). The six variables are normalized, thus taking values in the real interval $[0, 1]$.

With the aim of not biasing the learning, we have randomly obtained ten different partitions of the mentioned set, composed by 75 pieces of data in the training set and 30 in the test one, for generating ten qualitative models in each experiment. To solve the problem, we use the two GFRBSs based on the IRL approach introduced in this paper, and two qualitative modeling processes with different characteristics as well:

D1. The inductive learning process proposed by Nozaki et al. in [32].

D2. The inductive learning process proposed by Wang and Mendel (WM) in [39].
D3. The SLAVE GFRBS introduced in Section 4.1.
D4. The GFRBS obtained from MOGUL introduced in Section 4.2.

As was done in [32], we have worked with fuzzy partitions composed by a different number of linguistic labels for the six variables considered. These fuzzy partitions have been obtained from a normalization process in which the universe of discourse of each variable has been equally divided into 2 and 3 parts, and a triangular fuzzy set has been associated to each one of them. Figure 3 shows an example of a fuzzy partition with five linguistic labels. The reason why we have not considered fuzzy partitions with a higher number of labels is that there is a need to obtain simple qualitative models with FRBs composed by a small number of rules in order to make them interpretable.

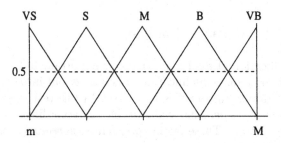

Fig. 3. Example of fuzzy partition with five linguistic labels

The results obtained in the experiments developed are collected in Table 1. The values shown in columns SE_{tra} and SE_{tst} have been computed as an average of the mean square error values obtained in the approximation of the training and test data sets, respectively, by the ten qualitative models generated in each case. The column $\#R$ stands for the average number of fuzzy rules in the FRBs of the models generated from each process. We should remember that these fuzzy rules are simple in GFRBSs **D1**, **D2** and **D4**, and present the disjunctive normal form in the case of GFRBS **D3**. Finally, as may be observed, GFRBS **D4**, the one based on MOGUL, has two rows associated, one for each one of the learning stages: generation and postprocessing.

In view of these results, many interesting conclusions may be drawn. On the one hand, as regards the accuracy in the problem solving, the qualitative model generated by the GFRBS obtained from SLAVE, **D3**, has obtained the best training result and MOGUL, **D4**, has obtained the best test result when working with 2 labels, with the second best result being obtained by SLAVE. With respect to MOGUL, the good behaviour of the cooperation encouraged by the postprocessing stage is demonstrated in the light of the results obtained: it not only significatively reduces the number of rules in the models generated but

Process	2 labels			3 labels		
	#R	SE_{tra}	SE_{tst}	#R	SE_{tst}	SE_{tst}
D1	64	0.00862	0.00985	364.8	0.00251	0.00322
D2	15	0.013284	0.013118	23	0.003339	0.003758
D3	2.0	0.004111	0.007288	3.0	0.003866	0.006533
D4 (gen.)	10.1	0.013601	0.012508	21.2	0.005157	0.006579
D4 (post.)	6	0.004861	0.0037	10.6	0.00281	0.004169

Table 1. Results obtained in the rice taste analysis problem by the different learning processes

improves their accuracy to a high degree (see rows **D4** (gen.) and **D4** (post.)). With respect to SLAVE the results are very close to the previous system and the main difference corresponds to the simplicity of the final model.

In the case of 3 labels, the best results are obtained by GFRBS **D1**, which obtains the best overall global results in this case as well. The problem is that the qualitative models generated from this GFRBS are not useful in practice due to the number of rules in their FRBs (364.8 in average) is excessively high in order to interpret them. We should remember that the goal is not only to obtain accurate fuzzy models solving the problem but to make sure these models can be interpreted by human beings.

Focusing on this second aspect, it may be observed that the simplest models are obtained by the SLAVE GFRBS, **D3**, presenting an average of 2.0 and 3.0 rules when considering 2 and 3 labels, respectively. This is a key aspect due to the fact that the interpretability of the model will depend directly on the number of fuzzy rules in the FRB. It will be very easy for an expert to interpret a qualitative model composed by only two rules. The cooperation induced in the rule generation in this GFRBS (see Section 4.1) allows it to generate very simple qualitative models with an adequate accuracy according to its simplicity. On the other hand, the behaviour of the GFRBS obtained from MOGUL, **D4**, is also good in this aspect. It allows us to design qualitative models with a very good balance between interpretability (generates simple models with 6 rules in the case of 2 labels, and 10.6 in the case of 3 labels) and accuracy.

In Tables 2 and 3, as an example, the composition of the FRB is shown for one of the models generated from each one of the GFRBSs based in the IRL introduced in this contribution. The specific values obtained by them in both measures are $SE_{tra} = 0.0041$ and $SE_{tst} = 0.0061$ for the GFRBS **D3** (SLAVE), and $SE_{tra} = 0.005681$ and $SE_{tst} = 0.001782$ for the GFRBS **D4** (MOGUL).

6 Concluding Remarks

In this contribution, the IRL approach, one of the existing genetic learning approaches to design GFRBSs, has been briefly reviewed, and the problem of ob-

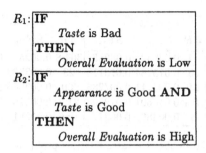

R_1: | **IF**
| *Taste* is Bad
| **THEN**
| *Overall Evaluation* is Low
R_2: | **IF**
| *Appearance* is Good **AND**
| *Taste* is Good
| **THEN**
| *Overall Evaluation* is High

Table 2. FRB of one of the qualitative models generated from the GFRBS **D3** using 2 labels

	Flavor	*Appearance*	*Taste*	*Stickness*	*Toughness*	**Overall Evaluation**
R_1:	Good	Good	Good	Sticky	Tender	High
R_2:	Good	Good	Good	Sticky	Tender	High
R_3:	Good	Good	Good	Sticky	Tender	High
R_4:	Good	Bad	Bad	Not sticky	Tough	Low
R_5:	Bad	Bad	Bad	Not sticky	Tough	Low
R_6:	Bad	Good	Good	Sticky	Tender	Low

Table 3. FRB of one of the qualitative models generated from the GFRBS **D4** using 2 labels

taining the best possible cooperation between the generated fuzzy rules in the genetic learning processes based on it has been analyzed. Two different ways for encouraging cooperation between rules in them have been presented: the inclusion of the cooperation between rules inside of the iterative rule learning, used in SLAVE, and the creation of a postprocessing stage obtaining different simplified FRB definitions with good cooperation from the rules generated in the genetic learning stage, used in MOGUL.

Both GFRBSs have been applied to solve a qualitative modeling problem, rice taste analysis, and the results obtained by them have been compared with two other design processes with different characteristics. They have performed well, showing the good behaviour of both alternatives presented to encourage the cooperation between rules in GFRBSs based on the IRL approach.

On the other hand, we should note that these GFRBSs have been applied to solve other real-world problems as well. In [16], SLAVE was used in a medical application, the diagnosis of myocardial infarction, while a real-world Spanish electrical engineering problem was solved by the GFRBS obtained from MOGUL in [12].

References

[1] T. Bäck, Evolutionary Algorithms in Theory and Practice (Oxford University Press, 1996).

[2] A. Bardossy, L. Duckstein, Fuzzy Rule-Based Modeling With Application to Geophysical, Biological and Engineering Systems (CRC Press, 1995).

[3] D. Beasly, D.R. Bull, R.R. Martin, A sequential niche technique for multimodal function optimization, Evolutionary Computation 1:2 (1993) 101-125.

[4] A. Bonarini, Evolutionary learning of fuzzy rules: competition and cooperation, in: W. Pedrycz, Ed., Fuzzy Modelling: Paradigms and Practice (Kluwer Academic Press, 1996) 265-283.

[5] L. Booker, Intelligent Behaviour as an Adaption to the Task Environment, PhD thesis, University of Michigan (1982).

[6] B. Carse, T.C. Fogarty, A. Munro, Evolving fuzzy rule based controllers using genetic algorithms, Fuzzy Sets and Systems 80 (1996) 273-294.

[7] Cordón, O., Herrera, F., A General Study on Genetic Fuzzy Systems. In: G. Winter, J. Periaux, M. Galan, P. Cuesta (Eds.), Genetic Algorithms in Engineering and Computer Science, Wiley and Sons, (1995), 33-57.

[8] O. Cordón, F. Herrera, M. Lozano, A classified review on the combination fuzzy logic-genetic algorithms bibliography: 1989-1995, in: E. Sanchez, T. Shibata, L. Zadeh, Eds., Genetic Algorithms and Fuzzy Logic Systems. Soft Computing Perspectives (World Scientific, 1997) 209-241.

[9] O. Cordón, F. Herrera, M. Lozano, On the combination of fuzzy logic and evolutionary computation: a short review and bibliography, in: W. Pedrycz, Ed., Fuzzy Evolutionary Computation (Kluwer Academic Press, 1997) 57-77.

[10] O. Cordón, F. Herrera, A three-stage evolutionary process for learning descriptive and approximate fuzzy logic controller knowledge bases, International Journal of Approximate Reasoning 17:4 (1997) 369-407.

[11] O. Cordón, M.J. del Jesus, F. Herrera, M. Lozano, MOGUL: A Methodology to Obtain Genetic fuzzy rule-based systems Under the iterative rule Learning approach. Technical Report DECSAI-98101, Dept. Computer Science and Artificial Intelligence, University of Granada, Granada (Spain, January 1998).

[12] O. Cordón, F. Herrera, L. Sánchez, Computing the Spanish Medium Electrical Line Maintenance Costs by means of Evolution-Based Learning Processes, Eleventh International Conference on Industrial & Engineering Applications of Artificial Intelligence & Expert Systems (IEA-98-AIE) Castellón (Spain, 1998).

[13] K. Deb, D.E. Goldberg, An investigation of niche and species formation in genetic function optimization, Proc. of the Second International Conference on Genetic Algorithms, Lawrence Erlbaum (Hillsdale, NJ, 1989) 42-50.

[14] D.E. Goldberg, Genetic Algorithms in Search, Optimization, and Machine Learning. Addison-Wesley (1989).

[15] A. González, R. Pérez, J.L. Verdegay, Learning the structure of a fuzzy rule: a genetic approach. Proc. EUFIT'93 vol. 2 (1993) 814-819. Also in Fuzzy System and Artificial Intelligence 3(1) (1994) 57-70.

[16] A. González, R. Pérez, A. Valenzuela, Diagnosis of myocardial infarction through fuzzy learning techniques, Proceedings of IFSA'95 vol.I, Sao Paulo (1995) 273-276.

[17] A. González, R. Pérez, Completeness and Consistency Conditions for Learning Fuzzy Rules. Fuzzy Sets and Systems (1998, to appear).

116

[18] A. González, R. Pérez, A Learning System of Fuzzy Control Rules. In: F. Herrera, J.L. Verdegay (Eds.), Genetic Algorithms and Soft Computing, Physica-Verlag (1996) 202-225.

[19] A. González, R. Pérez, SLAVE: a genetic learning system based on an iterative approach, Technical Report #DECSAI-97111 (1997).

[20] A. González, F. Herrera, Multi-stage genetic fuzzy systems based on the iterative rule learning approach, Mathware & Soft Computing 4 (1997) 233-249.

[21] J.J. Grefenstette, (Ed.), Genetic Algorithms for Machine Learning. Kluwer Academic, (1994).

[22] F. Herrera, J.L. Verdegay (Eds.), Genetic Algorithms and Soft Computing (Physica-Verlag, 1996).

[23] F. Herrera, L. Magdalena, Genetic fuzzy systems, in: R. Mesiar, B. Riecan, Eds., Tatra Mountains Mathematical Publications 13 (1997) 93-121. Vol. "Fuzzy Structures. Current Trends". Lecture Notes of the Tutorial: Genetic Fuzzy Systems. Seventh IFSA World Congress (IFSA'97).

[24] F. Herrera, M. Lozano, J.L. Verdegay, A learning process for fuzzy control rules using genetic algorithms, Fuzzy Sets and Systems (1998, to appear).

[25] J.H. Holland. Adaptation in Natural and Artificial Systems. Ann Arbor, 1975. (MIT Press (1992)).

[26] J.H. Holland, S. Reitman, Cognitive systems based on adaptive algorithms, in: D. A. Waterman and F. Hayes-Roth, Eds., Pattern-Directed Inference Systems (Academic Press, 1978).

[27] C.C. Lee, Fuzzy logic in control systems: fuzzy logic controller - parts I and II, IEEE Transactions on Systems, Man, and Cybernetics 20 (1990) 404-435.

[28] L. Magdalena, F. Monasterio, A Fuzzy Logic Controller with Learning Through the Evolution of its Knowledge Base, International Journal of Approximate Reasoning, 16 (1997) 335-358.

[29] L. Magdalena, Adapting the Gain of an FLC with Genetic Algorithms, International Journal of Approximate Reasoning, 17 (1997) 327-349.

[30] Z. Michalewicz. Genetic Algorithms + Data Structures = Evolution Programs. Springer-Verlag, (1992).

[31] R.S. Michalski, Understanding the nature of learning, Machine Learning: An artificial intelligence approach (Vol II). San Mateo, CA: Morgan Kaufmann (1986).

[32] K. Nozaki, H. Ishibuchi, H. Tanaka, A Simple but Powerful Heuristic Method for Generating Fuzzy Rules from Numerical Data, Fuzzy Sets and Systems 86 (1997) 251-270.

[33] W. Pedrycz (Ed.), Fuzzy Evolutionary Computation (Kluwer Academic Press, 1997).

[34] E. Sanchez, T. Shibata, L. Zadeh (Eds.), Genetic Algorithms and Fuzzy Logic Systems. Soft Computing Perspectives (World Scientific, 1997)

[35] S.F. Smith, A Learning System Based on Genetic Adaptive Algorithms, PhD thesis, University of Pittsburgh (1980).

[36] M. Sugeno, T. Yasukawa, A Fuzzy-logic-based Approach to Qualitative Modeling, IEEE Transactions on Fuzzy Systems 1(1) (1993) 7-31.

[37] T. Takagi, M. Sugeno, Fuzzy identification of systems and its application to modeling and control, IEEE Transactions on Systems, Man, and Cybernetics 15(1) (1985) 116-132.

[38] G. Venturini, SIA: a Supervised Inductive Algorithm with Genetic Search for Learning Attribute Based Concepts. Proc. European Conference on Machine Learning, Vienna, (1993), 280-296.

[39] L.X. Wang, J.M. Mendel, *Generating Fuzzy Rules by Learning from Examples*, IEEE Transactions on Systems, Man, and Cybernetics 22(6) (1992) 1414-1427.

[40] L. Zadeh, *The Concept of a Linguistic Variable and its Applications to Approximate Reasoning*. (1975) Part I, Information Sciences 8, 199-249, Part II, Information Sciences 8, 301-357, Part III, Information Sciences 9 43-80.

2

TOOLS FOR LINGUISTIC DATA MODELING AND ANALYSIS

Fuzzy Graphs with Linguistic Inputs-Outputs by Fuzzy Approximation Models

Haekwan Lee & Hideo Tanaka

Department of Industrial Engineering, Osaka Prefecture University
Gakuencho 1-1, Sakai, Osaka 599-8531, JAPAN
{leehk, tanaka}@ie.osakafu-u.ac.jp

Abstract: This paper proposes an approach to construct fuzzy graphs with linguistic inputs-outputs by fuzzy approximation models. Linguistic inputs can be transformed into linguistic outputs through fuzzy systems. In this paper, we consider fuzzy approximation models as fuzzy relations to represent linguistic inputs-outputs. In fuzzy regression, two approximation models, i.e. the possibility and necessity models, can be considered. Always there exist a possibility model when a linear system with fuzzy coefficients is considered, but it is not assured to attain a necessity model in a fuzzy linear system. The absence of a necessity model is caused by adopting a model not fitting to the given data. Thus we consider polynomials to find a more refined regression model. If we can find a proper necessity model, the necessity and possibility models deserve more credit than the previous models in the former studies. The measure of fitness is used to gauge the degree of approximation of the obtained models to the given data. The obtained approximation models themselves can be regarded as fuzzy graphs. Furthermore, by the obtained approximation models, we can construct another fuzzy graphs which represent linguistic inputs-outputs relations. The possibility and necessity models in fuzzy regression analysis can be considered as the upper and lower approximations in rough sets. Similarities between the fuzzy regression and the rough sets concept are also discussed.

1. Introduction

Zadeh [19] defined *computing with words* as a methodology where numbers are replaced with words for computing and reasoning. Fuzzy sets enable to transfer linguistic variables to numerical values which are easy for computing [18]. Then, the computed results can be transferred to linguistic variables for reasoning. This can be explained well with fuzzy relations which effectively represent linguistic input-output relations. A fuzzy relation obtained from the given input-output data can be regarded as approximation models which give linguistic input-output relation.

Fuzzy regression is introduced by Tanaka et al. [9] where a fuzzy linear system was used as a regression model. Since then, many developments have been continued in possibilistic regression [10-14]. Furthermore, based on the identification method, possibilistic coefficients in fuzzy linear systems are identified [16]. Recently, regression analysis using the quadratic programming problem [15] and several methods dealing with outliers [17] are introduced. Fuzzy regression for fuzzy input-output data is dealt in [8]. As a simpler version of fuzzy regression, interval regression analyses [3, 4] are studied.

If the given output values are fuzzy numbers, we can formulate two approximation models, i.e., the possibility and necessity models. It is well known that there are possibility models even if the assumed models are linear. However, we do not know whether there exists a necessity model when the assumed models are linear systems. The non-existence of a necessity model is caused by adopting a model not fitting to the given data. To cope with that, we suggest polynomials to find approximate regression models. By increasing the number of terms of the polynomials, any function can be expressed. Thus finally we can obtain the optimal necessity model. We also introduce the measure of fitness to gauge the degree of approximation of the given data to the obtained models.

The obtained approximation models themselves can be regarded as fuzzy graphs. Furthermore, by the obtained fuzzy approximation models, we can obtain linguistic outputs corresponding to linguistic inputs. From these linguistic inputs-outputs, another fuzzy graphs can be constructed. For the concept of fuzzy graphs, see Zadeh [19, 20].

Pawlak [6, 7] introduced a new concept of approximate data analysis based on rough sets. Rough sets can be described as approximate inclusion of sets and provide a systematic framework for the study of the problems arising from imprecise and insufficient knowledge. The possibility and necessity models in fuzzy regression analysis can be considered as the upper and lower approximations in rough sets. The similarities between the fuzzy approximation models and the rough sets concept are discussed and compared.

2. Fuzzy relations

A fuzzy relation R can be defined as a fuzzy collection of ordered pairs. Let $X \times Y = \{(x, y) \mid x \in X, y \in Y\}$, then a fuzzy relation from X to Y is a fuzzy subset of $X \times Y$ characterized by a membership function μ_R, namely

$$\mu_R : X \times Y \to [0, 1]. \tag{1}$$

For example, a fuzzy equivalence relation can be represented as

$$\mu_R(x, y) = 1 - |x-y| / 2, \quad \text{if } |x-y| \leq 2,$$
$$= 0, \quad \quad \text{if } |x-y| > 2, \tag{2}$$

which is a fuzzification of $y = x$. The h-level relation of a fuzzy relation R can be denoted as

$$R_h = \{(x, y) \mid \mu_R(x, y) \geq h\} \tag{3}$$

which is equivalent to the h-level set of a fuzzy set.

A fuzzy relation is an effective tool to represent fuzzy input-output relations which occur frequently in real life phenomena. Let a crisp input x_0 be given, then we can consider a fuzzy output B through the fuzzy relation $R(x, y)$ as

$$\mu_B(y) = \mu_R(x_0, y). \tag{4}$$

If an input is a fuzzy set A on X, using the extension principle [18], we can define the fuzzy output B as

$$\mu_B(y) = \max_x \; [\mu_A(x) \wedge \mu_R(x, y)] \tag{5}$$

where $\wedge$ represents a *min*. Thus, a fuzzy relation is a fuzzy system where, given a crisp or fuzzy input, a fuzzy output is obtained. Fig. 1 explains a fuzzy system representing a fuzzy relation $R(x, y)$.

As shown in Fig. 2, given a fuzzy relation $R(x, y)$, a fuzzy output B can be obtained for the crisp input (4) and the fuzzy input (5). A fuzzy relation can be obtained by fuzzy regression analysis.

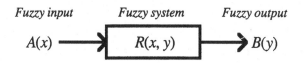

Fig. 1. A fuzzy system with a fuzzy relation $R(x, y)$

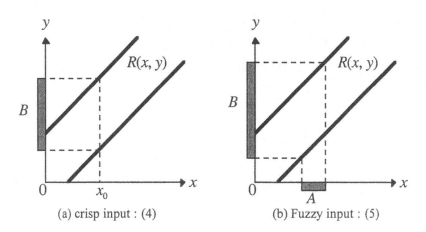

Fig. 2. Examples of input-output relations through a fuzzy relation $R(x, y)$

3. Fuzzy regression analysis for fuzzy relations

In this section, we consider fuzzy regression analysis as one of methodologies to represent the linguistic input-output relations.

3.1 Fuzzy regression models representing fuzzy input-output relations

A fuzzy regression model can be written as

$$Y(x) = A_0 + A_1 x_1 + \cdots + A_n x_n = A\,x \tag{6}$$

where $x = (1, x_1, \ldots, x_n)'$ is an input vector, $A = (A_0, \ldots, A_n)$ is a fuzzy coefficient vector, and $Y(x)$ is the estimated fuzzy output. If the coefficient A_i is assumed to be a symmetric fuzzy number, A_i denoted as $A_i = (a_i, c_i)_L$ can be defined by

$$\mu_{A_i}(x) = L((x - a_i)/c_i), \quad c_i > 0, \tag{7}$$

where a_i is a center and c_i is a spread, and $L(x)$ is a shape function of the fuzzy number.

For a symmetric triangular fuzzy number A_i defined by $L(x) = \max(0, 1 - |x|)$, the membership function of A_i can be denoted as

$$\mu_{A_i}(x) = 1 - |x - a_i|/c_i \tag{8}$$

Since regression coefficients A_i, $(i = 0, \dots, n)$ in (6) are fuzzy numbers, the estimated output $Y(x)$ also becomes a fuzzy number. Therefore, using the extension principle, (2) can be expressed as

$$Y(x) = (a_0, c_0)_L + (a_1, c_1)_L x_1 + \cdots + (a_n, c_n)_L x_n \tag{9}$$
$$= (a'x, c'|x|)_L$$

where $a'x$ and $c'|x|$ represent a center and a spread of the fuzzy output $Y(x)$, respectively. The membership function of $Y(x)$ can be denoted as

$$\mu_{Y(x)}(y) = L((y - a'x)/c'|x|) \quad \text{if } x \neq 0,$$
$$= 1 \qquad\qquad \text{if } x = 0, y = 0, \tag{10}$$
$$= 0 \qquad\qquad \text{if } x = 0, y \neq 0.$$

Let the h-level set of $Y(x)$ is defined as

$$[Y(x)]_h = \left\{ y \mid \mu_{Y(x)}(y) \geq h \right\} = [y_h^L, y_h^U] \tag{11}$$

where y_h^L and y_h^U represent the lower and the upper bounds of $[Y(x)]_h$, respectively. To obtain $[Y(x)]_h = [y_h^L, y_h^U]$, consider

$$L((y - a'x)/c'|x|) = h, \tag{12}$$

which is equivalent to

$$(y - a'x)/c'|x| = \pm |L^{-1}(h)|. \tag{13}$$

From (13), the lower and the upper bounds of $[Y(x)]_h$ are

$$y_h^L = a'x - |L^{-1}(h)| |c'| |x|,$$
$$y_h^U = a'x + |L^{-1}(h)| |c'| |x|. \tag{14}$$

For a symmetric triangular fuzzy number, $|L^{-1}(h)|$ can be denoted as

$$|L^{-1}(h)| = 1 - h. \tag{15}$$

Through this paper, fuzzy numbers are assumed to be symmetric triangular ones. Thus, the h-level set of $Y(x)$ (11) can be expressed as an interval

$$[Y(x)]_h = \left[a'x - (1 - h)c'|x|, \ a'x + (1 - h)c'|x| \right]. \tag{16}$$

For the threshold h given by an analyst, if we put a large value h, we consider only intervals of data which have high possibilities. Conversely, if we put a small value h, we consider intervals of low possibilities.

Assume that input- output data (x_j, Y_j) are given as

$$(x_j; Y_j) = (1, x_{j1}, \dots, x_{jn}; Y_j), \quad j = 1, \dots, m \tag{17}$$

where x_j is the j-th input vector, Y_j is the corresponding fuzzy output that consist of a center y_j and a spread e_j denoted as $Y_j = (y_j, e_j)$, and m is a data size.

From the data set expressed by (17) two estimation models can be considered, i.e., the possibility and the necessity estimation models denoted as

$$Y^*(x_j) = A_0^* + A_1^* x_{j1} + \cdots + A_n^* x_{jn}, \quad j = 1, \ldots, m, \tag{18}$$

$$Y_*(x_j) = A_{*0} + A_{*1} x_{j1} + \cdots + A_{*n} x_{jn}, \quad j = 1, \ldots, m, \tag{19}$$

where the fuzzy coefficients A_i^* and A_{*i} are denoted as $A_i^* = (a_i^*, c_i^*)_L$ and $A_{*i} = (a_{*i}, c_{*i})_L$ respectively. The h-level set of the estimated output $Y^*(x_j)$ by the possibility model always includes the h-level set of the observed output Y_j, whereas the h-level set of $Y_*(x_j)$ by the necessity model should be included in the h-level set of Y_j. These relations can be expressed as follows:

$$\left[Y^*(x_j)\right]_h \supseteq \left[Y_j\right]_h \Leftrightarrow \left\{ \begin{array}{l} a^{*\,\prime} x_j - (1-h) c^{*\,\prime} |x_j| \leq y_j - (1-h) e_j, \\ a^{*\,\prime} x_j + (1-h) c^{*\,\prime} |x_j| \geq y_j + (1-h) e_j \end{array} \right\} \tag{20}$$

$$\left[Y_*(x_j)\right]_h \subseteq \left[Y_j\right]_h \Leftrightarrow \left\{ \begin{array}{l} a_*^{\prime} x_j - (1-h) c_*^{\prime} |x_j| \geq y_j - (1-h) e_j, \\ a_*^{\prime} x_j + (1-h) c_*^{\prime} |x_j| \leq y_j + (1-h) e_j \end{array} \right\} \tag{21}$$

$$\left[Y_*(x_j)\right]_h \subseteq \left[Y_j\right]_h \subseteq \left[Y^*(x_j)\right]_h. \tag{22}$$

Our main concern is to obtain fuzzy coefficients A_i^* and A_{*i}, $(i = 0, \ldots, n)$ satisfying the above inclusion relations. Followings are LP problems to obtain approximation models:

Possibility model;

$$\operatorname*{Min}_{a^*, c^*} \quad J^* = \sum_{j=1}^m c^{*\,\prime} x_j$$

subject to $\left[Y^*(x_j)\right]_h \supseteq \left[Y_j\right]_h, \quad j = 1, \ldots, m,$ (23)

$$c_i^* \geq 0, \quad i = 0, \ldots, n.$$

Necessity model;

$$\operatorname*{Max}_{a_*, c_*} \quad J_* = \sum_{j=1}^m c_*^{\prime} x_j$$

subject to $\left[Y_*(x_j)\right]_h \subseteq \left[Y_j\right]_h, \quad j = 1, \ldots, m,$ (24)

$$c_{*i} \geq 0, \quad i = 0, \ldots, n.$$

Constraint conditions in (23) and (24) are referred to (20) and (21) respectively.

3.2 Fuzzy regression analysis with polynomials

LP problems obtaining two approximation models are explained in Section 3.1. Since two approximation models are obtained by separate optimization problems (23) and (24), the inclusion relation (22) is not always satisfied for new inputs even if inclusion relations (20) and (21) are satisfied. But it is desirable to obtain approximation models which satisfy (22). If all necessity coefficients are included in the corresponding possibility coefficients such that $A_i^* \supseteq A_{i*}, i = 0, \ldots, n$, then the necessity model is also included in the possibility model as $Y^*(x) \supseteq Y_*(x)$ for any x. This can be proved easily by simple arithmetic (see Alefeld and Herzberger [1]).

Therefore, to obtain the possibility and necessity models simultaneously, the following unified LP problem can be considered (see Ishibuchi and Tanaka [4]):

$$\text{Min}_{a^*,c^*,a_*,c_*} \sum_{j=1}^{m} c^{*\,t}x_j - \sum_{j=1}^{m} c_*^t x_j$$

subject to
$$\left[Y^*(x_j) \right]_h \supseteq \left[Y_j \right]_h,$$
$$\left[Y_*(x_j) \right]_h \subseteq \left[Y_j \right]_h, \qquad j = 1, \dots, m,$$
$$a_{*\,i} + c_{*\,i} \leq a_i^* + c_i^*,$$
$$a_i^* - c_i^* \leq a_{*\,i} - c_{*\,i},$$
$$c_i^*, c_{*\,i} \geq 0, \qquad\qquad i = 0, \dots, n. \tag{25}$$

This LP problem is combining (23) and (24) under consideration of the inclusion relations $A_i^* \supseteq A_{i*}, i = 0, \dots, n$ between the possibility and necessity regression coefficients. By adding $A_i^* \supseteq A_{i*}, i = 0, \dots, n$ in LP problem (25), we obtain two models satisfying $Y^*(x) \supseteq Y_*(x)$ for any x.

There always exist possibility models, but the necessity models can not be obtained if we fail to assume a proper regression model. In case of no solution of a necessity model by a linear system, we can take a following polynomial:
$$Y = A_0 + \sum A_i x_i + \sum A_{ij} x_i x_j + \sum A_{ijk} x_i x_j x_k + \cdots. \tag{26}$$
Since a polynomial such as (26) can represent any function, the center of a necessity model $Y_*(x_j)$ can meet the center of the observed output Y_j. Thus, one can obtain a necessity model by increasing the number of terms of the polynomial until a solution is found. Here it should be noted that this polynomial (26) is such a linear system as (6) with respect to parameters. Thus we can use LP problem with no difficulty to obtain the parameters in (26).

The existence of the necessity model means that the assumed model is somewhat reliable. Thus, the *measure of fitness for the j-th data* $\varphi_Y(x_j)$ can be defined as
$$\varphi_Y(x_j) = \frac{c_*^t |x_j|}{c^{*\,t} |x_j|} \tag{27}$$
which indicates how closely the possibility output for the j-th input approximates to the necessity output for the j-th input. Then the *measure of fitness for all data* φ_Y can be defined as
$$\varphi_Y = \frac{1}{m} \sum_{j=1}^{m} \varphi_Y(x_j) = \frac{1}{m} \sum_{j=1}^{m} \frac{c_*^t |x_j|}{c^{*\,t} |x_j|} \tag{28}$$
where $0 \leq \varphi_Y \leq 1$. Even if a necessity model does not exist, φ_Y can be defined because we can set zero for c_*. The larger the value of φ_Y, the more the model is fitting to the data. φ_Y is an average over ratios being spread of necessity outputs divided by spread of possibility outputs for m data.

Now assuming that an analyst may consider a tolerance limit ω such that $\varphi_Y \geq \omega$, we propose a new algorithm which gives two approximate models.

Algorithm obtaining two approximation models:
Step 1 : Take a linear function as regression model:

$$Y = A_0 + \sum A_i x_i. \tag{29}$$

Step 2 : Solve the unified LP problem (25) and calculate the measure of fitness φ_Y of the two models. If $\varphi_Y \geq \omega$, then go to Step 4 (We already have the optimal possibility model $Y^*(x)$ and the optimal necessity model $Y_*(x)$ satisfying $Y^*(x) \supseteq Y_*(x)$ for any x). Otherwise, go to Step 3.

Step 3 : Increase the number of terms of the polynomials, i.e.

$$Y = A_0 + \sum A_i x_i + \sum A_{ij} x_i x_j. \tag{30}$$

Go to Step 2.

Step 4 : End.

3.3 A numerical example

Let us apply the proposed approach using numerical data. A data set of crisp inputs and fuzzy outputs is shown in Table 1. Assuming that a tolerance limit is $\omega = 0.25$, let us explain our proposed method as the following sequences. For simplicity, we set the threshold $h = 0$.

Table 1. Numerical data

No.(j)	1	2	3	4	5
x	1	2	3	4	5
$Y = (y, e)_L$	(3.75, 1.75)	(4.25, 1.75)	(4.75, 1.75)	(6.5, 1.5)	(7.5, 2.5)
No.(j)	6	7	8	9	10
x	6	7	8	9	10
$Y = (y, e)_L$	(10.5, 2.5)	(15.5, 3.5)	(15.5, 2.5)	(22.0, 6.0)	(21.5, 4.5)

First, we assumed a linear function as a regression model:

$$Y = A_0 + A_1 x. \tag{31}$$

Using the unified LP problem (25), we obtained the possibility model $Y^*(x)$ and the necessity model $Y_*(x)$ as

$$Y^*(x) = (-0.6563, 2.7813)_L + (2.2813, 0.5938)_L x, \tag{32}$$
$$Y_*(x) = (0.8125, 0)_L + (1.7422, 0.0547)_L x, \tag{33}$$

which are depicted in Fig. 3 (a) where the outer two solid lines represent the possibility model and the inner two dotted lines represent the necessity model. From (32) and (33) we obtained $\varphi_Y(x_j)$ as shown in Table 2 (a), but the measure of fitness is less than the tolerance limit, i. e., $\varphi_Y (= 0.0458) < \omega (= 0.25)$. Thus we rejected models (32) and (33), and reassumed a quadratic function as a model:

$$Y = A_0 + A_1 x + A_2 x^2. \tag{34}$$

By solving the unified LP problem (25), we obtained

$$Y^*(x) = (3.7118, 0.8507)_L + (-0.1958, 0.3625)_L x + (0.2340, 0.0368)_L x^2, \tag{35}$$
$$Y_*(x) = (3.3417, 0.4806)_L + (0.0597, 0.1347)_L x + (0.1972, 0)_L x^2, \tag{36}$$

which are depicted in Fig. 3 (b). From (35) and (36) we obtained $\varphi_Y(x_j)$ as shown in Table 2 (b), and the measure of fitness is greater than the tolerance limit, i.e., $\varphi_Y (= 0.3281) > \omega (= 0.25)$. Thus we accept (35) and (36) as optimal models which satisfy $Y^*(x) \supseteq Y_*(x)$ for any x. The obtained models (35) and (36) can be considered as an upper approximation model and a lower approximation model, respectively.

In Table 2, it can be observed that the values of $\varphi_Y(x_j)$ increased greatly when we use a quadratic model than a linear model. Also the measure of fitness for all data φ_Y is increased from 0.0458 to 0.3281.

In this example, even if the possibility and necessity models exist simultaneously, those models are rejected if the measure of fitness φ_Y is less than the tolerance limit ω. By increasing the number of terms of the polynomials, it can be concluded that approximate models in Fig. 3 (b) are more fitting to the given data than those in Fig. 3 (a). This fact is reflected in the measure of fitness φ_Y.

Table 2. The obtained $\varphi_Y(x_j)$ for numerical data

Model	No.(j)	1	2	3	4	5
(a) Linear	$\varphi_Y(x_j)$	0.0162	0.0276	0.0360	0.0424	0.0476
(b) Quadratic	$\varphi_Y(x_j)$	0.4922	0.4353	0.3898	0.3528	0.3221
Model	No.(j)	6	7	8	9	10
(a) Linear	$\varphi_Y(x_j)$	0.0517	0.0552	0.0581	0.0606	0.0627
(b) Quadratic	$\varphi_Y(x_j)$	0.2962	0.2742	0.2552	0.2386	0.2241

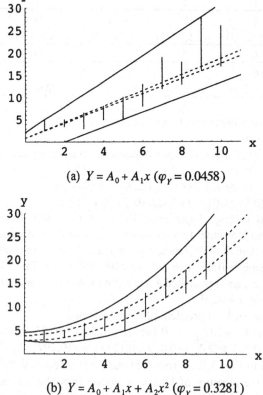

(a) $Y = A_0 + A_1 x$ ($\varphi_Y = 0.0458$)

(b) $Y = A_0 + A_1 x + A_2 x^2$ ($\varphi_Y = 0.3281$)

Fig. 3. Obtained possibility and necessity models for numerical data

4. Linguistic inputs-outputs for fuzzy graphs

4.1 Fuzzy graphs with linguistic inputs-outputs relations

In this section, we will consider fuzzy graphs with linguistic inputs-outputs by fuzzy approximation models obtained by the method in Section 3. Consider a fuzzy model

$$Y(x) = A_0 + A_1 x_1 + \cdots + A_n x_n = A\,x \tag{37}$$

where $x = (1, x_1, \dots, x_n)^t$ is an input vector, the coefficient A_i is a symmetric triangular fuzzy number denoted as $A_i = (a_i, c_i)_L$. Then, (37) is defined by the fuzzy relation $R(x, y)$ as

$$R(x, y) = \mu_R(x, y) = L((y - a^t x)/c^t|x|) = 1 - |y - a^t x| / c^t|x|. \tag{38}$$

If fuzzy inputs $X = (1, X_1, \dots, X_n)$ where $X_i = (x_i, d_i)_L$ is defined by

$$\mu_{X_i}(x) = 1 - |x - x_i|/d_i, \tag{39}$$

are given, we can consider a fuzzy model

$$Y(X) = A_0 + A_1 X_1 + \cdots + A_n X_n. \tag{40}$$

By extension principle [18], the membership function of $Y(X)$ is

$$\mu_{Y(X)}(y) = \max_x\ [\mu_X(x) \wedge \mu_R(x, y)] \tag{41}$$

which does not give a clear explicit form. But, by considering h-level set of A_i and X_i, we can obtain the h-level set of (40) represented by an interval as

$$[Y(X)]_h = [AX]_h = [y_h^L,\ y_h^U], \tag{42}$$

where a lower bound y_h^L and an upper bound y_h^U are

$$y_h^L = \sum_{i=0}^{n} \big[(a_i - (1 - h)c_i)(x_i - (1 - h)d_i) \wedge (a_i - (1 - h)c_i)(x_i + (1 - h)d_i)$$
$$\wedge (a_i + (1 - h)c_i)(x_i - (1 - h)d_i) \wedge (a_i + (1 - h)c_i)(x_i + (1 - h)d_i)\big],$$

$$y_h^U = \sum_{i=0}^{n} \big[(a_i - (1 - h)c_i)(x_i - (1 - h)d_i) \vee (a_i - (1 - h)c_i)(x_i + (1 - h)d_i) \tag{43}$$
$$\vee (a_i + (1 - h)c_i)(x_i - (1 - h)d_i) \vee (a_i + (1 - h)c_i)(x_i + (1 - h)d_i)\big],$$

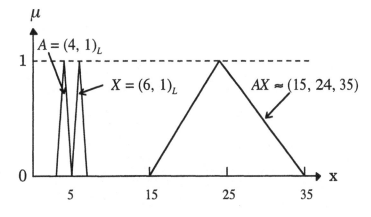

Fig. 4. Multiplication of fuzzy numbers $A = (4, 1)_L$ and $X = (6, 1)_L$

where $\wedge$ and $\vee$ are *min* and *max* operators. Furthermore, the center of (42) can be obtained by replacing $h = 1$ to (43) as

$$y^C = y^L_{h=1} = y^U_{h=1} = \sum_{i=0}^{n} a_i x_i. \tag{44}$$

Now, for example, let us consider multiplication of two fuzzy numbers $A = (4, 1)_L$ and $X = (6, 1)_L$. The h-level set of AX is obtained by (43) as

$$[15 + 8h + h^2, 35 - 12h + h^2]. \tag{45}$$

Putting $h = 0$, $AX = [15, 35]$ and the center is $[AX]_{h=1} = [24, 24] = 24$.

It should be mentioned that multiplication of two triangular fuzzy numbers is not an exact triangular shape, but approximately it can be regarded as a triangular fuzzy number as shown in Fig. 4 (see Kaufmann and Gupta [5]). Thus, (42) can be denoted approximately as a non-symmetric fuzzy number as

$$[Y(X)]_h \approx (y^L_h, y^C, y^U_h) \tag{46}$$

where $y^L_h, y^C_h,$ and y^U_h are referred to (43) and (44). Therefore, given the two approximation models by the proposed unified LP problem (25), two fuzzy outputs can be obtained for a new fuzzy input X denoted as

$$\begin{aligned} [Y^*(X)]_h &\approx (y^{*L}_h, y^{*C}, y^{*U}_h), \\ [Y_*(X)]_h &\approx (y^L_{*h}, y^C_*, y^U_{*h}). \end{aligned} \tag{47}$$

It should be mentioned that the inclusion relation

$$[Y^*(X)]_h \supseteq [Y_*(X)]_h \tag{48}$$

is always satisfied because the approximation models (18) and (19) by the unified LP problem (25) always satisfies the inclusion relation (22) at the h-level. The h-level set of a fuzzy number can be considered as an interval.

Since $a_i, c_i, x_i, d_i, (i = 0, \ldots, n)$ are given values, it is very simple to obtain above values (47). In other words, if a linguistic value which is transferred to a fuzzy input $X = (X_1, \ldots, X_n)$ is given, we can obtain two fuzzy outputs (47) through fuzzy approximation models. The obtained fuzzy outputs can be transferred to linguistic values for reasoning. Fig. 5 explains the concept of a linguistic input-output relation through a fuzzy approximation model. A fuzzy graph can be constructed by accumulating these fuzzy inputs-outputs which represent linguistic inputs-outputs.

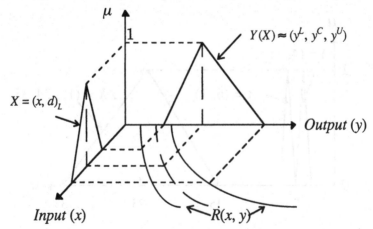

Fig. 5. Linguistic input-output through a fuzzy approximation model

4.2 A numerical example (continued)

Now, we return to the numerical example. We already obtained two approximation models (35) and (36) in Section 3. Let us consider a linguistic value *about 4* which can be transferred into a fuzzy number $X = (4, 1)_L$. Then, from the approximation models (35) and (36), two fuzzy outputs can be obtained as defined in (47). By (43) and (44), we obtained

$$Y^*(X) \approx (y^{*L}, y^{*C}, y^{*U}) = (2.961, 6.673, 12.166),$$
$$Y_*(X) \approx (y_*^L, y_*^C, y_*^U) = (4.411, 6.736, 9.724). \tag{49}$$

Given the input $X = (4, 1)_L$, the two fuzzy outputs in (49) can be approximately represented with triangular fuzzy numbers as shown in Fig. 6. In Fig. 6, $Y^*(X)$ is regarded as an upper approximation output, and $Y_*(X)$ as a lower approximation output for the input $X = (4, 1)_L$. We can interpret this as "if an input is *about 4*, then the output will be *about 6.7* with a lower approximation between 4.4 and 9.7 products, and an upper approximation between 3 and 12.2".

In short, when certain inputs-outputs data are given like Table 1, we can construct two approximation models. These models can be regarded as fuzzy graphs representing the given crisp inputs - fuzzy outputs relations. Furthermore, for a new linguistic input, we can get the lower and upper approximation outputs as shown in Fig. 6 which can be transferred to linguistic values for reasoning. In Fig. 6, the small rectangle represents the lower linguistic input-output relation denoted as $(X, Y_*(X))$, while the bigger one represents the upper linguistic input-output relation denoted as $(X, Y^*(X))$.

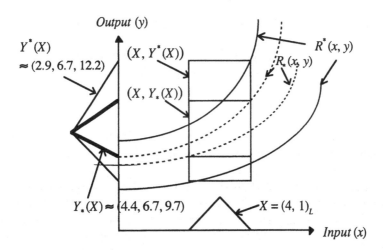

Fig. 6. Fuzzy outputs (46) obtained through two approximation models (35) and (36) for the linguistic input *about 4* represented as $X = (4,1)_L$

With same respect, we can obtain linguistic outputs through the approximation models (35) and (36) for linguistic inputs *about 2*, *about 4*, *about 6*, and *about 8* which are represented with fuzzy numbers $X_2 = (2, 1)_L$, $X_4 = (4, 1)_L$, $X_6 = (6, 1)_L$, and $X_8 = (8, 1)_L$ respectively. In Fig. 7, the inner small rectangles represent the lower linguistic input-output relations

$$(X_2, Y_*(X_2)), (X_4, Y_*(X_4)), (X_6, Y_*(X_6)), (X_8, Y_*(X_8)) \tag{50}$$

while the outer big ones represent the upper linguistic input-output relations

$$(X_2, Y^*(X_2)), (X_4, Y^*(X_4)), (X_6, Y^*(X_6)), (X_8, Y^*(X_8)). \tag{51}$$

Consequently, the inner small rectangles defined as (50) constitute a lower approximation fuzzy graph, while the outer big ones defined as (51) constitute an upper approximation fuzzy graph.

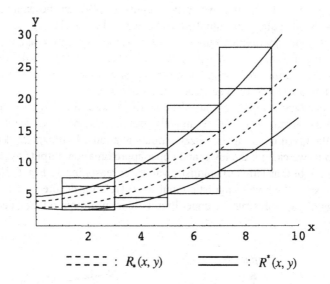

Fig. 7. Fuzzy graphs with linguistic inputs-outputs
by fuzzy approximation models (35) and (36)

5. Similarities between fuzzy regression and rough sets concept

Rough sets, introduced by Pawlak [6, 7], can be described as approximate inclusion of sets and provide a systematic framework for the study of the problems arising from imprecise and insufficient knowledge.

Let U denote the universe of discourse, and let R denote an equivalence relation on U which will be considered to be an indiscernibility relation. Then the ordered pair $A = (U, R)$ is called an approximation space. Equivalence classes of the relation R are called elementary sets in A. Any finite union of elementary sets in A is called a definable set in A.

Let a set $X \subset U$ be given. Then an upper approximation of X in A denoted as $A^*(X)$ means the least definable set containing X, and a lower approximation of X in A denoted as $A_*(X)$ means the greatest definable set contained in X. The upper approximation $A^*(X)$ and the lower approximation $A_*(X)$ can be defined as

$$A^*(X) = \bigcup_{E_i \cap X \neq \varnothing} E_i,$$
$$A_*(X) = \bigcup_{E_i \subseteq X} E_i, \tag{52}$$

where E_i is the i-th elementary set in A, and the following inclusion relation should be satisfied:

$$A^*(X) \supseteq A_*(X). \tag{53}$$

An accuracy measure of a set X in the approximation space $A = (U, R)$ is defined as

$$\alpha_A(X) = \frac{\text{Card}\,(A_*(X))}{\text{Card}\,(A^*(X))} \tag{54}$$

which lies between 0 to 1 and Card $(A_*(X))$ is the cardinality of $A_*(X)$. This accuracy measure $\alpha_A(X)$ corresponds well to the measure of fitness $\varphi_Y(x)$ in the fuzzy regression analysis. When the classification $C(U) = \{X_1, \dots, X_n\}$ are given, the accuracy of the classification $C(U)$ is defined as

$$\beta_A(U) = \text{Card}(\bigcup A_*(X_j)) \,/\, \text{Card}(\bigcup A^*(X_j)) \tag{55}$$

which is corresponding to φ_Y.

Assume that an approximation space A is composed of 9 elementary sets, i.e. $U / R = \{E_1, \dots, E_9\}$, and the set X is depicted with a thicker rectangle as shown in Fig. 8 (a). Then the upper approximation $A^*(X)$ and the lower approximation $A_*(X)$ are

$$A^*(X) = \{E_i \mid E_i \cap X \neq \varnothing\} = \{E_1, \dots, E_6\},$$
$$A_*(X) = \{E_i \mid E_i \subseteq X\} = \varnothing. \tag{56}$$

which means that the set X is internally indefinable in A. From (56) we obtain $\alpha_A(X) = 0$.

On the other hand, if elementary sets E_i's are classified in more detail as shown in Fig. 8 (b) then we obtain

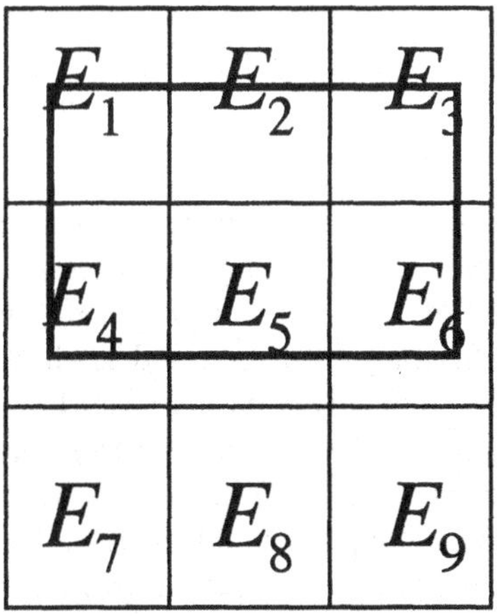

	E_1	E_2	E_3	E_4	E_5	E_6
	E_7	E_8	E_9	E_{10}	E_{11}	E_{12}
	E_{13}	E_{14}	E_{15}	E_{16}	E_{17}	E_{18}
	E_{19}	E_{20}	E_{21}	E_{22}	E_{23}	E_{24}
	E_{25}	E_{26}	E_{27}	E_{28}	E_{29}	E_{30}
	E_{31}	E_{32}	E_{33}	E_{34}	E_{35}	E_{36}

(a) $A_*(X)$ does not exist 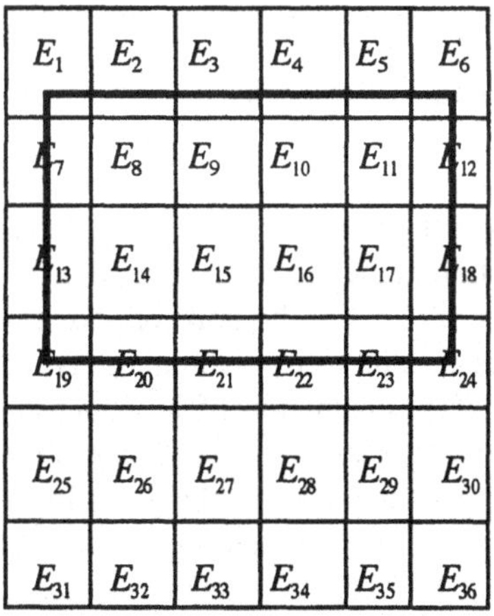   (b) $A_*(X)$ exists

Fig. 8. The lower approximations of X ($A_*(X)$) in two different elementary sets

$$A^*(X) = \{E_i \mid E_i \cap X \neq \varnothing\} = \{E_1, \dots, E_{24}\},$$
$$A_*(X) = \{E_i \mid E_i \subseteq X\} = \{E_8, \dots, E_{11}, E_{14}, \dots, E_{17}\}, \tag{57}$$

and $\alpha_A(X) = 0.33$. In this case it is said that the set X is roughly definable in A. By (56) and (57), we can notice that the accuracy measure of the set X is improved much by giving the more refinely partitioned elementary sets.

Let us compare the concepts of the upper and lower approximations of rough sets with the approximation models of fuzzy regression analysis. The lower approximation $A_*(X)$ and the upper approximation $A^*(X)$ of a set X are quite similar concept to the outputs $Y_*(x_j)$ and $Y^*(x_j)$ from the necessity and the possibility approximation models, respectively. Also, the inclusion relation (53) between the rough set approximations corresponds well to the inclusion relation (22) between the fuzzy approximation models. Furthermore, the concept of adopting a polynomial (26) as a model corresponds to Fig. 8 (b) in rough sets since the polynomials are more rich in the expression of a model than linear equations whereas more refined elementary sets like Fig. 8 (b) are better in the approximation of a set than those like Fig. 8 (a). Table 3 compares the concepts between fuzzy regression analysis and rough sets.

Table 3. Similarities of the concepts between fuzzy regression and rough sets

Fuzzy regression	Rough sets
Possibility estimation model: $Y^*(x)$	Upper approximation: $A^*(X)$
Necessity estimation model: $Y_*(x)$	Lower approximation: $A_*(X)$
Spread of $Y^*(x)$: $c^{*t}\lvert x \rvert$	Cardinality of $A^*(X)$: $\mathrm{Card}\,(A^*(X))$
Spread of $Y_*(x)$: $c_*^{t}\lvert x \rvert$	Cardinality of $A_*(X)$: $\mathrm{Card}\,(A_*(X))$
Inclusion relation: $Y^*(x) \supseteq Y_*(x)$	Inclusion relation: $A^*(X) \supseteq A_*(X)$
Measure of fitness for j-th input: $\varphi_Y(x_j)$	Accuracy measure of X_j: $\alpha_A(X_j)$
Measure of fitness for all data: φ_Y	Accuracy measure of classification $C(U)$:
(The higher, the better.)	$\beta_A(U)$ (The higher, the better.)

6. Concluding remarks

An approach to construct fuzzy graphs with linguistic inputs-outputs by fuzzy approximation models is proposed. In fuzzy regression analysis, there is no necessity estimation model if a model not fitting to the given data is adopted. By increasing the number of terms of the polynomials, any shape of curve can be represented. Thus, fuzzy regression with polynomials give more refined approximation models where the degree of approximation of the obtained models to the given data is gauged by the measure of fitness. The obtained approximation models themselves can be regarded as fuzzy graphs representing the given inputs-outputs relations. With same respect, we can construct fuzzy graphs representing the linguistic inputs-outputs relations by the obtained fuzzy approximation models. Similarities between fuzzy regression and rough sets concept are also discussed.

References

[1] G. Alefeld and J. Herzberger, *Introduction to interval computations*, Academic Press, New York, 1983.

[2] D. Dubois and H. Prade, Twofold fuzzy sets and rough sets - some issues in knowledge representations of expert's inference models, *Int. J. of Fuzzy Sets and Systems*, vol. 23, pp. 3-18, 1987.

[3] M. Inuiguchi, N. Sakawa, and S. Ushiro, Interval regression based on Minkowski's subtraction, *Proc. of Fifth IFSA World Congress*, Seoul, Korea, pp. 505-508, 1993.

[4] H. Ishibuchi and H. Tanaka, A unified approach to possibility and necessity regression analysis with interval regression models, *Proc. of Fifth IFSA World Congress*, Seoul, Korea, pp. 501-504, 1993.

[5] A. Kaufmann and M. M. Gupta, *Fuzzy mathematical models in engineering and management science*, Elsevier Science Publishers, Amsterdam, 1988.

[6] Z. Pawlak, Rough sets, *Int. J. of Information and Computer Sciences*, vol. 11, pp. 341-356, 1982.

[7] Z. Pawlak, Rough classification, *Int. J. of Man-Machine Studies*, vol. 20, pp. 469-483, 1984.

[8] M. Sakawa and H. Yano, Multiobjective fuzzy linear regression analysis for fuzzy input-output data, *Int. J. of Fuzzy Sets and Systems*, vol. 47, pp. 173-181, 1992.

[9] H. Tanaka, S. Uejima, and K. Asai, Linear regression analysis with fuzzy model, *IEEE Trans. Systems Man Cybernet*, vol. 12, pp. 903-907, 1982.

[10] H. Tanaka, Fuzzy data analysis by possibilistic linear models, *Int. J. of Fuzzy Sets and Systems*, vol. 24, pp. 363-375, 1987.

[11] H. Tanaka and J. Watada, Possibilistic linear systems and their application to the linear regression model, *Int. J. of Fuzzy Sets and Systems*, vol. 27, pp. 275-289, 1988.

[12] H. Tanaka, I. Hayashi, and J. Watada, Possibilistic linear regression analysis for fuzzy data, *European J. of Operational Research*, vol. 40, pp. 389-396, 1989.

[13] H. Tanaka and H. Ishibuchi, Identification of possibilistic linear systems by quadratic membership functions of fuzzy parameters, *Int. J. of Fuzzy sets and Systems*, vol. 41, pp. 145-160, 1991.

[14] H. Tanaka and H. Ishibuchi, Possibilistic regression analysis based on linear programming, in J. Kacprzyk and M. Fedrizzi, Eds. *Fuzzy Regression Analysis*, Omnitech press, Warsaw and Physica-Verlag, Heidelberg, pp. 47-60, 1992.

[15] H. Tanaka, K. Koyama, and H. Lee, Interval Regression Analysis based on Quadratic Programming, *Proc. of Fifth IEEE Int. Conf. on Fuzzy Systems*, New Orleans, USA, pp. 325-329, 1996.

[16] H. Tanaka, H. Lee, and T. Mizukami, Identification of possibilistic coefficients in fuzzy linear systems, *Proc. of Fifth IEEE Int. Conf. on Fuzzy Systems*, New Orleans, USA, pp. 842-847, 1996.

[17] H. Tanaka and H. Lee, Fuzzy linear regression combining central tendency and possibilistic properties, *Proc. of Sixth IEEE Int. Conf. on Fuzzy Systems*, Barcelona, Spain, pp. 63-68, 1997.

[18] L. A. Zadeh, The concept of a linguistic variable and its application to approximate reasoning-I, *Information Sciences*, vol. 8, pp. 199-249, 1975.

[19] L. A. Zadeh, Fuzzy logic = Computing with words, *IEEE Trans. Fuzzy Systems*, vol. 4, pp. 103-111, 1996.

[20] L. A. Zadeh, Toward a theory of fuzzy information granulation and its centrality in human reasoning and fuzzy logic, *Int. J. of Fuzzy sets and Systems*, vol. 90, pp. 111-127, 1997.

FUZZY RANDOM VARIABLES: MODELING LINGUISTIC STATISTICAL DATA

María Angeles Gil [1], Pedro A. Gil [1] and Dan A. Ralescu [2]

[1] Departamento de Estadística, I.O. y D.M.
Universidad de Oviedo
33071 Oviedo, SPAIN
(e-mail: angeles@pinon.ccu.uniovi.es, pedro@pinon.ccu.uniovi.es)

[2] Department of Mathematical Sciences
University of Cincinnati
Cincinnati, OH 45221-0025, USA
(e-mail: Dan.Ralescu@math.uc.edu)

Abstract. This paper deals with a concept which connects Probability and Fuzzy Set Theories: the fuzzy random variable. Fuzzy random variables represent an operational and rigorous model to formalize linguistic variables associated with numerical quantification processes (like measurements or counting). This paper offers a review of Puri and Ralescu's definition of fuzzy random variables and gathers most of the probabilistic and statistical results and methods based on it.

1. Introduction

Statistics and Probability Theory are concerned with the outcomes of real or conceptual experiments. By a *random experiment* we usually mean some well-defined act or process that leads to a well-defined outcome, and involves randomness (which is the uncertainty associated with the occurrence of the possible outcomes).

Experimental outcomes may be expressed in terms of numbers or they may be expressed in nonnumerical terms. It is operational to unify the nature of experimental outcomes by converting them into elements of certain spaces.

In this way, experimental outcomes can be converted into numerical (or vectorial) values, by assigning to each possible outcome a real (or vectorial) value. Alternatively, experimental outcomes can be converted into categories or subsets of real (or vectorial) values. These assignment processes are formalized, respectively, by means of the concepts of *random variables* (or *random vectors*) and *random sets*.

An intermediate level of precision in this assignment is that corresponding to processes converting experimental outcomes into fuzzy subsets of finite-dimensional Euclidean spaces, which has been formalized throughout *fuzzy random variables*.

The concept of fuzzy random variable provides us with a valuable mathematical model to deal with statistical problems involving certain linguistic variables: those which can be properly described by means of fuzzy subsets of the set of real numbers or vectors. Thus, fuzzy random variables can take on values like LOW, QUITE EXPENSIVE, VERY TALL, WARM, A FEW HOURS, etc.

In this work, we will first recall the notion of fuzzy random variable, as introduced by Puri and Ralescu (1986) and some related concepts and results. We then summarize some of the probabilistic aspects concerning this notion, as well as some of the recent statistical applications based on it. We will illustrate the concepts and applications with a few examples.

2. Preliminaries

Consider a *random experiment* and let $(\Omega, \mathcal{A}, P)$ be a probability space modeling this experiment, that is, Ω is the sample space (or set of the possible experimental outcomes), $\mathcal{A}$ is a σ-field of events of interest (which can be identified with subsets of Ω), and P is a probability measure defined on $\mathcal{A}$.

In the model above, the nature of elements in Ω or in $\mathcal{A}$ can be diverse. To unify this nature and make the model more operational, the experimental outcomes can be converted into elements of some well-known spaces.

Depending on the degree of precision in the conversion of outcomes, we can consider different spaces, like the Euclidean ones, the spaces of certain subsets of Euclidean spaces, or the spaces of certain functions defined on Euclidean spaces.

The rules establishing the conversion of outcomes into elements of the above mentioned spaces are formalized as mappings from the sample space Ω to the considered space, which are assumed to be measurable to guarantee the induction of a probability measure and hence ensure that useful probabilities can be computed.

If we consider the highest degree of precision, we obtain the concept of *random variable* (or *random vector*), which is a Borel-measurable mapping

$$X : \Omega \to \mathbb{R} \ \ (\text{or } \mathbb{R}^p, \, p = 2, 3, \ldots).$$

The expected value of X is intended for random variables or vectors in the sense of Bochner (1933). A random variable or vector X is said to have an *expected value in Bochner's sense* if there exists a sequence of simple random variables (or vectors) $X_1, X_2, \ldots$, such that $\lim_{n \to \infty} X_n = X$ almost surely w.r.t. P, and $\lim_{n \to \infty} \int_\Omega \|X_n - X\| \, dP = 0$ ($\| \cdot \|$ being the norm on $\mathbb{R}^p$), and this expected value is given by

$$E(X) = \int_\Omega X \, dP = \lim_{n \to \infty} \int_\Omega X_n \, dP,$$

where if X_n takes on the values $x_{n1}, \ldots, x_{nN_n}$ over $C_1, \ldots, C_{N_n}$, respectively, ($\{C_1, \ldots, C_{N_n}\}$ being a partition of Ω by elements of $\mathcal{A}$) then $\int_\Omega X_n \, dP = \sum_{i=1}^{N_n} x_{ni} P(C_i)$. The existence of $E(X)$ can be ensured if $E(\|X\|)$ exists.

A much lower degree of precision is that corresponding to compact random sets. In contrast to the case of random variables or vectors, in random sets each experimental outcome is not necessarily converted into a real or vector value but into a nonempty compact subset of real or vector values. Thus, if $\mathcal{K}(\mathbb{R}^p)$ ($p = 1, 2, \ldots$) denotes the class of nonempty compact subsets of $\mathbb{R}^p$, a *compact random set* is a Borel-measurable mapping

$$\mathsf{S} : \Omega \to \mathcal{K}(\mathbb{R}^p)$$

when $\mathcal{K}(\mathbb{R}^p)$ is assumed to be endowed with a linear structure induced by the product with a scalar and the Minkowski addition, that is,

$$\lambda A = \{\lambda a \mid a \in A\}, \quad A + B = \{a + b \mid a \in A, b \in B\},$$

for all $A, B \in \mathcal{K}(\mathbb{R}^p)$, and $\lambda \in \mathbb{R}$, and the Hausdorff metric, which for $A, B \in \mathcal{K}(\mathbb{R}^p)$ is given by

$$d_H(A, B) = \max \left\{ \sup_{a \in A} \inf_{b \in B} \|a - b\|, \sup_{b \in B} \inf_{a \in A} \|a - b\| \right\}.$$

If S is a compact random set, the *expected value of S in Aumann's sense* (1965) is given by the set

$$E(\mathsf{S}) = \left\{ E(f) \mid f \in L^1(\Omega, \mathcal{A}, P), f \in \mathsf{S} \text{ a.s. } [P] \right\},$$

where $E(f)$ is the expected value of f in Bochner's sense.

The condition $\|\mathsf{S}\| \in L^1(\Omega, \mathcal{A}, P)$ (which is referred to as the *integrable boundedness* condition for S), with $\|\mathsf{S}(\omega)\| = d_H(\{0\}, \mathsf{S}(\omega)) = \sup_{x \in \mathsf{S}(\omega)} \|x\|$ for all $\omega \in \Omega$, guarantees the existence of $E(\mathsf{S})$. Actually, if S is integrably bounded, then we can ensure that $E(\mathsf{S}) \in \mathcal{K}_c(\mathbb{R}^p)$ (class of convex elements in $\mathcal{K}(\mathbb{R}^p)$).

An intermediate degree of precision (although a higher level of generalization) is that associated with fuzzy-valued random variables. In contrast to the preceding two situations, in fuzzy-valued random variables each experimental outcome is not necessarily converted either into a real or vector value, or into a fuzzy subset of this space, but it can be converted into a fuzzy subset of this space. Assume that $\mathcal{F}(\mathbb{R}^p)\,(p = 1, 2, \ldots)$ denotes the class of all fuzzy subsets V of $\mathbb{R}^p$, $V : \mathbb{R}^p \to [0,1]$, such that $V_\alpha \in \mathcal{K}(\mathbb{R}^p)$ for all $\alpha \in [0,1]$, where V_α is the α-level set of V for all $\alpha \in (0,1]$ and $V_0 = \mathrm{cl}(\mathrm{supp}\,V)$. Then, a *fuzzy random variable* in Puri and Ralescu's sense (1986) is a Borel-measurable mapping

$$\mathcal{X} : \Omega \to \mathcal{F}(\mathbb{R}^p)$$

when $\mathcal{F}(\mathbb{R}^p)$ is assumed to be endowed with the addition $\oplus$ and the product by a scalar $\odot$ based on Zadeh's extension principle (Zadeh, 1975), in accordance with which

$$(\lambda \odot V)_\alpha = \lambda V_\alpha, \quad (V \oplus W)_\alpha = V_\alpha + W_\alpha,$$

for all $V, W \in \mathcal{F}(\mathbb{R}^p)$, $\lambda \in \mathbb{R}$, and $\alpha \in [0,1]$, and the metric d_∞ defined (Puri and Ralescu, 1981) as follows:

$$d_\infty(V, W) = \sup_{\alpha \in (0,1]} d_H(V_\alpha, W_\alpha), \quad \text{for all} \quad V, W \in \mathcal{F}(\mathbb{R}^p).$$

$\mathcal{X}$ is a fuzzy random variable if, and only if, the mapping $X_\alpha : \Omega \to \mathcal{K}(\mathbb{R}^p)$, defined by $X_\alpha(\omega) = (X(\omega))_\alpha$ is a (compact) random set for all $\alpha \in [0,1]$.

If X is a fuzzy random variable, the *expected value of $\mathcal{X}$ in Puri and Ralescu's sense* is given by the fuzzy set $\widetilde{E}(\mathcal{X})$ (sometimes denoted alternatively by $\widetilde{E}(\mathcal{X}|P)$) such that $\left(\widetilde{E}(\mathcal{X})\right)_\alpha = E(\mathcal{X}_\alpha)$ for all $\alpha \in (0,1]$. The condition $\|\mathcal{X}_0\| \in L^1(\Omega, \mathcal{A}, P)$ (which is referred to as the *integrable boundedness* condition for $\mathcal{X}$) guarantees the existence of $\widetilde{E}(\mathcal{X})$. Actually, if $\mathcal{X}$ is integrably bounded, then we can ensure that $\widetilde{E}(\mathcal{X}) \in \mathcal{F}_c(\mathbb{R}^p)$ (class of convex elements in $\mathcal{F}(\mathbb{R}^p)$) (see Puri and Ralescu, 1986).

To illustrate the types of random variables we have just described and formalized, we can consider for instance the population of all the hotels in a big city and examine the variable "price of a single room per night (breakfast and taxes included)" by consulting some guides for hotel information. According to the degree of precision of the information supplied for each guide, variable values can be either the exact price (say \$50) which gives a classical random variable, or a range of prices for different seasons (say \$50-\$60) which gives a compact random set, or a linguistic quantification of the prices (say MODERATELY CHEAP) which represents a fuzzy random variable.

On the other hand, the computation of the expected value of a fuzzy random variable is also illustrated now by means of the following example (see Gil *et al.*, 1997a):

Example 2.1: Consider the populations associated with two university classes, the first one of 106 Biology undergraduate students and the second one of 76 Mathematics undergraduate students, both taking a course in Introductory Statistics.

The University is interested in examining the point of view of the preceding classes on the importance of this course. To this purpose, an opinion poll has been conducted and students have been requested to indicate the "degree of importance of Statistics for their scientific/professional training." The results of the poll have been the following:

BIOLOGY STUDENTS' ANSWERS:

There have been 11 'very lows', 24 'lows', 31 'mediums', 25 'highs', 8 'very highs', and 6 'don't knows.'

MATHEMATICS STUDENTS' ANSWERS:

There have been 5 'lows', 13 'mediums', 32 'highs', 25 'very highs', and 1 'don't know.'

It is a practical use in the analysis of the results of this type of polls, to identify most of the answers with some real values (like 'very low' = 1, ..., 'very high' = 5), and ignore the 'don't knows'. However, this identification/ignorance is too rigid, and a more realistic and suitable description is that which identifies these answers with fuzzy numbers (Figure 1) whose supports are contained, for instance, in the real interval [1, 10] and such numbers are assumed to be expressed in terms of the S-curve (sigmoid/logistic) representations (see Zadeh, 1976) as follows:

$$\text{'low'} = \tilde{x}_2^* = \begin{cases} 1-S(1,2.5,4) & \text{on } [1,4] \\ 0 & \text{otherwise,} \end{cases}$$

$$\text{'medium'} = \tilde{x}_3^* = \begin{cases} S(2,3.5,5) & \text{on } [2,5] \\ 1-S(5,7,9) & \text{on } [5,9] \\ 0 & \text{otherwise,} \end{cases}$$

$$\text{'high'} = \tilde{x}_4^* = \begin{cases} S(4,7,10) & \text{on } [4,10] \\ 0 & \text{otherwise,} \end{cases}$$

$$\text{'don't know'} = \tilde{x}_6^* = \begin{cases} S(1,2,3) & \text{on } [1,3] \\ 1 & \text{on } [3,7] \\ 1-S(7,8.5,10) & \text{on } [7,10] \\ 0 & \text{otherwise,} \end{cases}$$

and 'very low' $= \tilde{x}_1^*$ and 'very high' $= \tilde{x}_5^*$ are obtained from $\tilde{x}_2^*$ and $\tilde{x}_4^*$, respectively, by applying the linguistic modifier 'very' as suggested by Zadeh (1976), that is,

$$\tilde{x}_1^*(x) = \left(\tilde{x}_2^*(x)\right)^2 \quad \text{for all } x \in (0, +\infty),$$

$$\tilde{x}_5^*(x) = \left(\tilde{x}_4^*(x)\right)^2 \quad \text{for all } x \in (0, +\infty),$$

with

$$S(\alpha,\beta,\gamma)(x) = \begin{cases} 0 & \text{if } x \leq \alpha \\ 2\left(\frac{x-\alpha}{\gamma-\alpha}\right)^2 & \text{if } \alpha \leq x \leq \beta \\ 1-2\left(\frac{\gamma-x}{\gamma-\alpha}\right)^2 & \text{if } \beta \leq x \leq \gamma \\ 1 & \text{if } x \geq \gamma. \end{cases}$$

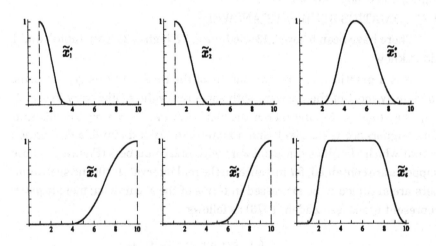

Fig.1. Fuzzy values of the variable "degree of importance of
Statistics for the scientific/professional training."

If $\mathcal{X}$ is the fuzzy random variable defined on the corresponding populations and taking on the values $\tilde{x}_1^*, \tilde{x}_2^*, \tilde{x}_3^*, \tilde{x}_4^*, \tilde{x}_5^*,$ and $\tilde{x}_6^*$, then some summary measures of interest in the study the University is developing would be the expected value of $\mathcal{X}$ in both populations, which are given in Figure 2.

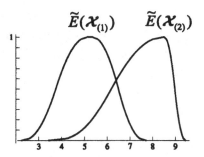

Fig.2. Expected value of the variable "degree of importance of Statistics for the scientific/professional training"in the populations of Biology students, $\widetilde{E}(\mathcal{X}_{(1)})$, and Mathematics Students, $\widetilde{E}(\mathcal{X}_{(2)})$.

It should be emphasized that fuzzy random variables have been introduced by Puri and Ralescu (1986) in a quite general way, since they are defined so that they can take on values which are fuzzy subsets of $\mathbb{R}^p$ with $p \in \mathbb{N}$ (i.e., p can be greater than 1), or more generally fuzzy subsets of a Banach space. Furthermore, these fuzzy subsets are not necessarily assumed to be convex.

In consequence, this concept of fuzzy random variable is an extension ofcompact random sets (and hence of classical random variables and vectors) and the considered measurability involves all all the α-levels and all the elements in each α-level. For previous or alternative definitions of fuzzy random variables, one can refer to Ralescu (1995a).

3. Probabilistic results concerning fuzzy random variables

There is a wide literature investigating metric and probabilistic structures and results concerning fuzzy random variables.

With respect to the *metric structure*, Puri and Ralescu (1986) and Klement *et al.* (1986) have shown that

Theorem 3.1. $\left(\mathcal{F}(\mathbb{R}^p), d_\infty\right)$ *is a metric space which is complete but nonseparable.*

An *extension of the Lebesgue dominated convergence Theorem* can be given when the convergence is intended in the d_∞ sense. Thus, Puri and Ralescu (1986) have proved that

Theorem 3.2. *Let $(\Omega, \mathcal{A}, P)$ be a probability space with P being a nonatomic probability measure. Let $\mathcal{X}, \mathcal{X}_1, \mathcal{X}_2, \ldots$ be a sequence of integrably bounded fuzzy random variables such that $\lim_{n \to \infty} d_\infty(\mathcal{X}_n(\omega), \mathcal{X}(\omega)) = 0$ for almost all $\omega \in \Omega$ with respect to P. If $\mathcal{X}_1, \mathcal{X}_2, \ldots$ is a sequence dominated by a function $h \in L^1(\Omega, \mathcal{A}, P)$ (more precisely, $\|\mathcal{X}_{n\alpha}(\omega)\| \le h(\omega)$ for all $n \in \mathbb{N}$, $\omega \in \Omega$ and $\alpha \in (0, 1]$), then*

$$\lim_{n \to \infty} d_\infty(\widetilde{E}(\mathcal{X}_n), \widetilde{E}(\mathcal{X})) = 0.$$

Recently, López-Díaz and Gil (1997ab) have stated two *constructive definitions of integrably bounded fuzzy random variables* as "limits" of sequences of special types of fuzzy random variables. These limits are intended in the d_H and d_∞ senses. The result characterizing integrably bounded fuzzy random variables as certain d_H limit has been presented (López-Díaz and Gil, 1997a) as follows:

Theorem 3.3. *Given a probability space $(\Omega, \mathcal{A}, P)$, a function $\mathcal{X} : \Omega \to \mathcal{F}(\mathbb{R}^p)$ is an integrably bounded fuzzy random variable associated with this space if, and only if, there exists a sequence of simple fuzzy random variables (i.e., taking on a finite number of different values) $\mathcal{X}_1, \mathcal{X}_2, \ldots$, with $\mathcal{X}_n : \Omega \to \mathcal{F}(\mathbb{R}^p)$, associated with the same probability space, and a function $h : \Omega \to \mathbb{R}$, $h \in L^1(\Omega, \mathcal{A}, P)$, such that $\|\mathcal{X}_{n0}(\omega)\| \le h(\omega)$ for all $\omega \in \Omega$ and $n \in \mathbb{N}$, and*

$$\lim_{n \to \infty} d_H(\mathcal{X}_{n\alpha}(\omega), \mathcal{X}_\alpha(\omega)) = 0$$

for all $\omega \in \Omega$ and for each $\alpha \in (0, 1]$.

Alternatively, integrably bounded fuzzy random variables can be characterized as a d_∞-limit (see López-Díaz and Gil, 1997b) as follows:

Theorem 3.4. *Given a probability space $(\Omega, \mathcal{A}, P)$, a function $\mathcal{X} : \Omega \to \mathcal{F}(\mathbb{R}^p)$ is an integrably bounded fuzzy random variable associated with this space if, and only if, there exists a sequence of fuzzy random variables $\mathcal{X}_1, \mathcal{X}_2, \ldots$, with $\mathcal{X}_n : \Omega \to \mathcal{F}(\mathbb{R}^p)$, associated with the same probability space and having simple α-level functions (i.e., each of the α-level functions takes on a finite number of different values), and a function $h : \Omega \to \mathbb{R}$, $h \in L^1(\Omega, \mathcal{A}, P)$, such that $\|\mathcal{X}_{n0}(\omega)\| \le h(\omega)$ for all $\omega \in \Omega$ and $n \in \mathbb{N}$, and*

$$\lim_{n \to \infty} d_\infty(\mathcal{X}_n(\omega), \mathcal{X}(\omega)) = 0$$

for all $\omega \in \Omega$.

The preceding definitions has allowed (López-Díaz and Gil, 1997ab) to give two *constructive definitions of the expected value of an integrably bounded fuzzy random variable* in Puri and Ralescu's sense. Thus,

Theorem 3.5. *Let $(\Omega, \mathcal{A}, P)$ be a probability space and let $\mathcal{X}$ be an integrably bounded fuzzy random variable. Then, there exists a sequence of simple fuzzy random variables $\mathcal{X}_1, \mathcal{X}_2, \ldots$ such that*

$$\lim_{n \to \infty} d_H \left(\big(\widetilde{E}(\mathcal{X}_n) \big)_\alpha, \big(\widetilde{E}(\mathcal{X}) \big)_\alpha \right) = 0,$$

for all $\alpha \in (0, 1]$.

Theorem 3.6. *Let $(\Omega, \mathcal{A}, P)$ be a probability space and let $\mathcal{X}$ be an integrably bounded fuzzy random variable. Then, there exists a sequence of integrably bounded fuzzy random variables $\mathcal{X}_1, \mathcal{X}_2, \ldots$ with simple α-level functions such that*

$$\lim_{n \to \infty} d_\infty \big(\widetilde{E}(\mathcal{X}_n), \widetilde{E}(\mathcal{X}) \big) = 0.$$

The results in Theorems 3.3-3.6 can be also established for $\mathcal{F}_c(\mathbb{R}^p)$-valued fuzzy random variables. In this case, both variables, the limit one and those in the convergent sequence, will be $\mathcal{F}_c(\mathbb{R}^p)$-valued.

It should be emphasized that, due to the added convexity, the Aumann integral of a simple random set can be easily computed by means of the use of the scalar product and the Minkowski addition (see Debreu, 1966, Byrne, 1978). Consequently, the expected value of a simple fuzzy random variable can be easily computed by means of the use of the fuzzy product by a scalar $\odot$ and the fuzzy addition $\oplus$ based on Zadeh's extension principle (1975). If we combine the last assertions with Theorems 3.5 and 3.6, we obtain an operational procedure to compute the expected value of a general integrably bounded fuzzy random variable.

The result in Theorem 3.3 has been also used to give conditions to compute *iterated expected values* of fuzzy random variables, irrespectively of the order of integration. In this way, López-Díaz and Gil (1997c) have proven that

Theorem 3.7. *Consider the probability space $(\Omega_1 \times \Omega_2, \mathcal{A}_1 \otimes \mathcal{A}_2, P)$, and assume that the "marginal" probability spaces $(\Omega_1, \mathcal{A}_1, P_1)$ and $(\Omega_2, \mathcal{A}_2, P_2)$ are complete. Let $\mathcal{X}$ be an integrably bounded fuzzy random variable associated with $(\Omega_1 \times \Omega_2, \mathcal{A}_1 \otimes \mathcal{A}_2, P)$ and such that there exists a function $f \in L^1(\Omega_1 \times \Omega_2, \mathcal{A}_1 \otimes \mathcal{A}_2, P)$ satisfying for all $(\omega_1, \omega_2) \in \Omega_1 \times \Omega_2$ that* *i)* the projections $f_{\omega_1} \in L^1(\Omega_2, \mathcal{A}_2, P_{\omega_1})$, $f_{\omega_2} \in L^1(\Omega_1, \mathcal{A}_1, P_{\omega_2})$,

ii) $g_1 \in L^1(\Omega_1, \mathcal{A}_1, P_1)$, $g_2 \in L^1(\Omega_2, \mathcal{A}_2, P_2)$,

with $g_1(\omega_1) = \int_{\Omega_2} f_{\omega_1} \, dP_{\omega_1}$, $g_2(\omega_2) = \int_{\Omega_1} f_{\omega_2} \, dP_{\omega_2}$, and P_{ω_1} and P_{ω_2} being the regular conditional probabilities given ω_1 and ω_2, respectively. Then,

$$\widetilde{E}\left(\widetilde{E}(\mathcal{X}_{\omega_1}|P_{\omega_1})|P_1\right) = \widetilde{E}\left(\widetilde{E}(\mathcal{X}_{\omega_2}|P_{\omega_2})|P_2\right) = \widetilde{E}(\mathcal{X}|P).$$

An important investigation in this framework is that of limit theorems for fuzzy random variables. Regarding the *strong law of large numbers*, Klement *et al.* (1986) have stated a result generalizing the Artstein and Vitale SLLN for random sets (1975), by using the d_1 metric, which is given by

$$d_1(V, W) = \int_{(0,1]} d_H(V_\alpha, W_\alpha) \, d\alpha \text{ for all } V, W \in \mathcal{F}(\mathbb{R}^p),$$

and which induces a complete and separable metric space on $\mathcal{F}(\mathbb{R}^p)$ (see Klement *et al.*, 1986). Thus, in accordance with Klement *et al.* (1986), we have that

Theorem 3.8. *Let $(\Omega, \mathcal{A}, P)$ be a probability space. Let $\mathcal{X}_1, \mathcal{X}_2, \ldots$ be a sequence of fuzzy random variables independent and identically distributed and satisfying that $E(\|\mathcal{X}_{10}\|) < \infty$. Then,*

$$\lim_{n \to \infty} d_1\left(\frac{1}{n} \odot (\mathcal{X}_1(\omega) \oplus \ldots \oplus \mathcal{X}_n(\omega)), \widetilde{E}(\mathrm{co}\,\mathcal{X}_1)\right) = 0$$

for almost all $\omega \in \Omega$ w.r.t. P (with $(\mathrm{co}\,\mathcal{X}_1(\omega))_\alpha$ denoting the convex hull of $(\mathcal{X}_1(\omega))_\alpha$ for all $\alpha \in [0,1]$, and $\widetilde{E}(\mathrm{co}\,\mathcal{X}_1) = \widetilde{E}(\mathcal{X}_1)$ if $\mathcal{X}_1$ is nonconstant).

Quite recently, Colubi *et al.* (1997) have generalized the last SLLN by using the d_∞ metric. To drop the nonseparability of the metric space $(\mathcal{F}(\mathbb{R}^p), d_\infty)$, the constructive definition of integrably bounded fuzzy random variables in Theorem 3.4 has been employed. In this way, Colubi *et al.*'s result indicates that

Theorem 3.9. *Let $(\Omega, \mathcal{A}, P)$ be a probability space. Let $\mathcal{X}_1, \mathcal{X}_2, \ldots$ be a sequence of integrably bounded fuzzy random variables pairwise independent and identically distributed. Then,*

$$\lim_{n \to \infty} d_\infty\left(\frac{1}{n} \odot (\mathcal{X}_1(\omega) \oplus \ldots \oplus \mathcal{X}_n(\omega)), \widetilde{E}(\mathrm{co}\,\mathcal{X}_1)\right) = 0$$

for almost all $\omega \in \Omega$ w.r.t. P. Conversely, if $\mathcal{X}_1, \mathcal{X}_2, \ldots$ is a sequence of fuzzy random variables pairwise independent and identically distributed, and satisfying that

$$\lim_{n \to \infty} d_\infty \left(\frac{1}{n} \odot (\mathcal{X}_1(\omega) \oplus \ldots \oplus \mathcal{X}_n(\omega)), V \right) = 0$$

for almost all $\omega \in \Omega$ w.r.t. P, and for certain $V \in \mathcal{F}(\mathbb{R}^p)$, then $\mathcal{X}_1, \mathcal{X}_2, \ldots$ are integrably bounded and $\mathrm{co}\, V = \widetilde{E}(\mathrm{co}\, \mathcal{X}_1)$.

On the other hand, Klement *et al.* (1986) have also proved a *central limit theorem* for fuzzy random variables which extends the classical CLT:

Theorem 3.10. *Let $(\Omega, \mathcal{A}, P)$ be a probability space. Let $\mathcal{X}_1, \mathcal{X}_2, \ldots$ be a sequence of integrably bounded fuzzy random variables independent and identically distributed, whose values are Lipschitz functions of the level α w.r.t. the Hausdorff distance (i.e., there exists $M \in \mathbb{R}^+$ such that $d_H(\mathcal{X}_{n\alpha}, \mathcal{X}_{n\alpha'}) \leq M |\alpha - \alpha'|$ for every $\alpha, \alpha' \in (0,1]$). Assume also that*

i) $E\left[(\|\mathcal{X}_{10}\|)^2 \right] < \infty,$

ii) $E\left[\left(\sup_{\alpha, \alpha' \in (0,1] | \alpha \neq \alpha'} \frac{d_H(\mathcal{X}_{1\alpha}, \mathcal{X}_{n\alpha'})}{|\alpha - \alpha'|} \right)^2 \right] < \infty.$

Then, there exists a gaussian random element Z which is a continuous function on $[0,1] \times S^{p-1}$ (with $S^{p-1} = \{x \in \mathbb{R}^p \mid \|x\| = 1\}$), such that $\sqrt{n}\, d_\infty \left(\frac{1}{n} \odot (\mathcal{X}_1 \oplus \ldots \oplus \mathcal{X}_n), \widetilde{E}(\mathcal{X}_1) \right)$ converges in law to $\|Z\|_\infty$.

Puri and Ralescu (1985) introduced the concept of *normality* for fuzzy random variables, which extends that normality of classical random variables (or vectors) and that for random sets. If a fuzzy random variable $\mathcal{X}$ takes on values which are Lipschitz functions of the level α w.r.t. the Hausdorff distance, $\mathcal{X}$ is said to be a *normal fuzzy random variable* if there exists a classical normal random variable (or vector) η with mean zero such that $\mathcal{X} = \widetilde{E}(\mathcal{X}) \oplus \eta$.

Finally, some inequalities involving the expected value of a fuzzy random variable have been established by Ralescu (1995ab). The first one is an *extension of the Brunn-Minkowski inequality* for fuzzy random variables, in accordance with which we have

Theorem 3.11. *Let (Ω, A, P) be a probability space, and let $\mathcal{X} : \Omega \to \mathcal{F}(\mathbb{R}^p)$ be an integrably bounded fuzzy random variable associated with it. If for any $U \in \mathcal{F}(\mathbb{R}^p)$ the volume of U is given by*

$$V_p(U) = \left[\int_{(0,1]} \left(V_p(U_\alpha) \right)^{1/p} d\alpha \right]^p$$

(where $V_p(U_\alpha)$ denotes the "classical volume of U_α), then

$$V_p \left(\widetilde{E}(\mathcal{X}) \right) \geq \left[E(V_p \circ \mathcal{X})^{1/p} \right]^p.$$

The second inequality is an *extension of Jensen's inequality* and asserts (Ralescu, 1995ab) that

Theorem 3.12. *Let (Ω, A, P) be a probability space, and let $\mathcal{X} : \Omega \to \mathcal{F}(\mathbb{R}^p)$ be an integrably bounded fuzzy random variable associated with it. Let $\varphi : \mathcal{F}(\mathbb{R}^p) \to \mathbb{R}$ be a convex function (that is, $\varphi((\lambda \odot V) \oplus ((1 - \lambda) \odot W)) \leq \lambda \varphi(V) + (1 - \lambda) \varphi(W)$). Then, we have that*

$$\varphi \left(\widetilde{E}(\mathcal{X}) \right) \leq E \left(\varphi(\mathcal{X}) \right).$$

4. Statistical techniques concerning fuzzy random variables

The concepts and results in Sections 2 and 3 of this paper have been used extensively to study some problems of Statistics concerning fuzzy random variables.

In this way, Ralescu (1982, 1995c, 1996), Ralescu and Ralescu (1984, 1986) have analyzed several *inferential problems about fuzzy parameters of fuzzy random variables*.

This analysis involves certain discussions on: the *fuzzy "point" estimation* of fuzzy parameters based on either fuzzy or crisp sample information (like, for instance, the estimation of an unknown parameter representing the 'probability of being TALL in a population of size N' on the basis of the sample information 'there are MANY TALL people in this population'); the *fuzzy confidence estimation* of a fuzzy population parameter based on a fuzzy statistic (which means a single fuzzy random variable based on a random sample from either a fuzzy or a crisp variable), where confidence is measured in terms of fuzzy probabilities.

In the *fuzzy testing of hypotheses* some or all of the hypotheses, parameters, statistics, sample information and probabilities of different errors are assumed to be fuzzy. In this sense, if $(X_1, \ldots, , X_n)$ denotes a random sample from a variable whose distribution is given by the probability measure P_θ, where θ is an unknown parameter of interest, and we want to test a null hypothesis of the form $H_0 : \text{'}\theta$ is $V\text{'}$, where V is a fuzzy set, it seems natural to consider statistical procedures as follows: 'reject H_0 if $\delta(X_1, \ldots, , X_n)$ is $W\text{'}$, where $\delta(X_1, \ldots, , X_n)$ is a fuzzy statistic and W is a fuzzy subset. The *probabilities of Type I error* of such tests (and hence the so-called *size* of these tests) will be given by

$$P_{H_0}\big(\delta(X_1, \ldots, , X_n) \text{ is } W\big),$$

and it is clear that such a probability shoud be fuzzy rather than exact. Concerning the "supremum" of the probabilities of Type I error of a given test, this supremum will be now taken over a fuzzy set so that we can set the corresponding test size at a fixed (but fuzzy) value π. In specific cases π will stand for SMALL, VERY SMALL, and so on.

More importantly, still, is the calculation of the *power function of a fuzzy test of hypotheses*,

$$P_{H_1}\big(\delta(X_1, \ldots, , X_n) \text{ is } W\big),$$

where H_1 stands for the alternative hypothesis. This power function must be now fuzzy-valued and it is definitely a nontrivial matter that of comparing two testing procedures on the basis of their (fuzzy) power functions.

Some other statistical problems have been examined, and methods have been suggested in the literature to solve them.

An immediate application of Theorem 3.7 has been developed by López-Díaz and Gil (1997c) to get an *extension of the double expectation theorem*, in accordance with which

Theorem 4.1. *Let $(\Omega, \mathcal{A}, P)$ be a complete probability space and let $\mathcal{X} : \Omega \to \mathcal{F}_c(\mathbb{R}^p)$, $\mathcal{Y} : \Omega \to \mathcal{F}_c(\mathbb{R}^p)$ be two integrably bounded fuzzy random variables. Let $\sigma_\mathcal{X}$ and $\sigma_\mathcal{Y}$ be the σ-fields in $\mathcal{F}_c(\mathbb{R}^p)$ induced from $\mathcal{A}$ by $\mathcal{X}$ and $\mathcal{Y}$, respectively, and let $P_\mathcal{X}$ and $P_\mathcal{Y}$ be the probability measures induced from P by $\mathcal{X}$ and $\mathcal{Y}$, respectively. Consider the product probability space $(\mathcal{F}_c(\mathbb{R}^p) \times \mathcal{F}_c(\mathbb{R}^p), \sigma_\mathcal{X} \otimes \sigma_\mathcal{Y}, P_\mathcal{X} \otimes P_\mathcal{Y})$, and let $\mathcal{X}^* : \mathcal{F}_c(\mathbb{R}^p) \times \mathcal{F}_c(\mathbb{R}^p) \to \mathcal{F}_c(\mathbb{R}^p)$ be the integrably bounded fuzzy random variable such that $\mathcal{X}^*(\tilde{x}, \tilde{y}) = \tilde{x}$, for all $\tilde{x}, \tilde{y} \in \mathcal{F}_c(\mathbb{R}^p)$. Assume that when $\mathcal{Y} = \tilde{y}$ the conditional probability distribution induced by $\mathcal{X}$ is given by a regular conditional probability distribution on*

$(\mathcal{F}_c(\mathbb{R}^p), \sigma_{\mathcal{X}})$ denoted by $P_{\tilde{y}}$. Then, if we identify $\widetilde{E}(\mathcal{X}/\mathcal{Y} = \tilde{y}) = \widetilde{E}(\mathcal{X}_{\tilde{y}}^*/P_{\tilde{y}})$ and $\widetilde{E}\left(\widetilde{E}(\mathcal{X}/\mathcal{Y})/P_{\mathcal{Y}}\right) = \widetilde{E}\left(\widetilde{E}(\mathcal{X}/\mathcal{Y} = \tilde{y})/P_{\mathcal{Y}}\right)$, we obtain that

$$\widetilde{E}(\mathcal{X}/P_{\mathcal{X}}) = \widetilde{E}\left(\widetilde{E}(\mathcal{X}/\mathcal{Y})/P_{\mathcal{Y}}\right).$$

The last result becomes especially useful when we consider *mixture distributions of fuzzy random variables*, like in the following example (cf. López-Díaz and Gil, 1997c) in which one of the variables in the mixture is real-valued:

Example 4.1: Let $\mathcal{X}$ be a fuzzy random variable which in a population of N sampling units, $U_1, \ldots, U_N$, takes on the values $\tilde{x}_1 = \mathcal{X}(U_1), \ldots, \tilde{x}_N = \mathcal{X}(U_N)$, with $\tilde{x}_1, \ldots, \tilde{x}_N \in \mathcal{F}_c(\mathbb{R})$.

If a sample $[\tau]$ of size n is chosen at random and without replacement from the overall population, and $U_{\tau 1}, \ldots, U_{\tau n}$ are the units in it, then the *fuzzy sample mean* $\overline{\mathcal{X}}_n$ which associates with $[\tau]$ the fuzzy value

$$\overline{\mathcal{X}}_n[\tau] = \frac{1}{n} \odot \left(\mathcal{X}(U_{\tau 1}) \oplus \ldots \oplus \mathcal{X}(U_{\tau n})\right),$$

is a fuzzy unbiased estimator of the *fuzzy population mean*, $\overline{\mathcal{X}} = \frac{1}{N} \odot \left(\mathcal{X}(U_1) \oplus \ldots \oplus \mathcal{X}(U_N)\right)$. Thus, $\widetilde{E}(\overline{\mathcal{X}}_n) = \overline{\mathcal{X}}$, where $\widetilde{E}(\overline{\mathcal{X}}_n)$ is the expected value of the sample mean $\overline{\mathcal{X}}_n$ computed on the space of the $\binom{N}{n}$ distinct possible random samples without replacement of size n from the given population.

Assume that a sample of size n is now chosen at random and with replacement from the overall population, and let ν be the "effective sample size", which is the number of distinct units contained in the sample. Let $\overline{\mathcal{X}}_\nu$ denote the sample mean for the distinct units. $\overline{\mathcal{X}}_\nu$ is a fuzzy random variable whose distribution depends on a classical random variable ν, and $\overline{\mathcal{X}}_\nu$ and ν satisfy the conditions in Theorem 4.1, and the application of this result entails that $\overline{\mathcal{X}}_\nu$ is a fuzzy unbiased estimator of $\overline{\mathcal{X}}$.

In connection with the example above the problem of estimating some population characteristics associated with fuzzy random variables in samplings from finite populations has been analyzed. Thus, Lubiano and Gil *et al.* (1997) have developed the *estimation of the expected value of an $\mathcal{F}_c(\mathbb{R})$-valued random variable in random samplings from finite populations*. To this purpose, a measure quantifying the average dispersion of an $\mathcal{F}_c(\mathbb{R})$-valued random variable $\mathcal{X}$ from a given fuzzy number has been introduced previously (see Lubiano *et al.*, 1997). This measure has been called the $\vec{\lambda}$-*mean square dispersion* ($\vec{\lambda}$-*MSD*) associated with $\mathcal{X}$ about a fuzzy number

$V \in \mathcal{F}_c(\mathbb{R})$, and is given by the real value

$$MSD_{\vec{\lambda}}(\mathcal{X}, V) = E\left(\left[D_{\vec{\lambda}}(\mathcal{X}, V)\right]^2\right)$$

with $D_{\vec{\lambda}}$ the metric on $\mathcal{F}_c(\mathbb{R})$ introduced by Bertoluzza *et al.* (1995), so that for all V, $W \in \mathcal{F}_c(\mathbb{R})$

$$D_{\vec{\lambda}}(V, W) = \left\{ \int_{(0,1]} \left[\lambda_1 \left(\sup V_\alpha - \sup W_\alpha \right)^2 \right. \right.$$
$$\left. \left. + \lambda_2 \left(\text{mid } V_\alpha - \text{mid } W_\alpha \right)^2 + \lambda_3 \left(\inf V_\alpha - \inf W_\alpha \right)^2 \right] d\alpha \right\}^{1/2},$$

mid denoting the mid-point of the corresponding compact interval, and $\vec{\lambda} = (\lambda_1, \lambda_2, \lambda_3)$ with $\lambda_i \in [0, 1)$ for $i = 1, 2, 3$, and $\lambda_1 + \lambda_2 + \lambda_3 = 1$.

Lubiano *et al.* (1997) have examined the properties of $MSD_{\vec{\lambda}}(\mathcal{X}, V)$ which confirm the suitability of this measure to quantify how much "in error" the number V is expected to be a description of variable values of $\mathcal{X}$, and serves as an extension and a counterpart to the classical Mean Square Error for real-valued random variables.

The $\vec{\lambda}$-*MSD* has been applied to determine the precision of (fuzzy) unbiased (in Puri and Ralescu's expected value sense) estimators of a *fuzzy parameter* of a fuzzy random variable: the expected value of this variable. Thus, Lubiano and Gil (1997) have proved that

Theorem 4.2. *Let $\mathcal{X}$ be a fuzzy random variable which in population of N sampling units, $U_1, \ldots, U_N$, takes on the values $\tilde{x}_1 = \mathcal{X}(U_1), \ldots, \tilde{x}_N = \mathcal{X}(U_N)$, with $\tilde{x}_1, \ldots, \tilde{x}_N \in \mathcal{F}_c(\mathbb{R})$.*

If a sample $[\tau]$ of size n is chosen at random and with or without replacement from the overall population, and $U_{\tau 1}, \ldots, U_{\tau n}$ are the units in this sample, then the fuzzy sample mean $\overline{\mathcal{X}}_n$ which associates with $[\tau]$ the fuzzy value

$$\overline{\mathcal{X}}_n[\tau] = \frac{1}{n} \odot \left(\mathcal{X}(U_{\tau 1}) \oplus \ldots \oplus \mathcal{X}(U_{\tau n}) \right),$$

is a (fuzzy) unbiased estimator of the population mean, $\overline{\mathcal{X}} = \tilde{E}(\mathcal{X}) = \frac{1}{N} \odot \left(\mathcal{X}(U_1) \oplus \ldots \oplus \mathcal{X}(U_N) \right)$.

Moreover, the $\vec{\lambda}$-MSD of $\overline{\mathcal{X}}_n$ in the random sampling of size n with replacement is given by

$$MSD_{\vec{\lambda}}(\overline{\mathcal{X}}_n, \overline{\mathcal{X}}) = \frac{MSD_{\vec{\lambda}}\left(\mathcal{X}, \tilde{E}(\mathcal{X})\right)}{n},$$

whereas the $\vec{\lambda}$-MSD of $\overline{X}_n$ in the random sampling of size n without replacement is given by

$$MSD_{\vec{\lambda}}\left(\overline{X}_n, \overline{X}\right) = \frac{(N-n)\,MSD_{\vec{\lambda}}\left(X, \widetilde{E}(X)\right)}{n(N-1)}.$$

Consequently, from Theorem 4.2 we arrive at the obvious conclusion that the random sampling without replacement is more precise than the random sampling with replacement, in estimating the population expected value of a fuzzy random variable.

The $\vec{\lambda}$-*MSD* defines a quantification of the variation of a fuzzy random variable in an absolute way. Nevertheless, sometimes one can be interested in measuring this variation in a relative way. This objective can be achieved by studying the problem of *quantifying (fuzzily) the relative inequality associated with fuzzy random variables*. This study has been developed in Gil *et al.* (1997a) and López-García (1997), in which some measures of the extent of the inequality associated with an $\mathcal{F}_c(\mathbb{R})$-valued random variable have been introduced. In the literature, inequality indices are commonly used in fields like Economics (income inequality, wealth inequality, etc.) and Industry (industrial concentration). The extension of these indices for fuzzy random variables entails an enlargement of the classes of variables and fields of application the quantification of inequality can be employed for. In this way, the fuzzy quantification of inequality can be applied to many linguistic variables and fields like Medicine, Social Sciences, and so on.

The *fuzzy inequality ϕ-index* associated with an $\mathcal{F}_c(\mathbb{R})$-valued random variable X such that $X_0(\Omega) \subset (0, +\infty)$ has been defined by López-García (1997) as an extension of Gastwirth's indices, as follows:

$$\widetilde{I}_\phi(X) = \widetilde{E}\left[\phi(X) \oslash \phi(\widetilde{E}(X))\right] \ominus 1,$$

with $\oslash$ and $\ominus$ the fuzzy quotient and substraction based on Zadeh's extension principle (1975), $\phi : (0, +\infty) \rightarrow (0, +\infty)$ being a monotonic strictly convex function, and $\phi(X)$ being obtained also by using Zadeh's extension principle.

Properties of $\widetilde{I}_\phi(X)$, and in particular of $\widetilde{I}_H(X)$ (which equals $\widetilde{I}_\phi(X)$ when $\phi(x) = 1/x$ for all $x \in (0, +\infty)$), corroborate the suitability of these indices and have been analyzed in Gil *et al.* (1997a) and López-García (1997).

In López-García *et al.* (1997), *unbiased (up to additive equivalences) estimators of $\widetilde{I}_H(X)$ in random samplings from finite populations* have been constructed.

We now illustrate the computation of $\tilde{I}_H(\mathcal{X})$ by means of an example (see Gil *et al.*, 1997a):

Example 4.2: The decision-makers in a University are interested in estimating the inequality associated with the variable "mean time spent daily in the study of Mathematics", $\mathcal{X}$, in a class of 100 students who take a course in Mathematics in this university. For this purpose, the students in the class are asked about their values for variable $\mathcal{X}$, and among the answers obtained, there have been 8 'not too much time,' 15 'less than 1 hour,' 9 'a bit less than 1 hour,' 12 'around 1 hour,' 11 'much more than 1 hour,' 17 '1 to 2 hours,' 10 'a bit more than 1 hour and a half,' 6 'approximately 2 hours,' 10 'not much more than 2 hours,' and 2 'more than 2 hours.'

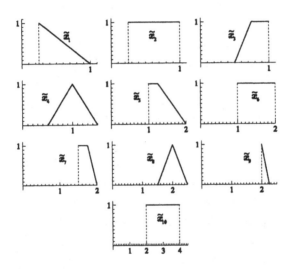

Fig. 3. Fuzzy numbers $\tilde{x}_1=$ 'not too much time,' $\tilde{x}_2=$ less than 1 hour,' $\tilde{x}_3=$ 'a bit less than 1 hour,' $\tilde{x}_4=$ 'around 1 hour,' $\tilde{x}_5=$ 'much more than 1 hour,' $\tilde{x}_6=$ '1 to 2 hours,' $\tilde{x}_7=$ 'a bit more than 1 hour and a half,' $\tilde{x}_8=$ 'approximately 2 hours,' $\tilde{x}_9=$ 'not much more than 2 hours,' and $\tilde{x}_{10}=$ 'more than 2 hours.'

If these answers are described by means of the triangular Tri and trapezoidal Tra fuzzy numbers whose support is contained in $[.25, 4]$ (with $.25 = 15$ minutes) and given by (see Figure 3):

$$\tilde{x}_1 = \text{'not too much time'} = Tri(.25, .25, 1),$$
$$\tilde{x}_2 = \text{'less than 1 hour'} = Tra(.25, .25, 1, 1),$$
$$\tilde{x}_3 = \text{'a bit less than 1 hour'} = Tra(.5, .75, 1, 1),$$
$$\tilde{x}_4 = \text{'around 1 hour'} = Tri(.5, 1, 1.5),$$
$$\tilde{x}_5 = \text{'much more than 1 hour'} = Tra(1, 1, 1.25, 2),$$

$$\tilde{x}_6 = \text{'1 to 2 hours'} = Tra(1, 1, 2, 2),$$
$$\tilde{x}_7 = \text{'a bit more than 1 hour and a half'} = Tra(1.5, 1.5, 1.75, 2),$$
$$\tilde{x}_8 = \text{'approximately 2 hours'} = Tri(1.5, 2, 2.5),$$
$$\tilde{x}_9 = \text{'not much more than 2 hours'} = Tri(2, 2, 2.25),$$
$$\tilde{x}_{10} = \text{'more than 2 hours'} = Tra(2, 2, 4, 4),$$

then, the value of the fuzzy hyperbolic index $\tilde{I}_H(\mathcal{X})$ is given by the fuzzy number represented in Figure 4.

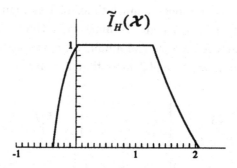

Fig. 4. Fuzzy hyperbolic inequality index associated with $\mathcal{X}$.

Finally, fuzzy random variables have been used to establish a handy *model for single-stage statistical decision problems involving fuzzy-valued utilities or losses* assessed to the consequences of the decisions.

Gil and López-Díaz (1996) have presented the concept of *fuzzy utility function*, so that if we consider a single-stage decision problem with state space Θ and action space A, then a function $\mathcal{U} : \Theta \times A \to \mathcal{F}_c(\mathbb{R})$ is said to be a *fuzzy utility function* if

- $\mathcal{U}_a$ is a fuzzy random variable associated with the measurable space $(\Theta, \mathcal{E})$, for all $a \in A$, and

- if a prior distribution π on $(\Theta, \mathcal{E})$ is assumed, then for any two actions a_1, $a_2 \in A$ for which the projections $\mathcal{U}_{a_1}$ and $\mathcal{U}_{a_2}$ are integrably bounded fuzzy random variables associated with $(\Theta, \mathcal{E}, \pi)$, a_2 is considered to be not preferred to a_1 if, and only if, $\tilde{E}(\mathcal{U}_{a_1}/\pi) \succeq \tilde{E}(\mathcal{U}_{a_2}/\pi)$, where $\succeq$ is an appropriate ranking of fuzzy numbers.

Given a random experiment $X \equiv (\mathbb{X}, \mathcal{B}_{\mathbb{X}}, P_\theta)$, $\theta \in \Theta$, with $\mathbb{X} \subset \mathbb{R}^p$, and a *decision rule* $\delta : \mathbb{X} \to A$ associated with the decision problem, we can define the mapping $\mathcal{U}^\delta : \Theta \times \mathbb{X} \to \mathcal{F}_c(\mathbb{R})$ such that $\mathcal{U}^\delta(\theta, x) = \mathcal{U}(\theta, \delta(x))$.

Then, the use of Theorem 3.7 allows us to obtain decision rules "maximizing" the expected (fuzzy) utility for each experimental outcome $x \in X$. More precisely (see Gil and López-Díaz (1996),

Theorem 4.3. *Consider a statistical decision problem with state space* Θ, *action space* A, *and a random experiment* $X \equiv (X, \mathcal{B}_X, P_\theta)$, $\theta \in \Theta$, *and assume that we have defined a fuzzy utility function* $\mathcal{U}$ *to represent decision maker's preferences. Let* π *be the prior distribution on the measurable space* $(\Theta, \mathcal{E})$. *Then, if* $\mathcal{U}^\delta$ *satisfies the conditions in Theorem 3.7, the decision rule* $\delta_B : X \to A$ *such that* $\delta_B(x) = a_x$ *for each* $X \in X$, *where*

$$\tilde{E}(\mathcal{U}_{a_x}/\pi_x) \succeq \tilde{E}(\mathcal{U}_a/\pi_x) \quad \text{for all } a \in A,$$

(π_x being the posterior distribution given x) is an optimal decision rule for this problem.

Some examples illustrating the determination of optimal decision rules in Bayesian decision problems (and, in particular, in point estimation and hypothesis testing), and the comparison of random experiments in this context, can be found in Gil and López-Díaz (1996), Gil *et al.* (1997b) and López-Díaz and Gil (1997c).

Acknowledgments. The research in this paper has been supported in part by DGICYT Grant No. PB94-1328 and DGES Grant No. PB95-1049 from the Spanish Ministry of Education and Culture. Dan Ralescu was supported by Grant US 97016 from the Japan Society for the Promotion of Science and by a Grant from Faculty Development at the University of Cincinnati. Their financial support is gratefully acknowledged.

REFERENCES

Artstein, Z. and Vitale, R.A. (1975). A strong law of large numbers for random compact sets. *Ann. Probab.* **3** 879-882.

Aumann, R.J. (1965). Integrals of set-valued functions. *J. Math. Anal. Appl.* **12** 1-12.

Bertoluzza, C., Corral, N. and Salas, A. (1995). On a new class of distances between fuzzy numbers. *Mathware & Soft Computing* **2** 71-84.

Bochner, S. (1933). Integration von funktionen, deren werte die elemente eines vektorraumes sind. *Fundamenta Math.* **20** 262-176.

Byrne, C. (1978). Remarks on the set-valued integrals of Debreu and Aumann. *J. Math. Anal. Appl.* **78** 243-246.

Colubi, A., López-Díaz, M., Domínguez-Menchero, J.S. and Gil, M.A. (1997). A generalized Strong Law of Large Numbers. *Tech. Rep.* University of Oviedo, June 1997.

Debreu, G. (1966). Integration of correspondences. *Proc. Fifth Berkeley Symp. Math. Statist. Prob.* 351-372. Univ of California Press, Berkeley.

Gil, M.A. and López-Díaz, M. (1996). Fundamentals and Bayesian Analyses of decision problems with fuzzy-valued utilities. *Int. J. Approx. Reason.* 15 203-224.

Gil, M.A., López-Díaz, M. and López-García, H. (1997a). The fuzzy hyperbolic inequality index associated with fuzzy random variables. *European J. Oper. Res.* (in press).

Gil, M.A., López-Díaz, M. and Rodríguez-Muñiz, L.J. (1997b). An improvement of a comparison of experiments in statistical decision problems with fuzzy utities. *IEEE Trans. Syst. Man, Cyb.* (in press).

Klement, E.P., Puri M.L. and Ralescu, D.A. (1986). Limit theorems for fuzzy random variables. *Proc. R. Soc, Lond.* A 407, 171-182.

López-Díaz, M. and Gil, M.A. (1997a). Constructive definitions of fuzzy random variables. *Stat. Probab. Lett.* (in press).

López-Díaz, M. and Gil, M.A. (1997b). Approximating integrably bounded fuzzy random variables in terms of the "generalized" Hausdorff metric. *Inform. Sci.* (in press).

López-Díaz, M. and Gil, M.A. (1997c). Reversing the order of integration in iterated expectations of fuzzy random variables, and some statistical applications. *Tech. Rep.* University of Oviedo, January 1997.

López-García, H. (1997). *Cuantificación de la desigualdad asociada a conjuntos aleatorios y variables aleatorias difusas.* PhD Thesis, University of Oviedo.

López-García, H., Gil, M.A., Corral, N. and López, M.T. (1997). Estimating the fuzzy inequality associated with a fuzzy random variable in random samplings from finite populations. *Kybernetika* (in press).

Lubiano, A., Gil, M.A., López-Díaz, M. and López, M.T. (1997). The real-valued mean squared dispersion associated with a fuzzy random variable. *Tech. Rep.* University of Oviedo, April 1997.

Lubiano, A. and Gil, M.A. (1997). Estimating the expected value of fuzzy random variables in random samplings from finite populations. *Tech. Rep.* University of Oviedo, July 1997.

Puri, M.L. and Ralescu, D. (1981). Différentielle d'une fonction floue. *C.R. Acad. Sci. Paris, Sér. I* 293 237-239.

Puri, M.L. and Ralescu, D. (1985). The concept of normality for fuzzy random variables. *Ann. Probab.* 13 1373-1379.

Puri, M.L. and Ralescu, D. (1986). Fuzzy random variables. *J. Math. Anal. Appl.* 114 409-422.

Ralescu, A. and Ralescu, D.A. (1984). Probability and fuzziness. *Information Sciences* 17 85-92.

Ralescu, A. and Ralescu, D.A. (1986). Fuzzy sets in statistical inference. *The Mathematics of Fuzzy Systems* (A. Di Nola and A.G.S. Ventre, Eds.), Verlag TÜV Rheinland, Köln, pp. 273-283.

Ralescu, D.A. (1982). Fuzzy logic and statistical estimation. *Proc. 2nd World Conference on Mathematics at the Service of Man* 605-606, Las Palmas-Canarias.

Ralescu, D.A. (1995a). Fuzzy random variables revisited. *Proc. IFES'95 and Fuzzy IEEE Joint Conference, Vol. 2* 993-1000, Yokohama.

Ralescu, D.A. (1995b). Inequalities for fuzzy random variables. *Proc. 26th Iranian Mathematical Conference* 333-335, Kerman.

Ralescu, D.A. (1995c). Fuzzy probabilities and their applications to statistical inference. *Advances in Intelligent Computing — IPMU'94, Lecture Notes in Computer Science* **945** 217-222.

Ralescu, D.A. (1996). Statistical Decision-Making without numbers. *Proc. 27th Iranian Mathematical Conference* 403-417, Shiraz.

Zadeh, L.A. (1975). The concept of a linguistic variable and its application to approximate reasoning. Parts 1,2, and 3. *Inf. Sci.* **8** 199-249; **8** 301-357; **9** 43-80.

Zadeh, L.A. (1976). A fuzzy-algorithmic approach to the definition of complex or imprecise concepts. *Int. Jour. Man-Machine Studies,* **8** 249-291.

3

LINGUISTIC MODELS IN SYSTEM RELIABILITY, QUALITY CONTROL AND RISK ANALYSES

Linguistic Model of System Reliability Analysis

Takehisa Onisawa* and Akio Ohmori**

*Institute of Engineering Mechanics
University of Tsukuba
1-1-1, Tennodai
Tsukuba, 305 Japan
E-mail: onisawa@esys.tsukuba.ac.jp

**Master's Program in Science and Engineering
Institute of Engineering Mechanics, Onisawa Lab
University of Tsukuba
1-1-1, Tennodai
Tsukuba, 305 Japan
E-mail: oomori@fhuman.esys.tsukuba.ac.jp

Abstract

This paper presents a system reliability analysis method with natural language based on consideration that expert's experienced engineering judgement plays an important role in system reliability analysis. It is necessary to have component reliability estimate including human reliability estimate, and knowledge about system functional relation in order to analyze system reliability using components reliability estimates. However, component and human reliability estimates, and system functional relations including failure dependence and procedure failure are expressed by linguistic terms better than by numerical values since we have not enough amount of data to represent reliability and knowledge on system functional relations by numerical values. The meaning of linguistic terms is expressed by a fuzzy set defined on a unit interval. Especially, the fuzzy set representing reliability is called a subjective measure of reliability. Parametrized *and* operation and *or* operation of fuzzy sets are employed which can reflect analyst's subjectivity toward an analyzed system. The analysis results are also expressed by linguistic expressions. The analysis example is shown and it is found that analyst's subjectivity is reflected well and that analysis results are comprehensible for discussion of system reliability since they are expressed by linguistic expressions.

1. Introduction

Reliability is associated with probability theory. In fact, many probability distributions are applied to reliability of machinery equipment and electronic component. Probabilistic methods have a ground that the failure occurrence of the same component usually has a statistical regularity under same conditions. This ground is based on the assumption that the state of a component is either good or bad. Equipment reliability is defined as the probability of its good state during a fixed time interval. The probabilistic method is also adopted into system reliability analysis based on consideration that complex systems are made up of many components and that a system state has only one of two states corresponding to components states.

The introduction of the probabilistic method to the reliability engineering field has many reasons. One of the reasons is the following. A component failure and a system accident are rare events from the viewpoint of our daily life. It is necessary to evaluate the occurrence of rare events numerically, i.e., objectively. By the probability it is possible to assess component reliability and system reliability rationally, i.e., objectively, and to compare a failure probability and an accident probability with probabilities of other rare events. There have been many applications of the probabilistic method to system reliability analysis. For example, U.S. Atomic Energy Comission presents WASH-1400[1] which is known as risk assessment of nuclear power plants. Swain presents THERP(Technique for Human Error Rate Prediction)[2] as a model of human reliability analysis. A handbook of human reliability in nuclear power plants is also published[3].

However, assumptions of the conventional reliability engineering have many questions[4,5]. There have been many applications of fuzzy theory to the reliability engineering field for the answer to the questions[6–10].

As one of viewpoints of applications of fuzzy theory to the reliability engineering field, this paper has the following frameworks. Expert's experienced judgement plays an important role in system reliability analysis[11] even if the probabilistic method is employed. We usually have not enough amount of data on components failures and human errors to assess their reliabilities by probability. The estimation of the probability is often dependent on expert's experienced engineering judgement. And it is necessary to know system functional structure including failure dependence and the procedure of component failure for analyzing system reliability with components reliability estimates. In practice, however, the system structure is described based on expert's experienced and engineering judgement, who are familiar with an analyzed system. Although a fault tree is often employed to analyze system reliability, it is said that the construction of a fault tree is dependent on expert's subjectivity. In these situations, information on the data and experienced engineering judgement for system analysis can be expressed with linguistic terms better than with numerical values[12].

In this paper linguistic expressions about components failures including human errors, and about system functional structure are used, and the meaning of linguistic terms is expressed by a fuzzy set defined on a unit interval [0,1]. System reliability is analyzed by the use of fuzzy sets operations, and expert's subjectivity is included in the analysis. In this paper, especially, the procedure of failure is considered in the analysis. Results of analysis are also expressed by linguistic expressions.

2. System Reliability Analysis with Words

2.1 Natural Language Expressions

This paper takes a system reliability analysis approach which uses system component reliability estimation, human reliability estimation and system functional relation. In practice, however, it is often difficult for even experts to estimate component reliability and human reliability, and to represent system functional relation by numerical values. In these situations it is easier with linguistic terms. For example, when experts have not enough amount of data about system component reliability, its reliability estimate by numerical values such as 10^{-4} [1/hr] is unreasonable and difficult. However, they estimate it more easily by natural language based on their experienced engineering judgement such as *it has rather high reliability* since in this situation fuzziness rather than randomness becomes important, and fuzziness in the estimation is contained in linguistic terms.

This paper expresses system component reliability, human reliability and system reliability with natural language in the form of reliability estimate and its fuzziness. Table 1 shows natural language expressions of reliability estimate and Table 2 shows natural language expressions of its fuzziness. *"System, component or human reliability is standard"* means that its reliability is evaluated to be equal

Table 1 Natural Language Expressions of Reliability Estimate and Corresponding Parameter Values

Class	Expressions of Reliability Estimate	Parameter x_0 (Representative Value)
	(System, subsystem, component or human operator has:)	
1	no reliability	–
2	very low reliability	0.9 – 1.0 (0.95)
3	low reliability	0.7 – 0.9 (0.8)
4	rather low reliability	0.55 – 0.7 (0.625)
5	standard reliability	0.45 – 0.55 (0.5)
6	rather high reliability	0.3 – 0.45 (0.375)
7	high reliability	0.2 – 0.3 (0.25)
8	quite high reliability	0.1 – 0.2 (0.15)
9	extremely high reliability	0.05 – 0.1 (0.075)
	(Accident, failure or human error is:)	
10	next to impossible	0.0 – 0.05 (0.025)
11	Impossible	–

Table 2   **Natural Language Expressions of Fuzziness of Reliability Estimate and Corresponding Parameter Values**

Class	Expressions of Fuzziness	Parameter m
1	low fuzziness	2.0
2	medium fuzziness	2.5
3	rather high fuzziness	3.0
4	high fuzziness	3.5

to expert's standard. "*System, component or human reliability is high*" means that its reliability is evaluated to be higher than expert's standard.

2.2   Fuzzy Set Representation of Natural Language about Reliability: Subjective Measure of Reliability

The meaning of natural language expressions is represented by a fuzzy set better than by numerical values since the meaning is fuzzy by itself. The presented approach uses a fuzzy set defined on a unit interval [0, 1] which means subjective evaluation of reliability. Then a numerical value in the unit interval is not probability but subjective evaluation. The fuzzy set is called a *subjective measure of reliability* in this paper. The subjective measure of reliability is a non-probabilistic reliability measure in the sense that it does not satisfy axiomatic laws of probability such as additivity. Eq. (1) is given by its membership function[13]

$$F(x) = \frac{1}{1 + 20 \times |x - x_0|^m} \, , \tag{1}$$

where x_0 and m are parameters, and $0 \le x, x_0 \le 1$. The parameter x_0 gives a maximal grade of $F(x)$ and the parameter m is related to fuzziness. Fig. 1 shows an example of a subjective measure of reliability. It is interpreted that the smaller the numerical value of the abscissa, the higher the subjective reliability. The ordinate means the grade of membership. Then the larger the numerical value of m, the fuzzier the subjective measure of reliability. The middle point 0.5 means subjective standard evaluation of reliability.

The fuzzy set (1) has the following properties[13]:

1. The fuzzy set is normal and convex[14]. This implies that it is easy to translate natural language expressions as shown in Tables 1 and 2 to fuzzy sets.
2. $F(0) \ne 0$ and $F(1) \ne 0$. These imply that even if reliability is quite low, a system component does not necessarily fail, or a human operator does not necessarily make an error in a given task, and that even if reliability is quite high, a component does not always work without failure, or a human operator does not always perform the task without error.

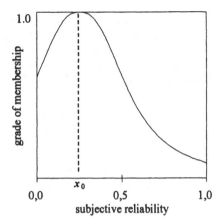

Fig. 1 Subjective Measure of Reliability

The parameter x_0 and m correspond to natural language expressions of reliability estimate and its fuzziness, respectively, as shown in Tables 1 and 2. Especially, the subjective measure of reliability in class 1 and that in class 11 are defined as follows:

$$F(x) = \begin{cases} 1, & x = 1 \\ 0, & x \neq 1 \end{cases},$$ (2)

$$F(x) = \begin{cases} 0, & x \neq 0 \\ 1, & x = 0 \end{cases}.$$ (3)

Fuzziness is not taken into consideration for natural language expressions in classes 1 and 11.

The correspondence of parameters x_0 and m to linguistic terms is defined subjectively. However, correspondence relationships are consistent in the following sense. The $x < 0.5$ part of the abscissa in Fig. 1 means higher reliability. Therefore, the expressions such as *rather low reliability*, or *low reliability* do not correspond to numerical values which are smaller than 0.5. And as mentioned above, the larger the numerical value of m, the fuzzier the subjective measure of reliability. Once the correspondence relationships are defined, they are consistently employed through the analysis.

2.3 Fault Tree Analysis by Subjective Measure of Reliability

In this paper the failure of a component is assumed to include human error. In a fault tree analysis basic operations are an *and* operation and an *or* operation. The process in which failures of all components lead to the failure of a system is expressed by an *and*-gate in a fault tree. This system corresponds to a parallel system(task) as shown in Fig. 2 (1). On the other hand the process in which the failure of at least one of components leads to the failure of a system is expressed by an *or*-gate in a fault tree. This system corresponds to a series system(task) as shown in Fig. 2 (2). In the fault tree analysis by the subjective measure of reliability the following parametrized *t*-norm and *t*-conorm are used as the *and* and the *or* operations of subjective measures of reliability, respectively. The extension principle[14] is applied to these operations as follows:

$$H(x, y) = \frac{1}{1 + \left\{ \left(\frac{1-x}{x}\right)^{1/nH} + \left(\frac{1-y}{y}\right)^{1/nH} \right\}^{nH}} , \qquad (4)$$

where $0 < x, y \le 1$, $H(0, y) = H(x, 0) = 0$, and nH is a non-negative parameter.

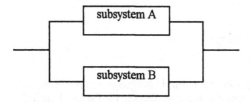

(1) parallel system(task)

(2) series system(task)

Fig. 2   Parallel System(Task) and Series System(Task)

$$G(x, y) = \frac{\left\{ \left(\frac{x}{1-x}\right)^{nG} + \left(\frac{y}{1-y}\right)^{nG} \right\}^{1/nG}}{1 + \left\{ \left(\frac{x}{1-x}\right)^{nG} + \left(\frac{y}{1-y}\right)^{nG} \right\}^{1/nG}} , \qquad (5)$$

where $0 \le x, y < 1$, $G(1, y) = G(x, 1) = 1$, and nG is a non-negative parameter.

The operation H and the operation G are the so-called Dombi *t*-norm and Dombi *t*-conorm, respectively[15]. The operations H and G have the following properties[15]. The operation H becomes the drastic product when nH is infinite,

$$H(x, y) = \begin{cases} x, & y = 1 \\ y, & x = 1 \\ 0, & \text{otherwise} \end{cases} , \qquad (6)$$

and the min operation when nH is zero.

$$H(x, y) = \min(x, y). \qquad (7)$$

On the other hand the operation G is the max operation when nG is infinite,

$$G(x, y) = \max(x, y),$$ (8)

and the drastic sum when nG is zero

$$G(x, y) = \begin{cases} x, & y = 0 \\ y, & x = 0 \\ 1, & \text{otherwise} \end{cases}.$$ (9)

From the viewpoint of reliability analysis, the above properties imply that the operations H and G can cover the range of reliability estimate from the most pessimistic estimate through the most optimistic estimate[13]. The larger the parameters nH and nG are, the more optimistic the reliability estimate is. That is, the parameters nH and nG can reflect analyst's subjectivity toward an analyzed system whether the system should be analyzed pessimistically or not. Parameter determination is mentioned below.

2.4 Functional Relations of Analyzed System

2.4.1 Procedure Failure

The error in a procedure is often observed in a human task. For example, let us consider a task such as opening two valves A and B, and let us assume that according to a given procedure, a human operator must open valve B after opening valve A. If the operator opens valve B in the beginning, the error in the procedure may lead to a system accident . That is, even if the operator opens valve A and valve B successfully, if the operator makes an error in the task procedure, the task is estimated to be error. This kind of error is called a procedure failure in this paper. In the above example of opening valves, if the procedure failure is not considered, only *not opening valves* leads to an error in the task. As abovementioned, however, when the procedure is considered, even if a human operator opens the valves, if the operator opens the valve B in the beginning, the task becomes error. The procedure failure is peculiar to human error and is regarded as one of functional relations in human tasks.

We usually have not enough amount of data to estimate the probability of the procedure failure. Therefore, the procedure failure is also estimated by natural language better than by numerical values. In this paper linguistic terms about the procedure failure are assumed to be the same as the ones in Table 1 and Table 2. That is, the estimation of the procedure failure is expressed by reliability estimate of the procedure failure and its fuzziness. The meaning of linguistic terms of estimation of the procedure failure is expressed by a fuzzy set with the same membership function as that of the subjective measure of reliability.

Subjective measure of reliability considering the procedure failure is obtained by the operation G and the extension principle[14].

$$F' = G(F, F_p),$$ (10)

where F is the subjective measure of reliability of a given task without consideration of the procedure failure and F_p is a fuzzy set representing estimation of the procedure failure. This implies that the failure in a given task occurs when the procedure failure happens or not the procedure failure but the failure in the task itself happens.

2.4.2 Dependence Analysis

Let us consider the system as shown in Fig. 3. Fig. 3 implies that the failure of subsystem A(B) has an influence on that of subsystem B(A), where failures of subsystems include human errors. Dependence situations are related to functional structure of an anlalyzed system and are dependent on it. Therefore, knowledge on dependence situations is obtained by experts based on their engineering experienced judgements, who are familiar with the system. In this paper dependence evaluation is expressed by linguistic terms in the form of dependence level estimate and its fuzziness. Table 3 shows linguistic terms about dependence level estimate referring to [3]. With regard to linguistic expressions of fuzziness of dependence level estimate, the same terms as the ones in Table 2 are used.

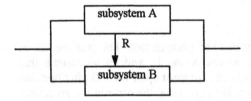

(1) with failure procedure

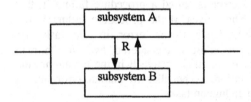

(2) without failure procedure

Fig. 3   Dependence among Subsystems

Table 3   Linguistic Terms about Dependence Level Estimate

Level	Expressions of Dependence Level Estimate
1	complete dependence
2	high dependence
3	moderate dependence
4	low dependence
5	zero dependence

For the sake of simplicity, the meaning of linguistic terms of dependence evaluation is expressed by a fuzzy set with the same membership function as the subjective measure of reliability

$$R(r) = \frac{1}{1 + 20 \times |r - r_0|^{m_r}} \, , \tag{11}$$

where $0 \leq r$, $r_0 \leq 1$, and r_0 and m_r are parameters. With regard to numerical values of m_r, the same numerical values as shown in Table 2 are used. Determination of the parameter r_0 is mentioned below. In the dependence analysis only a parallel system including a parallel human task as shown in Fig. 3 is considered since the failure of a series system including a series human task leads to a system accident whether or not the dependence exists.

The dependence analysis considers two situations. In one of two situations the procedure failure must be considered as shown in Fig. 3 (1). In another situation the procedure failure is not considered as shown in Fig. 3 (2). In both situations as far as the dependence level is not complete, the failure of subsystem A(B) does not always have an influence on the failure of subsystem B(A). Then the following two cases are considered: (*Case I*) Failure of subsystem A(B) has an influence on failure of subsystem B(A), and (*Case II*) failure of subsystem A(B) has no influence on failure of subsystem B(A). Let F_A and F_B be subjective measures of reliability of subsystems A and B, respectively, and R be a fuzzy set representing the dependence level.

(1)   Situation in which the procedure failure must be considered

Let us consider Fig. 3 (1) and assume that the failure of subsystem A has an influence on the failure of subsystem B. Therefore, a human operator must perform the task A in the beginning. Only human error of the procedure in a parallel task is applied to this situation.

Case I

The subjective measure of reliability of the whole system is estimated by F_A and R, i.e.,

$$F_1' = H(F_A, R) . \tag{12}$$

Case II

The portion of the subjective measure of reliability of subsystem A, which is estimated not to have any influence on the failure of subsystem B, is estimated by

$$F_A = G(F_A', F_1') , \tag{13}$$

where F_A' corresponds to the portion. The subjective measure of reliability of the whole system in *Case II* is estimated by

$$F_1'' = H(F_A', F_B).\qquad(14)$$

The subjective measure of reliability of the whole system considering both *Case I* and *Case II* is estimated by

$$F_1 = G(F_1', F_1'').\qquad(15)$$

Considering the procedure failure, the subjective measure of reliability of the whole system in the situation (1) is estimated by

$$F_{1p} = G(F_1, F_p),\qquad(16)$$

where F_p is a fuzzy set representing estimation of the procedure failure.

(2) Situation in which the procedure failure must not be considered

Let us consider Fig. 3 (2). It is not necessary to consider which failure of subsystem A or subsystem B occurs first since the procedure failure is not considered. Components failures in a parallel system and human errors in a parallel task without the procedure failure are applied to this situation.

Case I

When the failure of subsystem A occurs first and the failure of subsystem A has an influence on the failure of subsystem B, the subjective measure of reliability is obtained by

$$F_{0A}' = H(F_A, R).\qquad(17)$$

On the other hand, when the failure of subsystem B occurs first and the failure of subsystem B has an influence on the failure of subsystem A, the subjective measure of reliability is obtained by

$$F_{0B}' = H(F_B, R).\qquad(18)$$

Considering both equations the subjective measure of reliability of the whole system in *Case I* is estimated by

$$F_0' = G(F_{0A}', F_{0B}').\qquad(19)$$

Case II

The portion of the subjective measure of reliability of subsystem A, which is estimated not to have any influence on the failure of subsystem B, is estimated by

$$F_A = G(F_A', F_{0A}'),$$ (20)

where F_A' corresponds to the portion. And the portion of the subjective measure of reliability of subsystem B, which is estimated not to have any influence on the failure of subsystem A, is estimated by

$$F_B = G(F_B', F_{0B}'),$$ (21)

where F_B' corresponds to the portion. The subjective measure of reliability of the whole system in *Case II* is estimated by

$$F_0'' = H(F_A', F_B').$$ (22)

The subjective measure of reliability of the whole system considering both *Case I* and *Case II* in this situation is estimated by

$$F_1 = G(F_0', F_0'').$$ (23)

It is found that in this situation when the dependence level is complete, a parallel system(task) is only apparent and a parallel system(task) is equal to a series system(task), that is, the system does not work redundantly at all.

2.5 Natural Language Expressions of Analysis Results

Results of system reliability analysis are expressed by natural language in the form of reliability estimate and its fuzziness. Let F_R be a subjective measure of reliability obtained by the presented analysis method, and F_s be a subjective measure of reliability with the membership function (1). Let α-cuts of F_R and F_s be $(F_R)_\alpha = (x_{1R}(\alpha), x_{2R}(\alpha))$ and $(F_s)_\alpha = (x_{1S}(\alpha), x_{2S}(\alpha))$, respectively. The distance between F_R and F_s is defined as

$$d = \int_0^1 [\{x_{1R}(\alpha) - x_{1S}(\alpha)\}^2 + \{x_{2R}(\alpha) - x_{2S}(\alpha)\}^2]^{1/2} d\alpha$$ (24)

The parameter x_0 ($0 \leq x_0 \leq 1$) and m (= 2.0, 2.5, 3.0, 3.5) of F_s are selected so as to minimize the distance d. Table 1 and Table 2 are used in order to express results with linguistic terms according to the selected parameters x_0 and m.

2.6 Determination of Parameters nH, nG and r_0

2.6.1 Parameters nH and nG

Let us consider a parallel system(task) and a series system(task) as shown in Fig. 2. And let reliability estimate of each subsystem and its fuziness be *standard* and *medium*, respectively, where subsystems are assumed to be independent of each other functionally. The parameters nH and nG are determined according to each analyst's reliability estimate of the parallel system(task) and the series system(task), respectively, assuming that each subsystem(subtask) constructs the part of an analyzed system. For example, if an analyst estimates reliability of the parallel system(task) and that of the series system(task) as *extremely high* (x_0=0.075) and *rather low* (x_0=0.625), respectively, these estimates lead to determination of parameters nH=3.45 and nG=1.05 . This estimation depends on an analyst and an analyzed system whether system reliability should be evaluated optimistically or not. Therefore, the parameters nH and nG reflect analyst's subjectivity toward an analyzed system. These parameters play an important role in the analysis.

2.6.2 Parameter r_0

Let us consider the system shown in Fig. 3 (1), where the procedure failure, i.e., Eq. (16), is not considered. Or let us consider the system shown in Fig. 3 (2). Let reliability estimates of subsytems and their fuzziness be *standard* and *medium*, respectively. When the dependence level is estimated to be *complete*, in the situation of Fig. 3 (1) reliability estimate of the whole system is *standard* and its fuzziness is *medium*. In the situation of Fig. 3 (2), reliability estimate of the whole system is obtained using the operation G with the determined parameter nG. On the other hand, when the dependence level is estimated to be *zero*, reliability estimate is obtained using the operation H with the determined parameter nH in both situations of Fig. 3 (1) and Fig. 3 (2). Let x_{0i} be the parameter x_0 of the subjective measure of reliability F_s of the whole system with the dependence level i, and let r_{0i} be the parameter r_0 of R representing the dependence level i, where i = 1 implies *complete dependence*, i = 2, *high dependence*, i = 3, *moderate dependence*, i = 4, *low dependence*, i = 5, *zero dependence*. Therefore, the numerical value of the parameter x_{01} in the situation of Fig. 3 (1) is equal to 0.5. And the numerical value of the parameter x_{01} in the situation of Fig. 3 (2) is obtained by the operation G, extension principle and Eq. (24). The numerical value of the parameter x_{05} is obtained by the operation H, the extension principle, and Eq. (24). Numerical values of parameters x_{0i} (i = 2, 3, 4) in the situation of Fig. 3 (1) are obtained by Eq. (15), extension principle and Eq. (24). In the situation of Fig. 3 (2), parameter values x_{0i} (i = 2, 3, 4) are obtained by Eq. (23), the extension principle and Eq. (24). The parameters r_{0i} (i = 2, 3, 4) are determined so as to satisfy the following:

$$(x_{0i} - x_{05}) : (x_{01} - x_{0i}) = \begin{cases} 3:1 & (i=2) \\ 1:1 & (i=3) \\ 1:3 & (i=4) \end{cases} \qquad (25)$$

That is, two kinds of parameters values (r_{0i} ; i = 1, 2, 3, 4, 5), which correspond to situations of Fig. 3 (1) and Fig. 3 (2), are obtained.

3. Analysis Example

3.1 Fault Tree

Fig. 4 shows a fault tree to be analyzed by the presented method. Let us assume the following:

(1) There are dependences with the procedutre failure between basic events (4–1) and (4–2), and between basic events (4–5) and (4–6). These events are concerned with human errors. There are dependences without the procedure failure between basic events (4–3) and (4–4), and between basic events (4–7) and (4–8).

(2) Reliability estimate of each basic event in the fault tree is *standard reliability* and its fuzziness is *medium*. Each dependence level estimate is *moderate dependence*, and its fuzziness is *medium*. Each procedure failure estimate is *standard*, and its fuzziness is *medium*.

(3) Two analysts A and B analyze the fault tree. The analyst A is more optimistic than the analyst B toward the analyzed sysytem. The analyst A estimates reliability of a parallel system(task) and that of a series system(task) as *high* and *standard*, respectively, where reliability estimate of each subsystem (subtask) is *standard* and its fuzziness is *medium*. That is, the analyst A selects numerical values 2.05 and 3.0 as the parameters nH and nG, respectively. On the other hand the analyst B estimates reliability of the same parallel system(task) and the same series system(task) as *rather high* and *rather low*, respectively. Numerical values 1.03 and 1.05 are chosen as the parameters nH and nG.

3.2 Analysis Results and Remarks

Fig. 5 shows the analysis result by the analyst A. The result is *"System reliability is **high** and its fuzziness is **medium**"*. On the other hand the analyst B estimates system reliability as *"System reliability is **standard** and its fuzziness is **medium**"* as shown in Fig. 6. These results reflect analyst's subjectivity toward the analyzed system, that is, the analyst A is more optimistic than the analyst B toward the analyzed system. In this example, reliability estimate of each basic event, dependence level estimate and procedure failure estimate are assumed to be the same among the two analysts for the sake of simplicity. In a practical analysis, however, there is a possibility that each analyst has different estimate for these kinds of estimates as well as numerical values of parameters nH and nG. Therefore, analysis results reflect analyst's subjectivity toward an analyzed system more clearly. Therefore, it is necessary to consider mutual agreement[13] or an estimation support system among analysts. This is a future problem.

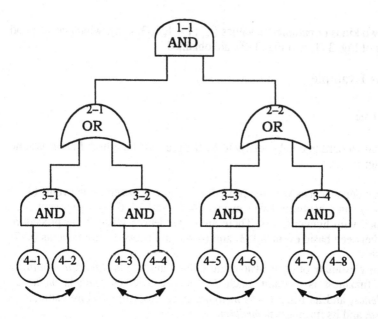

Fig. 4 Fault Tree

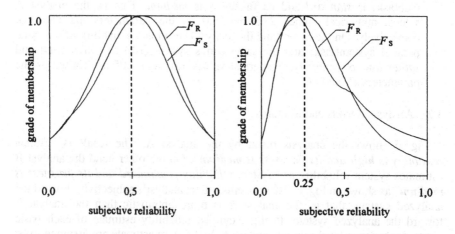

Fig. 5 Result by Analyst A　　　　**Fig. 6 Result by Analyst B**

4 Conclusions

This paper presents an analysis method of system reliability using natural languages. The presented method is based on the following frameworks. We usually have not enough amount of data on components failures and human errors to assess their reliabilities by probability. Estimation of these probabilities is often dependent on expert's experienced engineering judgement. It is also necessary to know system functional relations including failure dependence and the failure procedure to analyze system reliability by the use of components reliability estimates. This kind of knowledge is also dependent on expert's experienced engineering judgement. In these situations, information on the data and the knowledge on the system structure are expressed by linguistic expressions better than by numerical values.

The meaning of linguistic expressions is expressed by a fuzzy set on a unit interval in this paper. Especially, the fuzzy set representing reliability is called a subjective measure of reliability in this paper. The presented analysis method uses parametrized *and* operation and *or* operation of fuzzy sets which can reflect analyst's subjectivity toward an analyzed system. The presented method especially considers the failure dependence and the procedure failure besides an *and* system and an *or* system as system functional relations. The procedure failure is peculiar to human error. The dependence analysis with the procedure failure becomes important in human reliability analysis. The analysis results are also expressed by linguistic expressions. The analysis example shows that analyst's subjectivity toward an analyzed system can be reflected by the method and that analysis results are comprehensible for discussion of system reliability since linguistic expressions are employed in sysytem reliability analysis.

In a future it becomes necessary to consider an estimation support system which unifies analysis results reflecting analyst's subjectivity toward an analyzed system since the results are different among analysts because of their subjectivity.

References

[1] U.S. Atomic Energy Commission, Reactor Safety Study: An Assessment of Accident Risks in US Commercial Nuclear Power Plants, WASH-1400 (1975).

[2] A.D. Swain, A Method for Performing a Human Factors Reliability Analysis, Report SCR-685, Sandia Corporation (1963).

[3] A.D. Swain and H.E. Guttmann, Handbook of Human Reliability Analysis with Emphasis on Nuclear Power Plant Applications, NUREG/CR-1278 (1983).

[4] T. Onisawa and K.B. Misra, Use of Fuzzy Sets Theory (Part-II: Applications), in: K.B. Misra, Ed., *New Trends in System Reliability Evaluation*, pp. 551-586, Elsevier, Amsterdam (1993).

[5] T. Onisawa, System Reliability from the Viewpoint of Evaluation and Fuzzy Sets Theory Approach, in: T. Onisawa and J. Kacprzyk, Eds., *Reliability and Safety Analyses under Fuzziness*, pp. 43-60, Physica-Verlag, A Springer-Verlag Company, Heidelberg (1995).

[6] Special Issue on Fuzzy Methodology in System Failure Engineering, *Fuzzy Sets and Systems*, Vol. 83, No. 2 (1996).

[7] K.Y. Cai, C.Y. Wen and M.L. Zhang, Fuzzy Reliability Modelling of Gracefully Degradable Computing Systems, *Reliability Engineering and System Safety*, Vol. 33, pp. 141-157 (1991).

[8] B.K. Cappelle, Multistate Structure Functions and Possibility Theory : An Alternative Approach to Reliability, in: E.E. Kerre Ed., *Introduction to the*

Lifetime Tests for Vague Data

Przemysław Grzegorzewski, Olgierd Hryniewicz

Systems Research Institute, Polish Academy of Sciences,

ul. Newelska 6, 01-447 Warsaw, Poland,

e-mail: {pgrzeg, hryniewi}&ibspan.waw.pl

Abstract

Life tests for vague data expressed, e.g. by plain words, are considered. It is shown how to handle with fuzzy lifetimes and fuzzy censoring in order to find estimates, fuzzy confidence intervals and verify hypotheses concerning the mean lifetime. Different strategies corresponding to the decision-maker's attitude to the life data is considered.

Key words: censoring, confidence interval, fuzzy data, hypothesis testing, life data, lifetime

1 Introduction

Statistical analysis is frequently used in all areas of human activity where decision-makers are faced with data of a stochastic nature. Various statistical methods have been developed during the last 200 years in order to cope with such data. In nearly all cases it is assumed that available data are described precisely (usually by real numbers). Thus the only source of uncertainty is the randomness of data. The results of statistical analysis of such "exact" data are presented in a rather unambiguous form which is usually understandable only for people trained in statistics, who know such notions as, e.g., confidence interval, statistical test or significance level. However, in many real life situations the data are not precise and we have to analyze not only exact numbers but vague statements as well. Moreover, the results of statistical reasoning should be presented in a form which is understandable not only for experts in statistics but also for usual decision-makers. Thus classical methods are sometimes not sufficient and there is a need to apply some theories which, at least in statistics, are considered as non-standard. The theory of fuzzy sets is such a theory, which has been successfully applied in many cases where we deal with vague data, and the results of a rigorous mathematical analysis have to be presented to people in a plain language.

Many statistical methods for fuzzy data have been developed during the last twenty years. The most important theoretical and practical results have been published in books by Kruse and Meyer [8] and Viertl [15]. However, there are still many unsolved problems, especially in the area of statistical testing (see, e.g., Grzegorzewski and Hryniewicz [4]). The majority of problems arise when data are really very vague, and are described in words. The existing theory does not provide us with completely satisfactory results.

In this paper we restrict ourselves only to problems which arise in the statistical analysis of vague reliability data. We assume that the input data may be presented in an everyday language. We also assume that the output should be presented in a form which is easy to understand for a usual decision-maker. In Section 2 we discuss basic concepts of the lifetime statistical analysis. In Section 3 we present how to cope with vague data. Point estimation of the mean lifetime in the presence of vague data is presented in Section 4. In Section 5 and Section 6 we discuss the problems of interval estimation and hypotheses testing. We consider here different strategies corresponding to the decision-maker's attitude to vague life data. Last of all we present a numerical example which illustrates some new concepts introduced in this paper.

2 Basic concepts

One of the most important problems of reliability analysis is testing requirements for the *mean lifetime*. In technical applications this parameter is also called *mean time to failure* ($MTTF$) and is often included in the specification of a product. For example, producers are interested whether this time is sufficiently large, as large $MTTF$ allows them to extend a warranty time. The mean lifetime may be efficiently estimated by the sample average from the sample of the lifetimes $T_1, T_2, \ldots, T_n$ of n tested items. In such a case $MTTF$ may be estimated as

$$MTTF = \frac{T_1 + T_2 + \cdots + T_n}{n} \tag{1}$$

However, in the majority of practical cases the lifetimes of all tested items are not known, as the test is usually terminated before the failure of all items. It means that exact lifetimes are known for only a portion of the items under study, while remaining lifetimes are known only to exceed certain values. This feature of lifetime data is called *censoring*. More formally, we have a random sample of n items with lifetimes $T_1, T_2, \ldots, T_n$ such that a fixed censoring time $Z_i > 0$, $i = 1, \ldots, n$ is also associated with each item. We observe T_i only if $T_i \leq Z_i$. Therefore our lifetime data consist of pairs

$$(X_1, Y_1), \ldots, (X_n, Y_n), \tag{2}$$

where

$$X_i = \min\{T_i, Z_i\} \tag{3}$$

and

$$Y_i = \begin{cases} 1, & \text{if} \quad X_i = T_i \\ 0, & \text{if} \quad X_i = Z_i. \end{cases} \tag{4}$$

Numerous parametric models are used in the lifetime data analysis. Among them the most widely used are the exponential, Weibull, gamma and lognormal distribution models. Historically, the exponential model was the first lifetime model extensively developed and widely used in many areas of lifetime analysis: from studies on the lifetimes of various types of manufactured items to research involving survival or remission times in chronic diseases. In this model the lifetime T is described by the probability density function

$$f(t) = \begin{cases} \frac{1}{\theta} e^{-\frac{t}{\theta}}, & \text{if } t > 0 \\ 0, & \text{if } t \le 0. \end{cases} \tag{5}$$

where $\theta > 0$ is the mean lifetime. It is worth to notice that the hazard function in the considered model is constant. However this assumption is very restrictive, the exponential model is still frequently used in practice because of two important features:

$1°$ its parameter θ is easily estimated;

$2°$ for lifetimes described by a probability distribution with increasing hazard (e.g. product which reliability, roughly speaking, deteriorates in time) it gives conservative approximation for the mean lifetime.

Thus in this paper we assume that the exponential distribution model is the mathematical model which describes lifetimes of tested items. Note that

$$T = \sum_{i=1}^{n} X_i = \sum_{i \in D} T_i + \sum_{i \in C} Z_i \tag{6}$$

is the total survival time (the sum of lifetimes of all observed items), where D and C denote the sets of items for whom lifetimes are observed and censored, respectively. Moreover let

$$r = \sum_{i=1}^{n} Y_i \tag{7}$$

denote the number of observed failures.

In the considered exponential model the statistic (r, T) is minimally sufficient statistic for θ and the maximum likelihood estimator of the mean lifetime θ is (assuming $r > 0$)

$$\widehat{\theta} = \frac{T}{r}. \tag{8}$$

It can be shown (see Cox [1]) that statistic $\frac{2r\widehat{\theta}}{\theta}$ is approximately chi-square distributed with $2r + 1$ degrees of freedom. It appears that this approximation can be used for constructing satisfactory confidence intervals and tests even for quite small sample sizes (see. Lawless [11]). Namely, the two-sided confidence interval for the mean lifetime θ on the confidence level $1 - \delta$ is

$$\left[\frac{2T}{\chi^2_{2r+1, 1-\frac{\delta}{2}}}, \frac{2T}{\chi^2_{2r+1, \frac{\delta}{2}}} \right], \tag{9}$$

where $\chi^2_{m,p}$ is the pth quantile of the chi-square distribution with m degrees of freedom. Similarly, the one-sided confidence interval with upper limit for θ on the confidence level $1 - \delta$ is

$$\left(0, \frac{2T}{\chi^2_{2r+1,\delta}}\right]. \tag{10}$$

Practitioners are usually interested in testing hypothesis $H : \theta \geq \theta_0$ that the mean lifetime is not smaller than given θ_0 (e.g. given requirement on $MTTF$) against $K : \theta < \theta_0$. The desired test can be constructed easily using (10). Namely the hypothesis H should be rejected on the significance level δ if

$$\frac{2T}{\theta_0} \leq \chi^2_{2r+1,\delta}. \tag{11}$$

All statistical procedures described above can be used for strictly controlled reliability tests (for example, those performed by a producer at his laboratory). In such a case a failure should be precisely defined, and all tested items should be continuously monitored. However, in real situation these test requirements might not be fulfilled. In the extreme case, the reliability data comes from users whose reports are expressed in a vague way. The vagueness of reliability data coming from the users has many different sources. We could divide these sources into three groups:

1° vagueness caused by subjective and imprecise perception of failures by a user,

2° vagueness caused by imprecise records of reliability data,

3° vagueness caused by imprecise records of the rate of usage.

First source of vagueness is typical for so called non-catastrophic failures. The tested item may be considered as failed, or - strictly speaking - as nonconforming, when at least one value of its parameters falls beyond specification limits. In practice, however, a user does not have a possibility to measure all parameters, and is not able to define precisely the moment of a failure. For example, if there exists a requirement for an admissible level of noise it usually may be verified by a user only subjectively. The user can usually indicate only a moment when he noticed that the level of noise had increased, and the moment when he (or she) considered it as obviously excessive. Thus, it might be assumed that the first moment describes the time when the tested item (say, a car) may be considered as failed, and the second moment indicates the time of a sure failure. As the result, we obtain an imprecise information about the real lifetime. Moreover, this type of vagueness causes situations in which even at the end of a test (i.e. at a censoring time) a user is not sure whether the tested item has failed or not. In such a case, we have not only imprecise values of lifetimes, but we have imprecise information about the number of observed failures as well. This type of imprecise reliability data was considered in [5].

Second source of vagueness is typical to retrospective data. Users do not record precisely the moments of failures, especially when they are not sure if they observed a real failure (see above). So when they are asked about failures which occurred some time ago, they sometimes provide an imprecise information.

A lifetime of an individual is the actual length of life of that individual measured from some particular starting point. However it may happen that the user cannot specify this starting point precisely but only in a vague way. In such situation the lifetime of the item under study is also vague.

Third source of vagueness is related to the fact that users, who report their data in days (weeks, months),use the tested items with different intensity. Two reports about items that failed after 20 weeks of work may have completely different meaning for the measurement of $MTTF$ expressed in hours of continuous work, when the intensity of usage significantly differs in both these cases. In practice, the users are asked about the intensity of usage (for example, in hours per day), and their responses are, from obvious reasons, very often imprecise.

The lack of precision of reliability field data comes from all these sources, and in many cases cannot be even identified. Precise probability models can be seldom applied only for clearly identified sources of vagueness, and they are very often impractical, because of many parameters which are either unknown or difficult to estimate. Therefore, we have to admit, that we often deal with really vague data expressed by imprecise words, and it is the only source of information which can be used for the verification of hypotheses about the mean lifetime of tested items.

In the present paper we will restrict our consideration to situations with vague lifetimes and vague censoring times. However, we will assume that the number of failures would be known precisely.

3 Vague data

Suppose that the results of life tests of n individuals are available. It means that starting points O_i, failure times U_i and censoring moments W_i for each individual $i = 1, \ldots, n$ are known. If all these values are precise we can easily find lifetimes and censoring times of each individual, namely $T_i = U_i - O_i$, $Z_i = W_i - O_i$ and we can perform statistical inference about the mean life as it was shown in the previous section. In the mentioned classical theory one usually assume that O_i, U_i and W_i are nonnegative random variables so their realizations are nonnegative real numbers. However if we admit vagueness in the reliability data we have to make a good beginning by indicating a mathematical model for these vague data.

In this paper we assume that the theory of fuzzy sets gives us tools appropriate for modelling and handle with vague data. Next, we assume that vague (fuzzy) starting points, failure times and censoring times are nonnegative fuzzy random variable, i.e. - roughly speaking - mappings which assign to each random event a nonnegative fuzzy number (as random variables are, by analogy, mappings which assign to each random event a real number). Thus we begin by recalling some basic concepts and notation connected with the mentioned notions.

Definition 1 *The fuzzy subset A of the real line $\mathcal{R}$, with the membership function $\mu_A : \mathcal{R} \to [0,1]$, is a fuzzy number iff*

(a) *A is normal, i.e. there exists an element x_0 such that $\mu_A(x_0) = 1$;*

(b) *A is fuzzy convex, i.e. $\mu_A(\lambda x_1 + (1 - \lambda)x_2) \geq \mu_A(x_1) \wedge \mu_A(x_2)$,*

  $\forall x_1, x_2 \in \mathcal{R}, \quad \forall \lambda \in [0,1]$;

(c) *μ_A is upper semicontinuous;*

(d) *$\operatorname{supp} A$ is bounded.*

This definition is due to Dubois and Prade (see [2]). It is easily seen that if A is a fuzzy number then its membership function has the following form:

$$\mu_A(x) = \begin{cases} 0 & \text{for } x < a_1 \\ r_l(x) & \text{for } a_1 \leq x < a_2 \\ 1 & \text{for } a_2 \leq x \leq a_3 \\ r_u(x) & \text{for } a_3 < x \leq a_4 \\ 0 & \text{for } x > a_4, \end{cases} \tag{12}$$

where $a_1, a_2, a_3, a_4 \in \mathcal{R}$, $a_1 \leq a_2 \leq a_3 \leq a_4$, $r_l : [a_1, a_2] \to [0,1]$ is a nondecreasing upper semicontinuous and $r_u : [a_3, a_4] \to [0,1]$ − is a nonincreasing upper semicontinuous function. Functions r_l and r_u are called sometimes the left and the right arms (or sides) of the fuzzy number, respectively.

Similarly as in classical arithmetic we can also add, subtract, multiply and divide fuzzy numbers (for more details we refer the reader to [2] or [12]). Since all these operations become rather complicated if the sides of fuzzy numbers are not very regular, simple fuzzy numbers - e.g. with linear or piecewise linear sides - are preferred in practice. Such fuzzy numbers with simple membership functions also have more natural interpretation. Therefore the most often used fuzzy numbers are, so called, *trapezoidal fuzzy numbers*, i.e. fuzzy numbers which both sided are linear. Trapezoidal fuzzy numbers can be used for the representation of such expressions as, e.g., "more or less between 5 and 7", "approximately between 10 and 15", etc. Trapezoidal fuzzy numbers with $a_2 = a_3$ are called *triangular fuzzy numbers* and are often used for modelling such expressions as, e.g., "about 6", "more or less 8", etc. Triangular fuzzy numbers with only one side may be useful for describing situations like "just before 50" ($a_2 = a_3 = a_4$) or "just after 30" ($a_1 = a_2 = a_3$). If $a_1 = a_2$ and $a_3 = a_4$ then we get, so called, *rectangular fuzzy numbers* which may represent such expressions as, e.g., "between 20 and 25". If $a_1 = a_2 = a_3 = a_4 = a$ than we get a crisp number, i.e. a fuzzy number which is no longer vague but represents precise value and can be identified with the proper real number a.

A useful tool for dealing with fuzzy numbers are their α—cuts. The α—cut of a fuzzy number A is a nonfuzzy set defined as

$$A_\alpha = \{x \in R : \mu_A(x) \geq \alpha\}. \tag{13}$$

A family $\{A_\alpha : \alpha \in [0,1]\}$ is a set representation of the fuzzy number A. Basing on the resolution identity, we get:

$$\mu_A(x) = \sup\{\alpha I_{A_\alpha}(x) : \alpha \in [0,1]\}, \tag{14}$$

where $I_{A_\alpha}(x)$ denotes the characteristic function of A_α. Definition 1 implies that every α—cut of a fuzzy number is a closed interval. Hence we have $A_\alpha = [A_\alpha^L, A_\alpha^U]$, where

$$\begin{aligned} A_\alpha^L &= \inf\{x \in \mathcal{R} : \mu_A(x) \geq \alpha\}, \\ A_\alpha^U &= \sup\{x \in \mathcal{R} : \mu_A(x) \geq \alpha\}. \end{aligned} \tag{15}$$

Hence, by (12) we get $A_\alpha^L = r_l^{-1}$, $A_\alpha^U = r_u^{-1}$.

A space of all fuzzy numbers will be denoted by $\mathcal{FN}$. Of course, $\mathcal{FN} \subset \mathcal{F}(\mathcal{R})$, where $\mathcal{F}(\mathcal{R})$ denotes a space of all fuzzy sets on the real line.

Definition 2 *Fuzzy number $A \in \mathcal{FN}$ is nonnegative if $\mu_A(x) = 0$ for all $x < 0$ and is positive if $\mu_A(x) = 0$ for all $x \leq 0$.*

Equivalently, we may say that $A \in \mathcal{FN}$ is nonnegative if $A_{\alpha=0}^L \geq 0$ and is positive if $A_{\alpha=0}^L > 0$. A space of all nonnegative fuzzy numbers will be denoted by $\mathcal{NFN}$, while a space of all positive fuzzy numbers will be denoted by $\mathcal{PFN}$ ($\mathcal{PFN} \subset \mathcal{NFN} \subset \mathcal{FN}$).

A notion of fuzzy random variable was introduced by Kwakernaak [10]. Other definitions of fuzzy random variables are due to Kruse [7], Puri and Ralescu [13], Stein and Talati [14]. Our definition is similar to those of Kwakernaak and Kruse (see [3]). Suppose a random experiment is described as usual by a probability space $(\Omega, \mathcal{A}, P)$, where Ω is a set of all possible outcomes of the experiment, $\mathcal{A}$ is a σ—algebra of subsets of Ω (the set of all possible events) and P is a probability measure

Definition 3 *A mapping $X : \Omega \to \mathcal{FN}$ is called a fuzzy random variable if it satisfies the following properties:*

(a) $\{X_\alpha(\omega) : \alpha \in [0,1]\}$ *is a set representation of $X(\omega)$ for all $\omega \in \Omega$,*

(b) *for each $\alpha \in [0,1]$ both $X_\alpha^L = X_\alpha^L(\omega) = \inf X_\alpha(\omega)$ and $X_\alpha^U = X_\alpha^U(\omega) =$*

$= \sup X_\alpha(\omega)$, are usual real-valued random variables on $(\Omega, \mathcal{A}, P)$.

Thus a fuzzy random variable X is considered as a perception of an unknown usual random variable $V : \Omega \to \mathcal{R}$, called an *original* of X. Let $\mathcal{V}$ denote a set of all possible originals of X. If only vague data are available, it is of course impossible to show which of the possible originals is the true one. Therefore we can define a fuzzy set on $\mathcal{V}$, with a membership function $\iota : \mathcal{V} \to [0,1]$ given as follows:

$$\iota(V) = \inf\{\mu_{X(\omega)}(V(\omega)) : \omega \in \Omega\}, \tag{16}$$

which corresponds to the grade of acceptability that a fixed random variable V is the original of the fuzzy random variable in question (see Kruse and Meyer [8]).

Similarly n–dimensional fuzzy random sample $X_1, \ldots, X_n$ may be treated as a fuzzy perception of the usual random sample $V_1, \ldots, V_n$ (where $V_1, \ldots, V_n$ are independent and identically distributed crisp random variables). A set $\mathcal{V}^n$ of all possible originals of that fuzzy random sample is, in fact, a fuzzy set with a membership function

$$\iota(V_1, \ldots, V_n) = \min_{i=1,\ldots,n} \inf\{\mu_{X_i(\omega)}(V_i(\omega)) : \omega \in \Omega\}. \tag{17}$$

Although a random variable is characterized completely by its probability distribution very often we are interested only in some parameters of the distribution. Let us consider a parameter $\theta = \theta(V)$ of a random variable V. This parameter may be viewed as an image of a mapping $\Gamma : \mathcal{P} \to \mathcal{R}$, which assigns each random variable V having distribution $P_\theta \in \mathcal{P}$ the considered parameter θ, where $\mathcal{P} = \{P_\theta : \theta \in \Theta\}$ is a family of distributions. However, if we deal with a fuzzy random variable we cannot observe parameter θ but only its vague image. Using this reasoning together with Zadeh's extension principle Kruse and Meyer [8] introduced the notion of *fuzzy parameter of fuzzy random variable* which may be considered as a *fuzzy perception* of the unknown parameter θ. It is defined as a fuzzy set with a membership function

$$\mu_{\Lambda(\theta)}(t) = \sup\{\iota(V) : V \in \mathcal{V}, \theta(V) = t\}, \quad t \in \mathcal{R}, \tag{18}$$

where $\iota(V)$ is given by (16). This notion is well defined because if our data are crisp, i.e. $X = V$, we get $\Lambda(\theta) = \theta$. Similarly, for a random sample of size n we get

$$\mu_{\Lambda(\theta)}(t) = \sup\{\iota(V_1, \ldots, V_n) : (V_1, \ldots, V_n) \in \mathcal{V}^n, \theta(V_1) = t\}, \quad t \in \mathcal{R}. \tag{19}$$

One can easily obtain α–cuts of $\Lambda(\theta)$:

$$\Lambda_\alpha(\theta) = \{t \in \mathcal{R} : \exists (V_1, \ldots, V_n) \in \mathcal{V}^n, \theta(V_1) = t, \text{ such that } \\ V_i(\omega) \in (X_i(\omega))_\alpha \text{ for } \omega \in \Omega \text{ and for } i = 1, \ldots, n\}. \tag{20}$$

For more information we refer the reader to Kruse, Meyer [8].

Now, suppose that instead of precise starting points of the life test, precise failure times and precise censoring moments we deal with their fuzzy counterparts O_i, U_i and W_i ($i = 1, \ldots, n$) described by nonnegative fuzzy numbers. It would be natural to assume additionally that $(O_i)_{\alpha=0}^U \leq (U_i)_{\alpha=0}^L$ and $(O_i)_{\alpha=0}^U \leq (W_i)_{\alpha=0}^L$ for every $i = 1, \ldots, n$. Now we have to calculate fuzzy lifetimes and fuzzy censoring times necessary in further statistical inference. Thus in order to get $T_i = U_i - O_i$ or $Z_i = W_i - O_i$ we have to subtract fuzzy numbers. By the extension principle subtraction of two fuzzy numbers A and B with membership functions μ_A and μ_B, respectively, is also a fuzzy number $A - B$ with the membership function defined as follows

$$\mu_{A-B}(z) = \sup_{\{(x,y)\in\mathcal{R}^2 : x-y=z\}} (\mu_A(x) \wedge \mu_B(x)), \qquad \forall z \in \mathcal{R}. \qquad (21)$$

Sometimes it is easier to find α–cuts of $A - B$ using the Minkowski operation

$$(A - B)_\alpha = A_\alpha - B_\alpha = \{z \in \mathcal{R} : z = x - y, \text{ where } x \in A_\alpha, \, y \in B_\alpha\}. \qquad (22)$$

Thus using formulas (21) or (22) we get fuzzy lifetimes $T_1, \ldots, T_n$ described by their membership functions $\mu_1(t), \ldots, \mu_n(t) \in \mathcal{NFN}$ and fuzzy censoring times $Z_1, \ldots, Z_n$ with membership functions $v_1(t), \ldots, v_n(t) \in \mathcal{NFN}$.

4 Estimation of the mean lifetime from vague data

If we admit vague results we have to redefine notions (2)–(4). Now we consider fuzzy lifetimes $T_1, \ldots, T_n$ described by their membership functions $\mu_1(t), \ldots, \mu_n(t)$ $\in \mathcal{NFN}$ and fuzzy censoring times $Z_1, \ldots, Z_n$ with membership functions $v_1(t),$ $\ldots, v_n(t) \in \mathcal{NFN}$. Our data set consist of pairs

$$(X_1, Y_1), \ldots, (X_n, Y_n), \qquad (23)$$

however now $X_1, \ldots, X_n$ are no longer real numbers but fuzzy numbers such that

$$X_i = \min\{T_i, Z_i\}, \quad i = 1, \ldots, n \qquad (24)$$

which means that their membership functions are

$$\zeta_i(t) = \sup_{\{(x,y)\in\mathcal{R}^2 : \min\{x,y\}=t\}} \min\{\mu_i(x), v_i(y)\}, \quad \forall t \in \mathcal{R}^+, \quad i = 1, \ldots, n \qquad (25)$$

(see, e.g., Klir, Yuan [6]), while $Y_1, \ldots, Y_n$ remain integers defined as follows

$$Y_i = \begin{cases} 1, & \text{if } X_i = T_i \\ 0, & \text{otherwise.} \end{cases} \qquad (26)$$

It is easily seen that the problem described by equations (23)–(26) reduces to that given by (2)–(4) if all lifetimes and censoring times are not fuzzy but precisely defined.

Using the extension principle, we may find a fuzzy total survival lifetime $T = \sum_{i=1}^n X_i$ with a membership function

$$\mu_T(t) = \sup_{x_1,\ldots,x_n \in \mathcal{R}^+ : x_1+\ldots+x_n=t} \{\zeta_1(x_1) \wedge \ldots \wedge \zeta_n(x_n)\}. \qquad (27)$$

Using the Minkowski operation on α−cuts we may find a set representation of T as follows

$$T_\alpha = (X_1)_\alpha + \ldots + (X_n)_\alpha =$$
$$= \{t \in \mathcal{R}^+ : t = x_1 + \ldots + x_n, \text{ where } x_i \in (X_i)_\alpha, \ i = 1, \ldots, n\}, \tag{28}$$

where $\alpha \in (0, 1]$. Now, using the extension principle once more, we may define a fuzzy estimator of the mean lifetime $\hat{\Theta}$ in the presence of vague data as

$$\hat{\Theta} = \frac{T}{r}. \tag{29}$$

Since r is a real number we can easily find a set representation of $\hat{\Theta}$:

$$\hat{\Theta}_\alpha = \frac{1}{r} S_\alpha = \left\{ t \in \mathcal{R}^+ : t = \frac{x}{r}, \text{ where } x \in T_\alpha \right\}. \tag{30}$$

It is seen at once that since all $T_i \in \mathcal{NFN}$ and $Z_i \in \mathcal{NFN}$, $i = 1, \ldots, n$, then $T \in \mathcal{NFN}$ and $\hat{\Theta} \in \mathcal{NFN}$. Moreover, our fuzzy estimator $\hat{\Theta}$ is a natural generalization of the estimator $\hat{\theta}$ of the mean lifetime because if all the lifetimes and censoring times are crisp, not vague, fuzzy estimator (29) reduces to the classical one (8).

5 Confidence intervals for the mean lifetime

Besides finding the fuzzy estimator of the mean lifetime we can also show how to construct fuzzy confidence intervals for the mean lifetime on a given confidence level $1-\delta$. We can derive both one-sided and two-sided fuzzy confidence intervals but because of the nature of our problem we will restrict ourselves to the one-sided fuzzy confidence interval with upper limit.

First of all we should realize what information is yielded with the one-sided confidence interval with upper limit for the mean lifetime. Roughly speaking it tells us that with high probability (confidence) the true mean lifetime of the individual under study does not exceed the given value (upper confidence limit). For the crisp case this confidence limit can be easily found from (10), i.e.

$$\pi = \frac{2T}{\chi^2_{2r+1,\delta}}. \tag{31}$$

For example, if $\pi = 100$ hours it means that the true mean lifetime "almost surely" does not exceed 100 hours − it is possible that the mean lifetime is equal to 99.5 hours, or 57.3 or 13.2 or even 0.5 hour − it remains unknown, although it is "almost sure" that it is not equal to, e.g., 150 hours (expression "almost surely" might be a linguistic interpretation of the confidence level equal to, e.g., 0.95).

Unfortunately in the presence of fuzzy data T is no longer crisp but fuzzy and therefore π would be also fuzzy ($\pi \in \mathcal{NFN}$, because $T \in \mathcal{NFN}$). Moreover, if our data are fuzzy we loose that natural and simple interpretation of the one-sided confidence interval with upper limit for the mean lifetime given above. Since if we get, e.g., $\pi = $ " about 100 hours" (described by the triangular fuzzy number with $a_1 = 95$, $a_2 = a_3 = 100$ and $a_4 = 105$) it is possible that the true mean lifetime is equal, e.g., 5 hours or 50 hours, it is "almost sure" that it is not equal to, e.g., 150 hours, but it is not clear whether it is possible or not that it is equal to 97 or 103 hours. An optimist would say: "yes, it is possible that the true mean lifetime is equal to 97 hours" and "it might be possible that the true mean lifetime is equal to 103 hours", however a pessimist would be more cautious and would answer: "no, it might be possible that the true mean lifetime is equal to 97 hours" but "it is not possible that the true mean lifetime is equal to 103 hours". This example shows that we have neither clear nor unique interpretation of the upper confidence limit for vague life data. Below we will suggest how to handle situations like these described above. Our proposal is based on the mentioned difference in attitude: i.e. optimism and pessimism.

To make a good begining we have to consider vague data again. It is seen at once that there are doubts, analogous to that mentioned above, how to qualify our conviction about survival time of any individual whose vague lifetime is, e.g., $X = $ " between 1000 and 1050 hours" (described by the following rectangular fuzzy number: $a_1 = a_2 = 1000$, $a_3 = a_4 = 1050$). And again, according to optimistic or pessimistic attitude to that lifetime one may be convinced or not that it is possible that the individual under discussion survived, for example, 1020 hours. Hence together with given vague life data $X_1, \ldots, X_n$ we will also consider, so called, survival data of two types: optimistic and pessimistic.

It is evident that any fuzzy number A with α-cuts $A_\alpha = [A_\alpha^L, A_\alpha^U]$ can be obtained as a fuzzy intersection of two fuzzy subsets B and C of the real line $\mathcal{R}$ such that $B_\alpha = (-\infty, A_\alpha^U]$ and $C_\alpha = [A_\alpha^L, +\infty)$. Let us consider a fuzzy complement of the fuzzy set C. It is known that the membership function of that complement $\neg C$ is $\mu_{\neg C}(x) = 1 - \mu_C(x)$ for all $x \in \mathcal{R}$. Thus the set representation of $\neg C$ is $C_\alpha = (-\infty, A_{1-\alpha}^L]$ for $\alpha \in (0, 1]$.

Now let $X_1, \ldots, X_n$, $X_i \in \mathcal{NFN}$, denote a sample of vague life data and $(X_i)_\alpha = [(X_i)_\alpha^L, (X_i)_\alpha^U]$ is an α-cut of X_i, $\alpha \in (0, 1]$, $i = 1, \ldots, n$. Consider two operators: $Opt, Pes : \mathcal{NFN} \rightarrow \mathcal{NFN}$ defined as follows

$$Opt(X_i) = \overline{X_i} \quad \text{such that}$$
$$(\overline{X_i})_\alpha = (0, X_\alpha^U], \quad \alpha \in (0, 1] \tag{32}$$

and

$$Pes(X_i) = \underline{X_i} \quad \text{such that}$$
$$(\underline{X_i})_\alpha = (0, \overline{X_{1-\alpha}^L}], \quad \alpha \in (0, 1]. \tag{33}$$

Definition 4 *If $X_1, \ldots, X_n$ denotes vague life data then $\overline{X_1}, \ldots \overline{X_n}$ defined by (32) and $\underline{X_1}, \ldots, \underline{X_n}$ defined by (33) are optimistic survival times and pessimistic survival times, respectively.*

Remark 1 *If all the data are crisp then both optimistic and pessimistic survival times are identical and might be identified with life data.*

Kruse and Meyer (see [8], [9]) showed the general method for deriving fuzzy confidence intervals for fuzzy data $X_1, \ldots, X_n$ if one knows how to construct usual (i.e. crisp) confidence interval for the parameter under discussion. Particularly, if $(-\infty, \pi]$ is the crisp one-sided confidence interval with upper limit for θ, where $\pi = \pi(V_1, \ldots, V_n)$, on a confidence level $1 - \delta$ then a fuzzy set $\Pi = \Pi(X_1, \ldots, X_n)$ with the membership function

$$\mu_\Pi(t) = \sup \left\{ \alpha I_{(-\infty, \Pi_\alpha^U]}(t) : \alpha \in (0, 1] \right\}, \tag{34}$$

where

$$\Pi_\alpha^U = \Pi_\alpha^U(X_1, \ldots, X_n) =$$
$$= \sup \left\{ u \in \mathcal{R} : \forall i \in \{1, \ldots, n\} \exists x_i \in (X_i)_\alpha \text{ such that } \pi(x_1, \ldots, x_n) \geq u \right\} \tag{35}$$

is the one-sided fuzzy confidence interval with upper limit for θ on a confidence level $1 - \delta$. For the details we refer the reader to [8], [9].

In the case of our vague life data we will construct two one-sided fuzzy confidence intervals with upper limits for the mean lifetime based on either optimistic or pessimistic survival times. According to the method of Kruse and Meyer the *optimistic one-sided fuzzy confidence interval with upper limit* $\Pi^{opt} = \Pi^{opt}(\overline{X_1}, \ldots \overline{X_n})$ for the mean lifetime on the confidence level $1 - \delta$ has following membership function:

$$\mu_{\Pi^{opt}}(t) = \sup \left\{ \alpha I_{(0, (\Pi^{opt})_\alpha^U]}(t) : \alpha \in (0, 1] \right\}, \tag{36}$$

where

$$(\Pi^{opt})_\alpha^U = \frac{2}{\chi_{2r+1, \delta}^2} (\overline{T})_\alpha^U, \tag{37}$$

and

$$\overline{T} = \sum_{i=1}^n \overline{X_i}, \tag{38}$$

while the *pessimistic one-sided fuzzy confidence interval with upper limit* $\Pi^{pes} = \Pi^{pes}(\underline{X_1}, \ldots, \underline{X_n})$ for the mean lifetime on the confidence level $1 - \delta$ has following membership function:

$$\mu_{\Pi^{pes}}(t) = \sup \left\{ \alpha I_{(0, (\Pi^{pes})_\alpha^U]}(t) : \alpha \in (0, 1] \right\}, \tag{39}$$

where

$$(\Pi^{pes})_\alpha^U = \frac{2}{\chi_{2r+1, \delta}^2} T_{1-\alpha}^U. \tag{40}$$

and

$$\underline{T} = \sum_{i=1}^n \underline{X_i}. \tag{41}$$

One may check easily that $(\overline{T})_\alpha^U = T_\alpha^U$ and $(\underline{T})_\alpha^U = T_{1-\alpha}^L$, so α-cuts (37) and (40) of the optimistic and pessimistic one-sided confidence interval with upper limit for the mean lifetime, respectively, might be calculated from the equations:

$$(\Pi^{opt})_\alpha^U = \frac{2}{\chi_{2r+1, \delta}^2} T_\alpha^U, \tag{42}$$

$$(\Pi^{pes})_\alpha^U = \frac{2}{\chi_{2r+1,\delta}^2} T_{1-\alpha}^L.$$ (43)

Hence it is seen that the optimistic one-sided fuzzy confidence interval with upper limit Π^{opt} is entirely based on the right side of the total lifetime T and disregards completely the left side of T. So it corresponds only to that optimistic attitude to life data described in the example given above. Π^{pes} contrary to Π^{opt} is based solely on the left side of the total lifetime T and disregards the right side of T, thus it represents the pessimistic attitude to the life data.

It is not surprising that $\Pi^{pes} \subseteq \Pi^{opt}$, since $\underline{X_i} \subseteq \overline{X_i}$ for each $i = 1,\ldots,n$. Moreover, if all life data are crisp both optimistic and pessimistic fuzzy confidence intervals coincide and reduce to the traditional crisp one-sided confidence interval with upper limit. One may also notice that our optimistic one-sided fuzzy confidence interval with upper limit Π^{opt} coincides with the one-sided confidence interval with upper limit proposed by Kruse and Meyer.

6   Testing hypotheses on the mean lifetime

In the present section we will consider the problem how to design a statistical test to verify a hypothesis that the mean lifetime of the individual under study is not smaller than a certain fixed value. Thus we are interested in testing a hypothesis $H : \theta \geq \theta_0$, where θ_0 is a given requirement for the mean lifetime, against $K : \theta < \theta_0$. Since now our data are not crisp but fuzzy we cannot use directly the test described in Sec. 2 (see (11)). Grzegorzewski in [3] showed the general method for deriving fuzzy tests for testing hypotheses with vague data. In the case of testing one-sided null hypothesis $H : \theta \geq \theta_0$ against $K : \theta < \theta_0$ with vague data $X_1,\ldots,X_n$, $X_i \in \mathcal{FN}$, $i = 1,\ldots,n$, we get a fuzzy test $\varphi : (\mathcal{FN})^n \to \mathcal{F}(\{0,1\})$ on the significance level δ with a membership function

$$\begin{aligned}\mu_\varphi(t) &= \mu_\Pi(\theta_0)I_{\{0\}}(t) + \mu_{\neg\Pi}(\theta_0)I_{\{1\}}(t) = \\ &= \mu_\Pi(\theta_0)I_{\{0\}}(t) + (1 - \mu_\Pi(\theta_0))I_{\{1\}}(t), \qquad t \in \{0,1\},\end{aligned}$$ (44)

where Π denotes the one-sided fuzzy confidence interval with upper limit for the parameter θ on the confidence level $1 - \delta$ given by (34) and (35) and I is an indicator function. Since in our case of vague life data we have to consider two kinds of one-sided fuzzy confidence intervals with upper limits Π^{opt} and Π^{pes} we may also consider two tests which correspond to the optimistic and pessimistic attitude to the life data, respectively. Namely, we have two tests $\phi^{opt}, \phi^{pes} : (\mathcal{NFN})^n \to \mathcal{F}(\{0,1\})$ on the significance level δ with membership functions

$$\begin{aligned}\mu_{\phi^{opt}}(t) &= \mu_{\Pi^{opt}}(\theta_0)I_{\{0\}}(t) + \mu_{\neg\Pi^{opt}}(\theta_0)I_{\{1\}}(t) = \\ &= \mu_{\Pi^{opt}}(\theta_0)I_{\{0\}}(t) + (1 - \mu_{\Pi^{opt}}(\theta_0))I_{\{1\}}(t), \qquad t \in \{0,1\}\end{aligned}$$ (45)

and

$$\begin{aligned}\mu_{\phi^{pes}}(t) &= \mu_{\Pi^{pes}}(\theta_0)I_{\{0\}}(t) + \mu_{\neg\Pi^{pes}}(\theta_0)I_{\{1\}}(t) = \\ &= \mu_{\Pi^{pes}}(\theta_0)I_{\{0\}}(t) + (1 - \mu_{\Pi^{pes}}(\theta_0))I_{\{1\}}(t), \qquad t \in \{0,1\},\end{aligned}$$ (46)

where Π^{opt} and Π^{pes} are given by equations (42) and (43), respectively.

As one may expect $\mu_{\phi^{opt}}(1) \leq \mu_{\phi^{pes}}(1)$ and $\mu_{\phi^{opt}}(0) \geq \mu_{\phi^{pes}}(0)$ for any life data. Moreover, if all life data are crisp both optimistic and pessimistic fuzzy tests coincide and reduce to the traditional test for one-sided hypotheses.

Both tests ϕ^{opt} and ϕ^{pes} represent "pure strategies" which correspond to optimistic and pessimistic attitude to the life data, respectively. A decision-maker should choose his own strategy (i.e. declare his attitude to the data) in advance, before proceeding any calculations, similarly as he has to choose the significance level δ. However it may happen that he cannot declare himself as optimist or pessimist. In such a case we recommend "mixed strategy" which balances both pure strategies. This mixed strategy corresponds to following, so called, *neutral* fuzzy test ϕ^{neu} with membership function

$$\mu_{\phi^{neu}}(t) = \frac{1}{2}\left(\mu_{\phi^{opt}}(0) + \mu_{\phi^{pes}}(0)\right)I_{\{0\}}(t) + \frac{1}{2}\left(\mu_{\phi^{opt}}(1) + \mu_{\phi^{pes}}(1)\right)I_{\{1\}}(t),$$
(47)

where $t \in \{0, 1\}$. Of course, if all life data are crisp, that neutral test coincide with both optimistic and pessimistic fuzzy tests and reduce to the traditional test for one-sided hypotheses.

It is easily seen that our fuzzy tests, contrary to the classical crisp test, do not lead to the binary decision − to accept or to reject the null hypothesis − but to a fuzzy decision. We may get $\varphi = 1/0 + 0/1$ which indicates that we shall accept H, or $\varphi = 0/0 + 1/1$ which means that H must be rejected. But we may also get $\varphi = \mu_0/0 + (1-\mu_0)/1$, where $\mu_0 \in (0,1)$, which can be interpreted as a degree of conviction that we should accept (μ_0) or reject $(\mu_1 = 1 - \mu_0)$ the hypothesis H. We suggest to categorize all possible outcomes of our fuzzy tests in a following way:

if	$0 \leq \mu_0 < 0.1$	(i.e. $0.9 < \mu_1 \leq 1$)	then	H must be rejected
if	$0.1 \leq \mu_0 < 0.2$	(i.e. $0.8 < \mu_1 \leq 0.9$)	then	H should be rejected
if	$0.2 \leq \mu_0 < 0.3$	(i.e. $0.7 < \mu_1 \leq 0.8$)	then	H may be rejected
if	$0.3 \leq \mu_0 < 0.4$	(i.e. $0.6 < \mu_1 \leq 0.7$)	then	H might be rejected
if	$0.4 \leq \mu_0 \leq 0.6$	(i.e. $0.4 \leq \mu_1 \leq 0.6$)	then	we do not know what to do
if	$0.6 < \mu_0 \leq 0.7$	(i.e. $0.3 \leq \mu_1 < 0.4$)	then	H might be accepted
if	$0.7 < \mu_0 \leq 0.8$	(i.e. $0.2 \leq \mu_1 < 0.3$)	then	H may be accepted
if	$0.8 < \mu_0 \leq 0.9$	(i.e. $0.1 \leq \mu_1 < 0.2$)	then	H should be accepted
if	$0.9 < \mu_0 \leq 1$	(i.e. $0 \leq \mu_1 < 0.1$)	then	H shall be accepted.

Situation when μ_0 is close to μ_1 was classified as "we do not know what to do". It means that using our data we can neither reject nor accept H. These data are simply too vague.

7 Numerical example

Manufacturer of a certain type of car has analyzed the economic consequences of a given warranty period for this type of car. The result of this analysis shows, that the mean time to failure $(MTTF)$ should be greater than 75000 km. The data from 20000 km maintenance at one maintenance station are used to verify if this requirement is really fulfilled.

Failure records of $n = 16$ cars have been examined. Ten of these cars have had no failure till the 20000 km maintenance. However, their precise mileage at the moment of the maintenance has not been recorded. The technicians at the maintenance station say that car users arrive at the station when their cars have: "About 20000 km, usually more, but not more than 21000km".

For $r = 6$ cars that have had failures only three have been serviced at this service station, and their times to failure were recorded exactly as

$$T_1 = 2798 \text{ km}, \; T_2 = 8808 \text{ km}, \; T_3 = 19356 \text{ km}$$

The third failure (after 19356 km) has been revealed during the 20000 km maintenance. The remaining time to failures have been reported by the users in the following way:

- "My car had a failure between 2000 and 3000 kilometers"
- "My car failed after about 11000 kilometers"
- "My car failed just before the 10000 km maintenance"

To proceed with these data all verbal descriptions should be converted into fuzzy numbers. After receiving some information from the technicians, the censoring times for all $n - r = 10$ cars may be described by an asymmetric triangular fuzzy number with $a_1 = 19500$, $a_2 = a_3 = 20000$, and $a_4 = 21000$.

The descriptions of time to failures may be converted to fuzzy numbers after acquiring some additional (but also verbal) information. Using these information, first verbal description of a failure time may be described by a rectangular fuzzy number with $a_1 = a_2 = 2000$, and $a_3 = a_4 = 3000$; second, by a symmetric triangular fuzzy number with $a_1 = 10500$, $a_2 = a_3 = 11000$, and $a_4 = 11500$; and the last, by a one-sided triangular fuzzy number with $a_1 = 9500$, and $a_2 = a_3 = a_4 = 10000$.

Using the rules for adding fuzzy numbers we easily could find that the total survival time T, calculated as (6), can be described by a trapezoidal fuzzy number with $a_1 = 247942$, $a_2 = 253962$, $a_3 = 254962$, and $a_4 = 264962$. Thus,using (8), the mean time to failure (the mean lifetime) may be estimated by a trapezoidal fuzzy number with $a_1 = 247942/6 = 41323.6$, $a_2 = 253962/6 = 42327$, $a_3 = 254962/6 = 42493.7$, $a_4 = 264962/6 = 44160.3$ and -using colloquial language - expressed as "more or less between 42327 and 42493.7 km".

First look at this result suggests that the $MTTF$ of tested cars is significantly smaller than 75000 km, and the requirement is not fulfilled. However, the sample size $n = 16$ is rather small, so a rigorous statistical test has to be applied in order to confirm that the reliability requirement is not fulfilled.

In order to test the hypothesis that the $MTTF$ is not smaller than 75000 km we have to declare our attitude to the life data. Then, in compliance with our choice, we would find either optimistic or pessimistic fuzzy confidence interval with upper limit, as it was proposed in Sec. 5. However, in this example we design both optimistic and pessimistic fuzzy confidence interval to show the relationship between the considered strategy and final results. The α-cuts (37) and (40) of the optimistic and pessimistic fuzzy confidence interval with upper limit can be calculated from the equations (42) and (43). For the observed fuzzy total survival time we have:

$$T_\alpha^U = 264962 - 10000\alpha \tag{48}$$

$$T_{1-\alpha}^L = 253962 - 6000\alpha \tag{49}$$

For the confidence level $1 - \delta = 0.90$ and $r = 6$ we have $\chi^2_{13,0.10} = 7.042$. Hence

$$(\Pi^{opt})_\alpha^U = 75251.9 - 2840.1\alpha \tag{50}$$

$$(\Pi^{pes})_\alpha^U = 72127.8 - 1704.1\alpha \tag{51}$$

Thus for the optimistic attitude the membership function $\mu_{\Pi^{opt}}(t)$ has the following form:

$$\mu_{\Pi^{opt}}(t) = \begin{cases} 1 & \text{for } t < 72411.8 \\ \frac{75251.9-t}{2840.1} & \text{for } 72411.8 \le t \le 75251.9 \\ 0 & \text{for } t > 75251.9, \end{cases} \tag{52}$$

while for the pessimistic attitude we get

$$\mu_{\Pi^{pes}}(t) = \begin{cases} 1 & \text{for } t < 70423.7 \\ \frac{72127-t}{1704.1} & \text{for } 70423.7 \le t \le 72127.8 \\ 0 & \text{for } t > 72127.8 \end{cases} \tag{53}$$

Now, we are ready for testing our hypothesis that $MTTF$ is not smaller than 75000 km. It means, we are interested in testing the null hypothesis H : $\theta \ge \theta_0 = 75000$ km, against the alternative hypothesis $K : \theta < \theta_0$. According to the considered strategy (i.e. according to our attitude to the life data) we may apply ϕ^{opt} or ϕ^{pes}. The membership functions of these tests are

$$\mu_{\phi^{opt}}(75000) = 0.0887|0 + 0.9113|1 \tag{54}$$

and

$$\mu_{\phi^{pes}}(75000) = 0|0 + 1|1. \tag{55}$$

For an "optimistic" decision-maker the odds are strongly for the rejection of the null hypothesis. He could say that the hypothesis H should be rejected. A "pessimistic" decision-maker has any doubts: the hypothesis must be rejected. Of course, it is not surprising, that a mixed strategy would also lead to rejection.

Consider now the other, slightly weaker, null hypothesis for $MTTF$, say $H' : \theta \ge \theta_0 = 72000$ km. For such a case "optimistic" and "pessimistic" decisions are described, respectively, as

$$\mu_{\phi^{opt}}(72000) = 1|0 + 0|1 \tag{56}$$

and

$$\mu_{\phi^{pes}}(72000) = 0.075|0 + 0.925|1 \tag{57}$$

Now, for an "optimistic" decision-maker the decision is evident. He does not see any reason to reject the null hypothesis H', so for him it *shall be accepted*. However, for a "pessimistic" decision-maker, the odds are strongly in favor of rejection. He would decide: "the hypothesis H' *must be rejected*". Both decisions are obviously contradictory. However, a "neutral" decision-maker would apply ϕ^{neu} and get

$$\mu_{\phi^{neu}}(72000) = 0.5375|0 + 0.4625|1 \tag{58}$$

Despite the slight evidence in favor of acceptance, he would not be able do decide whether accept or reject H'. So his answer is, simply, "*I do not know*". It is necessary to stress that this ambiguity is due entirely to the vagueness of data and not to any uncertainty of a probabilistic nature.

8 Conclusions

In the present paper we have suggested how to handle with vague life data. We have considered only the generalization of the most popular exponential model. Thus it is worth to notice that the suggested methodology can be also used for other models. Moreover we have assumed that we admit vagueness in lifetimes or censoring times but we have precise information about the number of observed failures (i.e. we know whether given item has failed or it has survived). However in real life we sometimes face situations when the number of observed failures is also vague. It may be due, for example, to imprecise definition of the failure. Similarly, we can also consider partial failures or information about the scale of the failure expressed by colloquial words. Next, we can use plain words to set requirements for admissible errors (e.g. for the significance level δ), etc. All these problems have to be solved with the help of soft techniques which enable to include imprecision modelled by, e.g., fuzzy sets, to traditional reliability. We hope that these new soft reliability models would be more flexible and thus more useful in real life problems.

References

[1] Cox D.R., *Some Simple Approximate Tests for Poisson Variates*, Biometrika **40** (1953), 354-360.

[2] Dubois D., Prade H., *Operations on Fuzzy Numbers*, Int. J. Syst. Sci. **9** (1978), 613-626.

[3] Grzegorzewski P., *Testing Statistical Hypotheses with Vague Data*, submitted.

[4] Grzegorzewski P., Hryniewicz O., *Testing Hypotheses in Fuzzy Environment*, Mathware and Soft Computing (to appear).

[5] Hryniewicz O. , Lifetime Tests for Imprecise Data and Fuzzy Reliability Requirements, In: Reliability and Safety Analyses under Fuzziness, Eds. T. Onisawa, J. Kacprzyk, Physica-Verlag, Heidelberg, 1995, 169-179.

[6] Klir G.J., Yuan B., Fuzzy Sets and Fuzzy Logic. Theory and Applications, Prentice-Hall PTR, 1995.

[7] Kruse R., *The Strong Law of Large Numbers for Fuzzy Random Variables*, Inform. Sci. **28** (1982), 233-241.

[8] Kruse R., Meyer K.D., *Statistics with Vague Data*, D. Riedel Publishing Company, 1987.

[9] Kruse R., Meyer K.D., *Confidence Intervals for the Parameters of a Linguistic Random Variable*, In: Kacprzyk J., Fedrizzi M. (Eds.), Combining Fuzzy Imprecision with Probabilistic Uncertainty in Decision Making, Springer-Verlag, 1988, 113-123.

[10] Kwakernaak H., *Fuzzy Random Variables*, Part I: *Definitions and Theorems*, Inform. Sci. **15** (1978), 1-15; Part II: *Algorithms and Examples for the Discrete Case*, Inform. Sci. **17** (1979), 253-278.

[11] Lawless J.F., *Statistical Models and Methods for Lifetime Data*, Wiley, New York, 1982.

[12] Mizumoto M., Tanaka K., *Some Properties of Fuzzy Numbers*, In: Gupta M.M., Ragade R.K., Yager R.R. (Eds.), Advances in Fuzzy Theory and Applications, North−Holland, Publ., Amsterdam, 1979, 153-164.

[13] Puri M.L., Ralescu D.A., *Fuzzy Random Variables*, J. Math. Anal. Appl. **114** (1986), 409-422.

[14] Stein W.E., Talati K., *Convex Fuzzy Random Variables*, Fuzzy Sets and Systems **6** (1981), 271-283.

[15] Viertl R., *Statistical Methods for Non-Precise Data*, CRC Press, Boca Raton, 1996.

Systems Analytic Models for Fuzzy Risk Estimation

Chongfu Huang[†] and Da Ruan[††]

[†]Institute of Resource Sciences, Beijing Normal University, China
[††] Nuclear Research Centre (SCK•CEN), B-2400 Mol, Belgium

Abstract

In this contribution we analyse the difficulties of risk estimation on natural disasters in the real world and present a fuzzy mathematical model, based on the principle of information diffusion, to estimate fuzzy risk of natural disasters. Moreover, we illustrate an example, in earthquake engineering, to demonstrate how to use the model. Finally, we show that the model is effective for assessing natural disaster risk.

1 Introduction

Most of countries, whose natural disasters strike frequently and cause heavy damage, have all along paid close attention to natural disaster reduction and obtained remarkable achievement. However, they cannot support every project concerning to natural disaster reduction due to the fund shortage. It forces their scientists to develop technologies of risk analyse for reducing the blindness of strategy. For example, before Tangshan Great˜Earthquake in 1976, whose magnitude is 7.8 in the Richter scale, the buildings in Tangshan, an important industry city located in Hebei province of China, were not designed for resisting earthquake because there was no strong earthquake before that. After that, Chinese earthquake engineers had to employ probability method to zone seismic intensity instead of traditional method which takes maximum intensity in historical earthquakes to be zoning intensity. Probability intensity is a kind of compensatory estimators and is appropriate to model the compensation tendencies in human aggregation in seismology and geology. The core problem of probability zoning is that, for ever, it is impossible to find a crisp value as a probability estimator which approximately agrees with the real situation. Indeed, any seismic system is extreme

---

*Project Supported by China Natural Science Foundation, No.495710001

complex. And, needless to say, we cannot collect sufficient records of strong earthquakes for statistical models employed.

Facing competition from opponents and fierce change of society structure and natural environment, any insurance company which deals with natural disaster such as earthquakes, floods, droughts, winds and so on has to carefully assess risks of natural disasters from recent data. Now, obsolete data is non-utility. In this case, we will meet the complexity of systems and the problem of small samples. So it may be argued that, it is impossible to get a reasonable probability estimator by any traditional statistical method such as histogram method [1], parameter method (maximum likelihood estimators [2]). The problem of small samples stimulates empirical Bayes methods [3] and kernel methods [1, 4, 5, 6, 7, 8, 9] to our further development.

To coordinate our activities with the complexity of a risk system in the real world, we have to again consider if employing a crisp value to be a probability estimator is reasonable. To find a much better approach for solving the problem of small samples, we have to ponder if we can do some thing to take over for use all information which may hide in a few of observations.

In this chapter, based on the principle of information diffusion which is employed to deal with fuzzy information of incomplete data, we mathematically develop a system analyse model to get a fuzzy risk of a complex natural disaster system. In Section 2, we outline the principle of information diffusion and concern two models, one is the linear information distribution, another is the normal diffusion function. In Section 3, we discuss fuzzy risk estimation on natural disasters. In Section 4, we describe system analyse models for analysing fuzzy risk of natural disasters. In Section 5, we give two examples to show how to use the model. The chapter is then summarized with a conclusion in Section 6.

2 Principle of Information Diffusion

The principle of the information diffusion [10, 11] is an assertion that there must exist reasonable information diffusion functions to change an observation into a fuzzy set to partly fill the gaps caused by incomplete data and improve non-diffusion estimator.

In the framework of the information diffusion, data is defined as verifiable facts about the real world. We generally strict data to be observations. Meanwhile, information is defined as the data organized to reveal patterns, and to facilitate search. In this framework, the concept of incomplete data has a narrow sense.

Let X consist of observations $x_1, x_2, \cdots, x_n$, and we suppose that X will be employed to analyse some relations between objects. If the observations cannot provide sufficient evidences for discovering the relations precisely, X is called incomplete data.

For example, tossing a coin n times, we obtain:

$$X = \{x_1, x_2, \cdots, x_n\}, \quad x_i \in \{0, 1\}, i = 1, 2, \cdots, n.$$

If we employ X to estimate the probability of tail occurrence of the coin, for any $n < \infty$, the estimation is not the true value in statistics terms. Therefore, X is incomplete data.

Another example is that, collecting all earthquake records in China in earthquake magnitude, M, and epicentre intensity, I_o, we may obtain:

$$\begin{aligned} X &= \{x_1, x_2, \cdots, x_n\} \\ &= \{(M_1, I_{o1}), (M_2, I_{o2}), \cdots, (M_n, I_{on})\}. \end{aligned}$$

If we use X to discover the relation between magnitude and epicentre intensity, for any $n < \infty$, the relation obtained from X must suffer from some drawbacks. And hence, X is incomplete data.

In fact, there are many reasons to cause data to be incomplete, such as mistaking, losing, lacking, and roughing. In principle, mistaking and losing can be overcome if we carefully collect the data, and roughing might be studied by the standard fuzzy methods as linguistic variables.

The models of the information diffusion are established to deal with incompleteness of data caused by lacking.

Now, we give the formal definition of the information diffusion.

Unless stated otherwise, it is assumed that we are given a set of observations $X = \{x_1, x_2, \cdots, x_n\}$ on a given universe $U = \{u\}$.

Definition 2.1 A mapping μ_x from $X \times U$ to [0,1]:

$$\begin{aligned} \mu_x : \quad & X \times U \to [0, 1] \\ & (x, u) \mapsto \mu_x(u), \forall (x, u) \in X \times U \end{aligned}$$

is called an information diffusion of X on U, if and only if it satisfies:

(1) For $x \in X$, $\exists u_0 \in U$ such that $|u_0 - x| = \inf\{|u - x| \,|u \in U\}$ and $\mu_x(u_o) = \sup\{\mu_x(u)|u \in U\}$;

(2) For every $x \in X$, $\mu_x(u)$ is a convex function about u;

$\mu_x(u)$ is called an information diffusion function of X on U.

For example, let X be a batch of middle and strong earthquake data which includes 134 seismic records [12] observed in China from 1900 to 1975 with magnitudes, M, in the range $4.3 - 8.5$ and intensities, I, in range VI-XII degree. Let its universe of discourse be:

$$\begin{aligned} U = M \times I &= \{m_1, \cdots, m_{14}\} \times \{I_1, \cdots, I_7\} \\ &= \{4.6, \cdots, 8.5\} \times \{VI, \cdots, XII\} \end{aligned}$$

For an observation $x_i = (M_i, I_{oi}) \in X$, the formula of the linear information distribution [13]:

$$\mu_{x_i}(m_t, I_j) = \begin{cases} 1 - \frac{|M_i - m_t|}{0.3}, & \text{if } I_j = I_{oi} \text{ and } |M_i - m_t| \leq 0.3; \\ 0, & \text{otherwise.} \end{cases} \tag{2.1}$$

is an information diffusion function of the records on $M \times I$.

The linear information distribution as an information diffusion function can be formally described as the following.

Given a discrete universe of discourse of observations set $X = \{x_1, x_2, \cdots, x_n\}$ as $U = \{u_1, u_2, \cdots, u_m\}$, where u_j is called a controlling point. If $\Delta = u_{i+1} - u_i, i = 1, 2, \cdots, m-1$, is a constant, the linear information distribution is defined by a mapping μ_x from $X \times U$ to $[0, 1]$ as

$$\begin{aligned}
\mu_x : \quad & X \times U \quad \to [0, 1] \\
& (x, u) \quad \mapsto 1 - \frac{|u-x|}{\Delta}, \quad \text{if } |u - x| \leq \Delta; \\
& (x, u) \quad \mapsto 0, \quad\quad\quad \text{otherwise.}
\end{aligned}$$

It can be expressed as a linear information distribution function which is

$$\mu_x(u) = \begin{cases} 1 - \frac{|u-x|}{\Delta}, & \text{if } |u - x| \leq \Delta; \\ 0, & \text{otherwise.} \end{cases} \tag{2.2}$$

The function divides observation, x_i carrying information as measure value 1, into two parts. If $x_i \in [u_j, u_{j+1}]$, one part is distributed to u_j by gain at $q_{ij} = 1 - \frac{x_i - u_j}{\Delta}$, another part to u_{j+1} at $q_{ij+1} = 1 - \frac{x_i - u_{j+1}}{\Delta}$. Obviously, $q_{ij} + q_{ij+1} = 1$.

In fact, the linear information distribution function fuzzifies the observation x_i as

$$\underset{\sim}{X_i} = 0/u_1 + \cdots + 0/u_{j-1} + q_{ij}/u_j + q_{ij+1}/u_{j+1} + 0/u_{j+2} + \cdots + 0/u_m$$

The information distribution method possesses the advantage of keeping the data structure of the original information unreformed, so a better result can be obtained. However, it needs some experts' experience to choose the universe, U.

Definition 2.2 If a relation $\widehat{R}$ is constructed by X with an operation γ directly, then $\widehat{R}$ is called a non-diffusion estimator, which is written as $\widehat{R} = \gamma(X)$.

For example, using the earthquake data X with the linear-regression operation LR, we obtain a relation between M and I as:

$$\widehat{R} : \quad I = a + bM.$$

That is a non-diffusion estimator.

Definition 2.3 If a relation $\widetilde{R}$ is constructed by X with an information diffusion function μ_x of X on U and an operation β, then $\widetilde{R}$ is called an information diffusion estimator, which is written as $\widetilde{R} = \beta \circ \mu_x(X)$.

For example, let μ_x be an information diffusion function expressed by the linear information distribution as in (2.1), and an operation β be described as the following:

$$q_{tj} = \sum_{i=1}^{134} \mu_{x_i}(m_t, I_j) \tag{2.3}$$

$$s_j = \sum_{t=1}^{14} q_{tj} \tag{2.4}$$

$$r_{tj} = \begin{cases} \frac{q_{tj}}{s_j}, & \text{if } s_j > 0; \\ 0, & \text{if } s_j = 0. \end{cases} \tag{2.5}$$

Then, $\tilde{R} = \beta \circ \mu_x(X) = \{r_{tj}\}$ is an information diffusion estimator about the relation between magnitude and intensity. In paper [12], the author had given the $\tilde{R}$ by a fuzzy relation.

In the viewpoint of discovering a relation between objects, a more generalizing description about the principle of information diffusion is as the following.

The Principle of Information diffusion: Let $X = \{x_1, x_2, \cdots, x_n\}$ be a set of some observations which obey a relation R on the universe $U = \{u\}$. If X is incomplete, there must exist a function $\mu_{x_i}(u)$, $i = 1, 2, \cdots, n$, $u \in U$, such that the information, which is provided by i-th observation at the place x_i, can be diffused to the place u in quantity $\mu_{x_i}(u)$. Meanwhile there must exist a reasonable operation β, which deal with set-value sample $\mu_{x_i}(u)$, such that we can produce an information diffusion estimator $\tilde{R}$ which is more near R than any non-diffusion estimator $\hat{R}$.

In the framework of the information diffusion, a relation is defined by a mathematical mapping from the input space to the output space. In this viewpoint, a probability density function is just a relation between events and probabilities of occurrence.

The principle of information diffusion holds, at least, in the case of estimating a probability relation. To prove it, it is sufficient to normalize a reasonable kernel function to be an information diffusion function and revise slightly the formulae which are employed in the kernel estimator.

The simplest information diffusion function is the normal diffusion function, which is suggested by the study of the similarities of molecules diffusion and information diffusion. Given a universe $U = \{u\} = R^1$ and a set of observations $X = \{x_1, x_2, \cdots, x_n\}$, $x_i \in R^1$, the normal diffusion function is defined as:

$$\mu_x(u) = \exp[-\frac{(u-x)^2}{2h^2}], \quad \text{for } x \in X \text{ and } \forall u \in U \tag{2.6}$$

where, h is called normal diffusion coefficient.

Not mathematically, but by computer simulation, we suggested a formula to calculate the diffusion coefficient, that is,

$$h = \begin{cases} 1.6987(b-a)/(n-1), & \text{for } 1 < n \le 5; \\ 1.4456(b-a)/(n-1), & \text{for } 6 \le n \le 7; \\ 1.4230(b-a)/(n-1), & \text{for } 8 \le n \le 9; \\ 1.4208(b-a)/(n-1), & \text{for } 10 \le n. \end{cases} \tag{2.7}$$

where $b = \max\{x_i\}$, $a = \min\{x_i\}$.

When we apply the normal diffusion function to estimate the probability density function $p(x)$, we can use the following operation:

$$\beta = \frac{1}{nh\sqrt{2\pi}} \sum_{i=1}^{n} \tag{2.8}$$

That is,

$$\widetilde{R}: \quad \tilde{p}(u) = \frac{1}{nh\sqrt{2\pi}} \sum_{i=1}^{n} \exp[-\frac{(u-x_i)^2}{2h^2}], \quad \forall u \in U \tag{2.9}$$

3 Fuzzy Risk Estimation

In general, risk is, at minimum, a two-dimensional concept involving (1) the possibility of an adverse outcome, and (2) uncertainty over the occurrence, timing, or magnitude of that adverse outcome. People talk about risk when there is the chance, but not the certainty, that something they do not want may happen. In fact, risk means many things to many people. The Webster [14], for example, defines risk as "exposure to the chance of injury or loss." In terms of insurance, risk is defined as "the hazard or chance of loss."

On the technical level, we prefer a simple definition to more complete. Natural-disaster risk can be defined as a probability distribution or similar measures that describe the uncertainty about the magnitude, timing, and other relevant features of a disaster.

A major challenge in estimating risk of natural disasters is to find a scientific approach for the probability-distribution estimation. Ignoring this problem is to assume implicitly that either no disaster will occur or, if they do occur, they will be strictly determined by some physical laws captured in deterministic mathematical models.

If we possess sufficient knowledge about the physical process of a natural disaster, we can use stochastic models to represent a random law of the natural disaster. For example, in earthquake engineering, the frequency distribution of earthquake magnitudes, especially those in the middle range, can be approximated reasonably well by the exponential distribution [15].

In many cases, we only know a little about the physical process. For example, the structural mechanisms of various types of buildings being destroyed by earthquakes are unknown [16]. In these cases, statistical methods are employed to estimate the probability distribution from whatever is available in historical data. For example, although flood disasters in river basins are ubiquitous throughout the United States, local variables are of such importance and yet so diversified among river basins so that it is difficult. It is impossible to use a single national disaster model to describe individual flood plains. Therefore, using historical materials of individual cities being modeled, some researchers had developed a model of the Monte Carlo approach [17] to determine which cities would be affected by a flood in any given year.

In fact, the difficulties of estimating risk of natural disasters does not only lie in studying risk sources, but also transforming the risk to embodiment. In some sense, the latter is more difficult because we have to deal with complex natural disaster systems involving natural risks, environments, vulnerabilities, and losses.

Even if there is some possibility of reasonably estimating natural risk in crisp values, there is no possibility of practically estimating system risk in crisp values. The relations related to system risk must be fuzzy relations. For example, in the future, scientists may more precisely give the probabilities of floods occurrence about the magnitude, timing and place. However, it is impossible to practically estimate the probabilities of losses. Natural risk may change slowly, but environment and society can change more quickly.

All difficulties in estimating risk of natural disasters force us to develop a more practical approach to analyse the problems of risk of natural disasters. Because any crisp relation between events and probabilities of occurrence cannot represent practical situation of risk of natural disasters, the only way we can choose is to employ fuzzy relation to represent this kind of risk.

In fact, since the publication of the first paper on fuzzy sets, there have been many researchers [18, 19, 20, 21] who use fuzzy methods to analyse the problems of natural disasters. Their work has led to a universal acceptance of the belief that natural disaster systems must be dealt with by the methods provided by fuzzy sets theory.

The traditional approaches to study risk problems in fuzzy viewpoint [22, 23, 24] are based on the premise that one can provide the input of natural language estimate as probability of failure, severity of loss, and reliability of the estimate. Indeed, they only tell us how to combine the risk of each subsystem to calculate the risk of the entire system.

The theory of falling shadows of random sets [25] extends the concept of usual statistic sample, and a fuzzy set can be considered as a sample employed to estimate probability distribution in a super-space. Besides this, the theorem of great numbers of fall-shadow is also available [26]. In some sense, the falling shadows theory may be more suitable for risk problem in fuzzy viewpoint. However, it has not provided yet any method to analyse a risk system.

It may be argued that the risk estimation in fuzzy viewpoint is more complex than the imagine. Obviously, it is necessary to study what the fuzzy feature of risk is.

We have to mention that there may be many researchers to prefer traditional fuzzy probability [27], defined as the probability of fuzzy events, to others. With respect to a natural disaster system, even if the sense of risk is restricted to probability, the fuzzy feature of risk cannot be characterized by traditional fuzzy probability which is based on the probability distribution of non-fuzzy events. If we could get the probability distribution agreeing with a practical system, the problems in risk estimation on natural disasters would not be so severe. In many cases, it is very difficult to get a reasonable probability distribution. In these cases, we can only obtain an approximate estimator. The fuzzy feature of risk is due to the approximation. If we could get a precise estimator, the fuzzy feature of risk would automatically disappear. Based on the analyse, we give our definition of the fuzzy risk of natural disasters as the following.

Definition 3.1 Let x be a natural disaster event and $P = \{p\} = [0, 1]$ be the universe of discourse of probability, a mapping $\mu_x(p)$ from $\{x\} \times P$ to $[0, 1]$ is called a fuzzy risk about x if and only if $\mu_x(p)$ is convex.

For example, if we have a given definition of "small probability" represented by a fuzzy set A_1 in P as the following:

$$A_1(p) = e^{-100p^2}, \quad p \in [0, 1]$$

then

$$\mu_x(p) = A_1(p), \quad p \in [0, 1]$$

is a fuzzy risk about x.

Definition 3.2 Let x be a random variable on the universe R^1 and $P = \{p\} = [0, 1]$ be the universe of discourse of probability, a mapping $\mu_x(p)$ from $R^1 \times P$ to $[0, 1]$ is called a fuzzy probability distribution if and only if, for every $x \in R^1$, $\mu_x(p)$ is convex.

Using an interval estimator [28] of a parameter, we can get a fuzzy probability distribution.

For example, let x obey a normal distribution:

$$p(x) = \frac{1}{\sigma\sqrt{2\pi}} e^{[-(x-\mu)^2/(2\sigma^2)]}, \quad \sigma > 0, -\infty < x < \infty$$

Suppose that parameter $\mu = 0$ and σ is a 95% confidence interval estimator $[0.8, 1.2]$, then

$$\mu_x(p) = \begin{cases} 1, & \text{if } \exists \sigma \in [0.8, 1.2] \text{ such that } p = \frac{1}{\sigma\sqrt{2\pi}} e^{-x^2/(2\sigma^2)} \\ 0, & \text{otherwise.} \end{cases}$$

is a fuzzy probability distribution.

Definition 3.3 Let $M = \{m\}$ be the universe of discourse of natural disaster z and $P = \{p\} = [0, 1]$ be the universe of discourse of probability, a mapping

$\mu_z(m, p)$ from $M \times P$ to $[0, 1]$ is called a fuzzy risk of z if and only if $\mu_z(m, p)$ is convex about p.

If we have also given definitions of "middle probability" and "large probability" respectively as

$$A_2(p) = e^{-100(0.5-p)^2}, \quad p \in [0, 1],$$

$$A_3(p) = e^{-100(1-p)^2}, \quad p \in [0, 1],$$

then any result of risk estimation characterized by A_1, A_2, A_3 is a fuzzy risk. For example, a statement "In the city C, in the near future days, some slight earthquakes will occur in a large probability, a middle earthquake may occur in a middle probability, a strong earthquake might occur in a small probability" is a fuzzy risk estimator.

If we have given definitions of "slight earthquake," "middle earthquake," and "strong earthquake" respectively as

$$B_1(m) = \begin{cases} 1, & \text{for } m \in (0, 4] \\ 0, & \text{otherwise,} \end{cases}$$

$$B_2(m) = \begin{cases} 1, & \text{for } m \in (4, 6.5] \\ 0, & \text{otherwise,} \end{cases}$$

$$B_3(m) = \begin{cases} 1, & \text{for } m > 6.5 \\ 0, & \text{otherwise,} \end{cases}$$

the fuzzy risk statement about earthquake occurrence is

$$\mu_z(m, p) = \begin{cases} e^{-100(1-p)^2}, & \text{for } m \in (0, 4] \text{ and } p \in [0, 1] \\ e^{-100(0.5-p)^2}, & \text{for } m \in (4, 6.5] \text{ and } p \in [0, 1] \\ e^{-100p^2}, & \text{for } m > 6.5 \text{ and } p \in [0, 1] \end{cases}$$

where z means earthquake occurrence, namely, $\mu_z(m, p)$ is a fuzzy risk of earthquake occurrence.

In many cases, we are more interested in the risk of exceeding magnitude m. For a sake of convenience, we give a special symbol, $\pi_z(m, p)$, to represent this kind of fuzzy risk. Namely, $\pi_z(m, p)$ means the possibility of that probability value of exceeding magnitude m is p.

For example, a statement "In the region C, in 3 days, the probability of that rainfall will exceed 100 mm is small" is a fuzzy risk estimator of exceeding rainfall of flood disaster.

For a random variable ξ, a probability distribution F of exceeding m is defined as

$$F = \{p(\xi \geq m) \mid m \in M\}$$

According to the definition and statement "The probability of exceeding m_0 is middle," we can obtain the following fuzzy reasoning:

(1) For $m < m_0$, the probability of exceeding m is not smaller than middle.

(2) For $m > m_0$, the probability of exceeding m is not larger than middle.

The final goal of risk analyses is to provide scientific basis for management decision. In general, a manager is more interested in a more comprehensive risk concerning properties and people. There may be some scientists who pay attention to a strong earthquake occurring in a desert far from any civilization societies, but there may be no such manager to do it. By contrast, a manager is interested in earthquakes occurring near cities, even slight and middle earthquakes. They want to know what kind of risks a civilization society is facing, including how many buildings will collapse, how much property will be lost, and how many people will die.

Therefore, besides natural risks such as earthquake occurrence risk and flood occurrence risk, we have to study other risks such as the building damage risk, the property loss risk, and the death risk. These risks depend not only on natural risks, but also on society systems. Where, we regard an environment as a society factor because, generally, people can coordinate their environment to avoid or reduce natural disasters.

A risk of natural disasters is called a consequence risk if and only if it is not a natural risk. A consequence risk must depend on both a natural risk and other factors such as the environment, the vulnerability of buildings, the capability in monitoring, and the urgency in dealing with natural disasters.

Obviously, calculating a consequence risk is more difficult than doing a natural risk. A consequence risk must be more fuzzy because both a natural risk and a society system are fuzzy. Any society system is a fuzzy system due to its complex and scanty of detailed materials.

Therefore, it is necessary to choose the fuzzy risk for representing a consequence risk. A fuzzy consequence risk estimator is a fuzzy relation between consequence events and their probabilities of occurrence. Next section, we will discuss how to calculate a fuzzy consequence risk estimator from a fuzzy natural risk estimator and society factors.

4　System Analyse Models

In general, when we analyse a system of natural disasters, we consider all kinds of natural disasters which may be met in the future. However, the core problem of system analyse for natural disasters is to study a single disaster such as earthquakes, floods, droughts, winds, and so on. Combining different disaster risks to a comprehensive disaster risk is relative easy.

A system of a natural disaster consists of four subsystems: (1) disaster source risk, (2) site intensity risk, (3) damage risk, and (4) loss risk.

4.1 Disaster Source Risk

Let s be a risk source such as earthquake, flood, drought, wind, and so on. Let m be a magnitude of s. For example, when s is earthquake, m may be the earthquake magnitude in the Richter scale. If s is flood, m may be a rainfall or a water level of a river.

Definition 4.1 Let $M = \{m\}$ be the universe of discourse s, and $\pi_s(m, p)$ be the possibility of that probability value of exceeding m is p. We call

$$\Pi_s = \{\pi_s(m, p) | m \in M, p \in [0, 1]\} \tag{4.1}$$

a fuzzy risk of natural disaster source s.

Generally, getting $\pi_s(m, p)$ is a physical analysing procedure, or one of historical data analysis processes. Sometimes, the work involves both of them. It may be given by experts in relevant special departments.

If we have nothing but a few of data observed natural disaster source s in the region C, we suggest the following model, based on the linear information distribution, to estimate the risk.

We suppose to have a given set of observations as

$$X = \{M_1, M_2, \cdots, M_{n_0}\} \tag{4.2}$$

Let u_{min} be the minimum magnitude which is used in the decision, and u_{max} be the maximum possible magnitude. The universe of discourse magnitude which is used in the decision is $[u_{min}, u_{max}]$. According to the size of set X, take step Δ, and let

$$u_1 = u_{min}, u_2 = u_1 + \Delta, u_3 = u_2 + \Delta, \cdots, u_{m_0} = u_{max}$$

Then, the universe $[u_{min}, u_{max}]$ of discourse magnitude can be changed into a discrete universe as

$$U = \{u_1, u_2, \cdots, u_{m_0}\}$$

Using the linear information distribution function, we can diffuse information of X on U to show the information structure of X.

Using formula (2.2), we can diffuse the observation M_i to controlling the point u_j in an information gain

$$q_{ij} = \begin{cases} 1 - \frac{|M_i - u_j|}{\Delta}, & |M_i - u_j| \leq \Delta \\ 0, & \text{otherwise.} \end{cases}$$

After n_0 data have been treated with this simple process and information gains at each controlling point have been summed up, a distribute of information gains will turn out. That is,

$$Q = \{Q_1, Q_2, \cdots, Q_{m_0}\}$$

where $Q_j = \sum_{i=1}^{n_0} q_{ij}$.

Q_j can be interpreted as that, if we are only allowed to record disaster events in one of $u_1, u_2, \cdots, u_{m_0}$, from X we know that there are approximately Q_j disaster events with the magnitude u_j have occurred. Namely, Q_j is the number of disaster events with the magnitude u_j.

Using Q, the number of disaster events with the magnitude greater than or equal to u_j can be obtained as:

$$N_j = \sum_{i=j}^{m_0} Q_i$$

They can constitute a number distribution of exceeding u_j as:

$$N = \{N_1, N_2, \cdots, N_{m_0}\}$$

Obviously, an estimator of the probability value of exceeding u_j is

$$P_j = \frac{N_j}{n_0}$$

where n_0 is the number of the observations in (4.2). We can obtain an exceeding probability distribution estimator as

$$P = \{P_1(\xi \geq u_1), P_2(\xi \geq u_2), \cdots, P_{m_0}(\xi \geq u_{m_0})\} \tag{4.3}$$

Because we only have n_0 samples, an exceeding probability distribution estimator in (4.3) is unreliable. The reason is that the knowledge sample set in (4.2) is incomplete which carries on fuzzy information. Using the two-dimension information distribution method [29], P can be changed to a fuzzy risk.

Let discrete universe of discourse magnitude with step Δ_1 be

$$\{m_1, m_2, \cdots, m_n\},$$

and discrete universe of discourse probability with step Δ_2 be

$$\{p_1, p_2, \cdots, p_m\}.$$

We use the simplest formula as (4.4) to diffuse sample (u_k, P_k) to the discrete point (m_i, p_j), namely,

$$\mu_k(m_i, p_j) = \begin{cases} (1 - \frac{|m_i - u_k|}{\Delta_1})(1 - \frac{|p_j - P_k|}{\Delta_2}), & |m_i - u_k| \leq \Delta_1 \text{ and } |p_j - P_k| \leq \Delta_2 \\ 0, & \text{others} \end{cases}$$

$$\tag{4.4}$$

Let

$$f(m_i, p_j) = \sum_{k=1}^{m_0} \mu_k(m_i, p_j) \tag{4.5}$$

and

$$g_i = \max\{f(m_i, p_j)|j = 1, 2, \cdots, m\} \tag{4.6}$$

If $g_i = 0$, let $g_i = 1$. Then,

$$\pi_s(m_i, p_j) = \frac{f(m_i, p_j)}{g_i} \tag{4.7}$$

is a fuzzy risk estimator of the natural disaster source s.

4.2 Site Intensity Risk

In many cases, a natural risk is with respect to a special place such as a seismic active belt or a river. We have to use a so-called attenuation relation of intensity to calculate a site risk with respect to an object in a given society system. A site risk depends on natural risks and the environment.

Let c be a site where there are some buildings, properties, or people. Let w be an intensity of s in sites. For example, when s is earthquake, w may be an earthquake intensity in I-XII scale or a level acceleration. If s is flood, w may be a water level and a current velocity.

Definition 4.2 Let $W = \{w\}$ be the universe of discourse of intensity of s, and $\pi_c(w, p)$ be the possibility of that probability value of exceeding w is p. We call

$$\Pi_c = \{\pi_c(w, p)|w \in W, p \in [0, 1]\} \tag{4.8}$$

a fuzzy risk of the site c.

We suggest the following model to estimate a fuzzy risk of the site c when it only needs to consider distance from the source place to the site.
Let the universe of discourse distance be $D = \{d\}$.
Assume that the attenuation relation can be expressed as:

$$w = f(m, d) \tag{4.9}$$

where w is the site intensity, m is the magnitude at the source, and d is the distance from the source to the site.
In general, the relation can be improved by using a fuzzy relation of M, D, and W:

$$R_1 = R_{M,D,W} = \{r^{(1)}(m, d, w)\} \tag{4.10}$$

which can be obtained by experts. Where M, D, and W is the universe of discourse m, d, and w, respectively.
R_1 can also be obtained from (4.9) directly by using the following formula.

$$r^{(1)}(m, d, w) = \begin{cases} 1, & \text{if } w = f(m, d) \\ 0, & \text{otherwise.} \end{cases}$$

We suppose that the nearest and farthest distance from the site to the source is d_1 and d_2, respectively. In fact, the distance from the source to the site is fuzzy. The fuzzy distance $\underset{\sim}{D}$ can be expressed simply by using a bell function:

$$\mu_D(d) = \exp[-\frac{(\frac{d_2+d_1}{2} - d)^2}{\frac{(d_2-d_1)^2}{6}}] = \exp[-1.5(\frac{d_2 + d_1 - 2d}{d_2 - d_1})^2] \tag{4.11}$$

Therefore, we can get the fuzzy risk of the site intensity as the following:

$$\pi_c(w,p) = \sup_{m \in M, d \in D} \{r^{(1)}(m, d, w) \wedge \pi_s(m, p) \wedge \mu_D(d)\} \tag{4.12}$$

Next step, we transform an intensity to a damage consequence.

4.3   Damage Risk

Let o be an object which will be struck by a destructive force in the intensity w. An object may be a building, a bridge, a group of people, or others.

Definition 4.3 Let $V = \{v\}$ be the universe of discourse of damage of o, and $\pi_o(v, p)$ be the possibility of that probability value of exceeding v is p. We call

$$\Pi_o = \{\pi_o(v, p) | v \in V, p \in [0, 1]\} \tag{4.13}$$

a fuzzy risk of damage of the object o.

The principal type of damage assessment models is the dose-response model, which is a relation between the dose (i.e., measure of site intensity of a natural disaster) and an adverse object response (i.e., the measure of damage). Most dose-response models are derived from statistical data such as that from monitoring or testing. Examples are the linear dose-response models used to estimate human health effects and materials damage of buildings. Alternatively, dose-response models may be derived from theoretical considerations with little or no basis in empirical data.

Dose-response models have many limitations, including the availability of the data or the knowledge and understanding needed to set their parameters and verify their accuracy.

Assume that the relation between the dose and an adverse object response can be expressed as:

$$v = g(w) \tag{4.14}$$

where w is the site intensity, v is the measure of damage concerning the object's vulnerability. The relation can be improved by using a fuzzy relationship of W, and V

$$R_2 = R_{w,v} = \{r^{(2)}(w, v)\} \tag{4.15}$$

which can be obtained by the experts. Where W, and V is the universe of discourse w, and v, respectively.

R_2 can also be obtained from (4.14) directly by using the following formula.

$$r^{(2)}(w, v) = \begin{cases} 1, & \text{if } v = g(w) \\ 0, & \text{otherwise.} \end{cases}$$

More generally, if we have nothing but a few of historical disaster records with the site intensity, W, and damage degree, V, in the region C for a kind of objects, we suggest the following model, based on the normal diffusion function, to estimate the risk.

We suppose to have a given set of observations as

$$X = \{x_1, x_2, \cdots, x_{n_0}\} = \{(W_1, V_1), (W_2, V_2), \cdots, (W_{n_0}, V_{n_0})\} \tag{4.16}$$

Let w_{min} be the minimum intensity which is used in the decision, and w_{max} be the maximum possible intensity.

The universe of discourse intensity used in the decision is $[w_{min}, w_{max}]$. According to the precision we want and the computer time we can spend, take step Δ_1, and let

$$w_1 = w_{min}, w_2 = w_1 + \Delta_1, w_3 = w_2 + \Delta_1, \cdots, w_n = w_{max}$$

Then, the universe $[w_{min}, w_{max}]$ of discourse intensity can be changed into a discrete universe as

$$W = \{w_1, w_2, \cdots, w_n\} \tag{4.17}$$

which is called an input universe.

Using the same way, we choose a discrete universe for damage as

$$V = \{v_1, v_2, \cdots, v_m\} \tag{4.18}$$

which is called an output universe. Using the normal diffusion function, we can diffuse information of X on $W \times V$ to show the information structure of X. Using formula (2.7) with respect to $\{W_1, W_2, \cdots, W_{n_0}\}$ and $\{V_1, V_2, \cdots, V_{n_0}\}$, we can obtain diffusion coefficients h_1 and h_2, respectively.

A two-dimension normal diffusion function [29] as in (4.19) can diffuse information carried by the record $x_k = (W_k, V_k)$ to any point $(w_j, v_j) \in W \times V$.

$$\mu_k(w_i, v_j) = \exp[-\frac{(w_i - W_k)^2}{2h_1^2}] \exp[-\frac{(v_j - V_k)^2}{2h_2^2}] \quad \text{for } (W_k, V_k) \in X \tag{4.19}$$

Let

$$q_{ij} = \sum_{k=1}^{n_0} \mu_k(w_j, v_j), \quad \text{and } t_j = \max\{q_{ij} | i = 1, 2, \cdots, n\}$$

If $t_j = 0$, let $t_j = 1$. Then, $\tilde{R} = \{r(w_i, v_j) | i = 1, 2, \cdots, n, j = 1, 2, \cdots, m\}$

$$= \{\frac{q_{ij}}{t_j} | i = 1, 2, \cdots, n, j = 1, 2, \cdots, m\}$$

is a fuzzy dose-response estimator about the kind of objects.

Now, using the fuzzy risk of the site intensity $\pi_c(w,p)$, we obtain the fuzzy risk of damage of the object o as the following.

$$
\begin{aligned}
\pi_o(v,p) &= \sup_{w\in W}\left\{r^{(2)}(w,v)\wedge\pi_c(w,p)\right\}\\
&= \sup_{w\in W}\left\{r^{(2)}(w,v)\wedge\sup_{m\in M,d\in D}\left\{r^{(1)}(m,d,w)\wedge\pi_s(m,p)\right.\right.\\
&\quad\left.\left.\wedge\mu_D(d)\right\}\right\}
\end{aligned}
$$

(4.20)

Finally, let us analyse a loss risk.

4.4   Loss Risk

Definition 4.4 Let $L = \{l\}$ be the universe of discourse of loss of city C, and $\pi_c(l,p)$ be the possibility of that probability value of exceeding l is p. We call

$$\Pi_c = \{\pi_c(l,p)|l\in L, p\in[0,1]\} \tag{4.21}$$

a fuzzy risk of loss of the city C.

We strictly discuss the losses in buildings. Suppose that the loss of a building is indirect proportion to its area and damage index. Generally, a damage index of a building is defined as the damage percentage. The universe of discourse damage index is:

$$Y = \{y_1, y_2, \cdots, y_n\} \tag{4.22}$$

There is some fuzzy relation between the damage degree and the damage index. For example, earthquake disasters in China, let fuzzy damages be

$$
\begin{aligned}
v_1 &= \text{"Good condition"}\\
v_2 &= \text{"Light destruction"}\\
v_3 &= \text{"General destruction"}\\
v_4 &= \text{"Heavy destruction"}\\
v_5 &= \text{"Collapse"}
\end{aligned}
$$

and

$$Y = \{y_1, y_2, \cdots y_{11}\} = \{0, 0.1, 0.2, \cdots, 1\}$$

Using historical data, we can get a fuzzy relation as the following:

$$
R_{v,y} = \begin{array}{c} \\ v_1 \\ v_2 \\ v_3 \\ v_4 \\ v_5 \end{array}
\begin{array}{c}
\begin{array}{ccccccccccc} y_1 & y_2 & y_3 & y_4 & y_5 & y_6 & y_7 & y_8 & y_9 & y_{10} & y_{11} \end{array}\\
\left(\begin{array}{ccccccccccc}
1 & 0.7 & 0.2 & 0 & 0 & 0 & 0 & 0 & 0 & 0 & 0\\
0.2 & 0.7 & 1 & 0.7 & 0.2 & 0 & 0 & 0 & 0 & 0 & 0\\
0 & 0 & 0.2 & 0.7 & 1 & 0.7 & 0.2 & 0 & 0 & 0 & 0\\
0 & 0 & 0 & 0 & 0.2 & 0.7 & 1 & 0.7 & 0.2 & 0 & 0\\
0 & 0 & 0 & 0 & 0 & 0 & 0.2 & 0.7 & 1 & 0.7 &
\end{array}\right)
\end{array}
\tag{4.23}
$$

Moreover, let us presume that every square meter is worth e dollars in the city C. If the area of all buildings in the city C totalled S square meters, the buildings in the city C are worth $E = e \cdot S$ dollars. Corresponding with the universe Y of discourse damage index in (4.22), we can obtain the universe of discourse losses of the city as:

$$L_C = \{l_1, l_2, \cdots, l_n\} = \{E \cdot y_1, E \cdot y_2, \cdots, E \cdot y_n\} \qquad (4.24)$$

By using (4.23) and (4.24), it is easy to obtain the fuzzy relationship between the fuzzy damage and loss as the following:

$$R_{V,L} = \begin{array}{c} \\ v_1 \\ v_2 \\ v_3 \\ v_4 \\ v_5 \end{array} \begin{array}{c} \begin{matrix} l_1 & l_2 & l_3 & l_4 & l_5 & l_6 & l_7 & l_8 & l_9 & l_{10} & l_{11} \end{matrix} \\ \left(\begin{matrix} 1 & 0.7 & 0.2 & 0 & 0 & 0 & 0 & 0 & 0 & 0 & 0 \\ 0.2 & 0.7 & 1 & 0.7 & 0.2 & 0 & 0 & 0 & 0 & 0 & 0 \\ 0 & 0 & 0.2 & 0.7 & 1 & 0.7 & 0.2 & 0 & 0 & 0 & 0 \\ 0 & 0 & 0 & 0 & 0.2 & 0.7 & 1 & 0.7 & 0.2 & 0 & 0 \\ 0 & 0 & 0 & 0 & 0 & 0 & 0.2 & 0.7 & 1 & 0.7 & \end{matrix} \right) \end{array} \qquad (4.25)$$

In general, the relation between the damage and loss is denoted as:

$$R_3 = R_{V,L} = \{r^{(3)}(v,l)\} \qquad (4.26)$$

Therefore, we get the fuzzy risk of loss of the city C as the following:

$$\begin{aligned} \pi_C(l,p) &= \sup_{v \in V} \{r^{(3)}(v,l)\} \wedge \pi_o(v,p)\} \\ &= \sup_{v \in V} \left\{ r^{(3)}(v,l)\} \wedge \sup_{w \in W} \{r^{(2)}(w,v) \wedge \sup_{m \in M, d \in D} \right. \\ &\left. \{r^{(1)}(m,d,w) \wedge \pi_s(m,p) \wedge \mu_D(d)\}\} \right\} \end{aligned} \qquad (4.27)$$

5 Fuzzy Risk of Earthquake Disasters for a City in China

In this section, we will give an example of earthquake engineering for showing how to calculate fuzzy risks. Earthquake engineering is concerned with the design and construction of all kinds of civil and building engineering systems to withstand earthquake shaking. Earthquake engineers, in the course of their work, are faced with many uncertainties and must use sound engineering judgement to develop safe solutions to challenging problems.

The studied city is the authors' imagination according to characteristics of Chinese cities. Suppose the disaster is earthquake. Let us calculate its fuzzy risk.

Let there be 50 objects in the city C. And suppose all objects are buildings. That is,

$$C = \{c_1, c_2, \cdots, c_{50}\}$$

5.1 Earthquake Risk

The risk source can be regarded as a seismic active belt around or nearby the city. In the belt, 12 epicenters of historic earthquakes with $M \geq 5.0$ in T years were recorded. The set of these historic earthquakes is:

$$X = \{M_1, M_2, \cdots, M_{12}\} = \{5.5, 6.8, 5.1, 5.7, 5.0, 6.5, 6.5, 6.0, 6.0, 5.2, 7.4, 5.2\}$$
$$(5.1)$$

which is called a sample set.

Let $M_0 = 4.9$ be the minimum magnitude which used in engineering, and $M_\mu = 7.4$ be the maximum magnitude in the belt. The universe of discourse earthquake magnitude in the belt is $[M_0, M_\mu] = [4.9, 7.4]$. According to the capacity of the set of these historic earthquakes, take step $\Delta = 0.5$, and let

$$U = \{u_1, u_2, \cdots, u_6\} = \{4.9, 5.4, 5.9, 6.4, 6.9, 7.4\}$$

Then, the universe $[M_0, M_\mu]$ of discourse earthquake magnitude has been changed into the discrete universe U. Employing the information distribution method, we can use U to absorb information from the set of these historic earthquakes and show its information structure.

We use the linear information distribution formula as (2.2) to diffuse the observation, M_i, to, with gain q_{ij}, the controlling point, u_j. Namely,

$$q_{ij} = 1 - \frac{|M_i - u_j|}{0.5}, \quad |M_i - u_j| \leq 0.5.$$

For example, for $M_1 = 5.5$ and $u_2 = 5.4$, we obtain:

$$q_{12} = 1 - |5.5 - 5.4|/0.5 = 1 - 0.2 = 0.8$$

The information gain of u_2 from M_1 is 0.8.

After 12 earthquake data have been treated with this simple process and information gains at each controlling point have been summed up, a distribute of information gains will turn out. That is

$$Q = \{Q_1, Q_2, \cdots, Q_6\} = \{2.2, 3.0, 2.4, 2.2, 1.2, 1\}$$

where $Q_j = \sum_{i=1}^{12} q_{ij}$.

Using Q, we can obtain the number of earthquakes with magnitude greater than or equal to u_j as:

$$N_j = \sum_{i=j}^{6} Q_i$$

They can constitute a number distribution of exceeding magnitude as:

$$N = \{N_1, N_2, \cdots, N_6\} = \{12, 9.8, 6.8, 4.4, 2.2, 1\}$$

Obviously, the probability value of exceeding u_j is

$$p_j = \frac{N_j}{12}$$

where 12 is the number of the observations in (5.1). We can obtain an exceeding probability distribution as

$$P = \{P_1(\xi \geq u_1), P_2(\xi \geq u_2), \cdots, P_1(\xi \geq u_6)\} = \{1, 0.82, 0.57, 0.37, 0.18, 0.08\}$$

We can change P into a fuzzy risk. Let the discrete universe of discourse magnitude, with $\Delta_1 = 0.3$, be

$$\{m_1, m_2, \cdots, m_{14}\} = \{4.6, 4.9, 5.2, 5.5, 5.8, 6.1, 6.4, 6.7, 7.0, 7.3, 7.6, 7.9, 8.2, 8.5\} \tag{5.2}$$

and the discrete universe of discourse probability, with $\Delta_1 = 0.2$, be

$$\{p_1, p_2, \cdots, p_6\} = \{0, 0.2, 0.4, 0.6, 0.8, 1\} \tag{5.3}$$

We use formula as (4.4) to diffuse the observation (u_k, P_k) to the discrete point (m_i, p_j), namely,

$$f_k(m_i, p_j) = \begin{cases} (1 - \frac{|m_i - u_k|}{0.3})(1 - \frac{|p_j - P_k|}{0.2}), & |m_i - u_k| \leq 0.3 \text{ and } |p_j - P_k| \leq 0.2 \\ 0, & \text{others} \end{cases}$$

Employing formulae (4.5), (4.6), and (4.7), we can obtain the fuzzy risk of earthquake in the seismic active belt as the following.

$$\Pi_s = \begin{array}{c} \\ m_1 \\ m_2 \\ m_3 \\ m_4 \\ m_5 \\ m_6 \\ m_7 \\ m_8 \\ m_9 \\ m_{10} \\ m_{11} \\ m_{12} \\ m_{13} \\ m_{14} \end{array} \begin{pmatrix} p_1 & p_2 & p_3 & p_4 & p_5 & p_6 \\ 0.00 & 0.00 & 0.00 & 0.00 & 0.00 & 1.00 \\ 0.00 & 0.00 & 0.00 & 0.00 & 0.15 & 1.00 \\ 0.00 & 0.00 & 0.00 & 0.00 & 1.00 & 0.94 \\ 0.00 & 0.00 & 0.07 & 0.38 & 1.00 & 0.11 \\ 0.00 & 0.00 & 0.18 & 1.00 & 0.42 & 0.05 \\ 0.00 & 0.13 & 0.93 & 1.00 & 0.00 & 0.00 \\ 0.02 & 0.34 & 1.00 & 0.16 & 0.00 & 0.00 \\ 0.10 & 1.00 & 0.63 & 0.00 & 0.00 & 0.00 \\ 0.32 & 1.00 & 0.00 & 0.00 & 0.00 & 0.00 \\ 0.84 & 1.00 & 0.00 & 0.00 & 0.00 & 0.00 \\ 1.00 & 0.67 & 0.00 & 0.00 & 0.00 & 0.00 \\ 1.00 & 0.67 & 0.00 & 0.00 & 0.00 & 0.00 \\ 0.00 & 0.00 & 0.00 & 0.00 & 0.00 & 0.00 \\ 0.00 & 0.00 & 0.00 & 0.00 & 0.00 & 0.00 \end{pmatrix} \tag{5.4}$$

5.2 Intensity Risk

In earthquake engineering, we usually use the attenuation relationship of the seismic intensity to a site. The first of all is to transform an earthquake magnitude into an epicentral intensity. In China, the fuzzy relation [30] is:

$$R_{M,I_0} = \begin{array}{c} \\ m_1 \\ m_2 \\ m_3 \\ m_4 \\ m_5 \\ m_6 \\ m_7 \\ m_8 \\ m_9 \\ m_{10} \\ m_{11} \\ m_{12} \\ m_{13} \\ m_{14} \end{array} \begin{pmatrix} VI & VII & VIII & IX & X & XI & XII \\ 0.25 & 0.04 & 0 & 0 & 0 & 0 & 0 \\ 1.00 & 0.15 & 0 & 0 & 0 & 0 & 0 \\ 0.90 & 0.33 & 0 & 0 & 0 & 0 & 0 \\ 0.56 & 1.00 & 0.16 & 0 & 0 & 0 & 0 \\ 0.03 & 0.67 & 0.73 & 0 & 0 & 0 & 0 \\ 0 & 0.37 & 0.91 & 0.05 & 0 & 0 & 0 \\ 0 & 0.14 & 1.00 & 0.56 & 0 & 0 & 0 \\ 0 & 0 & 0.36 & 1.00 & 0 & 0 & 0 \\ 0 & 0 & 0.31 & 0.74 & 0.18 & 0 & 0 \\ 0 & 0 & 0 & 0.51 & 1.00 & 0 & 0 \\ 0 & 0 & 0 & 0.21 & 0.35 & 0 & 0 \\ 0 & 0 & 0 & 0 & 0.59 & 1.00 & 0 \\ 0 & 0 & 0 & 0 & 0 & 0.50 & 0 \\ 0 & 0 & 0 & 0 & 0 & 0 & 1.00 \end{pmatrix} \quad (5.5)$$

where the universe of the epicentral intensity is $I_0 = \{VI, VII, VIII, \cdots, XII\}$, and the universe of the earthquake magnitude is $M = \{m_1, m_2, \cdots, m_{14}\}$ as (5.2). We denote $R_{M,I_0} = \{r'(m,i) | m \in M, i \in I_0\}$.

Obviously, the fuzzy risk of the epicentral intensity in the seismic active belt can be obtained by using the following formula:

$$\pi_{I_0}(i,p) = \sup_{m \in M} \{\pi_s(m,p) \wedge r'(m,i)\} \quad (5.6)$$

where $\pi_s(m,p) \in \Pi_s$ in (5.4), $p \in \{p_1, p_2, \cdots, p_6\}$ in (5.3), and $i \in I_0$.

From (5.4) and (5.5), we obtain the fuzzy risk of the epicentral intensity as the following:

$$\Pi_{I_0} = \begin{array}{c} \\ VI \\ VII \\ VIII \\ IX \\ X \\ XI \\ XII \end{array} \begin{pmatrix} p_1 & p_2 & p_3 & p_4 & p_5 & p_6 \\ 0.00 & 0.00 & 0.07 & 0.38 & 0.90 & 1.00 \\ 0.02 & 0.14 & 0.37 & 0.67 & 1.00 & 0.33 \\ 0.31 & 0.36 & 1.00 & 0.91 & 0.42 & 0.11 \\ 0.51 & 1.00 & 0.63 & 0.16 & 0.00 & 0.00 \\ 0.84 & 1.00 & 0.00 & 0.00 & 0.00 & 0.00 \\ 1.00 & 0.67 & 0.00 & 0.00 & 0.00 & 0.00 \\ 0.00 & 0.00 & 0.00 & 0.00 & 0.00 & 0.00 \end{pmatrix} \quad (5.7)$$

Let the universe of discourse site intensity be $I = \{V, VI, VII, VIII, IX\}$, and the universe of discourse distance be

$$D = \{v_1, v_2, \cdots, v_6\} = \{9, 15, 20, 40, 80, 140\}$$

Suppose the nearest and farthest distance from the city to the belt is $d_1 = 0$ km, and $d_2 = 30$ km, respectively. Recall (4.11). Then, the fuzzy distance is

$$\underset{\sim}{D} = 0.79/9 + 1/15 + 0.85/20 + 0.02/40 + 0/80 + 0/140$$

According to the materials of the intensity attenuation relating to the seismic active belt, we can obtain an intensity attenuation relation [31] as the following.

$$
R_{I_0,D,I} =
\begin{array}{c}
\\ VI\ v_1 \\ VI\ v_2 \\ VI\ v_3 \\ VI\ v_4 \\ VI\ v_5 \\ VI\ v_6 \\ \cdots \\ XII\ v_1 \\ XII\ v_2 \\ XII\ v_3 \\ XII\ v_4 \\ XII\ v_5 \\ XII\ v_6
\end{array}
\begin{pmatrix}
V & VI & VII & VIII & IX \\
0.91 & 0.56 & 0.00 & 0.00 & 0.00 \\
0.90 & 0.56 & 0.00 & 0.00 & 0.00 \\
0.90 & 0.56 & 0.00 & 0.00 & 0.00 \\
0.82 & 0.37 & 0.00 & 0.00 & 0.00 \\
0.31 & 0.01 & 0.00 & 0.00 & 0.00 \\
0.01 & 0.00 & 0.00 & 0.00 & 0.00 \\
\cdots & \cdots & \cdots & \cdots & \cdots \\
0.00 & 0.00 & 0.00 & 0.00 & 0.36 \\
0.00 & 0.00 & 0.00 & 0.09 & 1.00 \\
0.00 & 0.00 & 0.01 & 0.51 & 1.00 \\
0.00 & 0.02 & 0.18 & 1.00 & 0.00 \\
0.02 & 0.22 & 0.83 & 0.00 & 0.00 \\
0.69 & 0.97 & 1.00 & 0.00 & 0.00
\end{pmatrix}
\tag{5.8}
$$

Using formula (4.12), so we see that the fuzzy risk of the site intensity might be

$$
\Pi_c =
\begin{array}{c}
\\ V \\ VI \\ VII \\ VIII \\ IX
\end{array}
\begin{pmatrix}
p_1 & p_2 & p_3 & p_4 & p_5 & p_6 \\
0.51 & 0.56 & 0.85 & 0.85 & 1.00 & 0.90 \\
0.51 & 0.82 & 0.91 & 0.91 & 1.00 & 0.56 \\
0.66 & 0.92 & 1.00 & 0.91 & 0.42 & 0.14 \\
0.85 & 1.00 & 0.63 & 0.36 & 0.36 & 0.11 \\
0.79 & 0.79 & 0.51 & 0.16 & 0.00 & 0.00
\end{pmatrix}
\tag{5.9}
$$

5.3 Earthquake Damage Risk

Suppose that every object in the city C is a single layer brick pillar factory-building.

Generally, damage index of building is defined as the damage percentage. The universe of discourse damage index is:

$$
Y = \{y_1, y_2, y_3, \cdots y_6\} = \{0, 0.2, 0.4, \cdots, 1\} \tag{5.10}
$$

From (4.23), we can define the fuzzy damage as:

$$
\begin{cases}
A_1 = \text{Good condition} = 1/y_1 + 0.2/y_2 \\
A_2 = \text{Light destruction} = 0.2/y_1 + 1/y_2 + 0.2/y_3 \\
A_3 = \text{General destruction} = 0.2/y_2 + 1/y_3 + 0.2/y_4 \\
A_4 = \text{Heavy destruction} = 0.2/y_3 + 1/y_4 + 0.2/y_5 \\
A_5 = \text{Collapse} = 0.2/y_4 + 1/y_5 + 0.2/y_6
\end{cases}
\tag{5.11}
$$

In China, the fuzzy relationship [16] between the site intensity and the fuzzy damage of a single layer brick pillar factory-building is:

$$R_{I',A} = \begin{array}{c} \\ VI \\ VII \\ VIII \\ IX \end{array} \begin{array}{ccccc} A_1 & A_2 & A_3 & A_4 & A_5 \\ \left(\begin{array}{ccccc} 1.00 & 0.43 & 0.14 & 0.00 & 0.00 \\ 0.21 & 1.00 & 0.36 & 0.00 & 0.00 \\ 0.21 & 0.36 & 1.00 & 0.14 & 0.13 \\ 0.00 & 0.14 & 0.43 & 1.00 & 0.57 \end{array} \right) \end{array} \qquad (5.12)$$

where $I' = \{VI, VII, VIII, IX\}$, and $A = \{A_1, A_2, A_3, A_4, A_5\}$.
Using formula (4.20) and according to (5.9), we can obtain the fuzzy risk of an object response as the following:

$$\Pi_o = \begin{array}{c} \\ A_1 \\ A_2 \\ A_3 \\ A_4 \\ A_5 \end{array} \begin{array}{cccccc} p_1 & p_2 & p_3 & p_4 & p_5 & p_6 \\ \left(\begin{array}{cccccc} 0.51 & 0.82 & 0.91 & 0.91 & 1.00 & 0.56 \\ 0.66 & 0.92 & 1.00 & 0.91 & 0.43 & 0.43 \\ 0.85 & 1.00 & 0.63 & 0.36 & 0.36 & 0.14 \\ 0.79 & 0.79 & 0.51 & 0.16 & 0.14 & 0.11 \\ 0.57 & 0.57 & 0.51 & 0.16 & 0.13 & 0.11 \end{array} \right) \end{array} \qquad (5.13)$$

5.4 Earthquake Loss Risk

Suppose that the loss of a building is indirect proportion to its area and damage index. Moreover, let us presume that every square meter is worth 490 dollars in the city C. If the area of all buildings in the city C totalled 50,000 square meters, the buildings in the city C are worth 24.5 million dollars. Corresponding with the universe Y of discourse damage index in (5.10), we can obtain the universe of discourse losses of the city as:

$$L_C = \{l_1, l_2, l_3, \cdots l_6\} = \{0, 4.9, 9.8, 14.7, 19.6, 24.5\} \qquad (5.14)$$

where a unit of loss is million dollars.
By using (5.11) and (5.13), it is easy to obtain the fuzzy relationship between the loss and fuzz damage as the following:

$$R_{L,A} = \begin{array}{c} \\ y_1 \\ y_2 \\ y_3 \\ y_4 \\ y_5 \\ y_6 \end{array} \begin{array}{ccccc} A_1 & A_2 & A_3 & A_4 & A_5 \\ \left(\begin{array}{ccccc} 1 & 0.2 & 0 & 0 & 0 \\ 0.2 & 1 & 0.2 & 0 & 0 \\ 0 & 0.2 & 1 & 0.2 & 0 \\ 0 & 0 & 0.2 & 1 & 0.2 \\ 0 & 0 & 0 & 0.2 & 1 \\ 0 & 0 & 0 & 0 & 0.2 \end{array} \right) \end{array} \qquad (5.15)$$

Employing formula as in (4.27), we obtain the fuzzy risk of loss of the city

C as the following.

$$\Pi_C = \begin{array}{c} \\ l_1 \\ l_2 \\ l_3 \\ l_4 \\ l_5 \\ l_6 \end{array} \begin{array}{cccccc} p_1 & p_2 & p_3 & p_4 & p_5 & p_6 \\ \left(\begin{array}{cccccc} 0.51 & 0.82 & 0.91 & 0.91 & 1.00 & 0.56 \\ 0.66 & 0.92 & 1.00 & 0.91 & 0.43 & 0.43 \\ 0.85 & 1.00 & 0.63 & 0.36 & 0.36 & 0.20 \\ 0.79 & 0.79 & 0.51 & 0.20 & 0.20 & 0.14 \\ 0.57 & 0.57 & 0.51 & 0.16 & 0.14 & 0.11 \\ 0.20 & 0.20 & 0.20 & 0.16 & 0.13 & 0.11 \end{array} \right) \end{array} \qquad (5.26)$$

According to Π_C, we know that the probability of exceeding losses is not one value but a fuzzy set. For example, when $l = l_3 = 9.8$ (million dollars), the fuzzy probability of loss is:

$$\underset{\sim}{P}(\xi \geq 9.8) = 0.85/0 + 1.00/0.2 + 0.63/0.4 + 0.36/0.6 + 0.36/0.8 + 0.20/0.9$$

The benefit of this result is that one can easily understand impreciseness of the risk estimator of earthquakes due to the complexity of a system and insufficient data. It might be useful to set a flexible and more economical strategy, plan, and action on disaster reduction.

If the region C faces several kinds of natural disasters, we can use fuzzy probabilities addition formula to get a synthesizing disasters risk.

Let there be n_0 natural disasters as

$$S = \{s_1, s_2, \cdots, s_{n_0}\}$$

For s_k, we have obtained the loss risk as

$$\Pi_C(s_k) = \{\pi_C^{(k)}(l_i, p_j) | i = 1, 2, \cdots, n, j = 1, 2, \cdots, m\}$$

For every i, we can get n_0 fuzzy quantities as

$$A_k^{(i)}(p_j) = \pi_C^{(k)}(l_i, p_j), \quad j = 1, 2, \cdots, m \quad, k = 1, 2, \cdots, n_0$$

In general, these n_0 natural disasters are independent mutually, hence the probability of loss l_i occurrence is the sum of all fuzzy quantities with respect to l_i. Namely, synthesizing probability of l_i is:

$$A^{(i)}(p_j) = A_1^{(i)}(p_j) \oplus A_2^{(i)}(p_j) \oplus \cdots \oplus A_{n_0}^{(i)}(p_j)$$

where operator $\oplus$ is a fuzzy addition.

Let

$$\pi_C(l_i, p_j) = A^{(i)}(p_j)$$

then

$$\Pi_C = \{\pi_C(l_i, p_j) | i = 1, 2, \cdots, n, j = 1, 2, \cdots, m\}$$

is the synthesizing disasters risk we need.

6 Conclusion

In this chapter, we all-around set forth the concept of fuzzy risk of natural disasters and analyse the reasons why we make a fuzzy risk estimation for a natural disaster system.

Fuzzy risk, in a probability fashion, is a fuzzy relation between events and probabilities. It differs from the tradition fuzzy probability which is defined by fuzzy events. The complexity of a natural disaster system leads to that crisp risks agreeing with the real situation cannot come out of today's knowledge about natural disasters.

We put forward a fuzzy mathematical model, based on the principle of information diffusion, to estimate fuzzy risk of natural disasters. From the case calculation, we know that, in this model, we can analyse the fuzzy uncertainty of various parts. Therefore a better assessment can be achieved.

If we say that the probabilistic method reduces the degree of blindness and provides more information, it is true that the fuzzy risk method can offer more information which enhances our understanding of probability to avoid acting rashly.

In our model, we only use the maximum and minimum operator. In fact, it can be replace by other powerful operators if we want analyse fuzzy risks more carefully. And, information diffusion functions can also be improved for obtaining much better results.

References

[1] Silverman B.W. (1986): Density Estimation for Statistics & Data Analysis. Chapman & Hall, London

[2] Fisher R.A. (1921): On the mathematical foundations of theoretical statistics. Phil. Trans. A **222**, 308–368

[3] Carlin B.P. and Louis T.A. (1996): Bayes and Empirical Bayes Methods for Data Analysis. Chapman & Hall, London

[4] Parzen E. (1962): On estimation of a probability density function and mode. Ann. Math. Statist. **33**, 1065–1076

[5] Wertz W. (1978): Statistical Density Estimation: a Survey. Vandenhoeck & Ruprecht in Göttingen

[6] Devroye L. and Györfi L. (1985): Nonparametric Density Estimation. John Wiley & Sons

[7] Hand D.J. (1982): Kernel Discriminate Analysis. Research Studies Press

[8] Breiman L., Meisel W., and Purcell E. (1977): Variable kernel estimates of multivariate densities. Technometrics **19**, 135–144

[9] Chen X. et al. (1989): Non-Parametric Statistics. Shanghai Science and Technology Press (in Chinese)

[10] Huang C.F. (1997): Principe of information diffusion. Fuzzy Sets and Systems **91**, 69–90

[11] Huang C.F. and Ruan D. (1996): Information diffusion principle and application in fuzzy neuron, in: Ruan D., ed., Fuzzy Logic Foundations and Industrial Applications. Kluwer Academic Publishers, Massachusetts, 165–189

[12] Liu Z. (1988): Application of information distribution concept to the estimation of earthquake intensity, in: Bezdek J.C., ed., Analysis of Fuzzy Information **3**. CRC. Press, Boca Raton, Florida, 67–73

[13] Liu Z. and Huang C.F. (1990): Information distribution method relevant in fuzzy information analysis. Fuzzy Sets and Systems **36**, 67–76

[14] Anon. (1989): Webster's Encyclopedic Unabridged Dictionary of the English Language. Gramercy Books, New York

[15] Lomnitz C. and Rosenblueth E. (1976): Seismic Risk and Engineering Decisions. Elsevier Scientific Publishing Company, Amsterdam

[16] Xiu X. and Huang C.F. (1989): Fuzzy identification between dynamic response of structure and structural earthquake damage. Earthquake Engineering and Engineering Vibration **9** (2), 57–66 (in Chinese)

[17] William J.P. and Arthur A. (1982): Natural Hazard Risk Assessment and Public Policy-Anticipating the Unexpected. Springer-verlag, New York

[18] Brown C.B. (1979): A fuzzy safety measure. J. Engineering Mechanics **105** (5), 855–872

[19] Dong W.M. et al. (1986): Fuzzy computation in risk and decision analysis. Civil Engineering Systems **2**, 201–208

[20] Hadipriono F.C. (1991): A rule-based fuzzy logic deduction technique for damage assessment of protective structures. Fuzzy Sets and Systems **44**, 459–468

[21] Esogbue A.O. et al. (1992): On the application of fuzzy sets theory to the optimal flood control problem arising in water resources systems. Fuzzy Sets and Systems **48**, 155–172

[22] Hoffman L.J., Michelmen E.H., and Clements D.P. (1978): SECURATE–Security evaluation and analysis using fuzzy metrics. Proc. of the 1978 National Computer Conference **47**. AFIPS Press, Montvale, New Jersey, 531–540

[23] Clement D.P. (1977): Fuzzy Ratings for Computer Security Evaluation. PhD Dissertation, University of California at Berkeley

[24] Schmucker K.J. (1984): Fuzzy Sets, Natural Language Computations, and Risk Analysis. Computer Science Press, Rockvill, Maryland

[25] Wang P.Z. (1985): Fuzzy Sets and Falling Shadows of Random Sets. Beijing Normal University Press, Beijing

[26] Luo C. (1992): Random fuzzy sets and the theorem of great number of fall-shadow. Fuzzy Systems and Mathematics 6 (2), 93–102

[27] Zadeh L.A. (1968): Probability measures of fuzzy events. Journal of Mathematical Analysis and Application 23, 421–427

[28] Govindarajulu Z. (1981): The Sequential Statistical Analysis of Hypothesis Testing, Point and Interval Estimation, and Decision Theory. American Sciences Press, Columbus, Ohio

[29] Huang C.F. (1993): The Principle of Information Diffusion and Thought Computation and Their Applications in Earthquake Engineering. PhD Dissertation, Beijing Normal University, Beijing

[30] Huang C.F. and Wang J. (1995): Technology of Fuzzy Information Optimization Processing and Applications. Beijing University of Aeronautics and Astronautics Press, Beijing

[31] Huang C.F. and Liu Z. (1985): Isoseimal area estimation of Yunnan Province by fuzzy mathematical method, in: Feng D. and Liu X., Eds., Fuzzy Mathematics in Earthquake Researches. Seismological Press, Beijing, 185–195

4

LINGUISTIC MODELS IN DECISION MAKING, OPTIMIZATION AND CONTROL

Decision Analysis by Advanced Fuzzy Systems

H. Kiendl
University of Dortmund
Faculty of Electrical Engineering
D-44221 Dortmund
Phone: +49.231.755-2760
Fax: +49.231.755-2752
e-mail: kiendl@esr.e-technik.uni-dortmund.de

1. Introduction

Human beings live in a world that shows a multitude of phenomena, which can vary continuously. Think of colours that can be characterized by wavelengths or frequencies of the real valued electromagnetic spectrum. The development of language has produced an inestimable tool to find one's way in this cosmos of phenomena. For instance, a language offers different words such as red, yellow, green or blue to distinguish colours. Each of these words is used to label an infinite set of different pure colours that belong to a certain interval of the frequency spectrum. Thus, words allow us to handle the huge cosmos of phenomena by dividing it into suitable 'granules' where the words can be considered as the labels of the granules (Zadeh, 1997). To continue the example of the colours, it is interesting to note that the language of certain peoples who live in a mainly green environment contains dozens of words to distinguish slightly different kinds of green but no word that summarizes all these green colours. Obviously in the development of languages, the precision of the words that correspond to the granules adapts constantly to changing needs.

The words of a language reduce the complexity of the surrounding world, allowing us to handle it, and form the basis for intelligent decisions that serve for finding one's way. Indeed, now, as always, most decisions we make are based on reasoning using words.

It is a constant challenge to delegate more and more human activities requiring intelligence to computers. To do this in the field of decision analysis (making intelligent decisions) the fuzzy approach introduced in [1, 2] has proven to be useful. On the one hand the concept of linguistic values modelled by membership functions serves to divide the continua of possible real values of real world variables into granules and thus reduces complexity. On the other hand errors induced by this reduction can be compensated for to some extent as the membership functions may assume arbitrary values μ with $0 \leq \mu \leq 1$, and these values can be processed appropriately by fuzzy logic. Thus it is possible to reach a favourable compromise between the desired simplification and the required accuracy and flexibility.

In recent years the author has pointed out that conventional fuzzy systems have certain structural drawbacks that restrict their domain of application for decision analysis. Furthermore, he has introduced advanced fuzzy systems that overcome these drawbacks. Extending [18] the essential concepts are summarized here together with examples of applications and new ideas.

2. The fuzzy philosophy and conventional fuzzy systems

There are two fields of application for decision analysis: The first is the field of process control, where the problem is to select a favourable value of the manipulated variable u, which influences the controlled process in a desired way (Fig. 1, top). The second is the domain of process analysis that covers tasks such as prediction, quality rating, estimation and classification. Here the problem is to select a meaningful value of a variable u, which characterizes a feature of the considered process (Fig. 1, middle). We consider here the frequently given case that all values u of a continuous spectrum $u_{min} \leq u \leq u_{max}$ are admitted in principle as output values. In many applications the required decision module (Fig. 1, grey) can be characterized as a transfer system without memory and can thus be described by a nonlinear function $u = F(x_1, x_2, ..., x_n)$ (Fig. 1, bottom). We consider this special case.

For the design of such a decision module the fuzzy approach may be useful if qualitative knowledge (expert or empirical knowledge) is available rather than analytical knowledge. In this case, the qualitative knowledge can be expressed in the form of rules and put into fuzzy machinery, thereby creating the desired fuzzy system (Fig. 2). As this design process allows us to make more use of different types of available qualitative knowledge, it is more efficient. We will show that conventional fuzzy systems have some structural restrictions in this respect.

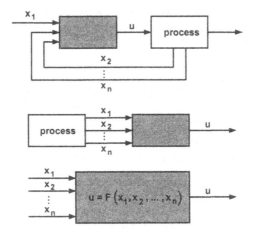

Figure 1: Two fields of application for decision modules: process control and process analysis (top and bottom, respectively) and the special case considered here of a decision module without memory.

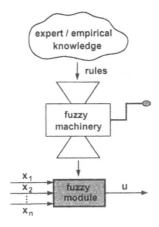

Figure 2: The fuzzy philosophy.

3. Conventional fuzzy systems

The Mamdani fuzzy system is widely used for decision analysis purposes (Fig. 3) [3]. A favourable feature is that this system represents an universal approximator and thus can *realize* any nonlinear function $u = F(x_1, x_2, ..., x_n)$. However, this flexibility—which incidentally is also shown by artificial neural networks or polynomials—is not the key feature that determines the practical value of a fuzzy system. The essential point is that with this system we can make purposeful use of available qualitative knowledge for *finding* a favourable function $u = F(x_1, x_2, ..., x_n)$, which solves the given decision problem.

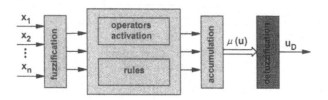

Figure 3: Conventional fuzzy system.

To see which type of qualitative knowledge can be made use of by the above fuzzy system we realize that such a fuzzy system can process rules of the form

$$\text{IF } <\text{condition}> \text{ THEN } <u = L_j \text{ RECOMMENDED}> , \qquad (1)$$

where the condition describes a special input situation and L_j is a linguistic value such as *small* or *large*. If this rule is activated it *recommends* the linguistic value L_j. In the case of a controller, this rule recommends an appropriate *action*. If the system is used for process analysis, such as supervision or prediction, the rule recommends a *statement* concerning the process. By evaluating all activated rules, the fuzzy system generates the output membership function $\mu(u)$. It is obtained by evaluating the formula

$$\mu(u) = \bigvee_k \left[p_k(x_1, x_2, ..., x_n) \wedge c_k(u) \right]. \qquad (2)$$

Here $p_k(x_1, x_2, ..., x_n)$ and $c_k(u)$ are the truth values of the premise and the conclusion, respectively, of the k-th rule, which depend on the values of the input variables x_i and the output variable u. From this, the defuzzification stage produces the output value u_D, which represents the most recommended value considering the recommendations of all individual rules.

4. Two-way fuzzy systems with hyperinference

We notice that conventional fuzzy systems can process only *positive* rules that express recommendations. This is a serious drawback of conventional fuzzy systems. In many applications, both positive experience, in the form of recommendations, and also negative experience, in the form of warnings and prohibitions to avoid undesirable operating situations, are important. In the interests of safety in particular, or for protecting facilities or cutting costs or for avoiding unacceptable product qualities, it may be essential to adhere strictly to certain prohibitions or it may be desirable to take appropriate heed of certain warnings.

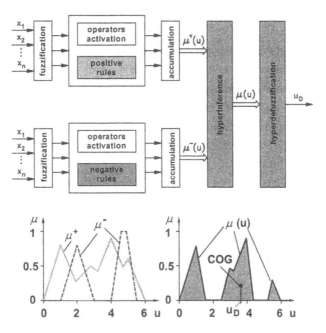

Figure 4: Two-way fuzzy system with hyperinference and hyperdefuzzification (top) and an example of the processing of $\mu^+(u)$ and $\mu^-(u)$ (bottom).

To make use of such warnings or prohibitions in a systematic and transparent manner we introduce *negative rules* (warning rules) of the type

$$\text{IF } <\text{condition}> \text{ THEN } <u = L_j \text{ FORBIDDEN}> . \tag{3}$$

Such a rule warns against generating output values u that are associated with the linguistic value L_j. To process such negative rules, together with positive rules, the two-way fuzzy system has been proposed [4, 5, 6]. It is made up of two conventional fuzzy systems without a defuzzification unit (Fig. 4, top). The first branch is used to process *positive rules* forming a membership function $\mu^+(u)$, which indicates the degree to which each admissible output value u is recommended. The second branch processes *negative rules* forming a membership function $\mu^-(u)$ indicating the degree of warning against each value u. The function $\mu^-(u)$ is obtained by evaluating Eq. (2) for the negative rules. A *hyperinference* strategy such as

$$\mu(u) = \mu^+(u) \wedge \neg \mu^-(u) , \tag{4}$$

where $\wedge$ is a selectable fuzzy operator, computes a resulting function $\mu(u)$ from the membership functions $\mu^+(u)$ and $\mu^-(u)$, which represents a reasonable compromise between recommendations and warnings. Finally, a well-motivated crisp output value u_D of the output variable is determined from $\mu(u)$ by means of *hyperdefuzzification*. This process takes place in two stages. If the support for $\mu(u)$ consists of several disjoint intervals I_i the function $\mu(u)$ is first decomposed into partial functions $\mu_i(u)$, each having an interval I_i as its support. The partial function having the greatest 'weight' (area below the functional graph or maximum functional value of $\mu_i(u)$) is defuzzified by applying conventional methods (Fig. 4, bottom). The key feature of the two-way fuzzy system is that it is now possible to make allowance for recommendations and warnings separately and to find an acceptable compromise between them.

The addition of a few negative rules can bring about a decisive improvement in performance compared with conventional fuzzy controllers. As a simple illustrative example we consider a ship going on a river (Fig. 5).

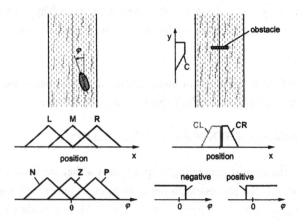

Figure 5: Course control of a ship on a river with and without an obstacle (right and left, respectively), together with the membership functions used for the controller design.

The aim is to maintain course in the middle of the river. If there is no obstacle in the river (Fig. 5, left) this aim is reached using a conventional fuzzy system with the three positive rules

IF position = L THEN φ = negative (N)
IF position = M THEN φ = zero (Z)
IF position = R THEN φ = positive (P)

(Fig. 6, left). In the case of an obstacle in the river (Fig. 5, right) we have the additional aim of preventing collision. To meet this aim the two negative rules

IF (position = CL) AND ($Y = C$)   THEN φ = negative FORBIDDEN
IF (position = CR) AND ($Y = C$)   THEN φ = positive FORBIDDEN

are added to the above three positive rules and processed together by a two-way fuzzy system. Obviously the resulting course always corresponds to the desired specifications, namely, to keep the ship in the middle of the river *and* to prevent collision (Fig. 6, right).

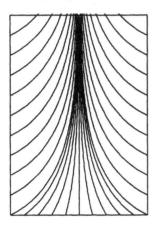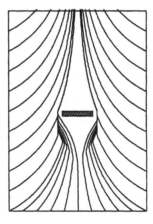

Figure 6: Courses of a ship using a conventional fuzzy system with three positive rules (left) and using a two-way fuzzy system with two additional negative rules (right). Collision is prevented due to the negative rules.

Fig. 7 shows the characteristic surfaces for both cases.

In [6] it was shown that by introducing negative rules that forbid undesired performance due to static friction of an electromechanical plant, it is possible to produce nonlinear characteristic surfaces (Fig. 8) that compensate for plant nonline-arities and therefore considerably improve performance. By employing two-way fuzzy systems for event detection purposes, it is possible to observe rules speaking in favour of or against the presence of an event. For example, it has been revealed in pattern recognition (letter detection) that the rate of detection can be distinctly increased by this means [7]. In rating the quality of complex processes it is possible to resort to rules speaking in favour of the rating 'good' and rules speaking against it.

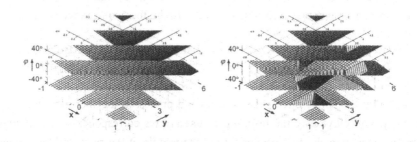

Figure 7: Characteristic surfaces for the conventional fuzzy system (left) and the two-way fuzzy system (right) that produce the ship courses shown in Fig. 6.

In the above examples (Figs. 6, 7) the resulting characteristic surfaces of the fuzzy system F were not known *in advance*. If they were known in advance, the system could be designed without making use of the fuzzy approach simply by defining the characteristic surface in the form of a look-up table and providing a suitable interpolation function. The significant point to note is that the two-way fuzzy system allows us to *find* a favourable characteristic surface by making appropriate use of recommendations *and* warnings.

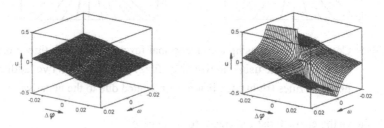

Figure 8: Part of a characteristic surface $u = f(\Delta\varphi, \omega)$ of a conventional fuzzy controller with 25 positive rules (left) and of a two-way fuzzy controller with the same 25 positive and two additional negative rules (right).

5. Fuzzy systems with inference filters

Conventional fuzzy systems offer only a limited spectrum of defuzzification methods, most commonly the COG method (centre of gravity) and the MOM method (mean of maxima). These are more or less well motivated, *ad hoc* approaches. In each special application, these options are interactively tested to determine which supplies the best results. This procedure does not favour sensitive optimization. To overcome this second drawback of conventional fuzzy systems, the concept of the *inference filter* has been introduced [2, 8, 9].

In conventional fuzzy systems, the membership function $\mu(u)$ is interpreted as being an *attractivity function*: the functional value of $\mu(u)$ indicates the degree to which each potential value u of the output variable is recommended, based on the conclusions drawn from the rules. Following this interpretation strictly, it is only justifiable to define a value u_D as a crisp output value if the function $\mu(u)$ assumes its maximum with that value. This is achieved by the MOM method. However, the COG defuzzification method, which is successful in many applications, does not meet this interpretation (Fig. 9, left). To overcome this discrepancy, we introduce the idea that the attractivity of a possible output value u_D depends not only on the functional value of $\mu(u)$ for the value u_0 but also on the functional values of $\mu(u)$ in the neighbourhood of u_0. This means that the functional values of $\mu(u)$ for all $u' \neq u_0$ should influence the attractivity of the value u_0, according to the distance d between u' and u_0 and the size of the functional value $\mu(u')$ (Fig. 9, right). To make this idea precise we say that the attractivity is not represented by the function $\mu(u)$, but by a function $\hat{\mu}(u)$ resulting from the *transformation*

$$\hat{\mu}(u) = \int_{-u_{max}}^{+u_{max}} \mu(u')h(u-u')du' \tag{5}$$

in which case, $h(u-u')$ is a selectable *distance function*. If the linguistic values of u are modelled by singletons and therefore $\mu(u)$ consists of a family of r singletons, the transformation is given by

$$\hat{\mu}(u) = \sum_{k=1}^{r} \mu_i \, h(u-u_i) \; , \tag{6}$$

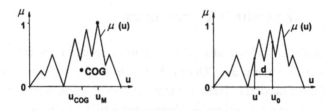

Figure 9: Motivation of the inference filter.

where u_i is the degree of activation of the singleton located in u_i. This distance function h determines the nature and size of the distance effect to be apportioned to each functional value of the membership function $\mu(u)$. The value determined as being the output of the fuzzy controller is u_D, for which the attractivity function is $\hat{\mu}(u)$ after Eq. (4) or Eq. (5) assumes its global maximum. Fig. 10 shows the resulting one-way fuzzy system where the transformation which supplies $\hat{\mu}(u)$ is called inference filter. This system includes the traditional COG, MOA and MOM (mean of area) defuzzification approaches as special cases if square, linear or δ-function is used as the distrance function (Fig. 11). By using an approach $h_\gamma (u - u')$ with a parameter γ, where for $\gamma = 2$, $\gamma = 1$ or $\gamma = 0$ the distance function $h_\gamma (u - u')$ is square, linear or a δ-function, respectively, we can produce conventional defuzzification methods or, by choosing a suitable value of γ, make an arbitrary compromise between these methods (Fig. 12). This feature allows a much more sensitive optimization than conventional fuzzy systems [10].

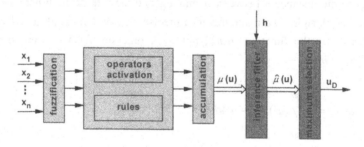

Figure 10: Structure of a one-way fuzzy system with inference filter.

By incorporating an inference filter into the two-way fuzzy system we can combine the advantages of both approaches (Fig. 11). The membership functions $\mu^+(u)$ and $\mu^-(u)$ are filtered and hyperdefuzzification is replaced by maximum selection [11].

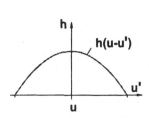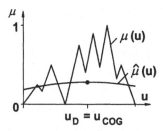

Figure 11: Equivalence of COG defuzzification and applying a quadratic filter function h in the fuzzy system of Fig. 10.

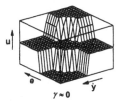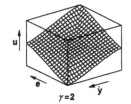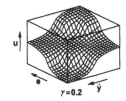

Figure 12: Characteristic surfaces $u = F(e, \dot{y})$ of a fuzzy controller with inference filter for different values of the filter parameter γ. The values $\gamma \approx 0$ and $\gamma = 2$ correspond to MOM and COG defuzzification. The value $y = 0.2$ represents a compromise and supplies the best performance.

Fig. 13 (top) shows a fuzzy system that supplies an estimated value $\hat{R}$ for the radius R of sheet metal after passing through a bending machine. Applying an optimized inference filter the relative error of $\hat{R}$ becomes considerably smaller compared with COG defuzzification (Fig. 13, bottom).

As in this example, use of an inference filter can often give considerably better performance than conventional defuzzification methods (another example is presented in [12]). This is plausible if we consider the following analogy: a car that is equipped with continuously adjustable gearing can adapt better to particular situations than a car with conventional gearing, which offers only some discrete options.

Fuzzy systems are very suitable for rating the performance of a process. In particular, we can use a fuzzy system that supplies a performance index for stepwise optimization of performance by suitable variations of the process parameters. However, such an optimization procedure may become trapped in an uninteresting side optimum if the characteristic surface produced by the fuzzy system exhibits many local optima. We can guard against this difficulty by making use of a fuzzy system with an inference filter. Assume that the fuzzy system supplies the correct value of the performance index with the nominal value γ_0 for the filter parameter. In this case we can make the characteristic surface 'softer' so that it exhibits less local optima by working with a value $\gamma_1 > \gamma_0$ (Fig. 14). The price for this measure is that the softened characteristic surface no longer describes the desired performance index *exactly*. Therefore it makes sense to work in the beginning of the optimization process with a value $\gamma_1 > \gamma_0$ and to decrease γ_1 gradually until it finally assumes the nominal value γ_0.

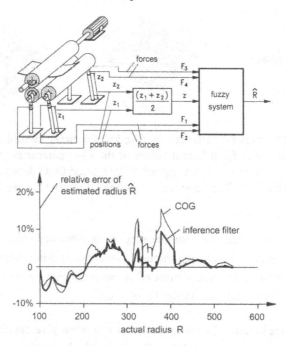

Figure 13: Machine for bending sheet metal with a fuzzy system for estimating the resulting bending radius R (top). Error of the estimation $\hat{R}$ with COG defuzzification and with an optimized inference filter (bottom).

By incorporating inference filters into the two-way fuzzy system we can combine the advantages of both approaches (Fig. 15). To illustrate the resulting advantages we consider the use of a fuzzy system for rating the performance of a process. The scale of values of the output u of the fuzzy system ranges from $u = 0$ (*excellent*) to $u = 6$ (*very bad*) (Fig. 16). We consider two different situations. In situation 1 two activated positive rules recommend the ratings *very good* and *bad*, respectively, and produce together the membership function $\mu^+(u)$ (Fig. 16, left). Furthermore, a negative rule forbids the rating *better than medium* and thus produces the output membership function $\mu^-(u)$. Situation 2 is different, as now two positive rules recommend the ratings *medium* and *bad*, respectively (Fig. 16, right). If we process $\mu^+(u)$ and $\mu^-(u)$ by the two-way fuzzy system according to Fig. 4 we obtain the implausible result that in situation 2 the resulting output u_D expresses a better rating than that in situation 1 (Fig. 16, top). If we use a two-way fuzzy system with inference filter according to Fig. 15 we obtain a worse rating in situation 2 than that in situation 1 (Fig. 16, bottom), a result that makes sense. A deeper reason for the superiority of the two-way fuzzy system with inference filter in this example is that in this fuzzy system, *first* the degree of attractivity due to the reasonings of *all* positive rules is evaluated and *afterwards* the inference of the negative rules is considered. This order of operations prevents the contribution of an *individual* positive rule being cancelled completely if the positive rule recommends forbidden output values.

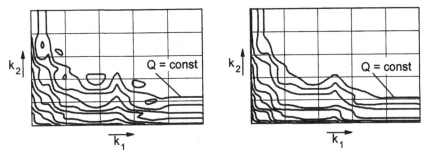

Figure 14: Niveau curves of a performance index $Q(k_1, k_2)$ supplied by a fuzzy system with inference filter for the nominal value γ_0 and for a value $\gamma_1 > \gamma_0$ (left and right, respectively).

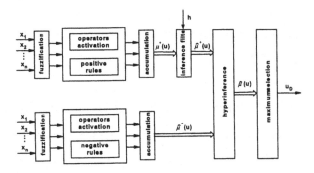

Figure 15: Two-way fuzzy system with inference filter.

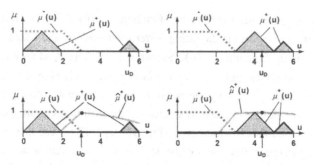

Figure 16: Example showing the performance of a two-way fuzzy system without an inference filter (top), and the superior performance with one (bottom).

6. The torque method

In the following section we point out a somewhat more hidden drawback of conventional fuzzy systems and we show how to overcome it. For this we consider first a situation where two rules of a fuzzy system, which recommend the linguistic output values *bad* and *good,* respectively, are activated (Fig. 17, left). In this situation, conventional defuzzification methods generate a crisp output value u_D for which (loosely written)

$$bad \le u_D \le good \tag{7}$$

holds. This shows that conventional defuzzification methods have the property:

(i) *opposed-directional* recommendations of the rules are superimposed so as to *compensate* one another.

Now, we consider a second situation where two rules, which recommend the linguistic output values *good* and *very good*, are activated (Fig. 17, right). In this case, conventional defuzzification methods generate a crisp output value u_D for which (loosely written)

$$good \le u_D \le very\ good \tag{8}$$

is valid. This shows that conventional defuzzification methods have the property:

(ii) *equi-directional* recommendations of the rules are superimposed in the sense of a *compromise.*

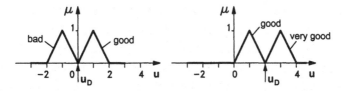

Figure 17: Translation invariance property of conventional defuzzification methods.

The property (ii) is adequate if each rule considers all main factors and therefore can make an *absolute* recommendation (type 1 rules). For example, in rating the value of a second-hand car, the main factors are the type, the age and the mileage reading of the car. However, it may be that a rule does not consider all the main factors or considers only additional factors (type 2 rules). In the above example, such rules may consider whether the car is fitted with a new engine or with new tyres or has had an accident. Type 2 rules cannot make absolute but only *incremental* or *decremental* recommendations (increasing or decreasing the value of the car). For processing type 2 rules, property (i) remains adequate. However, for processing type 2 rules that supply equi-directional incremental recommendations, instead of Eq. (8), an output value u_D is desired for which (loosely written)

$$u_D > very \ good \tag{9}$$

is valid. This shows that in this case we would need the following property:

(iii) *equi-directional* recommendations are superimposed so as to *amplify* one another.

Conventional defuzzification methods do not have property (iii), as they are *translation-invariant*: if u_D is the output corresponding to $\mu(u)$ then $u_D + d$ is the output corresponding to the shifted function, $\mu(u - d)$. This invariance property makes it impossible to meet both of the requirements (i) and (ii) simultaneously.

This observation supplies the key to overcoming this third drawback of a conventional fuzzy system and leads to the concept of the inference filter introduced in [13, 14]. The central idea is that we must look for a mechanism that is not translation-invariant. One possibility is the formula

$$u_D = \frac{1}{p} \int_{u_{min}}^{u_{max}} \mu(u) u \, du \ , \tag{10}$$

where p is a scaling factor. It is obvious that this formula meets the properties (i) and (ii). By applying the scaling factor $p = 1$, the resulting value u_D can be interpreted as being the *torque* corresponding to the neutral point $u_0 = 0$ induced by $\mu(u)$. Therefore, we call this formula the TOR method (torque). By using output membership functions in the form of singletons, defuzzification according to

$$u_D = \frac{1}{p} \sum_{k=1}^{r} \mu_k u_k \tag{11}$$

supplies the desired properties (i) and (ii). Here, r is the number of the rules, μ_k is the activation of rule k and u_k is the position of the corresponding output singleton.

We see now that we should distinguish between those rules that are based on *comprehensive knowledge* and therefore express *absolute recommendations* and those that are based on *partial knowledge* and therefore can express only *incremental* or *decremental recommendations*. The first type should be processed by COG, the second type by TOR defuzzification.

For output membership functions in the form of singletons, the conventional COG defuzzification can be combined with the torque method. To do this, each rule R_k is provided with a factor λ_k with $0 \le \lambda_k \le 1$, having the meaning that a rule R_k with $\lambda_k = 1$ must be processed conventionally (in the sense of the COG defuzzification), while a rule with $\lambda_k = 0$ must be processed in the sense of the torque method. By using output singletons, the formulas

$$u_D = q \frac{\sum_{k=1}^{r} \mu_k u_k}{\sum_{k=1}^{r} \mu_k} + (1-q) \frac{1}{p} \sum_{k=1}^{r} \mu_k u_k \quad \text{with} \quad q = \frac{\sum_{k=1}^{r} \lambda_k u_k}{\sum_{k=1}^{r} \mu_k} \tag{12}$$

correspond for $\lambda_k = 1$, $k = 1, 2, \ldots, r$ and $\lambda_k = 0$, $k = 1, 2, \ldots, r$ to the COG method or to the torque method, respectively. For $0 \le \lambda_k \le 1$, the factor λ_k determines the way each rule is processed.

To decide the type of a rule, the expert or operator who has laid down the rules should be asked, if possible. Otherwise, we can choose the values λ_k according to the heuristic that a more general premise of the rule k (i.e., when a smaller number of variables enters the premise) should be associated with a smaller λ_k, or we can use the λ_k as tuning parameters.

7. Fuzzy systems for processing rules generated from data

There are two possible approaches for the generation of rules. Firstly, a process expert or human operator can lay down his/her knowledge or experience in the form of if-then-rules, or these rules can be extracted by interviews. (With this method of rule generation, the resulting rule basis considers only the experience of which the expert is conscious.) Secondly, the rules can be generated from data by analysing the input data and the resulting decisions of a human operator. (With this method we gain access to unconscious knowledge.)

The Fuzzy-ROSA method for generating rules from data is based on the following idea [6, 15]. Consider a hypothesis

$$\text{IF <spinach eaten> THEN <allergic reaction>} . \tag{13}$$

In order to test whether this is a statistically relevant rule, we can record, for all days of a year, how often an allergic reaction is observed *in general* and how often after eating spinach. Evaluating these data statistically, we can find out whether the above hypothesis is a relevant (positive) rule, whether there is no statistically significant relationship between spinach and allergic reaction or whether, in contradiction to the hypothesis, eating spinach *prevents* allergic reaction so that the hypothesis is a relevant *negative* rule. In addition, by evaluating the above data a *relevance index* can be calculated that rates the relevance of each established rule. This relevance concept can also be applied in the fuzzy case, i.e., when the premise and conclusion of the hypothesis, respectively, are met by the data to a degree μ with $0 < \mu < 1$.

To illustrate the mechanism of the Fuzzy-ROSA method, we consider the following problem: a human operator adjusts at each time instant the value $u(t)$ of a manipulated variable, e.g. a dosing rate, depending on current and past values $x_i(t)$ of certain process variables. For generating rules that describe his/her behaviour the following main steps are executed:

(i)   recording the values $x_i(t_j)$, $u(t_j)$ for a sequence $t_1, t_2, \ldots$ of time instants;

(ii) specification of a search space consisting of hypotheses of the form IF <premise> THEN $<u = L_j>$, where the premise depends on the values $x_i(t_j)$ and L_j is a linguistic value of u;

(iii) selection of membership functions, which model the linguistic values provided in the hypotheses;

(iv) statistical tests of all hypotheses of the search spaces or of the most promising ones (this supplies a set of positive rules and a set of negative rules where each rule is rated by a corresponding relevance index);

(v) combination of all relevant rules to a rule base and, if possible, reduction of the rule base.

We see that this method quite naturally supplies both positive *and* negative rules. Using both types of rules usually improves the performance considerably when compared with those using positive rules only. For instance, we used this approach to model a human operator who controls a chemical semi-batch reactor (Fig. 18). Another example is the data-based generation of rules for a situation-dependent adaptation of the controller parameters of a robot in order to improve positioning accuracy [12, 16].

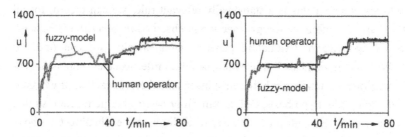

Figure 18: Data-based modelling of a human operator using only positive rules (left) and using positive and negative rules (right).

8. Conclusions and future development

Fuzzy systems can be useful in exploiting qualitative conscious or unconscious knowledge for the design of intelligent decision systems. The efficiency of this approach is improved if the fuzzy system allows us to make appropriate use of the different types of available knowledge. We have shown that conventional fuzzy systems have some drawbacks in this respect: they cannot process knowledge adequately in the form of vetoes and warnings, they offer only a discrete spectrum of defuzzification strategies, and they cannot superimpose equi-directional recommendations of different rules so as to amplify one another. These drawbacks are overcome by advanced fuzzy systems. Two-way fuzzy systems can process positive and negative rules. The concept of the inference filter generalizes classical defuzzification methods. It allows an adjustable compromise between a crisp and a soft interpretation of the rules. This may be used for better modelling of the available qualitative knowledge or for more sensitive optimization. With TOR defuzzification, the rules can be processed so that equi-directional recommendations are superimposed so as to amplify one another and opposed-directional recommendations are superimposed so as to compensate for one another. Negative rules can either be laid down by hand or can be obtained quite naturally by data-based rule generation. The practical advantages of the advanced fuzzy systems presented here are obvious from the theoretical viewpoint and have been demonstrated in various applications [2, 4, 7, 11, 12].

In this paper the input variables of the fuzzy system were considered as given. However, great potential for further improvement of fuzzy decision systems lies in strategies in which a great number of weakly relevant original input variables x_i are condensed to a smaller number of more relevant secondary input variables μ_j. Hints for proceeding in this direction can be derived from the process of development of languages. The word 'strawberry' for instance labels a cluster of various features that together characterize how a strawberry looks, smells and tastes. The word has evolved firstly as patterns of features belonging to this cluster are *observed frequently* and secondly as this word is perceived to be *relevant* in the sense that we can find *successful* rules such as 'IF object = strawberry AND colour = red THEN object = eatable'. Fuzzy systems could incorporate a similar mechanism. For this we set up an adaptive clustering procedure that identifies the relevant clusters consisting of frequently observed and relevant patterns formed by the current values of the variables x_i. Instead of the original variables x_i we now use the variables μ_j which express the degrees of similarity between an observed pattern, formed by the values of the variables x_i, and each cluster j as input values of the desired fuzzy decision system. The first results we have obtained are presented in [17].

References

[1] Zadeh, L. A.: Fuzzy Sets. Information and Control 8, 1965, pp. 338 – 353

[2] Zadeh, L. A.: Probability Measures of Fuzzy Events. Journal of Mathematical Analysis and Applications 23, 1968, pp. 421 – 427

[3] Driankov, D., Hellendoorn, H., Reinfrank, M.: An Introduction to Fuzzy

Control. Springer-Verlag, Berlin 1993

[4] Kiendl, H.: Verfahren zur Erzeugung von Stellgrößen am Ausgang eines Fuzzy-Reglers und Fuzzy-Regler hierfür. Patent DE 43 08 083, 1994

[5] Kiendl, H.: System of controlling or monitoring processes or industrial plants employing a dual-line fuzzy unit. U.S. Patent Number 5,826,251, 1998

[6] Kiendl, H.: Fuzzy Control methodenorientiert, Oldenbourg-Verlag, München, Wien 1997

[7] Lakewand, H.: Erkennen handgeschriebener Ziffern mit Hilfe der Fuzzy-Logik. Diplomarbeit Fachhochschule der Deutschen Bundespost Telekom, Berlin 1994

[8] Kiendl, H.: Verfahren zur Defuzzifizierung für signalverarbeitende Fuzzy-Baueinheiten und Filtereinrichtung hierfür. Patent DE 44 16 465, 1995

[9] Kiendl, H.: The inference filter. in: ELITE (Ed.), Proceedings EUFIT '94, Verlag der Augustinus Buchhandlung, Aachen 1994, pp. 438 – 447

[10] Reil, G., Jessen, H.: Fuzzy contour modelling of roll bent components using inference filter. in: ELITE (Ed.): Proceedings EUFIT '95, Verlag der Augustinus Buchhandlung, Aachen 1995, pp. 771 – 774

[11] Kiendl, H., Knicker, R., Niewels, F.: Two-way fuzzy controllers based on hyperinference and inference filter. In: Jamshidi, M., Yuh, J., Danchez, P. (eds.), Proceedings Second World Automation Congress, Vol. 4, Intelligent Automation and Control, TSI Press, Montpellier 1996, pp. 387 – 394

[12] Schwane, U.: Datenbasierte Generierung von Adaptionsregeln und Anwendung zur Erhöhung der Bahngenauigkeit eines Industrieroboters. Dissertation Universität Dortmund 1998. Fortschritt-Berichte VDI Reihe 8: Meß-, Steuerungs- und Regelungstechnik, VDI-Verlag Düsseldorf 1998

[13] Kiendl, H.: Verfahren zur Defuzzifizierung für signalverarbeitende Fuzzy-Baueinheiten. Patent DE 19 640 635, 1996

[14] Kiendl, H.: Non-translation-invariant Defuzzification. In: Proceedings of the sixth IEEE International Conference on Fuzzy Systems (FUZZ-IEEE '97), Barcelona 1997, pp. 737 – 742

[15] Krone, A., Schwane, U.: Generating fuzzy rules form contradictory data of different control strategies and control performances. In: Proceedings FUZZ-IEEE '96, New Orleans 1996, pp. 492 – 497

[16] Schwane, U., Praczyk, J., Kiendl, H.: Adaption von Reglerparametern unter Verwendung von datenbasiert generierten positiven und negativen Fuzzy-Regeln mit Konklusionen mit mehreren Ausgangsgrößen. 7. GMA-Workshop Fuzzy Control, Forschungsbericht der Fakultät für Elektrotechnik Nr. 0397, ISSN 0941-4169, 1997, pp. 53 – 67

[17] Kiendl, H.: Self-organising Adaptive Moment-based Clustering. FUZZ-IEEE '98, Anchorage (Alaska) 1998, Paper #1237, pp. 1470 – 1475

[18] Kiendl, H.: Next Generation Fuzzy Systems. in ELITE (Ed.): Proceedings EUFIT '98, Verlag der Augustinus Buchhandlung, Aachen 1998, pp. 779 - 788

Group Decision Making and a Measure of Consensus under Fuzzy Preferences and a Fuzzy Linguistic Majority

Janusz Kacprzyk*, Hannu Nurmi** and Mario Fedrizzi***

* Systems Research Institute, Polish Academy of Sciences
ul. Newelska 6, 01–447 Warsaw, Poland

Email: kacprzyk@ibspan.waw.pl

** Department of Political Science, University of Turku
20500 Turku, Finland

Email: hnurmi@sara.utu.fi

*** Department of Computer and Management Sciences, University of Trento
Via Inama 5, 38100 Trento, Italy
Email: fedrizzi@cs.unitn.it

Summary. The essence of group decision making is: there is a group of individuals (decisionmakers, experts, . . .) who provide their testimonies concerning an issue in question. These testimonies are assumed here to be individual preference relations over some set of option (alternatives, variants, . . .). The problem is to find a solution, i.e. an alternative or a set of alternatives, from among the feasible ones, which best reflects the preferences of the group of individuals as a whole. In this paper we will survey main developments in group decision making under fuzziness, mainly under fuzzy preference relations and a fuzzy (linguistic) majority. We will concentrate on how to derive solutions under individual fuzzy preference relations, and a fuzzy majority equated with a fuzzy linguistic quantifier (e.g., most, almost all, . . .) and dealt with in terms of a fuzzy logic based calculus of linguistically quantified statements or via the ordered weighted averaging (OWA) operators. Finally, we will discuss a related issue of how to define a "soft" degree of consensus in the group under individual fuzzy preference relations and a fuzzy majority.

Keywords: fuzzy logic, linguistic quantifier, fuzzy preference relation, fuzzy majority, group decision making, social choice, consensus.

1. Introduction

The essence of *group decision making* is basically as follows. There is a set of alternatives and a set of individuals who provide their testimonies concerning the alternatives. Usually, these testimonies are assumed to be *preferences* over the set of options, and this is also the case in this paper. The problem is to find a *solution*, i.e. an alternative (or a set of alternatives) which is best acceptable by the group of individuals as a whole. For a different point of departure, involving choice sets or utility functions, we may refer the interested reader to, e.g., Kim (1993), Salles (1996), Seo and Sakawa (1985) or Tanino (1990).

Unfortunately, this problem, which may seem to be trivial, is certainly not. Since its very beginning group decision making has been plagued by negative results. Their essence is that no "rational" choice function satisfies all "natural", or plausible, requirements; so, each choice function has at least one serious drawback. By far the best known negative result is the so-called Arrow's impossibility theorem (cf. Arrow, 1963) which says that there is no social choice (welfare) function which satisfies a set of plausible conditions of: an unrestricted domain, independence of irrelevant options, Pareto condition, and non-dictatorship.

Another well-known negative result is due to Gibbard and Satterthwaite (cf. Gibbard, 1973) which states then that all (universal and non-trivial) social decision functions are either manipulable or dictatorial; that is, first of all, there is no election system that may encourage the voters to reveal their true preferences.

In this context one can also cite, e.g., McKelvey's and Schofield's findings on the instability of solutions in spatial contexts (for more detail, see, e.g., Nurmi, 1982, 1983, 1987, 1988; Nurmi, Fedrizzi and Kacprzyk, 1990; Nurmi, Kacprzyk and Fedrizzi, 1996).

Basically, all these negative results might be summarized as follows: no matter which group choice procedure we employed, it would satisfy one set of plausible conditions but not another set of equally plausible ones. Unfortunately, this general property pertains to all possible choice procedures, so that attempts to develop new, more sophisticated choice procedures do not seem very promising in this respect. Much more promising seems to be to modify some basic assumptions underlying the group decision making process. This line of reasoning is also basically assumed here. Namely, we assume fuzzy preferences and a fuzzy linguistic majority. For a deeper analysis of these issues we refer the reader to Kacprzyk and Nurmi (1998).

Basically, suppose that we have a set of $n \geq 2$ options, $S = \{s_1, \ldots, s_n\}$, and a set of $m \geq 2$ individuals, $I = \{1, \ldots, m\}$. Then, an individual's $k \in I$ individual fuzzy preference relation in $S \times S$ assigns a value in the unit interval for the preference of one alternative over another.

We assume that the individual and social fuzzy preference relations are defined in $S \times S$, i.e. assign to each pair of options a strength of preference of one over another as a value from $[0, 1]$. This will also be assumed in this paper. However, one should be aware that it may be viewed counter-intuitive, and a better solution would be to assume the values of the strength of preference belonging to some ordered set (exemplified by a set of linguistic values). This gives rise to some non-standard notions of soft preferences, orderings, etc. The best source for information on these and other related topics is Salles (1996). In this paper the fuzzy preferences will be employed only instrumentally, i.e. as a point of departure for procedures to find group decision making (social choice) solutions.

Another basic element underlying group decision making is the concept of a *majority* – notice that a solution is to be an option(or options) best acceptable by the group as a whole, that is by (at least!) *most* of its members since in practically no real nontrivial situation it would be accepted by all. Though a strict majority as, e.g., at least a half, at least 2/3, ..., is traditionally employed, very often the human perception of what majority should be taken into account is often different. A good, often cited example in a biological context may be found in Loewer and Laddaga (1985):

" ...It can correctly be said that there is a consensus among biologists that Darwinian natural selection is an important cause of evolution though there is currently no consensus concerning Gould's hypothesis of speciation. This means that there is a widespread agreement among biologists concerning the first matter but disagreement concerning the second ... "

and it is clear that a rigid majority as, e.g., more than 75% would evidently not reflect the essence of the above statement. However, it should be noted that there are naturally situations when a strict majority is necessary, for obvious reasons, as in all political elections.

A natural manifestations of such a "soft" majority are the so-called *linguistic quantifiers* as, e.g., most, almost all, much more than a half, etc. Such linguistic quantifiers can be, fortunately enough, dealt with by fuzzy-logic-based calculi of linguistically quantified statements as proposed by Zadeh (1983) and Yager (1983). Moreover, Yager's (1988) ordered weighted averaging (OWA) operators can be used for this purpose.

These calculi have been applied by the authors to introduce a fuzzy majority (represented by a fuzzy linguistic quantifier) into group decision making and consensus formation models (Fedrizzi and Kacprzyk, 1988; Kacprzyk, 1984, 1985b,c, 1986a, 1987a; Kacprzyk and Fedrizzi, 1986, 1988, 1989; Kacprzyk, Fedrizzi and Nurmi, 1990; Kacprzyk and Nurmi, 1988; Nurmi and Kacprzyk, 1990; Nurmi, Fedrizzi and Kacprzyk, 1990), and also in an implemented decision support system for consensus reaching (Fedrizzi, Kacprzyk and Zadrożny, 1988; Kacprzyk, Fedrizzi and Zadrożny, 1988).

In this paper we will present how fuzzy preference relations and fuzzy majorities can be employed for deriving solution of group decision making, and of degrees of consensus. Our discussion will be kept simple and constructive in the sense of discussing algorithms for determining solutions, and referring the interested reader to the source papers for more theoretical results.

2. Fuzzy Linguistic Quantifiers and the Ordered Weighted Averaging (OWA) Operators

A *linguistically quantified statement* may be exemplified by, say, "most experts are convinced" or "almost all good cars are expensive", and may be generally written as

$$Qy\text{'s are } F \tag{2.1}$$

where Q is a linguistic quantifier (e.g., most), $Y = \{y\}$ is a set of objects (e.g., experts), and F is a property (e.g., convinced).

We may assign to the particular y's (objects) a different importance (relevance, competence, ...), B, which may be added to (2.1) yielding a *linguistically quantified statement with importance qualification* generally written as

$$QBy\text{'s are } F \tag{2.2}$$

which may be exemplified by "most (Q) of the important (B) experts $(y$'s) are convinced (F)".

From our point of view, the main problem is now to find the truth of such statements, i.e. truth(Qy's are F) or truth(QBy's are F) knowing truth(y is F), for each $y \in Y$. Two basic fuzzy logic based calculi may be employed for this purpose: the ones due to Zadeh (1983) and to Yager (1983a, b). In the following we will present the essence of Zadeh's (1993) calculus since it is simpler and more transparent, hence better suited for the purposes of this paper. Our discussion will be kept as simple as possible, tailored to our particular needs. More information on fuzzy linguistic quantifiers, and their various representations and methods of handling, can be found in Part I, Chaptre 2 in this volume.

2.1 A Fuzzy-Logic-Based Calculus of Linguistically Quantified Statements

In Zadeh's (1983) method, a fuzzy linguistic quantifier Q is assumed to be a fuzzy set defined in $[0, 1]$. For instance, $Q = $ "most" may be given as

$$\mu_Q(x) = \begin{cases} 1 & \text{for } x \geq 0.8 \\ 2x - 0.6 & \text{for } 0.3 < x < 0.8 \\ 0 & \text{for } x \leq 0.3 \end{cases} \tag{2.3}$$

which may be meant as that if at least 80% of some elements satisfy a property, then *most* of them certainly (to degree 1) satisfy it, when less than 30% of them satisfy it, then *most* of them certainly do not satisfy it (satisfy to degree 0), and between 30% and 80% – the more of them satisfy it the higher the degree of satisfaction by *most* of the elements.

This is an example of a *proportional* fuzzy linguistic quantifier (e.g., most, almost all, etc.), and we will deal with such quantifiers only since they are obviously more important for the modeling a fuzzy majority than the absolute quantifiers (e.g., about 5, much more than 10, etc.). The reasoning for the absolute quantifiers is however analogous.

Property F is defined as a fuzzy set in Y. For instance, if $Y = \{X, W, Z\}$ is the set of experts and F is a property "convinced", then F may be exemplified by $F =$ "convinced" $= 0.1/X + 0.6/W + 0.8/Z$ which means that expert X is convinced to degree 0.1, expert W to degree 0.6 and expert Z to degree 0.8. If now $Y = \{y_1, \ldots, y_p\}$, then it is assumed that truth(y_i is F) $= \mu_F(y_i)$, $i = 1, \ldots, p$.

The value of truth(Qy's are F) is determined in the following two steps (Zadeh, 1983):

$$r = \frac{1}{p} \sum_{i=1}^{p} \mu_F(y_i) \tag{2.4}$$

$$\text{truth}(Qy\text{'s are } F) = \mu_Q(r) \tag{2.5}$$

Basically, the expression (2.4) determines some mean proportion of elements satisfying the property under consideration, and (2.5) determines the degree to which this percentage satisfies the meaning of the fuzzy linguistic quantifier Q.

In the case of importance qualification, B is defined as a fuzzy set in Y, and $\mu_B(y_i) \in [0,1]$ is a degree of importance of y_i: from 1 for definitely important to 0 for definitely unimportant, through all intermediate values. For instance, $B =$ "important" $= 0.2/X + 0.5/W + 0.6/Z$ means that expert X is important (e.g., competent) to degree 0.2, expert W to degree 0.5, and expert Z to degree 0.6.

We rewrite first "QBy's are F" as $Q(B$ and $F)y$'s are B" which leads to the following counterparts of (2.4) and (2.5):

$$r' = \frac{\sum_{i=1}^{p} [\mu_B(y_i) \wedge \mu_F(y_i)]}{\sum_{i=1}^{p} \mu_B(y_i)} \tag{2.6}$$

$$\text{truth}(QBY\text{'s are } F) = \mu_Q(r') \tag{2.7}$$

Example 2.1. Let $Y =$ "experts" $= \{X, Y, Z\}$, $F =$ "convinced" $= 0.1/X + 0.6/Y + 0.8/Z$, $Q =$" most" be given by (2.3), $B =$ "important" $= 0.2/X + 0.5/Y + 0.6/Z$. Then: $r = 0.5$ and $r' = 0.92$, and truth("most experts are convinced")=0.4 and truth("most of the important experts are convinced")=1. □

The method presented is simple and efficient, and has proven to be useful in a multitude of cases, also in this paper.

2.2 The Ordered Weighted Averaging (OWA) Operators

Quite recently, Yager (1988) [see also Yager and Kacprzyk's (1997) book] has proposed a special class of aggregation operators, called the *ordered weighted averaging* (or OWA, for short) operators, which seem to provide an even better and more general aggregation in the sense of being able to simply and uniformly model a large class of fuzzy linguistic quantifiers.

An OWA operator of dimension p is a mapping $F : [0,1]^p \to [0,1]$ if associated with F is a weighting vector $W = [w_1, \ldots, w_p]^T$ such that: $w_i \in [0,1]$, $w_1 + \cdots + w_p = 1$, and

$$F(x_1, \ldots, x_p) = w_1 b_1 + \cdots + w_p b_p \qquad (2.8)$$

where b_i is the i-th largest element among $\{x_1, \ldots, x_p\}$. B is called an ordered argument vector if each $b_i \in [0,1]$, and $j > i$ implies $b_i \geq b_j$, $i = 1, \ldots, p$.

Then

$$F(x_1, \ldots, x_p) = W^T B \qquad (2.9)$$

Example 2.2. Let $W^T = [0.2, 0.3, 0.1, 0.4]$, and calculate $F(0.6, 1.0, 0.3, 0.5)$. Thus, $B^T = [1.0, 0.6, 0.5, 0.3]$, and $F(0.6, 1.0, 0.3, 0.5) = W^T B = 0.55$; and $F(0.0, 0.7, 0.1, 0.2) = 0.21$. □

For our purposes it is relevant how the OWA weights are found from the membership function of a fuzzy linguistic quantifier Q; an approach given in Yager (1988) may be used here:

$$w_k = \begin{cases} \mu_Q(k) - \mu_Q(k-1) & \text{for } k = 1, \ldots, p \\ \mu_Q(0) & \text{for } k = 0 \end{cases} \qquad (2.10)$$

Some examples of the w_i's associated with the particular quantifiers are:

- If $w_p = 1$, and $w_i = 0$, for each $i \neq p$, then this corresponds to $Q =$ "all";
- If $w_i = 1$ for $i = 1$, and $w_i = 0$, for each $i \neq 1$, then this corresponds to $Q =$ "at least one",

and the intermediate cases as, e.g., a half, most, much more than 75%, a few, almost all, etc. may be obtained by a suitable choice of the w_i's between the above two extremes.

Thus, we will write

$$\text{truth}(Qy's \text{ are } F) = \text{OWA}_Q(\text{truth } y_i \text{ is } F) = W^T B \qquad (2.11)$$

An important, yet difficult problem is the OWA operators with importance qualification, i.e. with importance coefficients associated with the particular data.

Suppose that we have a vector of data (pieces of evidence) $A = [a_1, \ldots, a_n]$, and a vector of importances $V = [v_1, \ldots, v_n]$ such that $v_i \in [0,1]$ is the importance of a_i, $i = 1, \ldots, n$, $(v_1 + \cdots + v_n \neq 1$, in general), and the OWA weights $W = [w_1, \ldots, w_n]^T$ corresponding to Q is determined via (2.10).

The case of an *ordered weighted averaging* operator with importance qualification, denoted OWA$_I$, is unfortunately not trivial. In a recent Yager's (1993) approach to be used here – which seems to be highly plausible, simple and efficient – the problem boils down to some redefinition of the OWA's weights w_i into $\overline{w}_i$. Then, (2.8) becomes

$$F_I(a_1, \ldots, a_n) = \overline{W}^T \cdot B = \sum_{j=1}^{n} \overline{w}_j b_j \tag{2.12}$$

We order first the pieces of evidence a_i, $i = 1, \ldots, n$, in descending order to obtain B such that b_j is the j-th largest element of $\{a_1, \ldots, a_n\}$. Next, we denote by u_j the importance of b_j, i.e. of the a_i which is the j-th largest; $i, j = 1, \ldots, n$. Finally, the new weights $\overline{W}$ are defined as

$$\overline{w}_j = \mu_Q \left(\frac{\sum_{k=1}^{j} u_k}{\sum_{k=1}^{n} u_k} \right) - \mu_Q \left(\frac{\sum_{k=1}^{j-1} u_k}{\sum_{k=1}^{n} u_k} \right) \tag{2.13}$$

Example 2.3. If $A = [a_1, a_2, a_3, a_4] = [0.7, 1, 0.5, 0.6]$, $U = [u_1, u_2, u_3, u_4] = [1, 0.6, 0.5, 0.9]$, and $Q=$"most" is given by (2.3), then $B = [b_1, b_2, b_3, b_4] = [1, 0.7, 0.6, 0.5]$, $\overline{W} = [0.04, 0.24, 0.41, 0.31]$, and $F_I(A) = \sum_{j=1}^{4} \overline{w}_j b_j = 0.067 \cdot 1 + 0.4 \cdot 0.7 + 0.333 \cdot 0.6 + 0.2 \cdot 0.5 = 0.6468$. □

For more information on the OWA operators we refer the reader to the recent Yager and Kacprzyk's (1997) book.

Let us also mention that OWA-like aggregation operators may be defined in an ordinal setting, i.e. for non-numeric data (which are only ordered, and we will refer the interested reader to, e.g., Delgado, Verdegay and Vila (1993) or Herrera, Herrera-Viedma and Verdegay (1996).

We have now the necessary formal means to proceed to our discussion of group decision making and consensus formation models under fuzzy preferences and a fuzzy majority.

3. Group Decision Making under Fuzzy Preferences and a Fuzzy Linguistic Majority

Group decision making proceeds here as follows. We have a set of $n \geq 2$ options, $S = \{s_1, \ldots, s_n\}$, and a set of $m \geq 2$ individuals, $I = \{1, \ldots, m\}$. Each individual $k \in I$ provides his or her testimony as to the alternatives in S. These testimonies are assumed to be individual fuzzy preference relations defined over the set of alternatives S (i.e. in $S \times S$).

An *individual fuzzy preference relation* of individual k, R_k, is given by its membership function $\mu_{R_k} : S \times S \longrightarrow [0, 1]$ such that

$$\mu_{R_k} = \begin{cases} 1 & \text{if } s_i \text{ is definitely preferred to } s_j \\ c \in (0.5, 1) & \text{if } s_i \text{ is slightly preferred to } s_j \\ 0.5 & \text{in the case of indifference} \\ d \in (0, 0.5) & \text{if } s_j \text{ is slightly preferred to } s_i \\ 0 & \text{if } s_j \text{ is definitely preferred to } s_i \end{cases} \tag{3.1}$$

If card S is small enough (as assumed here), an individual fuzzy preference relation of individual k, R_k, may conveniently be represented by an $n \times m$

matrix $R_k = [r_{ij}^k]$, such that $r_{ij}^k = \mu_{R_k}(s_i, s_j)$; $i, j = 1, \ldots, n$; $k = 1, \ldots, m$. R_k is commonly assumed (also here) to be reciprocal in that $r_{ij}^k + r_{ji}^k = 1$; moreover, it is also normally assumed that $r_{ii}^k = 0$, for all i, j, k.

The individual fuzzy preference relations, similarly as their nonfuzzy counterparts in traditional (non-fuzzy) group decision making, are a point of departure for most procedures for the derivation of solutions. As we have already mentioned, we will not deal with group decision making taking as a point of departure choice sets or utility functions (cf. Tanino, 1990).

Basically, two lines of reasoning may be followed here (cf. Kacprzyk, 1984–1986):

– a direct approach

$$\{R_1, \ldots, R_m\} \longrightarrow \text{solution} \tag{3.2}$$

that is, a solution is derived directly (without any intermediate steps) just from the set of individual fuzzy preference relations, and
– an indirect approach

$$\{R_1, \ldots, R_m\} \longrightarrow R \longrightarrow \text{solution} \tag{3.3}$$

that is, from the set of individual fuzzy preference relations we form first a social fuzzy preference relation, R (to be defined later), which is then used to find a solution.

A solution is here, unfortunately, not clearly understood – see, e.g., Nurmi (1981, 1982, 1983, 1987, 1988) for diverse solution concepts. More details related to the use of fuzzy preference relations as a point of departure in group decision making can also be found in, e.g., Nurmi (1981, 1982, 1988) and in many articles in Kacprzyk and Roubens (1988), Kacprzyk and Fedrizzi (1990), and Kacprzyk, Nurmi and Fedrizzi (1996).

In this paper we will only sketch the derivation of some fuzzy cores and minimax sets for the direct approach, and some fuzzy consensus winners for the indirect approach. In addition to fuzzy preference relations, which are usually employed, we will also use a fuzzy majority represented by a linguistic quantifier as proposed by Kacprzyk (1984–1986a).

3.1 Direct Derivation of a Solution

We will first employ the direct approach (3.2), i.e.

$$\{R_1, \ldots, R_m\} \longrightarrow \text{solution}$$

to derive two popular solution concepts: fuzzy cores and minimax sets.

3.1.1 Fuzzy Cores. Conventionally, the core is defined as a set of *undominated alternatives*, i.e. those not defeated in *pairwise comparisons* by a required majority (strict!) $r \leq m$, i.e.

$$C = \{s_j \in S : \neq \exists s_i \in S \text{ such that } r_{ij}^k > 0.5 \text{ for at least } r \text{ individuals}\} \tag{3.4}$$

The first attempt at a fuzzification of the core is due to Nurmi (1981) who has extended it to the *fuzzy α-core* defined as

$$C_\alpha = \{s_j \in S : \neq \exists s_i in S \text{ such that } r_{ij}^k > \alpha \geq 0.5 \text{ for at least } r \text{ individuals}\} \tag{3.5}$$

that is, as a set of alternatives not sufficiently (at least to degree α) defeated by the required (still strict!) majority $r \leq m$.

As we have already indicated, in many group decision making related situations is may be more adequate to assume that the required majority is imprecisely specified as, e.g., given by a fuzzy linguistic quantifier as, say, *most* defined by (3). This concept of a fuzzy majority has been proposed by Kacprzyk (1984–1986a), and it has turned out that it can be quite useful and adequate.

To employ a fuzzy majority to extend (fuzzify) the core, we start by denoting

$$h_{ij}^k = \begin{cases} 1 & \text{if } r_{ij}^k < 0.5 \\ 0 & \text{otherwise} \end{cases} \tag{3.6}$$

where here and later on in this section, if not otherwise specified, $i, j = 1, \ldots, n$ and $k = 1, \ldots, m$.

Thus, h_{ij}^k just reflects if alternative s_j defeats (in pairwise comparison) alternative s_i ($h_{ij}^k = 1$) or not ($h_{ij}^k = 0$).

Then, we calculate

$$h_j^k = \frac{1}{n-1} \sum_{i=1, i \neq j}^{n} h_{ij}^k \tag{3.7}$$

which is clearly the extent, from 0 to 1, to which individual k is not against alternative s_j, where 0 standing for definitely not against to 1 standing for definitely against, through all intermediate values.

Next, we calculate

$$h_j = \frac{1}{m} \sum_{k=1}^{m} h_j^k \tag{3.8}$$

which expresses to what extent, from 0 to 1 as in the case of (3.7), *all* the individuals are not against alternative s_j.

And, finally, we calculate

$$v_Q^j = \mu_Q(h_j) \tag{3.9}$$

is to what extent, from 0 to 1 as before, Q (say, most) individuals are not against alternative s_j.

The *fuzzy Q-core* is now defined (Kacprzyk, 1984–1986a, 1987a) as a fuzzy set

$$C_Q = v_Q^1/s_1 + \cdots + v_Q^n/s_n \tag{3.10}$$

i.e. as a fuzzy set of alternatives that are not defeated by Q (say, most) individuals.

Notice that in the above basic definition of a fuzzy Q-core we do not take into consideration to what degrees those defeats of one alternative by another are. They can be accounted for different ways. First and most straightforward is the introduction of a threshold into the degree of defeat in (3.6), for instance by denoting

$$h_{ij}^k(\alpha) = \begin{cases} 1 & \text{if } r_{ij}^k < \alpha \le 0.5 \\ 0 & \text{otherwise} \end{cases} \tag{3.11}$$

where, again, $i, j = 1, \ldots, n$ and $k = 1, \ldots, m$.

Thus, $h_{ij}^k(\alpha)$ just reflects if alternative s_j sufficiently (i.e. at least to degree $1 - \alpha$) defeats (in pairwise comparison) alternative s_i or not.

Then, by following (3.7)–(3.9), we arrive at the *fuzzy α/Q-core* defined (Kacprzyk, 1984–1986a, 1987a) as a fuzzy set

$$C_{\alpha/Q} = v_Q^1(\alpha)/s_1 + \cdots + v_Q^n(\alpha)/s_n \tag{3.12}$$

i.e. as a fuzzy set of alternatives that are not sufficiently (at least to degree $1 - \alpha$) defeated by Q (say, most) individuals.

We can also explicitly introduce the strength of defeat into (3.6). Namely, we can introduce a function exemplified by

$$\hat{h}_{ij}^k = \begin{cases} 2(0.5 - r_{ij}^k) & \text{if } r_{ij}^k < 0.5 \\ 0 & \text{otherwise} \end{cases} \tag{3.13}$$

where, again, $i, j = 1, \ldots, n$ and $k = 1, \ldots, m$.

Thus, by following (3.7)–(3.9), we arrive at the *fuzzy s/Q-core* defined (Kacprzyk, 1984–1986a, 1987a) as a fuzzy set

$$C_{s/Q} = \hat{v}_Q^1/s_1 + \cdots + \hat{v}_Q^n/s_n \tag{3.14}$$

i.e. as a fuzzy set of alternatives that are not strongly defeated by Q (say, most) individuals.

Example 3.1. Suppose that we have four individuals, $k = 1, 2, 3, 4$, whose individual fuzzy preference relations are:

$R_1 =$		$j = 1$	2	3	4
	$i = 1$	0	0.3	0.7	0.1
	2	0.7	0	0.6	0.6
	3	0.3	0.4	0	0.2
	4	0.9	0.4	0.8	0

$R_2 =$		$j = 1$	2	3	4
	$i = 1$	0	0.4	0.6	0.2
	2	0.6	0	0.7	0.4
	3	0.4	0.3	0	0.1
	4	0.8	0.6	0.9	0

	$j=1$	2	3	4		$j=1$	2	3	4
$i=1$	0	0.5	0.7	0.1	$i=1$	0	0.4	0.7	0.8
2	0.5	0	0.8	0.4	2	0.6	0	0.4	0.3
3	0.3	0.2	0	0.2	3	0.3	0.6	0	0.1
4	1	0.6	0.8	0	4	0.7	0.7	0.9	0

$R_3 =$ (left table), $R_4 =$ (right table)

Let the fuzzy linguistic quantifier be $Q =$ "most" defined by (2.3). Then, say:

$$C_{\text{"most"}} \cong 0.06/s_1 + 0.56/s_2 + 1/s_4$$
$$C_{0.3/\text{"most"}} \cong 0.56/s_4$$
$$C_{s/\text{"most"}} \cong 0.36/s_4$$

to be meant as follows: in case of $C_{\text{"most"}}$ alternative s_1 belongs to to the fuzzy Q-core to the extent 0.06. s_2 to the extent 0.56, and s_4 to the extent 1, and analogously for the $C_{0.3/\text{"most"}}$ and $C_{s/\text{"most"}}$. Notice that though the results obtained for the particular cores are different, for obvious reasons, s_4 is clearly the best choice which is evident if we examine the given individual fuzzy preference relations. □

Clearly, the fuzzy linguistic quantifier based aggregation of partial scores in the above definitions of the fuzzy Q-core, α/Q-core and s/Q-core, may be replaced by an ordered weighted averaging (OWA) operator based aggregation given by (2.10) and (2.11). This was proposed by Fedrizzi and Kacprzyk (1993), and Kacprzyk and Fedrizzi (1995a, b).

First, to derive the fuzzy Q-core, we start with h_{ij}^k (3.6) which reflects if alternative s_j defeats (in pairwise comparison) alternative s_i ($h_{ij}^k = 1$) or not ($h_{ij}^k = 0$). Then, we calculate h_j^k (3.7) which is the extent, from 0 to 1, to which individual k is not against alternative s_j. Next, we calculate h_j (3.8) which expresses to what extent, from 0 to 1 as in the case of (3.7), *all* the individuals are not against alternative s_j. And, finally, we calculate

$$\overline{v}_Q^j = \text{OWA}_Q(h_j) \tag{3.15}$$

is to what extent, from 0 to 1 as before, Q (say, most) individuals are not against alternative s_j, and $\text{OWA}_Q(.)$ is the OWA based aggregation given by (2.11) where the OWA weights corresponding to Q are given by (2.10).

The *fuzzy Q-core* is then defined (cf. Kacprzyk, 1984–1986a, 1987a) as a fuzzy set

$$C_Q = \overline{v}_Q^1/s_1 + \cdots + \overline{v}_Q^n/s_n \tag{3.16}$$

i.e. as a fuzzy set of alternatives that are not defeated by Q (say, most) individuals.

And, analogously, by introducing a threshold into the degree of defeat in (3.6), $\alpha \in [0, 0.5)$, we start with $h_{ij}^k(\alpha)$ (3.11) which reflects if alternative s_j sufficiently (i.e. at least to degree $1 - \alpha$) defeats (in pairwise comparison) alternative s_i or not.

Then, we calculate $h_j^k(\alpha)$ which is the extent, from 0 to 1, to which individual k is not sufficiently (at least to degree $1 - \alpha$) against alternative s_j, where 0 standing for definitely not against to 1 standing for definitely against, through all intermediate values. Next, we calculate $h_j(\alpha)$ which expresses to what extent, from 0 to 1 as in the case of (3.7), *all* the individuals are not sufficiently (at least to degree $1 - \alpha$) against alternative s_j. And, finally, we calculate

$$\overline{v}_Q^j(\alpha) = \text{OWA}_Q[h_j(\alpha)] \tag{3.17}$$

is to what the extent, from 0 to 1 as before, Q (say, most) individuals are not sufficiently (at least to degree $1 - \alpha$) against alternative s_j, and $\text{OWA}_Q(.)$ is the OWA based aggregation given by (2.11) where the OWA weights corresponding to Q are given by (2.10).

The *fuzzy α/Q-core* is then defined (cf. Kacprzyk, 1984–1986a, 1987a) as a fuzzy set

$$C_{\alpha/Q} = \overline{v}_Q^1(\alpha)/s_1 + \cdots + \overline{v}_Q^n(\alpha)/s_n \tag{3.18}$$

i.e. as a fuzzy set of alternatives that are not sufficiently (at least to degree $1 - \alpha$) defeated by Q (say, most) individuals.

Finally, we can also explicitly introduce the strength of defeat by using $\hat{h}_{ij}^k$ (3.13) which reflects how strongly (from 0 to 1) alternative s_j defeats (in pairwise comparison) alternative s_i. Then, we calculate $\hat{h}_j^k$ which is how strongly, from 0 to 1, individual k is not against alternative s_j, where 0 standing for definitely not against to 1 standing for definitely against, through all intermediate values. Next, we calculate $\hat{h}_j$ which expresses the strength, from 0 to 1, to which *all* the individuals are not against alternative s_j. And, finally, we calculate

$$\hat{w}_Q^j = \text{OWA}_Q(\hat{h}_j) \tag{3.19}$$

is the strength, from 0 to 1, to which Q (say, most) individuals are not against alternative s_j,and $\text{OWA}_Q(.)$ is the OWA based aggregation given by (2.11) where the OWA weights corresponding to Q are given by (2.10).

The *fuzzy s/Q-core* is then defined (cf. Kacprzyk, 1984–1986a, 1987a) as a fuzzy set

$$C_{s/Q} = \hat{w}_Q^1/s_1 + \cdots + \hat{w}_Q^n/s_n \tag{3.20}$$

i.e. as a fuzzy set of alternatives that are not strongly defeated by Q (say, most) individuals.

The results obtained by using the OWA operators are similar to those for the usual fuzzy linguistic quantifiers.

3.1.2 Minimax Sets. Another intuitively justified solution concept may be the minimax (opposition) set which may be defined for our purposes as follows.

Let $w(s_i, s_j) \in \{1, 2, \ldots, m\}$ be the number of individuals who prefer alternative s_i to alternative s_j, i.e. for whom $r_{ij}^k < 0.5$. If now $v(s_i) = \max_{j=1,\ldots,n} w(s_i, s_j)$ and $v^* = \min_{i=1,\ldots,n} v(s_i)$, then the *minimax set* is defined as

$$M(v^*) = \{s_i \in S : v(s_i) = v^*\} \tag{3.21}$$

i.e. as a (nonfuzzy) set of alternatives which in pairwise comparisons with any other alternative are defeated by no more than v^* individuals, hence by the least number of individuals.

Nurmi (1981) extends the minimax set, similarly in spirit to his extension of the core (3.5), to the α-*minimax set* as follows. Let $w_\alpha(s_i, s_j) \in \{1, 2, \ldots, m\}$ be the number of individuals who prefer alternative s_i to alternative s_j at least to degree $1 - \alpha$, i.e. for whom $r_{ij}^k < \alpha \leq 0.5$. If now $v_\alpha(s_i) = \max_{j=1,\ldots,n} w_\alpha(s_i, s_j)$ and $v_\alpha^* = \min_{i=1,\ldots,n} v_\alpha(s_i)$, then the α-*minimax set* is defined as

$$M_\alpha(v_\alpha^*) = \{s_i \in S : v_\alpha(s_i) = v_\alpha^*\} \tag{3.22}$$

i.e. as a (nonfuzzy) set of alternatives which in pairwise comparisons with any other alternative are defeated (at least to degree $1 - \alpha$) by no more than v^* individuals, hence by the least number of individuals.

A fuzzy majority is introduced into the above definitions of minimax sets as follows (Kacprzyk, 1985c, 1986a).

We start with (3.6), i.e.

$$h_{ij}^k = \begin{cases} 1 & \text{if } r_{ij}^k < 0.5 \\ 0 & \text{otherwise} \end{cases} \tag{3.23}$$

and

$$h_i^k = \frac{1}{n-1} \sum_{j=1, j \neq i}^n h_{ij}^k \tag{3.24}$$

is the extent, between 0 and 1, to which individual k is against alternative s_i.

Then

$$h_i = \frac{1}{m} \sum_{k=1}^m h_i^k \tag{3.25}$$

is the extent, between 0 and 1, to which all the individuals are against alternative s_i, while

$$t_i^Q = \mu_Q(h_i) \tag{3.26}$$

is the extent, from 0 to 1, to which Q (say, most) individuals are against alternative s_i, and

$$t_Q^* = \min_{i=1,\ldots,n} t_i^Q \tag{3.27}$$

is the least defeat of any alternative by Q individuals.

Finally, the Q-minimax set is

$$M_Q(t_Q^*) = \{s_i \in S : t_I^Q = t_Q^*\} \tag{3.28}$$

And analogously as for the α/Q-core (3.12), we can explicitly introduce the degree of defeat $\alpha < 0.5$ into the definition of the Q-minimax set. We start with (3.11), i.e.

$$h_{ij}^k(\alpha) = \begin{cases} 1 & \text{if } r_{ij}^k < \alpha \leq 0.5 \\ 0 & \text{otherwise} \end{cases} \tag{3.29}$$

and

$$h_i^k(\alpha) = \frac{1}{n-1} \sum_{j=1, j \neq i}^n h_{ij}^k(\alpha) \tag{3.30}$$

is the extent, between 0 and 1, to which individual k is sufficiently (at least to degree $1 - \alpha$) against alternative s_i.

Then, by following (3.25)–(3.27), we arrive at the α/Q-minimax set defined as

$$M_{\alpha/Q}[t_Q^*(\alpha)] = \{s_i \in S : t_I^Q(\alpha) = t_Q^*(\alpha)\} \tag{3.31}$$

We can also introduce explicitly the strength of defeat similarly as in the case of the fuzzy s/Q-core (3.14). We start with (3.13), i.e.

$$\hat{h}_{ij}^k = \begin{cases} 2(0.5 - r_{ij}^k) & \text{if } r_{ij}^k < 0.5 \\ 0 & \text{otherwise} \end{cases} \tag{3.32}$$

and

$$\hat{h}_i^k = \frac{1}{n-1} \sum_{j=1, j \neq i}^n \hat{h}_{ij}^k \tag{3.33}$$

is the extent, between 0 and 1, to which individual k is strongly against alternative s_i.

Then, by following (3.25)–(3.27), we arrive at the s/Q-minimax set defined as

$$M_{s/Q}(\hat{t}_Q^*) = \{s_i \in S : \hat{t}_I^Q = \hat{t}_Q^*\} \tag{3.34}$$

Example 3.2. For $R_1, \ldots, R_4$ as in Example 3.1, we obtain for instance:

$$M_{\text{"most"}}(0) = \{s_4\}$$
$$M_{0.3/\text{"most"}}(0) = \{s_1, s_2, s_4\}$$
$$M_{s/\text{"most"}} = \{s_1, s_2, s_4\}$$

□

The OWA based aggregation can also be employed for the derivation of fuzzy minimax sets given above.

First, we start with h_{ij}^k (3.23) and h_i^k (3.24) is the extent, between 0 and 1, to which individual k is against alternative s_i. Then, h_i (3.25) is the extent, between 0 and 1, to which all the individuals are against alternative s_i. Next, we calculate

$$\bar{t}_i^Q = \text{OWA}_Q(h_i) \tag{3.35}$$

which is the extent, from 0 to 1, to which Q (say, most) individuals are against alternative s_i, with $OWA_Q(.)$ being the OWA based aggregation defined by (2.10) and (2.11), and

$$\bar{t}_Q^* = \min_{i=1,\dots,n} \bar{t}_i^Q \tag{3.36}$$

is the least defeat of any alternative by Q individuals.

Finally, the Q-minimax set is

$$M_Q(\bar{t}_Q^*) = \{s_i \in S : \bar{t}_I^Q = \bar{t}_Q^*\} \tag{3.37}$$

And, analogously, we can explicitly introduce the degree of defeat $\alpha < 0.5$, and start with $h_{ij}^k(\alpha)$ (3.29), and $h_i^k(\alpha)$ (3.30) is the extent, between 0 and 1, to which individual k is sufficiently (at least to degree $1 - \alpha$) against alternative s_i. Then, $h_i(\alpha)$ is the extent, between 0 and 1, to which all the individuals are sufficiently (at least to degree $1 - \alpha$) against alternative s_i. Next

$$\bar{t}_i^Q(\alpha) = OWA_Q[h_i(\alpha)] \tag{3.38}$$

is the extent, from 0 to 1, to which Q (say, most) individuals are sufficiently (at least to degree $1 - \alpha$) against alternative s_i, and

$$\bar{t}_Q^*(\alpha) = \min_{i=1,\dots,n} \bar{t}_i^Q(\alpha) \tag{3.39}$$

is the least sufficient (at least to degree $1 - \alpha$) defeat of any alternative by Q individuals.

Finally, the α/Q-minimax set is

$$M_{\alpha/Q}[\bar{t}_Q^*(\alpha)] = \{s_i \in S : \bar{t}_I^Q(\alpha) = \bar{t}_Q^*(\alpha)\} \tag{3.40}$$

We can also introduce explicitly the strength of defeat, and start with $\hat{h}_{ij}^k$ (3.32), and $\hat{h}_i^k$ (3.33) is the extent, between 0 and 1, to which individual k is strongly against alternative s_i. Then, $\hat{h}_i$ is the extent, between 0 and 1, to which all the individuals are strongly against alternative s_i. Next

$$\hat{u}_i^Q = OWA(\hat{h}_i) \tag{3.41}$$

is the extent, from 0 to 1, to which Q (say, most) individuals are strongly against alternative s_i, and

$$\hat{u}_Q^* = \min_{i=1,\dots,n} \hat{u}_i^Q \tag{3.42}$$

is the least strong defeat of any alternative by Q individuals.

Finally, the s/Q-minimax set is

$$M_{s/Q}(\hat{u}_Q^*) = \{s_i \in S : \hat{u}_I^Q = \hat{u}_Q^*\} \tag{3.43}$$

And, again, the results obtained by using the OWA based aggregation are similar to those obtained by directly employing Zadeh's (1983) calculus of linguistically quantified statements.

3.2 Indirect Derivation of a Solution – the Consensus Winner

Now we follow the scheme (3.3), i.e.

$$\{R_1, \ldots, R_m\} \longrightarrow R \longrightarrow \text{solution}$$

i.e. from the individual fuzzy preference relations we determine first a social fuzzy preference relation, R, which is similar in spirit to its individual counterpart but concerns the whole group of individuals, and then find a solution from such a social fuzzy preference relation.

The above scheme involves in fact two problems:

– how to find a social fuzzy preference relation from the individual fuzzy preference relations, i.e.

$$\{R_1, \ldots, R_m\} \longrightarrow R$$

– how to find a solution from the social fuzzy preference relation, i.e.

$$R \longrightarrow \text{solution}$$

Here we will assume that $R = [r_{ij}]$ is given by

$$r_{ij} = \begin{cases} \frac{1}{m} sum_{k=1}^{m} a_{ij}^k & \text{if } i \neq j \\ 0 & \text{otherwise} \end{cases} \tag{3.44}$$

where

$$a_{ij}^k = \begin{cases} 1 & \text{if } r_{ij}^k > 0.5 \\ 0 & \text{otherwise} \end{cases} \tag{3.45}$$

Notice that R obtained via (3.44) need not be reciprocal, i.e. $r_{ij} \neq 1 - r_{ji}$, but it can be shown that $r_{ij} \leq 1 - r_{ji}$, for each $i, j = 1, \ldots, n$. For other definitions of R, see, e.g., Blin and Whinston (1973) or Ovchinnikov (1990).

A solution concept of much intuitive appeal is here the consensus winner (Nurmi, 1981) which will be extended under a social fuzzy preference relation and a fuzzy linguistic majority.

We start with

$$g_{ij} = \begin{cases} 1 & \text{if } r_{ij} > 0.5 \\ 0 & \text{otherwise} \end{cases} \tag{3.46}$$

which expresses whether alternative s_i defeats (in the whole group's opinion!) alternative s_j or not.

Next

$$g_i = \frac{1}{n-1} \sum_{j=1, j \neq i}^{n} g_{ij} \tag{3.47}$$

which is a mean degree to which alternative s_i is preferred, by the whole group, over all the other alternatives.

Then

$$z_Q^i = \mu_Q(g_i) \tag{3.48}$$

is the extent to which alternative s_i is preferred, by the whole group, over Q (e.g., most) other alternatives.

Finally, we define the *fuzzy Q-consensus winner* as

$$W_Q = z_Q^1/s_1 + \cdots + z_Q^n/s_n \tag{3.49}$$

i.e. as a fuzzy set of alternatives that are preferred, by the whole group, over Q other alternatives.

And analogously as in the case of the core, we can introduce a threshold $\alpha \geq 0.5$ into (3.46), i.e.

$$g_{ij}(\alpha) = \begin{cases} 1 & \text{if } r_{ij} > \alpha \geq 0.5 \\ 0 & \text{otherwise} \end{cases} \tag{3.50}$$

which expresses whether alternative s_i sufficiently (at least to degree α) defeats (in the whole group's opinion!) alternative s_j or not.

Next, by following (3.47) and (3.48), we arrive at the *fuzzy α/Q-consensus winner* defined as

$$W_{\alpha/Q} = z_Q^1(\alpha)/s_1 + \cdots + z_Q^n(\alpha)/s_n \tag{3.51}$$

i.e. as a fuzzy set of alternatives that are sufficiently (at least to degree α) preferred, by the whole group, over Q other alternatives.

Furthermore, we can also explicitly introduce the strength of preference into (3.46) similarly as in (3.13), for instance by defining

$$\hat{g}_{ij} = \begin{cases} 2(r_{ij} - 0.5) & \text{if } r_{ij} > 0.5 \\ 0 & \text{otherwise} \end{cases} \tag{3.52}$$

which expresses whether alternative s_i defeats (in the whole group's opinion!) alternative s_j or not, and if so (i.e. if $\hat{g}_{ij} > 0$), then $\hat{g}_{ij}$ gives the strength of this defeat.

Next, by following (3.47) and (3.48), we arrive at the *fuzzy s/Q-consensus winner* defined as

$$W_{s/Q} = \hat{z}_Q^1/s_1 + \cdots + \hat{z}_Q^n/s_n \tag{3.53}$$

i.e. as a fuzzy set of alternatives that are strongly preferred, by the whole group, over Q other alternatives.

Example 3.3. For the same individual fuzzy preference relations as in Example 3.1, and using (3.44) and (3.45), we obtain the following social fuzzy preference relation

$$R = \begin{array}{c|cccc} & j=1 & 2 & 3 & 4 \\ \hline i=1 & 0 & 0 & 1 & 0.25 \\ 2 & 0.75 & 0 & 0.75 & 0.25 \\ 3 & 0 & 0.25 & 0 & 0 \\ 4 & 1 & 0.75 & 1 & 0 \end{array}$$

If now the fuzzy majority is given by Q = "most" defined by (2.3) and $\alpha = 0,8$, then we obtain

$$W_{\text{"most"}} = \tfrac{1}{15}/s_1 + \tfrac{11}{15}/s_2 + 1/s_4$$
$$W_{0.8/\text{"most"}} = \tfrac{1}{15}/s_1 + \tfrac{11}{15}/s_4$$
$$W_{s/\text{"most"}} = \tfrac{1}{15}/s_1 + \tfrac{1}{15}/s_2 + 1/s_4$$

which is to be read similarly as for the fuzzy cores in Example 3.1. Notice that here once again alternative s_4 is clearly the best choice which is obvious by examining the social fuzzy preference relation. □

One can evidently use here the OWA based aggregation defined by (2.10) and (2.11), and denoted generically as $\text{OWA}_Q(.)$. This was proposed by Fedrizzi and Kacprzyk (1993), and Kacprzyk and Fedrizzi (1995a, b).

First, we start with g_{ij} (3.46) which expresses whether alternative s_i defeats (in the whole group's opinion!) alternative s_j or not.

Next, g_i (3.47) is a mean degree to which alternative s_i is preferred, by the whole group, over all the other alternatives.

Then,

$$\overline{z}_Q^i = \text{OWA}_Q(g_i) \tag{3.54}$$

is the extent to which alternative s_i is preferred, by the whole group, over Q (e.g., most) other alternatives.

Finally, we define the *fuzzy Q-consensus winner* as

$$\overline{W}_Q = \overline{z}_Q^1/s_1 + \cdots + \overline{z}_Q^n/s_n \tag{3.55}$$

i.e. as a fuzzy set of alternatives that are preferred, by the whole group, over Q other alternatives.

We can also introduce a threshold $\alpha \geq 0.5$ into (3.46) to obtain $g_{ij}(\alpha)$ (3.50) which expresses whether alternative s_i sufficiently (at least to degree α) defeats (in the whole group's opinion!) alternative s_j or not. Next, $g_i(\alpha)$ is a mean degree to which alternative s_i is sufficiently (at least to degree α) preferred, by the whole group, over all the other alternatives. Then, $\overline{z}_Q^i(\alpha) = \text{OWA}_Q[g_i(\alpha)]$ is the extent to which alternative s_i is sufficiently (at least to degree α) preferred, by the whole group, over Q (e.g., most) other alternatives.

Finally, we define the *fuzzy α/Q-consensus winner* as

$$W_{\alpha/Q} = \overline{z}_Q^1(\alpha)/s_1 + \cdots + \overline{z}_Q^n(\alpha)/s_n \tag{3.56}$$

i.e. as a fuzzy set of alternatives that are sufficiently (at least to degree α) preferred, by the whole group, over Q other alternatives.

Furthermore, we can also explicitly introduce the strength of preference into (3.46) by defining $\hat{g}_{ij}$ (3.52) which expresses whether alternative s_i defeats (in the whole group's opinion!) alternative s_j or not, and if so (i.e. if $\hat{g}_{ij} > 0$), then $\hat{g}_{ij}$ gives the strength of this defeat. Next, $\hat{g}_i$ is a mean degree to which alternative s_i is strongly preferred, by the whole group, over all the other alternatives alternatives. Then, $\hat{y}_Q^i = \text{OWA}_Q(\hat{g}_i)$ is the extent to which alternative s_i is strongly preferred, by the whole group, over Q (e.g., most) other alternatives.

Finally, we define the *fuzzy s/Q-consensus winner* as

$$W_{s/Q} = \hat{y}_Q^1/s_1 + \cdots + \hat{y}_Q^n/s_n \qquad (3.57)$$

i.e. as a fuzzy set of alternatives that are strongly preferred, by the whole group, over Q other alternatives.

Again, the results obtained by using the OWA based aggregation are similar to those via the traditional Zadeh's (1983) calculus of linguistically quantified statements.

This concludes our brief exposition of how to employ fuzzy linguistic quantifiers to model the fuzzy majority in group decision making. For readability and simplicity we have only shown the application of Zadeh's (1983) calculus of linguistically quantified propositions. The use of Yager's (1983) calculus is presented in the source papers by Kacprzyk (1985b, c).

We will not present some other solution concepts as, e.g., minimax consensus winners (cf. Nurmi, 1981, Kacprzyk, 1985c) or those based on fuzzy tournaments which have been proposed by Nurmi and Kacprzyk (1991).

4. Degrees of Consensus under Fuzzy Preferences and Fuzzy Linguistic Majority

Fuzzy linguistic quantifiers as representations of a fuzzy majority will now be employed to define a degree of consensus as proposed in Kacprzyk (1987), and then advanced in Kacprzyk and Fedrizzi (1986, 1988, 1989), and Fedrizzi and Kacprzyk (1988) [see also Kacprzyk, Fedrizzi and Nurmi (1990, 1992a, b)]. This degree is meant to overcome some "rigidness" of the conventional concept of consensus in which (full) consensus occurs only when "all the individuals agree as to all the issues". This may often be counterintuitive, and not consistent with a real human perception of the very essence of consensus (see, e.g., the citation from a biological context given in the beginning of the paper).

The new degree of consensus proposed can be therefore equal to 1, which stands for full consensus, when, say, "most of the individuals agree as to almost all (of the relevant) issues (alternatives, options)".

Our point of departure is again a set of individual fuzzy preference relations which are meant analogously as in Section 3. [see, e.g., (refeq8)].

The degree of consensus is now derived in three steps:

− first, for each pair of individuals we derive a degree of agreement as to their preferences between *all* the pairs of alternatives,

— second, we aggregate these degrees to obtain a degree of agreement of each pair of individuals as to their preferences between Q_1 (a linguistic quantifier as, e.g., "most", "almost all", "much more than 50%", ...) pairs of relevant alternatives, and

— third, we aggregate these degrees to obtain a degree of agreement of Q_2 (a linguistic quantifier similar to Q_1) pairs of important individuals as to their preferences between Q_1 pairs of relevant alternatives, and this is meant to be the *degree of consensus* sought.

The above derivation process of a degree of consensus may be formalized by using Zadeh's (1983) calculus of linguistically quantified statements and Yager's (1988, 1994) OWA based aggregation outlined in Section 1..

We start with the degree of strict agreement between individuals k_1 and k_2 as to their preferences between alternatives s_i and s_j

$$v_{ij}(k_1, k_2) = \begin{cases} 1 & \text{if } r_{ij}^{k_1} = r_{ij}^{K_2} \\ 0 & \text{otherwise} \end{cases} \tag{4.1}$$

where here and later on in this section, if not otherwise specified, $k_1 = 1, \ldots, m - 1$; $k_2 = k_1 + 1, \ldots, m$; $i = 1, \ldots, n - 1$; $j = i + 1, \ldots, n$.

The relevance of alternatives is assumed to be given as a fuzzy set defined in the set of alternatives S such that $\mu_B(s_i) \in [0, 1]$ is a *degree of relevance* of option s_i, from 0 for fully irrelevant to 1 for fully relevant, through all intermediate values.

The relevance of a pair of alternatives, $(s_i, s_j) \in S \times S$, may be defined, say, as

$$b_{ij}^k = \frac{1}{2}[\mu_B(s_i) + \mu_B(s_j)] \tag{4.2}$$

which is clearly the most straightforward option; evidently, $b_{ij}^B = b_{ji}^k$, and b_{ii}^k do not matter; for each i, j, k.

And analogously, the *importance of individuals*, I, is defined as a fuzzy set in the set of individuals such that $\mu_I(k) \in [0, 1]$ is a *degree of importance* of individual k, from 0 for fully unimportant to 1 for fully important, through all intermediate values.

Then, the importance of a pair of individuals, (k_1, k_2), b_{k_1,k_2}^I, may be defined in various ways, e.g., analogously as (4.2), i.e.

$$b_{k_1,k_2}^I = \frac{1}{2}[\mu_I(k_1) + \mu_I(k_2)] \tag{4.3}$$

The degree of agreement between individuals k_1 and k_2 as to their preferences between *all* the pairs of alternatives is [cf. (2.6)]

$$v_B(k_1, k_2) = \frac{\sum_{i=1}^{n-1} \sum_{j=i+1}^{n} [v_{ij}(k_1, k_2) \wedge b_{ij}^B]}{\sum_{i=1}^{n-1} \sum_{j=i+1}^{n} b_{ij}^B} \tag{4.4}$$

The degree of agreement between individuals k_1 and k_2 as to their preferences between Q_1 relevant pairs of alternatives is

$$v_{Q_1}^B(k_1, k_2) = \mu_{Q_1}[v_B(k_1, k_2)] \tag{4.5}$$

In turn, the degree of agreement of *all* the pairs of important individuals as to their preferences between Q_1 pairs of relevant alternatives is

$$v_{Q_1}^{I,B} = \frac{2}{m(m-1)} \frac{\sum_{k_1=1}^{m-1} \sum_{k_2=k_1+1}^{m} [v_{Q_1}^B(k_1, k_2) \wedge b_{k_1,k_2}^I]}{\sum_{k_1=1}^{m-1} \sum_{k_2=k_1+1}^{m} b_{k_1,k_2}^I} \tag{4.6}$$

and, finally, the degree of agreement of Q_2 pairs of important individuals as to their preferences between Q_1 pairs of relevant alternatives, called the *degree of $Q1/Q2/I/B$-consensus*, is

$$con(Q_1, Q_2, I, B) = \mu_{Q_2}(v_{Q_1}^{I,B}) \tag{4.7}$$

Since the strict agreement (4.1) may be viewed too rigid, we can use the degree of sufficient agreement (at least to degree $\alpha \in (0,1]$ of individuals k_1 and k_2 as to their preferences between options s_i and s_j, defined by

$$v_{ij}^{\alpha}(k_1, k_2) = \begin{cases} 1 & \text{if } |r_{ij}^{k_1} - r_{ij}^{k_2}| \le 1 - \alpha \le 1 \\ 0 & \text{otherwise} \end{cases} \tag{4.8}$$

where, $k_1 = 1, \ldots, m-1; k_2 = k_1+1, \ldots, m; i = 1, \ldots, n-1; j = i+1, \ldots, n$.

Then following (4.4)–(4.6), we arrive at the degree of sufficient (at least to degree α) agreement of Q_2 pairs of important individuals as to their preferences between Q_1 pairs of relevant alternatives, called the *degree of $\alpha/Q1/Q2/I/B$-consensus*, which is defined as

$$con^{\alpha}(Q_1, Q_2, I, B) = \mu_{Q_2}(v_{Q_1}^{I,B,\alpha}) \tag{4.9}$$

We can also explicitly introduce the strength of agreement into (4.1), and analogously define the degree of strong agreement of individuals k_1 and k_2 as to their preferences between options s_i and s_j, e.g., as

$$v_{ij}^s(k1, k2) = s(|r_{ij}^{k_1} - r_{ij}^{k_2}|) \tag{4.10}$$

where $s : [0,1] \longrightarrow [0,1]$ is some function representing the degree of strong agreements as, e.g.,

$$s(x) = \begin{cases} 1 & \text{for } x \le 0.05 \\ -10x + 1.5 & \text{for } 0.05 < x < 0.15 \\ 0 & \text{for } x \ge 0.15 \end{cases} \tag{4.11}$$

such that $x' < x'' \implies s(x') \ge s(x'')$, for each $x', x'' \in [0,1]$, and there is no such an $x \in [0,1]$ that $s(x) = 1$.

Then, following (4.4)–(4.6), we arrive at the degree of agreement of Q_2 pairs of important individuals as to their preferences between Q_1 pairs of relevant alternatives, called the *degree of s/Q1/Q2/I/B-consensus*, which is defined as

$$con^s(Q_1, Q_2, I, B) = \mu_{Q_2}(v_{Q_1}^{I,B,s}) \qquad (4.12)$$

Example 4.1. Suppose that $n = m = 3$, $Q_1 = Q_2 = $ "most" are given by (2.3), $\alpha = 0.9$, $s(x)$ is defined by (4.11), and the individual preference relations are:

$$R_1 = [r_{ij}^1] = $$

	$j = 1$	2	3
$i = 1$	0	0.1	0.6
2	0.9	0	0.7
3	0.4	0.3	0

$$R_2 = [r_{ij}^2] = $$

	$j = 1$	2	3
$i = 1$	0	0.1	0.7
2	0.9	0	0.7
3	0.3	0.3	0

$$R_3 = [r_{ij}^3] = $$

	$j = 1$	2	3
$i = 1$	0	0.2	0.6
2	0.8	0	0.7
3	0.4	0.3	0

If we assume the relevance of the alternatives to be $b_i^B = 1/s_1 + 0.6/s_2 + 0.2/s_3$, the importance of the individuals to be $b_k^I = 0.8/1 + 1/2 + 0.4/3$, $\alpha = 0.9$ and $Q = $ "most" given by (2.3), then we obtain the following degrees of consensus:

$$con(\text{"most"}, \text{"most"}, I, B) \cong 0.35$$
$$con^{0.9}(\text{"most"}, \text{"most"}, I, B) \cong 0.06$$
$$con^s(\text{"most"}, \text{"most"}, I, B) \cong 0.06$$

$\square$

And, similarly as for the group decision making solutions shown in Section 3., the aggregation via Zadeh's (1983) calculus of linguistically quantified propositions employed above may be replaced by the OWA based aggregation given by (2.10) and (2.11). The procedure is analogous as that presented in Section 3., and will not be repeated here.

5. Concluding Remarks

In this paper we have briefly presented the use of some elements of computing with words, mainly the use of a fuzzy linguistic majority, handled by a fuzzy logic based calculus of linguistically quantified propositions, for a further extension of group decision making models under fuzzy preferences.

BIBLIOGRAPHY

Arrow, K.J. (1963). *Social Choice and Individual Values*. Second Edition. Wiley, New York.

Barrett, C.R. and Pattanaik, P.K. (1990). Aggregation of fuzzy preferences. In J. Kacprzyk and M. Fedrizzi, (Eds.): *Multiperson Decision Making Models using Fuzzy Sets and Possibility Theory*, Kluwer, Dordrecht, pp. 155–162.

Barrett, C.R., Pattanaik, P.K. and Salles, M. (1986). On the structure of fuzzy social welfare functions. *Fuzzy Sets and Systems*, 19, 1–10.

Barrett, C.R., Pattanaik, P.K. and Salles, M. (1990). On choosing rationally when preferences are fuzzy. *Fuzzy Sets and Systems*, 34, 197–212.

Barrett, C.R., Pattanaik, P.K. and Salles, M. (1992). Rationality and aggregation of preferences in an ordinally fuzzy framework. *Fuzzy Sets and Systems*, 49, 9–13.

Bezdek, J.C., Spillman, B. Spillman, R. (1978). A fuzzy relation space for group decision theory, *Fuzzy Sets and Systems*, 1, 255–268.

Bezdek, J.C., Spillman, B. and Spillman, R. (1979). Fuzzy relation space for group decision theory: An application, *Fuzzy Sets and Systems* 2, 5–14.

Blin, J.M. (1974). Fuzzy relations in group decision theory, *J. of Cybernetics*, 4, 17–22.

Blin, J.M. and Whinston, A.P. (1973). Fuzzy sets and social choice, *J. of Cybernetics*, 4, 17–22.

Carlsson, Ch. et al. (1992). Consensus in distributed soft environments, *Europ. J. of Operational Research*, 61, 165–185.

Delgado, M., Verdegay, J.L. and Vila, M.A. (1993). On aggregation operations of linguistic labels, *Int. J. of Intelligent Systems*, 8, 351–370.

Fedrizzi, M. and Kacprzyk, J. (1988). On measuring consensus in the setting of fuzzy preference relations. In J. Kacprzyk and M. Roubens (Eds.): *Non-Conventional Preference Relations in Decision Making*, pp. 129–141.

Fedrizzi, M. and Kacprzyk, J. (1993). Consensus degrees under fuzzy majorities and preferences using OWA (ordered weighted average) operators", *Proc. of Fifth IFSA World Congress '93* (Seoul, Korea, July 1993), Vol. I, pp. 624–626.

Fedrizzi, M., Kacprzyk, J. and Nurmi, H. (1993). Consensus degrees under fuzzy majorities and fuzzy preferences using OWA (ordered weighted average) operators, *Control and Cybernetics*, 22, 71–80.

Fedrizzi, M., Kacprzyk, J. and Nurmi, H. (1996). How different are social choice functions: a rough sets approach, *Quality and Quantity*, 30, 87–99.

Fedrizzi, M., Kacprzyk, J., Owsiński, J.W. and Zadrożny, S. (1994). Consensus reaching via a GDSS with fuzzy majority and clustering of preference profiles, *Annals of Operations Research*, 51, 127–139.

Fedrizzi, M., Kacprzyk, J. and Zadrożny, S. (1988). An interactive multi-user decision support system for consensus reaching processes using fuzzy logic with linguistic quantifiers, *Decision Support Systems*, 4, 313–327.

Fishburn, P.C. (1990). Multiperson decision making: a selective review. In J. Kacprzyk and M. Fedrizzi (Eds.): *Multiperson Decision Making Models using Fuzzy Sets and Possibility Theory*, Kluwer, Dordrecht, pp. 3–27.

Gibbard A. (1973). Manipulation of schemes that mixvoting with chance, *Econometrica*, 45, 665–681.

Herrera, F., Herrera-Viedma, E. and Verdegay, J.L. (1996). A model of consensus in group decision making under linguistic assessments, *Fuzzy Sets and Systems*, 78, 73–88.

Herrera, F. and Verdegay, J.L. (1995). On group decision making under linguistic preferences and fuzzy linguistic quantifiers. In B. Bouchon-Meunier, R.R. Yager and L.A. Zadeh (Eds.): *Fuzzy Logic and Soft Computing*, World Scientific, Singapore, pp. 173–180.

Intriligator, M.D. (1973). A probabilistic model of social choice, *Review of Economic Studies*, 40, 553–560.

Intriligator, M.D. (1982). Probabilistic models of choice, *Mathematical Social Sciences*, 2, 157–166.

Kacprzyk, J. (1984). Collective decision making with a fuzzy majority rule, *Proc. of WOGSC Congress*, AFCET, Paris, pp. 153–159.

Kacprzyk, J. (1985a). Zadeh's commonsense knowledge and its use in multicriteria, multistage and multiperson decision making. In M.M. Gupta et al. (Eds.): *Approximate Reasoning in Expert Systems*, North-Holland, Amsterdam, pp. 105–121.

Kacprzyk, J. (1985b). Some 'commonsense' solution concepts in group decision making via fuzzy linguistic quantifiers. In J. Kacprzyk and R.R. Yager (Eds.): *Management Decision Support Systems Using Fuzzy Sets and Possibility Theory*, Verlag TÜV Rheinland, Cologne, pp. 125–135.

Kacprzyk, J. (1985c). Group decision-making with a fuzzy majority via linguistic quantifiers. Part I: A consensory-like pooling; Part II: A competitive-like pooling, *Cybernetics and Systems: an Int. J.*, 16, 119–129 (Part I), 131–144 (Part II).

Kacprzyk, J. (1986a). Group decision making with a fuzzy linguistic majority, *Fuzzy Sets and Systems*, 18, 105–118.

Kacprzyk, J. (1986b). Towards an algorithmic/procedural 'human consistency' of decision support systems: a fuzzy logic approach. In W. Karwowski and A. Mital (Eds.): *Applications of Fuzzy Sets in Human Factors*, Elsevier, Amsterdam, pp. 101–116.

Kacprzyk, J. (1987a). On some fuzzy cores and 'soft' consensus measures in group decision making. In J.C. Bezdek (Ed.): *The Analysis of Fuzzy Information*, Vol. 2, CRC Press, Boca Raton, pp. 119–130.

Kacprzyk, J. (1987b). Towards 'human consistent' decision support systems through commonsense-knowledge-based decision making and control models: a fuzzy logic approach, *Computers and Artificial Intelligence*, 6, 97–122.

Kacprzyk, J. and Fedrizzi, M. (1986). 'Soft' consensus measures for monitoring real consensus reaching processes under fuzzy preferences, *Control and Cybernetics*, 15, 309–323.

Kacprzyk, J. and Fedrizzi, M. (1988). A 'soft' measure of consensus in the setting of partial (fuzzy) preferences, *Europ. J. of Operational Research*, 34, 315–325.

Kacprzyk, J. and Fedrizzi, M. (1989). A 'human-consistent' degree of consensus based on fuzzy logic with linguistic quantifiers, *Mathematical Social Sciences*, 18, 275–290.

Kacprzyk, J. and Fedrizzi, M., Eds. (1990). *Multiperson Decision Making Models Using Fuzzy Sets and Possibility Theory*, Kluwer, Dordrecht.

Kacprzyk, J. and Fedrizzi, M. (1995a). A fuzzy majority in group DM and consensus via the OWA operators with importance qualification, *Proc. of CIFT'95 – Current Issues in Fuzzy Technologies* (Trento, Italy), pp. 128–137.

Kacprzyk, J. and Fedrizzi, M. (1995b). Consensus degrees under fuzziness via ordered weighted average (OWA) operators. In Z. Bien and K.C. Min (Eds.): *Fuzzy Logic and its Applications in Engineering, Information Sciences and Intelligent Systems*, Kluwer, Dordrecht, pp. 447–454.

Kacprzyk, J., Fedrizzi, M. and Nurmi, H. (1990). Group decision making with fuzzy majorities represented by linguistic quantifiers. In J.L. Verdegay and M. Delgado (Eds.): *Approximate Reasoning Tools for Artificial Intelligence*, Verlag TÜV Rheinland, Cologne, pp. 126–145.

Kacprzyk, J., Fedrizzi, M. and Nurmi, H. (1992a). Fuzzy logic with linguistic quantifiers in group decision making and consensus formation. In R.R. Yager and L.A. Zadeh (Eds.): *An Introduction to Fuzzy Logic Applications in Intelligent Systems*, Kluwer, Dordrecht, 263–280.

Kacprzyk, J., Fedrizzi, M. and Nurmi, H. (1992b). Group decision making and consensus under fuzzy preferences and fuzzy majority, *Fuzzy Sets and Systems*, 49, 21–31.

Kacprzyk, J., Fedrizzi, M. and Nurmi, H. (1996). "Soft" degrees of consensus under fuzzy preferences and fuzzy majorities. In J. Kacprzyk, H. Nurmi i M. Fedrizzi (Eds.): *Consensus under Fuzziness*, Kluwer, Boston, pp. 55–83.

Kacprzyk, J., Fedrizzi, M. and Nurmi, H. (1997). OWA operators in group decision making and consensus reaching under fuzzy preferences and fuzzy majority. In R.R. Yager and J. Kacprzyk (Eds.): *The Ordered Weighted Averaging Operators: Theory and Applications*, Kluwer, Boston, pp. 193–206.

Kacprzyk, J. and Nurmi, H. (1989). Linguistic quantifiers and fuzzy majorities for more realistic and human-consistent group decision making. In G.

Evans, W. Karwowski and M. Wilhelm (Eds.): *Fuzzy Methodologies for Industrial and Systems Engineering*, Elsevier, Amsterdam, pp. 267–281.

Kacprzyk J. and Nurmi H. (1998). Group decision making under fuzziness. In R. Słowiński (Ed.): *Fuzzy Sets in Decision Analysis, Operations Research and Statistics*, Kluwer, Boston, pp. 103–136.

Kacprzyk, J., Nurmi, H. and Fedrizzi, M., Eds. (1996). *Consensus under Fuzziness*, Kluwer, Boston.

Kacprzyk, J. and Roubens, M., Eds. (1988). *Non-Conventional Preference Relations in Decision Making*, Springer–Verlag, Heidelberg.

Kacprzyk, J. and Yager, R.R. (1984a). Linguistic quantifiers and belief qualification in fuzzy multicriteria and multistage decision making, *Control and Cybernetics*, 13, 155–173.

Kacprzyk, J. and Yager, R.R. (1984b). 'Softer' optimization and control models via fuzzy linguistic quantifiers, *Information Sciences*, 34, 157–178.

Kacprzyk, J., Zadrożny, S. and Fedrizzi, M. (1988). An interactive user-friendly decision support system for consensus reaching based on fuzzy logic with linguistic quantifiers. In M.M. Gupta and T. Yamakawa (Eds.): *Fuzzy Computing*, Elsevier, Amsterdam, pp. 307–322.

Kacprzyk, J., Zadrony, S. and Fedrizzi, M. (1997). An interactive GDSS for consensus reaching using fuzzy logic with linguistic quantifiers. In D. Dubois, H. Prade and R.R. Yager (Eds.): *Fuzzy Information Engineering- A Guided Tour of Applications*, Wiley, New York, pp. 567–574.

Kelly, J.S. (1978) *Social Choice Theory*, Springer–Verlag, Berlin.

Kuzmin, V.B. and Ovchinnikov, S.V. (1980a). Group decisions I: In arbitrary spaces of fuzzy binary relations, *Fuzzy Sets and Systems*, 4, 53–62.

Kuzmin, V.B. and Ovchinnikov, S.V. (1980b). Design of group decisions II: In spaces of partial order fuzzy relations, *Fuzzy Sets and Systems*, 4, 153–165.

Loewer, B. and Laddaga, R. (1985). Destroying the consensus, in Loewer B., Guest Ed., Special Issue on Consensus, *Synthese*, 62 (1), pp. 79–96.

Nurmi, H. (1981). Approaches to collective decision making with fuzzy preference relations, *Fuzzy Sets and Systems*, 6, 249–259.

Nurmi, H. (1982). Imprecise notions in individual and group decision theory: resolution of Allais paradox and related problems, *Stochastica*, VI, 283–303.

Nurmi, H. (1987). *Comparing Voting Systems*, Reidel, Dordrecht.

Nurmi, H. (1988). Assumptions on individual preferences in the theory of voting procedures. In J. Kacprzyk and M. Roubens (Eds.): *Non-Conventional Preference Relations in Decision Making*, Springer–Verlag, Heidelberg, pp. 142–155.

Nurmi, H., Fedrizzi, M. and Kacprzyk, J. (1990). Vague notions in the theory of voting. In J. Kacprzyk and M. Fedrizzi (Eds.): *Multiperson Decision Making Models Using Fuzzy Sets and Possibility Theory*, Kluwer, Dordrecht, pp. 43–52.

Nurmi, H. and Kacprzyk, J. (1991). On fuzzy tournaments and their solution concepts in group decision making, *Europ. J. of Operational Research*, 51, 223–232.

Nurmi, H., Kacprzyk, J. and Fedrizzi, M. (1996). Probabilistic, fuzzy and rough concepts in social choice, *Europ. J. of Operational Research*, 95, 264–277.

Ovchinnikov, S.V. (1990). Means and social welfare functions in fuzzy binary relation spaces. In J. Kacprzyk and M. Fedrizzi (Eds.): *Multiperson Decision Making Models using Fuzzy Sets and Possibility Theory*, Kluwer, Dordrecht, pp. 143–154.

Roubens, M. and Vincke, Ph. (1985). *Preference Modelling*, Springer–Verlag, Berlin.

Salles, M. (1996). Fuzzy utility. In S. Barbera, P.J. Hammond and C. Seidl (Eds.): *Handbook of Utility Theory*, Kluwer, Boston (forthcoming).

Szmidt, E. and Kacprzyk, J. (1996). Intuitionistic fuzzy sets in group decision making, *Notes on Intuitionistic Fuzzy Sets*, 2, 15–32.

Tanino, T. (1984). Fuzzy preference orderings in group decision making, *Fuzzy Sets and Systems*, 12, 117–131.

Tanino, T. (1990). On group decision making under fuzzy preferences. In J. Kacprzyk and M. Fedrizzi (Eds.): *Multiperson Decision Making Models using Fuzzy Sets and Possibility Theory*, Kluwer, Dordrecht, pp. 172–185.

Yager, R.R. (1983). Quantifiers in the formulation of multiple objective decision functions, *Information Sciences*, 31, 107–139.

Yager, R.R (1988). On ordered weighted averaging aggregation operators in multicriteria decision making, *IEEE Trans. on Systems, Man and Cybernetics*, SMC-18, 183–190.

Yager, R.R. (1993). On the Issue of Importance Qualifications in Fuzzy Multi-Criteria Decision Making. Tech. Report MII-1323, Machine Intelligence Institute, Iona College, New Rochelle, NY.

Yager, R.R. and Kacprzyk, J. (Eds.) (1997). *The Ordered Weighted Averaging Operators: Theory and Applications*, Kluwer, Boston.

Zadeh, L.A. (1983). A computational approach to fuzzy quantifiers in natural languages, *Computers and Maths. with Appls.*, 9, 149–184.

Linear Programming with Words

Stefan Chanas and Dorota Kuchta

Institute of Industrial Engineering and Management
Wroclaw University of Technology
Wybrzeże Wyspiańskiego 27
50-370 Wrocław, Poland
E-mail: CHANAS@iozi23n.ioz.pwr.wroc.pl

1. Introduction

Linear programming is the part of operational research, which is most widely used in practical applications. There are many classical algorithms in this domain (the most important one is the well known simplex method) and many new ones, together with corresponding software, are being developed for specific applications, which often solve problems of enormous dimensions.

The problem is that all these algorithms, however good they are, will give a wrong results if they are run on wrong data. Such data include various estimates and forecasts (like the expected demand, prices etc.) and a considerable amount of them are rather rarely exactly true. People responsible for delivering data for linear programming software are asked to give certain values and they do so, because they are required to. But how often these people simply do not know exact values? The only thing a sales manager can often say, when asked about the demand for the product in the next month, is: it will be *about 7000*. When asked for a specific value he gives the value *7000*, knowing that it may be wrong, but he has no possibility of transmitting another kind of information. The same thing is true for goals and constraints. In this case it may even be hard for the decision maker to speak in the language of numbers. We read in [9] about some decision makers: "If only they could merely describe their values and uncertainties by using the English language instead of 'reducing everything to numbers', then decision analysis would be very useful to them." So, in many cases we may hear verbal statements that something should be rather high or medium instead of a ready constraint for a linear programming problem.

For this reason a new domain was born, that of linguistic values (Zadeh [12], Dubois and Prade [4]), in which the user can transmit the information that a certain unknown value will be "around something", "probably not greater than something", "should be big" etc. "One is much less likely to be wrong when one is using linguistic values instead of numerical ones. (...) Instead of being almost certainly wrong, we resort to vagueness as a hedge" [10].

Linguistic reasoning has already been used for some time with success, also in practical application (see [7], [11]). However, most of the them use this way of reasoning in other kind of problems, which are not solved by linear programming. The aim of this paper is to present some results making it possible to use linguistic values in linear programming problems.

In order to solve a linear programming problem stated verbally, we have to express it in a mathematical form. What is more, this mathematical form has to be solvable by existing algorithms – otherwise the approach would not be practical. In order to arrive at a manageable form of the problem, it is necessary to co-operate with the decision maker and get from him a more exact explanation of his verbal statements. The way he understands his statements will then be expressed by means of the fuzzy set based possibility theory introduced by Zadeh ([13]). This means that the coefficients, the objective and the constraints of the linear programming problem to be solved are expressed as fuzzy numbers, and then we show how this formulation can be reduced to a classical one, which can be solved without any problems.

Being aware that the understanding of ones imprecise statements may be imprecise too and as a result we may have problems while trying to link a decision maker's statement to a fuzzy problem, we extend the classical fuzzy approach and admit a "fuzzy understanding of fuzzy statement", which we model by what we call interval valued fuzzy numbers.

The imprecision in the model formulation often implies an imprecision in the definition of the solution. Therefore we see our approach as just a proposition, indicating open ways to other definitions of solutions.

2. Selected notions concerning fuzzy numbers

Let us start with a general definition of fuzzy number:

Definition 2.1. *A fuzzy number $\tilde{A}$ is a function $A : \Re \to [0,1]$ (where $\Re$ denotes real space) which is*

(i) *upper semicontinuous.*
(ii) *quasi-concave, i.e. fulfilling the following condition*

$$A(z) \geq min\{A(x), A(y)\} \text{ for each } x, y, z \text{ such that } z \in [x, y].$$

Function A is called the membership function of the fuzzy number $\tilde{A}$. If there exists $z \in \Re$ such that $A(z) = 1$ then $\tilde{A}$ is called a normal fuzzy number.

For each $z \in \Re$ the value $A(z)$ denotes the degree to which z belongs – or the possibility to which it may belong – to the set (notion, group, etc.) modelled by the fuzzy number $\tilde{A}$. The biggest degree is 1, the smallest – 0. For example, if $\tilde{A}$ stands for a value which at present is known only approximately and will be known exactly only in the future, then $A(z)$ is the possibility degree of z being this value. Another example: if $\tilde{A}$ models the decision maker's understanding of what it means to fulfil the relation "z should not significantly exceed 5", then $A(z)$ is the degree to which z fulfils this relation according to the decision maker. For example, $A(5)$, $A(4.8)$ would probably always be 1, but $A(5.1)$ does not have to be 0. It can even be 1, but most probably it will be a value from the interval $(0, 1)$.

Definition 2.2. *Let $\tilde{A}$ be a fuzzy number. For each $\lambda \in [0, 1]$ the set $A^\lambda = \{z : A(z) \geq \lambda\}$ is called $\lambda - level$ of the fuzzy number $\tilde{A}$.*

It is well known fact that a fuzzy number $\tilde{A}$ is fully determined by its λ−levels:

$$A(z) = sup\{\lambda : \lambda \in [0, 1] \text{ and } z \in A^\lambda\}.$$

It is easy to prove the following lemma:

Lemma 2.1. *Let $\tilde{A}$ be a fuzzy number. For each $\lambda \in (0, 1]$ the λ−level is a closed set: an interval of one of the forms $[-\infty, a_R(\lambda)]$, $[a_L(\lambda), \infty]$, $[a_L(\lambda), a_R(\lambda)]$ or empty set $\emptyset$.*

In this paper we will use special types of fuzzy numbers. Here are the corresponding definitions:

Definition 2.3. *A fuzzy number $\tilde{A}$ is called a number of the $L - R$ type if it is a function A of the following form:*

$$A(x) = \begin{cases} r_A & \text{for } x \in [\underline{a}, \overline{a}], \\ L\left(\frac{\underline{a}-x}{\alpha_A} + L^{-1}(r_A)\right) & \text{for } x \leq \underline{a}, \\ R\left(\frac{x-\overline{a}}{\beta_A} + R^{-1}(r_A)\right) & \text{for } x \geq \overline{a}, \end{cases} \quad (2.1)$$

where L and R are continuous non-increasing functions, called shape function, defined on $[0, \infty)$ and strictly decreasing to zero in those subintervals of the interval $[0, \infty)$ in which they are positive, and fulfilling the conditions $L(0) = R(0) = 1$. The parameters α_A and β_A are non-negative real numbers. The parameter $r_A \in (0, 1]$ is called the height of $\tilde{A}$. Symbols L^{-1} and R^{-1} stand for reverse functions to L and R, respectively, reduced to the subintervals in which they are strictly decreasing.

The following notation for a fuzzy number $\tilde{A}$ with a membership function A given by formula (2.1) will be assumed:

$$\tilde{A} = (\underline{a}, \ \overline{a}, \ r_A, \ \alpha_A, \ \beta_A)_{L-R}. \quad (2.2)$$

If we assume in (2.1) $r_A = 1$ then we receive the normal fuzzy number of the $L - R$ type as introduced by Dubois and Prade [3]. It is enough to notice that $L^{-1}(1) = R^{-1}(1) = 0$.

For example the following functions are among those fulfilling the conditions for being a shape function:

$$S(y) = max\{0, 1 - y\} - \text{linear}, \tag{2.3}$$
$$S(y) = exp(-py), \ p \geq 1 - \text{exponential}, \tag{2.4}$$
$$S(y) = max\{0, 1 - y^p\}, \ p \geq 1 - \text{power}, \tag{2.5}$$
$$S(y) = \frac{1}{1 + y^p}, \ p \geq 1 - \text{rational}. \tag{2.6}$$

For a fuzzy number $\tilde{A}$ of the $L - R$ type, $\tilde{A} = (\underline{a}, \bar{a}, r_A, \alpha_A, \beta_A)_{L-R}$, the following relationship holds:

$$
\begin{aligned}
A^\lambda &= [a_L(\lambda), a_R(\lambda)] = \\
&= [\underline{a} - \alpha_A(L^{-1}(\lambda) - L^{-1}(r_A)), \bar{a} + \beta_A(R^{-1}(\lambda) - R^{-1}(r_A))]
\end{aligned} \tag{2.7}
$$

for $\lambda \in (0, r_A]$ and $A^\lambda = \emptyset$ for $\lambda \in (r_A, 1]$.

For a normal fuzzy number of the $L - R$ type the formula (2.7) is reduced to:

$$A^\lambda = [a_L(\lambda), a_R(\lambda)] = [\underline{a} - \alpha_A L^{-1}(\lambda), \bar{a} + \beta_A R^{-1}(\lambda)]. \tag{2.8}$$

In the paper we will use extended operations of the addition of two fuzzy numbers and of multiplication of a fuzzy number with a scalar. Let us remind the definitions of those operations, which are a consequence of the extension principle of Zadeh.

Definition 2.4. Let $\tilde{A}$, $\tilde{B}$ be fuzzy numbers and $r \in \Re$. Then:

(i) $\tilde{A} + \tilde{B}$ is a fuzzy number with the membership function

$$(A + B)(z) = \sup_{z = x + y} \min\{A(x), B(y)\}, \qquad x, y, z \in \Re,$$

(ii) for $r \neq 0$ $r\tilde{A}$ is a fuzzy number with the membership function

$$(rA)(z) = A(z/r), \qquad z \in \Re,$$

(iii) for $r = 0$ $r\tilde{A}$ is zero, i.e. $(rA)(z) = 1$ for $z = 0$ and $(rA)(z) = 0$ for $z \neq 0$.

The operations defined in Definition 2.4 preserve the fuzzy numbers type. Let $\tilde{A} = (\underline{a}, \bar{a}, r_A, \alpha_A, \beta_A)_{L-R}$ and $\tilde{B} = (\underline{b}, \bar{b}, r_B, \alpha_B, \beta_B)_{L-R}$ be two fuzzy numbers of the same $L - R$ type. The following equalities hold:
if $r_B < r_A$ then

$$\tilde{A} + \tilde{B} = \tilde{C} = (\underline{c}, \ \bar{c}, \ r_B, \ \alpha_A + \alpha_B, \ \beta_A + \beta_B)_{L-R}, \tag{2.9}$$

where

$$\underline{c} = \underline{a} + \underline{b} - \alpha_A(L^{-1}(r_B) - L^{-1}(r_A)), \tag{2.10}$$
$$\bar{c} = \bar{a} + \bar{b} + \beta_A(R^{-1}(r_B) - R^{-1}(r_A)), \tag{2.11}$$

if $r_B > r_A$ then

$$\tilde{A} + \tilde{B} = \tilde{C} = (\underline{c}, \ \overline{c}, \ r_A, \ \alpha_A + \alpha_B, \ \beta_A + \beta_B)_{L-R}, \qquad (2.12)$$

where

$$\underline{c} = \underline{a} + \underline{b} - \alpha_B(L^{-1}(r_A) - L^{-1}(r_B)), \qquad (2.13)$$
$$\overline{c} = \overline{a} + \overline{b} + \beta_B(R^{-1}(r_A) - R^{-1}(r_B)), \qquad (2.14)$$

if $r_B = r_A = r$ then

$$\tilde{A} + \tilde{B} = \tilde{C} = (\underline{a} + \underline{b}, \ \overline{a} + \overline{b}, \ r, \ \alpha_A + \alpha_B, \ \beta_A + \beta_B)_{L-R}. \qquad (2.15)$$

Theorem 2.1. *The following conditions hold true for any fuzzy numbers $\tilde{A}$ and $\tilde{B}$:*

$$(A+B)^\lambda = A^\lambda + B^\lambda = [a_L(\lambda) + b_L(\lambda), \ a_R(\lambda) + b_R(\lambda)], \\ \lambda \in (0, r_A \wedge r_B], \qquad (2.16)$$

$$(rA)^\lambda = rA^\lambda = [ra_L(\lambda), \ ra_R(\lambda)], \ r \geq 0, \ \lambda \in (0, r_A]. \qquad (2.17)$$

The symbol $\wedge$ stands in (2.16) and everywhere in the paper for the minimum operation.

There are many ways of comparing two fuzzy numbers $\tilde{A}$ and $\tilde{B}$ (see eg. [1],[2]). Let us use an index of possibility, denoted by $\mu(\tilde{A}, \tilde{B})$, which is a measure of credibility of the fact that $\tilde{B}$ is large than $\tilde{A}$ (see [13]):

$$\mu(\tilde{A}, \tilde{B}) = Poss(\tilde{B} \geq \tilde{A}) = \sup{}_{x \leq y} [A(x) \wedge B(y)]. \qquad (2.18)$$

The following theorem is very easy to prove:

Theorem 2.2. *Let $\tilde{A}$ and $\tilde{B}$ be two arbitrary fuzzy numbers. For each $\lambda \in (0, 1]$ the following condition is fulfilled:*

$$\mu(\tilde{A}, \tilde{B}) = Poss(\tilde{B} \geq \tilde{A}) \geq \lambda \Leftrightarrow b_R(\lambda) \geq a_L(\lambda). \qquad (2.19)$$

We will use also the notion of the L type (R type) fuzzy number.

Definition 2.5. *A fuzzy number $\tilde{A}$ is called a number of the L (R) type if its membership function is of the following form:*

$$A(x) = \begin{cases} r_A & \text{for} \ x \geq \underline{a}, \\ L\left(\frac{\underline{a}-x}{\alpha_A} + L^{-1}(r_A)\right) & \text{for} \ x \leq \underline{a}, \end{cases} \qquad (2.20)$$

$$\left(A(x) = \begin{cases} r_A & \text{for} \ x \leq \overline{a}, \\ R\left(\frac{x-\overline{a}}{\beta_A} + R^{-1}(r_A)\right) & \text{for} \ x \geq \overline{a}. \end{cases} \right) \qquad (2.21)$$

We assume the following notations for fuzzy numbers of the L and R type, respectively:

$$\tilde{A} = (\underline{a},\ \infty,\ r_A,\ \lambda_A, 0)_L\,,$$

$$\tilde{A} = (-\infty,\ \overline{a},\ r_A,\ 0,\ \beta_A)_R\,.$$

The λ levels of fuzzy numbers of the L (R) type are intervals similar to those given by formulae (2.7) and (2.8). It is enough to replace in them the right (left) end with the symbol ∞ $(-\infty)$.

3. Interval valued fuzzy numbers

In this section we will define so called interval valued fuzzy numbers, which allow a more flexible formulation of linear programming problems.

Definition 3.1. *An interval valued fuzzy number $\tilde{\overline{A}}$ is any function $\overline{A} : \Re \to I^{[0,1]}$ (where $I^{[0,1]}$ denotes the set of closed intervals contained in the interval $[0,1]$). For each $x \in \Re$, the value $\overline{A}(x)$ will be denoted as $[\overline{A}_D(x), \overline{A}_U(x)]$.*

An interval valued fuzzy number can be used to model such a situation where the membership degrees cannot be determined unequivocally (this problem will be discussed more thoroughly in the next section). If the decision maker, when asked for example to which possibility degree a given real number can be the value of a certain coefficient, is not able to give a number from the interval [0,1], but says something like "it will be around 0.9", or if several experts have different opinions about the membership degree, then we can ask them to give it in the form of an interval.

For each $x \in \Re$, the value $\overline{A}_D(x)$ denotes the smallest membership (possibility) degree given by the experts (decision maker), and the value $\overline{A}_U(x)$ — the biggest one. The smallest degree may correspond to the opinion of the most cautious or the most requiring expert, the biggest one — to that of the least cautious or the least requiring one.

In order to make it possible to carry out calculations and arrive at a result in the practice, we will consider special cases of interval valued fuzzy numbers:

Definition 3.2. *An interval valued fuzzy number $\tilde{\overline{A}}$ is called regular if the functions $\overline{A}_D(x)$ and $\overline{A}_U(x)$ are fuzzy numbers, i.e. fulfil the conditions of Definition 2.1. The ends of the $\lambda-$levels of the fuzzy numbers $\overline{A}_D(x)$ and $\overline{A}_U(x)$ will be denoted, respectively, as*

$$(a_D)_L(\lambda),\ (a_D)_R(\lambda),\ (a_U)_L(\lambda),\ (a_U)_R(\lambda).$$

Definition 3.3. *An interval valued fuzzy number $\tilde{\overline{A}}$ is called an interval valued fuzzy number of the $L-R$ (L,R) type if it is regular and if both functions $\overline{A}_D(x)$ and $\overline{A}_U(x)$ are of the L-R (L,R) type. The shape functions of $\overline{A}_D(x)$ and $\overline{A}_U(x)$ do not have to be identical.*

Let us define operations on regular interval valued fuzzy numbers:

Definition 3.4. *Let $\tilde{\overline{A}}$, $\tilde{\overline{B}}$ be regular interval valued fuzzy numbers and $r \in \Re$. Then:*

(i) *$\tilde{\overline{A}} + \tilde{\overline{B}}$ is an interval valued fuzzy number defined in the following way:*

$$(\overline{A} + \overline{B})(x) = [(\overline{A}_D + \overline{B}_D)(x), (\overline{A}_U + \overline{B}_U)(x)] \text{ for } x \in \Re,$$

(ii) *for $r \in \Re$ $r\tilde{\overline{A}}$ is an interval valued fuzzy number defined as*

$$(r\overline{A})(x) = [(r\overline{A}_D))(x), (r\overline{A}_U)(x)] \text{ for } x \in \Re.$$

where the operations of addition and multiplication on the right-hand side of both formulae are understood as in Definition 2.4.

It is obvious that the results of the operations defined above are regular interval valued fuzzy numbers. Like in the case of fuzzy numbers, both operations preserve the type of the interval valued fuzzy numbers.

The operations defined in this way can be interpreted as follows (let us explain it for the sum): for each $x \in \Re$, the possibility (membership) degree that x will be the notion represented by $\tilde{\overline{A}} + \tilde{\overline{B}}$ (e.g. that x will be the sum of two coefficients $\tilde{\overline{A}}$ and $\tilde{\overline{B}}$) is the interval $[(\overline{A}_D + \overline{B}_D)(x), (\overline{A}_U + \overline{B}_U)(x)]$, whose lowest end represents the possibility (membership) in question corresponding to the opinion of the most cautious or the most requiring expert, defined according to the extension-principle of Zadeh, and the upper end — to that of the least cautious or the least requiring expert, defined on the basis of the same principle.

In previous section we mentioned that the problem of comparing two fuzzy numbers can be solved in many different ways. This is even more true for interval valued fuzzy numbers: each method of comparing fuzzy numbers may generate several methods of comparing interval valued fuzzy numbers. Here we will pursue the idea of the index of possibility, extending it to interval valued fuzzy numbers.

Let us consider two interval valued fuzzy numbers $\tilde{\overline{A}}$ and $\tilde{\overline{B}}$. The index of possibility, measuring the credibility of the fact that $\tilde{\overline{B}}$ is larger than $\tilde{\overline{A}}$, will be denoted by $\tilde{\mu}(\tilde{\overline{A}}, \tilde{\overline{B}})$ or $\text{Poss}(\tilde{\overline{B}} \geq \tilde{\overline{A}})$ and calculated in the following way:

$$\tilde{\mu}(\tilde{\overline{A}}, \tilde{\overline{B}}) = min(Poss(\overline{B}_D \geq \overline{A}_U), Poss(\overline{B}_U \geq \overline{A}_D)) \tag{3.1}$$

The following theorem is a direct consequence of Theorem 2.1:

Theorem 3.1. *Let $\tilde{\overline{A}}$ and $\tilde{\overline{B}}$ be two arbitrary interval valued fuzzy numbers. For each $\lambda \in (0,1]$ the following condition is fulfilled:*

$$\tilde{\mu}(\tilde{\overline{A}}, \tilde{\overline{B}}) = Poss(\tilde{\overline{B}} \geq \tilde{\overline{A}}) \geq \lambda \Leftrightarrow$$
$$(b_D)_R(\lambda) \geq (a_U)_L(\lambda) \text{ and } (b_U)_R(\lambda) \geq (a_D)_L(\lambda). \tag{3.2}$$

4. Words and fuzziness in linear programming

In this chapter we will show the passage between verbal statements of the decision maker in problems solved by linear programming to fuzzy numbers and interval values fuzzy numbers (and more exactly, to $L - R$ (L,R) fuzzy numbers and $L - R$ (L,R) interval valued fuzzy numbers.

A linear programming problem consists of an objective, of coefficients and of relations in the constraints. Each one of the three elements can be understood or known in an imprecise form, expressed in a verbal statement "bigger than 700", "not too much smaller than 40", "around 50", "as big as possible". Let us thus start with the coefficients. We assume that the coefficients are not known exactly yet (they may be unit prices or incomes from the future). The verbal statements about such coefficients that we are most likely to hear are the "around something", "more or less something" ones.

In order to solve linear programming problems with coefficients given as such verbal statements, we require that the person (or persons) giving such a piece of information has a more precise understanding of his or her statement. For each coefficient C of the problem in question, we try to obtain from people describing it its possibility distribution. A possibility distribution is simply a function determined on the set of real numbers with values in the interval [0,1], which for each real number x gives the possibility degree (according to the decision maker) that this number will be the coefficient C (that the coefficient C will assume the value x).

There are several procedure (see [8]) allowing to get the corresponding possibility distributions (fuzzy numbers) from the decision maker. He may be directly asked, for selected values of x, to give the possibility degree of the event that the coefficient in question will take on value x ("direct rating",[8]). He may also be asked to give, for several selected possibility degrees (from the interval [0,1] of course), the values x which can be the coefficient C to the given possibility degree ("reverse rating",[8]).

If the values we obtain in applying one from the above procedures form a well-shaped, i.e. an $L - R$ fuzzy number (or can be approximated by such without losing much information), we have done our job and can apply the results from section 5.1. We need the special form of fuzzy numbers in order to arrive, in the final analysis, at a problem which can be solved in the practice. However, this will usually be not the case.

The first problem is that the values we get do not have to form an $L - R$ membership function. In such a case we propose to find the "best-fitting" interval valued $L - R$ fuzzy number such that the membership function we have obtained is completely included in its "interior". In this way we are sure that we have not lost any information. It is true that in doing this, we admit for some x some possibility degrees that were not given by the experts (and for some possibility degrees some values x which were not assigned by the experts to them), but we are proceeding in a cautious way, trying to keep any expert information that has been given, and the $L - R$ form of the interval valued fuzzy numbers still assures the simplicity of calculation while solving the final problem.

The second problem is that the results of the procedures will not be clear. This is a consequence of the fact that the determination of the membership function is difficult, not unequivocal and therefore very often done by several persons who usually disagree. What is more, as it is indicated in [8], even one person, when asked repeatedly (with breaks in between) to give the possibility degree for a given x or the value x for a given possibility degree, contradicts himself or herself very often.

In a very practical paper [5] we read: "there is no way to determine the membership functions uniquely, because (...) several experts may choose different membership function to represent the same value. The definition of the membership function is therefore a somewhat heuristic approach which may be iterative and interactive between experts, knowledge engineers and test results". The authors of [5] propose, in case of disagreement, to try to find a compromise, being "as simple as possible". This means, according to the authors, determining a sort of a "mean" membership function, which necessarily implies that some opinions of some of the experts are not taken into account in the final analysis (e.g. the extreme values of the searched possibility degree for a given x). Also probabilistic procedures are proposed for such a case ([8]) - the final membership function will be obtained as the expected value of a distribution determined on the basis of the answers given by the experts and the decision maker.

In any attempt to get a unique membership function from the multiplicity of data, we have to lose something. Thus, we propose to take all the answers of the experts into account and if there are differences, to find the best fitting $L - R$ interval valued number which contains all the data for each coefficient.

In fact, it may even be convenient for the expert to have the possibility, in both procedures described above, to give an interval instead of a value (expressing in this way either his own uncertainty or the verbal-imprecise opinion of a group or both). In such a case we obtain interval valued fuzzy numbers directly from the experts. However, we may still be forced to find a best-fitting L-R interval valued fuzzy number "containing" the one we have from the procedure itself.

Another possible procedure of determining the membership functions on the basis of the knowledge of the experts consists in asking them to give λ-levels with the corresponding λ-s or in presenting them several closed intervals and asking to say to which λ-level they correspond ("set valued statistics", [8]). The λ-levels can correspond to the estimation of the unknown value in question made by various experts (some are more certain about this value and give a narrower interval as its estimation, some are less certain). Here too it is not very likely that the λ-levels we obtain in this way will form a $L - R$ fuzzy number. But again we have the possibility of "wrapping" these levels in a best-fitting interval valued fuzzy number. What is more, here too the expert is allowed to give an interval instead of a single number λ.

It would also be possible to develop a procedure which, on the basis of the answers obtained by means of the procedures described above, proposes certain L-R fuzzy numbers or interval valued fuzzy numbers to the experts/decision maker, asking them to find the one which best expresses their understanding of the verbal statement they have formulated.

Let us now pass to the objective. We assume that the decision maker can express his objective in a verbal statement of the following form: "the objective function (which can be profit, cost etc.) should be big, small, not really big etc" Again, we require him to be more exact, so that he can help us to formulate the objective in a form which expresses his understanding of it and at the same time can be included into a solvable mathematical problem. He will be asked to give a "target value": a small number (according to his understanding) for a minimisation problem and a big number for a maximisation problem. This target value will be around the parameter $\bar{a}$ of a fuzzy number or around the parameters $\bar{a}_D$ and $\bar{a}_U$ of an interval-valued fuzzy number of the R-type for a minimisation problem and around the corresponding parameters of a fuzzy number or an interval valued fuzzy number of the L-type for a maximisation problem. These fuzzy numbers or interval fuzzy numbers have to express his understanding of the satisfaction of the objective. Again, if the information of the decision maker does not give the desirable form of the fuzzy number or interval fuzzy number, we have to "fit" this information into the form we need.

As matter of fact, when the decision maker is asked to give the coefficients for the right-hand sides of the constraints, he may reason exactly as in the case of the objective. He may formulate his constraints not in terms of a ready right-hand side coefficient, but in statements like "the left hand side should be rather not smaller etc than something", "it should not exceed something, but if it does so, it should not be by too much" etc. Then he will be asked to give a target value, which will constitute the basis for the construction of a fuzzy number or an interval fuzzy number of the L-type (usually corresponding to a "$\geq$" relation), R-type ("$\leq$" relation) or $L - R$-type ("$=$" relation).

In the next section we will present concepts of solutions and methods of their determination for linear programming problems in which the coefficients are given in the form of fuzzy numbers or interval valued fuzzy numbers.

5. Fuzzy linear programming with linguistic coefficients

5.1 Linguistic coefficients as fuzzy numbers

Let us consider the following linear programming problem, in which the co-efficients are normal fuzzy numbers:

$$\min \tilde{F}(x) = \sum_{j=1}^{n} \tilde{C}_j x_j,$$
$$\sum_{j=1}^{n} \tilde{A}_{ij} x_j \geq \tilde{B}_i, \quad i = 1, \ldots, m, \tag{5.1}$$
$$x_j \geq 0, \quad j = 1, \ldots, n.$$

The following relationships follow from Theorem 2.1:

$$(F(x))^\lambda = \sum_{j=1}^{n} C_j^\lambda x_j = \left[\sum_{j=1}^{n} c_{j_L}(\lambda) x_j, \sum_{j=1}^{n} c_{j_R}(\lambda) x_j \right], \tag{5.2}$$

$$\left(\sum_{j=1}^{n} A_{ij} x_j \right)^\lambda = \sum_{j=1}^{n} A_{ij}^\lambda x_j =$$
$$= \left[\sum_{j=1}^{n} a_{ij_L}(\lambda) x_j, \sum_{j=1}^{n} a_{ij_R}(\lambda) x_j \right], \quad i = 1, \ldots, m. \tag{5.3}$$

With the objective function in (5.1) let us associate a fuzzy goal (expressing the decision maker's understanding of the satisfaction of the objective), being a fuzzy number $\tilde{B}_o$ and let us replace problem (5.1) with the following system of fuzzy inequalities:

$$\sum_{j=1}^{n} \tilde{C}_j x_j \leq \tilde{B}_o,$$
$$\sum_{j=1}^{n} \tilde{A}_{ij} x_j \geq \tilde{B}_i, \quad i = 1, \ldots, m, \tag{5.4}$$
$$x_j \geq 0, \quad j = 1, \ldots, n,$$

where $\tilde{B}_o$ is a normal fuzzy number of R type: $\tilde{B}_o = (-\infty, \bar{b}_o, 1, 0, \beta_o)_{R_0}$.

Definition 5.1. *The fuzzy solution of the system of inequalities (5.4) (and also of problem (5.1)) is the fuzzy set $\tilde{D}$ in the space of solutions $X = \{x = (x_1, \ldots, x_n): x_j \geq 0, j = 1, \ldots, n\}$ with the following membership function:*

$$D(x) = \mu(\tilde{F}(x), \tilde{B}_o) \wedge \min_{1 \leq i \leq m} \mu\left(\tilde{B}_i, \sum_{j=1}^{n} \tilde{A}_{ij} x_j \right), \quad x \in X. \tag{5.5}$$

Definition 5.2. *The optimising solution of problem (5.1) is the vector $x_o \in$* *X fulfilling the condition:*

$$D(x_o) = \max_{x \in X} \; D(x). \tag{5.6}$$

Now we will present an algorithm determining the optimising solution according to Definition 5.2.

Making use of Definition 5.2, Theorem 2.2 and relationships (5.2) and (5.3), it is easy to come to the conclusion that in order to find the optimising solution of problem (5.1) it is enough to solve the following mathematical programming problem:

$$\begin{aligned}
&\max \; \lambda, \\
&\textstyle\sum_{j=1}^{n} c_{j_L}(\lambda)x_j \le b_{o_R}(\lambda), \\
&\textstyle\sum_{j=1}^{n} a_{ij_R}(\lambda)x_j \ge b_{i_L}(\lambda), \quad i = 1,\ldots,m, \\
&x_j \ge 0, \quad j = 1,\ldots,n, \quad \lambda \in [0,1].
\end{aligned} \tag{5.7}$$

We will concentrate on the case when all the parameters in problem (5.1) are normal fuzzy numbers of $L-R$ types, but this assumptions can be alleviated without any problems: the fuzzy numbers do not necessarily have to be normal and the coefficients representing the right-hand side of the constraints can be of the R-type (L-type for the $\le$ relation). But for the presentation of the calculations we assume that the coefficients have the following form:

$$\begin{aligned}
\tilde{C}_j &= \left(\underline{c}_j,\; \overline{c}_j,\; 1,\; \alpha_{C_j},\; \beta_{C_j}\right)_{L_j - R_j}, \quad j = 1,\ldots n, \\
\tilde{A}_{ij} &= \left(\underline{a}_{ij},\; \overline{a}_{ij},\; 1,\; \alpha_{A_{ij}},\; \beta_{A_{ij}}\right)_{S_{ij} - T_{ij}}, \quad i = 1,\ldots m,\; j = 1,\ldots n, \\
\tilde{B}_i &= \left(\underline{b}_i,\; \overline{b}_i,\; 1,\; \alpha_{B_i},\; \beta_{B_i}\right)_{W_i - Z_i}, \quad i = 0,1,\ldots m,
\end{aligned}$$

problem (5.7) takes the following form:

$$\begin{aligned}
&\max \; \lambda, \\
&\textstyle\sum_{j=1}^{n} \left(\underline{c}_j - L_j^{-1}(\lambda)\alpha_{C_j}\right) x_j \le \overline{b}_o + Z_o^{-1}(\lambda)\beta_0, \\
&\textstyle\sum_{j=1}^{n} \left(\overline{a}_{ij} + T_{ij}^{-1}(\lambda)\beta_{A_{ij}}\right) x_j \ge \underline{b}_i - W_i^{-1}(\lambda)\alpha_{B_i}, \quad i = 1,\ldots,m, \\
&x_j \ge 0, \quad j = 1,\ldots,n, \quad \lambda \in [0,1].
\end{aligned} \tag{5.8}$$

Problem (5.7) (also (5.8)) is non-linear, but it has a useful property. If the value of the variable λ is fixed, then the problem constraints become linear with respect to the other variables x_j, $j = 1,\ldots,n$. Making use of this property and combining the bisection method with phase one of the simplex algorithm of the linear programming, we can propose the following algorithm solving problem (5.7). A fixed value $\lambda \in [0,1]$ is called feasible if by substituting it in constraints of problem (5.7) we obtain a system of inequalities which is not contradictory with respect to variables x_j, $j = 1,\ldots,n$. The solutions of this system obtained with the help of the simplex method is denoted in the algorithm by $x(\lambda)$. Solving problem (5.7) consists thus in determining the greatest feasible value of the parameter λ - this value will be denoted by λ_{max}. The vector $x(\lambda_{max})$ is of course the maximising solution and it holds $D(x(\lambda_{max})) = \lambda_{max}$.

Algorithm solving problem (5.7):

Step 1. Check if $\lambda = 0$ is a feasible value. If so, set $\lambda_{max} = 0$ and go to step 2. Otherwise STOP – the initial problem is infeasible (the fuzzy solution is an empty set, i.e. $D(x) = 0$ for each $x \in X$).

Step 2. Check if $\lambda = 1$ is a feasible value. If so, STOP – vector $x(1)$ is the maximising one and $\lambda_{max} = 1$. Otherwise go to step 3.

Step 3. For the sequence λ_k, $k = 1, \ldots K$, build up gradually according to the recurrence formula:

$$\lambda_1 = 0.5$$
$$\lambda_k = \begin{cases} \lambda_{k-1} + 1/2^k & \text{if } \lambda_{k-1} \text{ feasible,} \\ \lambda_{k-1} - 1/2^k & \text{if } \lambda_{k-1} \text{ infeasible,} \end{cases}$$
$$k = 2, \ldots, K,$$

check if λ_k is feasible value of parameter λ. If so, set each time $\lambda_{max} = \lambda_k$. Go to step 4.

Step 4. Assume vector $x(\lambda_{max})$ as the solution and $D(x(\lambda_{max})) = \lambda_k$.

The length K of the sequence $k = 1, \ldots, K$, built up in step 3 of the algorithm, depends of the assumed precision for λ_{max}. If the absolute error is to be greater than 10^N, then K should fulfil the condition $K \geq N/\log_{10} 2 = N/0.3010299$.

A similar algorithm was proposed for triangular fuzzy numbers in [6].

Example:

Let us consider the following fuzzy linear programming problem:

$$\min \tilde{F}(x) = \tilde{C}_1 x_1 + \tilde{C}_2 x_2 + \tilde{C}_3 x_3,$$
$$\tilde{A}_{11} x_1 + \tilde{A}_{12} x_2 + \tilde{A}_{13} x_3 \geq \tilde{B}_1,$$
$$\tilde{A}_{21} x_1 + \tilde{A}_{22} x_2 + \tilde{A}_{23} x_3 \geq \tilde{B}_2,$$
$$x_1, x_2, x_3 \geq 0,$$

(5.9)

in which the coefficients are normal fuzzy numbers of the exponential type with the shape functions $L(y) = \exp(-2y)$ and $R(y) = \exp(-y)$:

$$\tilde{C}_1 = (22, 25, 1, 4, 3)_{L-R}, \qquad \tilde{C}_2 = (35, 42, 1, 6, 8)_{L-R},$$
$$\tilde{C}_3 = (28, 32, 1, 5, 6)_{L-R},$$
$$\tilde{A}_{11} = (24, 26, 1, 3, 5)_{L-R}, \qquad \tilde{A}_{12} = (5, 6, 1, 2, 3)_{L-R},$$
$$\tilde{A}_{13} = (12, 12, 1, 4, 2)_{L-R}, \qquad \tilde{A}_{21} = (5, 6, 1, 2, 3)_{L-R},$$
$$\tilde{A}_{22} = (14, 16, 1, 4, 4)_{L-R}, \qquad \tilde{A}_{23} = (9, 9, 1, 3, 5)_{L-R},$$
$$\tilde{B}_1 = (120, 120, 1, 20, 20)_{L-R}, \quad \tilde{B}_2 = (100, 110, 1, 20, 10)_{L-R}.$$

Let us suppose that the decision maker has formulated his objective as the fuzzy goal $B_o = (220, 230, 1, 50, 40)_{L-R}$ being a normal fuzzy number of the same type as previous data. Then problem (5.7) corresponding to problem (5.9) has the following form:

$$\max \lambda,$$
$$(22 + 2\ln\lambda)x_1 + (35 + 3\ln\lambda)x_2 + (28 + 2.5\ln\lambda)x_3 \le 230 - 40\ln\lambda,$$
$$(26 - 5\ln\lambda)x_1 + (6 - 3\ln\lambda)x_2 + (12 - 2\ln\lambda)x_3 \ge 120 + 10\ln\lambda,$$
$$(6 - 3\ln\lambda)x_1 + (16 - 4\ln\lambda)x_2 + (9 - 5\ln\lambda)x_3 \ge 100 + 10\ln\lambda,$$
$$x_1, x_2, x_3 \ge 0, \ \lambda \in (0, 1].$$

In the considered example we have $L^{-1}(\lambda) = -0.5\ln\lambda$ and $R^{-1}(\lambda) = -\ln\lambda$.

Applying our algorithm to the above problem, we will obtain, at the assumed precision $\varepsilon = 10^{-4}$, the following optimising solution: $\lambda_{max} = 0.8816$, $x(\lambda_{max}) = (3.33479, 4.69402, 0)$.

5.2 Linguistic coefficients as interval valued fuzzy numbers

In this subsection we assume that the coefficients of the linear programming problem in question are given as interval valued fuzzy numbers. Let us consider such a problem:

$$\min \tilde{\tilde{F}}(x) = \sum_{j=1}^{n} \tilde{\tilde{C}}_j x_j,$$
$$\sum_{j=1}^{n} \tilde{\tilde{A}}_{ij} x_j \ge \tilde{\tilde{B}}_i, \ i = 1, \dots, m, \tag{5.10}$$
$$x_j \ge 0, \ j = 1, \dots, n.$$

The following relationships follow from Theorem 2.1:

$$(\overline{F}(x)_D)^{\lambda} = \sum_{j=1}^{n}((\overline{C}_j)_D)^{\lambda} x_j = $$
$$= \left[\sum_{j=1}^{n}((c_j)_D)_L(\lambda)x_j, \ \sum_{j=1}^{n}((c_j)_D)_R(\lambda)x_j \right], \tag{5.11}$$

$$\left(\left(\sum_{j=1}^{n} \overline{A}_{ij} x_j \right)_D \right)^{\lambda} = \sum_{j=1}^{n}((\overline{A}_{ij})_D)^{\lambda} = $$
$$= \left[\sum_{j=1}^{n}((a_{ij})_D)_L(\lambda)x_j, \ \sum_{j=1}^{n}((a_{ij})_D))_R(\lambda)x_j \right], \ i = 1, \dots, m. \tag{5.12}$$

$$(\overline{F}(x)_U)^\lambda = \sum_{j=1}^n ((\overline{C}_j)_U)^\lambda x_j =$$
$$= \left[\sum_{j=1}^n ((c_j)_U)_L(\lambda)x_j, \ \sum_{j=1}^n ((c_j)_U)_R(\lambda)x_j \right], \tag{5.13}$$

$$\left(\left(\sum_{j=1}^n \overline{A}_{ij}x_j \right)_U \right)^\lambda = \sum_{j=1}^n ((\overline{A}_{ij})_U)^\lambda x_j =$$
$$= \left[\sum_{j=1}^n ((a_{ij})_U)_L(\lambda)x_j, \ \sum_{j=1}^n ((a_{ij})_U))_R(\lambda)x_j \right], \ i = 1,\dots,m. \tag{5.14}$$

With the objective function in (5.10) let us associate a fuzzy goal, an interval valued fuzzy number $\tilde{\bar{B}}_o$ expressing the decision maker's understanding of the goal satisfaction, and let us replace problem (5.10) with the following system of fuzzy inequalities:

$$\sum_{j=1}^n \tilde{\bar{C}}_j x_j \leq \tilde{\bar{B}}_o,$$
$$\sum_{j=1}^n \tilde{\bar{A}}_{ij}x_j \geq \tilde{\bar{B}}_i, \ i = 1,\dots,m, \tag{5.15}$$
$$x_j \geq 0, \ j = 1,\dots,n,$$

where $\tilde{\bar{B}}_0$ is an interval valued fuzzy number of the R type:

$$(\underline{B}_0)_D = (-\infty, \ (\bar{b}_0)_D, \ r_{0_D}, \ 0; \beta_{0_D})_{(R_0)_D},$$

$$(\underline{B}_o)_U = (-\infty, \ (\bar{b}_o)_U, \ r_{0_R}, \ 0; \beta_{0_R})_{(R_0)_U}.$$

Definition 5.3. *The fuzzy solution of the system of inequalities (5.15) (and also of problem (5.10)) is the fuzzy set $\tilde{D}$ in the space of solutions $X = \{x = (x_1,\dots,x_n) : x_j \geq 0, \ j = 1,\dots,n\}$ with the following membership function:*

$$D(x) = \tilde{\mu}(\overline{F}(x), \tilde{\bar{B}}_o) \wedge \min_{1 \leq i \leq m} \tilde{\mu}\left(\tilde{\bar{B}}_o, \sum_{j=1}^n \tilde{\bar{A}}_{ij}x_j \right), \ x \in X. \tag{5.16}$$

Definition 5.4. *The optimising solution of problem (5.10) is the vector $x_o \in X$ fulfilling the condition:*

$$D(x_o) = \max_{x \in X} D(x). \tag{5.17}$$

Making use of Definition 5.4, Theorem 3.1 and relationships (5.11), (5.13), (5.12) and (5.14), it is easy to come to the conclusion that in order to find the optimising solution of problem (5.10) it is enough to solve the following mathematical programming problem:

$$\max \lambda,$$
$$\sum_{j=1}^{n}((c_j)_D)_L(\lambda)x_j \leq ((b_0)_U)_R(\lambda),$$
$$\sum_{j=1}^{h}((c_j)_U)_L(\lambda)x_j \leq ((b_0)_D)_R(\lambda),$$
$$\sum_{j=1}^{h}(((a_{ij})_D)_R)(\lambda)x_j \geq ((b_i)_U)_L(\lambda), \quad i=1,\ldots,m, \qquad (5.18)$$
$$\sum_{j=1}^{h}(((a_{ij})_U)_R)(\lambda)x_j \geq ((b_i)_D)_L(\lambda), \quad i=1,\ldots,m,$$
$$x_j \geq 0, \quad j=1,\ldots,n, \quad \lambda \in [0,M].$$

where M is the minimum of the heights of all the fuzzy numbers appearing in the above problem.

As in section 5.1, we do not consider the case when the coefficients representing the right-hand side of the constraints are of the R-type (L-type for the $\leq$ relation), in which the calculations would be identical, but assume that all the parameters in problem (5.10) are interval valued fuzzy numbers of $L-R$ types, i.e.

$$(\overline{C}_j)_D = ((\underline{c}_j)_D, \ (\overline{c}_j)_D, \ (r_{C_j})_D, \ (\alpha_{C_j})_D, \ (\beta_{C_j})_D)_{(L_j)_D-(R_j)_D}, \quad j=1,\ldots n,$$
$$(\overline{C}_j)_U = ((\underline{c}_j)_U, \ (\overline{c}_j)_U, \ (r_{C_j})_U \ (\alpha_{C_j})_U, \ (\beta_{C_j})_U)_{(L_j)_U-(R_j)_U}, \quad j=1,\ldots n,$$

$$(\overline{A}_{ij})_D = ((\underline{a}_{ij})_D, \ (\overline{a}_{ij})_D, \ (r_{A_{ij}})_D \ (\alpha_{A_{ij}})_D, \ (\beta_{A_{ij}})_D)_{(S_{ij})_D-(T_{ij})_D},$$
$$i=1,\ldots m, \ j=1,\ldots n,$$
$$(\overline{A}_{ij})_U = ((\underline{a}_{ij})_U, \ (\overline{a}_{ij})_U, \ (r_{A_{ij}})_U \ (\alpha_{A_{ij}})_U, \ (\beta_{A_{ij}})_U)_{(S_{ij})_U-(T_{ij})_U},$$
$$i=1,\ldots m, \ j=1,\ldots n,$$

$$(\overline{B}_i)_D = ((\underline{b}_i)_D, \ (\overline{b}_i)_D, \ (r_{B_i})_D, \ (\alpha_{B_i})_D, \ (\beta_{B_i})_D)_{(W_i)_D-(Z_i)_D}, \quad i=0,1,\ldots m,$$
$$(\overline{B}_i)_U = ((\underline{b}_i)_U, \ (\overline{b}_i)_U, \ (r_{B_i})_U, \ (\alpha_{B_i})_U, \ (\beta_{B_i})_U)_{(W_i)_U-(Z_i)_U}, \quad i=0,1,\ldots m.$$

Problem (5.18) takes now the following form:

$$\max \lambda,$$
$$\sum_{j=1}^{n}\left((\underline{c}_j)_D - [(L_j)_D^{-1}(\lambda) - ((L_j)_D^{-1}(r_{C_j})_D))](\alpha_{C_j})_D\right)x_j \leq$$
$$(\overline{b}_0)_U + [((R_0)_U)^{-1}(\lambda) - ((R_0)_U)^{-1}((r_0)_U)](\beta_0)_U,$$
$$\sum_{j=1}^{n}\left((\underline{c}_j)_U - [(L_j)_U^{-1}(\lambda) - ((L_j)_U^{-1}(r_{C_j})_U))](\alpha_{C_j})_U\right)x_j \leq$$
$$(\overline{b}_0)_D + [((R_0)_D)^{-1}(\lambda) - ((R_0)_D)^{-1}((r_0)_D)](\beta_0)_D,$$
$$\sum_{j=1}^{n}\left((\overline{a}_{ij})_D + [(T_{ij})_D^{-1}(\lambda) - ((T_{ij})_D^{-1}(r_{A_{ij}})_D))](\alpha_{A_{ij}})_D\right)x_j \geq \qquad (5.19)$$
$$(\underline{b}_i)_U - [(W_i)_U^{-1}(\lambda) - ((W_i)_U^{-1}(r_{B_i})_U))](\alpha_{B_i})_U,$$
$$\sum_{j=1}^{n}\left((\overline{a}_{ij})_U + [(T_{ij})_U^{-1}(\lambda) - ((T_{ij})_U^{-1}(r_{A_{ij}})_U))](\alpha_{A_{ij}})_U\right)x_j \geq$$
$$(\underline{b}_i)_D - [(W_i)_D^{-1}(\lambda) - ((W_i)_D^{-1}(r_{B_i})_D))](\alpha_{B_i})_D, \quad i=1,\ldots,m,$$
$$x_j \geq 0, \quad j=1,\ldots,n, \quad \lambda \in [0,M],$$

where

$$M = \min\{(r_0)_D, (r_{C_j})_D, (r_{A_{ij}})_D, (r_{B_i})_D, i=1,\ldots,m; j=1,\ldots,n\}$$

Problem (5.18) (as well as (5.19)) can be solved by means of the algorithm similar to that presented in section 5.1.

Example:

Let us consider the following fuzzy linear programming problem:

$$\min \tilde{F}(x) = \tilde{C}_1 x_1 + \tilde{C}_2 x_2 + \tilde{C}_3 x_3,$$
$$\tilde{A}_{11} x_1 + \tilde{A}_{12} x_2 + \tilde{A}_{13} x_3 \geq \tilde{B}_1,$$
$$\tilde{A}_{21} x_1 + \tilde{A}_{22} x_2 + \tilde{A}_{23} x_3 \geq \tilde{B}_2, \qquad (5.20)$$
$$x_1, x_2, x_3 \geq 0,$$

in which the coefficients are normal fuzzy numbers of the exponential type with the shape functions $L(y) = \exp(-2y)$ and $R(y) = \exp(-y)$:

$$
\begin{aligned}
(\overline{C}_1)_D &= (22, 25, 0.5, 4, 3)_{L-R}, & (\overline{C}_1)_U &= (22, 25, 1, 4, 3)_{L-R}, \\
(\overline{C}_2)_D &= (35, 42, 0.5, 6, 8)_{L-R}, & (\overline{C}_2)_U &= (35, 42, 1, 6, 8)_{L-R} \\
(\overline{C}_3)_D &= (28, 32, 0.5, 5, 6)_{L-R}, & (\overline{C}_3)_U &= (28, 32, 1, 5, 6)_{L-R} \\
(\overline{A}_{11})_D &= (24, 26, 0.5, 3, 5)_{L-R}, & (\overline{A}_{11})_U &= (24, 26, 1, 3, 5)_{L-R}, \\
(\overline{A}_{12})_D &= (5, 6, 0.5, 2, 3)_{L-R}, & (\overline{A}_{12})_U &= (5, 6, 1, 2, 3)_{L-R}, \\
(\overline{A}_{13})_D &= (12, 12, 0.5, 4, 2)_{L-R}, & (\overline{A}_{13})_U &= (12, 12, 1, 4, 2)_{L-R}, \\
(\overline{A}_{21})_D &= (5, 6, 0.5, 2, 3)_{L-R}, & (\overline{A}_{21})_U &= (5, 6, 1, 2, 3)_{L-R}, \\
(\overline{A}_{22})_D &= (14, 16, 0.5, 4, 4)_{L-R}, & (\overline{A}_{22})_U &= (14, 16, 1, 4, 4)_{L-R}, \\
(\overline{A}_{23})_D &= (9, 9, 0.5, 3, 5)_{L-R}, & (\overline{A}_{23})_U &= (9, 9, 1, 3, 5)_{L-R}, \\
(\overline{B}_1)_D &= (120, 120, 0.5, 20, 20)_{L-R}, & (\overline{B}_1)_U &= (120, 120, 1, 20, 20)_{L-R}, \\
(\overline{B}_2)_D &= (100, 110, 0.5, 20, 10)_{L-R}, & (\overline{B}_2)_U &= (100, 110, 1, 20, 10)_{L-R},
\end{aligned}
$$

Let us suppose that the decision maker has associated with the objective the following fuzzy goal

$$(\overline{B}_o)_D = (220, 230, 0.5, 50, 40)_{L-R},$$
$$(\overline{B}_o)_U = (220, 230, 1, 50, 40)_{L-R},$$

being an interval valued fuzzy number of the same type as previous data. Then problem (5.18) corresponding to problem (5.20) has the following form:

$$\max \lambda,$$
$$(22 + 2\ln(2\lambda))x_1 + (35 + 3\ln(2\lambda))x_2 + (28 + 2.5\ln(2\lambda))x_3 \leq 230 - 40\ln \lambda,$$
$$(22 + 2\ln \lambda)x_1 + (35 + 3\ln \lambda)x_2 + (28 + 2.5\ln \lambda)x_3 \leq 230 - 40\ln(2\lambda),$$
$$(26 - 5\ln(2\lambda))x_1 + (6 - 3\ln(2\lambda))x_2 + (12 - 2\ln(2\lambda))x_3 \geq 120 + 10\ln \lambda,$$
$$(26 - 5\ln \lambda)x_1 + (6 - 3\ln \lambda)x_2 + (12 - 2\ln \lambda)x_3 \geq 120 + 10\ln(2\lambda),$$
$$(6 - 3\ln(2\lambda))x_1 + (16 - 4\ln(2\lambda))x_2 + (9 - 5\ln(2\lambda))x_3 \geq 100 + 10\ln \lambda,$$
$$(6 - 3\ln \lambda)x_1 + (16 - 4\ln \lambda)x_2 + (9 - 5\ln \lambda)x_3 \geq 100 + 10\ln(2\lambda),$$
$$x_1, x_2, x_3 \geq 0, \ \lambda \in (0, 0.5].$$

Applying the algorithm presented in the previous section to the above problem, we will obtain, at the assumed precision $\varepsilon = 10^{-4}$, the following optimising solution: $\lambda_{max} = 0.5$, $x(\lambda_{max}) = (1.51418, 9.43155, 0)$.

6. Conclusions

We have presented one approach to the case when a linear programming problem is to be solved, but the coefficients and/or relations can only be given in a verbal form. We have shortly discussed the transition from such problems to ones with coefficients/relations are expressed as fuzzy numbers or a generalisation of the latter, interval valued fuzzy numbers. Then we show how to reduce the problems created as a result of this transition, to classical linear programming problems, which can be solved by means of the generally accessible software.

Our approach is based on several assumptions, and a future research may go in the direction of dropping or alleviating them. The first one is that the coefficients, the objective and the constraints are determined by the decision maker/experts (or a group them) in verbal statements and a correspondence can be established (or rather already exist in the mind of the persons formulating such statements) between them and fuzzy numbers or a generalisation of them that we have introduced, so called interval valued fuzzy numbers. This correspondence equals to saying for each real number x to which degree it is possible that this number will be the coefficient in question or to which degree this number satisfies the objective or a constraint, whereas this degree can given in a more or less precise form. The procedures of establishing such correspondences are briefly described in the text.

These procedures are in turn based on two assumptions. The first one is that we try not to lose any information we get from the experts. If there are contradictory statements as to the possibility or satisfaction degree, we keep all the data, making the possibility/satisfaction degree less precise. We also give individual experts the possibility to give the possibility/satisfaction degree in the form of an interval. The other assumption is that, in order to make the calculation practicable, we force the verbal statement to be expressed in a special form (which is, however, rather general and seems sufficient in most applications) of fuzzy numbers or interval valued fuzzy number. If the expert(s) express(es) his(their) statements in other forms (i.e. the shape of the membership function, expressing for each $x \in \Re$ the possibility degree of x being the coefficient in question or the degree to which this x satisfies the objective or a constraint), we find an interval valued fuzzy number being the smallest "envelope" of the membership function given by the expert. In this way we keep to the principle not to lose any information obtained from the experts, making at the same time the calculations more manageable.

Another assumption is the way of comparing fuzzy numbers. We have adopted one of them, a so called possibility degree. It a fuzzy way of comparing fuzzy numbers, which gives the degree to which one fuzzy number is greater than (preferred to) another one. The possibility degree is a strong criterion in the sense that it is very "easy" for one fuzzy number to be greater to a positive degree than another fuzzy number. The literature proposes many other methods (approaches) of comparing fuzzy numbers, and each method can generate another concept of solving linear programming problems with coefficients given in a verbal form.

References

1. G. Bortolan, R. Degani, A review of some methods for ranking fuzzy subsets, *Fuzzy Sets and Systems* **15** (1985) 1–19.
2. Chen, S.J., Hwang, C.L., *Fuzzy Multiple Attribute Decision Making: Methods and Applications*, Springer Verlag, Berlin, Heidelberg, 1992
3. D. Dubois, H. Prade, Operations on fuzzy numbers, *Int. J. Systems Sci.* **30** (1978) 613–626.
4. D. Dubois, H. Prade, Fuzzy sets in approximate reasoning, Part 1: inference with possibility distributions, *Fuzzy Sets and Systems* **40** (1991) 143–202.
5. M. Locke, Fuzzy modelling in expert for process control, *Syst. Anal. Model. Simul.* **7** (1990) 715–719.
6. S. Tong, Interval number and fuzzy number linear programmings, *Fuzzy Sets and Systems* **66** (1994) 301–306.
7. I. B. Turksen, Approximate reasoning for production planning, *Fuzzy Sets and Systems* **4** (1988) 23–27.
8. I. B. Turksen, Measurement of membership function and their acquisition, *Fuzzy Sets and Systems* **4** (1991) 5–38.
9. S.R. Watson, J.J. Weiss and M.L. Donnell Fuzzy decision analysis, *IEEE Trans. on Syst., Man and Cyber.* **SMC-9(1)** (1979) 1–9.
10. F. Wenstop, Quantitative analysis with linguistic values, *Fuzzy Sets and Systems* **4** (1980) 99–115.
11. M.R. Wilhelm and H.R. Parsaei, A fuzzy linguistic approach to implementing a strategy for computer integrated manufacturing, *Fuzzy Sets and Systems* **42** (1991) 191–204.
12. L. A. Zadeh, The concept of a linguistic variable and its application to approximate reasoning I,II,III, *Inform. Sci.* **8** (1975) 199–249; 301–357; **9** 43–80.
13. L. A. Zadeh, Fuzzy sets as a basis for theory of possibility, *Fuzzy Sets and Systems* **1** (1978) 3–29.

Computing with Words in Control

James J. Buckley[1] and Thomas Feuring[2]*

[1] University of Alabama at Birmingham, Department of Mathematics, Birmingham, Alabama, 35294, USA
[2] Westfälische Wilhelms-Universität Münster, Institut für Informatik, Einsteinstraße 62, 48149 Münster, Germany

This chapter describes a supervisory fuzzy controller which is used to advise, or train, people who are in control of a complex plant. The supervisory fuzzy controller is designed to interact with the human operators through accepting verbal evaluations and producing verbal suggestions.

1. Introduction

A diagram of the supervisory fuzzy controller is shown in Figure 1.1. We will discuss, in detail, all parts of this figure in the next section. An example of a supervisory fuzzy controller is presented in the third section and the last section contains a brief summary.

Let us now present the notation we will employ in this chapter. We place a bar over a capital letter to denote a fuzzy subset of the real numbers. So $\overline{A}$, $\overline{B}$, ..., $\overline{L}$, etc. all represent fuzzy subsets of the real numbers. We write $\overline{A}(x)$, a number in $[0,1]$, for the membership function of $\overline{A}$ evaluated at x. A triangular fuzzy number $\overline{A}$ is defined by three numbers $a_1 < a_2 < a_3$ where the membership function is a triangle with base on the interval $[a_1, a_3]$ and vertex at $x = a_2$. We write triangular fuzzy number $\overline{A}$ as $(a_1/a_2/a_3)$.

Let us abbreviate a supervisory fuzzy controller as SFC. Notice that we have fuzzy controllers also in Figure 1.1 together with the SFC. Let us describe the possible interaction between the SFC and the fuzzy controllers.

In general, there are four possible situations: (1) no SFC; (2) no fuzzy controllers; (3) there are fuzzy controllers together with a SFC but they are "independent"; and (4) there is a SFC plus fuzzy controllers and they are "interactive". The first case is only about fuzzy controllers which we shall not discuss further in this chapter. In the second case we only have a SFC which will operate very slowly and so can be used for processes which do not require fast turn around time (for example sailing a sail boat in open waters through a calm sea). Anyway, case 2 is essentially contained in the next case so we will not discuss it further. In case three by "independent" we mean that the fuzzy controllers are independent from the fuzzy rules in the SFC. That is, no input to a fuzzy controller is also an input to the SFC

* This work was supported with a grant from the German Academic Exchange Service (DAAD) based on the Hochschulsonderprogramm III of Bund and Länder while staying at the University of Alabama at Birmingham.

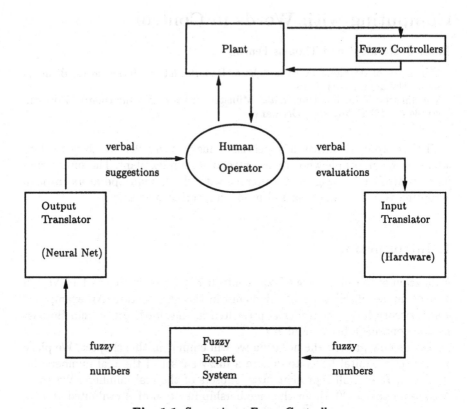

Fig. 1.1. Supervisory Fuzzy Controller

and vice versa, no input to the SFC is also an input to a fuzzy controller. In contrast to the "independent" case we have case 4, described in [1], where the two controller are "interactive". In the "interactive" case there is only one set of fuzzy rules for both the fuzzy controller and the SFC. That is, in case 4 the controller simultaneously processes error, change in error, and verbal evaluations to give defuzzified input to the plant and verbal suggestions to the human operators of the plant.

In this chapter we will only discuss case 3. In case 3 the fuzzy controllers and the SFC are not completely independent but can interact in the following way. Suppose the SFC gives the verbal suggestion "close valve # C3". If a human operator closes this valve, then the plant's output will change, producing different inputs to the fuzzy controllers, which changes their output-input to the plant, etc., which in term changes the verbal evaluation of the plant.

2. Supervisory Fuzzy Controller

We will give the details on the various components of the supervisory fuzzy controller shown in Figure 1.1.

2.1 Verbal Evaluation

The human operators are allowed to use a very limited vocabulary to communicate with the SFC. Let us take as an example the variable pressure (P) and the human operators may communicate two things concerning pressure: its current value and how it is changing. With respect to how it is changing they can say: decreasing rapidly, decreasing, decreasing very slowly, no change, increasing very slowly, increasing, or increasing rapidly. For the value of pressure they may communicate: very low, low, slightly low, good, slightly high, high, or very high. All of these descriptions are defined by fuzzy numbers. Notice that hedges are built into the system since very high is separately defined as a fuzzy number and not constructed out of the fuzzy number for high. So let the fuzzy numbers for the change in pressure be $\overline{D}_1$ = decrease rapidly, ..., $\overline{D}_7$ =increase rapidly and for the value of pressure $\overline{P}_1$ =very low, ..., $\overline{P}_7$ =very high.

The method of communication to the SFC may take various forms. The human operators could use a special keyboard, use a mouse to click on the words, touch the words on a computer screen, or as in [1] draw the fuzzy numbers on the computer screen. Also there could be a voice recognition system trained to recognize certain words from a few of the human operators.

In fact, there could be uncertainty as to which word to use so we will allow multiple word inputs for each variable. That is, for change in pressure the input could be "decreasing or decreasing very slowly" and for the value of pressure "slightly high or high".

At certain times the input to the input translator will be words describing the value of a variable and possibly how it is changing. Suppose the variables are pressure, temperature (T) and flow rate (FR). When the human operators wish to consult the SFC they do not have to input words for all the variables. If they input observations only for change in pressure, change in temperature and flow rate the system automatically takes the previous values for the other variables (value of pressure and value of temperature) to compute its suggestions.

2.2 Input Translator

The job of the input translator is to translate the words into fuzzy numbers for input to the fuzzy expert system. Since the human operators use a very limited vocabulary, and all the words have been previously defined by fuzzy numbers, this translation is basically trivial and could be accomplished by a specially designed piece of hardware. The only problem is when an operator uses multiple words for a single variable. When multiple words are used for a variable we sort of take the union of the corresponding fuzzy numbers for input to the fuzzy expert system.

For example, consider the example discussed above in 2.1 where an operator said, pressure is "decreasing and decreasing slowly" and the value of the pressure is "slightly high and high". We usually use triangular fuzzy numbers for the $\overline{D}_i$ and $\overline{P}_j$ which are shown in Figure 2.1. Then the automatic translation of these verbal evaluations is $\overline{D}$ for the change in pressure and $\overline{P}$ for the value of pressure. Notice that $\overline{D}$ and $\overline{P}$ will be trapezoidal (fuzzy intervals) fuzzy numbers showing the uncertainty of the human observer. The input translator sends $\overline{D}$ and $\overline{P}$ to the fuzzy expert system.

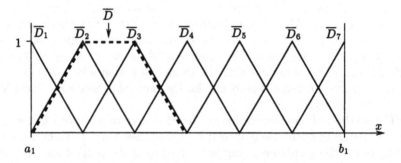

Fig. 2.1a: Fuzzy Numbers for Change in Pressure.

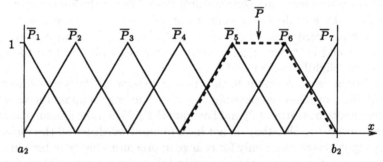

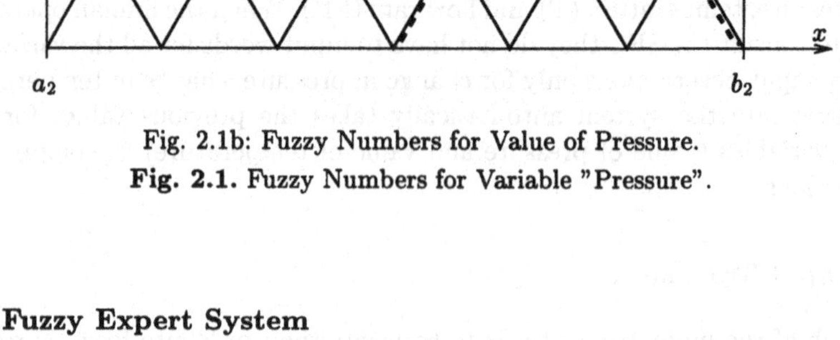

Fig. 2.1b: Fuzzy Numbers for Value of Pressure.

Fig. 2.1. Fuzzy Numbers for Variable "Pressure".

2.3 Fuzzy Expert System

The fuzzy expert system processes, through blocks of fuzzy rules, the fuzzy numbers it has received, for all the variables from the input translator, to produce discrete fuzzy sets for control actions. Suppose we have five input fuzzy sets, two for pressure (change and value), two for temperature (change and value) and one for flow rate. The fuzzy numbers are: (1) $\overline{D}$ for change in pressure and $\overline{P}$ for pressure; (2) $\overline{C}$ for change in temperature and $\overline{T}$ for value of temperature; and (3) $\overline{FR}$ for flow rate. Of course, $\overline{D}$ can be one of the $\overline{D}_i$ in Figure 2.1a and $\overline{P}$ may be a $\overline{P}_j$ in Figure 2.1b. There are M fuzzy rules of the type

R_s: If $[\overline{D} = \overline{Q}_{1i}]$ and $[\overline{P} = \overline{Q}_{2j}]$ and $[\overline{C} = \overline{Q}_{3k}]$ and $[\overline{T} = \overline{Q}_{4l}]$ and $[\overline{FR} = \overline{Q}_{5m}]$, then $CA_1 = \overline{A}_n$ and $CA_2 = \overline{B}_p$,

where CA_1 = control action #1, CA_2 = control action #2 and the fuzzy numbers $\overline{Q}_{ij}$ are specially defined for each variable, $1 \le s \le M$. Also, the CA_i are discrete fuzzy sets

$$CA_1 = \left\{ \frac{\alpha_1}{\overline{A}_1}, \cdots, \frac{\alpha_N}{\overline{A}_N} \right\} , \tag{2.1}$$

$$CA_2 = \left\{ \frac{\beta_1}{\overline{B}_1}, \cdots, \frac{\beta_P}{\overline{B}_P} \right\} , \tag{2.2}$$

where the α_i (β_j) are the membership values of the fuzzy sets $\overline{A}_i$ $(\overline{B}_j)$ in CA_1 (CA_2). Given the inputs $\overline{D}, \overline{P}, \overline{C}, \overline{T}$ and $\overline{FR}$ the fuzzy expert system is to construct the discrete fuzzy sets CA_i, $i = 1, 2$.

First we need to specify the $\overline{Q}_{ij}$. Consider the $\overline{Q}_{2j}$ for the value of pressure. The $\overline{Q}_{2j}$ give a qualitative evaluation of pressure and possible definitions are shown in Figure 2.2. In Figure 2.2 linguistic translations of the $\overline{Q}_{2i}$ are: $\overline{Q}_{21} =$ out-of-control, stop; $\overline{Q}_{22} =$ danger; $\overline{Q}_{23} =$everything is OK; $\overline{Q}_{24} =$ danger; and $\overline{Q}_{25} =$ out-of-control, stop. These $\overline{Q}_{ij}$ are defined for all the input fuzzy sets.

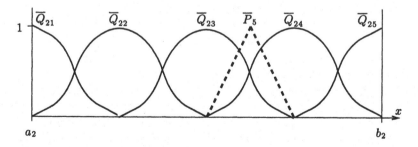

Fig. 2.2. Fuzzy Sets for the Value of Pressure in the Fuzzy Expert System.

Next we need to define the meaning of the $\overline{A}_n$ $(\overline{B}_p)$ for the control actions. These fuzzy sets represent suggestions for the human operators. Let $I_{1i} = \overline{A}_i$, $1 \le i \le N$ and $I_{2i} = \overline{B}_i$, $1 \le i \le P$. For example, I_{12} could be "close valve V2" and I_{23} might be "empty contents of storage tank #2 into output tank".

Given the input fuzzy set $\overline{P}$, $\overline{D}$, $\overline{C}$, $\overline{T}$ and $\overline{FR}$ all the fuzzy rules are evaluated producing the discrete fuzzy sets CA_i, $1 = 1, 2$. Initially, all the α_i and β_j values are set to zero. To evaluate rule R_s we need to compute the value of all the comparisons $[\overline{D} = \overline{Q}_{1i}]$, $[\overline{P} = \overline{Q}_{2j}]$, etc. Let E be some fuzzy equality relation defined on the set of fuzzy numbers. Then the value of $[\overline{D} = \overline{Q}_{1i}]$, say λ_i, is

$$\lambda_i = E(\overline{D}, \overline{Q}_{1i}) . \tag{2.3}$$

One might consider using the height of the intersection of $\overline{D}$ and $\overline{Q}_{1i}$, which is

$$\lambda_i = \sup_x(\min(\overline{D}(x), \overline{Q}_{1i}(x))) , \tag{2.4}$$

for E. So we assume $E(\overline{P}, \overline{Q}_{2j}) = \lambda_j$, $E(\overline{C}, \overline{Q}_{3k}) = \lambda_k$, $E(\overline{T}, \overline{Q}_{4l}) = \lambda_l$, and $E(\overline{FR}, \overline{Q}_{5m}) = \lambda_m$ have all been computed.

We next evaluate[1]

$$\gamma_s = T(\lambda_i, \lambda_j, \lambda_k, \lambda_l, \lambda_m) , \tag{2.5}$$

for all rules, $1 \le s \le M$, for a t-norm T. The value for the antecedent of the rule R_s is γ_s. To obtain the α_i and β_j we have to aggregate the γ_s over the rules.

The memory update algorithm for the SFC now collects together all the rules that have the same $\overline{A}_n$, or the same $\overline{B}_p$, in their right hand side (consequence). Let Γ_n (Γ_p) be all s in $\{1, 2, \ldots, M\}$ whose consequence is $\overline{A}_n = CA_1$ ($\overline{B}_p = CA_2$) for $n = 1, 2, \ldots, N$ and $p = 1, 2, \ldots, P$. Then

$$\alpha_n = C\{\gamma_s \mid s \in \Gamma_n\} , \tag{2.6}$$

$$\beta_p = C\{\gamma_s \mid s \in \Gamma_p\} , \tag{2.7}$$

$1 \le n \le N$, $1 \le p \le P$, for a t-conorm[2] C. In this way the fuzzy expert system constructs the discrete fuzzy sets CA_i, $i = 1, 2$.

We could use more general fuzzy rules than always having equality between fuzzy numbers. That is, a rule could have $[\overline{P} \le \overline{Q}_{2j}]$ or $[\overline{C} \ne \overline{Q}_{3k}]$ or $[\overline{C} > \overline{Q}_{3k}]$, etc. The $\overline{Q}_{ij}$ could also be real numbers. All of these relations can be evaluated producing the γ_s numbers.

Where do these fuzzy rules come from? They come from the human observers who have been overseeing, and controlling, the complex process. For example, consider the control of a nuclear power plant. Many components of the plant can be individually controlled by controllers but the overall control is accomplished by human operators. The SFC acts as an advisor (back-up) for experienced human operators or as a training module for unexperienced operators.

---

[1] Any t-norm T is associative and may be extended to n arguments so that $T(x_1, \ldots, x_n)$ is defined.

[2] Any t-conorm C may be extended, though associativity, to n arguments so that $C(x_1, \ldots, x_n)$ is defined.

The last thing to do, before we go to the output translator, is aggregate the $\overline{A}_n$ ($\overline{B}_p$) into one fuzzy set. We will employ the following method (like the center of gravity defuzzifier)

$$\overline{A}^* = \frac{\sum_{n=1}^N \alpha_n \overline{A}_n}{\sum_{n=1}^N \alpha_n}, \tag{2.8}$$

$$\overline{B}^* = \frac{\sum_{p=1}^P \beta_p \overline{B}_p}{\sum_{p=1}^P \beta_p}. \tag{2.9}$$

The SFC sends $\overline{A}^*$ and $\overline{B}^*$ to the output translator.

2.4 Output Translator

The output translator translates the $\overline{A}^*$ ($\overline{B}^*$) into verbal suggestions (the I_{1i} and I_{2j}). This will be accomplished by a neural net. We require one neural net for each control action. The neural net for CA_1 is shown in Figure 2.3. This neural net is trained on the training set $(\overline{A}_i, I_{1i})$, $1 \leq i \leq N$. More

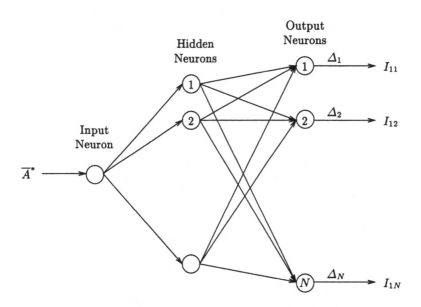

Fig. 2.3. Output Translator for First Control Action.

details are in Appendix B. This means if we input $\overline{A}^* = \overline{A}_3$ then the output should be I_{13}. Or, input $\overline{A}_3$, then $\Delta_3 \approx 1$, $\Delta_i \approx 0$, $1 \leq i \leq N$ with $i \neq 3$. The Δ_i are the strengths of the output signals at the ith output neuron. Once trained, we can input $\overline{A}^*$ from the fuzzy expert system.

We have a similar neural net for $\overline{B}^*$ and the I_{2i}, $1 \leq i \leq P$. The output translator will not output all the I_{ij} but will perform thresholding first before sending its verbal suggestions to the human operators. Let $\tau \in [0, 1)$, the thresholding constant. For CA_1, the output translator sends I_{1n} to the operators only if $\Delta_n \geq \tau$. Also, for CA_2 a I_{2p} is sent only when $\Delta_p \geq \tau$. So, for example, the operators could get only I_{12} for CA_1 but I_{23} and I_{24} for CA_2. The confidences (Δ_i) would also be given.

These verbal suggestions could be displayed on a computer screen or spoken through a voice box.

Why do we suggest a neural net for the output translator? The translation of an $\overline{A}^*$ back into I_{1n} is what has been called inverse linguistic approximation. Numerous papers have addressed the problem of inverse linguistic approximation ([2]-[4], [6] and its references, [7]). The procedure of inverse linguistic approximation is just non-linear interpolation and neural nets are perfect for this task. Hence, we propose a neural net, with fuzzy input and crisp output, for the output translator. In [6] the use of neural networks as output translators was also proposed. However, in that thesis another way of input coding was used. There the support of the fuzzy number, which is used as neural net input, was discretizied and the membership degrees at these points were put into the net. Due to the fact that $\overline{A}^* = (a_1^*/a_2^*/a_3^*)$ ($\overline{B}^* = (b_1^*/b_2^*/b_3^*)$) will be a triangular fuzzy number (discussed in the next section) in our SFC, if $\overline{A}_n$ ($\overline{B}_n$) are triangular for $1 \leq n \leq N$, we simply can use the a_1^*, a_2^* and a_3^* as input data for the neural net. The neural net is described in more detail in the example in the next section.

3. Example

In this section we implement the ideas of the previous section and construct a small scale SFC. We will need to limit the number of variables and the fuzzy sets $\overline{Q}_{ij}$ (Figure 2.2) so that the fuzzy rule table is not too large.

Our basic variables are pressure (P) and temperature (T), so we omit FR for flow rate. The variables will be P, D =change in P, T, and C =change in T. As in subsection 2.2 there will be seven fuzzy numbers (see Figure 2.1) for P, D, T, and C. The descriptions of each of these fuzzy numbers is the same as given in 2.2 for P (T) and for D (C).

The fuzzy rules are

R_s: If $[\overline{D} = \overline{Q}_{1i}]$ and $[\overline{P} = \overline{Q}_{2j}]$ and $[\overline{C} = \overline{Q}_{3k}]$ and $[\overline{T} = \overline{Q}_{4l}]$, then $CA_1 = \overline{A}_n$ and $CA_2 = \overline{B}_p$,

for $1 \leq s \leq 81$, $i = j = k = l = 1, 2, 3$ and n, p in the set $\{1, 2, 3\}$.

We first define the fuzzy sets $\overline{Q}_{ij}$. We will assume that all the fuzzy numbers (also for the variables P, D, T, C) have been scaled so that they lie in $[-1, 1]$. We will also use the same $\overline{Q}$'s for all the variables. That is, $\overline{Q}_{ij} = \overline{Q}_j$, $i = 1, 2, 3, 4$ and $j = 1, 2, 3$. The $\overline{Q}_j$ are specified in Figure 3.1.

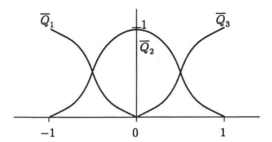

Fig. 3.1. The Fuzzy Numbers $\overline{Q}$ for the Fuzzy Expert System.

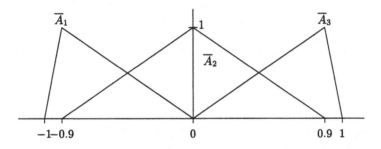

Fig. 3.2. Fuzzy Sets for the Control Actions.

Having only three $\overline{Q}$'s will greatly reduce the total number of fuzzy rules (now 81). The interpretation of the $\overline{Q}$'s is: (1) $\overline{Q}_1$ = danger, too low; (2) $\overline{Q}_2$ = variable OK; and (3) $\overline{Q}_3$ =danger, too high.

There will be three fuzzy numbers for each control action as shown in Figure 3.2. For simplicity we have assumed that $\overline{A}_i = \overline{B}_i$, $i = 1, 2, 3$. Recall that the meaning of $\overline{A}_i$ is I_{1i} and the suggestions corresponding to $\overline{B}_i$ is I_{2i}, $i = 1, 2, 3$. The statements corresponding to these I_{ij} are as follows: (1) I_{11} = close valve V3; (2) I_{12} = no action required; (3) I_{13} = open valve V3; (4) I_{21} = increase fuel rate R2; (5) I_{22} = no action required; and (6) I_{23} = decrease fuel rate R2.

To evaluate the fuzzy rules we will use $T = \min$, $C = \max$, and the height of the intersection (equation (2.4)) to compute the λ_i.

$$\overline{D}$$

		$\overline{Q}_1$	$\overline{Q}_2$	$\overline{Q}_3$
	$\overline{Q}_1$	$\overline{A}_1, \overline{B}_2$	$\overline{A}_1, \overline{B}_2$	$\overline{A}_2, \overline{B}_2$
$\overline{P}$	$\overline{Q}_2$	$\overline{A}_1, \overline{B}_2$	$\overline{A}_2, \overline{B}_2$	$\overline{A}_3, \overline{B}_2$
	$\overline{Q}_3$	$\overline{A}_2, \overline{B}_2$	$\overline{A}_3, \overline{B}_2$	$\overline{A}_3, \overline{B}_2$

Table 3.1. Fuzzy Rule Table for $\overline{C} = \overline{T} = \overline{Q}_2$.

$$\overline{D}$$

	$\overline{Q}_1$	$\overline{Q}_2$	$\overline{Q}_3$
$\overline{Q}_1$	$\overline{A}_1, \overline{B}_2$	$\overline{A}_2, \overline{B}_2$	$\overline{A}_2, \overline{B}_2$
$\overline{P}$ $\overline{Q}_2$	$\overline{A}_2, \overline{B}_2$	$\overline{A}_3, \overline{B}_2$	$\overline{A}_3, \overline{B}_2$
$\overline{Q}_3$	$\overline{A}_2, \overline{B}_2$	$\overline{A}_3, \overline{B}_2$	$\overline{A}_3, \overline{B}_2$

Table 3.2. Fuzzy Rule Table for $\overline{C} = \overline{Q}_3$ and $\overline{T} = \overline{Q}_1$.

We need to present all 81 fuzzy rules. They will be given in nine 3×3 tables. Two of the tables are given below and the other seven are in Appendix A. Notice, that the values of the variables can interact in producing the consequences of a rule. For example, consider Table 3.2 where $\overline{P} = \overline{Q}_2$ and $\overline{D} = \overline{Q}_2$. Normally, we would suggest $CA_1 = A_2$ but temperature is rising rapidly, so we would expect the pressure to be also increasing. We recommend $\overline{A}_3$ which opens the valve to decrease the pressure. This interaction of changes in temperature effecting pressure was incorporated in all the rule tables.

The interpretation of $\overline{Q}_1$ and $\overline{Q}_3$ on the change in pressure and the change in temperature must be further explained. $\overline{Q}_1$ for $\overline{D}$ $(\overline{C})$ means that pressure (temperature) is decreasing rapidly and $\overline{Q}_3$ for $\overline{D}$ $(\overline{C})$ is interpreted as pressure (temperature) is increasing rapidly.

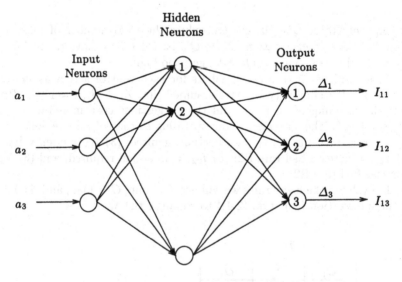

Fig. 3.3. Output Neural Network in the Example.

The neural net used for the output translator is the heart of the SFC. The neural net will have fuzzy input (the $\overline{A}^*$ and $\overline{B}^*$ of Section 2.3) and crisp output (Figure 2.3). But since the $\overline{A}_i$ $(\overline{B}_i)$ in Figure 3.2 are triangular fuzzy numbers the net can have crisp input (Figure 3.3). From Figure 3.2 we see that $\overline{A}_1 = \overline{B}_1 = (-1/-0.9/0)$, $\overline{A}_2 = \overline{B}_2 = (-0.9/0/0.9)$ and $\overline{A}_3 = \overline{B}_3 = (0/0.9/1)$. In Figure 3.3 $a_1 = -0.9$, $a_2 = 0$, $a_3 = 0.9$ for $\overline{A}_2$. Figure 3.3 shows the net for CA_1. The only changes for CA_2 would be at the output neurons where: (1) output neuron #1 has I_{21} with signal strength θ_1; (2) output neuron #2 has I_{22} with θ_2; and (3) output neuron #3 has signal θ_3 and I_{23}. The training set for CA_1 is: (1) $(-1/0.9/0)$ and $\Delta_1 = 1$, $\Delta_2 = 0$, $\Delta_3 = 0$; (2) $(-0.9/0/0.9)$ and $\Delta_1 = 0$, $\Delta_2 = 1$, $\Delta_3 = 0$; and (3) $(0/0.9/1)$ and $\Delta_1 = 0$, $\Delta_2 = 0$, $\Delta_3 = 1$. The training set for CA_2 is the same so the net only has to be trained once. Further details on the training of the net (number of hidden neurons, training algorithm, final error, etc.) is in Appendix B.

We input an $\overline{A}^* (\overline{B}^*)$ the same way because they are also triangular fuzzy numbers. From equation (2.8) we see that

$$\overline{A}^* = \sum_{n=1}^{3} \epsilon_n \overline{A}_n , \qquad (3.1)$$

where

$$\epsilon_n = \frac{\alpha_n}{\sum_{i=1}^{3} \alpha_i} , \qquad (3.2)$$

for $n = 1, 2, 3$. Therefore, $\epsilon_n \in [0,1]$ all n and $\sum_{n=1}^{3} \epsilon_n = 1$. If we set $\overline{A}_i = (a_{i1}/a_{i2}/a_{i3})$, $1 \le i \le 3$, then $\overline{A}^* = (\varphi_1/\varphi_2/\varphi_3)$ where

$$\varphi_i = \sum_{n=1}^{3} \epsilon_n a_{ni} , \qquad (3.3)$$

for $i = 1, 2, 3$. So, given an $\overline{A}^*$, output from the fuzzy expert system, we input φ_i for a_i, $1 \le i \le 3$, into the net in Figure 3.3. Similarly, we find values for η_i in $\overline{B}^* = (\eta_1/\eta_2/\eta_3)$ which will be inputs to the output translator for CA_2. For the thresholding constant we will use $\tau = 0.5$ for both CA_1 and CA_2.

Now we are ready to actually run our small scale SFC on some input data. The operation of the SFC is straightforward. We input values for P, D, T and C. These will be triangular, or trapezoidal, fuzzy numbers. Then the λ values (equation (2.5)) are all computed. We will explain below what membership functions we used for the $\overline{Q}_i$. From these λ values we compute the γ_s (equation (2.5) with min $= T$) and the α_n, β_n (equations (2.6), (2.7) with $C = $ max). Then the $\alpha_n (\beta_n)$ are used to obtain the $\varphi_i (\eta_i)$ as in equation (3.3). Finally, the $\varphi_i (\eta_i)$ are inputted to the neural net to obtain the verbal suggestions for the operators. The results are in Table 3.3.

Consider the first experiment in Table 3.3. The inputs are: pressure is low or slightly low; pressure is decreasing slightly; temperature is slightly high or high; and temperature is decreasing. The output translator states: (1) for control action #1 "close valve V3 (0.631) or no reaction required (0.582)"; and (2) for control action #2 "no action required (0.585)" or "decrease fuel rate (0.651)". Notice that the large uncertainties in the input ($\overline{P}_2$ or $\overline{P}_3$ and $\overline{T}_5$ or $\overline{T}_6$) produced large uncertainties in the verbal suggestions to the operators.

For the membership functions for the $\overline{Q}_i$ we pieced together quadratic polynomials. Let us specify $\overline{Q}_2$ of Figure 3.1. We used

$$\overline{Q}_2(x) = \begin{cases} 2(x+1)^2 & : & -1 \le x \le -0.5 \\ -2x^2 + 1 & : & -0.5 \le x \le 0.5 \\ 2(x-1)^2 & : & 0.5 \le x \le 1 \\ 0 & : & \text{otherwise} . \end{cases} \tag{3.4}$$

Verbal Evaluation	SFC Output
1. Pressure $= \overline{P}_2$ or $\overline{P}_3$	$\overline{A}^* = (-0.950/-0.450/0.450)$
Change in Pressure $= \overline{D}_3$	$\Delta_1 = 0.631,\ \Delta_2 = 0.582,\ \Delta_3 = 0.104$
Temperature $= \overline{T}_5$ or $\overline{T}_6$	$\overline{B}^* = (-0.450/0.450/0.950)$
Change in Temperature $= \overline{C}_2$	$\theta_1 = 0.138,\ \theta_2 = 0.585,\ \theta_3 = 0.651$
2. Pressure $= \overline{P}_1$ or $\overline{P}_2$	$\overline{A}^* = (-0.633/0.000/0.633)$
Change in Pressure $= \overline{D}_4$ or $\overline{D}_5$	$\Delta_1 = 0.259,\ \Delta_2 = 0.691,\ \Delta_3 = 0.249$
Temperature $= \overline{T}_2$ or $\overline{T}_3$	$\overline{B}^* = (-0.900/0.000/0.900)$
Change in Temperature $= \overline{C}_2$	$\theta_1 = 0.452,\ \theta_2 = 0.952,\ \theta_3 = 0.469$
3. Pressure $= \overline{P}_5$	$\overline{A}^* = (-0.633/0.000/0.633)$
Change in Pressure $= \overline{D}_3$ or $\overline{D}_4$	$\Delta_1 = 0.259,\ \Delta_2 = 0.691,\ \Delta_3 = 0.249$
Temperature $= \overline{T}_2$	$\overline{B}^* = (-0.450/0.450/0.950)$
Change in Temperature $= \overline{C}_6$	$\theta_1 = 0.138,\ \theta_2 = 0.585,\ \theta_3 = 0.651$
4. Pressure $= \overline{P}_6$	$\overline{A}^* = (-0.335/0.565/0.963)$
Change in Pressure $= \overline{D}_6$	$\Delta_1 = 0.098,\ \Delta_2 = 0.495,\ \Delta_3 = 0.751$
Temperature $= \overline{T}_4$	$\overline{B}^* = (-0.611/0.205/0.839)$
Change in Temperature $= \overline{C}_5$	$\theta_1 = 0.222,\ \theta_2 = 0.741,\ \theta_3 = 0.472$
5. Pressure $= \overline{P}_4$ or $\overline{P}_5$	$\overline{A}^* = (-0.611/0.205/0.839)$
Change in Pressure $= \overline{D}_2$ or $\overline{D}_3$	$\Delta_1 = 0.222,\ \Delta_2 = 0.741,\ \Delta_3 = 0.472$
Temperature $= \overline{T}_2$ or $\overline{T}_3$	$\overline{B}^* = (-0.937/-0.335/0.565)$
Change in Temperature $= \overline{C}_3$	$\theta_1 = 0.612,\ \theta_2 = 0.681,\ \theta_3 = 0.159$

Table 3.3. Results in the Example

4. Summary

This chapter described the design of a supervisory fuzzy controller (Figure 1.1) for human operators of a complex plant (nuclear reactor). The human operators are allowed to verbally describe the status of various variables used to control the plant. These verbal descriptions come from a very limited vocabulary recognized by the input translator. The input translator translates these descriptions into fuzzy numbers for input to a fuzzy expert system. The fuzzy expert system processes these fuzzy numbers into fuzzy number output describing suggestions to the human operators. The output translator, which is a neural net, takes the fuzzy number output from the fuzzy expert system, and produces the verbal suggestions, of what to do, for the human operators. An example was presented, with four variables and 81 rules, showing the basic operation of a supervisory fuzzy controller.

A main contribution of this design was the use of a neural net as the output translator. The translation of fuzzy numbers into words is called inverse linguistic approximation. We believe a neural net is ideal for this job.

We also suggested two main applications of a supervisory fuzzy controller: (1) as an advisor (back-up) for experienced human operators; and (2) for training inexperienced human operators. We feel that a supervisory fuzzy controller could have great potential as a trainig module.

References

1. J.J Buckley, *Fuzzy I/O Controller*, Fuzzy Sets and Systems, 43 (1991) 127-137.
2. R. Degani and G. Bortolan, *The Problem of Linguistic Approximation in Clinical Decision Making*, Int. J. Approximate Reasoning 2 (1988) 143-162.
3. A. Dvorak, *On Linguistic Approximation in the Frame of LFLC*, Proc. Seventh IFSA, Prague, June 25-29, Vol. 1, 413-417.
4. F. Eshragh and E. H. Mamdani, *A General Approach to Linguistic Approximation*, Int. J. Man-Machine Studies 11 (1979) 501-519.
5. E.E. Kerre, The use of fuzzy set theory in electrocardiological diagnostics, in: M.M. Gupta, E. Sanchez (eds.), Approximate Reasoning in Decision Analysis, 1982, 277-282
6. K. Lukas, *Linguistic Approximation and Fuzzy Logic: Current Methods and a New Approach using Neural Networks*, Johannes Kepler Univ., Austria, 1994.
7. M. Sugeno and T. Yakusawa, *A Fuzzy-Logic Based Approach to Qualitative Modeling*, IEEE Trans. Fuzzy Systems 1 (1993) 7-31.

Appendix A

This Appendix contains the rest of the rule tables for the example.

$$\overline{D}$$

		$\overline{Q}_1$	$\overline{Q}_2$	$\overline{Q}_3$
	$\overline{Q}_1$	$\overline{A}_1, \overline{B}_1$	$\overline{A}_1, \overline{B}_1$	$\overline{A}_1, \overline{B}_1$
$\overline{P}$	$\overline{Q}_2$	$\overline{A}_1, \overline{B}_1$	$\overline{A}_2, \overline{B}_1$	$\overline{A}_3, \overline{B}_1$
	$\overline{Q}_3$	$\overline{A}_2, \overline{B}_1$	$\overline{A}_3, \overline{B}_1$	$\overline{A}_3, \overline{B}_1$

Table A.1. Fuzzy Rule Table for $\overline{C} = \overline{Q}_1$ and $\overline{T} = \overline{Q}_1$.

$$\overline{D}$$

		$\overline{Q}_1$	$\overline{Q}_2$	$\overline{Q}_3$
	$\overline{Q}_1$	$\overline{A}_1, \overline{B}_1$	$\overline{A}_1, \overline{B}_1$	$\overline{A}_2, \overline{B}_1$
$\overline{P}$	$\overline{Q}_2$	$\overline{A}_1, \overline{B}_1$	$\overline{A}_2, \overline{B}_1$	$\overline{A}_3, \overline{B}_1$
	$\overline{Q}_3$	$\overline{A}_1, \overline{B}_1$	$\overline{A}_3, \overline{B}_1$	$\overline{A}_3, \overline{B}_1$

Table A.2. Fuzzy Rule Table for $\overline{C} = \overline{Q}_1$ and $\overline{T} = \overline{Q}_2$.

$$\overline{D}$$

		$\overline{Q}_1$	$\overline{Q}_2$	$\overline{Q}_3$
	$\overline{Q}_1$	$\overline{A}_1, \overline{B}_2$	$\overline{A}_1, \overline{B}_2$	$\overline{A}_2, \overline{B}_2$
$\overline{P}$	$\overline{Q}_2$	$\overline{A}_2, \overline{B}_2$	$\overline{A}_2, \overline{B}_2$	$\overline{A}_3, \overline{B}_2$
	$\overline{Q}_3$	$\overline{A}_2, \overline{B}_2$	$\overline{A}_3, \overline{B}_2$	$\overline{A}_3, \overline{B}_2$

Table A.3. Fuzzy Rule Table for $\overline{C} = \overline{Q}_1$ and $\overline{T} = \overline{Q}_3$.

$$\overline{D}$$

		$\overline{Q}_1$	$\overline{Q}_2$	$\overline{Q}_3$
	$\overline{Q}_1$	$\overline{A}_1, \overline{B}_1$	$\overline{A}_1, \overline{B}_1$	$\overline{A}_1, \overline{B}_1$
$\overline{P}$	$\overline{Q}_2$	$\overline{A}_1, \overline{B}_1$	$\overline{A}_2, \overline{B}_1$	$\overline{A}_3, \overline{B}_1$
	$\overline{Q}_3$	$\overline{A}_2, \overline{B}_1$	$\overline{A}_3, \overline{B}_1$	$\overline{A}_3, \overline{B}_1$

Table A.4. Fuzzy Rule Table for $\overline{C} = \overline{Q}_2$ and $\overline{T} = \overline{Q}_1$.

$$\overline{D}$$

		$\overline{Q}_1$	$\overline{Q}_2$	$\overline{Q}_3$
	$\overline{Q}_1$	$\overline{A}_1, \overline{B}_3$	$\overline{A}_1, \overline{B}_3$	$\overline{A}_2, \overline{B}_3$
$\overline{P}$	$\overline{Q}_2$	$\overline{A}_2, \overline{B}_3$	$\overline{A}_2, \overline{B}_3$	$\overline{A}_2, \overline{B}_3$
	$\overline{Q}_3$	$\overline{A}_2, \overline{B}_3$	$\overline{A}_2, \overline{B}_3$	$\overline{A}_3, \overline{B}_3$

Table A.5. Fuzzy Rule Table for $\overline{C} = \overline{Q}_2$ and $\overline{T} = \overline{Q}_3$.

$$\overline{D}$$

		$\overline{Q}_1$	$\overline{Q}_2$	$\overline{Q}_3$
	$\overline{Q}_1$	$\overline{A}_1, \overline{B}_3$	$\overline{A}_1, \overline{B}_3$	$\overline{A}_2, \overline{B}_3$
$\overline{P}$	$\overline{Q}_2$	$\overline{A}_2, \overline{B}_3$	$\overline{A}_2, \overline{B}_3$	$\overline{A}_3, \overline{B}_3$
	$\overline{Q}_3$	$\overline{A}_2, \overline{B}_3$	$\overline{A}_2, \overline{B}_3$	$\overline{A}_3, \overline{B}_3$

Table A.6. Fuzzy Rule Table for $\overline{C} = \overline{Q}_3$ and $\overline{T} = \overline{Q}_2$.

$$\overline{D}$$

		$\overline{Q}_1$	$\overline{Q}_2$	$\overline{Q}_3$
	$\overline{Q}_1$	$\overline{A}_1, \overline{B}_3$	$\overline{A}_1, \overline{B}_3$	$\overline{A}_2, \overline{B}_3$
$\overline{P}$	$\overline{Q}_2$	$\overline{A}_2, \overline{B}_3$	$\overline{A}_3, \overline{B}_3$	$\overline{A}_3, \overline{B}_3$
	$\overline{Q}_3$	$\overline{A}_2, \overline{B}_3$	$\overline{A}_3, \overline{B}_3$	$\overline{A}_3, \overline{B}_3$

Table A.7. Fuzzy Rule Table for $\overline{C} = \overline{Q}_3$ and $\overline{T} = \overline{Q}_3$.

Appendix B

In this appendix we describe how we trained the neural net so it can work as an output translater. Before we describe the process of generating a suitable training set and the training of a neural net operating as an output translator for the example (Section 3) we discuss the network architecture.

The neural net input is a triangular fuzzy number $\overline{A}^* = (a_1^*/a_2^*/a_3^*)$. As network output we want to have crisp numbers in $[0, 1]$ representing the confidence values of the input $\overline{A}^*$ to the corresponding output neuron I_{1i} (see Figure 3.3). We do not need to input the whole fuzzy number $\overline{A}^*$ into the net and perform fuzzy arithmetic within the net because, as explained in Section 3, $\overline{A}^*$ will be a triangular fuzzy number completely described by three numbers a_1^*, a_2^*, a_3^*. Hence, we input only a_1^*, a_2^*, a_3^* and we may use a feedforward net and the backpropagation algorithm can be used for training.

In order to train the neural net a training set is needed. Of course, we already have a few training patterns given by $\overline{A}^* = \overline{A}_i, \Delta_i = 1.0, \Delta_j = 0.0\, j \neq i$ but we need a larger training set because we cannot expect that $\overline{A}^*$ equals $\overline{A}_i$ for one i. So we randomly chose triangluar fuzzy numbers in $[-1.0, 1.0]$. In order to evaluate the corresponding target values (Δ_j) a metric E is needed which computes the confidence value that the generated triangular fuzzy number equals $\overline{A}_i$. The method we used is inspired by Kerre's inequality relation [5] and computes the area of the intersection between $\overline{A}_i$ and $\overline{A}^*$. The resulting value is normed by the area of $\overline{A}_i$ so we get a value in $E(\overline{A}^*, \overline{A}_i) \in [0, 1]$ where $E(\overline{A}^*, \overline{A}_i) = 0$ if the intersection of $\overline{A}^*$ and $\overline{A}_i$ is empty and $E(\overline{A}^*, \overline{A}_i) = 1$ if $\overline{A}^* = \overline{A}_i$. E is given by

$$E(\overline{A}^*, \overline{A}_i) = \frac{\int\limits_{-\infty}^{\infty} \min(\overline{A}^*(x), \overline{A}_i(x))dx}{\int\limits_{-\infty}^{\infty} \overline{A}_i(x)dx}. \tag{4.1}$$

Now, the training set can be generated by chosing a triangular fuzzy number $\overline{A} = (a_1/a_2/a_3)$ and computing the target values $\Delta_1 = E(\overline{A}, \overline{A}_1)$, ..., $\Delta_n = E(\overline{A}, \overline{A}_n)$. A subset of the training set used to train the output translator is given in Table B.1. Let us now explain the details of the output translator training. The training set consisted of 300 input output pairs. A randomly chosen input fuzzy number only was taken into the training set if at least one confidence value was larger than 0.5. The net had three input neurons, seven hidden units and three output neurons standing for I_{11}, I_{12} and I_{13}. The learning rate was set to 0.001. After 91145 iterations the mean squared error on the training set was 0.000124.

304

Input Data ($\overline{A} = (a_1/a_2/a_3)$)			Output Data		
a_1	a_2	a_3	Δ_1	Δ_2	Δ_3
-0.6484	0.5622	0.8717	0.1992	0.6304	0.6282
-0.8227	-0.4249	0.8618	0.5215	0.7820	0.3396
-0.8274	-0.7995	-0.2779	0.5337	0.1479	0.0000
-0.6132	0.1244	0.9942	0.2296	0.7768	0.5585
-0.9548	-0.9513	0.2568	0.9723	0.3527	0.0313
-0.1432	0.9603	0.9817	0.0102	0.3018	0.9809
-0.9872	-0.9585	0.0293	0.9618	0.2541	0.0005
-0.9854	-0.9692	0.9647	0.9952	0.6794	0.3284
-0.7154	-0.3040	0.6950	0.3902	0.7055	0.2543
-0.7046	0.2277	0.2489	0.2709	0.5127	0.0673

Table B.1. Subset of the Training Set for Training the Neural Net of Section 3.

On Linguistic Fuzzy Constraint Satisfaction Problems

Ryszard Kowalczyk

CSIRO Mathematical and Information Sciences
723 Swanston Street, Carlton 3053, Australia
ryszard.kowalczyk@cmis.csiro.au

Abstract. Fuzzy constraint satisfaction problems (FCSPs) extend standard (crisp) constraint satisfaction problems (CSPs) by introducing a notion of fuzzy constraints. Fuzzy constraints allow one to express the degrees to which the constraints are satisfied with a given instantiation of constrained variables. The main advantage of FCSPs is flexibility in handling the constraints including their representation, satisfaction and relaxation. However, similarly to CSPs, FCSPs consider the variable instantiations in the form of singletons only, i.e. the constrained variables take single, usually numerical, values from their domains. A solution of a FCSP consists of a complete instantiation of all the constrained variables together with a degree of satisfaction of the constraints with the instantiation. In some applications such as decision analysis and support it may be desirable to express possible instantiations and solutions in more qualitative or descriptive way taking into account imprecision and uncertainty of the solutions. A concept of linguistic variable in fuzzy logic and in particular in computing with words has been developed for that purpose and it can also be used in FCSPs to advantage. Linguistic FCSPs (LFCSPs) extend FCSPs by considering the constrained variables as linguistic variables taking linguistic values that are words or sentences in a natural or synthetic language rather then single numerical values. In this paper some aspects of LFCSPs that aim in providing flexibility in handling both constraints and solutions are presented.

1 Introduction

Constraint satisfaction problems (CSPs) have successfully been used as a general formalism in modeling and solving a wide range of real-world problems including decision support, making and optimization, design, scheduling and planning (e.g. [8, 14, 16]). In general CSPs are NP-complete problems involving a set of variables and a set of constraints acting on the variables with the objective of finding an instantiation of the constrained variables such that all constraints are satisfied at the same time. However CSPs are limited to problems that can be completely specified, i.e. the constraints can be precisely defined and fully satisfied. To soften those assumptions and take into account aspects of uncertainty and imprecision which characterize most real-world problems, elements of fuzzy set theory [18] have been introduced to CSPs. Fuzzy CSPs (FCSPs) extend standard CSPs by introducing a notion of fuzzy constraints that represent fuzzy relations between the constrained variables [4, 6, 17, 18]. This allows one to express the degrees to which the constraints are satisfied by a given instantiation of the constrained variables and the priority between the constraints.

The main advantage of FCSPs is flexibility in handling constraints including representation, satisfaction and relaxation of soft and prioritized constraints [4, 6]. However, similarly to CSPs, FCSPs consider the variable instantiations in the form of singletons only, i.e. the constrained variables take single, usually numerical, values from their domains. All possible instantiations are prescribed by sets of values from the domains of not yet instantiated variables together with the possible constraint satisfaction degrees for the values. Consequently a solution of a FCSP consists of a complete instantiation of all the constrained variables together with a degree of satisfaction of the constraints with the instantiation. Therefore it can be said that FCSPs are limited to problems where solutions can (have to) be precise which is sometimes very difficult to accomplish (e.g. problems with continuous real valued variables) [1, 15]. Moreover, in some applications such as interactive decision analysis and support (where the user may select variable instantiations, observe their effect on other variables and make decisions about new instantiations in order to satisfy/optimize some criteria) it may be desirable to express possible instantiations and solutions in more qualitative or descriptive way taking into account aspects of uncertainty and imprecision of the solutions. A concept in fuzzy logic and in particular in computing with words that has been developed to exploit the tolerance for imprecision and uncertainty is the linguistic variable [18, 19, 20]. It can also be used to represent possible options and solutions in FCSPs [12] to advantage. Linguistic FCSPs (LFCSPs) extend FCSPs by considering the constrained variables as linguistic variables taking linguistic values that are words or sentences in a natural or synthetic language rather then single numerical values. The main advantage of LFCSPs is flexibility in handling both constraints and solutions.

The LFCSP formalism can be considered as an instance of computing with words, a methodology of computation with fuzzy variables proposed by Zadeh [20]. In computing with words the objects of computing are words rather than numbers, with words playing the role of labels of information granules represented by fuzzy sets. The fundamental concepts in this methodology such as a linguistic variable, fuzzy inference, fuzzy restrictions (constraints) and fuzzy constraint propagation play an important role in LFCSPs. In general computing with words involves three main tasks [20] that can also be identified in the LFCSP context. The first task in computing with words is explicitation of propositions expressed in a natural language, i.e. representation of the linguistic propositions viewed as implicit constraints on variables in their canonical forms. In LFCSPs explicitation involves both predefined constraints relating the variables in the problem and unary restrictions associated with possible linguistic values for variable instantiations considered during the solving process. The second task involves reasoning about the propositions (fuzzy restriction propagation) with the use of rules of inference in fuzzy logic. Constraint propagation is an important mechanism in solving LFCSPs. It is usually used to provide constraint consistency, i.e. to determine possible values for instantiation of not yet instantiated variables and their possible constraint satisfaction degrees such that together with linguistic instantiations of other variables they are consistent with the constraints. The third task is a re-translation of induced conclusions into propositions expressed in a natural language. In the context of LFCSPs these propositions are both the induced possible instantiations of the variables during the solving process and the final solution.

The paper presents some aspects of LFCSPs based on the use of fuzzy constraints and linguistic variables that can be instantiated with linguistic values. After an overview of FCSPs, a concept of the linguistic variable is introduced to FCSPs and a linguistic FCSP (LFCSP) is defined. Then some aspects of solving strategies for LFCSPs are discussed and the final conclusion is presented.

2 Fuzzy constraint satisfaction problems

In general, constraint satisfaction problems (CSPs) [13, 14] are defined by a set of variables with the associated domains and a set of crisp constraints relating the variables. Fuzzy CSPs (FCSPs) [4, 6, 12, 17] extend CSPs by introducing a notion of fuzzy constraints that can be partially satisfied. Fuzzy constraints are considered as fuzzy relations between the variables and are represented by membership functions defining the degree of constraint satisfaction with the variable instantiations. An assignment satisfies a constraint fully if it is evaluated to 1 and violates a constraint when it is evaluated to 0. The intermediate values represent the degree of partial constraint satisfaction. Examples of fuzzy constraints are presented in Fig. 1.

More formally, a FCSP can be defined as follows:

- a set of variables $X = \{X_1, \ldots, X_n\}$,

- a set of domains $D = \{D_1, \ldots, D_n\}$ for the variables, where each domain $D_i, i = 1, \ldots, n$ consists of values $x_i \in D_i$ that the corresponding variable X_i can assume (the domains may be continuous or discrete in a particular case),

- a set of fuzzy constraints $C = \{C_1, \ldots, C_m\}$ between the variables, where each constraint $C_j, j = 1, \ldots, m$ relating a subset of the variables $\left\{X_{j_1}, \ldots, X_{j_k}\right\} \subseteq X$ represents a fuzzy relation defined on the Cartesian product space $D_{j_1} \times \ldots \times D_{j_k}$, $\left\{ D_{j_1}, \ldots, D_{j_k} \right\} \subseteq D$ characterized by a membership function $C_j\left(x_{j_1}, \ldots, x_{j_k}\right) \in [0,1]$ that represents satisfaction of the constraint with each assignment $\left(x_{j_1}, \ldots, x_{j_k}\right) \in D_{j_1} \times \ldots \times D_{j_k}$.

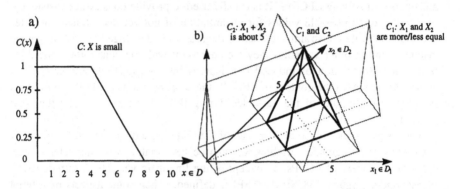

Fig. 1. Fuzzy constraints: a) unary C: X is small, b) binary C_1: X_1 and X_2 are more/less equal and C_2: $X_1 + X_2$ is about 5

A solution of a FCSP is a complete instantiation $x \in D$ of the variables X such that all constraints C are more or less satisfied. A set of all constraints C relating the variables X in a FCSP forms a global fuzzy relation $C(x) \in [0,1]$ defined on the Cartesian product space $D_1 \times \ldots \times D_n$. It represents a fuzzy set of solutions (i.e. complete instantiations of all variables) where each solution is characterized by the membership degree $C(x)$ to the fuzzy set. The global fuzzy relation is usually prescribed as a conjunctive combination of the fuzzy relations defined by each fuzzy constraint, i.e. $C(x) = \bigwedge_{j=1,\ldots,m} C_j(x)$, where $C_j(x) = Cyl_X\left[C_j\left(x_{j_1}, \ldots, x_{j_{kj}}\right)\right]$ is a cylindrical extension of the fuzzy relation representing the constraint C_j to X, and $\bigwedge_{j=1,\ldots,m}$ is a conjunctive combination represented usually by the minimum operation [4, 6, 12]. It should be noted that in general fuzzy relations can also be aggregated with the use of other operators such as t-norms and averages (e.g. [10, 17, 20]) that will not be considered in this paper.

An important concept in modeling and solving FCSPs is constraint consistency that similarly to constraint satisfaction is a matter of degree [4, 6]. An instantiation of a variable $X_i \in X$ is locally consistent if all constraints acting on the variable are fully or partially satisfied. The degree of local consistency estimates to what extent an instantiation x_i satisfies the constraints and it can be calculated as follows:

$$Cons(x_i) = \min_{C_j \in C(X_i) \subseteq C} \left(C_j(x_i) \right) \tag{1}$$

where $C(X_i)$ is a set of unary constraints acting on the variable X_i. In more general case the degree of local consistency for any partial or complete instantiation $x' \subseteq x = \{x_1, \ldots, x_n\}$ of variables $X' \subseteq X \in \{X_1, \ldots, X_n\}$ can be defined as follows:

$$Cons(x') = \min_{\substack{C_j \in C \\ x(C_j) \subseteq x'}} \left(C_j(x') \right) = \min_{\substack{C_j \in C \\ x(C_j) \subseteq x'}} \left(Cyl_X \cdot \left[C_j \left(x_{j1}, \ldots, x_{jn_j} \right) \right] \right) \tag{2}$$

where $X(C_j) = \left\{ X_{j1}, \ldots, X_{jn_j} \right\}$ is a set of variables related by a constraint C_j and $C_j(x') = Cyl_X \cdot \left[C_j \left(x_{j1}, \ldots, x_{jn_j} \right) \right]$ is a cylindrical extension of its fuzzy relation to X'.

Solutions of a FCSP are complete and consistent instantiations of the constrained variables that are not totally infeasible, i.e. $Cons(x) > 0$. The degrees of consistency provide an ordering of all possible solutions in respect to the satisfiability of the constraints in the problem. The satisfaction degree of the best complete instantiation of the constrained variables is the consistency degree of a FCSP as follows:

$$Cons(FCSP) = \max_{x \in D} \left(\min_{C_j \in C} \left(C_j(x) \right) \right). \tag{3}$$

The objective of solving of a FCSP may be to find the entire set of solutions, any solution or the best solution according to some criteria (typically maximal constraint satisfaction corresponding to $Cons(FCSP)$). Because FCSPs extend CSPs many CSP solving approaches can be adapted to solve FCSPs including heuristic search techniques (e.g. branch&bound, intelligent backtracking) and filtering methods (e.g. F-AC3, F-PC2) [4, 6]. Fuzzy constraint propagation based on rules of inference in fuzzy logic is often used to improve efficiency of solving FCSPs.

Fuzzy constraints can also be interpreted according to the principles of possibility theory [4, 5, 6, 19]. A fuzzy constraint C_j, $j = 1, \ldots, m$ relating a set of variables $X' \subseteq X \in \{X_1, \ldots, X_n\}$ can be viewed as a possibility distribution $\pi_{C_j}(x') = C_j(x')$ prescribing to what extent values $x' \in D' \subseteq D$ are suitable for instantiation of the constrained variables X'. Hence the degree of possibility $\pi_{C_j}(x')$ is the degree of preference for choosing x' for X', where $\pi_{C_j}(x') = 0$

means that x' is a forbidden instantiation of X', and $\pi_{C_j}(x') = 1$ means that x' is a definitely preferred instantiation of X'. The possibility distribution corresponding to the global fuzzy relation that relates all variables, i.e. $\pi_C(x) = C(x)$ gives a preference for each complete instantiation of the variables (solutions of a FCSP) with respect to the global constraint satisfiability. It should be noted that the possibility distribution corresponds to constraint consistency, i.e. $\pi_C(x') = Cons(x')$ for any partial or complete instantiation $x' \subseteq x = \{x_1, \ldots, x_n\}$.

To assess possible solutions of a FCSP two complementary measures based on the possibility distribution can be used, i.e. the possibility and necessity measures [4, 5, 6]. Given a possibility distribution $\pi_C(x)$ for possible instantiations of a variable X (a set of variables in general case), the occurrence of crisp events (i.e. $\underset{x \in A}{\forall} A(x) = 1$) of the form $x \in A$ can be assessed by means of the possibility and necessity (interpreted sometimes as certainty or belief) measures defined respectively as follows [3, 4]:

$$\Pi[A] = \max_{x \in A}\left(\pi_C(x)\right), \quad N[A] = \min_{x \notin A}\left(\overline{\pi_C(x)}\right), \tag{4}$$

where $\Pi[A] = 1$ means that A is consistent with the constraints represented by π_C and $N[A] = 1$ means that the satisfaction of the constraints entails the occurrence of A. In other words $N[A] = 1$ means that the fuzzy set of solutions which more or less satisfy the constraints represented by π_C is included in A. It should be noted that $N[A] = 1 - \Pi[\overline{A}]$ which means that an event necessarily occurs (certain instantiations) if its contrary (complement) is impossible. The concepts of the possibility and necessity measures are illustrated in Fig. 2.

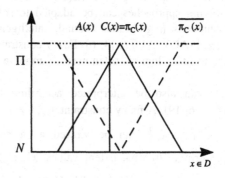

Fig. 2. Possibility and necessity measures

The possibility distribution corresponding to a constraint prescribes explicitly the suitability (preferences) of instantiations of all variables related by the constraint (complete instantiations for the global possibility distribution). It also implies an implicit suitability of values for instantiation of each variable involved in the constraint. Let us assume that each constrained variable X_i has associated a local possibility distribution $\pi_{X_i}(x_i) \in [0,1]$, $x_i \in D_i$ to estimate an extend to which the constraints can be possibly satisfied with the values from the domain of the variable. The local possibility distribution π_{X_i} can be defined as a conjunctive combination of possibility distributions implied by the constraints acting on the variable X_i, i.e. an intersection of projections of the constraint possibility distributions on the variable as follows:

$$\pi_{X_i}(x_i) = \min_{C_j \in C(X_i) \subseteq C} \left(\pi_{C_j}(x_i) \right) = \min_{C_j \in C(X_i) \subseteq C} \left(\mathrm{Proj}_{X_i} \left[\pi_{C_j}(x_{j1}, \ldots, x_{jn_j}) \right] \right) \tag{5}$$

where $\mathrm{Proj}_{X_i} \left[\pi_{C_j}(x_{j1}, \ldots, x_{jn_j}) \right] = \max_{x_{jl} \in \{D_{j1}, \ldots, D_{jnj}\} \setminus \{D_i\}} \left(\pi_{C_j}(x_{j_1}, \ldots, x_{j_{nj}}) \right)$ is a

projection of the constraint possibility distribution $\pi_{C_j} \left(x_{j_1}, \ldots, x_{j_{nj}} \right)$ on X_i and $C(X_i)$ is a set of constraints acting on the variable.

It should be noted that a cylindrical extension of any local possibility distribution to the complete instantiation forms an upper approximation of the global possibility distribution, i.e. $\pi_{X_i}(x) = Cyl_X \left[\pi_{X_i}(x_i) \right] \geq \pi_C(x)$. Therefore the local possibility distributions can be viewed as upper bounds of the global possibility distribution. Consequently, because the local possibility distributions bound the possibility distribution obtained from their conjunctive combination, i.e.

$$\forall X_i \in X' \subseteq X: \quad \pi_{X_i}(x') \geq \pi_{X'}(x') = \min_{X_i \in X' \subseteq X} \pi_{X_i}(x') \tag{6}$$

the upper bound of the global possibility distribution decreases (or more specifically does not increase) for more complete instantiations, i.e.

$$\pi_{X_i}(x) \geq \pi_{X'}(x) \geq \pi_{X''}(x) \geq \pi_X(x) \geq \pi_C(x), \quad X_i \in X' \subseteq X'' \subseteq X. \tag{7}$$

Therefore local possibility distributions can be used during solving FCSPs to guide the search through the partial instantiations of the variables and in particular to propagate effects of partial instantiations to not yet instantiated variables, i.e. to prune inconsistent instantiations. An example of the relationship between global and local possibility distributions for two constrained variables and an effect of partial instantiation are presented in Fig. 3.

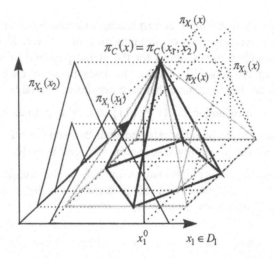

Fig. 3. Global and local possibility distributions for two constrained variables and an effect of partial instantiation

3 Linguistic FCSPs

FCSPs consider the variable instantiations in the form of singletons, i.e. single values from the domains of the variables that are in fact singleton fuzzifiers (e.g. x_1^0 in Fig. 3). To address aspects of imprecision and uncertainty that characterize many real-world problems singleton fuzzifiers can be extended to non-singleton (fuzzy) values and described in the linguistic terms.

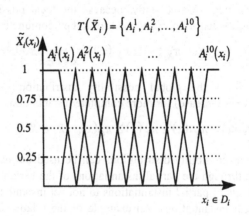

Fig. 4. A term set for a linguistic variable

The linguistic variable is a concept in fuzzy logic and in particular in computing with words that plays a central role in exploiting the tolerance for imprecision and uncertainty [2, 3, 7, 18, 19, 20]. The linguistic variable is a variable whose values are words or sentences in a natural or synthetic language rather than numeric. Linguistic values are represented by fuzzy sets called reference fuzzy sets. The reference fuzzy sets are defined on universes of discourse that are determined by the domains of the variables. A set of the linguistic values for one variable forms a term set for that variable. Fig. 4 shows an example of a term set $T\left(\tilde{X}_i\right)$ with associated reference fuzzy sets $A_i^l(x_i)$ for a linguistic variable $\tilde{X}_i$.

A notion of the linguistic variable can also be incorporated into FCSPs leading to linguistic FCSPs (LFCSPs) defined as follows:

- a set of linguistic variables $\tilde{X} = \left\{\tilde{X}_1, \tilde{X}_2, \ldots, \tilde{X}_n\right\}$, where each variable has an associated term set $T\left(\tilde{X}_i\right)$ of possible linguistic values,

- a set of domains $D = \left\{D_1, D_2, \ldots, D_n\right\}$ for the variables, where each domain is a base set for the reference fuzzy subsets $A_i^l(x)$ representing linguistic values A_i^l that a linguistic variable $\tilde{X}_i$ can assume,

- a set of fuzzy constraints $C = \left\{C_1, C_2, \ldots, C_m\right\}$ between the variables described by a fuzzy relation defined on the Cartesian product space $D_1 \times D_2 \times \ldots \times D_n$ characterized by a membership function $C(x) \in [0,1]$ which represents satisfaction of the constraints for each element of the Cartesian product of the base sets $x \in D_1 \times D_2 \times \ldots \times D_n$.

Solutions of a LFCSP are linguistic assignments $A = \left\{A_1^{l_1}, A_2^{l_2}, \ldots, A_n^{l_n}\right\}$ (for simplicity the superscripts l_i will be omitted later) to the variables $\tilde{X} = \left\{\tilde{X}_1, \tilde{X}_2, \ldots, \tilde{X}_n\right\}$ such that all constraints are more or less satisfied at the same time.

It should be noted that although linguistic assignments form implicit constraints on the variable, in the context of LFCSPs they differ from the fuzzy constraints. The fuzzy constraints are predefined static relations between the variables prescribing constraint satisfaction for all values of the constrained variables. Unary restrictions on the linguistic variables imposed by linguistic assignments can change by means of instantiations with the values (linguistic or numeric) that satisfy the fuzzy constraints to a degree defined by the fuzzy constraints and the characteristics of the linguistic values.

A notion of the constraint consistency in LFCSPs can be defined similarly as in FCSPs. The degree of local consistency for a linguistic instantiation A_i of a linguistic variable $\tilde{X}_i \in \tilde{X}$ can be defined as follows:

$$Cons(A_i) = \min_{C_j \in C(X_i) \subseteq C} \left[C_j(A_i) \right] \tag{8}$$

where $C(X_i)$ is a set of unary constraints acting on the variable X_i and $C_j(A_i)$ corresponds to the satisfaction of a constraint C_j with the linguistic instantiation.

Similarly the degree of local consistency of a partial or complete instantiation of the linguistic variables $\tilde{X}' \subseteq \tilde{X} = \{\tilde{X}_1, ..., \tilde{X}_n\}$ with linguistic values $A' \subseteq A = \{A_1, ... A_n\}$ can be defined as follows:

$$Cons(A') = \min_{\substack{C_j \in C \\ X(C_j) \subseteq X'}} \left(C_j(A') \right) = \min_{\substack{C_j \in C \\ X(C_j) \subseteq X'}} \left(Cyl_X \cdot \left[C_j \left(A_{j1}, ..., A_{jn_j} \right) \right] \right). \tag{9}$$

Solutions of LFCSPs are complete and consistent linguistic instantiations of the constrained variables that are not totally infeasible, i.e.:

$$Cons(A) = \min_{C_j \in C} \left(C_j(A) \right), \quad Cons(A) > 0 \tag{10}$$

and the consistency degree of a LFCSP is as follows:

$$Cons(LFCSP) = \max_{x \in D} \left(\min_{C_j \in C} \left(C_j(A) \right) \right). \tag{11}$$

A linguistic instantiation that corresponds to the consistency degree of a LFCSP is its the best solution.

Similarly to singleton instantiations constraint satisfaction with the linguistic instantiations of the variables can be quite naturally defined with the use of the concept of possibility distribution. A linguistic instantiation A of a constrained variable $\tilde{X}$ (a set of variables in general case) with the corresponding reference fuzzy set $A(x)$ is interpreted as a possibility distribution $\pi_A(x) = A(x)$ over the domain of the base variable. The suitability of the linguistic instantiation as a part of a possible solution can be assessed with the use of the possibility and necessity measures. The possibility measure $\Pi(A)$ gives a measure of the possibility that the fuzzy set of solutions represented by the possibility distribution $\pi_C(x) = Cons(x)$ is in the set specified by the possibility distribution $\pi_A(x)$ as follows:

$$\Pi[A] = \max_{x \in D} \left(\pi_A(x) \wedge \pi_C(x) \right). \tag{12}$$

The above interpretation allows one to consider the possibility measure as a degree of the constraint satisfaction with a linguistic instantiation and to use it in the definition of the constraint consistency for a linguistic instantiation $A' \subseteq A = \{A_1, \ldots, A_n\}$ as follows:

$$Cons(A') = \min_{\substack{C_j \in C \\ x(C_j) \subseteq x'}} \Pi[A'].$$ (13)

The necessity measure $N[A]$ of a linguistic instantiation A qualifies the certainty that A is implied by the constraints with the corresponding possibility distribution $\pi_C(x) = Cons(x)$ to degree as follows:

$$N[A] = 1 - \Pi[\overline{A}] = 1 - \max_{x \in D}\left(\pi_{\overline{A}}(x) \wedge \pi_C(x)\right).$$ (14)

The necessity measure can also be interpreted as a degree to which the situation that A is not suitable for instantiation is impossible.

It should also be noted that if A is a non-fuzzy (crisp) subset then the above formulas reduce to:

$$\Pi[A] = \max_{x \in A}\left(\pi(x)\right), \qquad N[A] = \min_{x \notin A}\left(\overline{\pi(x)}\right)$$ (15)

which corresponds to a specific case of FCSPs (see 4).

The principles of the possibility distribution allow also for another interpretation of the relationship between the fuzzy constraints and the linguistic instantiations in defining the possibility and necessity measures. The possibility measure can be treated as a measure of possibility that a linguistic value is in the set of possible solutions represented by $\pi_C(x) = Cons(x)$. The necessity measure can be interpreted as a degree to which a linguistic value cannot satisfy the complementary constraints. According to this interpretation the possibility and necessity measures can be defined as follows:

$$\Pi[A] = \max_{x \in D}\left(\pi_A(x) \wedge \pi_C(x)\right), \qquad N[A] = 1 - \max_{x \in D}\left(\pi_A(x) \wedge \overline{\pi_C(x)}\right).$$ (16)

Fig. 5 shows an example of fuzzy constraint satisfaction with a linguistic instantiation and the corresponding measures of possibility and necessity according to those two interpretations (indexed 1 and 2 respectively). It should be noted that although the second interpretation differs from one proposed for FCSPs [3] it may be more intuitive in the context of solving LFCSPs.

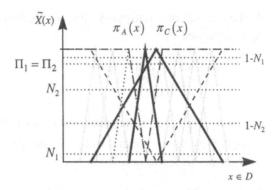

Fig. 5. Constraint satisfaction with a linguistic value

4 Solving LFCSPs

A common objective in solving FCSPs is to find a solution (a complete instantiation) that maximizes the satisfaction degree of fuzzy constraints. Most methods for solving standard CSPs such as the filtering [4, 6, 13, 14] and tree search algorithms [4, 6, 13, 14] can be adapted to take into account the fuzzy constraints in solving FCSPs. For example, Dubois et al. [4, 6] show how FCSPs can be solved with the use of the standard branch and bound search algorithm controlled by local consistency to prune the search for a predetermined sequence of the variable instantiations. They also extended some standard local consistency algorithms for fuzzy constraints including arc-consistency (F-AC3) and path-consistency (F-PC2) [4, 6]. Although those techniques consider singleton instantiations of the constrained variables it seems that the same principles can also be used in solving LFCSPs with linguistic instantiations.

For example the standard branch and bound algorithm in a LFCSP can search through partial linguistic instantiations of the linguistic variables in a similar way as in FCSPs [4, 6, 12]. Because, similarly to a crisp instantiation, local consistency for a partial linguistic instantiation is an upper bound of its extension to complete instantiations, i.e.

$$Cons\left(A_{k_1}, A_{k_2}, \ldots, A_{k_{nk}}\right) \geq Cons(A_k), \quad \left(A_{k_1}, A_{k_2}, \ldots, A_{k_{nk}}\right) \subseteq A_k \qquad (17)$$

the search can be bounded by the consistency degree of the best solution found so far. This bound can be used to prune the search for less consistent branches (partial and complete instantiations). For more detailed description of this algorithm used in FCSPs for a predetermined sequence of the variables refer to [4, 6].

The search can be extended with the use of additional control strategies for ordering the variables and selecting values for instantiation of a given variable. The control strategies can use information provided by the possibility distribution that can also be useful in performing constraint propagation to support the search. Similarly to the singleton instantiations in FCSPs the linguistic instantiations can also be ordered according to their suitability (possibility and necessity) to be solutions of a LFCSP.

As discussed before each constrained variable X_i has an associated local possibility distribution $\pi_{X_i}(x_i) \in [0,1]$, $x_i \in D_i$ to express the degree to which all constraints can be possibly satisfied with the values from the domain of the variable. The local possibility distribution π_{X_i} can be viewed as an upper bound of the global possibility distribution π_C (initially equal to the fuzzy relation representing the constraints, i.e. $\pi_C(x) = C(x)$) and therefore defined as its projection as follows:

$$\pi_{X_i}(x_i) = \text{Proj}_{X_i}\left(\pi_C(x)\right) = \max_{x \in D \setminus \{D_i\}}\left(\pi_C(x)\right) \geq \pi_C(x) \tag{18}$$

When a variable is instantiated then its local possibility distribution changes to reflect possible constraint satisfaction with the instantiation. Because it is an upper bound of the global possibility distribution the local possibility distributions of other variables can also change to ensure that they are consistent with the instantiation (i.e. they are the least upper bounds). The process of changing the possibility distributions to keep them consistent with the constraints and variable instantiations is called constraint propagation. Both automatic and interactive search for linguistic solutions in a LFCSP can be supported by constraint propagation to provide constraint consistency, i.e. eliminate inconsistent values during the search.

Given a linguistic instantiation A_i for the linguistic variable X_i, where A_i is a linguistic value characterized by a possibility distribution $\pi_{A_i}(x_i) = A_i(x_i)$, new local possibility distribution $\pi_{X_i}(x_i)$ of the variable can be calculated as follows:

$$\pi_{X_i}(x_i) \leftarrow \min\left[\pi_{X_i}(x_i), \pi_{A_i}(x_i)\right] \tag{19}$$

Then the global possibility distribution is effectively reduced to:

$$\pi_C(x) \leftarrow \min\left[\pi_C(x), Cyl_X\left(\pi_{X_i}(x_i)\right)\right] \tag{20}$$

Consequently, the local possibility distributions for other variables change as follows:

$$\mathop{\forall}_{\substack{x_j \in x \\ x_j \neq x_i}} \pi_{X_j}\left(x_j\right) \leftarrow \min\left[\pi_{X_j}\left(x_j\right), \mathop{\max}_{x \in D \backslash \{D_j\}} \pi_C(x)\right] \tag{21}$$

In general, the above formulas provide a mechanism for propagating the effects of any variable instantiation to other variables, or more specifically to their local possibility distributions. It is illustrated in Fig. 6.

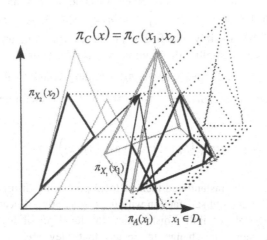

Fig. 6. Constraint propagation with linguistic instantiation

The local possibility distribution can be useful in guiding the search in LCSPs, i.e. in selecting the variables and linguistic values for instantiations. For example all variables can be ordered according to the possibility and necessity measures of the local possibility distribution as follows:

$$\mathop{\forall}_{\substack{i,j=1,\ldots,n \\ i \neq j}} \Pi\left(X_i\right) \geq \Pi\left(X_j\right), \qquad \mathop{\forall}_{\substack{i,j=1,\ldots,n \\ i \neq j}} N\left(X_i\right) \geq N\left(X_j\right) \tag{22}$$

where $\Pi[X_i] = \mathop{\max}_{x_i \in D_i}\left(\pi_{X_i}\left(x_i\right)\right)$ and $N[X_i] = 1 - \Pi[X_i]$. The variables are chosen for instantiation according to the above order with the preferences given to ones with higher possibility and necessity measures.

Similarly linguistic values A_i for instantiation of the chosen variable X_i can be selected on the basis of their possibility $\Pi[A_i]$ and necessity $N[A_i]$ measures with the preference given to the values with higher possibility and necessity (certainty) to satisfy constraints as follows:

$$\underset{\substack{A_{ik},A_{il}\in T(X_i)\\k\neq l}}{\forall}\ \Pi\!\left(A_{ik}\right)\geq\Pi\!\left(A_{il}\right),\qquad\underset{\substack{A_{ik},A_{il}\in T(X_i)\\k\neq l}}{\forall}\ N\!\left(A_{ik}\right)\geq N\!\left(A_{il}\right)\tag{23}$$

where $\Pi\!\left[A_i\right]=\underset{x_i\in D_i}{\max}\!\left(\pi_{A_i}(x_i)\wedge\pi_{X_i}(x_i)\right)$ and $N\!\left[A_i\right]=1-\underset{x_i\in D_i}{\max}\!\left(\pi_{A_i}(x_i)\wedge\overline{\pi_{X_i}(x_i)}\right)$.

The LFCSP framework seems to be especially suitable for interactive problem solving where the user is iteratively presented with the available variable instantiations (local possibility distributions), makes the decision on the variable instantiation, observes the effects of the instantiation on other variables (their local possibility distributions) and accepts/rejects a partial or complete solution. Linguistic approximation can be used here to interpret the local possibility distributions and present them to the user in the linguistic terms.

Linguistic approximation is a technique in fuzzy logic to describe an arbitrary fuzzy relation (possibility distribution) in the most appropriate linguistic terms. More formally the problem of linguistic approximation consists of associating a label with a membership distribution on the basis of semantic similarity [2, 7, 11, 18, 20]. Many approaches to process linguistic values and linguistic approximation exist that may also be used in LFCSPs. They usually use sets of primary terms (e.g. small, large), linguistic modifiers or hedges (e.g. not, much, very, more or less) and their connectives (e.g. and, or). For example Bonissone [2] developed a linguistic approximation method based on feature extraction and pattern recognition techniques. A more general approach to linguistic approximation has been proposed by Eshragh and Mamdani [7] which uses a combination of segments of the membership function with well defined characteristics. The segments are labeled with the use of linguistic modifiers (hedges) of the generated primitive terms and the final approximation is a combination of these labels. Some aspects of linguistic approximation in the context of FCSPs are presented in [11]. Fig. 7 illustrates an example of linguistic approximation in LFCSPs.

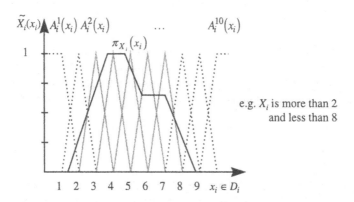

Fig. 7. Linguistic approximation

In this example the local possibility distribution can be linguistically approximated to more than 2 and less than 8. In the context of solving a LFCSP the user can accept this as a linguistic value for the variable or decide to try a more specific linguistic value from its term set (e.g. about 4) or a composed sequence (e.g. more less about 4 or about 6).

5 Conclusion

The paper presents an attempt to extend FCSPs to so-called linguistic FCSPs (LFCSPs) based on the use of the linguistic variables that can be instantiated with linguistic values rather than singletons such as numerical values in standard FCSPs. Therefore in addition to flexibility in handling constraints provided by FCSPs, LFCSPs introduce more flexibility in expressing solutions too. It seems that LFCSPs can especially be useful in interactive problem solving often required in many real-world problems characterized by imprecision and uncertainty (e.g. decision analysis and making, design, scheduling, planning etc.).

In addition the use of linguistic variables has the potential to extend the scope of the search and optimization in solving constrained problems modeled as LFCSPs. The common objective of FCSPs (LFCSPs) is to find the solution with the maximal degree of constraint satisfaction. LFCSPs for example may also allow one to search for solutions that are robust in respect to some changes in the environment (e.g. objectives, constraints).

The presented approach may be seen as the first step in defining more general framework for flexible CSPs regarding both constraints and solutions. However further research is required on the framework including the use of linguistic variables in consistency analysis, constraint propagation and optimization. Linguistic instantiations provide approximate solutions to LFCSPs with the singleton fuzzifiers corresponding to the most specific solution (that may be too precise and difficult to find in some cases) and the local possibility distributions corresponding to the least specific solutions (that may be in many cases too rough approximation to be acceptable solutions). A research question is how to measure the quality of the approximated solutions and how to determine the optimal level of approximation given some optimization criteria (e.g. robustness of solutions). Another issue is efficiency of search and constraint propagation (global and local) with the use of fuzzy instantiations.

References

1. Aberth, O.: Precise Numerical Analysis. Wm. C. Brown, Dubuque (1988)
2. Bonissone, P.: A fuzzy set based linguistic approach: Theory and applications. In: Gupta, M.M. and Sanchez, E. (eds.): Approximate Reasoning in Decision Analysis, North-Holland (1982) 329-339

3. Bonissone, P.P. and Decker, K.S.: Selecting uncertainty calculi and granularity: an experiment in trading off precision and complexity. In: Kanal, L.N. and Lemmer, J.F. (Eds): Uncertainty in Artificial Intelligence, Elsevier Science Publishers North-Holland (1986) 217-247

4. Dubois, D., Fargier, H. and Prade, H.: Flexible constraint satisfaction with application to scheduling problems. Report IRIT/93-30-R, Institute de Recherche en Informatique de Toulouse (1993)

5. Dubois, D. and Prade, H.: Possibility Theory: An Approach to Computerized Processing of Uncertainty. Plenum Press, NY (1988)

6. Dubois, D. Fargier, H. and Prade, H.: Propagation and Satisfaction of Flexible Constraints. In: Yager, R. and Zadeh, L. (eds.): Fuzzy Sets, Neural Networks and Soft Computing. Van Nostrand Reinhold, NY (1994) 166-187

7. Eshragh, F. and Mamdani, H.: A general approach to linguistic approximation. In: Mamdani, E.H. and Gaines, B.R. (eds.): Fuzzy Reasoning and its Applications, Academic Press (1981) 169-187

8. Fox, M.S. and Sadeh, N.: Why Is Scheduling Difficult? A CSP Perspective. Proceedings of the 9th European Conference on AI, August 6-10. Stockholm, Sweden (1990) 754-767

9. Freuder, E.C. and Wallace, R.J.: Partial constraint satisfaction. Artificial Intelligence 58 (1992) 21-70

10. Kaufman, A. and Gupta, M.: Introduction to Fuzzy Arithmetics. Theory and Applications. Van Nostrand Reinhold, New York (1985)

11. Kowalczyk, R., Czogala, E.: On linguistic approximation in fuzzy constraint satisfaction. The Fifth Congress on Intelligent Techniques and Soft Computing EUFIT'97, Aachen, Germany (1997) 1064-1068

12. Kowalczyk, R.: Fuzzy Constraint Satisfaction Problems with Linguistic Variables. The World Congress of International Fuzzy Systems Association IFSA'97, Prague, Czech Republic, vol. 4 (1997) 423-428

13. Kumar, V.: Algorithms for Constraint-Satisfaction Problems: A Survey. AI Magazine, Spring (1992) 32-44

14. Mackworth, A.K.: Constraint satisfaction. In: S.C. Shapiro (Ed.): Encyclopedia of Artificial Intelligence, John Wiley & Sons (1990) 205-211

15. Older, W., Vellino, A.: Constraint arithmetic on real intervals. In: Benhamou, F. & Colmerauer, A. (Eds.): Constraint Logic Programming, Collected Research. MIT Press, Cambridge, MA (1993)

16. Raughunathan, S.: A Planning Aid: An Intelligent Modelling System for Planning Problems Based on Constraint Satisfaction. IEEE Transactions on Knowledge and Data Engineering, Vol. 4, No. 4, August (1992) 317-335

17. Slany, W.: Scheduling as a fuzzy multiple criteria optimization problem. Fuzzy Sets and Systems, vol. 78 (1996) 197-222

18. Zadeh, L.A.: Outline of a new approach to the analysis of complex systems and decision processes. IEEE Trans. Man. Cybernetics, No.3 (1973) 28-44

19. Zadeh, L.A.: Fuzzy sets as a basis for a theory of possibility. Fuzzy Sets and Systems, vol.1 (1978) 3-28

20. Zadeh, L.A.: Fuzzy Logic = Computing with Words. IEEE Transactions on Fuzzy Systems, vol. 4, no. 2, May (1996) 103-111

5

LINGUISTIC AND IMPRECISE INFORMATION IN DATABASES AND INFORMATION SYSTEMS

Data Models for Dealing with Linguistic and Imprecise Information

Guoqing Chen

[1] Tsinghua University, School of Economics and Management, MIS Division, Beijing 100084, P. R. China

Abstract. *Data models play an important role in dealing with linguistic and imprecise information. This paper first describes fuzzy extensions to ER/EER concepts so that uncertainty and imprecision in data and semantics can be dealt with at a conceptual level. Fuzzy extensions to the concepts such as superclass/subclass, generalization/specialization, and shared subclass/category are discussed. The attribute inheritance is investigated in a fuzzy context, including multiple inheritance, selective inheritance, and the inheritance for derived attributes. Furthermore, certain constraints on relationships are explored in terms of the inheritance constraint, the participation constraint, and the cardinality constraint. At the (ordinary) data level, imprecision and uncertainty inherent in attribute values, database queries and integrity constraints are dealt with in fuzzy relational database models. The issues concerned center around fuzzy data representation and storage, data manipulation and extended algebraic operators, update anomalies, and information maintenance.*

1. Introduction

Management decision making and problem solving often involves uncertain and imprecise information in forms of linguistic terms. To represent and manipulate such information has been regarded as one of the basic characteristics of modern intelligent systems. Certain linguistic data/information can be dealt with from different perspectives within the frameworks of data models. For example, in various circumstances, managers may be concerned with (1) employees who are *young;* (2) the queries to find out the *most reliable* products; (3) the business rules such as "*close* performance levels lead to *close* salaries"; (4) the *degree* of relationship between the company and its suppliers; (5) the properties of a *specific* product (e.g., CAR) belonging to a *more general* product class (e.g., VEHICLE); etc.

In more technical terms, these management concerns are related to the following issues: (1) imprecise attribute values (e.g., AGE = "young"); (2) fuzzy queries with linguistic terms (e.g., most, reliable); (3) integrity constraints represented by fuzzy functional dependencies (e.g., Performance $\sim>$ Salary); (4) the entities that may be partially associated with each other (e.g., (Company, Supply, 0.9)); (5) attribute inheritance of a subclass (CAR) from its superclass (VEHICLE); etc.

These issues, along with many others, can be addressed by data models at two levels: namely, the conceptual level, and the (ordinary) data level. At the conceptual level, imprecision and uncertainty inherent in such concepts as entity, relationship, attribute, subclass/superclass, generalization/specialization, category, inheritance, participation, cardinality, etc., can be dealt with in fuzzy ER/EER models. At the data level, imprecision and uncertainty inherent in attribute values, integrity constraints, data dependencies, queries, etc., can be dealt with in fuzzy relational database models. These two kinds of models, as well as some interested issues, will be discussed in the following sections.

2. Fuzzy Conceptual Modeling

Since its inception by P.P. Chen (1976), the entity-relationship (ER) model has played an important role in the fields of database design, information systems analysis, and object orientation. During the past decades, a number of new concepts have also been introduced into the ER model by various researchers (e.g., see Scheuermann et al., 1979; Dos Santos et al., 1979; Teorey et al., 1986; Gogolla and Hohenstein 1991; Elmasri et al., 1985; etc.), giving rise to the notion of the enhanced (or extended) entity-relationship (EER) models. These efforts have largely enriched the usefulness and expressiveness of ER/EER as a conceptual model in many respects.

In 1985, Zvieli and Chen (1985) applied fuzzy set theory to some of the basic ER concepts. They introduced three levels of fuzziness in model building. The first level refers to the sets of semantic objects, resulting in fuzzy entity sets, fuzzy relationship sets and fuzzy attribute sets. The second level concerns the occurrences of entities and relationships. The third level is related to the fuzziness in attribute values. Consequently, fuzzy extension to Chen's ER algebra has been sketched. Ruspini (1986) has also worked on the extension of the ER model. In his work, attribute values can be fuzzy sets, and a truth value can be associated with each relationship instance. Additionally, some special relationships such as same-object, subset-of, member-of, etc. have also be introduced. In a different approach to fuzzy ER/EER extensions, Vandenberghe (1991) has applied Zadeh's extension principle to calculate the truth value of propositions. For each proposition, a possibility distribution is defined on the doubleton {true, false} of the classical truth values. In this way, the concepts such as entity, relationship and attribute as well as subclass, superclass, category, generalization and specialization, etc. have been extended.

In the following subsections, however, discussions will be based on a framework compatible with that of Zvieli and Chen's, and are to present a more complete picture of fuzzy extensions to ER/EER concepts. Primary attention will be paid to the fuzzification of the concepts at different levels of abstraction, as well as to the attribute inheritance including multiple inheritance, selective inheritance, and the inheritance for derived attributes. Moreover, constraints on relationships are explored in terms of the inheritance constraint, the participation constraint, and the cardinality constraint.

2.1. Basic Fuzzy ER/EER Concepts

The traditional ER model describes certain aspects of the real-world semantics in terms of entities, relationships, and attributes. Usually, entities, relationships and attributes are referred to as types and their values (or interchangeably as instances or occurrences). Each type may have a number of values. For example, Employee is an entity type, and J. Smith is a value of Employee. Conventionally, we use capital letters such as E, R and A to denote entity types, relationship types and attribute types, and small letters such as e, r, and a to denote their values. Thus, an ER model M can be expressed as $M = (\mathcal{E}, R, A)$ where $\mathcal{E} = \{E1, E2,...,Em\}$ is a set of entity types, $R = \{R1, R2,..., Rn\}$ is a set of relationship types between entity types, and $A = \{A_{\mathcal{E}}, A_R\}$ with $A_{\mathcal{E}}$ = the set of attribute types associated with entity type E and A_R = the set of attribute types associated with relationship type R.

In incorporating fuzziness into ER, three levels of fuzzy extensions could be considered. At the first level (model/type), the sets of $\mathcal{E}$, R, A_E, and A_R can all be fuzzy sets, reflecting possible partial belonging of the corresponding types to the ER model. That is, let $D_{\mathcal{E}}$ be the domain of $\mathcal{E}$ composed of all possible entity types concerned,

$\mathcal{E} = \{\mu_{\mathcal{E}}(E)/E \mid E \in D_{\mathcal{E}} \text{ and } \mu_{\mathcal{E}}(E) \in [0,1]\}$,

$R = \{\mu_R(R)/R \mid R \text{ is a relationship type involving entity}$
    types in $D_{\mathcal{E}}$ and $\mu_R(R) \in [0,1]\}$,

$A_E = \{\mu_{AE}(A)/A \mid A \text{ is an attribute type of entity type}$
    E, and $\mu_{AE}(A) \in [0,1]\}$,

$A_R = \{\mu_{AR}(A)/A \mid A \text{ is an attribute type of relationship}$
    type R, and $\mu_{AR}(A) \in [0,1]\}$,

where $\mu_{\mathcal{E}}$, μ_R, μ_{AE}, μ_{AR} are membership functions of $\mathcal{E}$, R, A_E, A_R, respectively. For example, in a fuzzy ER model, $\mathcal{E}$ may look like: $\mathcal{E} = \{1/\text{Employee}, 1/\text{Department}, 1/\text{Project}, 0.9/\text{Customer}, ...\}$.

The second level of fuzzy extensions is referred to as the level of type/value. For each entity type E and relationship type R, the sets of their values can be fuzzy sets, which reflects possible partial belonging of
the corresponding values to their types. That is,

$E = \{\mu_E(e)/e \mid e \text{ is an entity value of E}\}$,

$R = \{\mu_R(r)/r \mid r \text{ is an relationship value of R}\}$,

where $\mu_E(e)$ ($\mu_R(r)$) is the degree of e (r) belonging to E (R).

The third level of fuzzy extensions concerns with attributes and their values. For each attribute type A, any of its values can be a fuzzy set. In this way, the imprecision or partial knowledge about an attribute value v(A) could be represented. That is, let D_A be the domain of A,

$v(A) \in F(D_A) = \{ X \mid X \text{ is a fuzzy set of A on } D_A \}$.

As an example, suppose A = "Age", two values of A could be v1(A) = "young", v2(A) = {21,22} (i.e., 21 or 22 years).

In addition to fuzzy extensions of such ER concepts as entities, relationships and attributes, fuzzy extension of EER concepts can also be made, and centers around the notion of superclass/subclass. In a traditional EER model, if there exist two entity types E1 and E2 such that for any entity value e, e $\in$ E2 implies e $\in$ E1, then E2 is called a subclass of E1, and E1 is called a superclass of E2. Now consider the case where E1 and E2 are all fuzzy sets with membership functions μ_{E1} and μ_{E2} respectively, then superclass/subclass can be defined as follows: E1 is a superclass of

E2 and E2 is a subclass of E1 if and only if for any entity value e, $\mu_{E2}(e) \leq \mu_{E1}(e)$ (i.e., $E2 \subseteq E1$). An example is : E1 = Employee, and E2 = Secretary with $E2 \subseteq E1$.

A pair of EER concepts related to superclass/subclass is the dual concepts of generalization/specialization. Generalization is the process of defining a superclass from a number of entity types, and specialization is the process of defining a number of subclasses from an entity type, both by identifying their common properties (e.g., using predicates). For instance, entity types CAR and TRUCK may be grouped (generalized) into a single entity type VEHICLE according to their common characteristic as "transportation means". Symmetrically, VEHICLE may be split (specialized) into CAR and TRUCK according to "transportation means". Mathematically, a superclass E and a number of subclasses E1, E2,..., Es via generalization/specialization satisfy the relationship:

$E1 \cup E2 \cup ... \cup Es \subseteq E$ with $\max(\mu_{E1}(e),\mu_{E2}(e),...,\mu_{Es}(e)) \leq \mu_E(e)$ ($\forall e$).

In many cases the common characteristics or properties used are referenced to attributes to which conditions for a superclass/subclass apply. Now consider specialization (though generalization can be discussed in the same manner.), if all subclasses in a specialization have the condition on the same attribute of their superclass, the specialization is then called an attribute-defined specialization. For example, subclass Secretary (S) can be formed by specialization based on the attribute JobType of superclass Employee(E). In other words, an entity value e of Employee (E) with JobType = "secretary" will belong to subclass Secretary (S). Note here that since E can be a fuzzy set, and the values of JobType can also be fuzzy sets, then S will be generally a fuzzy set. That is,

$\mu_S(e) = \mu_E(e) \wedge \text{Truth}(A(e) = \text{"secretary"})$

where Truth(A(e) = "secretary") may be obtained by a closeness measure between fuzzy sets. If further considering the degree of membership A being an attribute type of entity type E, then one may have

$\mu_S(e) = \mu_E(e) \wedge \mu_{AE}(A) \wedge \text{Truth}(A(e) = \text{"secretary"})$.

In addition to generalization/specialization, another pair of EER concepts related to superclass/subclass consists of the concepts of shared subclass and category. A shared subclass is a subclass with more than one superclass. For example, subclass EngineerManager has two superclasses Engineer and Manager. A category is a subclass of the union of the superclasses with (different) entity types. For example, subclass VehicleOwner is a category with superclasses Person, Bank, and Company. Notably, an entity of a shared subclass must exist in **all** corresponding superclasses, while an entity of a category must exist in **at least one** of the corresponding superclasses. Thus, if e1 is an engineer manager, he must be both an engineer **and** a manager; if e2 is a vehicle owner, e2 must be a bank, a person, **or** a company. Mathematically, let E1, E2, ..., En be n superclasses, and F be a subclass, then

F is a shared subclass if $F \subseteq E1 \cap E2 \cap ... \cap En$, and

F is a category if $F \subseteq E1 \cup E2 \cup ... \cup En$.

In terms of membership functions, we may have:

for shared subclass, $\mu_F(e) \leq \min (\mu_{E1}(e), \mu_{E2}(e), ..., \mu_{En}(e))$, and

for category, $\mu_F(e) \leq \max (\mu_{E1}(e), \mu_{E2}(e), ..., \mu_{En}(e))$.

2.2. Inheritance of Attributes

The attribute inheritance is an important concept in ER/EER models. First, let us consider a kind of attribute (type) A whose values can be derived from the values of another attribute (type) B. Conventionally, such A is called a derived attribute, and B is called a stored attribute. In a fuzzy ER/EER model, if the values of a stored attribute are fuzzy, then the values of its derived attribute will also be fuzzy. For instance, if BirthDate is a stored attribute, then Age is a derived attribute. An imprecise value for BirthDate (e.g., "about 1975") will lead to an imprecise value for Age (e.g., "about 23"). Thus, the fuzziness in a stored attribute is inherited by its derived attribute. Specifically, let B be a stored attribute, A be a derived attribute, D_A, D_B be domains of A and B respectively, and f be a mapping from B to A, i.e., A(e) = f(B(e)) (the value of A for e is a function of the value of B for e), then for any y in D_A, y = f(x), x in D_B, $\mu_A(y) = \mu_B(x)$. That is, if given

$$B(e) = \{\mu_B(x)/x \mid x \in D_B \text{ and } \mu_B(x) \in [0,1]\}$$

then A(e) could be derived as follows:

$$A(e) = \{\mu_A(y)/y \mid y = f(x), \mu_A(y) = \mu_B(x)\}.$$

Next, let us consider the attribute inheritance for superclass/subclass. In the traditional EER, all attributes of a superclass will be inherited by each of its subclasses. Suppose E is a superclass with E1, E2,...,En being its subclasses, we have $A_E \subseteq A_{Ei}$, i.e., subclass Ei has all attributes of E plus the attributes of its own. In a fuzzy context, we have $\mu_{AE}(A) \leq \mu_{AEi}(A)$. In specialization, the fuzzy set A_{Ei} of attributes associated with the resultant subclass Ei is composed of the fuzzy set A_E of attributes inherited from the superclass E and the fuzzy set A_{Oi} of attributes associated with Ei as its own. That is,

$$A_{Ei} \equiv A_E \cup A_{Oi}.$$

For example, for Ei = Secretary, A_{Oi} may look like {(TypingSpeed, 1), (NumberOfLanguages, 0.9), ...}. If the superclass/subclass relationship can be represented as a hierarchy (e.g., a tree structure) in the model, the inheritance of attributes for a subclass can be traced back to the root.

Furthermore, consider the attribute inheritance in the case of shared subclasses, which then gives rise to the notion of multiple inheritance. For a shared subclass with multiple superclasses, each of superclass's attribute sets is inherited as the attributes of the subclass. Let F be a shared subclass of superclasses E1, E2,...,En, then

$$A_F = A_{E1} \cup A_{E2} \cup ... \cup A_{En} \cup A_{OF}$$

where A_F is the fuzzy set of attributes of shared subclass F, A_{Ei} is the fuzzy set of attributes of Ei, and A_{OF} is the fuzzy set of attributes associated with F as its own. Finally, consider another kind of inheritance, namely, selective inheritance, which is related to categories. A category inherits the attributes of its superclasses in a way that each category instance (value) selectively inherits all attributes of the superclass to which this category instance belongs. Let F be a category of superclasses E1, E2, ..., En, then $\forall e \in F$,

$$A_F(e) = (A_{Ej1}(e) \cup A_{Ej2}(e) \cup ... \cup A_{Ejm}(e)) \cup A_{OF}(e)$$

where $A_{Ejk}(e)$ is the fuzzy set of attributes of Ejk with $e \in Ejk$ (k=1,2,...m, and j1, j2,..., jm $\in$ {1,2,...n}).

2.3. Relationships and the Constraints

In this subsection, three kinds of constraints with respect to relationships will be discussed: namely, the inheritance constraint, the participation constraint, and the cardinality constraint. The inheritance constraint means that, in the case of subclass/superclass, an entity value e of a subclass inherits all relationship instances in which e has participated as a superclass entity. For example, consider a relationship type Course-Selection connecting two entity types Student and Course. Suppose there is a relationship instance (s1, c7, 0.9) for Course-Selection representing a 0.9-possibility that student s1 selects course c7. Now, Student has been specialized into two subclasses Undergraduate and Graduate. If s1 belongs to Graduate, according to the truth of predicate (StudentType = "graduate"), at a degree of 0.8, then (s1, c7, min(0.9, 0.8)) is inherited with s1. Generally, let R be a relationship type, $R: ExF \rightarrow [0,1]$, $(e_i, f_j, \mu_R(i,j))$ be a relationship instance of R with $\mu_R(i,j)$ being the degree of membership that $(e_i, f_j,)$ is compatible with R, and e_i be specialized into a subclass by predicate p, then e_i inherits the relationship between e_i and f_j with a degree of $\mu_R(i,j) \wedge \text{Truth}(p)$. In other words, e_i inherits $(e_i, f_j, \mu_R(i,j) \wedge \text{Truth}(p))$. Note that n-ary relationships may be extended similarly.

The participation constraint and the cardinality constraint are both related to the quantity (number) of entity instances of each participating entity type. Without loss of generality, we will only consider binary relationships in the following discussions. The participation constraint often refers to the completeness of participation. If every entity value of entity type E participates in the corresponding relationship R, then E is called totally participating in R. If there exists at least one entity value e of E such that e does not participates in R, then E is called partially participating in R. Now in a fuzzy context, total/partial participation may be extended as follows: Let R be a relationship type of entity types E and F, i.e., $R = \{(v, w, \alpha) \mid v \in E, w \in F, \text{and } \alpha \in [0,1]\}$, then E is called totally participating in R if $\forall e \in E$, we have
$e \in \{v \mid (v, w, \alpha) \in R \text{ and } \alpha > 0\}$.
E is called partially participating in R if $\exists e_0 \in E$ such that
$e_0 \notin \{v \mid (v, w, \alpha) \in R \text{ and } \alpha > 0\}$.

For example, if, according to the real-world semantics, every student must select at least one course, and some courses may be selected by nobody, then entity type Student totally participates in the relationship type Course-Selection, while entity type Course partially participates in Course-Selection.

Another constraint of concern for relationships is the cardinality constraint, which refers to the correspondence between the numbers of the related entities. A relationship R between entities E and F may have the cardinality of 1:1, 1:n, or n:m, meaning that
(1) one-to-one correspondence (1:1) - for each value e of E, there is at most one value of F corresponding to e, and vice versa;
(2) one-to-many correspondence (1:n) - for each value e of E, there may exist more than one value of F corresponding to e, and for each value f of F, there is at most one value of E corresponding to f;

(3) many-to-many correspondence (n:m) - for each value e of E, there may exist more than one value of F corresponding to e, and vice versa.

Sometimes it is possible or desirable to have and represent more information on the partial knowledge about the correspondence between related entities. For instance, in the cases of one-to-many and many-to-many correspondence, some information on the number of the "many" side may be represented. This may be done by using capital letters N or M to denote a fuzzy set (e.g., "about 40"). Accordingly, the cardinalities may be described as 1:N and N:M.

In addition, from the user's knowledge, expert's expertise, or the existing data, one may be able to obtain a pairwise correspondence between any particular e and f. When in the crisp case, the degree of correspondence is 0 or 1, while in the fuzzy case, the degree is a value in the interval $[0,1]$. For any e in E and any f in F, all such correspondences can be represented in a matrix, which is normally what R represents:

R:	f_1	f_2	...	f_m
e_1	r_{11}	r_{12}	...	r_{1m}
e_2	r_{21}	r_{22}	...	r_{2m}
...			...	
e_n	r_{n1}	r_{n2}	...	r_{nm}

where $E = \{e_1, e_2, ...e_n\}$, $F = \{f_1, f_2, ..., f_m\}$, and $r_{ij} \in [0,1]$. If there exists a row vector with all zero's, then a partial participation of E in R may be assumed. If there exists a column vector with all zero's then F partially participates in R. Moreover, in the case of 1:1 cardinality, each row i of the matrix can be viewed as a possibility distribution reflecting the possibility that any f_j corresponds to e_i. Similarly, each column can also be viewed as a possibility distribution reflecting the correspondence of E to F. Here by the possibility distribution we mean an excluding possibility distribution in which the domain elements are treated mutually exclusive. In the cases of 1:n and n:m, each row or column of R is not an (excluding) possibility distribution. Hence, if we have some more information on the possibilities that certain specific values of F correspond to a value of E (e.g., f_2 and f_3 correspond to e_1), this piece of information can hardly be represented by R. Instead, matrix $R^{(2)}$ may be introduced. For the cardinality of 1:n (from E to F), $R^{(2)} = R_{F|E}^{(2)}$ is to reflect the correspondence of F to E, where $R_{F|E}^{(2)}$ is a mapping from $Ex2^F$ to $[0,1]$. In the form of matrix,

$R_{F|E}^{(2)}$:	$\{f_1\}$	...	$\{f_m\}$	$\{f_1,f_2\}$	...	$\{f_1,..,f_m\}$
e_1		...			...	
e_2		...			...	
...		...		$r_{st}^{(2)}$	...	
e_n		...			...	

where $r_{st}^{(2)} \in [0,1]$, $s \in \{1,2,...,n\}$, and $t \in \{1,2,...,m, m+1,...,2^m\}$ with an (partial) ordering of the elements in 2^F. Each row i of the matrix is a (excluding) possibility distribution of the entity subsets of F corresponding to e_i. For the case of the n:m cardinality, both $R_{F|E}^{(2)}$ and $R_{E|F}^{(2)}$ may be used to represent the correspondences from both directions. It is worth mentioning that $R^{(2)}$ can also be used to represent the case of 1:1 with rows and columns of only singletons $\{e_i\}$ and $\{f_j\}$ $(i = 1, 2, ..., n; j = 1, 2, ...,m)$, i.e., $R^{(2)}$ $(R_{F|E}^{(2)}$ or $R_{E|F}^{(2)})$ degenerates to R in the case of 1:1 cardinality:

$R^{(2)}$:	$\{f_1\}$	$\{f_2\}$	...	$\{f_m\}$
$\{e_1\}$	r_{11}	r_{12}	...	r_{1m}
$\{e_2\}$	r_{21}	r_{22}	...	r_{2m}
...			...	
$\{e_n\}$	r_{n1}	r_{n2}	...	r_{nm}

Finally, it is important to notice that in many cases matrix $R^{(2)}$ $(R_{F|E}^{(2)}$ or $R_{E|F}^{(2)})$ may contain many cells whose values are zero, which means that $R^{(2)}$ $(R_{F|E}^{(2)}$ or $R_{E|F}^{(2)})$ may usually be a sparse matrix.

2.4. Fuzzy ER/EER Manipulation

As most of fuzzy ER/EER concepts are defined in terms of fuzzy sets or linguistic terms, they could be manipulated via fuzzy set operations (e.g., $\cup$, $\cap$, $\times$, ...). As a matter of fact, many fuzzy EER concepts discussed in previous subsections are defined based upon fuzzy set operations (e.g., subclass/superclass, specialization/generalization, category, inheritance, etc.). Currently, we are working on fuzzy extensions of ER/EER algebra, towards a fuzzy ER/EER manipulation language.

3. Fuzzy Database Models

The inception of fuzzy relational database models could be dated back to the early 1980's where Codd's model (Codd, 1970) was extended in various ways (Buckles and Petry, 1982; Prade and Testemale, 1983; Umano, 1983; Baldwin and Zhou, 1984). From the perspective of fuzzy data representation, three frameworks could be categorized (Kerre and Chen, 1995), namely, the similarity-based framework, the fuzzy-relation-based framework, and the possibility-based framework. In the following subsections, discussions will center around the roles that database models play in dealing with imprecise information represented by possibility distributions including linguistic terms. Primary attention will be paid to three respects, namely, imprecise attribute values, fuzzy data manipulation, and integrity constraints.

3.1. Imprecise Attribute Values

In relational databases where attributes are grouped into relation schemes, data are represented and stored as attribute values. Normally, it is implicitly assumed that any attribute value must be a single element of its domain. For instance, if attribute Age takes values from a domain [0, 200], then a value e assigned to Age must have e $\in$ [0, 200]. That is, Age = e. An example would be Age = 21. However, this assumption is relaxed when attribute values can be imprecise. For instance, in some cases, one's age may not be completely known, but partially known, such as "21 or 22 years", "young", 'middle-aged", or something represented by a possibility distribution. Generally, a n-tuple t in a database table may be of the form: $t(\pi_{A1}, \pi_{A2}, ..., \pi_{An})$, where π_{Ai}, as a value of attribute A_i, is a possibility distribution. In a customer database, for example, a table C with three tuples may look like the following:

C	Name	Sex	Age	Hair-color	Height
t1	J.S.	M	30	brown	175
t2	G.B.	M	{25,26}	dark-colored	185
t3	M.K.	F	middle-aged	black	{0.6/175, 0.8/177, 1.0/180, 0.8/183, 0.6/185}

tuple t1 has all attribute values which are precise, while tuples t2 and t3 contain imprecise attribute values such as "25 or 26 years", "dark-colored", "middle-aged", and {0.6/175, 0.8/177, 1.0/180, 0.8/183, 0.6/185}.

Since imprecise data now appear as attribute values, any two of attribute values are treated as being close to each other rather than being either identical or distinct. There are a number of ways to measure such kind of data closeness. For example, data closeness of two possibility distributions π_1 and π_2 may be measured based on the "height of $\pi_1 \cap \pi_2$":

$$\sup_{x} \min (\pi_1(x), \pi_2(x))$$

or based on the "distance" between π_1 and π_2:

$$\inf_{x} (1-| \pi_1(x) - \pi_2(x)|)$$

A more detailed discussion on data closeness can be found in Chen, Vandenbulcke and Kerre 1992.

Now consider how imprecise data could be represented and stored in database systems. Notably, although the standard and commercial products of fuzzy relational database management systems (FRDBMS) are still to emerge, one of the important components of the FRDBMS architecture is thought of to be data dictionary that stores "metadata" about the database (e.g., tables, elements, structures, relationships, etc.) as well as about anything related to fuzziness in the model (e.g., definitions, membership functions, fuzzy constraints, etc.). Recently, a general-purpose system called IFRDB was prototyped to support DBF-like database applications, allowing fuzzy data (e.g., fuzzy sets, linguistic terms, etc.) to be stored, fuzzy queries to be formulated, and fuzzy integrity constraints to be specified and then enforced (Chen and Kerre 1997). In IFRDB, attribute values can be linguistic terms such as "dark-colored", "middle-aged", or labels such as FS1 and FS2 representing the particular fuzzy data, where FS1= {1.0/25, 1.0/26}, and FS2 = {0.6/175, 0.8/177, 1.0/180, 0.8/183, 0.6/185}. Accordingly, the customer relation C may be realized as the following database file (i.e., table R1):

R1

Name	Sex	Age	Hair-color	Height
J.S.	N	30	brown	175
G.B.	M	FS1	dark-colored	185
M.K.	F	middle-aged	black	FS2

with the corresponding records in a data dictionary file (CD):

CD

TABLE	FIELD	ITEM	POINTER
R1	Age	FS1	a
R1	Age	middle-aged	b
R1	Hair-color	dark-colored	c
R1	Height	FS2	d

where TABLE is the name of entity database file, FIELD is the field/attribute name, ITEM is the name of fuzzy data appearing as an attribute value, and a, b, c d are labels or addresses for the definitions of FS1, "middle-aged", "dark-colored" and FS2 respectively. For example, at a: FS1 = {1.0/25, 1.0/26}, at b: "middle-aged" = trapezoidal (25, 35, 45, 55), at c: "dark-colored" = {0.7/brown, 0.9/red, 1.0/black}, and at d: FS2 = {0.6/175, 0.8/177, 1.0/180, 0.8/183, 0.6/185}.

3.2. Fuzzy Data Manipulation

Once a fuzzy database has been populates (e.g., via data entry, file import and transfer), data manipulation often deals with database queries and information maintenance. A database query is a request for retrieving interested information upon given criteria. If a query is formulated with fuzzy terms (e.g., linguistic terms, fuzzy conditions, etc.), it is usually referred to as a fuzzy query, regardless of the "nature" (i.e., fuzzy or crisp) of the data in the database. As precise data is a special case of fuzzy data, the evaluation of a fuzzy query can generally be carried out under the framework of fuzzy set and possibility theory.

Research on fuzzy queries has revealed two streams of efforts. One is to build interface systems or query languages to facilitate queries with fuzzy terms (Buckles and Petry 1982; Anvari and Rose 1984; Zemankova and Kandle 1984; Kacprzyk and Ziolkowski 1986; Kerre et al. 1986; Bosc and Pivert 1991; Yager 1988; Kacprzyk and Zadrozny 1994; Chen and Kerre 1997). For instance, In SQLf of Bosc and Pivert (1991), and in FQUERY for Access of Kacprzyk and Zadrozny (1994), users may issue queries that could be equivalently formulated in SQL:

> Select <list of fields>
> From <list of tables>
> Where <fuzzy conditions>

Logical operators AND and OR, and linguistic quantifiers (e.g., most, few, etc.) have also been incorporated in various ways. The other stream of efforts on fuzzy queries is to extend relational algebra (or calculus) to facilitate the manipulation of fuzzy elements (linguistic terms, fuzzy sets, etc.) (Buckles and Petry 1982; Prade and Testemale 1983; Yager 1991; Bosc and Pivert 1991; Chen, Kerre and Vandenbulcke 1993). Recall that, in classical databases, relational algebra serves as a foundation for a query language, and that a query language is called complete if it supports all the operations that can be performed by relational algebra (e.g., $\cap, \cup, \times, \div, -, \sigma, \Pi, *$). However, when attribute values are imprecise, fuzzy extensions of the classical relational algebra are inevitably necessary. For illustrative purposes, the following are some of the extended algebraic operators (Chen, Kerre and Vandenbulcke 1993):

Eight algebraic operators, namely, product($\times$), union($\cup$), intersection($\cap$), natural join($*$), projection(Π), selection(σ), minus(-) and division($\div$), are considered.

(i) $R \times S = \{ (\pi_{Ai1}, \pi_{Ai2},...,\pi_{Ain}, \pi_{Aj1}, \pi_{Aj2},...,\pi_{Ajm}) \mid (\pi_{Ai1}, \pi_{Ai2},...,\pi_{Ain}) \in R$ and $(\pi_{Aj1}, \pi_{Aj2},...,\pi_{Ajm}) \in S \}$.

(ii) $R \cup S = \{ (\pi_{A1}, \pi_{A2},...,\pi_{An}) \mid (\pi_{A1}, \pi_{A2},...,\pi_{An}) \in R$ or $(\pi_{A1}, \pi_{A2},...,\pi_{An}) \in S \}$.

(iii) $R \cap S = \{ (\pi''_{A1}, \pi''_{A2},...,\pi''_{An}) \mid r=(\pi_{A1}, \pi_{A2},...,\pi_{An}) \in R$ and $s=(\pi'_{A1}, \pi'_{A2},...,\pi'_{An}) \in S$ and $E_c(r,s) \geq \lambda$ and $\pi''_{Ai} = \pi_{Ai} \cup_F \pi'_{Ai}, i=1,2,...,n \}$. Note that here $R \cap S$ contains not only the common tuples in R and S but also the merging of the close tuples between R and S according to the closeness measure $E_c(r,s)$ and given threshold λ.

(iv) $R * S = \{t=(\pi_{A1},...,\pi_{AK-1},\pi_{AK},...,\pi_{An},\pi_{An+1},...,\pi_{Am}) \mid r$ in R and s in S and $E_c(r(D_K...D_n), s(D_K...D_n)) \geq \lambda$ and $t(D_1...D_{K-1}) = r(D_1...D_{K-1})$ and $t(D_j) = r(D_j) \cup_F s(D_j)$ for $j=k, ...,n$, and $t(D_{n+1}...D_m) = s((D_{n+1}...D_m) \}$. The join is performed not only on the common elements of R and S but also on the close elements of R and S. To form a tuple, close elements are merged by $\cup_F$.

(v) $\Pi_{Ai1...Aik}(R) = \{ (\pi_{Ai1}, \pi_{Ai2},..., \pi_{Aik}) \mid (\pi_{A1}, \pi_{A2},..., \pi_{An}) \in R, i_1, i_2,..., i_k \in \{1, 2,...,n \} \}$

(vi) Let P(t) be a single or composite predicate regarding the (components of) tuple t in R, and θ be a collection of comparison operators used in evaluating the truth value of P(t), such as E_c, $\cup_F$, arithmetic operators, etc. Then $\sigma_{P(t)|\theta}(R) = \{ t=(\pi_{A1}, \pi_{A2},..., \pi_{An}) \mid t \in R$ and $P(t)|_\theta \geq \lambda \}$.

(vii) $R-S = \{ r=(\pi_{A1}, \pi_{A2},..., \pi_{An}) \mid r \in R$ and $\neg(\exists s)(s \in S$ and $E_c(s,r) \geq \lambda) \}$. A tuple r in R belonging to R-S means that there does not exist any s in S such that s is close to r to a degree $\geq \lambda$.

(viii) $R \div S = \{ t=(\pi_{A1}, \pi_{A2},..., \pi_{Ak-1}) \mid t=r(D_1...D_{k-1})$ and $r \in R$ and $(\forall w)(\exists v)(w \in \Pi_{Ak...An}(S)$ and $v \in tR$ and $E_c(w,v) \geq \lambda) \}$. It is worth mentioning that $R \div S$ is an extension of the following: $\{ t \mid t=r(D_1...D_{k-1})$ and $r \in R$ and $\Pi_{Ak...An}(S) \subseteq tR \}$.

In addition to databases queries, information maintenance is also closely related to data manipulation. When there is a need for the database update by inserting, deleting and modifying some data in the database, which may happen frequently in real applications, three issues are worth considering. First, it is important to know whether or not the integrity constraints are not violated after the update. Particularly, a sort of constraints on attributes, expressed by fuzzy functional dependencies (FFDs), is usually desirable to be enforced. Second, it has been indicated (Chen, Kerre and Vandenbulcke, 1994b) that, in analogue to conventional databases, a fuzzy relational database may also suffer from the so-called update anomaly problem. Importantly, whether an attribute should be placed together with another attribute in a database scheme is a matter that has a serious impact on the existence of update anomalies. Third, for certain reasons, a database scheme may need to be decomposed into "simpler" schemes via projection (Π), and may also need to be recovered via join (*). This leads to the concerns for the possible information loss, where the information means both the data itself in the database and the semantic knowledge about the data. As a matter of fact, these three issues are all related to the notion of fuzzy functional dependencies, and will be discussed in detail in the next subsection.

3.3 Fuzzy Functional Dependencies as Integrity Constraints

As functional dependency (FD) is an important notion of nowadays database technology, its fuzzy extension has attracted more and more attention, especially since the late 1980's (Buckles and Petry, 1982; Prade and Testemale, 1983; Zemankova and Kandel, 1984; Raju and Majumdar, 1988; Kiss, 1990; Chen, Kerre and Vandenbulcke, 1991,1994a,1995a,1995b,1996a; Cubero and Vila, 1994; Dubios and Prade, 1992; Liu,1992). Hence, different definitions of fuzzy functional dependencies (FFDs) emerged, resulting from the application of fuzzy logic to the conventional FD in various manners, and to different extents.

Recall the classical FD: $X \rightarrow Y \Leftrightarrow \forall$ t, t' $\in$ R, if t(X)=t'(X) then t(Y)=t'(Y) where X and Y are two sets of attributes, t and t' are two tuples of a relation R. It says that equal X-values imply equal Y-values. In other words, $X \rightarrow Y$ means that equal Y-values correspond to equal X-values. Now considering the extended possibility-based framework of data representation in that possibility distributions can appear as attribute values and closeness relations can be associated with domain elements, the definition of FD can be extended using fuzzy implication operators (FIOs) I: $X \rightarrow_\theta Y$ $\Leftrightarrow$ I(t(X)$\approx$t'(X), t(Y)$\approx$t'(Y)) $\geq \theta$, where I: $[0,1] \times [0,1] \rightarrow [0,1]$, $\theta \in [0,1]$, and $\approx$ is a closeness relation (reflexive and symmetric) (Chen, Kerre and Vandenbulcke, 1991). This is a general form of fuzzy functional dependency, which expresses the semantics that close Y-values correspond to close X-values (to the degree θ). Choosing a particular FIO for I would lead to a specific form of FFD.

For example, with Gödel implication operator Ig (Ig(a, b)=1 if a$\leq$b; Ig(a, b)=b if a>b), $X \rightarrow_\theta Y$ means that (a) close Y-values correspond to close X-values, and (b) the degree of Y-values' closeness is at least the degree of X-values' closeness or at least θ. With Gödel implication operator Ig and the classical implication operator Ic, $X \rightarrow_\theta Y$ means that (a) identical Y-values correspond to identical X-values, (b) close Y-values correspond to close X-values, and (c) the degree of Y-values' closeness is at least the degree of X-values' closeness or at least θ. With the Standard Strict implication operator Is (Is(a, b)=1 if a$\leq$b; Is(a, b)=0 if a>b), $X \rightarrow_\theta Y$ means that (a) close Y-values correspond to close X-values, and (b) the degree of Y-values' closeness is at least the degree of X-values' closeness. With the Standard Sharp implication operator $I_\sqcap(I_\sqcap$(a, b) = 1 if a < 1 or b = 1; $I_\sqcap$(a, b) = 0 elsewhere), $X \rightarrow_\theta Y$ means that (a) close Y-values may correspond to close X-values, and (b) the degree of X-values' closeness is less that 1 (not totally close) or the degree of Y-values' closeness is 1 (totally close).

Like the conventional databases, it is desirable and important to have a FFD inference system that is both sound and complete. Therefore, the 3 well-known Armstrong's axioms have been extended accordingly:

A1': if $Y \subseteq X$, then $X \to_\theta Y$ for all θ.

A2': if $X \to_\theta Y$, then $XZ \to_\theta YZ$

A3': if $X \to_\alpha Y$ and $Y \to_\beta Z$, then $X \to_\chi Z$ with $\chi = \min(\alpha,\beta)$

Moreover, these extended Armstrong's axioms as a whole are both sound and complete. This result "equates" F^+ (= the set of FFDs logically implied by a pre-given FFD set F) and F^A (= the set of FFDs derived from F using the axioms) (Chen et al., 1991, 1994a), and is deemed as a fundamental step towards the use of FFDs in fuzzy databases and towards the theory of fuzzy database design. In the following discussions, for the purpose of convenience, we will use F^+ and F^A interchangeably.

3.3.1. Business Rules and Integrity Constraints

Databases constitute one of the main components of a modern information system (management information system, decision support system, office automation system, expert system, etc.). When modeling the real world, the conditions and constraints regarding an object's static aspects (object identity, attributes, relationships, etc.) and its dynamic aspects (processes, behavior, actions, events, etc.) are often referred to as the so-called business rules. These business rules reflect certain semantics of the problem, the nature of the behavior, the characteristics of the entities, the rules of the game, the status of the events, and/or the existent relationships, etc., therefore are usually desirable to be enforced. Particularly, FFDs are a sort of integrity constraints between the attributes (values) of objects, such as "identical names imply identical ages", "close salaries correspond to close performance levels", and so on. The enforcement of FFDs in a fuzzy relational database system may be realized by verifying the FFD specification against the data in the fuzzy database when the fuzzy database is populated (e.g., data entry, import, and file transfer.) or maintained (e.g., deletion, insertion, and modification).

In addition, FFDs, when their inference system is both sound and complete, can be used to define relation keys (θ-keys) in fuzzy databases (Chen, Kerre and Vandenbulcke, 1996b). For example, let us consider a specific form of FFD as defined using I_g and I_c. First, full FFDs can be defined as follows: $X \to_\theta Y$ *fully*: $X \to_\theta Y$ and there does not exist a subset X' of X ($X' \subset X$, $X' \ne \varnothing$) such that $X' \to_\theta Y$. Then, we will have relation keys in fuzzy terms: *θ-key (θ-candidate-key/θ-primary-key)* K: $K \to_\theta U \in F^+$ and $K \to_\theta U$ fully. *θ-superkey* S: S contains an θ-key. Here F^+ is the set of all FFDs logically implied by F. Notably, since FFD axioms together are proven to be both sound and complete, $F^+ = F^A \equiv$ the set of all FFDs that are inferred from F using the axioms. Furthermore, for $R(U)$ and $R'(U')$, we have *θ-foreign-key* K: $K \subseteq U$, K is not an θ-key of R but an θ-key of R'.

In fuzzy databases where fuzzy data appear as attribute values, the determination of an θ-key K can be described in terms of FFDs. That is, for every θ-key value t(K), there exists only one value of A_i, $t(A_i)$, corresponding to t(K). For any relation instance, $K \to_\theta A_i$ expresses the following: (a) for t(K), the corresponding $t(A_i)$ can be precisely known (a single element of D_i) or totally unknown (null), or anything in between (e.g., a possibility distribution on D_i). (b) *identical* A_i-values should correspond to *identical* K-values. (c) *close* A_i-values should correspond to *close* K-values. In addition, if two K-values are close, the corresponding A_i-values are also close to at least the same degree, or otherwise to at least the degree θ.

There are two kinds of integrity constraints which are related to the concepts of relation keys. One is called the entity integrity rule (EIR), whose fuzzy extension deals with the allowance of imprecise values for θ-keys. The other is called the referential integrity rule (RIR), whose fuzzy extension deals with the "matching" of the θ-foreign-key values with those in the corresponding parent relations.

3.3.2 Update Anomaly Avoidance

Update anomalies are undesirable consequences of database updates (insertion, deletion and modification) that updating a piece of data depends on the existence of another piece of data. For instance, an addition anomaly may result in the situation in that a newly enrolled student cannot have his biographic data recorded into the database until one day he starts to select some courses. This is due to the information "mix-up" (biographic data vs. course-selection data) in a single scheme.

There are two types of attribute relationships considered responsible for update anomalies. One is the partial functional dependency between attributes, and the other is the transitive functional dependency between attributes. In terms of FFDs, Y is called partially functionally dependent on X to the degree θ, denoted by $X \rightarrow_\theta Y$ partially, if and only if $X \rightarrow_\theta Y$ and there exists $X' \subset X$, $X' \neq \varnothing$, such that $X' \rightarrow_\theta Y$. Moreover, Z is called transitively functionally dependent on X to the degree θ, denoted by $X \rightarrow_\theta Z$ transitively, if and only if $X \rightarrow_\alpha Y$, $Y \rightarrow_\beta Z$ and $\min(\alpha, \beta) \geq \theta$.

Update anomalies due to partial/transitive FFDs can be avoided if the relation schemes conform to certain restrictions on attributes, namely, fuzzy normal forms (F1NF, F2NF, F3NF. FBCNF) (Chen, Kerre and Vandenbulcke, 1996a,1996c). More concretely, the restriction placed on F1NF is to obtain simple and plain relations and to avoid repeating groups. The restriction placed on the attributes of **R** in θ-F2NF disallows partial FFDs of θ-nonprime attributes on θ-keys. Further, the restriction placed on the attributes of **R** in θ-F3NF disallows partial and transitive FFDs of θ-nonprime attributes on θ-keys. Even further, the restriction placed on the attributes of **R** in θ-FBCNF disallows partial and transitive FFDs of θ-nonprime attributes on θ-keys, and disallows partial and transitive FFDs of θ-prime attributes on those θ-keys not containing them. In this way, update anomalies due to partial and transitive FFDs can be avoided by designing the schemes in corresponding fuzzy normal forms. That is, in fuzzy databases, fuzzy normal forms can be used to serve as guidelines for the scheme design such that undesired consequences (update anomalies) do not occur.

Usually, certain fuzzy normal forms can be obtained through scheme decomposition. That is, a scheme can be decomposed into a number of "simpler" schemes each of which is in a certain fuzzy normal form and free of partial or transitive FFDs. However, this is not sufficient. A proper design should also ensure that the information attached with the original scheme is maintained with the "simpler" schemes. This means that (i) the data with the original scheme can be recovered from the data with those "simpler" schemes; and (ii) the given FFDs with the original scheme can be preserved by the FFDs with those "simpler" schemes. These two aspects of information maintenance are usually referred to as the lossless-join property and the dependency-preserving property. It is desirable for a scheme decomposition to possess these properties while eliminating partial / transitive FFDs. Corresponding algorithms have been developed to obtain scheme decompositions into F3NFs with the dependency-preserving property, into F3NFs with both dependency-preserving and lossless-join properties, and into FBCNFs with the lossless-join property (Chen, Kerre and Vandenbulcke, 1996a,1996c).

3.3.3 Information Maintenance

As mentioned in the previous subsection, information maintenance has two aspects of concern. In this subsection, the FFD-preservation aspect will be discussed in some detail. The treatments of the lossless-join aspect can be found in Raju and Majumdar 1988; Kiss 1990; Chen, Kerre and Vandenbulcke 1993.

Usually, a scheme is associated with a set of FFDs. These FFDs are semantic knowledge and therefore desirable to be preserved. The preservation of FFDs in fuzzy databases is twofold. First, it refers to the preservation of FFDs associated with the original scheme ($\mathbf{R}$); second, it refers to the preservation of FFDs associated with the decomposed schemes ($\mathbf{R_i}$). Here a FFD being associated with the original scheme $\mathbf{R}$ means that this FFD either belongs to the pre-given FFD set, F, for the scheme $\mathbf{R}$ or is derivable from F using the extended Armstrong axioms. A FFD being associated with a "simple" scheme $\mathbf{R_i}$ means that this FFD either belongs to a subset of F with respect to $\mathbf{R_i}$, or is both derivable from F using the axioms and with respect to $\mathbf{R_i}$. These two respects of FFD preservation will be discussed in the following subsections respectively.

(a) Preservation of FFDs: the original scheme (R)

Similarly to the case of conventional databases, the preservation of FFDs means that when for certain reasons a scheme is decomposed into a number of "simpler" schemes, the FFDs derived from the union of the FFDs associated with each "simpler" scheme, using the extended Armstrong's axioms (A1', A2', A3'), should contain the FFDs associated with the original scheme. Symbolically, let F^A be the set of FFDs derived from F using the axioms, the preservation of FFDs for a decomposition $\rho = (\mathbf{R_1}, \mathbf{R_2}, ... \mathbf{R_k})$ means that $F^A = G^A$ where $G = \Pi_{R1}(F) \cup \Pi_{R2}(F) \cup...\cup \Pi_{Rk}(F)$, with $\Pi_{Ri}(F) = \{V\rightarrow_\alpha W \mid V\rightarrow_\alpha W$ in F^A and VW in $\mathbf{R_i}\}$. Such a decomposition is then called a dependency-preserving decomposition with respect to F.

Very often, a scheme needs to be decomposed to resolve possible data redundancy and update anomaly problems. However, not all decompositions are dependency-preserving. A decomposition, which leads to $G^A \subset F^A$, is usually not desirable because certain "information loss" (e.g., loss of some semantic knowledge-FFDs) occurs.

Example 1. Assume we have a scheme $R(A,B,C,D)$ and a given set of FFDs F = $\{A\rightarrow_{0.8}B, B\rightarrow_{0.9}C, C\rightarrow_{0.9}D, A\rightarrow_{0.9}D \}$. Now consider a decomposition: ρ = $\{ R_1(A,B), R_2(B,C), R_3(C,D)\}$. Then $A\rightarrow_{0.8}B$ in $\Pi_{R1}(F)$, $B\rightarrow_{0.9}C$ in $\Pi_{R2}(F)$, $C\rightarrow_{0.9}D$ in $\Pi_{R3}(F)$, and $A\rightarrow_{0.8}D$ can be derived from G = $\Pi_{R1}(F)\cup\Pi_{R2}(F)\cup \Pi_{R3}(F)$. But $A\rightarrow_{0.9}D$ $\notin G^A$. That is to say that ρ does not preserve all FFDs associated with **R** (i.e., $A\rightarrow_{0.9}D \in F \subseteq F^A$, but $A\rightarrow_{0.9}D \notin G^A$). $\square$

In order to tell whether or not any scheme decomposition is dependency-preserving, a testing algorithm (algorithm 1) has then been developed (Chen et al., 1995b). This is done by computing X^+_G for the left side X of each FFD in F where X^+_G is the transitive closure of X with respect to G. Notably, there is a computational algorithm for obtaining the FFD closure (Chen et al., 1994a).

Algorithm 1. Input: the scheme **R**, the decomposition of **R**: ρ = $\{ R_1, R_2,...,R_k\}$, and the FFD set F for **R**. Output: a decision to tell whether ρ is a dependency-preserving decomposition.

Method:

(1) Compute X^+_G if $X=X_1X_2...X_m$ is the left side of a FFD in F:

$Z = \{ (X_1,1), (X_2,1),..., (X_m,1) \}$

While changes to Z occur do   // do one pass //

  for i = 1 to k do

    begin

      $T_i = \{ (A,\phi) | (A,\phi) \in (Z_{Ri})^+_F$ and $A \in R_i\}$

      $Z = Z \cup_F T_i$ // U_i-operation //

    end

where $Z_{Ri} = \{ A | (A,\phi) \in Z$ and $A \in R_i\}$ is the set of those attributes which are both in Z and in R_i, $(Z_{Ri})^+_F$ is the transitive closure of Z_{Ri} with respect to F. Each time, $(Z_{Ri})^+_F$ is computed by starting with $\{ (A,\phi) | (A,\phi) \in Z$ and $A \in R_i\}$.

(2) If for every $X\rightarrow_\phi Y$ in F, $X=X_1X_2...X_m$, $Y=Y_1Y_2...Y_r$, we have (Y_i,ϕ) in X^+_G (i=1,2,...,r), then ρ is dependency-preserving, otherwise, ρ is not dependency-preserving. $\square$

Check example 1 with algorithm 1. For $A\rightarrow_{0.9}D$, the initial Z = $\{(A,1)\}$, and after AB-operation, Z = $\{(A,1), (B, 0.8)\}$, after BC-operation, Z = $\{(A,1), (B, 0.8), (C,0.8)\}$, after CD-operation, Z = $\{(A,1), (B, 0.8), (C,0.8), (D,0.8)\}$. As there is no further changes made to Z, the algorithm ends up with Z = $\{(A,1), (B, 0.8), (C,0.8), (D,0.8)\}$, which means that $A\rightarrow_{0.8}D$ is preserved but $A\rightarrow_{0.9}D$ is not preserved. It is worth mentioning, however, that if we have a decomposition ρ' = $\{ R_1(A,B), R_2(B,C), R_3(C,D), R_4(A,D)\}$ then all the FFDs associated with **R** will be preserved..

In fact, we could always obtain a dependency-preserving decomposition ρ by forming a $R_i(X,A)$ in ρ for each $X\rightarrow_\theta A$ in F. Without loss of generality, assume that F contains k FFDs, denoted as FFD_1, FFD_2, ..., FFD_k, and that all attributes in **R** are involved in F, then each FFD_i will lead to a scheme R_i in ρ , i.e., $\rho = \{R_1, R_2,..., R_k\}$.

It can be easily seen that since $\Pi_{Ri}(F) \supseteq FFD_i$ then $G \supseteq F$ and ρ is a dependency-preserving decomposition with respect to F.

(b) Preservation of FFDs: the decomposed "simpler" schemes (R_i)

In many cases, one may like to decompose an original scheme R into simpler schemes R_1, R_2,..., R_k , each of which is formed as $R_i(X,A)$ for each $X \rightarrow_\theta A$ in F. One reason for doing so is that such a decomposition ρ = $\{R_1, R_2,..., R_k\}$ is dependency-preserving with respect to F. Another reason is that each $R_i(X,A)$ obtained as such is in so-called fuzzy third normal form (θ-F3NF). Like its crisp counterpart, fuzzy third normal form disallows certain partial/transitive FFDs between attributes, therefore avoids certain data redundancy and update anomaly problems (Chen et al., 1996a).

However, R_i being in θ-F3NF is only with respect to a set of FFDs. That is, there is a set of FFDs associated with R_i. Apparently, this set is a subset of $\Pi_{Ri}(F)$. Furthermore, it has been proven that this set equals $\Pi_{Ri}(F)|_\theta = \{V \rightarrow_\alpha W \mid V \rightarrow_\alpha W$ in F^A and VW in R_i and $\alpha \geq \theta\} \subseteq \{V \rightarrow_\alpha W \mid V \rightarrow_\alpha W$ in F^A and VW in $R_i\}$ = $\Pi_{Ri}(F)$ (Chen et al., 1996a). In other words, the FFDs preserved for each R_i being in θ-F3NF are those FFDs in $\Pi_{Ri}(F)$ with the degree of each FFD (α) being at least θ. Now, a question may arise: can all FFDs in $\Pi_{Ri}(F)$ be preserved for the θ-F3NF R_i? The answer is "it depends". It depends on whether the given FFD set F is "partial-FFD-free".

Example 2. Let $R(A,B,C,D,E)$, $F=\{CD \rightarrow_\theta A, CD \rightarrow_\theta B, AD \rightarrow_\phi E, CD \rightarrow_\theta E, A \rightarrow_\alpha B, B \rightarrow_\beta E\}$, and ϕ > $\min(\alpha,\beta)$. The decomposition ρ = $\{R_1(C,D,A), R_2(C,D,B), R_3(A,D,E), R_4(C,D,E), R_5(A,B), R_6(B,E)\}$ leads to R_1, R_2, R_4, R_5, R_6, all in F3NF with the FFD set $\Pi_{Ri}(F)$, i = 1,2,4,5,6. But, $R_3(A,D,E)$ is in ϕ-F3NF with the FFD set $\Pi_{R3}(F)|_\phi$, not with $\Pi_{Ri}(F)$, because otherwise R_3 will not be in ϕ-F3NF due to $A \rightarrow_{\min(\alpha,\beta)} E \in \Pi_{Ri}(F)$. □

The problem as with R_3 in example 2 is caused by the existence of some $X' \rightarrow_\alpha A$ in F^A for some $X \rightarrow_\theta A$ in F such that $X' \subset X$ and $\alpha < \theta$. A FFD is called "partial-FFD-free" if such $X' \rightarrow_\alpha A$ does not exist. The given set F is called "partial-FFD-free" if every FFD in F is "partial-FFD-free". If F is "partial-FFD-free", then all FFDs in $\Pi_{Ri}(F)$ will be preserved to associate with the F3NF R_i.

In order to tell whether a give F is "partial-FFD-free", a computational testing algorithm is developed as follows.

Algorithm 2. Input: a given FFD set F. Output: Yes = F is "partial-FFD-free"; No = F is not "partial-FFD-free".

Method:

(1) for every FFD, $X \rightarrow_\phi Y$, in F and $Y = A_1 A_2 ... A_k$, then F = $(F \cup \{X \rightarrow_\phi Aj \mid j=1,2,...,k\}) - \{X \rightarrow_\phi Y\}$.

(2) for every FFD, $X \rightarrow_\alpha A$, in F, if (A,β) in X^+_F and $\beta > \alpha$, then F = F − $\{X \rightarrow_\alpha A\}$.

(3) for every FFD, $X \rightarrow_\alpha A$, in F, if (A,α) in X^+_G where G = F − $\{X \rightarrow_\alpha A\}$,

then $F = F - \{ X \rightarrow_\alpha A \}$.

(4) for every FFD, $X \rightarrow_\alpha A$, in F, and $X = B_1 B_2 ... B_m$ ($m \geq 2$), check each B_i ($i=1,2,...m$): if (A,α) in $(X - B_i)^+_F$ then $F = (F \cup \{(X - B_i) \rightarrow_\alpha A\}) - \{ X \rightarrow_\alpha A \}$.

(5) for every FFD, $X \rightarrow_\alpha A$, in F, and $X = B_1 B_2 ... B_m$ ($m \geq 2$), check each B_i ($i=1,2,...m$): if (A,β) in $(X - B_i)^+_F$ and $\beta > 0$ then goto (7).

(6) output "Yes", and stop.

(7) output "No", and stop. □

In fact, steps (1)-(4) result in a so-called minimal set of F. The efficiency of the algorithm is dominated by steps (4) and (5), which have the same level of computational complexity. Now without loss of generality, consider step (5): let $n = |R|$, and $m = |F|$, and $T = \max(n,m)$. The maximal number of iterations is $m \times n$, and for $X^+_F = \{(A,\alpha) \mid A$ in R and $\alpha = \sup\{\beta \mid X \rightarrow_\beta A$ in $F^+\}\}$, maximally, $X^+_F \sim o(T^3)$ according to the closure algorithm in (Chen et al., 1994a). Thus, maximally step (5) is of $o(T^5)$. Using algorithm 2 for example 2, at step (5), for $AD \rightarrow_\phi E$ in F, since $(E, \min(a,b))$ in A^+_F due to $A \rightarrow_\alpha B$ and $B \rightarrow_\beta E$, the algorithm stops with "No".

4. Conclusion

This paper has discussed data models in dealing with linguistic and imprecise information at two levels. At the conceptual level, fuzzy extensions have been shown to enhance the ER/EER concepts, as well as the notions of attribute inheritance (multiple inheritance, selective inheritance, and the inheritance for derived attributes) and the relationship constraints (the inheritance constraint, the participation constraint, and the cardinality constraint). At the data level, some of the issues of fuzzy database models (e.g., fuzzy data representation and storage, data manipulation, update anomalies, and information maintenance) have been discussed in various detail.

Acknowledgments

The work was partially supported by the International Projects of the Flemish Community Cooperation with China (No. 9704) and by China's National Natural Science Foundation (No.69573019).

References

Anvari M.; Rose G.F. 1984. Fuzzy relational databases. *Proc. of 1st Intl. Conf. on FIP*, Hawaii.

Baldwin, J. F.; Zhou, S. Q. 1984. A fuzzy relational inference language. *Fuzzy Sets & Sys.* Vol.14, pp.155-174.

Buckles, B.P.; Petry F.E. 1982. A fuzzy representation of data for relational databases. *Fuzzy Sets & Sys.* Vol.7, pp.213-226.

Bosc. P.; Pivert O. 1991. About equivalents in SQLf: a relational language· supporting imprecise querying. *Proc. of Intl. Fuzzy Engineering Symposium*, Japan, pp.309-320.

Chen, G.Q.; Vandenbulcke, J.; Kerre, E.E. 1991. A step towards the theory of fuzzy database design. *Proc. of IFSA'91*, Brussels, pp.44-47.

Chen G.Q.; Vandenbulcke J.; Kerre E.E. 1992. A general treatment of data redundancy in a fuzzy relational data model, *Journal of the American Society for Information Science*, 43, pp.304-311.

Chen G.Q.; Kerre E.E.; Vandenbulcke J. 1993. On the lossless-join decomposition in a fuzzy relational data model. *Proceedings of International Symposium on Uncertainty Modelling & analysis (ISUMA'93)*, IEEE Press, Maryland (USA), pp.440-446.

Chen, G.Q.; Kerre, E.E.; Vandenbulcke, J. 1994a. A computational algorithm for the FFD closure and a complete axiomatization of fuzzy functional dependency (FFD*). Int. J. of Intell. Sys.* Vol.9(5), pp.421-439.

Chen, G. Q.; Kerre, E. E.; Vandenbulcke, J. 1994b. Fuzzy normal forms and a dependency-preserving decomposition into θ-F3NF. *Proc. of WCCI:FUZZ-IEEE'94*, pp.156-161.

Chen G.Q.; Kerre E.E. 1996c. An extended Boyce-Codd normal form in fuzzy relational databases. *Proc. of FUZZ-IEEE'96*, New Orleans, pp.1546-1551.

Chen, G.Q., 1995a. Fuzzy functional dependencies and a series of design issues of fuzzy relational databases, in P. Bosc and J. Kacprzyk (eds.), *Studies in Fuzziness: fuzzy sets and possibility theory in database management systems*, Physica-Verlag (Springer-Verlag, Germany), pp.166-185.

Chen G.Q.; Kerre E.E.; Vandenbulcke J. 1995b. The dependency-preserving decomposition and a testing algorithm in a fuzzy relational data model. *Fuzzy Sets & Sys.* Vol.72, pp.27-37.

Chen, G. Q.; Kerre, E. E.; Vandenbulcke, J. 1996a. Normalization based on fuzzy functional dependency in a fuzzy relational data model. *Information Systems.* Vol.21(3), pp.299-310.

Chen G.Q.; Kerre E.E.; Vandenbulcke J. 1996b. Extended keys and integrity rules based on fuzzy functional dependency. *Proc. of EUFIT'96*, Verlag-Mainz, Germany, Vol.2, pp.806-810.

Chen G.Q.; Kerre E.E. 1997. Designing a general-purpose system for fuzzy data representation and queries. *Proc. of IFSA'97*, Prague, pp. 255-260.

Chen P. P., 1976, The entity-relationship model: towards a unified view of data. *ACM Transactions on Database Systems* (1)1, pp.9-36.

Codd, E.F. 1970. A relation model for large shared data banks. Comm. of. The ACM, Vol.(13)6, pp.377-387.

Cubero, J.C.; Vila, M.A. 1994. A new definition of fuzzy functional dependency in fuzzy relational databases, *Int. J. of Intell. Sys.* Vol.9(5), pp.441-448.

Dos Santos C.; Neuhold E.; Furtado A. 1979. A data type approach to the entity-relationship model. *Proceedings of ER Conference'79*.

Dubois, D.; Prade, H. 1992. Generalized dependencies in fuzzy data bases. *Proc. of IPMU'92*, pp.263-266.

Elmasri R.; Weeldreyer J.; Hevner A. 1985. The category concept: an extension to the entity-relationship model. *International Journal on Data and Knowledge Engineering* 1:1.

Gogolla M.; Hohenstein U. 1991.· Towards a semantic view of an extended entity-relationship model. *TODS* 16:3.

Kacprzyk J.; Ziolkowski A. 1986. Database queries with fuzzy linguistic quantifiers. *IEEE Trans. on Sys. Man and Cybern.*, 16:474-479.

Kacprzyk J.; Zadrozny S. 1994. Fuzzy querying for Microsoft Access. *Proc. of 3rd IEEE Conf. on Fuzzy Systems.* Orlando, 1.pp.167-171.

344

Kerre E.E.; Zenner R.B.R.C.; De Caluwe R.M.M. 1986. The use of fuzzy set theory in information retrieval and databases: a survey. *Journal of the American Society for Information Science*, 37(5),pp.341-345.

Kerre E. E.; Chen G. Q. 1995. An overview of fuzzy data models. In P. Bosc and J. Kacprzyk (eds.), Studies in Fuzziness: Fuzziness in Database Management Systems. *Physica-Verlag*, pp.23-41.

Kiss A., 1990. λ-decomposition of fuzzy relational databases. *Proc. of Int. Workshop on Fuzzy Sets and Systems*, December, Visegrad, Hungary.

Liu, W. Y. 1992. The reduction of the fuzzy data domain and fuzzy consistent join. *Fuzzy Sets & Sys*. Vol.50, pp.89-96.

Prade, H.; Testemale, C. 1983. Generalizing database relational algebra for the treatment of incomplete/uncertain information and vague queries. *Proc. of 2nd NAFIPS Workshop*, Schenectady, NY.

Raju, K. V. S. V. N.; Majumdar, A. K. 1988. Fuzzy functional dependencies and lossless join decomposition of fuzzy relational database systems. *ACM trans. on Database Systems*, Vol.13(2), pp.129-166.

Ruspini E., 1986, Imprecision and uncertainty in the entity-relationship model. In H. Prade and C. V. Negoita (eds.), Fuzzy Logic in Knowledge Engineering, *Verlag TUV* Rheinland, pp.18-22.

Scheuermann P.; Schiffner G.; Weber H. 1979. Abstraction capabilities and invariant properties modeling within the entity-relationship approach. *Proceedings of ER Conference '79*.

Teorey T.; Yang D.; Fry J. 1986. A logical design methodology for relational databases using the extended entity-relationship model. *ACM Computing Survey*, 18:2.

Umano, M. 1983. Retrieval from fuzzy databases by fuzzy relational algebra. In: Sanchez and Gupta (eds.), *Fuzzy Information Knowledge Representation and Decision Analysis*. Pergamon Press, Oxford, England. pp.1-6.

Vandenberghe R. M., 1991, An extended entity-relationship model for fuzzy databases based on fuzzy truth values. *Proceedings of IFSA '91*, Brussels, pp.280-283.

Yager R.R. 1988. On ordered weighted average aggregation operators in multicriteria decisionmaking. *IEEE Trans. on Sys.Man and Cyerbn*. 18(1),pp.183-190.

Yager R.R. 1991. Fuzzy quotient operators for fuzzy relational databases. *Proc. of Intl. Fuzzy Engineering Symposium*. Japan, pp. 289-296.

Zemankova; M.; Kandel, A. 1984. *Fuzzy Relational Database - a key to expert system*. Verlag TUV Rheinland.

Zvieli A.; Chen P. P. 1985. Entity-relationship modeling and fuzzy databases. *Proceedings of 2nd Conference on Data Engineering*, LA.

Fuzzy Set Approaches to Model Uncertainty in Spatial Data and Geographic Information Systems

Frederick E. Petry[1], Maria Cobb[2] and Ashley Morris[1]

[1] Center for Intelligent and Knowledge- Based Systems, Department of Electrical Engineering and Computer Science, Tulane University, New Orleans, LA 70118 USA, (petry, morrisa)@eecs.tulane.edu

[2] Department of Computer Science and Statistics, University of Southern Mississippi, Hattiesburg, MS 39406 USA, maria.cobb@usm.edu

Abstract. Issues of modeling uncertainty in spatial data is particularly suitable for the use of fuzzy set approaches. We survey the broader existing concerns on accuracy and uncertainty in the GIS community in the development of geographical information systems. In particular we note the current emphasis on the area by very significant government agencies and consortiums. Then we consider the issues involved in developing the modeling of uncertain spatial in the natural framework of object-oriented databases. Finally we give a specific approach for spatial directional relationships using an extension of Allen's temporal relationships with fuzzy modeling to provide a natural linguistic querying of a spatial database or geographic information system.

Keywords. geographical information systems, spatial databases, object-oriented databases, spatial accuracy, spatial relationships.

1 Introduction

The need to handle imprecise and uncertain information concerning spatial data has been widely recognized in recent years (e.g., Goodchild [1]), particularly in the field of geographical information systems (GIS). GIS is a rather general term for a number of approaches to the management of cartographic and spatial information. Most definitions of a geographic information system [2, 3] describe it as an organized collection of software systems and geographic data able to represent, store and provide access for all forms of geographically referenced information. At the heart of a GIS is a spatial database. The spatial information generally describes both the location and shape of geographic features in terms of points, lines and areas.

There has been a strong demand to provide approaches that deal with inaccuracy and uncertainty in GIS. The issue of spatial database accuracy has been viewed as critical to the successful implementation and long-term viability of GIS technology [1]. The value of a GIS as a decision-making tool is highly dependent on the ability of decision-makers to evaluate the reliability of the information on which their decisions are based. Users of geographic information system technology must therefore be able to assess the nature and degree of error in spatial databases, track this error through GIS operations and estimate accuracy for both tabular and graphic output products. There are a variety of aspects of potential errors in GIS encompassed by the general term "accuracy." However, here we are only interested in those aspects that lend themselves to modeling by fuzzy set techniques.

1.1 Sources of Imprecision in Spatial Data

There are a variety of sources of imprecision in a geographic information system that are manifested as several types of uncertainty: 1. uncertainty due to variability or error; 2. imprecision due to vagueness; 3. incompleteness due to inadequate sampling frequency for missing variables [4]. Both uncertainty of interpretation and inherent ambiguity are illustrated by the labeling of data such as that obtained from Landsat images. The images are initially processed by unsupervised classifications to obtain image classes and then the results are subjectively assigned land cover or resource class labels by a human interpreter. This is an inherently subjective task in which the interpreter is attempting to match objectively derived image classes with linguistic concepts that are represented by linguistic concepts in the mind of the interpreter. It is not surprising that there is variation in the interpretation of the very same data among interpreters. This is particularly troublesome when the result is stored in a database because at this point an inherently imprecise concept requires an specific representation.

In applications involving remote sensed information and typical multiple sources of information used to formulate geographical data, the problems of imprecision and uncertainty are of even more concern [5].

Many operations are applied to spatial data under the assumption that features, attributes and their relationships have been specified a priori in a precise and exact manner. However, this assumption is generally not justifiable, since inexactness is almost invariably present in spatial data. Inexactness exists in the positions of features and the assignment of attribute values and may be introduced at various stages of data compilation and database development. Moreover, inexactness may be propagated through GIS operations to appear in modified form on tabular and graphic output products. Inexactness is often inadvertent, as in the case of measurement error or imprecision in taxonomic definitions, but may also be intentional since generalization methods are frequently applied to enhance cartographic fidelity.

Models of uncertainty have been proposed for GIS information that incorporate ideas from natural language processing, the value of information concept, non-monotonic logic and fuzzy set, evidential and probability theory. For example in [6] there are reviews of four models of uncertainty based on probability theory, Shafer's theory of evidence, fuzzy set theory and non-monotonic logic. Each model is shown as appropriate for a different type of inexactness in spatial data. Inexactness is classified as arising primarily from three sources. "Randomness" may occur when an observation can assume a range of values. "'Vagueness" may result from imprecision in taxonomic definitions. "Incompleteness of evidence" may occur when sampling has been applied, there are missing values, or surrogate variables have been employed.

1.2 Previous Approaches to Fuzziness in GIS Systems

Robinson [7,8,9] has done extensive research on fuzzy data models for geographic information. He has considered several models as appropriate for this situation, the two early fuzzy database approaches using simple membership values in relations by Giardina [10] and Baldwin [11], and a similarity-based approach [12]. In modeling a situation in which both the data and relationships are imprecise he assesses that this situation entails imprecision intrinsic to natural language which is possibilistic in nature. A possibilistic relational (PRUF) model was chosen as providing a means of facilitating approximate machine inference [13]. In the PRUF model, queries and propositions are processed by identifying constraints induced by the query or proposition, performing tests on each constraint and then aggregating the individual test results to yield an overall test score. Consider a proposition stating that a specified location is on gentle slopes and is near a certain city. The constraints induced by the proposition, "gentle" and "near," are tested using a possibility distribution yielding test results indicating the degree to which the specified location satisfies each constraint. The two test results are then aggregated to produce an overall test score indicating the degree to which the proposition is satisfied.

Active recent research has extended these approaches to current geographic information system software [14], object-oriented approaches [15] and other GIS features [16]. A rather different technique uses fuzzy cognitive maps (FCM) in GIS systems ([17, 18]. The model developed was a hierarchy of generalized FCMs. Each FCM is a context graph of related object types called Object-FCMs. Since the object-oriented network of OFCMs captures fuzzy patterns, the network is useful for data mining as well as querying.

Several approaches to the use of fuzzy set theory in geographic modeling have been collected in the recent edited volume by Burrough and Frank [19]. These include a framework for fuzzy set implementation of geographic features [20], a consideration of the contrast between Boolean and fuzzy spatial regions [21], and a model for the semantics of fuzzy spatial objects [22]. Additionally specific features such soil types [23] and classification of bodies of water [24] that have been described by fuzzy approaches to model their imprecision are also in the collection

1.3 Significance of Uncertainty Modeling in Spatial Data

There have been a number of recent indications of the importance of uncertainty modeling in spatial data. Two in particular are of most significance. First NIMA, the National Imagery and Mapping Agency of the United States, announced for fiscal year 1997 a new program of University Research Initiatives. One of the major topics is uncertainty in geospatial information representation, analysis and decision support and the following are some of the main aspects:

i. *Elements of Uncertainty*: Geospatial information is extremely complex and includes several aspects that may have associated uncertainties. These include location, relationships and typologies. They requested proposals to identify and describe all aspects of uncertainty associated with geospatial information.

ii. *Models for Uncertainty:* The goal here was to develop extensions to existing geospatial data models that accommodate the elements of uncertainty.

iii. *Propagation of Uncertainty:* For this aspect of the proposed efforts they requested development of algorithms for determining how uncertainty is propagated through the fusion and analysis of geospatial information.

Secondly, the University Consortium for Geographic Information Science has published a major position paper [25] of research priorities for geographic information science. They state that the uncertainty information associated with a geographic data set can be conceived as a map depicting varying degrees of uncertainty associated with each of the features or phenomena represented in the data set, and potentially separable into three components: uncertainty in the typological attributes (describing the type of a geographic feature), uncertainty in the locational attributes, and uncertainty in spatial dependence (the spatial relationship with other features).

Uncertainty is seen as appearing in every part of the geographic data life cycle: data collection, data representation, data analyses, and final results.. The data that passes through the stages of observation to eventual archiving, may be handled by a variety of individuals/organizations, each of whom may provide their own distinct interpretations to the data. So the uncertainty is mostly a function of the relationship between the data and the user, i.e., a measure of the difference between the data and the meaning attached to the data by its current user. The University Consortium for Geographic Information Science emphasized that research was needed in studying in detail the sources of uncertainty in geographic data and the specific propagation processes of this uncertainty through GIS-based data analyses and in developing techniques for reducing, quantifying, and visualizing uncertainty in geographic data, and for analyzing and predicting the propagation of this uncertainty through GIS-based data analyses.

2 Fuzziness in an Object-Oriented Spatial Database / GIS

2.1 Introduction

We want to analyze spatial data uncertainty relative to its representation in a object-oriented database. Three basic forms of entities in a object-oriented geographic information system would consist of spatial (location) data (where an object is), temporal data (when an object is), and thematic (attribute) data (what an object is).

A geographic information system can include the use of fuzzy terms for queries, regardless of how the data is stored. Whether data, entities, or objects are stored with uncertainty or in fuzzy sets - they can still be queried using fuzzy terms. If this approach is taken, then the "back end"; that is, the database storage mechanism, does not need to directly represent fuzziness. This means that any traditional or any commercial spatial database may be used. The method for introducing fuzzy spatial queries could be a "plug in", a "front end", or an extension to the spatial DBMS. This front end could include the use of natural language or could consist of retrievals giving results with degree of membership or possibility of membership in a result query.

An example of the use of fuzzy queries on a spatial database could be "Display all elementary schools not within 100 meters of a fire hydrant". The location layer in the GIS that contains elementary schools probably contains very crisp data (for our purposes, "crisp" data refers to data at the maximum resolution available). However, fuzziness could exist in the thematic layer if, for example, there is a school which houses grades 1-12. Also, there may be fuzziness in the semantics of the person posing the query. Even though the query explicitly stated "within 100 meters", the user may actually desire to know which schools are within about 110 meters.

A more classic example of fuzzy queries for spatial databases would be to alter the query to actually include fuzzy terms. An example of such a query would be: "Display all elementary schools not near a fire hydrant". This query contains the fuzzy term "near", (and the Boolean inverse term "not") which could return a solution set with a degree of membership of 1 for every school more than 200 meters from a hydrant, and a degree of membership of 0 for every school less than 50 meters from a hydrant. Every school between 50 and 200 meters would have a variable degree of membership. This use of fuzzy terms can be definitely implemented in a spatial GIS whether or not the entities are stored in a fuzzy manner.

Another instance of where fuzziness may be included implicitly by the user would be in the above case in which the user asks for elementary schools "within 100 meters". The user is ambiguous in making the query so that we do not know if they mean 100 meters "as the crow flies", or 100 meters via a road, or 100 meters through a field.

2.2 Fuzzy Spatial Objects

There are many situations of how fuzziness can exist in objects in a spatial geographic information system. We will outline several of these.

2.2.1 Resolution

The resolution of the sample set can introduce fuzziness. When overlaying GIS layers of different resolution this can especially present problems. Also when an object is brought up to a very high degree of resolution when the data is at a coarser granularity, the geographic information system must introduce some form of fuzziness due to the inadequate set of sample points.

2.2.2 Missing Data

Dependent upon the implementation of the spatial geographic information system, this can be addressed by rounding or through other discriminate means. When queries are made against this object, however, fuzziness is introduced. Many GIS products tout one of their greatest selling points as the ability to "fill in the gaps" of missing data. While a necessary and useful feature, there are times when this technique will actually introduce errant data into the GIS. It is the domain of the GIS architect to determine what technique to use to determine what values the missing data may have. Many algorithms are available for this task, and some GIS allow the user to choose one particular algorithm out of many.

2.2.3 Uncertain Data

Objects can also consist of uncertain data. This may be simply because the human classifying the data does not exactly know which group into which to insert the object. If the classifier has selectable options of classification, they may be able to insert the object into several groups with a certain fuzzy degree of membership in each.

Consider an image, where classification has been done by a human using fuzzy grouping. For example, assume we have 4 classes, each class represented by a unique color: red, blue, black, and white. Each data cell has been grouped such that the denser the color, the more certain it is that the data fits into the classification represented by the color. It is easy to determine that some areas fit easily into groupings. However, most of the cells fit into several groups, with varying degrees of certainty. We must classify our objects so that we can, with a fair amount of certainty, determine the boundaries of the objects based upon the class to which they belong. At this point, we would borrow techniques from computer vision to detect the edges between the color groups. This would then give us a fair approximation of crisp boundaries between the different groups. We could once again bring in human intervention if we were not satisfied, or we could use other computer vision techniques, such as gaussian smoothing, laplacian transforms, and different edge detection algorithms in an attempt to determine our edges.

2.2.4 Object Identification

There is also a problem in actually discerning what individual objects are. A blob may be a simple blob, or may consist of a conglomeration of sub-blobs. This may have to do with indeterminate boundaries, or the actual identification and classification of the object. Every object in a database must be named. It is in this description of the objects that yet even more fuzziness may be introduced. This problem is particularly relevant to describing classes and inheritance in a spatial object-oriented database. In a picture of several blobs, it is difficult to determine if we are dealing with one large object, or with three smaller ones. The smaller blobs may have very uncertain boundaries, so that any two may also combine to be a unique object. So, often actually identifying the objects may introduce uncertainty into the equation.

2.2.5 Links/Indeterminate Boundaries

Links between objects can introduce fuzziness. The well known list of object intersections (equal, disjoint, etc.) can become fuzzy when the boundaries are indeterminate, are not concrete, or are subject to change. Consider two object with inexact/indeterminate boundaries. Perhaps we can say with some certainty where about two-thirds of the border of each object lies, but when there is overlap between the two objects, we cannot determine a crisp border. Our best solution in this case would probably be to use the technique we used with the classification of uncertain data, and run the image through an edge detector. Of course, while this would give us a crisp border, this would not necessarily give us a correct border. If the data was three dimensional, this would give us the possibility that one object could be on top of another. Of course, there are three dimensional edge-detectors that we could use. We might see that there are portions of the image where the first object predominates, yet there are obviously places in this object that consist of a large portion of data classified as belonging to the second class.

Boundaries of an object are the natural phenomena which is most difficult to introduce and also most important to represent in a spatial GIS. Even exact object boundaries can only be approximated due to the inaccuracy of the measurements when locating them. Also, there exist both natural phenomena as well as man made artifacts in which the borders are in a state of flux. An example of the natural phenomena would be any shoreline during a change in tides; and an example of the artifact would be the borders of the former Yugoslavia. Also, even when a border is determined to be crisp, the diffusion of an objects boundaries may vary along its border. For example, Israel has a crisp border with the Red Sea, but a fuzzier border with Jordan.

2.2.6 Temporality

Temporality must be addressed in a spatial geographic information system. Although it is agreed that an object's identity is immutable during its lifetime, the classes to which it belongs may change and vary and be interchanged as an object evolves. In our example above, the shoreline has two different boundaries, dependent upon whether the tide is in or out. This is due to the time at which we measure the border.

2.2.7 Object Grouping

Many Individual objects may be made of smaller sub-objects. These sub objects assume homogeneity within object boundaries, yet in certain spatial applications (i.e., soil coverage), at every level of resolution there will be variation within the objects. So in the case of land cover, this can particularly occur at the object borders.

2.2.8 Geostatistics

Objects may be replaced with continuous fields. This is the science of geostatistics. Once again, there is no completely unambiguous way of decomposing the complex irregular variation into unique sets of covariant structures.

2.2.9 Multi-dimensional Fuzziness

Objects may be crisp from one perspective, but fuzzy from another. For example, an object may have a crisp two dimensional border, but a fuzzy border in 3 dimensions. An example of this would be a border between two countries. On the ground, it is usually easy to determine the border, but when a border dispute is either below ground (mineral rights) or above ground (airspace), it becomes more difficult to determine exactly where the border is.

2.2.10 Fluid Boundaries

Boundaries may be fluid. For example, what if we are mapping the temperature of water in the gulf stream? Not only does the boundaries of the actual gulf stream itself move dynamically, but the sub-object of the common temperature group will constantly be shifting. This is a particularly heinous problem, which relies greatly on temporality; we will not address this problem further here.

2.2.11 Groups of Objects

Is a single pine tree a forest? If not, at what point does a group of pine trees become a forest? What if there are also ash trees mixed in with the pines. We then have a group of trees with a certain degree of membership in a "forest", and a certain degree of membership in "pine forest" and "ash forest", and possibly a very small degree of membership in "oak forest", assuming there is but a single oak tree in our group of trees.

2.3 Couclelis' Typography of Dimensions

Couclelis [26] has outlined three sets of dimensions which capture most of the ideas of where fuzziness or uncertainty may occur or can be represented in spatial data and geographic information systems. The first of these dimensions outlines where objects themselves in a GIS may involve fuzziness or uncertainty, this dimension deals with the empirical nature of the entity.

2.3.1 Objective Characteristics

atomic (vector) or plenum (raster) : In a vector-based world, objects inherently have crisp, well-defined borders. Just the opposite is true in a raster-based world. As geographic information systems become more hybrid, that is, they support both vector-based data and projection, and raster-based data and projection, the notion of crisp objects and object boundaries become blurred.

homogeneous or inhomogeneous: With a homogeneous object, for example, a steel anvil, the boundaries are crisp and clear. With an object such as soil, the boundaries are unclear. When differentiating among types of soil, we are dealing with inhomogeneous objects, and it is difficult to discern the differences between them.

continuous or discontinuous: It is fairly simple to determine the borders of a continuous object, such as our example of an anvil. When dealing with an object such as a forest, it becomes more difficult. Does the forest begin with the first tree, or do trees have to reach a certain density? What if there is an open area without trees in the middle of our forest? Is that area still included in our forest? And what if a fire burns down part of the forest? How do we classify that part of the forest which has been burned?

connected or distributed:: An example of a non-connected spatial object would be a city's historical downtown district, in which lines of demarcation have been drawn by the city. A more distributed spatial object would be a city's entire historical district. Portions of this object probably extend beyond the downtown area, and are not completely bounded by a conventional convex-hull type of classification.

solid or fluid:: Fluid objects are almost impossible to bound crisply, unless they are contained within crisply bounded entities (A cola still in the can). Fluid sub-objects within fluid objects are nightmares.

2 or 3 dimensional: As mentioned before, an object may have very crisp boundaries in two dimensions, which become less crisp in three dimensions.

actual or non-actual (temporality) : An actual object (as of today), could be the Czech Republic, and its borders are well defined (with some dispute). A non-actual object (again, as of today), would be Czechoslovakia, which ceased to exist in 1993. Most of this discussion deals with temporality, which we are, for the most part, avoiding in this current work.

permanent or variable: Given enough time, all entities are variable. For our purposes, an example of a permanent object would be the rock of Gibraltar, and a variable entity could be either a sand castle, or a trailer in south Florida during hurricane season.

fixed or moving: A herd of buffalo are an example of a moving object. To quote Couclelis: "It is questionable whether the very notion of boundary makes sense in such cases."

2.3.2 Mode of Observation

conventional or self-defining: Political boundaries are conventional, while self-defining boundaries could be exemplified by cultural or socio-economic regions. The second dimension pertains mainly to the representation of the objects in the spatial geographic information system, and the mode by which they are observed.

scale : Most of the problems of indeterminate boundaries due to the scale mode of observation. Because the final product of a GIS is typically a map (at a smaller scale than the object it models), users tend to think of the map as representing the real world fairly accurately. When there is fuzziness in the original model, it is usually discretized to the point where all fuzziness disappears, and we are only dealing with a crisp (well-bounded) representation of the fuzzy (indeterminate) model.

perspective An excellent example of how perspective can introduce uncertainty is by the use of different map projections. For example, the size of Greenland is extremely exaggerated in a Mercator projection map, while it is not in a conical projection map.

error : Error may be introduced into a spatial database at several points: sensing, measurement, conversion, observation, representation, or at any other point when converting the real world object into a representation. If the user or observer is aware of some such error, then the notion of uncertainty is introduced.

theory : Theoretical constructs and theoretical definitions may imply crisp or uncertain boundaries.

2.3.3 User Perception

The third dimension pertains to the user needs / user perception. Different users of spatial information have different needs. Couclelis defines three perspectives on boundaries: well bounded entities / not well bounded entities; mode of observation yields well bounded / not well bounded objects; user requires well bounded / user does not require well bounded object The needs of a user can be defined by selecting whether well bounded entities are required at each of the three perspectives. For example, data modelers do not require well bounded entities at any of the 3 perspectives.

3 Fuzzy Spatial Directional Relationships

3.1 Introduction

Assuming that we have some discrete representation of a geographic domain which is the best possible, yet another issue of uncertainty remains—that of determining relationships among the various geographic objects. The ability to discern spatial relationships is of particular importance to spatial reasoning systems which must utilize available topological, geometric and directional relationship information to infer missing or more complex relationships [27].

The ability to discriminate between similar spatial relationships, as well as the ability to communicate subtle differences in such relationships, is a remarkable human trait that is difficult to replicate in automated systems. Especially difficult is the determination of directions between 2-D features, as humans are able to adjust their assessment of directions according to variabilities in the relative sizes and shapes of, and distances between the features. The use of fuzzy methods associated with linguistic variables [28] is the most promising approach so far for duplicating the human reasoning process in the area of spatial relationship determination.

As an example, consider the three scenes pictured in figure 1. In figure 1(a) both objects are moderately sized, and it is unclear whether the statement "A is west of B" or "A is southwest of B" better describes the directional relationship between the two. In figure 1(b), however, where A is smaller and B is significantly larger than before, it is much less controversial to state simply that "A is west of B." Similarly, in figure 1(c), where A is much larger and B is much smaller, most would agree that now "A is southwest of B."

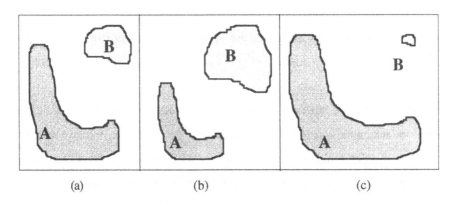

Figure 1. Example of effect of size on the directional relationship determination.

3.2 Minimum Bounding Rectangles

The work presented here, as well as that of Nabil [29], Sharma [30] and Clementini [31], relies upon the use of MBRs as approximations of the geometry of spatial objects. An MBR is defined as the smallest x-y parallel rectangle which completely encloses an object. The use of MBRs in geographic databases is widely practiced as an efficient way of locating and accessing objects in space [31]. In addition, numerous spatial data structures and indexing techniques have been developed that exploit the computationally efficient representation of spatial objects through the use of MBRs [32, 33]. Another advantage to the use of an MBR representation is that all objects can be dealt with at the same level of dimensionality—that is, point, line and area features are all represented as 2-D objects across which operations can be uniformly applied.

Of course, the use of MBRs is inherently problematic to some degree because an MBR is an approximation of an object's true geometry. One of the more significant challenges is the modeling of topological spatial relations using MBR representations. The problem is that the enclosure of false area (area not actually contained in the geometry of the object) within the MBR renders inconsistencies between the application of topological relations to the MBRs vs. the application of the relations to the objects themselves. This is especially evident in the case of overlapping relationships for which the MBRs may overlap, but for which no conclusion can be drawn about the corresponding relationship of their respective contained objects.

Clementini [31], however, shows how MBR relations can be used as a fast filter to determine whether it is possible for the object to satisfy a given topological relationship. This approach is based on the identification of a set of MBR relations for which a consistent mapping between these relations and object topological relations exists. For example, if two MBRs are disjoint, then the relationship between the objects must also be disjoint. An approach for ameliorating the topological consistency problem is the use of true MBRs proposed by Nabil [29]. A true MBR is not restricted by the x-y parallelism requirement, but is designed to represent the true maximum extent of an object unconstrained by orientation. This approach potentially results in less false area, thereby reducing the margin for error between MBR and object relationship mappings.

3.3 Abstract Spatial Graph Model

This section describes a data structure we have developed for representing topological and directional relationships, in addition to supplementary information needed for fuzzy query processing. The data structure, known as an abstract spatial graph (ASG), represents a transformation of 2-dimensional space (areas) into 0-dimensional space (points). A complete set of ASGs for the original relationships, including a graphical representation and specific property sets, was developed in [34].

First-level topological relationship definitions are based on an extension of Allen's temporal relations [35] to the spatial domain. In his work, Allen showed that the seven relationships before, meets, overlaps, starts, during, finishes and equal, along with their inverses, hold as the complete set of relationships between two intervals. Cobb [34] extended these to two dimensions by defining a spatial relationship as a tuple [rx, ry], where rx is the one of Allen's relationships that represents the spatial relationship between two objects in the x direction, and ry is likewise defined for the y direction. Relationships are often represented by their initial letter, for example [bo] stands for the relationship [before, overlaps]. Objects involved are assumed to be enclosed in MBRs.

The concept of extending Allen's temporal relations to two or more dimensions for spatial reasoning is not new. Examples of how this has been done can be found in [36, 37] to name a few. For each of these, the approach taken is somewhat different, based on the intent of the work. However, the concept of representing a 2-D object as a set of two intervals, an x and a y, and of having the resulting spatial relationship consist of some combination of the component 1-D relations seems to underlie most. In contrast, Egenhofer's well-known model for topological relations [38] utilizes a point-set approach in which relationships are based on combinations of intersections between boundaries and interiors of objects.

Directional relationships can be defined in a similar manner. Directional relationship definitions rely upon the partitioning of MBRs into object subgroups, which are created by extending the boundaries of the two MBRs so that they intersect one another. For those cases in which extensions do not intersect the other MBR, each MBR is considered to be an object sub-group. Overlapping areas are also considered object sub-groups.

The construction of an ASG for a binary spatial relationship relies heavily upon these object sub-groups. Each object sub-group is represented as a node on the ASG. Pictorially, ASG's are represented in a polar graph notation, where different node representations are used to distinguish between the objects involved in the relationship. The origin node represents the reference area of the relationship, which could be a sub-group of one of the objects, an overlapping area, or a common boundary. To provide support for fuzzy query processing, each node in an ASG has associated weights. These weights are used to define fuzzy qualifiers for the query language. Specifically, the weights are intended to support queries of the nature "To what degree is region A south of region B?," or "How much of region A overlaps region B (qualitatively speaking) ?".

Two types of weights are computed: area weights and total node weights. These provide information concerning the degree of participation in a relationship and relative direction, respectively. Area weights are computed simply as the ratio of the area of an object sub-group to the area of the entire MBR. The total node weight for an ASG node is defined as the product of the corresponding area weight and the normalized axis length of the directional axis which crosses the object subgroup. Normalization of axis lengths is accomplished separately for each object by first assigning a length of 1 to the longest axis crossing any object sub-group of the object. All other representational axes of the object are then given a value between 0 and 1, based on their lengths relative to the longest axis for that object.

From the above description, one can see that area weights are useful for answering how much of an object is involved in a relationship. By assigning ranges of area weights to linguistic terms we can provide a basis for processing queries concerning qualitatively defined relationships. The set given next is one example of how this may be done: {all (96-100%), most (60-95%), some (30-59%), little (6-29%), none (0-5%)}

This provides the capability to pose queries such as the following:

"Is object A surrounded-by most of object B?"

"Retrieve an object that is partially-surrounded-by little of object A."

Node weights are utilized in a similar manner to provide qualitative directional relationship information. The purpose of node weights is to answer the extent to which an object can be considered to be at a given direction in relation to another object. The definition of a node weight as the product of the area weight and the axis length means that this information is represented as a consideration of both the total relative amount of the object which lies in a given direction (represented by the area weight) tempered by how directly it lies in that direction (represented by the axis length). This implies that those directions which have both a large area representation and long axis length will have a higher weight than those which have either a large area representation but short axis length, or those that have a long axis length with lesser area representation. Again, ranges are provided that define a linguistic set useful for query purposes. These are : {directly (96-100%), mostly (60-95%), slightly (30--59%), somewhat (6-29%), not (0-5%)}

The use of these qualifiers is illustrated in the following:

"Is object B somewhat west of object A?"

"Retrieve an object that is directly northeast of object A"

3 Conclusions

We have surveyed here several of the issues pertaining to the development of fuzzy geographic information systems.   We have overviewed the issues of uncertainty, in particular as they have been perceived by the most relevant community - geographic information science researchers. Indeed there has been significant recognition in this community of the importance of uncertainty in representing spatial data and several approaches developed utilizing fuzzy set theory. It is clear that there is a significant demand in this user community for application of fuzzy database developments to spatial data and geographic information systems. It is quite possible this might be the area to finally validate the efforts of fuzzy database researchers as to the utility of their basic efforts in the area.   That is, it might represent the breakthrough application for this area (GIS), as fuzzy control has been in general for fuzzy set research.

We particularly believe that the most natural approach is to combine uncertainty modeling for GIS with fuzzy object oriented databases. The use of object-oriented databases for geographic information systems is particularly appropriate considering the structured nature of much of geographical information [39]. Additionally we expect the requirements for sharing geographic information over the Web will be greatly enhanced by the CORBA specifications for [40]. Also there have been significant advances in fuzzy object-oriented databases as can be seen the recent edited volume by deCaluwe [41]. We plan on focusing our research efforts strongly into this direction and to design prototypes of fuzzy object-oriented spatial databases for which the   technology that is developed can then be transferred into commercial systems.

REFERENCES

1. M. Goodchild and S. Gopal, eds. *The Accuracy of Spatial Databases*, 1990, Taylor and Francis, Basingstoke, UK.

2. __, *ARC / INFO " User's Guide: ARC / NFO " 6.0 Data Model. Concepts and Key Terms*, Environmental Systems Research Institute, Redlands, CA,

3. D. MaGuire, "An Overview and Definition of GIS", *Geographical Information Systems: Principles and Applications, VOL 1 - Principles*, (eds. D.MaGuire, M. Goodchild, and D. Rhind), 9-20, Longman, Essex GB, 1991.

4. H. Veregin, "A Taxonomy of Error in Spatial Databases", Technical Report 89-12, National Center for Geographic Information and Analysis, Santa Barbara, CA, 1989.

5. S. Kennedy, "The Small Number Problem and the Accuracy of Spatial Databases", Chapter 16, *The Accuracy of Spatial Databases*, (eds. M. Goodchild and S. Gopal), 1990, Taylor and Francis, Basingstoke, UK.

6. D. Stoms, "Reasoning with Uncertainty in Intelligent Geographic Information Systems", *Proc. GIS 87 - 2nd Annual Int. Conf on Geographic Information Systems*, 693-699, American Soc. for Photogrammetry and Remote Sensing, Falls Church VA, 1987.

7. V. Robinson and A. Frank, "About Different Kinds of Uncertainty in Geographic Information Systems", *Proc. AUTOCARTO 7 Conference*, 1985.

8. V. Robinson, "Implications of Fuzzy Set Theory for Geographic Databases", *Computers, Environment, and Urban Systems*, 12, 89-98, 1988.

9. V. Robinson, "Interactive Machine Acquisition of a Fuzzy Spatial Relation", *Computers and Geosciences*, 6, 857-872, 1990.

10. C. Giardina, "Fuzzy Databases and Fuzzy Relational Associative Processors," *Technical Report*, Stevens Institute of Technology, Hoboken NJ, 1979.

11. J. Baldwin, "Knowledge Engineering Using a Fuzzy Relational Inference Language", *Proc IFAC Symp. on Fuzzy Information Knowledge Representation and Decision Analysis*, 15-21, 1983.

12. B. Buckles and F. Petry, "A Fuzzy Model for Relational Databases", *Int. Jour. Fuzzy Sets and Systems*, 7, 213-226, 1982.

13. L. Zadeh,"Test-Score Semantics for Natural Languages and Meaning Representation via PRUF", *Empirical Semantics*, (ed. B. Rieger), 281-349, Brockmeyer, Bochum, GR, 1981.

14. F. Wang, G. Hall and S. Subaryono, "Fuzzy Information Representation and Processing In Conventional GIS Software: Database Design and Application", *Int. Jour. Geographical Information Systems*, 4, 261-283, 1990.

15. R. George, B Buckles, F Petry , and A. Yazici "Uncertainty Modeling in Object-Oriented Geographical Information Systems",*1992 Proceed.Conf Database & Expert System Applications.(DEXA)*, 77-86, 1992.

16. T. Dawson and C. Jones, "Representing and Analyzing Fuzzy Natural Features in GIS", 405-412, *Ninth Annual Symp. on Geographical Information Systems*, 1995.

17. B. Kosko, "Fuzzy Cognitive Maps", *Int. Jour. Man-Machine Studies*, 24, 65-75, 1986.

18. R. Satur and Z. Liu, "A·Context-driven Intelligent Database Processing System Using Object-Oriented Fuzzy Cognitive Maps", *Proc. FUZZ-IEEE'95 Workshop on Fuzzy Database Systems and Information Retrieval*, 97-102, 1995.

19. P. Burrough and A. Frank, eds, *Geographic Objects with Indeterminate Boundaries,* GISDATA Series Vol. 2, Taylor and Francis, London, UK, 1996.

20. E.L. Usery, "A Conceptual Framework and Fuzzy Set Implementation for Geographic Features", *Geographic Objects with Indeterminate Boundaries* (eds, P. Burrough and A. Frank), pp 71-86, GISDATA Series Vol. 2, Taylor and Francis, London, UK, 1996

21. P. Fisher, "Boolean and Fuzzy Regions", *Geographic Objects with Indeterminate Boundaries* (eds, P.Burrough and A. Frank), pp 87-94, GISDATA Series Vol. 2, Taylor and Francis, London, UK, 1996

22. M. Molenaar, "A Syntactic Approach for Handling the Semantics of Fuzzy Spatial Objects", *Geographic Objects with Indeterminate Boundaries* (eds, P. Burrough and A. Frank), pp 207-224, GISDATA Series Vol. 2, Taylor and Francis, London, UK, 1996

23. P. Lagacherie, P. Andrieux and R. Bouzigues, "Fuzziness and Uncertainty of Soil Boundaries: From Reality to Coding in GIS", *Geographic Objects with Indeterminate Boundaries* (eds, P. Burrough and A. Frank), pp 275-286, GISDATA Series Vol. 2, Taylor and Francis, London, UK, 1996

24. T. Sarjakoski, "How Many Lakes, Islands, and Rivers are There in Finland? A Case Study of Fuzziness in the Extent and Identity of Geographic Objects", *Geographic Objects with Indeterminate Boundaries* (eds, P. Burrough and A. Frank), pp 299-312, GISDATA Series Vol. 2, Taylor and Francis, London, UK, 1996

25. University Consortium on Geographic Information Science, "Research Priorities for Geographic Information Science," Cartography and Geographic Information Systems, Vol. 23, # 3, pp 115-127, 1996.

26. H. Couclelis, "Towards an Operational Typology of Geographic Entities with Ill-defined Boundaries", *Geographic Objects with Indeterminate Boundaries* (eds, P. Burrough and A. Frank), pp 45-56, GISDATA Series Vol. 2, Taylor and Francis, London, UK, 1996

27.M. Cobb and F. Petry, "Fuzzy Querying Binary Relationships in Spatial Databases", *Proceedings of 1995 IEEE International Conference on Cybernetics and Society* , 378-385, 1995.

28. L. Zadeh, "The Concept of a Linguistic Variable and it Application to Approximate Reasoning", *Fuzzy Sets and Systems*, 10, 211-245 (1975)..

29. M., Nabil, J. Shepherd and A.H.H. Ngu "2D Projection Interval Relationships: A Symbolic Representation of Spatial Relationships", *Advances in Spatial Databases: 42nd Symposium, SSD '95*, 292-309 (1995)..

30. J. Sharma, and D.M. Flewelling. "Inferences from Combined Knowledge about Topology and Direction", *Advances in Spatial Databases: 42nd Symposium, SSD '95*, 279-291 (1995).

31. E. Clementini, J. Sharma and M.J. Egenhofer "Modelling Topological and Spatial Relations: Strategies for Query Processing", *Computers and Graphics*, 18:6, 815-22 (1994)..

32. H.P.Kriegel, , Schiwietz, M., Schneider, R., and Seeger, B. "Performance comparison of Point and Spatial Access Methods," In A. Buchmann, O. Gunther,

T. Smith, and Y. Wang (Eds.), *Design and Implementation of Large Spatial Databases*, LNCS 409, 89-114, Santa Barbara, CA: Springer-Verlag (1989)..

33. H. Samet, . *Applications of Spatial Data Structures: Computer Graphics, Image Processing, and GIS.* Reading, MA: Addison-Wesley (1989).

34. M. Cobb, "An Approach for the Definition, Representation and Querying of Binary Topological and Directional Relationships Between Two-Dimensional Objects". Ph.D. thesis. Tulane University (1995).

35. J.F. Allen, "Maintaining Knowledge about Temporal Intervals", *Communications of the ACM*, Vol. 26, No. 11, 832-843 (1983).

36. H.W. Guesgen, "Spatial Reasoning Based on Allen's Temporal Logic", Technical Report TR-89-049, International Computer Science Institute, Berkeley, CA   (1989).

37. A. Mukerjee, and G. Joe "A Qualitative Model for Space", *AAAI-90: Proc. Eighth National Conference on Artificial Intelligence*, 721-727 (1990).

38. M.J. Egenhofer, "Spatial Query Languages", Ph.D. thesis, University of Maine (1989).

39. K. Shaw, M. Cobb, M. Chung and D. Arctur, "Managing the Navy's First Object-Oriented Digital Mapping Project," *IEEE Computer*, Vol. 2, #9, pp. 69-74, 1996.

40. J. Siegel, *CORBA Fundamentals and Programming*, J. Wiley, New York, 1996.

41. R. deCaulwe, ed. *Fuzzy and Uncertain Object-Oriented Databases,* World Scientific Press, Singapore, 1997

Computing Fuzzy Dependencies with Linguistic Labels

J.C. Cubero, J.M. Medina, O. Pons, M.A. Vila

Dpto. Ciencias de la Computación e Inteligencia Artificial Universidad de Granada.
18071 Granada, Spain.

Abstract. The relational database model is the most widely used in commercial systems. When we design a database, we must choose the attributes and properties that should appear in every relation. For this task, the concept of functional dependency (f.d) is a fundamental issue: roughly, the attributes which do not appear in a candidate key should not verify any kind of f.d. We extend this notion, for the case when the dependencies are not crisp but fuzzy. The use of linguistic labels will play a fundamental role in our approximation, so we advocate the spirit of *computing with words* in Zadeh's sense.

Keywords: *Fuzzy Dependencies, Relational Databases, Resemblance Relation, Fuzzy Projection, Fuzzy Join*

1 Statement of the Problem

The need to store big amount of information has given rise to the development of Database Systems capable to manage such data. These systems are based on theoretical models and implement some or all of the features of each one. One of the most widely used is the Relational Database Model [5, 14, 31] and several commercial systems have been developed to implement it. Other semantic models (like IFO model [1]) find their implementation in object based database systems, although these ones are currently in a research phase, and its intensive commercial use is still waiting.

Very briefly speaking, the relational model stores data in tables (also called *relations*) where each column represents a property or *attribute*, and each row (also called *tuple*) represents an object. A crucial issue is to establish the attributes each table should include, in order to avoid redundancy and updating problems. The mathematical tool to manage it is the concept of functional dependency, which is used to detect exact dependencies among the attributes appearing in a table.

The aim of this work is to see how we can benefit of the theory of fuzzy sets, in order to find not strict functional dependencies but weaker ones, which we shall call *fuzzy dependencies*. This will allow us to compress the information of a table satisfying such a fuzzy dependency. In our approach, we shall replace crisp data by fuzzy labels containing them, so that the role of fuzzy logic in this area is in the sense of computing with words as advocated by Zadeh [37].

1.1 Database Systems

Let us briefly introduce the basic relational notation and terminology used through this work (see [31, 14, 6]) We shall use capital letters at the beginning of the alphabet to denote single attributes $(A, B, \ldots)$. For compound (set of) attributes we shall use letters at the end of the alphabet $(X, Y, \ldots)$. Relations will be denoted by small letters such as $r, s \ldots$ and tuples by $t, u, \ldots$ The value for an attribute A in a tuple t, will be represented by $A(t)$. For instance, $X(t)$ is the set of tuple values for relation r and attributes X. REL will denote a relational scheme (a set of attributes), so that any relation r is an *instance* of a relational scheme REL (denoted by $REL(r)$ whenever we want to emphasize this connection). For example, the relation in figure 1, has as first tuple the following:

$$(\texttt{Smith103 , AB200 , 24\$})$$

The symbol $\times$ stands for the usual cartesian product, and $\Pi_Z(r)$ denotes the crisp projection operator over Z, applied to relation r. The *join* operator is denoted by $\bowtie_\Theta$ and is applied to two relations, r and s, with schemes given by $REL(r) = \mathbf{R}$ and $REL(s) = \mathbf{S}$, in the following way:

$$r \bowtie_\Theta s = \Pi_{\mathbf{R} \cup \mathbf{S}} \left(\sigma_\Theta(r \times s) \right) \tag{1}$$

where σ_Θ is a *selection* operator which selects those tuples in $r \times s$ satisfying a crisp condition given by Θ. On the other hand, if r and s share X as common attributes, then, the *natural join* of r and s is given by

$$r \bowtie s = \Pi_{\mathbf{R} \cup (\mathbf{S}-s.X)}(\sigma_{r.X=s.X}(r \times s)) = \Pi_{(\mathbf{R}-r.X) \cup \mathbf{S}}(\sigma_{r.X=s.X}(r \times s)) \tag{2}$$

1.2 The Role of Functional Dependencies in Relational Databases

One of the most important steps when deciding the attributes which should appear in a scheme in a relational database, consists of choosing such attributes in such a way that there are not non trivial dependencies among them. Let us remark that trivial dependencies are those which stem from the existence of a key in a relation: a key is a subset K of attributes such that there are not two tuples with the same values of K (*uniqueness property*) and such that no subset of K satisfies the uniqueness property.

If non trivial dependencies exist (the origin of the dependency is not a candidate key), then serious redundancy and updating problems appear. Let us consider the following example to show this. Let us suppose we want to store information about salesmen in a company. We design a relation with the following attributes:

$$(\texttt{Salesman-Code , Product-Code , Product-Price})$$

The following table (**Sales**) could be a legal instance of such relation: We can see that whenever we have **AB200** as product code, we have **24\$** as product price,

Salesman-Code	Product-Code	Product-Price
Smith103	AB200	24$
Ford200	AB200	24$
Stevenson001	GH300	19$
Stevenson001	AB200	24$

Sales =

Fig. 1. A bad scheme design

i.e, the same product is sold at the same price, no matter who the salesman is. Let us suppose that this relationship is supported by every product, i.e, the price of any product depends only on the product code (note that this is a semantic restriction of the real world). In this case, we have redundant information in our relation because we store, for instance, the pair (AB200 , 24$) each time such product is sold by someone. Even more, there are serious update problems. For instance, if we want to change the price of product AB200 to 25$, then we should change it wherever it appears in the relation. Formally, we say that there is a functional dependency from Product-Code to Product-Price in relation Sales. In general, we can give the following definition:

Definition 1. *A relational scheme* $REL = (A_i)_{i=1...n}$ *satisfies a -classical-* **functional dependency** *(f.d)* $X \to Y$ *with* $X, Y \subseteq REL$ *if and only if, every instance* r *of* REL *satisfies the following condition:*

$$\forall \, t_1, \, t_2 \in r \quad If \; X(t_1) = X(t_2) \quad then \; Y(t_1) = Y(t_2) \quad must \; hold$$

X represents the *antecedent* attributes and Y the *consequent* ones.

In our example, we have that relation Sales satisfies the following f.d:

$$(\text{Salesman-Code , Product-Code}) \to \text{Product-Price}$$
$$\text{Product-Code} \to \text{Product-Price}$$

The first one is the trivial dependency originated by the attributes appearing in the key, (Salesman-Code,Product-Code). The second one is the non trivial dependency we are looking at. In order to avoid the redundancy and updating problems, the relation should have been properly designed, so that it should not satisfy illegal functional dependencies as stated before. So, before proceeding to store data, the expert should construct two relations (named JustSales and Prices) with the following scheme:

$$(\text{Salesman-Code , Product-Code}) \quad and$$
$$(\text{Product-Code, Product-Price})$$

respectively, and the following data:

Salesman-Code	Product-Code
Smith103	AB200
Ford200	AB200
Stevenson001	GH300
Stevenson001	AB200

JustSales =

	Product-Code	Product-Price
Prices =	AB200	24$
	GH300	19$

Anyway, we could face with the problem that the relation Sales really exists in our database with a lot of tuples. In this case, the Heath's theorem [19] guarantees that the projections of Sales over (Salesman-Code,Product-Code) (yielding the relation JustSales) and over (Product-Code,Product-Price) (yielding the relation Prices) are such that the join of such projections is equal to the original relation Sales, i.e, JustSales ⋈ Prices = Sales. Thus, we have not lost any information in this decomposition process. In general, if a relation r with scheme XYZ satisfies the $X \to Y$ functional dependency, then the following equation holds:

$$\Pi_{XZ}(r) \bowtie \Pi_{XY}(r) = r$$

Roughly speaking, this is the interpretation we want to extend to the fuzzy case, when the dependency is not crisp but fuzzy.

1.3 The Role of Fuzzy Information in Databases

Fuzzy set theory represents a very useful tool for representing and managing imprecise information. We refer the reader to the works of Dubois, Prade and Zadeh [15, 36] for an introduction to this issue.

The treatment of non *crisp* information in databases has been accomplished over the last decade by several authors. The study of incomplete information has been addressed in [20–22, 26, 27]. Logic and imprecise information have been dealt with in [17, 24, 33], whereas fuzzy [36] relational data models have been introduced in [3, 23, 25, 28, 32]. One recent field of study is the incorporation of imprecise and uncertain information into object based data models [30, 34, 38]. This is a promising research area, but nowadays the main commercial database systems are relational ones, and that's the reason we shall focus on this type of models.

We are going to consider a general definition of Fuzzy Relational Database where a relation r is a subset of the cartesian product given by: $r \subseteq \times_{i=1}^{n} \mathbf{D}_i$, where $\mathbf{D}_i$ can be one of the following sets:

- A usual domain D_i
- A set $\tilde{\mathcal{P}}(D_i)$ of fuzzy subsets defined on D_i.

So, the tuple values allowed are scalar, possibility distributions, linguistic labels, etc. For instance, the following one could be a legal tuple in a fuzzy database:

(Stevenson001 , GH300 , normal)

where normal is a fuzzy set on the crisp domain of prices. It is worth mentioning that it is not necessary to build an ad hoc system to store fuzzy information: we propose to use a general relational data base management system, and properly design the relations and dictionaries to manage fuzzy information (see [25] for the theoretical aspects, and [23] for implementation details), so that we can take advantage of these efficient data storing and management systems.

1.4 The Role of Fuzzy Functional Dependencies in Relational Databases

There has been several attempts to smooth the concept of functional dependency to incorporate fuzzy information (see [4, 9, 13, 28, 29, 35]). In [13] we saw basic properties that a fuzzy extension of functional dependency should verify, and revised the behavior of several approaches to the definition of f.f.d (see for instance [4, 16, 35]) regarding these properties. In [2] a good comparative analysis can be found. We proceed to introduce now an outline of the process followed to define the concept of fuzzy dependency.

An immediate extension of definition 1 of classical functional dependency, for crisp databases, is given by:

If antecedent values are equal, the consequent ones should be resemblant. (3)

In order to define what is meant by *resemblant* we introduce the following definition:

Definition 2. *Let D be a crisp domain. A* **resemblance relation** *is a binary relation*
$R : D \times D \to [0,1]$, *satisfying reflexive and symmetric properties:* $R(x,x) = 1$, $R(x,y) = R(y,x)$. *Two values* $x, y \in D$ *are* **resemblant at level** θ, *if and only if* $R(x,y) \geq \theta$

In order to emphasize the resemblance relation and the threshold attached to each attribute, we include them in the definition of the relational scheme, as follows:

Definition 3. *An* **extended scheme** *is a triple:*

$$\mathcal{S} = (REL, \boldsymbol{\theta}, \boldsymbol{R})$$

where REL is a classic scheme, i.e., a set of attributes $(A_1, \ldots, A_n)$, $\boldsymbol{\theta}$ *is the set of associated thresholds* $(\theta_1, \ldots, \theta_n)$, *and* $\boldsymbol{R}$ *the set of associated resemblance relations* $(R_1, \ldots, R_n)$. *For the sake of simplicity, we shall talk about the* **extended scheme of an attribute** A_i *as the pair* (θ_i, R_i).

Remark. If we do not want to impose any resemblance for an attribute (for instance, Product-Code) we only have to choose $R(x,y) = 1$ if $x = y$ and 0 otherwise.

By using definition 2, we can translate the statement in equation 3 (see [11]). A relation r in a crisp database satisfies a fuzzy dependency between X and Y, considering a threshold of resemblance β, if and only if the next formula holds:

$$\forall \; t_1, t_2 \in r \;\; \text{if} \;\; X(t_1) = X(t_2) \;\; \text{then} \;\; R(Y(t_1), Y(t_2)) \geq \beta \;\; \text{must hold} \quad (4)$$

Now, it is important to realize that fuzzy dependencies have not a real application if we can not use them to decompose the original relation r. So, we should be able to store fuzzy data in order to summarize the information we had in r.

Let us now generalize equation 4 to work with fuzzy values. The idea is to construct a measure $R^{\approx}$ which can be applied when $Y(t_1)$ and $Y(t_2)$ are fuzzy labels, so that, the definition of fuzzy dependency would be like the following:

$$\forall\ t_1, t_2 \in \tilde{r}\ \text{ if }\ X(t_1) = X(t_2)\ \text{ then }\ R^{\approx}(Y(t_1), Y(t_2)) \geq \beta\ \text{ must hold} \quad (5)$$

This definition shall be applied to a relation $\tilde{r}$ derived from r by replacing the original data by fuzzy labels containing them. If such formula holds, then we shall be able to decompose r into two fuzzy projections, yielding two relations r_1 and r_2 in such a way that we can recover the information we had in r by a fuzzy join of r_1 and r_2. We shall not recover exactly the same information, but almost the same in a fuzzy sense. In order to quantify such loss, a granularity measure will be introduced. It is important to note that a very large relation r can be significantly reduced, in the sense that the amount of information to be stored in r_1 and r_2 will be significantly less than in r. This is the role we advocate a fuzzy dependency should play in classic databases.

2 Extending a Resemblance Relation

The first step to define a fuzzy dependency for a fuzzy database is to extend definition 2 of resemblance to the fuzzy case. It can be accomplished through two possible extensions [10, 12, 28], namely a weak resemblance and a strong one. We follow the strong approximation in this work.

Definition 4. *Let us consider a domain D of crisp values, and a resemblance relation R defined on $D \times D$. Two fuzzy values G and $G' \in \tilde{\mathcal{P}}(D)$, are **strongly resemblant** at level β, and will be denoted by:*

$$G \approx_\beta G'$$

if and only if

$$R^{\approx}(G, G') \geq \beta \quad (6)$$

with

$$R^{\approx}\ :\ \tilde{\mathcal{P}}(D) \times \tilde{\mathcal{P}}(D)\ \longrightarrow\ [0, 1]$$

$$R^{\approx}(G, G') \triangleq \inf_{x, y}\{R(x, y) \vee (1 - \mu_G(x)) \vee (1 - \mu_{G'}(y))\} \quad (7)$$

where $\vee$ stands for the maximum between numeric values, and inf *denotes the infimum. If we consider several domains $D_1 \times \ldots \times D_m$, fuzzy sets G_j, $G'_j \in \tilde{\mathcal{P}}(D_j)$, and thresholds β_j for each domain D_j, then, the definition of strong resemblance is applied to each component:*

$$G \approx_\beta G' \Leftrightarrow G_j \approx_{\beta_j} G'_j \quad \forall\ j = 1 \ldots m$$

where $G = (G_1 \ldots G_m)$, $G' = (G'_1 \ldots G'_m)$, and $\beta = (\beta_1 \ldots \beta_m)$

<u>Remark</u>. Strong resemblance was introduced in [28] and compute the extent to which all the crisp elements in G are resemblant to all the crisp elements in G'. It is easy to check that the extension given by $R^{\approx}$ is not reflexive even though the underlying crisp relation R is. So, we give the following definition:

Definition 5. *Let D be a crisp domain, R a resemblance relation defined on $D \times D$, and β a resemblance threshold. Under these hypotheses, a fuzzy value $G \in \widetilde{\mathcal{P}}(D)$ satisfies the* **level of granularity** *(or equivalently, the integrity restriction of granularity IR-G) if and only if:*

$$G \approx_\beta G \qquad (8)$$

When applied to trapezoidal fuzzy sets, we only have to compute special cuts and the resemblance between the crisp extremes:

$$G \approx_\beta G \Leftrightarrow R(x_{G_{1-\beta}}^{left}, x_{G'_{1-\beta}}^{right}) \wedge R(x_{G_{1-\beta}}^{right}, x_{G'_{1-\beta}}^{left}) \geq \beta \qquad (9)$$

where $x_{G_{1-\beta}}^{left} = \min\{x; \ x \in G_{1-\beta}\}$ and $x_{G_{1-\beta}}^{right} = \max\{x; \ x \in G_{1-\beta}\}$.

3 The Fuzzy Projection Operator

Let us suppose we have a relation r in a crisp database, and that the designer constructs a set of fuzzy linguistic labels on each (antecedent or consequent) attribute A_i. If A_i has D_i as domain, then we shall denote the set of linguistic labels as $\mathcal{L}_{D_i}$ or $\mathcal{L}_{A_i}$. Each label $L \in \mathcal{L}_{D_i}$ is a fuzzy set belonging to $\widetilde{\mathcal{P}}(D_i)$. Each set $\mathcal{L}_{D_i}$ must satisfy next restrictions:

Integrity Restriction of Separation IR-S.
A set of linguistic labels $\mathcal{L}_{D_i} \subseteq \widetilde{\mathcal{P}}(D_i)$ satisfies IR-S restriction, if and only if next condition holds:

$$\forall \, L, L' \in \mathcal{L}_{D_i} \quad ker(L) \cap ker(L') = \emptyset \qquad (10)$$

Integrity Restriction of Granularity IR-G.
A set of linguistic labels $\mathcal{L}_{D_i} \subseteq \widetilde{\mathcal{P}}(D_i)$ satisfies IR-G restriction (for a fixed threshold β), if and only if L satisfies the granularity level $\quad \forall \, L \in \mathcal{L}_{D_i}$

Now, we proceed to replace each $A_i(t)$ by the label $L \in \mathcal{L}_{D_i}$ which kernel contains it (it is unique because of the restriction stated in equation 10); if there is not such label, then, $A_i(t)$ remains with the same value.

Definition 6. *Let us consider a crisp relation r with scheme $REL \supseteq W = (A_1, \ldots, A_m)$, and $\mathcal{L}_{D_i}$ is a set of linguistic labels associated to each $A_i \in W$, satisfying IR-S restriction. We define the* **inclusion** *operator respect to W and $\mathcal{L} = \{\mathcal{L}_{D_i}\}_i$, as an operator which applied to a relation r yields another relation denoted by $\mathbb{E}^W(r)$, constructed in this way: each tuple $t \in r$ is modified according to:*

– If $\exists L \in \mathcal{L}_{D_i}$ such that $A_i(t) \in ker(L)$, then we replace $A_i(t)$ by L.
– In other case, $A_i(t)$ remains with the same value.

Definition 7. *Let us consider a crisp relation r with scheme $REL \supseteq XY$.
We define the **fuzzy projection** of r over XY and respect to X and $\mathcal{L}$,
denoted by $\widetilde{\Pi} \, {}^{X,\mathcal{L}}_{XY}(r)$ (or simply $\widetilde{\Pi} \, {}^X_{XY}(r)$ if there is no confusion), as the
next relation: $\widetilde{\Pi} \, {}^X_{XY}(r) = \Pi \, {}^X_{XY} \left(I\!E^{XY}(r) \right)$, where $\Pi \, {}^X_{XY}(s)$ merges through
fuzzy union the XY values of those tuples $\{t_i \in s\}$ with equal X-values, i.e.,
$X_h(t_j) = X_h(t_k) \quad \forall \, X_h \in X \quad \forall \, t_j, t_k \in \{t_i\}$. The merging of $\{t_i\}$ over
$XY = (X_1, \ldots, X_m, Y_1, \ldots, Y_k)$, is given by
$(\vee_i X_1(t_i), \ldots, \vee_i X_m(t_i), \vee_i Y_1(t_i), \ldots, \vee_i Y_k(t_i))$. Therefore, $\widetilde{\Pi} \, {}^X_{XY}(r)$ is a relation with scheme XY.*

This process of generalization has also been followed by other authors. Bosc
et al, address this issue in [2] but no quantification in the loss less process is given.
The paper by Han et al [18] also follows this idea as a step in their approach to
knowledge discovery.

Example 1. Let us consider the relation Sales given in figure 2

$$\text{Sales} = \begin{array}{|lll|} \hline \textbf{Salesman-Code} & \textbf{Product-Code} & \textbf{Product-Price} \\ \hline \texttt{Smith103} & \texttt{AB200} & \texttt{24.3\$} \\ \texttt{Ford200} & \texttt{AB200} & \texttt{24\$} \\ \texttt{Stevenson001} & \texttt{GH300} & \texttt{19\$} \\ \texttt{Stevenson001} & \texttt{AB200} & \texttt{24.2\$} \\ \texttt{Stevenson001} & \texttt{PG100} & \texttt{50\$} \\ \hline \end{array}$$

Fig. 2. Original relation

We can see that there is not a functional dependency between the attributes
Product-Code and Product-Price, but it seems that the price is more or less
independent from the salesman because a product is sold almost at the same
price. Let us consider the set of fuzzy labels $\mathcal{L} = \{\emptyset, \emptyset, \mathcal{L}_{\text{Prod-Price}}\}$, where

$$\mathcal{L}_{\text{Prod-Price}} = \{\textbf{very cheap}, \textbf{cheap}, \textbf{normal}, \textbf{expensive}\}$$

Let us suppose that $24, 24.2, 24.3 \in ker(\textbf{normal})$, $50 \in ker(\textbf{expensive})$ and 19
does not belong to any kernel. Then, the relation given by $I\!E^{PC,PP}(r)$ and the
fuzzy projection over PC and PP, i.e, $\widetilde{\Pi} \, {}^{PC}_{PC,PP}(\text{Sales})$ (named Prices) can be
found in figure 3.

4 Fuzzy Dependency

We propose the following criterion of fuzzy dependency: a relation r satisfies a
fuzzy dependency $X \overset{\beta}{\leadsto} Y$ whenever the tuple values in relation $I\!E^{XY}(r)$ verify
equation 5. So, the kind of dependency we are modeling is like the following:

$$IE^{\,PC,PP}(\text{Sales}) = $$

Salesman-Code	Product-Code	Product-Price
Smith103	AB200	normal
Ford200	AB200	normal
Stevenson001	GH300	19$
Stevenson001	AB200	normal
Stevenson001	PG100	expensive

$$\widetilde{\Pi}^{\,PC}_{PC,PP}(\text{Sales}) \equiv \text{Prices} = $$

Product-Code	Product-Price
AB200	normal
GH300	19$
PG100	expensive

Fig. 3. The IE and $\widetilde{\Pi}$ operators

If antecedent values are equal, then the consequent values are expected to be strong resemblant

Definition 8. *Let us consider a scheme REL, two sets of attributes* $X, Y \subseteq REL$, *with* $X, Y \neq \emptyset$, $X \cap Y = \emptyset$, *and associated thresholds for* Y *given by* β. *Let* r *be a relation in a database satisfying scheme REL, and let us consider a set of linguistic labels* $\mathcal{L}$ *satisfying IR-S and IR-G restrictions. Then,* r *satisfies a* β-**fuzzy dependency** *respect to* $\mathcal{L}$, *denoted by* $X \overset{\beta}{\leadsto}_{\mathcal{L}} Y$ *or simply* $X \overset{\beta}{\leadsto} Y$, *if and only if the following restriction is satisfied:*

$$\forall\ t_1, t_2 \in IE^{XY}(r)\ \ \text{if}\ \ X(t_1) = X(t_2)\ \ \text{then}$$

$$R^{\approx}(Y(t_1), Y(t_2)) \geq \beta\ \ \text{must hold}$$

An important issue is that testing the fuzzy dependency on $IE^{XY}(r)$ is equivalent to test only the granularity level for the Y-values on the relation $\widetilde{\Pi}^{X}_{XY}(r)$. This is stated in the following theorem:

Theorem 1. *Under the same hypotheses of definition 8, the relation* r *satisfies* $X \overset{\beta}{\leadsto} Y$, *if and only if all the* Y-*values in* $\widetilde{\Pi}^{X}_{XY}(r)$ *verify the level of granularity.*

Definition 9. *The proof is immediate if we consider that the relation* $\widetilde{\Pi}^{X}_{XY}(r)$ *is the merge through fuzzy union of those tuples in* $IE^{XY}(r)$ *with equal* X-*values. The corresponding* Y-*values have the format* $Y(t) = \vee_i Y(t_i)$ *with* $Y(t_i) \approx_\beta Y(t_{i'})$ *and thus* $Y(t) \approx_\beta Y(t)$ *if and only if*

$$(\vee_i Y(t_i)) \approx_\beta (\vee_i Y(t_i))$$

but this is equivalent (see [10]) to test whether $Y(t_i) \approx_\beta Y(t_{i'})\ \ \forall\ i, i'$

Example 2. Let us consider the relation in figure 2, with fuzzy projection given in figure 3. We want to test if **Sales** satisfies the fuzzy dependency **Product-Code** $\overset{\beta}{\leadsto}$ **Product-Price**. Then, according to theorem 1, the following restrictions must hold:

normal $\approx_\beta$ normal   expensive $\approx_\beta$ expensive

Both of them are satisfied, because we assumed that the linguistic labels satisfy the level of granularity. So, we can conclude saying that Sales satisfy the fuzzy dependency given by Product-Code $\overset{\beta}{\leadsto}$ Product-Price.

Let us suppose now that we had two more tuples in the original relation Sales, namely:

(Spencer01 , GH300 , 19.5\$) and (Spencer01 , PG100 , 56\$)

where 19.5 $\in$ker(normal) and 56 $\notin$ker(expensive). Then, the corresponding fuzzy projections can be found in the next tables:

$$\mathbb{E}^{\,PC,PP}(\text{Sales}) =$$

Product-Code	Product-Price
AB200	normal
AB200	normal
GH300	19\$
AB200	normal
PG100	expensive
GH300	19.5\$
PG100	56\$

$$\tilde{\Pi}^{PC}_{PC,PP}(\text{Sales}) \equiv \text{Prices} =$$

Product-Code	Product-Price
AB200	normal
GH300	(19∨19.5)\$
PG100	(expensive ∨ 56\$)

Now, we should test the following conditions:

- (19∨19.5) $\approx_\beta$ (19∨19.5), or equivalently $R(19, 19.5) \geq \beta$
- (expensive $\vee$ 56\$) $\approx_\beta$ (expensive $\vee$ 56\$), or equivalently,
  $R^{\approx}$(expensive, 56\$) $\geq \beta$. If we suppose that the extreme of the $(1-\beta)$-cut of expensive is equal to 48.8, then, by applying equation 9, we only have to test whether $R(48.8, 56) \geq \beta$

If both restrictions hold, then, we can conclude that Sales satisfies the Product-Code $\overset{\beta}{\leadsto}$ Product-Price fuzzy dependency

Let us remark that transitivity axiom does not hold, i.e, if $X \overset{\beta}{\leadsto} Y$ and $Y \overset{\gamma}{\leadsto} W$, then no fuzzy dependency like $X \overset{\min\{\beta,\gamma\}}{\leadsto} W$ can be derived. Formally, if $X(t) = X(t')$ then $Y(t) \approx_\beta Y(t')$ must hold, but this does not imply $Y(t) = Y(t')$, and then, we can not derive $Z(t) \approx_\theta Z(t')$ for any threshold θ. This is the price to pay for a softer restriction of dependency (see [7, 8] for alternative solutions).

5 The Loss Less Decomposition Issue

We have seen how to project into $r_2 = \widetilde{\Pi}\,{}^X_{XY}(r)$, the XY values of a relation r with scheme XYZ, satisfying a fuzzy dependency between X and Y. Now, the information appearing in Z in the original relation can be projected into the classic projection $r_1 = \Pi_{ZX}(r)$. So, we only have to introduce a special join operator which allows us to recover the values in relation r. Formally, we define the fuzzy natural join between r_1 and r_2 in the following sense:

$$r_1 \bowtie_X r_2 = \Pi_{r_1.(XY)\cup r_2.Z}\left(\sigma_{r_1.X \subseteq r_2.X}(r_1 \times r_2)\right)$$

where $\sigma_{r_1.X \subseteq r_2.X}(r_1 \times r_2)$ selects those tuples $t \in r_1$, $u \in r_2$ such that $r_1.X_i(t) \subseteq r_2.X_i(u)$ $\forall X_i \in X$, where $\subseteq$ stands for fuzzy set inclusion. Of course, this join operator is not symmetrical.

Example 3. Let us consider the relation in figure 2. The projection over the attributes Salesman-Code and Product-Code (r_1 = JustSales = $\Pi_{\text{SC,PC}}(\text{Sales})$) and the join of r_1 and r_2 = Prices = $\widetilde{\Pi}\,{}^{\text{PC}}_{\text{PC,PP}}(\text{Sales})$ are given below:

JustSales =

Salesman-Code	Product-Code
Smith103	AB200
Ford200	AB200
Stevenson001	GH300
Stevenson001	AB200
Stevenson001	PG100

JustSales $\bowtie$ Prices=

Salesman-Code	Product-Code	Product-Price
Smith103	AB2002	normal
Ford200	AB200	normal
Stevenson001	GH300	19$
Stevenson001	AB200	normal
Stevenson001	PG100	expensive

The relation so constructed, can be compared with the original relation r, and we see that the only loss we obtain, stem from the consequent values which are now fuzzier, but not too much because they satisfy the level of granularity (a condition imposed in the fuzzy dependency). So, we can conclude that the process of decomposition is fuzzy loss less. This is formally stated in next theorem.

The first and second conditions of the following theorem ensure that we recover the same information (without spurious tuples) as we had in r, i.e, if we had a tuple $t \in r$, we do not recover exactly the same values as in the classical case, but we can guarantee that $\exists\,\bar{t} \in r_1 \bowtie_X r_2$ such that $XZ(t) = XZ(\bar{t})$, $Y(t) \subseteq Y(\bar{t})$ (furthermore, all tuples in the join are of this type). On the other hand, the third condition guarantees the quality of such information in the following sense: the consequent values of each tuple $\bar{t}$ satisfy the same level of granularity (β) as the level of resemblance we allowed in $r.Y$, i.e, we do not obtain *too fuzzy* values in the attributes of Y.

Theorem 2. *Let us consider a relation r under the same conditions as in definition 8 and satisfying the fuzzy dependency $I = (X \overset{\beta}{\leadsto} Y)$. Then, the decomposition of r with respect to I given by:*

$$r_1 = \Pi_{XZ}(r) \quad , \quad r_2 = \widetilde{\Pi}_{XY}^X(r)$$

satisfy the following properties:

i) $\forall\, t \in r \;\; \exists\, \bar{t} \in r_1 \Join_X r_2 \quad$ *such that* $XZ(t) = XZ(\bar{t}) \;\;,\;\; Y(t) \in ker(Y(\bar{t}))$
ii) $\forall\, \bar{t} \in (r_1 \Join_X r_2) \;\; \exists\, t \in r \quad$ *such that* $XZ(t) = XZ(\bar{t}) \;\;,\;\; Y(t) \in ker(Y(\bar{t}))$
iii) *The Y-values in relation $r_1 \Join_X r_2$ satisfy the β-level of granularity.*

The proof of *i)* and *ii)* are straightforward and *iii)* follows from *i)*, *ii)* and the fact that the Y-values in r_2 satisfy the level of granularity because of theorem 1.

The previous theorem showed that if we replace the relation r by the projections $r_1 = \Pi_{ZX}(r)$ and $r_2 = \widetilde{\Pi}_{XY}^X(r)$, then, we can recover the same information we had in r. Once such decomposition has been done, there can be new tuples t entering to the database. We see in the next theorem that we can test whether t violates or not the fuzzy dependency just by looking at the values in the fuzzy projection. So, we can still test the dependency in the same way as we had used the old relation r.

Theorem 3. *Let us consider a relation r under the same conditions as in definition 8 of fuzzy dependency, and let us denote by $\widetilde{r}$ the fuzzy projection $\widetilde{\Pi}_{XY}^X(r)$. Let us consider a new tuple given by t. Then, we have:*

i) $\widetilde{\Pi}_{XY}^X(\widetilde{r} \cup XY(t)) = \widetilde{\Pi}_{XY}^X(r \cup t)$
ii) $r \cup t$ *satisfies* $X \overset{\beta}{\leadsto} Y$ *if and only if the Y-values of relation $\widetilde{\Pi}_{XY}^X(\widetilde{r} \cup XY(t))$ satisfy the level of granularity.*

Definition 10. *For the sake of simplicity, we shall omit X and Y, when denoting Π_{XY}^X and $\widetilde{\Pi}_{XY}^X$, and we shall denote $XY(t)$ by p. Part ii) is a direct consequence of part i) and theorem 1, so that we are going to prove i). We have $\mathbb{E}(r \cup t) = \mathbb{E}(r) \cup \mathbb{E}(t)$, and thus*

$$\Pi\,(\mathbb{E}(r \cup t)) = \Pi\,(\mathbb{E}(r) \cup \mathbb{E}(t)) \;\;\Leftrightarrow\;\; \widetilde{\Pi}\,(r \cup t) = \Pi\,(\mathbb{E}(r) \cup \mathbb{E}(t))$$

On the other hand, we have:

$$\Pi\,(\mathbb{E}(r) \cup \mathbb{E}(t)) = \Pi\,(\Pi\,(\mathbb{E}(r)) \cup \Pi\,(\mathbb{E}(t))) = \Pi\,(\widetilde{r} \cup \Pi\,(\mathbb{E}(t)))$$

As t is a single tuple, we obtain $\Pi\,(\mathbb{E}(t)) = \mathbb{E}(p)$, so, we find:

$$\widetilde{\Pi}\,(r \cup t) = \Pi\,(\mathbb{E}(r \cup t)) = \Pi\,(\widetilde{r} \cup \mathbb{E}(p))$$

Taking into account that $\tilde{r} = I\!\!E(\tilde{r})$, then we find:

$$\Pi\left(\tilde{r} \cup I\!\!E(p)\right) = \Pi\left(I\!\!E(\tilde{r}) \cup I\!\!E(p)\right) = \Pi\left(I\!\!E(\tilde{r} \cup p)\right) = \tilde{\Pi}\left(\tilde{r} \cup p\right)$$

By chaining these equalities, we finally obtain

$$\tilde{\Pi}\left(r \cup t\right) = \tilde{\Pi}\left(\tilde{r} \cup p\right)$$

6 Concluding Remarks

In this work we have introduced an approach to detect fuzzy dependencies among attributes in a classic relational database. This is done by using linguistic labels which should be given by the designer of the database. In addition, a projection operator is introduced, which permits to decompose such a relation r into two new ones, in such a way that the amount of information to be stored is less than the original one in r. In order to do this, we need to store fuzzy information, but this can be managed in classic relational database systems.

The advantage of our approach mainly relies on two points. First, we can quantify, through the granularity level, how much information we loose in the decomposition process. Second, we can benefit from the experience of the designer, who can supply the linguistic values to summarize the data appearing in the relation.

References

1. Hull R. Abiteboul S. Ifo: A formal semantic database model. *ACM Transactions on Database Systems*, 12(4):525–565, 1987.
2. P. Bosc, D. Dubois, and H. Prade. More results on functional dependencies and quotient operators in fuzzy databases. Technical Report IRIT/96-10-R, Institute de Recherche en Informatique de Toulouse, Mars 1996.
3. B.P. Buckles and F.E. Petry. Extending the fuzzy database with fuzzy numbers. *Information Sciences*, 34:145–155, 1984.
4. G. Chen, E.E. Kerre, and J. Vandenbulcke. A computational algorithm for the ffd transitivity closure and a complete axiomatization of fuzzy functional dependence (ffd). *International Journal of Intelligent Systems*, 9(5):421–440, 1994.
5. E.F. Codd. A relational model of data for large shared data banks. *Commun. ACM*, 13(6):377–387, 1970.
6. E.F. Codd. *The Relational Model for Database Management*. Addison-Wesley, Reading, Mass., 1990.
7. J.C. Cubero, J.M. Medina, O. Pons, and M.A. Vila. Non transitive fuzzy dependencies. *Fuzzy Sets and Systems*, to appear.
8. J.C. Cubero, J.M. Medina, O. Pons, and M.A. Vila. Transitive fuzzy dependencies. *Fuzzy Sets and Systems*, to appear.
9. J.C. Cubero, J.M. Medina, O. Pons, and M.A. Vila. Rules discovery in fuzzy relational databases. In *Conference of the North American Fuzzy Information Processing Society, NAFIPS'95. Maryland (USA)*. IEEE Computer Society Press, pages 414–419, 1995.

10. J.C. Cubero, J.M. Medina, O. Pons, and M.A. Vila. Extensions of a resemblance relation. *Fuzzy Sets and Systems*, 86(2):197–212, 1997.

11. J.C. Cubero, J.M. Medina, O. Pons, and M.A. Vila. Fuzzy loss less decompositions in databases. *Fuzzy Sets and Systems*, 97(2):145–167, 1998.

12. J.C. Cubero, J.M. Medina, and M.A. Vila. Influence of granularity level in fuzzy functional dependencies. In M. Clarke, R. Kruse, and S. Moral, editors, *Symbolic and Quantitative Approaches to Reasoning and Uncertainty. Lecture Notes in Computer Science 747*, pages 73–78. Springer Verlag, Berlin, 1993.

13. J.C. Cubero and M.A. Vila. A new definition of fuzzy functional dependencies in fuzzy relational databases. *International Journal of Intelligent Systems*, 9(5):441–448, 1994.

14. C.J. Date. *An Introduction to Data Bases Systems. Vol I*. Addison-Wesley, Reading, Mass., 1990.

15. D. Dubois and H. Prade. *Fuzzy Sets and Systems: Theory and Applications*. Academic Press, N.Y., 1979.

16. D. Dubois and H. Prade. Generalized dependencies in fuzzy databases. In *International Conference on Information Processing and Management of Uncertainty in Knowledge Based Systems, IPMU'92*, Palma de Mallorca, Spain, 1992.

17. H. Gallaire, J. Minker, and J. M. Nicolas. Logic and databases: A deductive approach. *ACM Computing Surveys*, 16(2):153–185, June 1984.

18. J. Han, Y. Cai, and N. Cercone. Knowledge discovery in databases: An attribute-oriented approach. In *Proceedings of the 18th VLDB Conference*, pages 547 – 559, Vancouver, British Columbia, Canada, 1992.

19. I.J. Heath. Unacceptable file operations in a relational database. In *ACM SIGFIDET Workshop on Data Description, Access, and Control. San Diego*, 1971.

20. T. Imielinski and W. Lipski. Incomplete information in relational databases. *Journal of ACM*, 31(4), 1984.

21. Jr. Lipski, W. On semantic issues connected with incomplete information databases. *ACM Transactions on Database Systems*, 4(3):262–296, September 1979.

22. K. C. Liu and R. Sunderraman. A generalized relational model for indefinite and maybe information. *IEEE Transactions on Knowledge and Data Engineering*, 3(1):65–76, 1991.

23. J.M. Medina, J.C. Cubero, O. Pons, and M.A. Vila. Towards the implementation of a generalized fuzzy relational database model. *Fuzzy Sets and Systems*, 75:273–289, 1995.

24. J.M. Medina, O. Pons, J.C. Cubero, and M.A. Vila. Freddi: A fuzzy relational deductive database interface. *International Journal of Intelligent Systems*, 12:597–613, 1997.

25. J.M. Medina, O. Pons, and M.A. Vila. GEFRED: A generalized model for fuzzy relational databases. *Information Sciences*, 76:87–109, 1994.

26. A. Ola and G. Ozsoyoglu. Incomplete relational database models based on intervals. *IEEE Transactions on Knowledge and Data Engineering*, 5(2):293–308, April 1993.

27. O. Pons, J.C. Cubero, J.M. Medina, and M.A. Vila. Dealing with disjunctive and missing information in logic fuzzy databases. *Int. Journal on Uncertainty and Fuzziness in Knowledge Based Systems*, 4(2):177–201, 1996.

28. H. Prade and C. Testemale. Generalizing database relational algebra for the treatment of incomplete/uncertain information and vague queries. *Information Sciences*, 34:115–143, 1984.

29. K. Raju and A. Majumdar. Fuzzy functional dependencies and loss less join decomposition on fuzzy relational database systems. *ACM Transactions on Database Systems*, 13(2):129–166, 1988.

30. K. Tanaka, M. Yoshikawa, and K. Ishihara. Schema design, views and incomplete information in object-oriented databases. *Journal of Information Processing*, 12(3):239–250, 1989.

31. J.D. Ullman. *Principles of Database and Knowledge-Base Systems, vol. I.* Computer Science Press., 1988.

32. M. Umano. Freedom-0: A fuzzy databases system. In M.M. Gupta and E. Sanchez, editors, *Fuzzy Information and Decision Processes.*, pages 339–347. North Holland, 1982.

33. M.A. Vila, J.C. Cubero, J.M. Medina, and O. Pons. A logic approach to fuzzy relational databases. *International Journal of Intelligent Systems*, 9(5):449–461, 1994.

34. M.A. Vila, J.C. Cubero, J.M. Medina, and O. Pons. A conceptual approach for dealing with imprecision and uncertainty in object-based data models. *International Journal of Intelligent Systems*, 11:791–806, 1996.

35. L. Weiyi. The reduction of the fuzzy data domain and fuzzy consistent join. *Fuzzy Sets and Systems*, 50:89–96, 1992.

36. L. Zadeh. Knowledge representation in fuzzy logic. *IEEE Transactions on Knowledge and Data Engineering*, 1(1):89–100, 1989.

37. L.A. Zadeh. Fuzzy logic = computing with words. *IEEE Transactions on Fuzzy Systems*, 4:103–111, 1996.

38. R. Zicari. Incomplete information in object-oriented databases. *Sigmod*, 19(3):5–16, September 1990.

The Paradigm of Computing with Words in Intelligent Database Querying

Janusz Kacprzyk and Sławomir Zadrożny
Systems Research Institute, Polish Academy of Sciences
ul. Newelska 6, 01-447 Warsaw, Poland
Email: {kacprzyk,zadrozny}@ibspan.waw.pl

Abstract. We present how the paradigm of computing with words may contribute to user-friendliness and effectiveness of database querying. We illustrate our exposition with the latest version of our FQUERY for Access system, a fuzzy querying user-friendly interface to Microsoft Access. The system accommodates fuzzy (imprecise) terms and linguistic quantifiers allowing for more human-consistent queries. The system employs Zadeh's (1983) fuzzy logic based calculus of linguistically quantified propositions. Alternatively, Yager's (1988) ordered weighted averaging (OWA) operators may be used to deal with fuzzy linguistic quantifiers.

Keywords: computing with words, database querying, flexible querying, fuzzy querying, fuzzy logic, fuzzy linguistic quantifiers, Microsoft Access.

1. INTRODUCTION

Database management systems (DBMSs) make it possible to organize and maintain huge collections of data. One of their basic functions is to provide for a quick access to relevant data. Requests may be precise and standardized like, e.g., in case of a payroll preparation subsystem – a typical part of systems supporting corporate financial departments. Then, the major effectiveness indicator is the speed of reaction secured by, e.g., sophisticated indexing schemes, an optimal physical layout of the data, etc. On the other hand, in case of casual, non-standardized requests, what mostly counts is the ease of their construction by the end user. Such an end user may be either a strategic planner in top management or a customer of, e.g., a real-estate agency. Typically, their requests will contain vague, highly aggregated terms, concepts and relations, which are rather cumbersome to translate into a form acceptable by traditional querying formalisms. Providing an additional layer responsible for dealing with linguistic elements in a query would be really worthwhile. Such a layer, a *querying system*, should provide for the maintenance of a dictionary of linguistic terms as well as for their proper interpretation when processing the query, i.e., should be capable of *computing with words*. FQUERY for Access is meant to be such a component working as an add-in for the commercial desktop DBMS, Microsoft Access.

Basically, in this paper we show how main elements of Zadeh's paradigm of computing with words: linguistic values (e.g., *high*), linguistic relations (e.g. *much more than a half*), linguistic modifiers (e.g., *very*), and linguistic quantifiers (e.g., *most*), can be used in devising more human-consistent and human-friendly querying interfaces to DBMSs. First, we discuss how the fuzzy sets (logic) based concepts may be included with the traditional querying language syntax. Second, we briefly present how the definition and processing of these fuzzy elements may be carried out. Third, we discuss some implementation details of the querying scheme proposed and implemented in the FQUERY for Access package.

2. TYPES OF LINGUISTIC TERMS IN FLEXIBLE QUERIES

Basically, the construction of a database query consists in spelling out conditions that should be met by the data sought. Very often, the meaning of these conditions is deeply rooted in natural language, i.e., their original formulation is available in the form of natural language utterances. It is then, often with difficulty, translated into mathematical formulas requested by the traditional query languages. For example, looking for a suitable house in a real estate agency database one may prefer a *cheap* one. In order to pose a query, the concept of "cheap" has to be expressed by an interval of prices. The bounds of such an interval will usually be rather difficult to assess. Thus, a tool to somehow define the notion of "being cheap" may essentially ease the construction of a query. The same definition may be then used, in other queries referring to this concept, also in the context of other words, as, e.g., *very*. The words of this kind, interpreted as so-called *modifiers*, modify the meaning of the original concept in a way that may be assumed context-independent and expressed by a strict mathematical formula.

Usually, a query comprises more than just one condition. In such a case, the user may require various combinations of conditions to be met, including:

- all conditions required (corresponds to the use of logical AND connective),
- any one condition met (corresponds to the use of logical OR connective),

In the first case, meeting each condition separately does contribute to the overall satisfaction of our query only in case all other conditions are also met. In the second case, meeting any, just one condition, is enough to satisfy the query. Sometimes a more flexible scheme of *aggregation*, positioned somewhere in between the two above extreme cases, may be useful. That is, we would like to consider each condition as determining a *partial* satisfaction of the query. Then, only meeting a predefined proportion of, e.g., *most*, of the conditions provides for a *complete* satisfaction of the query. Moreover, we can differentiate among the conditions as to their contribution to the overall satisfaction of the query. Some of them may be more *important* than others. Such flexible aggregation operators may be modeled using fuzzy (linguistic) quantifiers. In the framework of this model the importance degrees of the entities being aggregated may also be taken into account.

Our considerations will concentrate on the SQL language, the de facto industry standard. From that point of view, there is still room for an application of the fuzzy quantifiers mentioned above. Namely, they may be used instead of the classic quantifiers, represented by the SQL keywords ANY (SOME) and ALL in connection with subqueries placed in the WHERE clause. We will not discuss this possibility here as its implementation is rather difficult in our FQUERY for Access package. More on the use of fuzzy quantifiers in this context may be found in, e.g., Bosc, Lietard and Pivert (1995).

To summarize, various linguistic terms and their possible parameters which may be used in formulating queries may be classified in the following way:

1) terms representing inherent imprecision of some queries' conditions, including:
   a) numeric fuzzy values,
   b) modifiers,
   c) fuzzy relations,
   d) fuzzy sets of scalar values
2) terms corresponding to the non-standard aggregation operators, including:
   a) fuzzy (linguistic) quantifiers (or possibly OWA operators),
   b) importance coefficients

The query languages of classical DBMSs do not provide any means for representing such linguistic terms. Thus, in accordance with the *computing with words* paradigm, we will try to devise some extension of a classical query language, the SQL. In this section we will present a possible extension of its syntax. Obviously, this is not enough to extend the language alone – one must also provide for a proper interpretation of particular new linguistic constructs accompanied with some scheme for their representation, elicitation and manipulation. Thus, the next section will discuss these issues on the example of the FQUERY for Access package.

We will focus our attention on the well-known SELECT...FROM...WHERE command of the SQL. More precisely, we will deal only with its WHERE clause. Starting with its somehow simplified version, e.g., excluding subqueries, we propose the following additions to the usual syntax of this clause providing for the direct use of linguistic terms:

<WHERE-clause> ::= WHERE <condition>
<condition> ::= <linguistic quantifier> <sequence of subconditions> ;
<sequence of subconditions> ::= <subcondition> | <subcondition> OR
                                <sequence of subconditions>

```
<subcondition> ::= <importance coefficient> <linguistic quantifier>
                            <sequence of atomic conditions>
<sequence of atomic conditions> ::=  <atomic condition> |
                            <atomic condition> AND
                            <sequence of atomic conditions>
<atomic condition> ::=  <attribute> = <modifier> <fuzzy value> |
                        <attribute> <fuzzy relation> <attribute> |
                        <attribute> <fuzzy relation> <number> |
                        <single-valued-attribute> IN <fuzzy-set constant> |
                        <multi-valued-attribute> <compatibility operator>
                        <fuzzy-set constant> |
<attribute> ::= <numeric field>
<linguistic quantifier> ::= <OWA-tag> <quantifier name>
<OWA-tag> ::= OWA |
<modifier> ::= VERY | MORE OR LESS | RATHER | NOT |
<compatibility operator> ::= possible matching | necessary matching |
                            Jackard compatibility
```

Now, let us discuss particular categories of linguistic terms listed above. In what follows, we mainly use examples referring to a hypothetical database of a real estate agency. Particular houses are characterized by: price, land area, location (region), number of bedrooms and bathrooms and other life quality indicators as, e.g., an overall assessment of the environment, transportation infrastructure or shopping facilities.

Atomic condition

The basic building block of a query condition is the *atomic condition*. Basically, it contains a name of an attribute and a constraint imposed on the value of this attribute. Such a constraint may be a traditional, crisp one as, e.g., in

Price <= 200,000

It may also employ one of linguistic terms as, e.g.:

1. *Price = low*   (numeric fuzzy value)
2. *Land area = very large*   (numeric fuzzy value +
                                                                  modifier)
3. *Price is not much greater than 250,000*   (fuzzy relation)
4. *Location belongs to favorite regions*   (fuzzy set constant)
5. *Life quality indicators are compatible
   with high quality of life pattern*   (multi-valued-attribute +
                                                                  fuzzy set constant)

Numeric fuzzy values are to be used in connection with numeric fields as, e.g., with the field *Price*. Meaning of such a linguistic term is intuitively obvious, although rather subjective. Thus, it should be possible for each user to define his or her meaning of the linguistic term *low*. On the other hand, it would be advantageous to make it possible to use an already once defined term, like *low*, in various fields. Numeric fuzzy values may be accompanied by *modifiers* as, e.g., *very*, that directly correspond to the similar structures of the natural language.

Fuzzy relations make it possible to soften rigidness of crisp relations. In the third example given above, the atomic condition employs the *much greater than* fuzzy relation accompanied with the negation operator treated as a modifier. Thus, such a condition will accept the price of, e.g., 255,000, which seems to be much more practical than treating 250,000 as a sharp limit.

The examples discussed so far employed linguistic terms to be used along with the numeric data. The fourth example introduces a *fuzzy set constant* which is similar to numeric fuzzy values but meant to be used with scalar data. In this example, the *favorite regions* constant represents the user's preferences as to the location of the house sought. The concept of favorite regions will quite often turn out to be fuzzy, i.e., some regions will be perceived by the user as the best location, some will be completely rejected, and the rest will be acceptable to a degree. Obviously, such a concept is highly subjective.

Finally, the fifth example presents the concept of a *multi-valued attribute*. This concept emerged from the application of our fuzzy querying interface against a database of questionnaires on RTD institutions (see, e.g., Kacprzyk and Zadrożny, 1997c, Zadrożny and Kacprzyk, 1996). It can be best explained on the example given there. In brief, assume that each RTD institution is described by a set of obvious attributes, as, e.g., name, address etc. Usually, such an institution deals with a number of scientific disciplines. Some of them belong to the mainstream of activities of the institution, other may be more or less important. Thus, such an attribute, let us call it *subjects of activity*, may take on a set of values instead of just one as it is required in the classic relational approach. Moreover, quite often it may be advantageous to treat such a set as a fuzzy set, i.e., the institute's mainstream scientific disciplines will be assigned the membership degree 1 and the rest of them an appropriate degree from (0,1). Then, the user looking for an RTD institution in our database, may specify in his or her query another, possibly fuzzy, set of disciplines. Such a query should also employ one of the supported *compatibility operators*, making it possible to calculate the matching of (fuzzy) sets provided in the query and each of the relevant records from the database. Various compatibility operators may satisfy different requirements of the user. Namely, keeping up with our example, the user may be looking for an institution dealing:

• with at least one subject of activity specified in a query,

- with all activities specified in a query (and maybe some more),
- only with activities specified in the query, not necessarily all,
- with most activities specified in the query and not many other.

Obviously, appropriate queries may be constructed without calling for multi-valued attributes and compatibility operators concepts, but such a construction would be rather cumbersome.

We should stress here the difference between this concept of a multi-valued attribute and similar concepts used in the fuzzy databases. In the similarity based as well as in the possibility based models of the fuzzy database, a field may take on a set as its value. However, in both models, a set is used due to the imprecise knowledge of the real, *single* value of the field. Our multi-valued attribute, on the other hand, takes a set as its value by definition. As was mentioned earlier, we introduced the concept of a multi-valued attribute for practical reasons. This makes the use of our fuzzy querying interface more suitable in some situations. Although it seems to go beyond the paradigm of fuzzy querying against a crisp database, in fact it does not. As it is explained in the next section, multi-valued attribute is somehow a *virtual* concept and does not require any changes in the underlying, traditional DBMS. This virtual nature of our multi-valued attribute resembles the concept of an ambiguous attribute (cf. Nomura et al., 1992).

A traditional atomic condition, i.e., one without any linguistic terms, may be satisfied by a given record from the database (or, more precisely, by a given field from a row/record of a table in question) or not. Thus, binary logic applies. In the opposite case, an atomic condition may be satisfied to a *degree*. This is the essence of the linguistic approach. For example, the price may be definitely *low* or definitely *not low*, but also intermediate cases do exist.

Sequence of atomic conditions and a subcondition

The *sequence of atomic conditions* is just a conjunction of atomic conditions. Due to the fact that particular atomic conditions may be satisfied to a degree, we need to employ some generalization of the classical AND logical connective. For the fuzzy logic based approach, the natural choice is the *min* operator.

In the context considered here, the classical logical connective AND may be perceived as an aggregation operator. Namely, it aggregates the truth values of atomic conditions. This may however be sometimes counter-intuitive. Let us consider two cases. First, where all but one of n atomic conditions are met, and the second where just one atomic condition is satisfied. In both cases, the result of aggregation will be *False* (or 0). The *min* operator, making it possible to aggregate non-binary logical values, still preserves this behavior of the AND connective. In order to achieve a flexibility of the aggregation postulated at the beginning of this section, a linguistic quantifier may be applied for selected sequence of atomic conditions. Then, it replaces the AND connective as the aggregation operator. Linguistic quantifiers may be defined and interpreted in two ways, as it is explained in the next section. Here, we should only add that a *default* linguistic quantifier in the OWA operator form is automatically attached to each sequence of atomic conditions used in a query without explicitly specified quantifier. Originally, this default quantifier acts exactly like the AND connective, but may be easily manipulated by the user so as to reach a suitable aggregation behavior.

Each sequence of atomic conditions may be additionally assigned an importance coefficient. That way, the user may vary the degree to which given sequence contributes to the overall satisfaction degree of the whole query.

Finally, the sequence of atomic conditions, possibly accompanied by a linguistic quantifier and an importance coefficient, is called a *subcondition*.

Sequence of subconditions and a condition

The *sequence of subconditions* is the disjunction of subconditions. This structuring of various elements of the condition adheres to the scheme assumed in Microsoft Access. In fact, using this package, the user composes the query's condition in the disjunctive normal form.

As in case of the AND connective, the OR connective is replaced by the corresponding *max* operator of fuzzy logic. Again, sometimes it may be advantageous to apply another, more flexible scheme of aggregation. In such a case, a linguistic quantifier may be employed. The way a selected quantifier works may be guided by importance coefficients, possibly present in particular subconditions. The details are explained in the next section.

3. REPRESENTATION AND DEFINITIONS OF LINGUISTIC TERMS

Basically, all linguistic terms are represented as fuzzy sets. Obviously, the universe used to define particular fuzzy set depends on the type of their corresponding linguistic term. Namely, in order to represent terms used along with the *numeric* fields (attributes) we use trapezoidal fuzzy numbers. It seems obvious, that these fuzzy numbers are defined over the domains of corresponding fields. Namely, if the *price* of the house ranges from, say, 10,000 up to 100,000 USD, then the fuzzy value *low*, to be used in the atomic condition "price is low", should be defined as a fuzzy number over the interval [10,000, 100,000]. However, then if we strictly stick to this scheme, we have to define *low* separately for each field which we are going to use together with this linguistic term. In order to avoid this apparent inconvenience, we propose to use "context-free" definitions of numeric linguistic terms. Namely, the corresponding fuzzy numbers are defined over the universal interval, e.g., [-10, 10]. Additionally, for each relevant field, its range of variability, the [LowerLimit, UpperLimit] interval, has to be provided before a given linguistic term may be used along with this field in an atomic condition. Then, during the calculation of a matching degree – for details see next section – the definitions of relevant fuzzy numbers are translated into the domains of corresponding fields. In some cases, defining fuzzy numbers over the universal interval may be cumbersome. Thus, we provide the possibility to use, both, context-free as well as context-dependent definitions of fuzzy numbers.

Figure 1 shows an example of a trapezoidal fuzzy number, which may be a representation of a numeric fuzzy value *"moderate"*.

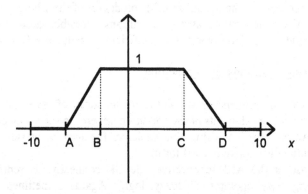

Figure 1. Trapezoidal membership function of a numeric fuzzy value

Thus, to define a fuzzy value, the four points A, B, C, and D are needed, and their interpretation is obvious.

The same approach is adopted for dealing with *fuzzy relations*. Basically, a fuzzy relation is a fuzzy set defined in the universe of the Cartesian product of two domains. In the context considered here, these are the domains of one or two *numeric* attributes involved. Obviously, it would be rather tedious to define a fuzzy relation directly on this Cartesian product. Thus, in our approach as the universe for the definition of a fuzzy relation we use the set of possible values of the difference of values of the two attributes involved. More precisely, the same universal interval [-10,10] is used for the definition which is then translated into the real interval of possible differences during the matching degree calculation. The definitions again take the form of trapezoidal fuzzy numbers.

The idea of a *universal* domain may also be applied for the definition of a linguistic quantifier. In fact, in this case it is then even more essential. Basically, linguistic quantifiers are defined in terms of Zadeh's (1983) approach. Again, the quantifier is represented as a fuzzy number – this time not trapezoidal but similar, defined by a piecewise linear membership function. As it is discussed in the previous section, the linguistic quantifier may be treated as an aggregation operator. Briefly speaking, in order to aggregate, we have to carry out the normalization using the number of propositions being aggregated, N. In case of our querying language syntax, the propositions correspond to the *atomic conditions* or *subconditions*. Thus, the number N will usually vary essentially between different queries. This, again, requires separate definitions of linguistic quantifiers for all queries posed. The solution is similar to that applied for numeric fuzzy terms but this time [0, 10] plays the role of the universal interval. We assume that the membership function of the fuzzy linguistic quantifier is piecewise linear as sketched in Figure 2.

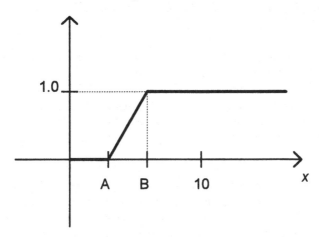

Figure 2. Example of the membership function of a fuzzy linguistic quantifier

In our approach, a linguistic quantifier has to be defined in the sense of Zadeh (1983). Then, for the matching degree calculation two options exist. First, the quantifier's original form may be employed directly. Second, an original definition may be automatically translated in order to obtain a corresponding Yager's OWA operator (cf. Yager, 1988, Yager and Kacprzyk, 1997). In the latter case, an OWA operator may be further fine tuned by the user so as to achieve a required aggregation functionality. More details will be given in the next section.

The linguistic terms envisaged for the use along with scalar attributes, i.e., *fuzzy set constants*, have to be defined directly in the appropriate universe of discourse corresponding to the domain of a given scalar attribute. More precisely, the set of given attribute values is taken as the universe of discourse. Thus, these constants are, by definition, context dependent. Their discrete membership functions are defined as arrays of numbers. Fuzzy set constants may be defined for any field of character (text) type. Since such a constant is dedicated for a selected field, no additional data about this field is required. This is in contrast to the case of context-independent numeric fuzzy values, where appropriate lower and upper limits have to be provided. Fuzzy set constants may also be defined for - and used together with - *multi-valued attributes*. Obviously, these attributes have to be separately defined, according to the explanation given in the previous section. The definition consists in indicating the list of fields which may then be treated jointly as a virtual attribute.

Basically, information regarding all linguistic terms is stored in some additional tables in the host relational database. Thus, it may be treated as part of *metadata* usually maintained by the relational database management system.

4. COMPUTATION OF A MATCHING DEGREE WITH WORDS (LINGUISTIC TERMS)

The answer to a classical query is a set of records matching the query, i.e., meeting conditions specified in the query. Classically, the notion of matching is binary: a record satisfies conditions or not. In case of flexible queries containing ambiguous and imprecise linguistic terms it is natural to consider a *degree of matching*. In previous sections we describe various linguistic terms, whose use in flexible queries we advocate. Here we briefly present algorithms for calculation of matching degree.

Real life corporate databases may contain hundreds of thousands of records and more. Queries have to be processed in a highly optimized way by, e.g., exploiting all existing and relevant indexes. However, for our purposes we will adopt more simplified a view of this procedure. Namely, we assume that query processing consists in scanning all relevant records, calculating for each of them the matching degree. Thus, while processing a query, a DBMS does the following:

1) fetches a record from the database,
2) evaluates all (or only a part of them, depending on the query structure and adopted optimization scheme) atomic conditions of the query using attributes' values present in the record,
3) aggregates partial matching degrees obtained in the previous step, thus producing the overall matching degree sought,
4) if this matching degree is high enough, includes the record in the answer to the query,
5) moves to the next record,
6) if there are no more records, stop,
7) otherwise, proceeds to step 1.

This procedure does not require any comments, except for steps 2 and 3. In what follows we explain the calculations carried out in these steps. We omit obvious operations on crisp data and focus on the computing with words, i.e., linguistic terms, possibly appearing in the query.

We assume the following notation:

AT_1, AT_2 – attributes,
$v(AT)$ – value of attribute AT in given record,

$[LL_{AT}, UL_{AT}]$ – lower and upper limit for the values of attribute AT (as defined by the user),

τ_{AT}– mapping from the interval $[LL_{AT}, UL_{AT}]$ onto the *universal interval* $[-10,10]$

τ_{AT1AT2}–mapping from the interval $[LL_{AT1}-UL_{AT2},\ UL_{AT1}-LL_{AT2}]$ onto the *universal interval* $[-10,10]$,

FV, μ_{FV} – numeric fuzzy value and its membership function; μ_{FV}: $[-10, 10] \rightarrow [0,1]$,

MOD, η– modifier and its associated function; η: $[0,1] \rightarrow [0,1]$,

FR, μ_{FR} – fuzzy relation and its membership function; μ_{FR}: $[-10, 10] \rightarrow [0,1]$,

FS, μ_{FS} – fuzzy set constant and its membership function defined on a custom domain,

MVAT – multi-valued attribute,

μ_{MVAT}– value of multi-valued attribute, i.e., membership function of corresponding fuzzy set

COMPOP– compatibility operator (label)

$\psi_{COMPOP}(\cdot,\cdot)$– function providing semantics for given compatibility operator (see comments under the table)

Q, μ_Q– fuzzy (linguistic) quantifier and its membership function; μ_Q: $[0, 10] \rightarrow [0,1]$

τ_N – mapping from the interval $[0,N]$ onto the *universal interval* $[0,10]$; N is the numebr of atomic conditions in a subcondition or the number of subconditions in the whole query

md_i – partial matching degree (for i-th atomic condition or subcondition)

κ_i – importance coefficient of the i-th subcondition

In the following table, we collected the formulas used to obtain a matching degree for atomic conditions containing particular linguistic terms:

Linguistic term type	Atomic condition form	Formula for the calculation of matching degree
Numeric fuzzy value	AT = FV	$\mu_{FV}(\tau_{AT}(v(AT))$
Numeric fuzzy value With modifier	AT = MOD FV	$\eta(\mu_{FV}(\tau_{AT}(v(AT)))$
Fuzzy relation	AT_1 FR AT_2	$\mu_{FR}(\tau_{AT_1AT_2}(v(AT_1)-v(AT_2)))$
Fuzzy relation	AT FR number	$\mu_{FR}(\tau_{ATAT}(v(AT)-number))$
Fuzzy set constant	AT in FS	$\mu_{FS}(v(AT))$
Fuzzy set constant with Multi-valued attribute	MVAT COMPOP FS	$\psi_{COMPOP}(\mu_{MVAT},\mu_{FS})$

The mappings τ are defined also outside the intervals previously mentioned. Namely, for arguments less than the lower limit of the interval they take on -10 as their value. Similarly, for arguments higher than the upper limit they take on 10. These additional assumptions are needed because it is possible that, e.g., $v(AT)$ for a certain record in a database lies outside of that interval. In other words, the interval corresponding to the range of variability of a particular attribute, <u>as perceived and specified by the user</u>, need not be identical with the actual range of variability of this attribute <u>in the database</u>.

Compatibility operators measure the compatibility of the value of a multi-valued attribute and a fuzzy set constant. The former may be a crisp set or a fuzzy set represented by a characteristic or membership function, respectively. The characteristic function may be treated as a special case of the membership function, thus, in what follows, we assume the latter is given. As it is discussed in the section 2, various compatibility operators are applicable depending on the intended meaning of a query. In a table below, we present formulas for computing ψ_{COMPOP} for four operators, whose use we advocate.

Compatibility operator	Formula for $\psi_{\text{COMPOP}}(\mu_{\text{MVAT}}, \mu_{\text{FS}})$
Degree of possibility of matching	$\Pi(FS \mid MVAT) = \sup\limits_{u \in U} \min(\mu_{\text{FS}}(u), \mu_{\text{MVAT}}(u))$
Degree of necessity of matching	$N(FS \mid MVAT) = \inf\limits_{u \in U} \max(1 - \mu_{\text{FS}}(u), \mu_{\text{MVAT}}(u))$
Degree of necessity of matching 2	$N(MVAT \mid FS) = \inf\limits_{u \in U} \max(1 - \mu_{\text{MVAT}}(u), \mu_{\text{FS}}(u))$
Generalized Jaccard coefficient	$\lvert FS \cap D \rvert / \lvert FS \cup D \rvert = $ $\sum\limits_{u \in U}(\mu_{\text{FS}}(u) \wedge \mu_{\text{MVAT}}(u)) / \sum\limits_{u \in U}(\mu_{\text{FS}}(u) \vee \mu_{\text{MVAT}}(u))$

The compatibility operator based on the degree of necessity of matching is not symmetric as to the arguments. Thus, its second version, given in the third entry of the table, has a different semantic which may be appropriate for some queries.

Finally, the partial matching degrees calculated for atomic conditions (subconditions) are aggregated in the following way:

$$md = \mu_Q(\tau_N(\frac{1}{N}\sum_i md_i)) \tag{1}$$

where md stands for subcondition (overall) matching degree.

For the overall matching degree calculation, the above formula may be extended to take into account the importance coefficients of particular subconditions (cf. Zadeh, 1983):

$$md = \mu_Q (\tau_N (\frac{\sum_i (md_i \wedge \kappa_i)}{\sum_i \kappa_i})) \tag{2}$$

In some cases other means of grasping the meaning of linguistic quantification (aggregation) are more suitable. For example, the OWA operators due to Yager (1988) [cf. Yager and Kacprzyk's (1997) volume] provide more flexibility in defining the range of aggregation operators. Also the fuzzy (linguistic) querying may benefit from the application of these operators. An OWA operator is characterized by its dimension, N, and a set of weights. Thus, the definition of such an operator is context dependent (depends on N). Fortunately, we can define OWA operator in terms of its corresponding fuzzy linguistic quantifier in the sense of Zadeh (1983) shown in Figure 2. Namely, starting with Zadeh's linguistic quantifier, we derive an OWA operator revealing similar aggregation behavior as the original quantifier (cf. Yager, 1988) via:

$$w_i = Q(i/N) - Q((i-1)/N) \tag{3}$$

As we employ the universal interval for the definition of Zadeh's quantifier, then its corresponding OWA operator defined by the above formula is also context independent. Moreover, the user may easily modify particular weights so as to obtain an aggregation behavior sought. This finetuning of the OWA operator may be guided by the measures of ORness and dispersion. These measures were introduced by Yager (1988) and are calculated for a given OWA operator F with the weight vector $[w_i]_{i=1,...,N}$ as follows:

$$\text{ORness}(F) = (\sum_{i=1}^{N} (N-i) * w_i)/(N-1) \tag{4}$$

$$\text{disp}(F) = -\sum_{i=1}^{N} w_j * \ln(w_j) \tag{5}$$

5. CONCLUDING REMARKS

We presented a framework for using the computing with words paradigm in the context of database querying. Formal languages devised for information retrieval from databases, are not well suited for this task. Basically, in querying decision makers usually try to obtain highly aggregated information from databases; this also holds for casual users. Fuzzy logic, originally conceived as a way to grasp ambiguity and imprecision of human thinking and perception, may help in these cases. Our proposal to extend the classic SQL query language with some linguistic elements has been implemented in a pilot system FQUERY for Access (cf. Kacprzyk and Zadrożny, 1994a – 1997c) which has proven the usefulness of the proposed approach and may also be viewed as a demonstration of the applicability of computing with words paradigm.

LITERATURE

Bordogna G., P. Carrara and G. Pasi (1995) Fuzzy approaches to extend Boolean information retrieval. In: P. Bosc and J. Kacprzyk (Eds.) Fuzziness in Database Management Systems, Physica-Verlag, Heidelberg, pp. 231 - 274.

Bosc P., M. Galibourg and G. Hamon (1988) Fuzzy querying with SQL: extensions and implementations aspects. Fuzzy Sets and Systems 28, 333 - 349.

Bosc P. and J. Kacprzyk, Eds. (1995) Fuzziness in Database Management Systems. Physica-Verlag, Heidleberg,

Bosc P. and O. Pivert (1992) Fuzzy querying in conventional databases. In L.A. Zadeh and J. Kacprzyk (Eds.): Fuzzy Logic for the Management of Uncertainty. Wiley, New York, pp. 645-671.

Bosc P. and O. Pivert (1994) SGL^f: a relational database language for fuzzy querying. IEEE Trans. on Fuzzy Systems (to appear).

Bosc P., L. Lietard and O. Pivert (1995) Quantified statements and database fuzzy querying. In P. Bosc and J. Kacprzyk (Eds.): Fuzziness in Database Management Systems. Physica-Verlag, Heidelberg, pp. 275-308.

Buckles B.P. and Petry F.E. (1982) A fuzzy representation of data for relational databases. Fuzzy Sets and Syst. 7, 213-226.

Chang S.K. and Ke J.S. (1978) Database skeleton and its application to fuzzy query translation. IEEE Trans. on Software Eng. SE-4, 31-43.

Chang S.K. and Ke J.S. (1979) Translation of fuzzy queries for relational database systems. IEEE Trans. on Pattern Anal. and Machine. Intel. PAMI-1, 281-294.

Kacprzyk J. (1995) Fuzzy logic in DBMSs and querying, in N.K. Kasabov and G. Coghill (Eds.): Proceedings of Second New Zealand International Two-Stream Conference on Artificial Neural Networks and Expert Systems (Dunedin, New Zealand), IEEE Computer Society Press, Los Alamitos, CA, USA, pp. 106 - 109.

Kacprzyk J. and S. Zadrożny (1994a) Fuzzy querying for Microsoft Access. Proceedings of the Third IEEE Conference on Fuzzy Systems (Orlando, USA), Vol. 1, pp. 167-171.

Kacprzyk J. and S. Zadrożny (1994b) Fuzzy queries in Microsoft Access: toward a 'more intelligent' use of Microsoft Windows based DBMSs, Proceedings of the 1994 Second Australian and New Zealand Conference on Intelligent Information Systems - ANZIIS'94 (Brisbane, Australia), pp. 492 - 496.

Kacprzyk J. and S. Zadrożny (1995a) FQUERY for Access: fuzzy querying for a Windows-based DBMS. In: P. Bosc and J. Kacprzyk (Eds.) Fuzziness in Database Management Systems, Physica-Verlag, Heidelberg, pp. 415 - 433.

Kacprzyk J. and S. Zadrożny (1995b) Fuzzy queries in Microsoft Access v. 2, Proceedings of 6th International Fuzzy Systems Association World Congress (Sao Paolo, Brazil), Vol. II, pp. 341 - 344.

Kacprzyk J. and S. Zadrożny (1997a) Fuzzy queries in Microsoft Access v. 2, in D. Dubois, H. Prade and R.R. Yager (Eds.): Fuzzy Information Engineering - A Guided Tour of Applications, Wiley, New York, 1997, pp. 223 - 232.

Kacprzyk J. and S. Zadrożny (1997b) Implementation of OWA operators in fuzzy querying for Microsoft Access. In: R.R. Yager and J. Kacprzyk (Eds.) The Ordered Weighted Averaging Operators: Theory and Applications, Kluwer, Boston, 1997, pp. 293 - 306.

Kacprzyk and S. Zadrożny (1997c) Flexible querying using fuzzy logic: An implementation for Microsoft Access, in T. Andreasen, H. Christiansen and H.L. Larsen (eds.): Flexible Query Answering Systems, Kluwer, Boston, 1997, pp. 247-275.

Kacprzyk J., Zadrożny S. and Ziółkowski A. (1989) FQUERY III+: a 'human consistent' database querying system based on fuzzy logic with linguistic quantifiers. Information Systems 6, 443 - 453.

Kacprzyk J. and Ziółkowski A. (1986a) Retrieval from databases using queries with fuzzy linguistic quantifiers. In H. Prade and C.V. Negoita (Eds.) Fuzzy Logics in Knowledge Engineering. Verlag TÜV Rheinland, Cologne, pp. 46-57.

Kacprzyk J. and Ziółkowski A. (1986b) Database queries with fuzzy linguistic quantifiers. IEEE Transactions on Systems, Man and Cybernetics SMC - 16, 474 - 479.

Larsen H.L. and Yager R.R. (1993) The use of fuzzy relational thesauri for classificatory problem solving in information retrieval and expert systems. IEEE Trans. On Syst., Man and Cybern. SMC-23, 31 - 41.

Miyamoto S. (1990) Fuzzy Sets in Information Retrieval and Cluster Analysis. Kluwer Academic Publishers. Dordrecht, Boston, London.

Nomura T., Odaka T., Ohki N., Yokoyama T. And Matsuhita Y. (1992) Generating ambiguous attributes for fuzzy queries. Proceedings of IEEE International Conference on Fuzzy Systems (FUZZ-IEEE '92), 1992, pp. 753-760.

Petry F.E. (1996) Fuzzy Databases: Principles and Applications. Kluwer, Boston.

Tahani V. (1977) A conceptual framework for fuzzy query processing: a step toward very intelligent data systems. Inf. Proc and Management 13, 289 - 303.

Vila M.A., Cubero J.C., Medina J.M. and Pons O. (1994) Logic and fuzzy relational databases: a new language and a new definition. In Bosc P. and J. Kacprzyk (Eds.) Fuzziness in Database Management Systems. Physica-Verlag, Heidleberg, pp. 114 - 138.

Yager R.R. (1988) On ordered weighted averaging aggregation operators in multi-criteria decision making. IEEE Transactions on Systems, Man and Cybernetics, 18, 183-190.

Yager R.R. and Kacprzyk J., Eds. (1997) The Ordered Weighted Averaging Operators: Theory and Applications. Kluwer, Boston.

Yazici A., R. George, B.P. Buckles and F.E. Petry (1992) A survey of conceptual and logical data models for uncertainty management. In L.A. Zadeh and J. Kacprzyk (Eds.): Fuzzy Logic for the Management of Uncertainty. Wiley, New York, pp. 607-643.

Yazici A. and R. George (1999) Fuzzy Database Modeling. Physica-Verlag, Heidelberg and New York.

Zadeh L.A. (1983) A computational approach to fuzzy quantifiers in natural languages. Computers and Maths. with Appls. 9, 149 - 184.

Zadrożny S. and J. Kacprzyk (1995) Fuzzy querying using the 'query-by-example' option in a Windows-based DBMS", Proceedings of Third European Congress on Intelligent Techniques and Soft Computing - EUFIT'95 (Aachen, Germany), vol. 2, pp. 733-736.

Zadrożny S. and J. Kacprzyk (1996) Multi-valued fields and values in fuzzy querying via FQUERY for Access, Proceedings of FUZZ–IEEE'96 - Fifth International Conference on Fuzzy Systems (New Orleans, USA), vol. 2, pp. 1351 - 1357.

Zemankova M. and J. Kacprzyk (1993) The roles of fuzzy logic and management of uncertainty in building intelligent information systems, Journal of Intelligent Information Systems 2, 311-317.

Zemankova-Leech M. and Kandel A. (1984) Fuzzy Relational Databases - a Key to Expert Systems. Verlag TÜV Rheinland, Cologne.

Linguistic Data Mining

Witold Pedrycz

Department of Electrical and Computer Engineering
University of Alberta
Edmonton, Alberta T6G 2G7 Canada

Abstract. Data mining emerges as a prudent and user - oriented sifting of data, qualitative observations and calibration of commonsense rules in an attempt to establish meaningful and useful relationships between system's variables. The role of fuzzy sets in knowledge discovery has not been visible even though fuzzy sets are inherently inclined towards coping with linguistic domain knowledge. This study re-examines the key issues of knowledge discovery by putting them in the context of the technology of fuzzy sets. Subsequently, we reveal several interesting conceptual and algorithmic links between linguistic data mining and fuzzy sets. The detailed investigations are geared toward inherently knowledge-oriented and context based modifications of well known techniques of fuzzy clustering.

Keywords knowledge discovery, data mining, context - dependent clustering, linguistic space, fuzzy modelling

1 Introduction

As commonly defined in the literature, " *knowledge discovery in databases is concerned with identifying interesting patterns and describing them in a concise and meaningful manner* " [4][5][6]. In particular, Knowledge Discovery (KD) helps:
- extract useful reports
spot interesting events and trends
- support decision- making procedures
- exploit the data to achieve scientific and business goals.
As such, the essence of efficient mechanisms of knowledge discovery (KD) even though some components of the process are or can be made autonomous and problem - independent to some extent, hinges on a prudent and well thought interaction with a user/analyst. The notion of data mining (DM) comes hand in hand with KD; as stipulated in the literature, DM is somewhat subsumed by KD. KD occurs in databases (hence we often refer to Knowledge Discovery id Databases, KDD, for short). In this sense, KDD embraces all activities including interfacing with databases and becomes broader than DM where the issue of

interaction with databases is not a crucial point of interest. The general paradigm of KD is portrayed in Figure 1.

The panoply of currently investigated discussed methodologies of KD, especially those emerging at the level of data mining, is impressive ranging from statistics, neurocomputing, set theory, machine learning, and rough sets, Figure 1. Data mining exploits various explanatory architectures including rules, decision trees, associations, etc. It exploits a diversity basic classes of models including classifiers, regression, link analysis, sequence analysis, to name a few of them.

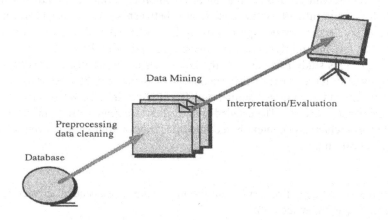

Figure 1. Knowledge Discovery: a general paradigm

The research agenda of KDD is very broad calling for a solution to a number of primordial problems such as
- handling massive datasets of high dimensionality
- an efficient incorporation of prior knowledge
- design of user interfaces
- supporting high understandability of patterns
- managing changing data and time - variant aspects of knowledge
- resolving integration tasks with databases (including query interfaces)

For the recent overview of the area of knowledge discovery the reader may refer to [5] as well as a special issue of Int. J. Intelligent Systems [11] and the Communications of the ACM [3]. Despite a growing versatility of KD systems, there is an important component of human interaction, that to a profound degree, is inherent to any process of knowledge representation, manipulation, and processing. The notion of interestingness embracing several main features such as validity, novelty, usefulness, and simplicity is central to all KD endeavors. What these properties imply is a growing and indisputable role of fuzzy set technology in this realm. Fuzzy sets are naturally suited to realize the notions such as information granularization and focus of attention supporting the development of the interestingness of the KD activities [13][8].

By no means, this study pretends to be exhaustive. The area of knowledge discovery itself is under continuous development and its eventual links with fuzzy sets are still to be established. This paper primarily addresses several key issues of KD carried out in the framework of fuzzy sets and neurocomputing. Our main objective is to discuss some constructive fuzzy - set driven computational vehicles of KD. In the sequel, we reveal relationships between data mining and fuzzy modeling and discuss how DM impacts fuzzy modelling in terms of new concepts and interpretation of the models themselves.

2 Data Mining and Fuzzy Sets

As already underlined, data mining is aimed at sifting data in order to reveal useful information required by a user while compressing huge records of data. It comes without saying that we are faced with a flood of data. Just to name a few of evident challenges in data mining let us refer to some evident facts:
- Walmart completes around 20 million transactions per day,
-the planned NASA earth observing system to be launched around 1999 will generate 50Gb of image data per hour,
- the rapidly expanding information highway will require advanced tools of mining through data; currently these are also referred to as intelligent agents. Pretty soon one may witness a call for building firewalls against excessive streams of data.
Indisputably, we live in a society that is data *rich* and knowledge *poor*. Having said that, any meaningful effort to distill and interpret revealing relationships becomes a must. This, in turn, implies a significant growth of KD in the near future.

As all these search and analysis procedures are highly user - oriented, there is a genuine need for the technology of fuzzy sets. In particular, fuzzy sets:
- support a focused search being defined linguistically through fuzzy sets of a relevant granularity
- help discover dependencies between the data; these relationships become again revealed in a qualitative or semi-qualitative format rather than in a purely numeric and quantitative way.

It is worth to elaborate on the notion of interestingness as being the central feature on an agenda of any KD endeavor. It entails several constituents :
validity This property pertains to significance of knowledge that has been discovered
novelty describes how much the discovered patterns deviate from prior knowledge that has already been gained
usefulness relates the finding of the KD activities to the goals of the user especially an impact these findings have on decisions to be made.
simplicity is primarily concerned with the aspects of syntactic complexity of the

presentation of a finding; higher simplicity promotes significant easiness of its interpretation
generality entails a fraction of the population a particular finding refers to.
Many of the above features (simplicity, in particular) are readily quantified through fuzzy sets. Overall, we emphasize that all the activities of data mining are essentially driven by some context within which any meaningful analysis should be accomplished.

To illustrate the very idea of data mining, let us consider a relational table (array) **X** comprising objects regarded as vectors of real numbers. We are interested in revealing (discovering) a structure and eventual quantify functional dependences manifesting throughout this table. What is commonly encountered in such a case is the use of standard methods of clustering, fuzzy clustering, correlation analysis or alike. The customization of the mechanism of data mining leads to a focused discovery of regularities and dependencies placed in the context already specified by the user. The focal nature of data mining is achieved by specifying linguistic term(s) prior to launching any detailed analysis and running computationally intensive algorithms. While a diversity of data mining processes is tremendous, below we highlight only a few of the most representative and interesting scenarios:
(a) Let us consider one of the attributes of interest as a context variable and define therein a fuzzy set (linguistic term of focus) A

$$A : \mathbf{Y} \rightarrow [0, 1]$$

here **Y** stands for a universe of discourse of this attribute (variable). The problem reads in the following way

reveal a structure in **X** in context A

where the context of KD is established as

$$A = \{ A: \mathbf{X} \rightarrow [0,1]\}$$

For instance, if the pressure variable has been selected as the context in which KD need to be carried out, the problem of data mining can be articulated in the following fashion

reveal a structure in **X** in context {pressure = *small*}

(b) Several attributes can form the context (more precisely, composite context). For instance, let A and B be two fuzzy sets defined in **Y** and **Z**, respectively. Then any composite context A is formed as a Cartesian product of A and B

$$A = \{ A \times B: \mathbf{Y} \times \mathbf{Z} \rightarrow [0,1]\}$$

Similarly, as before, we may arrive at the problem formulated as

reveal a structure in **X** in context {pressure = *small* and temperature = *medium*}

In addition to the two basic forms of the linguistic contexts, there are a number of interesting extensions, see Figure 2.

Contexts in Data Mining

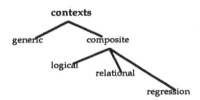

Figure 2. A taxonomy of contexts in Data Mining

The examples below illustrate each of these contexts:

☐   composite logical context: pressure is *small* and temperature is *low* or humidity is *medium*

☐   composite relational context: prices of product "a" and discount prices of product "b" are *similar*

☐   composite regression context: error of linear model $x_i = f(x_j, a)$ is negative *small*

It is instructive to recall that the problem of the form

reveal a structure in **X**

is context - free and comes exactly in the same format as commonly studied in the domain of data clustering. In the sequel, we discuss various clustering mechanisms and their KD - oriented modifications.

3 Context - Dependent Fuzzy Clustering

While clustering and fuzzy clustering have been already found a useful tool of data organization, data mining calls for some enhancements of the original methods along the line envisioned in Figure 3. The crux of this approach is to embark on some domain knowledge as an important guideline that help navigate throughout the data and focus any search mechanism. The prior mechanism of focusing prevents us from searching for meaningless or trivial patterns in a database.

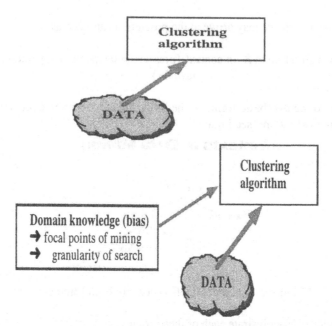

Figure 3. Clustering and KD - oriented clustering

In what follows, we concentrate on Fuzzy C - Means (FCM) [1] and discuss its two conceptual enhancements, namely context - based clustering and clustering in induced linguistic space. Firstly, we briefly summarize the generic method as usually encountered in the literature.

Assume that x_1, x_2, ..., x_N are n - dimensional patterns defined in $\mathbf{R}^n$. The objective function is defined as a sum of squared errors

$$Q = \sum_{i=1}^{c} \sum_{k=1}^{N} u_{ik}^2 \|x_k - v_i\|^2$$

(1)

with $U = [u_{ik}]$ being a partition matrix, $U \in \mathsf{U}$, and "c" standing for the number of the clusters; p >1 is often referred to as a fuzzification parameter. ‖.‖ forms a distance function being computed between x_k an the prototype (v_i) of the i-th cluster (group). U denotes a family of c × N partition matrices, namely

$$\mathsf{U} = \{\ u_{ik} \in [0, 1] |\ \sum_{i=1}^{c} u_{ik} = 1\ \forall_k\ \text{and}\ 0 < \sum_{k=1}^{N} u_{ik} < N\ \forall_i\}$$

(1')

Formally, the optimization problem becomes expressed in the form

$$\min_{U, v_1, v_2, ..., v_c} Q$$

subject to
$$U \in \mathbb{U}$$

The iterative scheme leading either to a local minimum or a saddle point of Q is well known and concerns a series of updates of the partition matrix that are written down as

$$u_{ik} = \frac{1}{\sum_{j=1}^{c} \left(\frac{\|\mathbf{x}_k - \mathbf{v}_i\|}{\|\mathbf{x}_k - \mathbf{v}_j\|} \right)^2}$$

$i = 1, 2, ..., c, k = 1, 2, ..., N$.
The prototypes of the clusters are obtained in the form of weighted averages of the patterns

$$\mathbf{v}_i = \frac{\sum_{k=1}^{N} u_{ik}^2 \mathbf{x}_k}{\sum_{k=1}^{N} u_{ik}^2}$$

3.1 Context - Sensitive FCM

The conditioning aspect (context sensitivity) of the clustering mechanism is introduced into the algorithm by taking into consideration the conditioning variable (context) assuming the values f_1, f_2, ..., f_N on the corresponding patterns. More specifically, f_k describes a level of involvement of $\mathbf{x}_k$ in the assumed context, $f_k = A(k)$. In other words, A acts as a data mining filter (or a focal element) by focusing attention on some specific subsets of data. The way in which f_k can be associated with or allocated among the computed membership values of $\mathbf{x}_k$, say $u_{1k}, u_{2k}, ..., u_{ck}$, is not unique. Two possibilities are worth exploring:
-we admit f_k to be distributed additively across the entries of the k-th column of the partition matrix meaning that

$$\sum_{i=1}^{c} u_{ik} = f_k$$

(2)

$k = 1, 2, ..., N$
-we may request that the maximum of the membership values within the corresponding column equals f_k,

$$\max_{i=1}^{c} u_{ik} = f_k$$

(3)

k=1, 2, ..., N.

We confine ourselves to the first way of distribution of the conditioning variable. Bearing this in mind, let us modify the requirements to be met by the partition matrices and define the family

$$U(f) = \{ u_{ik} \in [0, 1] | \sum_{i=1}^{c} u_{ik} = f_k \ \forall k \text{ and } 0 < \sum_{k=1}^{N} u_{ik} < N \ \forall i \}$$

Thus the standard normalization condition standing in (1') is replaced by the involvement (conditioning) constraint. The optimization problem is now reformulated accordingly [10]

$$\min_{U, v_1, v_2, ..., v_c} Q$$

subject to

$$U \in U(f)$$

(4)

Again the minimization of the objective function is carried out iteratively where

$$u_{ik} = \frac{f_k}{\sum_{j=1}^{c} \left(\frac{\|x_k - v_i\|}{\|x_k - v_j\|} \right)^2}$$

We arrive at the above formula by transforming (4) to a standard unconstrained optimization by making use of Lagrange multipliers and determining a critical point of the resulting function. The computations of the prototypes are the same as for the original FCM method. Moreover, the convergence conditions for the method are the same as discussed for the original FCM algorithm [1].

The context A has a dominant effect on the performance of the clustering mechanism. If $f < f'$ then the population of the patterns involved in grouping and placed under context f' is lower. Similarly, the number of eventual clusters could be lowered as well. The above inclusion relation between the contexts holds if the context fuzzy sets are made more specific or if the contexts consist of more constraints (focal points). In the first case we get $A \subset A'$ where f is implied by A and f' by A'. In the latter the ensuing f is associated with $A \times B \times C$ and f' comes with $A \times B$; here again $A \subset A'$.

Let us underline that the context of clustering plays an important role in discovering knowledge nuggets - rare yet essential pieces of evidence. Without any direction imposed on the clustering those could be be easily washed away in a mass of useless but frequent (and thus statistically meaningful) data. The filtering of data accomplished by the context prevents this from happening.

One should emphasize that the membership values of contexts do not sum up to

1; the similar phenomenon can be witnessed in possibilistic clustering [7] and clustering with noise cluster [2], however the origin of these two departures from the original constraint is completely different.

The results generated by the context - based clustering come in the form of entities that will be referred to as patterns. For instance, if the context defined for temperature is *low*, we get a Cartesian product of fuzzy sets

$$(\text{temperature} = low) \times (\Omega_1 \cup \Omega_2 \cup \ldots \cup \Omega_c)$$

where Ω_1, Ω_2, ... and Ω_c are fuzzy clusters (fuzzy relations) defined for the remaining variables and obtained via their clustering. The above is a union of the patterns

$$\bigcup_{i=1}^{c} (\text{temperature} = low \times \Omega_i)$$

The computations of their membership functions result directly from the FCM model. In particular,

$$u_i = \frac{1}{\sum_{j=1}^{c} \left(\frac{\|\mathbf{x} - \mathbf{v}_i\|}{\|\mathbf{x} - \mathbf{v}_j\|} \right)^2}$$

$j=1, 2, \ldots, c$, with the same distance function as encountered in the original method.

Interestingly enough, the patterns have nothing to do with any specific direction - what has been revealed are just plain associations between the relations and the context.

4 Fuzzy Modeling and Data Mining

System modeling (and fuzzy modeling, in particular) and data mining exhibit some interesting relationships. Let us elaborate on the three specific cases that show up as being of particular interest:

① well defined and highly visible relationships between variables. This scenario falls under a realm of system modeling and does not call for more sophisticated modeling methods.
② Data mining leading to a multivariable model in the form $y = f(x_1, x_2, \ldots, x_n)$. In this case we envision an important synergy between fuzzy models and methods of KD. The objectives of fuzzy modeling are also central items on an agenda of data mining in the sense that the models need to be easily comprehended

and fully interpretable. Bearing this in mind, the design of the model is highly influenced and substantially controlled by the developer/analyst. We discuss one of the specific types of the fuzzy models in the following sections.

③ no function - based model is available. An analysis of relational tables does not simply imply an existence of *functional* dependences between variables as usually encountered in the literature. From an operational standpoint, one can treat such models as a collection of rules with many conclusions,

-if condition then conclusion_a *or* conclusion_b *or*...

For a detailed discussion on so-called fuzzy multimodels refer to [9].

5 Data Mining as a Problem of Linguistic Data Compression

Multidimensional data to be represented through functions assume the form

$$z = f(x_1, x_2, ..., x_n)$$

where x_i are treated as independent variables. If z is in the unit interval (which assumption does not impose any loss of generality), the multidimensional data can be regarded as a fuzzy relation induced by the independent variables. To illustrate the very concept of data compression and how this leads to data mining, we confine ourselves to two argument fuzzy relation

$$R : X \times Y \to [0, 1]$$

where $card(X) = n_1$, $card(Y) = n_2$. The dimension of the fuzzy relation is linked with the assumed resolution of the numeric data. Furthermore, let r_{kl} denote the (k, l;) th entry of R. We consider two families of fuzzy sets (frames of cognition) A and B defined in X and Y, respectively. Let card (A) = p, card (B) = r. Moreover, $p \ll n_1$, and $r \ll n_2$.

The linguistic compression is carried out with the aid of the linguistic labels. We construct an induced fuzzy relation G defined over A × B with the entries

$$g_{ij} = \bigvee_{\substack{k = 1, 2 ... n_1 \\ l = 1, 2 ... n_2}} [A_i(x_k) \wedge B_j(y_l) \wedge R(x_l, x_k, y_l)]$$

i = 1, 2 ... p, j = 1, 2 ... r. In other words g_{ij} results as a sup-min composition (convolution) of the original fuzzy relation and the filtering fuzzy sets (A_i, B_j). Owing to the size of A and B, the dimension of G is far lower than the original data - hence the resulting effect of the linguistic compression, Figure 4.

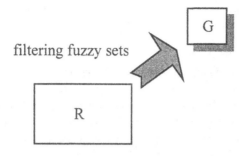

Figure 4. Linguistic compression of R realized with the aid of A and B

With any compression comes a decompression (inverse) scheme. One can look at the convolution formula as a fuzzy relational equation to be solved with respect to R for G and A and B provided.

The well - known maximal solution to this problem comes in the form

$$\hat{r}_{kl} = \bigwedge_{\substack{i=1,2\ldots p \\ j=1,2\ldots r}} \left[A_i(x_k) \wedge B_j(y_l) \rightarrow g_{ij} \right]$$

The implication operation is induced by the original max - t convolution used in the compression scheme. The maximal character of the solution means that R is included in the above reconstruction. The compression rate is determined based on the sizes of the fuzzy relation and the number of the fuzzy filters in A and B. More specifically, we compare the number of the elements of R, that is $n_1\, n_2$ and the size of the second relation G, that is p*r. In addition we have to take into consideration the fuzzy sets in **X** and **Y** whose dimensionality is $p*n_1$ and $r*n_2$. This leads to the compression ρ rate equal

$$\rho = \frac{n_1\, n_2}{pr + pn_1 + rn_2}$$

The difference between the original fuzzy relation R and its decompressed version $\hat{R}$ is regarded as the performance measure; our intent is to minimize the distance

$$\min \| R - \hat{R} \|$$

(where ||.|| stands for a suitable distance function). For fixed values of p and r (that induce a required compression rate) the minimization of this distance is accomplished by changing the family of the fuzzy filters A and B. Their parametric as well as structural optimization is completed with the aid of evolutionary computation. Here a GA search space comprises the parameters of the linguistic landmarks in A and B.

6 Evolutionary -Optimized Data Mining

By its nature, data mining subsumes classic modeling by focussing on patterns rather than precise functional relationships (functions) with a significant number of almost impossible to interpret parameters. It is appropriate to proceed with a relatively straightforward example, that is, however, quite representative for a broad class of systems. Let us discuss a series of triples of data

$$x(k), u(k), x(k+1)$$

$k = 1, 2, ..., N$ originating from a certain dynamic system. The usual modeling activities (as commonly envisioned in system identification) start from a certain form of the model, say

$$x(k+1) = f(x(k), u(k), \textbf{param})$$

The flexibility of the model stems from a vector of parameters (**param**); to cope with the available experimental data the model is optimized in a parametric fashion. In essence, data mining assumes no particular form of the functions but searches for patterns that could be eventually materialized into the number of functional dependences.

The experimental data can be arranged into a two-dimensional array indexed by $x(k)$ and $u(k)$ whose entries are just the corresponding values in the next time instant $x(k+1)$. An interpretation of the table calls for a suitable information granularity; this comes in the form of information granule defined for control $(u(k))$ and state variable $(x(k), x(k+1))$. To concentrate on the generic form of the method, we start with the codebooks A and B treated as sets. Let us now scan data, triple after triple, and converts it into the corresponding granulae. The entries of the resulting linguistic table defined over A × B can be multiple; the same combination (Cartesian product) of A_i and B_j may lead to different A_is, Figure 5.

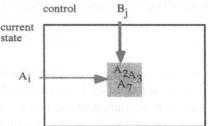

Figure 5. Linguistic table with multiplicity of entries

The same table can be interpreted as a collection of associations. For example, for the (i, j) -th entry we come up with the summarization of some experimental data, namely (A_i, B_j, A_2), (A_i, B_j, A_3), (A_i, B_j, A_7). The multiplicity of some of the patterns for the entries result in a nondeterministic behavior of the model; note also that so far we have not confined ourselves to any particular class of the function (say, linear, polynomials, trigonometric, etc.).

7 Linguistic Granules and Associations as Blueprints of Numeric Constructs

It is important to underline that linguistic granules deliver a useful and essential option of making sense of data by developing meaningful granules. The granules serve two important purposes:
- they help establish sound and meaningful chunks of information constructing a sound background for further refinements
- information granules support modularization of the data set that reduces a level of computing necessary to reveal detailed relationships at a numeric rather than linguistic level

Figure 6 contains a number of possible follow-ups dwelled on linguistic granules: they include correlation analysis, regression models, and neural networks.

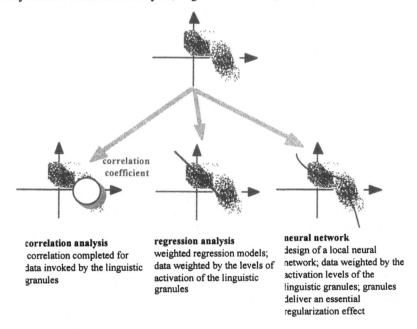

correlation analysis
correlation completed for data invoked by the linguistic granules

regression analysis
weighted regression models; data weighted by the levels of activation of the linguistic granules

neural network
design of a local neural network; data weighted by the activation levels of the linguistic granules; granules deliver an essential regularization effect

Figure 6. Refinements of associations between linguistic granules

8 Context-based Clustering and Databases

The context-based clustering carries some resemblances to standard queries in databases. Moreover, it rather generalizes the concept of a query that could be better described as a metaquery. In the standard querying process, one formulates a query and the database retrieves all pertinent records from the database that respond to the formulated request. Obviously, for the query of the type: "find all customers who have recently bought Ford Contour and are of middle age" the database retrieval mechanisms will produce a long (and perhaps in some cases useless) list of such individuals. The expectations are that we will be provided with a characterization (description) of this specific sector of the car market. This, in fact, what the discussed clustering method does, Figure 7. The generalized metaquery is just the imposed context while the characterization comes in the form of the induced clusters.

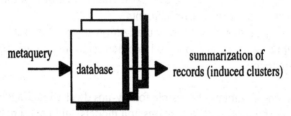

Figure 7. Context-based clustering as a process of summarization in a database

9 Numerical Studies

In this section we concentrate on several selected examples and carry out a complete analysis highlighting the key features of the clustering approach to data mining.

9.1 Auto mpg Example

The discussed data set, called auto mpg, comes from the repository of machine learning data sets situated at UC Irvine (http:// ftp.ics.edu/pub/machine-learning - databases/). The vehicles are characterized by 9 features such as fuel consumption (in miles per gallon), a number of cylinders, displacement, horse power, weight, acceleration, model year, and origin (USA, Europe, Japan), and the make of the vehicle. A short excerpt of this data set is shown in Figure 8. The origin of the vehicles are encoded as follows: 1-USA, 2-Europe, 3-Japan.

18.0	8	307.0	130.0	3504.	12.0	70	1	"chevrolet chevelle malibu"
15.0	8	350.0	165.0	3693.	11.5	70	1	"buick skylark 320"
18.0	8	318.0	150.0	3436.	11.0	70	1	"plymouth satellite"
16.0	8	304.0	150.0	3433.	12.0	70	1	"amc rebel sst"
17.0	8	302.0	140.0	3449.	10.5	70	1	"ford torino"
15.0	8	429.0	198.0	4341.	10.0	70	1	"ford galaxie 500"
14.0	8	454.0	220.0	4354.	9.0	70	1	"chevrolet impala"
14.0	8	440.0	215.0	4312.	8.5	70	1	"plymouth fury iii"
14.0	8	455.0	225.0	4425.	10.0	70	1	"pontiac catalina"
15.0	8	390.0	190.0	3850.	8.5	70	1	"amc ambassador dpl"
15.0	8	383.0	170.0	3563.	10.0	70	1	"dodge challenger se"
14.0	8	340.0	160.0	3609.	8.0	70	1	"plymouth 'cuda 340"
15.0	8	400.0	150.0	3761.	9.5	70	1	"chevrolet monte carlo"
14.0	8	455.0	225.0	3086.	10.0	70	1	"buick estate wagon (sw)"
24.0	4	113.0	95.00	2372.	15.0	70	3	"toyota corona mark ii"
22.0	6	198.0	95.00	2833.	15.5	70	1	"plymouth duster"
18.0	6	199.0	97.00	2774.	15.5	70	1	"amc hornet"
21.0	6	200.0	85.00	2587.	16.0	70	1	"ford maverick"
27.0	4	97.00	88.00	2130.	14.5	70	3	"datsun pl510"
26.0	4	97.00	46.00	1835.	20.5	70	2	"volkswagen 1131 deluxe sedan"

Figure 8. A excerpt from auto mpg dataset

For instance, take the first record (chevrolet). The features reads as:
- fuel consumption 18.0
- number of cylinders 8
- displacement 307.0
- horse power 130.0
- weight 3504
- acceleration 12.0
- model year 70
- origin USA

The first step is to formulate the point of view at the activity of data mining that is express a context variable and proceed with their granulation of interest. There are a number of possibilities. We choose the one that sounds quite useful: let us reveal relationships concerning vehicles of some categories of fuel efficiency. This naturally leads us to accepting the first variable as the context and work on clustering in the space of the remaining variables. The names of the cars are not used here. The granularity of the context variable is established via trapezoidal fuzzy sets with the membership functions of the form

$T(y, -1 \ 0 \ 10 \ 20)$

$T(y, 10 \ 20 \ 20 \ 30)$

$T(y, 20 \ 30 \ 30 \ 40)$

$T(y, 30 \ 40 \ 50 \ 80)$

where, as usual, the parameters standing there denote the characteristic points of the piecewise membership functions of these fuzzy sets, see Figure 9.

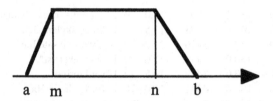

Figure 9. A class of trapezoidal fuzzy sets (fuzzy numbers) T(y, a, m, n, b)

In fact, as the two intermediate parameters are the same, we are dealing with triangular fuzzy sets. The first one can be regarded as a descriptor of vehicles of small efficiency while the last one characterizes vehicles of high fuel economy. The two intermediate categories deals with vehicles of medium fuel consumption. These linguistic fuzzy labels have been used to capture the meaning of the vehicles of some specific and meaningful nature. If necessary, these linguistic labels could be revised and modified according to the interest of the user. We should stress that the labels have not been optimized to meet some criteria discussed before (as, for instance, the equalization one). To illustrate that, the histogram of the context variable is shown in Figure 10.

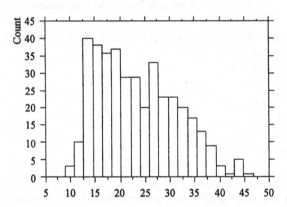

Figure 10. Distribution of the values of the context variable (mpg)

The calculations reveal the values of the s-count of the respective fuzzy labels to be equal

context$_1$	64.8300
context$_2$	168.0400
context$_3$	118.9800
context$_4$	38.1500

so it becomes apparent, as expected by eyeballing the histogram that some linguistic terms are quite dominant. The clustering is carried out for five clusters per context so, finally, we end up with 20 different associations between the resulting linguistic granules. The fuzzification parameter was set to 2. The resulting prototypes are summarized below. Based on their values one can easily generate the corresponding membership functions of the linguistic terms; each row describes an individual prototype (5 per context)

first context

7.9597	324.0681	147.4904	4141.4565	13.8119	74.7960	1.0077
7.9935	421.9014	206.9132	4576.3774	11.0116	71.7837	1.0015
7.9754	338.9013	156.0435	4179.1138	13.1936	72.4731	1.0045
7.9851	364.9198	175.4141	4402.2515	12.4981	72.0487	1.0031
6.0845	246.5758	101.6843	3509.3506	17.7591	74.4538	1.0451

second context

4.0874	117.2117	95.2903	2561.4968	15.3389	74.0668	2.3533
7.9295	328.2322	149.5903	3978.1433	12.9293	75.3593	1.0127
5.6790	207.2347	99.2230	3134.1489	16.5716	75.9661	1.1594
5.7946	212.4101	98.3907	2967.3010	15.6952	72.7827	1.0960
5.9282	219.8767	99.9425	3295.7715	17.1119	77.6124	1.0705

third context

4.1583	113.9076	78.9360	2294.1370	15.7431	76.9066	1.5600
4.1166	135.1387	85.3163	2584.2524	16.1681	80.4332	1.0853
4.0465	93.6141	72.0283	2087.6772	17.5755	73.4383	2.4799
4.0475	105.1029	73.0323	2239.2920	16.8227	79.4058	2.8950
4.0955	105.7471	78.8554	2214.5576	15.3149	76.0530	1.9204

fourth context

4.0219	90.2672	65.1666	1979.7280	16.5085	80.6769	2.9150
4.0585	105.6941	69.6008	2095.6660	15.2831	80.6091	1.0754
4.0386	103.6010	75.0548	2111.0115	14.7648	80.5556	2.7140
4.0186	88.0564	65.0256	2063.3794	18.5730	79.6490	2.9457
4.0252	92.8853	49.6662	2170.7195	22.7944	80.0778	1.9977

But even at this numeric level one can reveal a series of interesting facts. For instance:

- when it comes to low fuel economy, large and heavy American cars dominate in this category
- Japanese cars are placed in the fourth category with horsepower in the range of 88-100, four cylinder engines and weight of *about* 2 tons

9.2 Computer Performance Dataset

This example concerns a performance of various models of computers. These data describe various makes of computers using some basic hardware characteristics and summarize their performance through a single numeric index. The features of the patterns used therein are indicated below

MYCT: machine cycle time in nanoseconds
MMIN: minimum main memory in kilobytes
MMAX: maximum main memory in kilobytes
CACHE: cache memory in kilobytes
CHMIN: minimum channels in units
CHMAX: maximum channels in units
PERF: relative performance

To illustrate a variety of the computers under study, shown is an excerpt of this dataset

amdahl,470v/7,29,8000,32000,32,8,32,269
amdahl,470v/7a,29,8000,32000,32,8,32,220
amdahl,470v/7b,29,8000,32000,32,8,32,172
amdahl,470v/7c,29,8000,16000,32,8,16,132
amdahl,470v/b,26,8000,32000,64,8,32,318
amdahl,580-5840,23,16000,32000,64,16,32,367
...

sperry,80/6,180,512,4000,0,1,3,21,
sperry,80/8,124,1000,8000,0,1,8,42
sperry,90/80-model-3,98,1000,8000,32,2,8,46
sratus,32,125,2000,8000,0,2,14,52
wang,vs-100,480,512,8000,32,0,0,67

For instance, the first computer is characterized by the values of MYCT equal 29, MMIN 8000, MMAX 32000, etc. We complete the context-based clustering by defining contexts in the space of the relative performance. This allows us to discriminate between several linguistic categories of the computers as far as their performance is concerned and describe such categories of the machines. In the experiment we concentrate on four classes - context of the performance described by trapezoidal or triangular membership membership functions. They start with the computers of low performance, sweep through the machines of medium range and end up with the machines of high performance. More specifically, these corresponding membership functions are defined as

low performance	$T(x, 0, 0, 10, 20)$
...	$T(x, 10, 20, 150, 250)$
...	$T(x, 150, 250, 400, 500)$
high performance	$T(x, 400, 500, 2000, 2100)$

The experiments are carried out for three clusters per each context. Furthermore the fuzzification factor was set for 2, that is m = 2. First, we list the results by showing the prototypes of the individual contexts (note that we deal with a six-dimensional space of the parameters of the computers):

T(x, 0, 0, 10, 20)

prototype 1					
223.43	555.56	1829.82	2.35	1.07	3.92
prototype 2					
844.72	544.81	3624.26	0.16	0.99	2.64
prototype 3					
1213.89	645.31	1491.56	0.00	0.70	0.72

T(x, 10, 20, 150, 250)

prototype 1					
131.08	1634.28	7510.06 10.62	2.43	11.58	
prototype 2					
396.53	990.99	5571.41 5.93	1.80	9.35	
prototype 3					
88.20	3491.64	14788.85	34.78	5.24	19.96

T(x, 150, 250, 400, 500)

prototype 1					
50.31	3071.15	31762.39	112.58	50.99	102.67
prototype 2					
39.06	2377.62	9471.44	126.23	11.04	29.85
prototype 3					
34.65	8113.07	30338.65	52.14	9.57	25.94

T(x, 400, 500, 2000, 2100)

prototype 1					
29.94	8160.12	63610.66	113.23	12.08	173.02
prototype 2					
28.95	15996.53	36633.18	105.92	15.15	29.27
prototype 3					
23.36	30565.78	62270.66	132.00	30.56	60.71

The resulting linguistic labels in the space machine cycle and maximum main memory associated with the computers of low and high performance are shown in Figure 11.

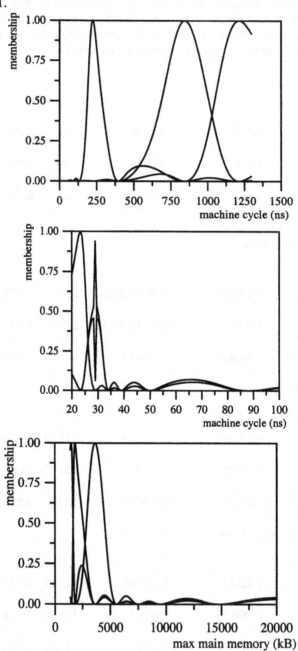

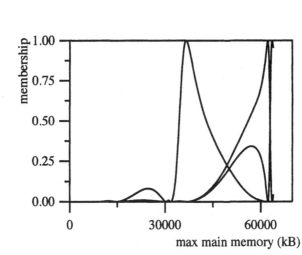

Figure 11. Linguistic terms associated with the computers of high and low performance

10 Conclusions

We have established some main links between the technology of fuzzy sets and knowledge discovery. It should be stressed that some of the key features of data mining can be strongly supported by fuzzy sets. As knowledge discovery is highly user - oriented, some interaction with the user is necessary and this facet is immensely supported through intensive linguistic processing. There are a number of synergistic links between data mining and fuzzy modelling. They have been discussed at the functional as well as algorithmic level. The latter has been realized via various context - dependent mechanisms of fuzzy clustering. The resulting context-based clustering not only becomes a useful data mining tool but computationally is far efficient than the standard tools of fuzzy clustering. This efficiency comes with the modularization effect being introduced by the use of the linguistic contexts. The experimental studies using widely accessible data sets strongly justify the use of fuzzy sets as a suitable information granulation vehicle supporting data mining. When studying KD and fuzzy modelling one can highlight an interesting hierarchy of models starting from the layer of KD and proceeding down to more specialized architectures along with their generic constructs:

> KD : *patterns*
> Multimodels: *rules and patterns*
> Fuzzy models: *rules*

An evident message originating from the KD methodology is the one about the direct bias of the developer to adhere to the famous Ockham's razor phenomenon (keep the model *simple*). The context - biased clustering supports this point of view and delivers a highly desired regularization effect. The study is not exhaustive; we have left out several design issues including fuzzy decision trees or the variety of problems dealing with a fuzzy quantification of probabilities.

Acknowledgement

Support from the Natural Sciences and Engineering Research Council of Canada (NSERC) is gratefully acknowledged.

11 References

1. J. C. Bezdek (1981). *Pattern Recognition with Fuzzy Objective Function Algorithms*, Plenum Press, N. York.

2. R. Dave (1992). Characterization and detection of noise in clustering, *Pattern Recognition Letters*, 12, 657 - 664.

3. *Communications of the ACM* - a special issue on Data Mining, 11, 1996.

4. U. M. Fayyad, G. Piatetsky - Shapiro, P. Smyth (1996). From data mining to knowledge discovery in databases, *AI Magazine*, 17, 37 - 54.

5. U. M. Fayyad, G. Piatetsky - Shapiro, P. Smyth, R. Uthurusamy (eds.) (1996). *Advances in Knowledge Discovery and Data Mining*, AAAI Press, Menlo Park, CA.

6. W. Frawley, G. Piatetsky - Shapiro, C. Matheus (1991). Knowledge discovery in databases: an overview. In: *Knowledge Discovery in Databases*, G. Piatetsky - Shapiro and W. Frawley (eds.), AAAI Press, Menlo Park, CA, pp. 1 -27.

7. R. Krishnapuram, J. M. Keller (1993). A possibilistic approach to clustering, IEEE Trans. on Fuzzy Systems, 1, 98- 110.

8. W. Pedrycz (1995). Fuzzy Sets Engineering, CRC Press, Boca Raton, FL.

9. W. Pedrycz (1996). Fuzzy multimodels, IEEE Trans. on Fuzzy Systems, 4, 139 - 148.

10. W. Pedrycz(1996). Conditional Fuzzy C - Means, Pattern Recognition Letters, 17, 625 - 632.

11. Special issue of *Int. J. Intelligent Systems* on Knowledge Discovery in Data - and Knowledge Bases, vol. 7, no. 7, 1992.

12. L. A. Zadeh (1979). Fuzzy sets and information granularity, In: advances in Fuzzy Set Theory and Applications (M. M. Gupta, R. K. Ragade, R. R. Yager, eds.) North Holland, Amsterdam, 3- 18.

Evaluation of Connectionist Information Retrieval in a Legal Document Collection

R.A. Bustos and T.D. Gedeon

School of Computer Science and Engineering
The University of New South Wales
Sydney, NSW 2052
Australia
E-mail: {robertb, tom} @cse.unsw.edu.au

Abstract

This paper describes the evaluation of a spreading activation model for information retrieval. Different configurations of this model were applied to the problem of discovering cross references for a hypertext version of a legal research textbook. The $cirs$ (Connectionist Information Retrieval System) is described. Six different weighting schemes for links between neurons were evaluated, using human indexed cross references.

1. Methodology

The aim of this experiment is to explore the effectiveness of spreading activation models of information retrieval when applied to a practical problem. A general model with a graphical user interface has been implemented in the $cirs$ system (Connectionist Information Retrieval System, Bustos, 1995). $Cirs$ allows users to interactively modify parameters of the system including indexing word selection criteria, network parameters, network models and query generation.

Using cirs, six different weighting schemes for links between neurons were evaluated, using a legal text document collection with human indexed cross references. The evaluation is carried out using the user oriented recall and precision measurement method [Savoy 1994]. The network models are described in full below. Recall and precision values for each model were recorded for 12 queries, selected to display varying levels of performance, from the 73 available. These results are in section 3 below.

The best precision / recall values over the 100 iterations of the network were selected on the basis that such a test would simulate the behaviour of a user operating the retrieval system, having the opportunity to decide whether or not to continue to search for more references at any point. The aim of this experiment was to compare the user oriented performance of the different models. Clearly, users would not have the prior knowledge of ideal retrieval results with which to measure performance and to help decide when to halt the search, however it is suggested users would approximate this by considering the number of relevant items, and their relative positions in the retrieved list. Parameter tuning heuristics, discovered by theoretical analysis and practical experience are in section 4 below.

2. Network Models

This section describes the six different network models which were implemented in `cirs`. Each of the models (including Smart Boolean) are implemented by defining the nature of the connections between word and document units.

2.1. Smart Boolean

Boolean full text retrieval systems rely on users' ability to choose appropriate words for queries, a task that they (usually) approach with knowledge of approximately how common particular words are in the domain of the search. Using these intuitions, users select words that they think will occur sufficiently often to retrieve relevant documents, yet not be so widespread as to cause retrieval of unwanted documents.

The present evaluation task requires that queries be constructed automatically from tutorial questions written to test understanding of the textbook that forms this document collection, without the intervention of a human user. One strategy would be to use every word·from each tutorial document and create links of constant weight between each word and the document that it occurs in, and consider retrieved any document neuron that received any activation. This process most accurately models the boolean retrieval method but fails to take into account the users' ability (and interest) in being more selective when choosing words for queries.

A weighting strategy as described above would demonstrate unrealistically poor performance, so modifications were implemented to make the model a more realistic simulation of the combination of users domain knowledge than the simple boolean retrieval method. Links from words to documents are created with constant weights, but an activation threshold is applied, with only document units of greater activation than the threshold considered to be retrieved. In this way, document with more of the query words will be retrieved first, thus performing a crude document relevance ranking.

Significantly, this retrieval method is the only one that does not have connections from documents to words, since boolean retrieval systems do not retrieve on the basis of shared words in any way. Inhibition between units is another feature of the other network models that is not included, as the traditional concordance implementation of boolean information retrieval does not include any facility such as this.

2.2. Binary Networks

The binary network model is a simple enhancement of the boolean network, by adding an extra link of constant weight in the opposite direction, from document neuron to word neuron, whenever a word occurs in a document. There are now two connections, which can also be described as a single bi-directional connection between the word and document units.

The binary network is a more powerful way of representing the relations between words and documents than the smart boolean method, since activation flowing from document to word neurons over the additional links can activate further new words, thus capturing context and eventually activating other document neurons. The use of the activation threshold maintains the retrieval ranking mechanism, and competition within the word and document unit pools limits the activation, with the effect of focussing the retrieval and reducing the effects of low frequency noise words.

2.3. Word Frequency Networks

Binary connections are, nevertheless, a relatively coarse way of representing relations between words and documents. The symmetric word frequency weighting method connects words and documents with bi-directional links, that are proportional to the word frequency of the indexed word in the given document. Weights are normalised by the total frequency of the word, thus reducing the relative effect of words which are highly frequent in the overall collection.

The frequency network is an improvement over the binary net, since the proportionality of the connection weights to document neurons allows for greater detail of this relation to be represented and used for retrieval. As the links in this method are bi directional, properties of the binary network method such as context capturing and use of inhibitory pools remain.

An asymmetric version of this interconnection method is also included. Weights from documents to words are calculated as above, thus the semantic meaning of documents is represented based on word frequencies in the document. However, the links from words to documents are proportional to the number of occurrences of the word in the document, normalised by the number of occurrences in the whole document collection. First described in [Rose and Belew, 1991], this interconnection method more accurately models the asymmetric nature of the relation between words and documents: a particular word may be of disproportionate value in describing the content of a particular document, however it does not follow that the word should retrieve that document any more readily than any other, as there may be several documents each containing this word with varying combinations of other terms that could influence strength of connection. The increased importance of the word in describing the content of the document becomes important however when activation begins to flow backwards from document to terms, when it is desirable that terms be activated in proportion to their semantic value for describing document content.

2.4. IDTW Networks

These networks with connection weights proportional to the inverse document - term weights of the document. This weighting method was developed by [Salton 1983] for vector retrieval, and takes account of the document frequency of words to assign term importance according to the discriminatory power of the word. Thus, words occurring very frequently in many documents, and those occurring only occasionally in very few documents are assigned less weight. The equation for the weighting method is:

$$TW_{ij} = \sqrt{\frac{F_{ij} \times \log\left(\frac{N}{DF_j}\right)}{\sum_{k=1}^{T}\left(F_{ik} \times \log\left(\frac{N}{DF_k}\right)\right)^2}}$$

where:

N = Number of documents

T = Number of terms

F_{ij} = Frequency of term j in document i.

DF_j = Document frequency of term j.

As with the word frequency networks, symmetric and asymmetric networks are constructed. The symmetric network consists of weights in both directions proportional to the IDTW value, whilst the asymmetric net uses IDTW values for connections from document to word neurons, and normalised document frequency values from words to documents (as was the case for the frequency networks described above).

Calculation of IDTW values for connection weights is significantly more computationally expensive than simply using normalised word frequencies values. This weighting method better models the relation, however, because the frequency of words over the whole collection is taken into account when assigning importance to terms in documents.

3. Network Evaluation

This section describes evaluation of the different network models using the user oriented recall and precision approach described above, in the Methodology section. Results presented are the best recall / precision points for each query, for each method (Tables 1 - 60.

3.1. Recall /Precision Performance Comparison

The 13 example queries displayed in these tables are a subset of the full collection of 73 queries, and were selected to display a wide variety of the properties of the collection, including varying query length, differing use of context in the query, and differing tutorial question style. Accordingly, these queries demonstrate the varying levels of performance of the models.

3.2. Smart Boolean Network

The Smart Boolean network demonstrated surprisingly good performance and was one of the most efficient networks, both for network generation time and cycling time. The activation threshold was set to 0.1. This parameter can have a dramatic effect on precision values for the retrieval method, since the combination of the activation threshold and number of cycles run effectively determines the number of items in the retrieved list.

Table 3.1. Boolean Network Results

Query	0	1	2	3	4	5	6	7	8	9	10	11	12
Recall	1.000	1.000	0.333	0.250	1	1.000	1.000	1.000	1.000	1.000	0.500	0.500	1.000
Precision	0.167	0.429	1.000	1.000	0.333	0.188	0.061	0.133	0.063	0.063	1.000	1.000	0.036
No. Ideal	1	3	3	4	1	3	2	2	2	6	2	2	7

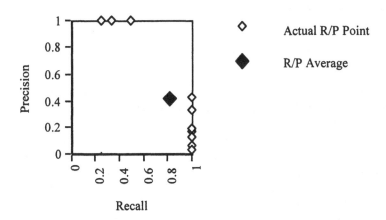

3.3. Binary Network

The binary network demonstrated the poorest performance and was the hardest to set the parameters well. Greater decay was required since the stronger interconnections between words and documents caused a very rapid increase in network total activation. Increasing decay has the effect of widening the separation between the activated units and units which are not activated, since units not receiving enough activation to overcome the decay end up being deactivated. The effects of inhibition, excitation and external input are also reduced by lowering these parameters.

Table 3.2. Binary Network Results

Query	0	1	2	3	4	5	6	7	8	9	10	11	12
Recall	0	0.667	0.333	0.250	1.0	1.000	0	0	0	0.167	0.5	0.5	0
Precision	0	0.333	0.500	0.125	0.25	0.2	0	0	0	0.33	0.5	0.2	0
No. Ideal	1	3	3	4	1	3	2	2	2	6	2	2	7

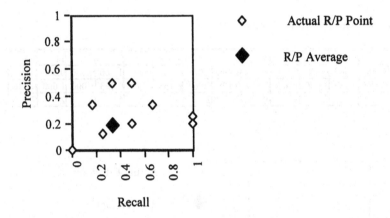

The crudeness of the associations between words and documents, when defined using only constant magnitude weights means that the first retrieval of the network is not particularly accurate, which greatly effects the final results.

With greater levels of total activation, retrieval results also end up being more dependent on the network topology than the query, so the same units keep on getting activated since they have the largest number of connections.

3.4. Symmetric Frequency Network

In general, the symmetric networks showed significantly worse performance when compared to the asymmetric versions. The normalised connections of this model made the task of setting parameters for the model easier, without the problem of rapid activation growth. However, after a number of cycles, the activation often did reach the maximum value and began to be scaled.

Table 3.3. Symmetric Frequency Network Results

Query	0	1	2	3	4	5	6	7	8	9	10	11	12
Recall	0.000	0.667	0.333	0.250	1.000	0.333	0.000	0.000	0.000	0.167	0.500	0.000	0.000
Precision	0.000	0.667	1.000	0.500	0.500	0.333	0.000	0.000	0.000	0.500	1.000	0.000	0.000
No. Ideal	1	3	3	4	1	3	2	2	2	6	2	2	7

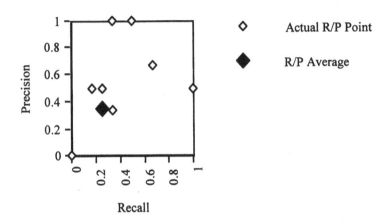

A significant feature of this network model is that the connections are not document size independent, so larger documents (with more connections) tended to be retrieved first.

3.5. Asymmetric Frequency Network

Performance improved significantly when using the asymmetric version of the frequency mode. Normalised connections again made the task of setting network parameters and easier one. It is interesting to note the performance with this model is generally at a lower level of recall than the Smart Boolean method, but with much improved precision.

Table 3.4. Asymmetric Frequency Network Results

Query	0	1	2	3	4	5	6	7	8	9	10	11	12
Recall	1.000	1.000	0.333	0.333	1.000	1.000	0.500	0.500	0.500	0.333	0.500	0.500	0.500
Precision	1.000	1.000	1.000	1.000	0.500	0.250	0.200	1.000	1.000	1.000	1.000	1.000	0.250
No. Ideal	1	3	3	4	1	3	2	2	2	6	2	2	7

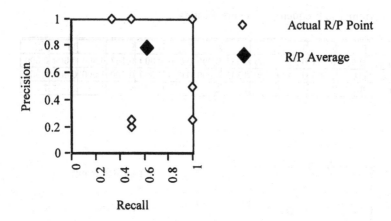

3.6. Symmetric IDTW Network

As with the other symmetric model, the Symmetric IDTW network shows disappointing performance, often failing to find any of the references for given tutorial. Greater effort was thus applied to finding the appropriate parameter settings for the asymmetric version of this model.

Table 3.5. Symmetric IDTW Network Results

Query	0	1	2	3	4	5	6	7	8	9	10	11	12
Recall	1.000	1.000	0.333	0.25	0.000	0.000	0.000	0	0	0.333	0.333	0	0.143
Precision	0.500	0.067	1.000	0.125	0.000	0.000	0.000	0	0	1.000	0.182	0	1.000
No. Ideal	1	3	3	4	1	3	2	2	2	6	2	2	7

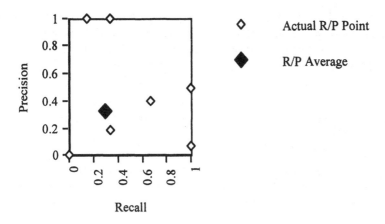

3.7. Asymmetric IDTW Network

This result is a significant improvement on the Smart Boolean network results, and is the best results over all the models. The same parameters that were applied to the model as were used in all the other networks; same 13 queries, activation

Table 3.6. Asymmetric IDTW Network Results

Query	0	1	2	3	4	5	6	7	8	9	10	11	12
Recall	1.000	1.000	0.333	0.500	1.000	1.000	0.500	0.500	0.500	0.500	0.500	1.000	0.429
Precision	1.000	0.750	1.000	0.500	0.500	0.150	0.250	1.000	1.000	1.000	1.000	0.286	0.250
No. Ideal	1	3	3	4	1	3	2	2	2	6	2	2	7

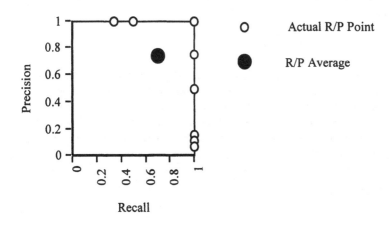

threshold and number of cycles, with the exception of those from the binary model, which required different settings due to the non-normalised nature of the word-document connections. Section 4 examines this network in a more qualitative light, and the 12 queries used here are tested with varying parameters for query length and sensitivity to stopword removal and stemming.

3.8. Comparison of Smart Boolean and Asymmetric IDTW over Full Collection.

The following scatter graph shows a comparison of the best retrieval results of the Smart Boolean and Asymmetric IDTW networks over the set of 13 testing queries used for the single network scatter graphs.

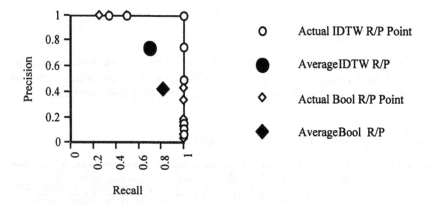

These results confirm the impression that the asymmetric IDTW spreading activation model appears to find a similar number of the references, however with greater precision.

4. Parameter Tuning Heuristics

This section records some observations during the parameter tuning process. The selection of network and word indexing parameters is an important, yet largely unguided process. A method of selecting indexed words was discussed in [Bustos and Gedeon, 1995], and it may be possible to use other machine learning techniques to discover correct network settings. Decisions about parameter settings were made with consideration of factors including machine resources, observed total activation levels and apparent retrieval performance (ie informal examination of results lists).

4.1. General Techniques

In general, parameters were adjusted to slow growth in total activation, since rapid growth often led to oscillation, and the negative effects of scaling to a total activation value which are described below.

The external input (*estr*) parameter can be decreased to reduce the effect of the initial query input on documents retrieved. A very high value for this parameter makes the retrieval process more closely resemble the underlying vector retrieval relations embodied in the weights, and total activation assumes a high value after just a single cycle.

The excitation parameter (*alpha*), may be increased to hasten the effect of documents activating other documents through the word units. Increasing alpha in combination with reducing the external input strength parameter emphasises the context capturing ability of the spreading activation model, however this can introduce problems of rapid activation growth and difficulty in achieving network convergence.

4.2. Decay and the Effects of Scaling to a Global Maximum Activation

It is necessary to prevent unbounded growth of total network activation, since effectively results in retrieval of all the documents in the collection, and thus very poor precision. Two approaches are built into cirs: a global decay term, and scaling to a constant total activation. Provision of a decay term was a strategy implemented in [McClelland and Rumelhart, 1988], while scaling of total activation was an extension examined by [Gedeon and Mital, 1991].

The inclusion of a decay term modifies the network algorithm to create a tendency for neuron activation to decrease, if the neuron does not have continuing support from neighbouring units. This has the effect of 'focussing' retrieval in the sense that low frequency connections are reduced further and activation growth (retrieval) proceed according to the most strongly connected units. Accordingly, use of a decay term removes some of the benefits of the accumulation of many smaller connections to retrieve documents, a feature of the spreading activation models.

Scaling the total network activation to a constant value allows control of the activation levels whilst maintaining the effects of low connection weight associations between words. This method is implemented in cirs with a single parameter for the total activation of document neurons, from which a proportional value for word units is calculated. When the total activation of a pool of unit exceeds these values, the activations are proportionally scaled down to the given total.

While this scaling has the desired effect of controlling activation, under conditions of total activation significantly greater than the scaling parameter, retrieval results become dependent on network topology only and the effect of the initially activated query words is lost. Activation is progressively spread over all the units in the pool, and in combination with a retrieval activation threshold, this has the effect of reducing the length of the retrieval list as fewer units reach the threshold.

5. Commentary and Conclusions

The aim of this work has been to implement and evaluate spreading activation models of information retrieval. The `cirs` system was designed and coded in object oriented C++ for this purpose and evaluated with the user oriented precision and recall approach.

The document collections used for this section are larger than any published study of spreading activation models, using more documents and indexing more words than any of the other reported systems. A number of weighting schemes were examined and the asymmetric approach to frequency, mentioned in [Rose and Belew, 1991] was implemented and evaluated, and extended to IDTW.

This large scale evaluation has achieved results significantly different to those expected from smaller scale implementations, since improved precision appears to be common result from use of the models. Expected improvements to absolute recall were not recorded, perhaps supporting the views of those [e.g., Blair 1990] who highlight the limitations of using word occurrence information to capture document meaning.

The specialised task of link generation for hypertext systems was examined, and problems with the large number of free parameters in the spreading activation model highlighted. Although beyond the scope of the evaluation project attempted here, the application of machine learning techniques to find appropriate parameter settings may be an area of research meriting future attention before these methods become practical enough to replace dominant retrieval technologies such as the boolean concordance.

The implementation of a network model combining connection weights proportional to word frequency in the document for document to word links, and weights proportional to word frequency normalised by total word occurrence for the whole document collection for word to document links, has not been described elsewhere.

The document collection view is shown in Exhibit 1.

References

Blair D.C. 1990 *Language and Representation in Information Retrieval*, Amsterdam, Elsevier.

Bustos, R.A. 1995 *Neural Networks in Law*, Thesis, School of Computer Science and Engineering, The University of New South Wales, Sydney.

Bustos, R.A. and Gedeon, T.D. 1995 "Learning Synonyms and Related Concepts in Document Collections," in Alspector, J, Goodman, R and Brown, TX

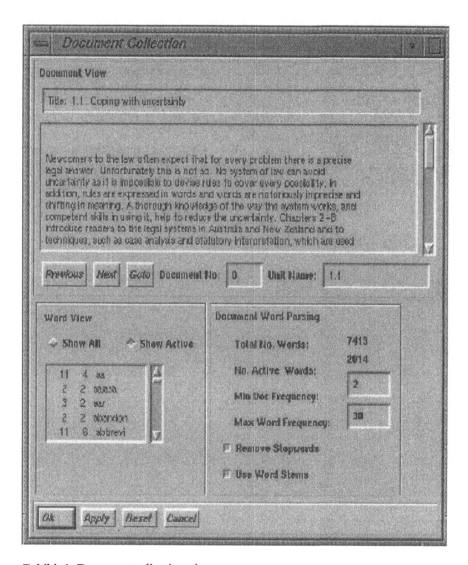

Exhibit 1. Document collection view

Applications of Neural Networks to Telecommunications 2, pp. 202-209, Lawrence Erlbaum.

Gedeon, T.D. and Mital V.J. 1991 "An Adaptive learning network for information retrieval in a litigation support application", *Proc AMSE International Conference on Neural Networks,* vol. 2, pp. 25-34, San Diego.

McClelland, J.L. and Rumelhart, D.E. 1988 *Explorations in Parallel Distributed Processing*, MIT Press, Cambridge, Massachusetts.

434

Rose, D.E., Belew, R.K. 1991 "A connectionist and symbolic hybrid for improving legal research", *International Journal of Man Machine Studies*, vol. 35, pp. 1-33.

Salton, G. 1983 "On the Representation of Query Term Relations by Soft Boolean Operators," *Proceedings of the Association for Computational Linguistics (ACL) European Chapter 2nd Conference*, pp. 116-122 Geneva.

Savoy, J. 1994 "Searching Information in Legal Hypertext Systems," *Artificial Intelligence and Law* , vol 2., pp. 205.

Wong, S.K.M., Cai, Y.J. and Yao, Y.Y. 1993 "An Application of neural Networks in Adaptive Information Retrieval" VOL 2, *Proceedings IEEE International Conference on Neural Networks*, San Francisco, CA , March 28-April 1.

6

APPLICATIONS
INFORMATION IN DATABASES AND
INFORMATION SYSTEMS

Using Linguistic Models in Medical Decision Making

Maurice E. Cohen and Donna L. Hudson

California State University, Fresno
University of California, San Francisco
2615 East Clinton Avenue
Fresno, California USA 93703
E-mails: {cohen, hudson}@ucsfresno.edu

Abstract

Medical records contain a wide variety of data types, including a sizable percentage in linguistic format including physician's notes, interpretations of medical images, impressions of pathological findings, and summaries of electrocardiogram and electroencephalogram recordings. Because of the complex nature of the medical record, development of practical computer-assisted medical decision making aids has met with numerous difficulties. In this article, a number of approaches for dealing with linguistic variables are presented and illustrated in a system for decision making in cardiology.

1 Introduction

Because of the nature of medical data, most early attempts at developing computer-based medical decision support systems were unsuccessful. The problems were many-fold. The nature of the medical record is complex, containing numerous data types including patient history, physical exam results, laboratory tests, electrocardiogram (ECG) or electroencephalogram (EEG) results, and medical images [1]. Although some of this information is in numeric terms, for example laboratory results, much of it is linguistic in nature, including notes written in patients' charts. In addition, even numeric results may be complex in nature, such as ECG or EEG recordings which are represented as time series data. The final complication is the inclusion of information in image form, such as radiographs, CT, MRI, and ultrasound scans.

The earliest medical decision making systems were based on pattern classification algorithms in which all information was represented numerically [2,3]. The major objection to these approaches was that the computer arrived at its decision in a black-box type fashion and was unable to explain the decision which it had reached [4]. As a reaction, symbolic processing approaches began to appear in the 1970's utilizing the knowledge-based approach [5]. These approaches flourished for the coming decade, but were superseded in the mid 1980's by neural network models which were again numerically based [6-8].

The latest approach to computer-assisted decision support is the hybrid system in which more than one approach is combined in the same system [9,10]. The objective of the hybrid system approach is to bring as many tools to bear as possible on the problem at hand. Traditionally, many researchers have become advocates of their methodology and have sought to promote it as the preferred method. The hybrid system approach requires a step back from this advocacy to a more pragmatic approach to problem solving. A typical argument of using hybrid systems is the ability to include both expert-derived and data-derived knowledge in the same system, thus allowing all information to incorporated.

In the next section, basic conflicts in structure which arise between numerical and symbolic approaches are discussed. Methods of using linguistic variables are then discussed, first in terms of symbolic processing and then in neural network models. Finally, an example using linguistic variables for decision support in cardiology is given.

2 Conflicts Between Numerical and Symbolic Processing

In symbolic processing approaches, linguistic variables are easily handled. For example, in a rule-based expert system, the knowledge base itself is expressed in English phrases. Note the following two formulations from the EMERGE rule-based system [11]:

Crisp Version

IF   Blood Pressure < 100/60
        Urinary Output < 30 cc/hr
THEN Patient is in Shock

Fuzzy Version

IF   Blood pressure low
        Urinary output very low
THEN Patient may be in shock

The limits stated in the rule on the left are obviously arbitrary cut-off values. The rule on the right allows for fuzzy interpretation in the reasoning process. Later in the article, the different reasoning strategies are compared.

On the other hand, in numerical processing systems such as neural networks or statistically-based systems, the knowledge base is generally in database format, containing on the whole numerical information. Thus knowledge is derived directly through accumulated numeric data. However, linguistic information can be incorporated into neural network models through pre-processing or post-processing.

In practice it is useful to include both expert-supplied information and data-derived information, so some method must be found for combining these sources. The major difficulty in combining different reasoning strategies arises in the combination of knowledge-based approaches and data-based approaches, as the sources of information are completely separate. It is, however, this combination which has the most to offer for the inclusion of all available information.

3 Linguistic Terms in Knowledge-Based Decision Paradigms

In knowledge-based systems, there are two sources of information: domain knowledge information which is contained in the knowledge base and case-specific information which is entered by the user for each case under consideration. The user interface is the means by which the case information enters the system.

3.1 User Interface

3.1.1 Binary Input

In traditional knowledge-based systems, the user was either asked to answer questions with a yes/no/? response, or in some data-driven systems the user was permitted to enter in word format the information which was known about the patient. Hence the following were equivalent methods of getting information into the system:

Questioning Mode	**Data-Driven Mode**
Blood pressure low? y	*Enter any clinical findings*
Syncope? n	Low blood pressure
Abnormal mental status? y	Abnormal mental state

The EMERGE system permits the data-driven entry of information, where the rule search commences with the first rule substantiated. Either of the above results in the confirmation of the follow rule [11]:

    IF Blood pressure low
        AND ANY OF
            abnormal mental status
            cold, clammy skin
            gray, cyanotic skin
            weak peripheral pulses
            very low urinary output
    THEN Patient should be admitted to CCU

The data-driven mode accomplished the matching using the following algorithm [12]:

Each word in a phrase is matched regardless of order.

Each word is matched by the computation in equation (1).
Each phrase is matched by the computation in equation (2).

$$WM(i,j) = 1/(\min[w_i,w_j]) \sum_{m=1}^{w_i} \sum_{n=1}^{\min(k,w_j)} \delta(m,n) \text{ for } |w_i-w_j| \leq 1 \qquad (1)$$

where $WM(i,j)$ is the attempted match for the ith word in phrase i with the jth word in phrase j, and

$$\delta(m,n) = \begin{cases} 1 \text{ if the mth letter of word i matches the nth letter of word j} \\ 0 \text{ if the mth letter does not match the nth letter} \end{cases}$$

w_i = length of the ith word in phrase 1

w_j = length of the jth word in phrase 2

k = position in word j where a match is found for the letters

$$WP = 1/(\min[p_1,p_2]) \sum_{j=1}^{p_1} \sum_{i=1}^{\min(l,p_2)} T(WM(i,j)) \qquad (2)$$

where:

p_1 = number of words in phrase 1
p_2 = number of words in phrase 2
l = position in phrase 2 where a match is found for the jth word in phrase i.
    A match occurs if $WP > T_2$ where
T_1 = threshold value for word match
T_2 = threshold value for phrase match, and

$$T(\alpha) = \begin{cases} \alpha \text{ if } \alpha \geq T_1 \\ 0 \text{ if } \alpha < T_1 \end{cases}$$

Note that WP and $WM(i,j)$ are values between 0 and 1, inclusive, with 1 indicating a perfect match. The threshold value T_1 accepts words where a slight misspelling has occurred. Words are compared only if there lengths differ by at most 1. Thus $T_1 = 0.8$ allows one out of five letters to differ. T_2 allows phrases to match even if every word does not match. The order of words in the phrases is not considered important.

For the example given above, assuming $T_1 = T_2 = 0.8$, comparing the questioning mode in which the phrases are taken directly from the rules with the data-driven information entered by the user, the first two phrases "blood pressure low" and "low blood pressure" match exactly since the order is not considered. In the second set of phrases, "abnormal mental status" and "abnormal mental state", "state" matches "status" to the degree 0.8, so consequently the phrases match according to

$$WP = (1/3) [1 + 1 + 0.8] = 0.93 > T_2$$

and the phrases are said to match. If the match is less than exact, the matched phrase is presented to the user for verification.

3.1.2 Degree of Presence Input

Although the above procedure utilizes fuzzy matching for words and phrases, the effect on the invocation of rules is still binary: either an antecedent is substantiated or it is not. A simple modification to this procedure is to allow a degree of presence to be entered instead of a yes/no/? response. Thus the questioning mode will change to

Questioning Mode

Blood pressure low? 8
Syncope? 3
Abnormal mental status? 9

and the data-driven mode:

Data-Driven Mode

Enter any clinical findings followed by a value between 0 and 10 indicating degree of presence
Low blood pressure 8
Abnormal mental state 9

The values are divided by 10 for normalization purposes. Note that the entry of these numbers does not change the word and phrase matching described above but does affect the operation of the inference engine to be discussed later.

3.1.3 Linguistic Input

Another possibility for user input is to present the questions in the following format:

Question Mode

Indicate the range of symptoms according to the following (low, medium, high), or (normal, abnormal)
Blood pressure: low
Mental status: abnormal

The first entry requires numeric interpretation which is most easily done by pre-defined membership functions as shown in Figure 1. The value obtained is then interpreted by the inference engine in the same manner as the values entered in the previous section. The second entry is treated simply as binary input.

3.2 Knowledge Base

The knowledge base itself traditionally contains production rules in the format illustrated above:

IF ALL OF
Antecedent 1
.
.
.
Antecedent n
THEN Conclusion

This structure can be altered by the introduction of linguistic quantifiers which were first introduced by Zadeh [13] There are two types of linguistic quantifiers: Kind 1 and Kind 2. Kind 1, or absolute quantifiers, represent a specified amount, such as about three, at least four, or all. Kind 2, or relative quantifiers, represent an approximate amount, such as most or some. An absolute quantifier can be expressed as a fuzzy subset of non-negative real numbers, while a relative quantifier can be expressed as a fuzzy subset of the unit interval.

Using kind 1 quantifiers, the rule structure can be changed to:

IF At least m of
Antecedent 1
.
.
.
Antecedent n
THEN Conclusion

where $1 \leq m \leq n$.

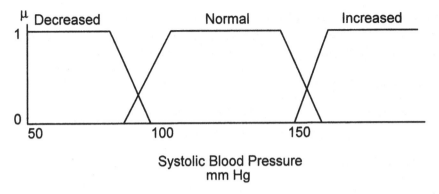

Figure 1: Membership Functions for Systolic Blood Pressure

Use of this type of quantifier results in minor modifications to the inference engine. If Kind 2 quantifiers are used:

IF Most of
    Antecedent 1
    .
    .
    .
    Antecedent n
THEN Conclusion

then more major modifications are required.

Further modifications to the rule base include the possibility that the antecedents do not contribute equally, i.e. quantifiers are associated with each antecedent and that each antecedent may be partially substantiated. Incorporation of this type of knowledge base is discussed below under other approximate reasoning techniques.

3.3 Inference Engine

The heart of the decision process in knowledge-based system is the inference engine. While rule searching may be done by a number of strategies, a particular rule is confirmed by matching the premises with case information.

3.3.1 Binary Logic Engines

Traditional rule-based system used binary logic inference engines with rules which were only conjunctions. Thus each antecedent had to be substantiated for the rule to fire. The original EMERGE system modified this structure to permit the inclusions of a subset of Kind 1 quantifiers represented by "at least m of" where $0 \le m \le n$, where n was the number of antecedents. Thus the input was still binary, but different degrees of substantiation were permitted.

3.3.2 Fuzzy Logic Engines

The normal production rule format as outlined above has unqualified antecedents. For a one-antecedent rule,

IF (X is A) THEN (Y is B)

the statements are considered all or nothing. However, membership functions $f_A(x)$ and $f_B(x)$ can be defined which describe to what degree X is A and Y is B, respectively, at every point x and y of the universes, U_X and U_Y, in other words to what degree these propositions are satisfied at each point. A possibility distribution can be defined by assigning to every element x in U_X a degree of possibility [14]

$$\pi_X(x) = f_A(x) \tag{3}$$

Let r(x,y) represent the strength of the implication. There are a number of possibilities for the definition of r(x,y), which are described in [15]. An example is the Mamdani implication:

$$r(x,y) = \min(f_A(x), f_B(y)) \tag{4}$$

As an example consider the rule

IF (blood pressure is low) THEN (shock is present)

and $f_A(x)$ and $f_B(y)$ must be defined. The respective universes of discourse are the range of all possible values, $U_X = [0,300]$, $U_Y = [0,1]$, where 0 indicates absent and 1 indicates present.

In order to implement a reasoning process, the above rules must be combined with data to produce conclusions. In ordinary binary logic, modus ponens is used for this purpose. Again, several possibilities have been proposed for a fuzzy modus ponens [15]. Assume the actual data for the above rule is

X is A'.

Define an operation T such that

$$g_{B'}(y) = \max (T(g_{A'}(x), r(x,y))) \tag{5}$$

where $g_A'(x)$ and $g_B'(x)$ are membership functions. Usually T is a t-norm [10], which is a function satisfying the following properties:

$$T(x,1) = x \qquad \text{(Boundary)} \qquad (6)$$
$$T(x,y) = T(y,x) \qquad \text{(Symmetry)} \qquad (7)$$
$$T(x,z) \leq T(y,z) \text{ if } x \leq y \quad \text{(Monotonicity)} \qquad (8)$$
$$T(x,T(y,z)) = T(T(x,y),z) \quad \text{(Associativity)} \qquad (9)$$

The most common choice for a t-norm is the minimum. T must be chosen in conjunction with r(x,y) to preserve the conclusion when the observation is identical with the premise.

Usually production rules have multiple antecedents and take the form

IF $(V_1$ is $A_1)$ and $(V_2$ is $A_2)$ ... and $(V_n$ is $A_n)$ THEN U is B [16].

The possibility distribution discussed above can be generalized to $\pi_{v_1,v_2,...,v_n,u}$ on $X_1 \times X_2 ... X_n \times Y$ such that

$$\pi_{v_1,v_2,...,v_n,u} = 1 \wedge (1-A_1(x_1)^\wedge A_2(x_2)...^\wedge A_n(x_n) + B(y)) \qquad (10)$$

where $\pi_i(x) = A_i(x)$ are the individual possibility measures and $\wedge$ is the min operator. For example:

IF (BP < 100/60) THEN (shock is present)

must be separated into the components

IF (Systolic BP < 100) AND (Diastolic BP < 60)
THEN (shock is present)

or alternately

IF (Systolic BP is low) AND (Diastolic BP is low)
THEN (shock is present)

3.3.3 Membership Function Computation

Medical variables can be defined as fuzzy sets, along with membership functions which indicate the degree to which an item belongs to a fuzzy set. For example, normal systolic blood pressure is a fuzzy subset of possible ranges of blood pressure. A particular value assumes a membership function in this fuzzy subset. A specific blood pressure value for a patient can be interpreted as a fuzzy number which accounts for the imprecision in the measurement (Figure 2.)

It is possible to use fuzzy matching as a direct means of classification [17]. Applying this method to the heart disease example, consider the three-category problem of differentiating among normal heart function, myocardial infarction, and angina pectoris. Assuming four possible variables apply, we get fuzzy set descriptions summarized in Table I using the variables: blood pressure (BP), pulse rate (PR), white blood count (WBC), and post-ventricular contractions (PVC's). The last of these (PVC's) is a type of arrhythmia. The corresponding membership functions are illustrated in Figure 3 [18].

The classification of a patient case using this information can be done through the use of a number of compatibility indices, which are illustrated in Figure 4. This figure shows the matching of patient data (triangle) with possible membership functions. The first measure is the possibility measure, as discussed above. It is defined as

$$\pi(M,F) = \text{Sup } (M \cap F) \tag{11}$$

The second is the necessity measure:

$$\nu(M,F) = 1 - \pi(M',F) = 1 - \text{Sup}(M' \cap F) = \text{Inf}(M \cup F') \tag{12}$$

The third is the truth-possibility index

$$\rho(M,F) = \pi(\tau_0, \tau_1) \tag{13}$$

With the fuzzy sets described here, the truth-possibility index is "around f" with the following holding

$$\nu \leq \rho \leq \pi$$

The index to be used is chosen according to optimistic or pessimistic considerations. These three indices yield slightly different results. It is up to the user to decide on the choice depending upon how conservative he or she wishes to be in the matching process. The characterizations given here can also be weighted according to relative importance, as with the rules described above, in which case relative heights are adjusted.

3.3.4 Other Approximate Reasoning Approaches

In order to accommodate kind 2 quantifiers, we need to change the rule structure. To use quantifiers, each proposition P in a rule is replaced with

P: QV's are A

or more commonly

Q(RV's) are A.

where the second type of statement can be interpreted as, for example,

(At least n) (important) objectives are satisfied by x

where Q is "at least n" and R is "important".

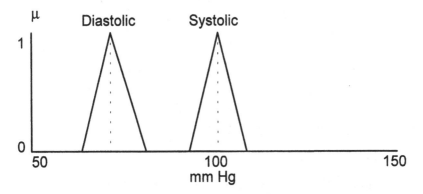

Figure 2: Fuzzy Numbers Representing Blood Pressure Case Data

Table I: Ranges for Angina and MI				
	BP	**PR**	**WBC**	**PVC's**
Angina Pectoris	Increased	Increased	Normal	None
Myocaridial Infarction	Decreased	Increased	Elevated	> 3

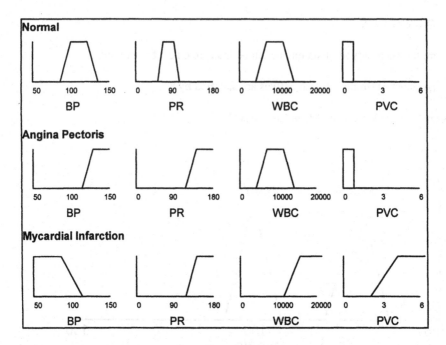

Figure 3: Membership Functions Corresponding to Table I

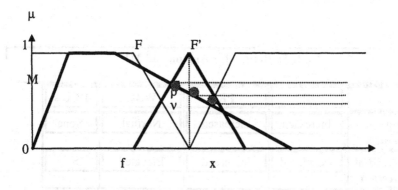

Figure 4: Compatibility Indices

Again, a number of possibilities exist. In order to determine the truth value of P, we consider some subset C of V such that 1) the number of elements in C satisfies Q, or 2) each element in C satisfies the property A. The degree to which P is satisfied by C will be denoted $V_P(C)$. The overall validity is then [19]:

$$V(P) = \max\{V_P(x)\} \qquad (14)$$
$$C \varepsilon 2^A$$

where 2^A is the power set of A. If Q is a kind 1 quantifier, then

$$V(P) = \max[Q \ (\ \sum_{i=1}^{n} c_i \wedge q_i) \wedge \min_{i=1,...,n} a_i^{c_i \wedge q_i}] \qquad (15)$$

$c \varepsilon [0,1]$ indicates the membership status, r_i is the weighting factor for the ith antecedent which indicates its relative importance and a_i is the degree of presence of the ith finding which is entered by the user. Determination of the values for the r_i's is discussed later. For an example corresponding to the rules in Figure 1, refer to Table I. In the general case, Q may also be a Kind 2 quantifier, in which case the summation in equation (1) is normalized by dividing by the summation over i of the r_i values.

3.4 Output

The output from rule-based systems is usually stated as the conclusion along with a degree of certainty in the conclusion. An explanation can be provided by re-tracing the rules which were substantiated, along with their degree of substantiation.

4 Symbolic Terms in Neural Network Models

4.1 Neural Network Algorithms

Neural networks can be used for a number of purposes, but the type which is of interest to decision making problems is the classification neural network. The heart of the neural network approach is the learning algorithm. There are two types of learning algorithms used in classification networks: supervised and unsupervised learning. In supervised learning the network is trained on data of known classification to develop a model which can be used to classify new cases. Classification can be into two or more categories. In unsupervised learning, the network is self-training, grouping data into categories through a process called clustering. By their nature, neural networks operate only on numerical data, either binary or continuous. However, there are a number of ways in which linguistic information can be used in conjunction with neural network models, usually either through pre-processing or post-processing. Many of these approaches use fuzzy techniques.

4.2 Fuzzy Neural Networks

Medical data often defy precise interpretation because diseases come in different states or in combination with other diseases. It is difficult to represent multi-class membership. Patients also suffer from a particular disease to different extents (e.g. mild, moderate, severe). The degree of illness can be expressed as the degree of membership of the patient in the class representing the disease. Furthermore, one disease my cause, complicate, or alleviate another. The dependence between classes corresponds to the dependence between diseases.

The overlapping nature of classes contributes to uncertainty. Fuzzy feature vectors can simultaneously have degrees of membership in these overlapping classes, exploiting the notion of similarity to conflicting classes. Crisp partitioning fails to exploit this similarity. A fuzzy partition algorithm indicates high partial memberships in multiple classes. Fuzzy sets are useful during feature analysis to represent input data with linguistic variables rather than exact numerical definitions. Fuzzy sets are also used for classification to maintain partial class memberships and to estimate missing information in terms of membership values [20].

4.2.1 Fuzzy Clustering

The purpose of clustering is to partition data into a number of subsets [21,22]. Within a set, the elements are as similar as possible to each other; elements from different sets are as different as possible. Given any finite data set, the purpose of clustering is to assign object labels that identify subsets within the given data set. Because the data are unlabeled, this problem is often called unsupervised learning, i.e. learning the correct labels for subsets. Fuzzy methods can be used for clustering in several ways. Relation Criterion Functions (clustering controlled by an optimization of a criterion function of the grouped date), Object Criterion Functions (clustering controlled by an optimization of an objective function based directly on the data in a n-dimensional feature space; this subdivision is the most popular with fuzzy c-means (number of classes known a priori) and fuzzy ISODATA (iterative, self-organizing data analysis techniques, number of classes unknown), Convex Decomposition (decomposing a set of fuzzy clusters into a combination of convex sets), Numerical Transitive (extracting crisp equivalence relations from fuzzy similarity relations), and Generalized Nearest Neighbor Rules (clustering version of the classifier, used after another clustering algorithm, such a fuzzy c-means.)

4.2.2 Fuzzy Classification

The difference between clustering and classification is that clustering algorithms label given data sets $X \varepsilon R^p$, whereas a classifier can label every data point in the entire space R^p. Usually classifiers are designed with labeled data (supervised learning). The partitioning decision functions may be computationally explicit discriminant functions, nearest prototype rules, or implicit multilayered perceptions, or k-nearest neighbor rules. Like fuzzy clustering, fuzzy classification preserves multiclass membership in similar classes and typically results in a hard design. This idea can be attributed to embedding: finding a better solution to a crisp problem by initially looking in a larger space with different constraints, allowing the algorithm more freedom to avoid errors by making hard decisions in intermediate stages. As an example, consider the crisp k-nearest neighbor algorithm as opposed to the fuzzy k-nearest neighbor algorithm (K-NN). Both the fuzzy and crisp algorithms search the labeled sample set for the K-nearest neighbors. Other than obtaining these K samples, the procedures differ considerable. The fuzzy K-NN algorithm assigns class membership to a sample vector rather than assigning the vector to a particular class. Thus, the algorithm makes no arbitrary assignments, assigning membership as a function of the vector's distance from its K-nearest neighbors and those neighbor's memberships in the possible classes.

4.2.3 Pre-Processing and Post-Processing Using Fuzzy Techniques

A traditional neuron sums weighted input values and fires if the summation exceeds a pre-specified threshold. The fuzzy neuron is similar except that it can process vague information via the membership function. The inputs to the fuzzy neuron, fuzzy sets $X_1, X_2, ..., X_N$ are weighted differently from those in the nonfuzzy case. The weighted inputs are then aggregated not by summation but by the fuzzy aggregation operation. The fuzzy output may remain with or without further operations.

At the final level, a decision must be made as to whether results should be de-fuzzified. Depending upon the algorithm employed, the de-fuzzification may have occurred at an earlier stage. In the case of the systems which use preprocessing of fuzzy information, the result will in general be de-fuzzified. In systems which use learning algorithms for interval data, the final result will in general be an interval which must be properly interpreted according to the application. Some neural network learning algorithms provide a classification as well as a degree of membership in that classification.

Another approach [23] concentrates on the aggregation at each neuron and its relationship to fundamental ideas from fuzzy logic. Specifically, a degree of membership is associated with the level of firing of a neuron. The process that determines the firing level of a neuron can be associated with the evaluation of the truth of a fuzzy proposition. This can be extended to define a model for competitive firing of neurons.

In a more complex structure [24] a fuzzy neuro-computational model is established in three steps: 1) quantization of the fuzzy variable spaces, definition of fuzzy sets, choice of model structure; 2) derivation of rules describing the system behavior, application of appropriate learning technique; 3) assessment of the model quality. Nonfuzzy and fuzzy data are transferred to the perception level determined by the primary fuzzy sets which are then processed by the neural network structure.

5 Hybrid Approaches

Basic strategies for combining two approaches include:

1. Using output of one method directly as input to another method
2. Re-structuring output of one method to produce input to another method
3. Running two methods independently and combining output information
4. Using of one methodology to significantly alter the structure of another

We will discuss some possible approaches to hybrid systems.

5.1 Use of Neural Networks to Produce Membership Functions for Knowledge-Based Systems

The determination of appropriate membership functions is not straightforward. Often they are defined in consultation with experts. For some parameters the normal values are well-known, as for the above example with blood pressure. However, a number of problems arise. Experts may disagree, and numbers may change with the discovery of new medical information. In some cases, there may be no known values, in which case a neural network learning algorithm can be used to extract information from a database [25]. Another use of the neural network approach is to determine relative weighting factors for antecedents, as mentioned above, and to derive thresholds for desired levels of substantiation of rules.

A learning algorithm developed by the authors [25] is run independently for each rule to determine the appropriate weighting of antecedents. In the simplest approximation, a hyperplane is obtained, generating an equation of the form

$$D_i(x) = \sum_{i=1}^{n} w_i x_i \qquad (16)$$

The weight a_i for the ith antecedent is then determined by

$$a_i = w_i / \sum_{i=1}^{n} w_i \qquad (17)$$

Note that these weights are normalized to sum to 1.

In addition, the neural network can be used to determine appropriate threshold levels for each rule using the nonlinear decision hypersurface. Thresholds replace the binary logical concept of AND's and OR's. The maximum and minimum values for the decision surface $D(x)$ must be determined. Let $A_i = \{m_1,...,m_k\}$, the set of all values which x_i can assume, where $m_i > 0$ for all i. Then to obtain the maximum value $D_{max}(x)$:

If $w_i > 0$, let $x_i' = \max [A_i]$ (18)
If $w_i < 0$, let $x_i' = 0$ for all i=1,...,n.

Then

$$D_{max}(x) = \sum_{i=1}^{m} w_i\, x_i' + \sum_{\substack{i=1\\i \neq j}}^{m} \sum_{j=1}^{m} w_{i,j}\, x_i' x_j' \tag{19}$$

Similarly, $D_{min}(x)$ is obtained by the following:

If $w_i > 0$, let $x_i' = 0$ (20)
If $w_i < 0$, let $x_i' = \max[A_i]$

and application of equation (19).
All decisions are then normalized by

$$D_n(x) = \begin{cases} D(x)/D_{max}(x) & \text{if } D(x) > 0 \quad (\text{class 1}) \\ D(x)/|D_{min}(x)| & \text{if } D(x) < 0 \quad (\text{class 2}) \\ 0 & \text{if } D(x) = 0 \quad (\text{indeterminate}) \end{cases} \tag{21}$$

The result is a value between -1 and 1, inclusive, which gives a degree of membership in that category. The values are then shifted to give an answer between 0 and 1, inclusive by

$$V(x) = [1 + D_n(x)]/2 \tag{22}$$

These values can be used in choosing appropriate implication operators to determine the degree of substantiation required, or in deciding among compatibility indices which range from pessimistic to optimistic considerations.

5.2 Neural Networks with Symbolic Layer

A traditional neural network has three layers, an input, output, and intermediate level as shown in Figure 6. In the method developed by the authors [26], the nonlinear decision function produces a normalized numerical value between 0 and

1, inclusive. A separate decision function $D_i(x)$ is attached to each of the output nodes at level three. The fourth-symbolic layer, can be used for non-numeric post-processing. A threshold value $T_i(x)$ (or values) is also attached to each level three node. If the value of the decision function exceeds the corresponding threshold value, a certain symbol is produced; if it does not, a different symbol is produced. This process can be extended by having any number of threshold values produce as many symbols as desired. An additional layer is added to the network which combines the symbols generated by adjacent nodes according to a well-structured grammar [27].

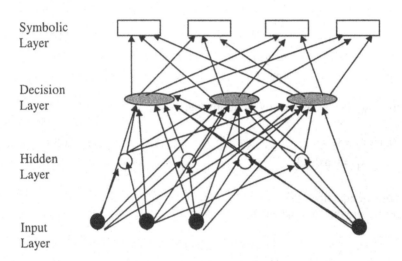

Symbolic
Layer

Decision
Layer

Hidden
Layer

Input
Layer

Figure 5: Neural Network with Symbolic Layer

Consider a medical application in which it is necessary to choose among three conditions. It is possible that none, one, or a combination of these conditions are present. A neural network is set up to learn on data of known classification, determining which variables are pertinent to making the decision and the appropriate weighting factors for each of these variables. In the case of medical decision making, level n-1 would determine which condition or conditions are present, and level n would determine what treatment or follow-up testing should be done based on these results. A possible interpretation is the following. Each node has an potential excitatory action (represented by a) or inhibitory action (represented by b). This is determined by threshold values.

If $D_i(x) > T_i$, then "a" else "b"

In the grammar, each node is numbered N_i. A response of "a" at node i indicates that condition C_i is present. To simplify the grammar, a sequential evaluation of nodes is assumed. If random evaluation is done, additional entries in the grammar are required. For the example, four possible actions are assumed:

r_1: No action
r_2: Re-do test
r_3: Do additional tests
r_4: Begin treatment

6 Sample Application: Decision Making in Cardiology

A hybrid system under development by our group over the past fifteen years, Hypermerge, is used to illustrate one possible approach for the incorporation of diverse data types as well as distributed information sources [28]. The system incorporates several decision strategies including knowledge-based reasoning, neural network modeling, image analysis, and summary techniques for medical times series. An illustration of the system applied to cardiology is given.

Computer-generated text is given in bold-face and user reply in regular type. The italicized information in parentheses is not part of the system but is included here to indicate which portion of the hybrid system is invoked.

Patient name: KZB
Age: 63
Chief complaint: chest pain
Hx of coronary problems y/n? y
Hx CAD y/n? y
Recent ETT data available y/n?: y
From ETT *(Neural Network)*
   Max ST depression in mm: 3.0
   HR at beginning of ETT: 87
   HR at end of ETT: 99
   BP at beginning of ETT: 148
   BP at end of ETT: 145
Hx of CHF y/n? y
Computer file of Holter data available y/n? y
Enter file name: KZBholter *(Chaotic Analysis)*
List current symptoms, followed by degree of severity between 0 and 10:
   Chest pain 8 *(Knowledge-Based System)*
   Nausea 9
   Abnormal mental state 7
   *

BP < 100/60? y

Dizziness? 6
Sweating? 8
Associated with onset? y

Patient should be admitted to hospital as inpatient.
ETT data indicate 2 vessel CAD
Holter data indicates significant chaos in R-R intervals related to CHF

Do you want an explanations of these conclusions? y

The following rules from the knowledge-based chest pain analysis were substantiated (in reverse order):

IF Sweating   .25
     Dizziness   .25
     Nausea   .25
     Associated with onset   .25
THEN   Patient should be admitted   (Threshold 0.5)

IF BP < 100/60   .5
     Abnormal Mental Status .1
     Cold, Clammy, Skin   .1
     Dry, Cyanotic Skin   .1
     Weak Peripheral Pulses   .1
     Urinary Output < 30cc/hr .1
THEN   Patient should be admitted to CCU (Threshold 0.6)

IF Chest pain
THEN   Proceed to other symptom analysis

The neural network model for ETT concluded 2-vessel disease based on change in HR during test, change in BP during test, double produce of HR and BP, and maximum ST depression.

Chaotic analysis of R-R intervals from the 24-hr Holter tape indicates a central tendency of 57%, indicating a high level of variability.

7 Conclusions

The techniques outlined above for the incorporation of linguistic variables have shown their practical usefulness in Hypermerge, a functioning medical expert system for the analysis of chest pain and other cardiac problems. The system has been demonstrated on a number of occasions at the Annual Meeting of the

American College of Cardiology with excellent results, particularly on the analysis of borderline cases [29]. The use of linguistic information not only makes the system more appealing to users, but also aids in fine-tuning the inference engine through the use of approximate reasoning techniques. Addition of the neural network component as well as time series analysis using chaos theory expands the system's ability to incorporate both linguistic and numeric data in the same reasoning process.

References

[1] M.E. Cohen, D.L. Hudson, Comparative Approaches to Medical Reasoning, World Scientific, 1995.

[2] Patrick, E., Stelmock, F., Shen, L., Review of pattern recognition in medical diagnosis and consulting relative to a new system model, IEEE Trans. Sys., Man, Cyber, SMC-4(1) (1974) 1-16.

[3] Kulikowski, C.A., 1979, Pattern recognition approach to medical diagnosis, IEEE Trans. Sys. Sci. Cyber., SS6(3), pp. 173-178.

[4] Gorry, G.A., Computer-assisted clinical decision making, Method. Inform. Med. 12 (1973) 45-51.

[5] Shortliffe EH, Computer-Based Medical Consultations, MYCIN, Elsevier/North Holland, New York, 1976.

[6] Sabbatini RME: Applications of connectionist systems in biomedicine. In: Lun KC, Degoulet P, Piemme TE, Rienhoff O (Eds): *MEDINFO 92*, Elsevier, pp. 418-425, 1992.

[7] Hudson, D.L., Cohen, M.E; Anderson, M.F., Use of neural network techniques in a medical expert system, Int. J. of Intel. Sys. **6,2** (1991) 213-223.

[8] Rummelhart, D.E., J.L. McClelland, Parallel Distributed Processing: Explorations in the Microstrucutre of Cognition, MIT Press, 1986.

[9] Kandel, A., Langholz, G., Eds., Hybrid Architectures for Intelligent Systems, CRC Press, Boca Raton, FL, 1992.

[10] Cohen, M. E. and D. L. Hudson, Integration of neural network techniques with approximate reasoning techniques in knowledge-based systems, in A. Kandel, G. Langholz, (Eds.): *Hybrid Architectures for Intelligent Systems*, CRC Press, (1992), 72-85.

[11] Hudson, D.L., Deedwania, P.C., Cohen, M.E., Watson, P.E., Prospective analysis of EMERGE, an expert system for chest pain analysis, *Computers in Cardiology* (1984) 19-24.

[12] Hudson, D.L, Rule-Based Computerization of Emergency Room Procedures Derived from Criteria Mapping, Ph.D. Dissertation, UCLA, 1981.

[13] Zadeh LA: The role of fuzzy logic in the management of uncertainty in expert systems. *Fuzzy Sets and Systems* (1983) 11:199-227.

[14] Zadeh LA: Fuzzy sets as a basis for a theory of possibilities. *Fuzzy Sets and Systems* (1978) 1:3-28.

[15] Bouchon-Meunier B: Inferences with imprecisions and uncertainties in

expert systems. In: Kandel A (Ed): *Fuzzy Expert Systems*, CRC Press, Boca Raton, FL, (1992) 43-54.

[16] Yager RR: General multiple-objective functions and linguistically quantified statements. *International Journal of Man-Machine Studies* (1984) 21:389-400.

[17] Sanchez E, Bartolin R: Fuzzy inference and medical diagnosis, a case study. *Proceedings, First Annual Meeting, Biomedical Fuzzy Systems Association*, (1989) 1-18.

[18] Hudson, D.L., Cohen, M.E., Fuzzy logic in medical expert systems, *IEEE EMBS Magazine*, (1994) 13(5), 693-698.

[19] Hudson DL, Cohen ME: Approaches to management of uncertainty in an expert system. *International J. of Intelligent Systems* 3:45-58, 1988.

[20] Bezdek, J.C., Some non-standard clustering algorithms, NATO ASI Series G14, Springer-Verlag, 1987.

[21] Akay, M., Cohen, M.E., Hudson, D.L., *Fuzzy Sets in Life Sciences*, Fuzzy Sets and Systems, 1997, 90(2), 221-224.

[22] Ruspini, E. A new approach to fuzzy clustering, Information and Control (1969), 15, 22-32.

[23] Yager, R.R., Modeling and formulating fuzzy knowledge bases using neural networks, Iona College Machine Intelligence Institute Report #MII-1111, (1991), 1-29.

[24] Gupta, M.M., Gorzalczany, in R.Lowen, M. Roubens (eds.), Proc. IFSA, (1991), 46-49.

[25] Cohen ME, Hudson DL: Approaches to handling of fuzzy input data in neural networks. *Proceedings, IEEE Conf. Fuzzy Systems*, (1992) 93-100.

[26] Hudson, D.L., Cohen, M.E., Anderson, M.F., Use of neural network techniques in a medical expert system, *Proceedings, International Fuzzy Set Association*, 3, (1989) 476-479.

[27] Hudson, D.L., Cohen, M.E., Deedwania, P.C., A neural network for symbolic processing, in *Engineering in Medicine and Biology*, A.Y.J. Szeto, R. M. Rangayyan, Eds., IEEE, (1993), 248-249.

[28] Hudson, D.L., Cohen, M.E., Deedwania, P.C, Hybrid system for diagnosis and treatment of heart disease, in ., *Comparative Approaches to Medical Reasoning*, World Scientific, Singapore, M. E. Cohen, D. L. Hudson, Eds., (1995), 289-310.

[29] Hudson, D.L., Cohen, M.E., Deedwania, P.C., Information integration for cardiology decision support, Journal of the American College of Cardiology, (1995), 759-4, 238A.

The Fuzzy Logic Advisor for Social Judgments: A First Attempt

Jerry M. Mendel*, Sheila Murphy**, Lynn C. Miller**, Matt Martin*, and Nilesh Karnik*

*Signal & Image Processing Institute, Department of Electrical Engineering-Systems, University of Southern California, Los Angeles, CA 90089-2564, mendel@sipi.usc.edu
**Annenberg School for Communication, University of Southern California, Los Angeles, CA 90089-0281, smurphy@rcf.usc.edu; lmiller@rcf.usc.edu

Abstract

A fuzzy logic advisor (FLA), which is a nonlinear device that accepts numeric measurements as inputs and provides a linguistic value at its output, is developed for one specific type of social judgment, judgments of flirtation. Qualitative and quantitative descriptions of the FLA and a nine step methodology for designing the FLA are given. The FLA is compared against traditional regression models; it provides at least an order of magnitude better performance, which demonstrates that a FLA may indeed be applied to enhance our predictability of social judgments above and beyond that provided using traditional linear models. The implications and applications of such FLAs for assessing social judgments are discussed. Finally, why this is just a "first attempt" is explained.

Introduction

In everyday social interaction, each of us is called upon to make judgments about the meaning of another's behavior. Such judgments are far from trivial, since often they affect the nature and direction of the subsequent social interaction and communications. But, how do we make this judgment? By *judgment* we mean an assessment of the *level* of the variable of interest. Although a variety of factors may enter into our decision, behavior is apt to play a critical role in assessing the level of the variable of interest. What models might be most useful in predicting individual's perceptions regarding the level of the variable of interest?

A prevailing paradigm for examining social judgments would be to examine the influence of various factors on the variable of interest using linear approaches, e.g., linear regression. Unfortunately, *perceptions* regarding the variable of interest may not be linear, but rather *step*-like, which are typically not captured with existing methods. Such a non-linear phenomenon might be better captured using a non-linear approach. The *purpose of this chapter* is to demonstrate how fuzzy logic may be applied to enhance our predictability of social judgments above and beyond that provided by using traditional linear models. To illustrate the utility of this fuzzy logic approach, we begin by focusing on one specific type of social judgment, judgments of *flirtation*.

Although in this chapter we only consider the social judgment of flirtation, we believe that the basic methodology that is described in the context of flirtation can also be applied to many other social judgments (e.g., sexual harassment). Flirtation judgments afford a fertile starting place for a variety of reasons. First, many of the behavioral indicators associated with flirtation have been well established (Koeffel, et al., 1993). Second, the indicators (e.g., smiling, touching, eye contact) are often ambiguous by themselves and with a changing level of the behavior (along with other cues), the meaning of the behavior is apt to shift from one inference (e.g., friendly) to another (flirtation, seductive, or harassing). Third, participants are apt to have had a great deal of experience with flirtation judgments, and be -- therefore-- apt to easily make them. Finally, inferences made about the meaning of these behaviors are often sensitive to both the gender of the perceiver and the genders of the interactants (Koeffel, et al., 1993). Although judgments in these domains are apt not to be linear ones, they have only been studied using linear methodologies.

The main difference between other models and a fuzzy logic system is that the former are determined only from numerical data (e.g., regression coefficients are fit to numerical data) whereas the latter are determined either from linguistic information, or from a combination of linguistic information and numerical data. By "linguistic information," we mean a collection of IF-THEN rules that are provided by people. These rules, if properly collected, convey the details of a *nonlinear* relationship between the antecedents of the rule and the consequent of the rule. A fuzzy logic system can directly quantify a linguistic rule; a regression model cannot. Regression models can, however include nonlinear regressors (e.g., interaction terms), which make them also nonlinear functions of their inputs; however, the structure of the nonlinearities in the fuzzy logic model is not prespecified, as it must be for a regression model; it is a direct result of fuzzy logic. A fuzzy logic system is also a variable structure model, in that it simultaneously provides excellent local and global approximations to social judgments, whereas a regression model can only provide global approximations to social judgments. Figure 1 compares the outputs of a two-antecedent fuzzy logic flirtation advisor and a two-variable regression flirtation advisor. It is clear from the two plots that the fuzzy logic advisor has the potential to indicate sharp jumps in behavior whereas the regression advisor does not. Although such jumps or steps may often occur in social judgments, regression tools are insufficient and non-linear methods are needed for assessing them. A crucial difference between a fuzzy logic system and linear models is the way in which uncertainty is dealt with. Typically, in a linear regression individuals are forced to translate their assessment into absolute numbers, e.g., 1, 2, 3, 4. In contrast a person can interact with the fuzzy logic system using normal linguistic phrases, for example, about eye contact (one of the indicators of flirtation), such as "eye contact is around a 4." Finally, if determining the level of flirtation were easy, we would all be experts; but it is not, and we are not. In fact, many times we get "mixed signals." Fuzzy logic leads to an explanation and potential resolution of "mixed signals." So our fuzzy logic system will also provide us with *insight* into why determining whether or not we are being flirted with is often difficult. The same should also be true for other social judgments. We do not believe that this is possible using a regression model.

In the psychological sphere, fuzzy logic systems have already been usefully applied in a few scattered domains, including perception and decision processes (Massaro and Friedman, 1990), and others have suggested their use in industrial/organizational settings (Hesketh, Smithson, and Hesketh, 1996). Many of the applications involve psychological questions of "fit" or pattern matching. For example, in the organizational domain, fit may involve assessing the match between the characteristics of the person and the demands of the environment. Although some have attempted to examine such fits or matches in traditional ways [e.g., (Edwards, 1991), (Edwards and Harrison, 1993)], non-linear approaches such as fuzzy logic systems are apt to provide better mapping between conceptual intent and methodological modeling. In fact, Massaro and Friedman (1990) found that a

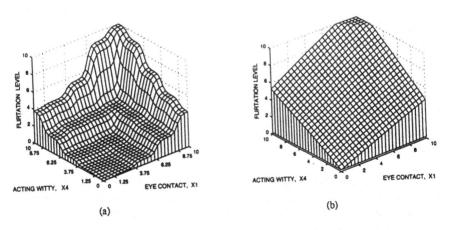

Figure 1. Flirtation surfaces versus the indicators *eye contact* and *acting witty*. (a) Fuzzy logic surface, and (b) Regression model surface.

fuzzy logic system "with truth values estimated from the data" (pg. 249) did as well as or outperformed alternative methods (e.g., a two-level connectionist model and more traditional linear integration models, including using ANOVA and multidimensional scaling methods) on a series of pattern recognition tasks.

The fuzzy-logic system's input and output numbers must be available through direct measurement. This is always the case in engineering applications of fuzzy logic; however, it is not necessarily the case for social judgments. A person does not measure flirtation directly, nor does a person measure the indicators of flirtation directly, e.g., eye contact and touching. This represents what might be called a "new twist" for the application of a fuzzy logic system.

In this study, we distinguish between quantities that can be measured directly and those that can be "sensed." Flirtation and its indicators can only be sensed (e.g., "you'll know it when you see it"); hence, there is a mismatch between a social judgment and its indicators and the use of a fuzzy logic system to make a social judgment. We rectify this mismatch by combining the fuzzy logic system with an *encoder* that converts sensed indicators of flirtation into numbers, and a *decoder* that converts a numerical value for flirtation into a meaningful linguistic judgment for flirtation. The interconnection of encoder, fuzzy logic system, and decoder is what we call a "Fuzzy Logic Advisor." It is described below and exemplifies what Zadeh (1996) calls "computing with words," although it was developed independently of Zadeh's more recent work.

Fuzzy Logic Advisor

Engineering applications of fuzzy logic, lead to a device called a fuzzy logic system (FLS) [e.g., Mendel (1995a)], one that accepts *numbers* at its input, which can be measured, and provides a *number* at its output, which can also be measured. Fuzzy logic [e.g., (Zadeh, 1965, 1973), (Klir and Yuan, 1996)] operates inside of the FLS. In essence, then, a FLS can be interpreted mathematically by the equation $y_m = f(\mathbf{x}_m)$, where y_m is the *measured* output of the FLS, $\mathbf{x}_m$ is a vector of *measured* inputs to the FLS, and $f(\cdot)$ is a nonlinear function whose exact structure is established by the tenets and precepts of fuzzy set theory and fuzzy logic.

There are a wide range of social judgment applications for a FLS. In this paper, we focus our attention at social judgments whose quantities of interest cannot be measured directly, they can only be *sensed*. We shall, therefore, think of a social judgment as obeying an equation like $y_s = d(\mathbf{x}_s)$, which represents an unknown transformation, $d(\cdot)$, from a collection (vector) of *sensed* indicators, $\mathbf{x}_s$, into a *sense* of the social judgment, y_s. For example, flirtation is an unknown function of some *indicators of flirtation*, x, such as **touch**, **eye contact**, **primping**, and **acting witty**. Flirtation, as well as these indicators of flirtation, cannot be measured directly; they can only be sensed.

As it stands, we can't use our FLS to model a social judgment because the FLS provides a transformation of a vector of *measured* social-judgment indicators into a *measured* level of the social-judgment. What is needed is an encoding device to the FLS that transforms x_s into x_m, and a decoding device to the FLS that transforms y_m into y_s. We refer to such a system as a *Fuzzy Logic Advisor*. Our encoder maps each sensed indicator of a social judgment onto a scale. For example, the flirtation indicators are all mapped onto a scale from zero to ten. Mathematically, this means that $x_m = g_{sm}(x_s)$, where $g_{sm}(\cdot)$ is a vector mapping, each of whose components works exclusively to map a particular component of x_s into its respective component in x_m. Although we can conceptualize such a mapping, we do not know its details ahead of time. It is established by each person (i.e., the user of the FLA) on an individual basis, for each occurrence of a specific social situation, e.g., what may be a touching value of 7 for one person may only be a touching value of 4 for another person. A person doesn't think about this mapping process in terms of a mathematical formula; they just do it! But, whatever it is that is done can indeed be conceptually *thought of* as the creation of $x_m = g_{sm}(x_s)$. Our decoder begins with the mapping of the social judgment onto a scale, which for flirtation is also a scale of zero to ten. This mapping is the output of the FLS, the number y_m. The decoder converts y_m into a linguistic statement that expresses the user's sense of the social judgment (flirtation) for this number, y_m. The intersection of y_m's vertical projection with the social issue fuzzy set membership functions establishes y_s. If more than one set is intersected, we choose the one associated with the largest membership function value. Mathematically, this means that $y_s = h_{ms}(y_m)$, where $h_{ms}(\cdot)$ is the decoder's mapping of y_m into y_s. The decoder puts labels (i.e., linguistic phrases) of the social judgment, along with associated levels (i.e., membership functions) on its appropriate y_m-scale. A label and its membership function constitute a *fuzzy set*. The labels for flirtation's and the indicators of flirtation's fuzzy sets that we used in this study are: *none to a little bit (NLB)*, *very little to a small amount (VLSA)*, *some to a fair amount (SFA)*, a *good amount to a lot (GAL)*, and *a large amount to a maximum amount (LAMA)*.

We can now put all of these mathematical formulas together (see Fig. 2) to give us a concise description of what the FLA is doing. Individually, we have:

$$x_m = g_{sm}(x_s), \ y_m = f(x_m), \text{and} \ y_s = h_{ms}(y_m);$$

hence, $y_s = h_{ms}(y_m) = h_{ms}[f(\mathbf{x}_m)] = h_{ms}[f(\mathbf{g}_{sm}(\mathbf{x}_s))]$.

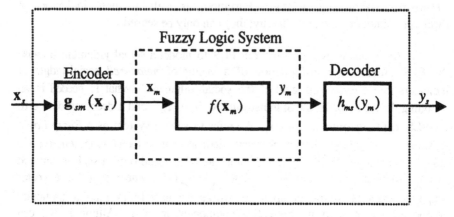

Fuzzy Logic Advisor

Figure 2. A *Fuzzy Logic Advisor* is an interconnection of three subsystems: encoder, fuzzy logic system, and decoder.

For all of this to work, we need a *cooperative environment*. Cooperation is needed to establish the FLS, $f(\mathbf{x}_m)$. The heart of this FLS is a collection of IF-THEN rules. An example of a possible flirtation rule is: IF there is *some to a fair amount* of touching and *very little to a small amount* of eye contact, THEN there is *some to a fair amount* of flirtation. The antecedents of a rule can be *all* the indicators of the social judgment or suitable subsets. The consequent of a rule is the social judgment (e.g., flirtation). The rules are established cooperatively by individual groups of people, and can be quite different for men and women, or even for different groups of men and women. The key, though, is that we must be able to meet with (i.e., survey) groups of people and get them to give us their social-judgment rules. Using fuzzy logic we can not only establish individual rules regarding flirtation, but we can also estimate across individuals to produce an average male or female response pattern.

The heart of the FL Advisor is the FLS (Fig. 3). We interpret a FLS mathematically [e.g., Mendel (1995a)] as

$$y_m(\mathbf{x}_m) = \sum_{l=1}^{M} \bar{y}^l \phi_l(\mathbf{x}_m) \tag{1}$$

where: x_m is a vector of p indicators (antecedents); $y_m(\mathbf{x}_m)$ is the output of the

FLS, namely a numerical value for the social judgment; M denotes the number of rules in the FL rule base; $\phi_l(\mathbf{x}_m)$ are *fuzzy basis functions*, whose exact mathematical structure is established through concepts from fuzzy logic, [see Mendel (1995a) and Mendel, et al. (1996)], and, $\bar{y}^l$ is the center (or shoulder) location of the fuzzy set that is associated with the consequent of the lth rule.

Fuzzy Logic System

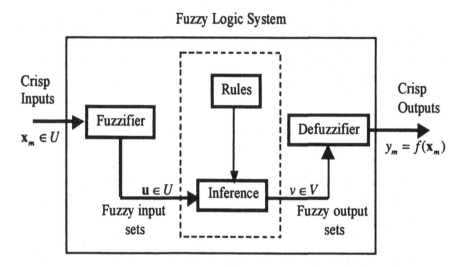

Figure 3. Fuzzy logic system (Mendel, 1995a).

In order to completely understand the FBF expansion in Eq. (1) we need to provide more details about the mathematical structure of the basis functions, $\phi_l(\mathbf{x}_m)$. The FLS is depicted in Fig. 3. It has been thoroughly described in many publications, including Mendel (1995a); hence, we shall not elaborate upon it here. In order to write down a formula for the fuzzy basis functions, very specific design choices must be made in the FLS. The choices we have made in this study are: nonsingleton fuzzification, max-product composition, product inference, modified height defuzzification, and Gaussian membership functions for rule antecedents as well as for fuzzy numbers. In this case, (Mendel, 1995a)

$$y_m(\mathbf{x}_m) = \frac{\sum_{l=1}^{M} \bar{y}^l \prod_{k=1}^{P} \left[\mu_{X_k}(x_{k,\max}) \mu_{F_k^l}(x_{k,\max}) \right] / \delta^{l^2}}{\sum_{l=1}^{M} \prod_{k=1}^{P} \left[\mu_{X_k}(x_{k,\max}) \mu_{F_k^l}(x_{k,\max}) \right] / \delta^{l^2}} \equiv \sum_{l=1}^{M} \bar{y}^l \phi_l(\mathbf{x}_{k,\max}) \quad (2)$$

where $\bar{y}^l$ is the center location of the fuzzy set that is associated with the consequent of the lth rule,

$$x_{k,\max} = \frac{\sigma_X^2 m_{F_k^l} + \sigma_{F_k^l}^2 x'_{m,k}}{\sigma_X^2 + \sigma_{F_k^l}^2},$$

(3)

and specific formulas for the Gaussian membership functions are given next. The equations that are needed to implement fuzzy basis functions are:

(1) <u>Indicator membership functions</u> (in order to simplify the notation, we drop the subscript m that was used to denote a measured quantity): Each of our 4 indicators, $x_1,...,x_4$, is treated as a fuzzy number with membership function $\mu_{X_k}(x_k)$, where

$$\mu_{X_k}(x_k) = \exp\left[-\frac{1}{2}\left(\frac{x_k - x'_k}{\sigma_X}\right)^2\right], \quad k = 1, ..., 4$$

(4)

in which x'_k denotes the measured value of x_k; observe that $\mu_{X_k}(x_k)$ is centered about x'_k. Measurement uncertainty is conveyed by standard deviation σ_X.

(2) <u>Antecedent membership functions</u>: Each antecedent in our one- and two-antecedent rules is described by a membership function; interior membership functions are described by

$$\mu_{F_k^l}(x_k) = \exp\left[-\frac{1}{2}\left(\frac{x_k - m_{F_k^l}}{\sigma_{F_k^l}}\right)^2\right], \quad k = 1, ..., 4$$

(5)

where $m_{F_k^l}$ is the point along the x_k-axis at which $\mu_{F_k^l}(x_k)$ is centered; shoulder membership functions are also assumed to be Gaussian [*all* antecedent membership functions must be Gaussian, or else Eq. (3) is not valid]; they are centered either at 0 or at 10; additionally, $l = 1, ..., 5$ for one-antecedent rules, and $l = 1, ..., 25$ for two-antecedent rules.

(3) <u>Prefilter to account for nonsingleton fuzzification</u>: A unique feature of a non-singleton FLS is that an uncertain numerical value for indicator x_k, x'_k, is first transformed by Eq. (3) into another value, $x_{k,\max}$, which accounts for its uncertainty, $k = 1, ..., 4$; and, $l = 1, ..., 5$ for one-antecedent rules, and $l = 1, ..., 25$ for two-antecedent rules [We have assumed that the same amount of uncertainty exists for all four of the

measured flirtation indicators; hence, the use of σ_X instead of σ_{X_k} in Eqs. (3) and (4). If this is not true, then change σ_X in their denominators to σ_{X_k}].

(4) <u>Product inference</u>: We have chosen product inference for our FLS, which means that the following functions of $x_{k,\max}$ must then be computed in Eq. (2):

$$\mu_{Q_k^l}(x_{k,\max}) \equiv \mu_{X_k}(x_{k,\max})\mu_{F_k^l}(x_{k,\max}), \quad k = 1, \dots, 4 \qquad (6)$$

where $l = 1, \dots, 5$ for one-antecedent rules, and $l = 1, \dots, 25$ for two-antecedent rules.

(5) <u>Fuzzy basis functions</u>: We use x_1 and x_2 as generic values for indicators 1 and 2. For one-antecedent rules (for which $p = 1$):

$$\phi_l(x) = \frac{\mu_{Q_1^l}(x_{1,\max}) / \delta^{l^2}}{\sum\limits_{j=1}^{5} \mu_{Q_1^j}(x_{1,\max}) / \delta^{l^2}} \quad l = 1, \dots, 5 \qquad (7a)$$

where δ^l is the measure of the spread of the consequent for rule $R^{(l)}$; For two-antecedent rules (for which $p = 2$):

$$\phi_l(x) = \frac{[\mu_{Q_1^l}(x_{1,\max})\mu_{Q_2^l}(x_{2,\max})] / \delta^{l^2}}{\sum\limits_{j=1}^{25}[\mu_{Q_1^j}(x_{1,\max})\mu_{Q_2^j}(x_{2,\max})] / \delta^{l^2}} \quad l = 1, 2, \dots, 25 \qquad (7b)$$

Once Eq. (7) has been computed, we compute $y_m(x_m)$ using Eq. (2).

The parameters that need to be specified in order to implement Eqs. (3) - (7) are: σ_X, which depends on the uncertainty associated with the measured inputs to the FLS; $m_{F_k^l}$ and $\sigma_{F_k^l}$, which are associated with antecedent membership functions; and, δ^l, which is associated with the consequent of rule $R^{(l)}$. Details regarding how to choose the first two sets of parameters and the choice for δ^l are discussed in subsequent sections below.

Equation (1) has the appearance of a regression equation model, where the regressors, the $\phi_l(x_m)$, are *nonlinear* functions of the indicators, and the weights (regression coefficients) are the $\bar{y}^l$'s. Although Eq. (1) looks like a regression equation, the $\bar{y}^l$'s are *not* determined by regression analysis. The structure of Eq. (1) is a direct result of the mathematics of fuzzy logic. There is yet another major difference between Eq (1) and a regression equation. In a standard regression model, *all* of its terms are activated for each x_m. Although it is not obvious by the way in which Eq. (1) is written, it is a *variable-structure model*, in the sense that all of its M terms are not activated by each x_m. The activated terms depend upon x_m. Each fired rule corresponds to a fuzzy basis function in Eq. (1), and, in general only a very small number of rules are fired for each x_m.

In order to make the FLA manageable (i.e., practical), we felt that rules with more than two antecedents are too complicated to deal with consciously, although we probably do this automatically all the time. So, we decided, for simplicity that it is not feasible to ask people to create rules involving social indicators taken three or four at a time. Based on our own experience, we felt that one- and two-antecedent rules were manageable, and so we asked men and women to create $5 \times 4 = 20$ rules for single-antecedents and $6 \times 5^2 = 150$ rules for pairs of antecedents; consequently, in this study $M = 170$. Doing this leads to 4 single-antecedent advisors and 6 two-antecedent advisors. Usual social science regression models do not account for correlation between indicators; our 2-antecedent FLAs do, and we believe that such correlation is very important to correctly model the dependence of flirtation on its indicators. We discuss a four-indicator FLA in the Conclusions.

Methodology for Design of a FLA

In developing a FLA for a social issue, it is very useful to follow the 9-step procedure (methodology) that is described next.

(1) <u>Identify a social judgment that cannot be measured directly, but can be 'sensed' to different degrees</u>.

(2) <u>Determine the 'indicators' of the social judgment</u>.

    (a) *Establish a list of candidate indicators*. For flirtation, our 6 candidate indicators were: touching, eye contact, acting witty, primping, smiling, and complimenting.

    (b) *Conduct a survey* in which a population is asked to rank order in importance the indicators on the list of candidate indicators. For flirtation, the indicators touching, eye contact, acting witty, and primping were always ranked above smiling and complimenting by both males and females.

(c) *Choose a meaningful subset of the indicators.* For flirtation, we chose touching, eye contact, acting witty, and primping. For some judgments, a factor analysis may be needed.

(3) Establish meaningful scales on which a person can easily convert a sensed value for each indicator, as well as the social judgment, into a number in their encoder. For example, all flirtation indicators, as well as flirtation, were scaled from zero to ten.

(4) Establish fuzzy sets for each of the indicators as well as the social judgment.

(a) *Establish how many fuzzy sets will be needed.* This can be done by means of a survey, or the number of sets can be chosen a priori.

(b) *Establish names for the fuzzy sets* (e.g., *very little to a small amount*). In some cases the names will be the same for all the indicators as well as for the social judgment. This was the case for flirtation and its four indicators. It is important that the names convey a sense of overlap of adjacent fuzzy sets (e.g., *very little* was felt to be to the left of *a little bit*, and *a small amount* was felt to be to the right of *some*). Choosing appropriate names whose intervals cover the entire range, from zero to ten, can be challenging, as we will explain in the Conclusions. See, also, Mendel (1998).

(c) *Check with experts and non-experts about the names* to be sure that they convey a clear and acceptable meaning, and make sense. A small survey may be needed in order to do this. An acceptable name for a set will often depend on the nature of the social judgment, e.g., *some to a fair amount* is acceptable for flirtation, but is unacceptable for sexual harassment. (because no amount of sexual harassment is "fair").

(5) Establish membership functions for the fuzzy sets (see Fig. 4). There are usually two distinctly different types of membership functions: end-of-range (shoulder) membership functions and interior membership functions. On a scale of zero to ten, there will be two end-of-range membership functions. How many interior membership functions there are will depend on how many fuzzy sets have been chosen in Step 4(a). In our flirtation study, because each indicator had 5 fuzzy sets associated with it, there were 3 interior membership functions. All membership functions range in value from zero to unity, and are "normal," meaning that they must have at least one value equal to unity.

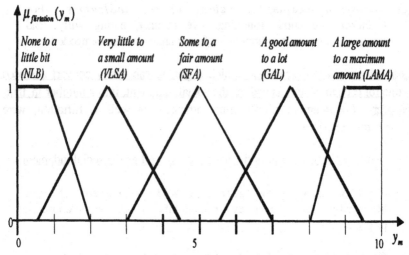

Figure 4. Hypothetical membership functions for the 5 fuzzy sets that characterize flirtation and the four indicators. For example, the triangle labeled very little to a small amount (VLSA) is actually $\mu_{VLSA}(y_m)$.

(a) *Choose shapes for the membership functions. In order to use the non-singleton fuzzy basis functions, given above, all membership functions must be Gaussians.* These basis functions are easy to compute and account for uncertainties in sensed values of the indicators. It is possible to use other shapes for the membership functions, especially if singleton fuzzy basis functions (which do not account for sensed indicator uncertainties) are used; however, Eq. (3) will not be applicable in those cases.

(b) *Establish length of interval for each fuzzy set, and then determine the parameters that are needed to specify the membership functions.* For Gaussian membership functions, which must be symmetrical about the interval's center location, determine: center value (which becomes the mean) and the standard deviation.

(6) <u>Establish rules between the indicators (the antecedents) and the social judgment (the consequent).</u>

(a) *Decide on how many antecedents the rules will have.* For flirtation, we felt that a person could comfortably handle one or two flirtation indicators at a time, but not 3 or 4 indicators. This does not mean that a person does not use all 4 flirtation indicators; it means that we believe that a person uses them one or two at a time. Note, also, that the total number of rules depends on the number of antecedents and the number of fuzzy sets associated with each antecedent. By using one- and two-antecedent rules, there are only 170 rules. It is manageable to ask a person to provide 170 rules.

(b) *Decide on how many rulebases will be established.* This can be done by a survey in which each respondent is asked to either rank-order all of the possible one-and two-antecedent rulebases, or to grade each of the possible rulebases on a scale of from zero to ten. A decision must then be made on how many of the rulebases will be used. For flirtation, there are 10 possible rulebases, and we established and used all of them. Later, when (and if) the outputs of the rulebases are combined, they can be weighted using the results of this step.

(c) *Establish the rulebases.* This is done using a survey and then some postprocessing.

(i) *Survey* - For flirtation, subsets of males and females were asked to establish all 10 rulebases (170 rules). An example of a question is: IF there is *none to a little bit* of touching and *a large amount to a maximum amount* of eye contact, THEN there is _____ flirtation. The respondent was given 5 numerical choices to fill in the blank space, and these were listed, as: 1-*none to a little bit*, 2-*very little to a small amount*, 3-*some to a fair amount*, 4-*a good amount to a lot*, and, 5-*a large amount to a maximum amount.*

(ii) *Postprocessing* - After the surveys were completed, we established consensus female and male rule bases, as follows: (a) we determined histograms for each of the 170 rules, and (b) we used the rule average as its consequent.

(7) Transfer the rules and membership function information into a mathematical fuzzy logic advisor. Details about this are given in Mendel, et al. (1996), and involve implementing the fuzzy basis functions in Eq. (1).

(8) Establish a vocabulary for the user of the FL Advisor. This is necessary in order to activate the FL Advisor after it is totally designed. Believing that people will not be able to specify precise numerical values for the indicators or the social judgment, we must provide them with an acceptable vocabulary that they can use to describe these quantities. Some phrases that can be used in the 'vocabulary' are (for example): 'exactly' 7, 'approximately' 7, 'close to'

7, 'near' 7, 'around' 7, etc. Modifiers like 'pretty' (e.g., pretty close to 7), 'very' (e.g., very close to 7), etc., can easily be handled as *hedges* (e.g., Mendel, 1995a).

(9) Map the vocabulary into quantitative measures of uncertainty for rule antecedents. Observed antecedents are treated as fuzzy numbers. Such numbers have a membership function associated with them, one that is centered at the exact value and is symmetrically distributed about that value. For a Gaussian membership function, one can choose its variance, for the vocabulary stated in item 8, as: σ_x^2(exactly) = 0, σ_x^2(approximately) = 0.05, σ_x^2(close to) = 0.1, σ_x^2(near) = 0.15, and σ_x^2(around) = 0.2.

In the present study we did not implement Steps 8 and 9.

Following these steps, all of the parameters in the FLA are fixed, i.e., the FLA has been completely designed, so that it can then be used.

Surveys

During this study, we conducted three surveys, to establish: (1) the most important indicators of flirtation, (2) names for the fuzzy sets of the indicators and flirtation, and, (3) the rules and relative weights for the rulebases. These surveys are described in Mendel, et al. (1996), and are beyond the scope of the present chapter.

Data Processing and Results

Tables 1 and 2 present histograms, obtained from 47 female respondents and 26 male respondents, for all of the rules associated with *touching and flirtation* and *acting witty and flirtation*. The rule numbering conforms to the following ordering of the antecedents: NLB, VLSA, SFA, GAL, and LAMA. These tables also include means and standard deviations for the survey flirtation levels for each rule. The statistics in these tables were used to generate synthetic surveys. 1,000 synthetic surveys were generated for both females and males in the following way: for each one-antecedent (or two-antecedent) rule, the survey mean and standard deviation were used in a Gaussian random number generator to produce 1,000 levels of flirtation and subsequently 1,000 surveys. The 1,000 surveys were then randomized, the first 700 of which were collected into a *training set* and the remaining 300 of which were collected into a *testing set*. The training set was used to determine fuzzy logic and regression models, whereas the testing set was used to test the models.

Table 1. Histogram of survey responses – **Touching**. 47 female surveys and 26 male surveys.

Rule #	FEMALES						
	NLB	VLSA	SFA	GAL	LAMA	Mean	Std. Dev.
1	36	7	4	0	0	0.7979	1.5731
2	26	17	4	0	0	1.3298	1.6361
3	2	16	27	2	0	4.0426	1.6112
4	1	3	11	22	10	6.9681	2.3275
5	0	3	7	17	20	7.8723	2.271
Rule #	MALES						
	NLB	VLSA	SFA	GAL	LAMA	Mean	Std. Dev.
1	24	1	1	0	0	0.2885	1.0786
2	14	11	1	0	0	1.25	1.4577
3	1	6	19	0	0	4.2308	1.3728
4	0	0	4	19	3	7.4038	1.3192
5	0	0	3	12	11	8.2692	1.6984

Table 2. Histogram of survey responses – **Acting witty**. 47 female surveys and 26 male surveys.

Rule #	FEMALES						
	NLB	VLSA	SFA	GAL	LAMA	Mean	Std. Dev.
1	39	8	0	0	0	0.4255	0.9497
2	24	22	0	1	0	1.3298	1.5509
3	2	21	23	1	0	3.7234	1.5527
4	4	15	13	14	1	4.6277	2.5526
5	2	11	11	15	8	5.8511	2.8683
Rule #	MALES						
	NLB	VLSA	SFA	GAL	LAMA	Mean	Std. Dev.
1	22	3	1	0	0	0.4808	1.2287
2	18	7	0	0	1	1.0577	2.1416
3	3	10	12	1	0	3.5577	1.8938
4	2	4	13	4	3	5.1923	2.6385
5	1	5	13	4	3	5.2885	2.4826

We computed 10 FLAs, four for single-antecedent rules, and six for two-antecedent rules. Each FLA was designed using the training set of 700 synthetic surveys by first determining an average female and male respondent. This was done by averaging the flirtation levels across the 700 surveys for each rule. In the sequel, we refer to these results as the "consensus female" and "consensus male." Hence, *our FLAs are consensus female or male advisors.* We assumed singleton fuzzification during the designs.

The FLA is a new type of a model for a social science application. How well does it do versus a more traditional quantitative social science model? To answer this question, we chose two standard regression models (SRMs). For *single-antecedent rule bases*, these SRMs are:

$$y_{RM1}(x) = C_0 + C_1 x \text{ and } y_{RM2}(x) = C_0 + C_1 x + C_2 x^2.$$

For *two-antecedent rule bases*, these SRMs are:

$$y_{RM1}(x_1, x_2) = C_0 + C_1 x_1 + C_2 x_2 + C_3 x_1 x_2$$

and

$$y_{RM2}(x_1, x_2) = C_0 + C_1 x_1 + C_2 x_2 + C_3 x_1 x_2 + C_4 x_1^2 + C_5 x_2^2.$$

In the first two equations, x denotes any one of the four flirtation indicators, whereas in the last two equations x_1 and x_2 denote the two flirtation indicators for a specific model. In the sequel, we refer to the SRMs in the first and third equations as SRM1 and the SRMs in the second and fourth equations as SRM2. We computed the regression coefficients in two ways. In one approach, we used least squares (LS) (Mendel, 1995b), whereas in the second approach we used best linear unbiased estimation (BLU) (Mendel, 1995b). The second approach makes use of the standard deviations for each rule, whereas LS does not.

Figures 5-7 were obtained by evaluating the FLA and SRM2 at uniformly spaced values of each indicator (or indicators). Figure 7, for example, depicts flirtation versus acting witty and touching for females and males, for the FLA and SRM2. The differences between the FLA and SRM2 models are striking; however, most of the differences are due to the interpolation between the 25 data points that were used to compute the models. The FLAs show an undulating transition from one level of flirtation to another, whereas the SRM2 looks quite linear, even though it includes three nonlinear terms (the coefficients for these terms were quite small). We also discern some differences between the consensus female and male FLAs, demonstrating, as expected, that females and males perceive flirtation differently. These differences are more obvious in some of the other rule base figures that can be found in Appendix F of Mendel, et al. (1996).

We compiled tables of mean-squared errors (MSEs)s for all of the computed models. Our tables include four MSEs, two related to consensus data and two related to population data. For each type of data we computed MSEs for test data and the actual survey data. Our two consensus MSEs were computed for the 300 test data and the N survey data, respectively, where $N = 47$ for females and

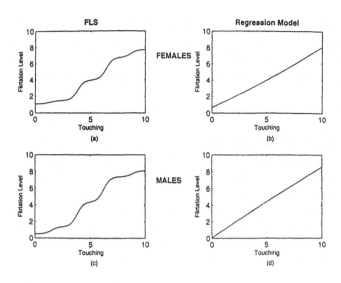

Figure 5. **Touching**: The outputs of fuzzy and regression models to continuous inputs: (a), (b) females; (c), (d) males.

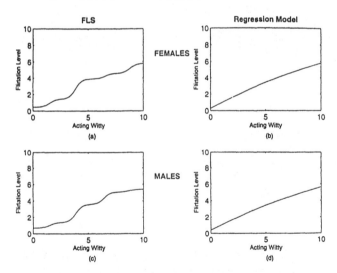

Figure 6. **Acting witty**: The outputs of fuzzy and regression models to continuous inputs: (a), (b) females; (c), (d) males.

$N = 26$ for males. We refer to the former consensus MSE as the *consensus testing MSE*, and to the latter consensus MSE as the *consensus survey MSE*. Our two population MSEs were also computed for the 300 test data and the N survey data, respectively, where $N = 47$ for females and $N = 26$ for males. We refer to the former population MSE as the *population testing MSE*, *MSE(S2)*, and to the latter population MSE as the *population survey MSE*, *MSE(Survey)*. Formulas for all these MSEs can be found in Mendel, et al. (1996). Tables 3 and 4 summarize the four flirtation MSEs for touching and acting witty, respectively.

Each table provides results for both females and males, and for 5 models: (1) *fuzzy* denotes the FLA; (2) *RM1 LS* denotes SRM1 whose coefficients have been computed using least squares; (3) *RM2 LS* denotes SRM2 whose coefficients have been computed using least squares; (4) *RM1 BLU* denotes SRM1 whose coefficients have been computed using best linear unbiased estimation; and, (5) *RM2 BLU* denotes SRM2 whose coefficients have been computed using best linear unbiased estimation. From these tables we observe the following: (1) there are hardly any significant differences between *RM1 LS*, *RM2 LS*, *RM1 BLU* and *RM2 BLU*; and, (2) *there is a substantial improvement in consensus MSEs for the FLA versus any of the SRMs.*

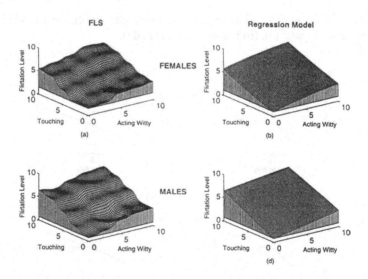

Figure 7. **Acting witty - Touching**: The outputs of fuzzy and regression models to continuous inputs: (a), (b) females; (c), (d) males.

A complete set of MSEs for all 10 rule bases is given in Appendix G of Mendel, et al. (1996). Because there is so much data, we summarize the winning models in Table 5, from which it is reasonable to conclude that on average *the FLA is an order of magnitude better than the next best model in terms of MSE*. This clearly demonstrates the superiority of the new FLA over the more traditional SRMs, in terms of MSE.

Table 3. Flirtation MSEs: **Touching**. Training was done on 700 randomly generated surveys for both females and males. Testing was done on 300 randomly generated surveys for both females and males and then on 47 (26) actual female (male) surveys.

	FEMALES			
	Population Testing MSE	Consensus Testing MSE	Population Survey MSE	Consensus Survey MSE
Fuzzy	3.3749	0.0152	3.62	0.0335
RM1 LS	3.7117	0.352	3.9821	0.3957
RM2 LS	3.717	0.3573	3.9715	0.385
RM1 BLU	3.7239	0.3642	4.0343	0.4478
RM2 BLU	3.7661	0.4064	4.0251	0.4385
	MALES			
	Population Testing MSE	Consensus Testing MSE	Population Survey MSE	Consensus Survey MSE
Fuzzy	2.093	0.0159	1.9042	0.02
RM1 LS	2.3823	0.3052	2.2777	0.3934
RM2 LS	2.3873	0.3102	2.279	0.3947
RM1 BLU	2.3904	0.3134	2.3101	0.4259
RM2 BLU	2.3851	0.3081	2.3064	0.4221

Table 4. Flirtation MSEs: **Acting witty**. Training was done on 700 randomly generated surveys for both females and males. Testing was done on 300 randomly generated surveys for both females and males and then on 47 (26) actual female (male) surveys.

	FEMALES			
	Population Testing MSE	Consensus Testing MSE	Population Survey MSE	Consensus Survey MSE
Fuzzy	3.9801	0.0266	4.0147	0.0095
RM1 LS	4.0276	0.074	4.1117	0.1065
RM2 LS	4.0094	0.0559	4.1045	0.0993
RM1 BLU	4.0245	0.0709	4.1165	0.1113
RM2 BLU	4.0076	0.054	4.1045	0.0993
	MALES			
	Population Testing MSE	Consensus Testing MSE	Population Survey MSE	Consensus Survey MSE
Fuzzy	4.0926	0.0087	4.4191	0.033
RM1 LS	4.3355	0.2516	4.7065	0.3204
RM2 LS	4.293	0.2091	4.6608	0.2747
RM1 BLU	4.338	0.2541	4.7057	0.3196
RM2 BLU	4.3268	0.2429	4.696	0.3099

Table 5. Summary of winning models. See Appendix G in Mendel, et al. (1996) for MSEs of all 10 rule bases. F denotes FLA. Number in parenthesis denotes the ratio of the MSE of the next best model to the MSE of the winning model.

	FEMALES		MALES	
	Consensus Testing MSE	Consensus Survey MSE	Consensus Testing MSE	Consensus Survey MSE
Eye Contact	F (5.5)	F (8.53)	F (53.49)	F (3.24)
Touching	F (23.16)	F (11.49)	F (19.19)	F (19.67)
Acting Witty	F (2.03)	F (10.4)	F (24)	F (8,32)
Primping	F (3.33)	F (2.16)	F (7.2)	F (11.03)
EC/T	F (6.15)	F (13.47)	F (14.8)	F (10)
EC/P	F (5.99)	F (7.47)	F (6.13)	F (8.49)
EC/AW	F (10.77)	F (12.76)	F (2.98)	F (6.53)
P/T	F (22.22)	F (28.27)	F (8.98)	F (14.63)
AW/T	F (9.72)	F (12.01)	F (20.59)	F (29.21)
P/AW	F (7.25)	F (9.66)	F (9.98)	F (14.36)

Discussion

We have entitled this chapter "a first attempt." Why? Because our work has actually led to more questions than it has answered; so, we do not want to leave the reader with the impression that our 9-step methodology is an end-all ... it is just the beginning. In this section, we briefly discuss some of the shortcomings of the present approach as well as some fixes to it.

Multi-antecedent rules: People do not like to take long surveys and have trouble answering complicated multi-antecedent questions. This is why we limited our surveys to one - and two -antecedent rules. The issue of how to combine flirtation levels from the outputs of more than one FLA remains to be studied, although it is discussed in Appendix A of Mendel, et al. (1996). Also, even though we have identified four indicators of flirtation, this does not mean that people focus on all four during an actual flirtation situation. How likely is it that someone will be touching, establishing eye contact, acting witty, and primping all at the same time? If only one or two of the indicators actually occur during a real flirtation situation, then one – and two- antecedent FLSs are sufficient.

If, however, flirtation, or any other judgment, really requires rules with more than two antecedents, then not only do we encounter the difficulties just mentioned, but, we also encounter rule-explosion, i.e., the number of questions that need to be asked becomes much too large. Perhaps, one way around this is to use the recent results of Combs and Andrews (1998), who have demonstrated a crisp logical equivalence between an intersection rule configuration (IRC) and a union rule configuration (URC). For a two-antecedent rule, the IRC and URC equivalence is: $[(p \wedge q) \Rightarrow r] \Leftrightarrow [(p \Rightarrow r) \vee (q \Rightarrow r)]$. Although this suggests that two-antecedent FLAs (the l. h. s. of the equivalence) could be constructed from one-antecedent FLAs (the r. h. s. of the equivalence), which would imply that we only have to ask people simple single-antecedent rule questions, it would seem that by doing this we lose the correlation information that people associate between indicators when they make a judgment. More work needs to be done to really understand how to (or if it can be done) apply this interesting equivalence to a FLA.

Rule uncertainties: As Mendel (1998) has recently noted, "words mean different things to different people." Since the rules that serve as the queries for people during a survey are comprised of words, these rules contain *linguistic uncertainties*. These uncertainties are associated with the labels of the antecedent and consequent fuzzy sets, and also with the histograms of the rule answers obtained during a rule-survey. In the present study we did not survey people about the intervals (on a scale of 0 – 10) that they associate with the 5 labels for our indicators. Perhaps, these labels do not completely cover the 0 - 10 range, or, some may not have sufficient overlap with their neighbors, or, their are gaps in the 0 - 10 range, or, it takes more than 5 labels to cover the range. When interval information about fuzzy set labels is collected from people during a survey, then there is uncertainty associated with the collected data. For example, the end points of an interval will each be described by a mean value and a standard deviation, because people do not, in general give the same numerical values for an interval. This is all discussed in great detail in Mendel (1998).

Unfortunately, it is not possible to use linguistic uncertainty in a FLA that is based on traditional type-1 FL. Recently, Karnik and Mendel (1998a – 1998d) have developed an entirely new theory of type-2 FLSs. In a type-2 FLS, rules have the same structure as they do in a type-1 FLS; however, some or all of the antecedent and consequent membership functions are type-2 fuzzy sets. Type-2 fuzzy sets treat our usual (type-1) membership functions as fuzzy; this lets us incorporate membership function uncertainties (which are associated with linguistic uncertainties) into a FLS. Just as fired rules in a type-1 FLS produce a type-1 fuzzy set, fired rules in a type-2 FLS produce a type-2 fuzzy set. Karnik and Mendel have developed an "extended" defuzzification procedure (based on Zadeh's Extension Principle) that transforms a type-2 set into a type-1 set. This operation is called *type-reduction*, and its associated type-1 set is called a *type-reduced set*. The type-reduced set is analogous to a confidence interval that is usually computed for stochastic uncertainty; but, it is for linguistic uncertainty.

It is very important to include and account for uncertainties in a FLA. A type-2 FLA will not provide a single judgment surface, such as the one in Fig. 7; it will provide a banded-surface (i.e., upper and lower intervals). When the FLA is actually used, such as a sensitivity training tool, knowing how close a person's flirtation-judgment level is in relation to that of a consensus models is not the real issue. The real issue is if an individual's response to a flirtation situation falls within the linguistic uncertainty band of a consensus FLA. If it does, then the individual does not need sensitivity training; if it doesn't , then the individual does.

The histograms of survey results, such as those in Tables 1 and 2, were averaged by us. Using type-2 FLSs, it is possible to even use the entire histogram. In this way, it is possible to account for this type of survey uncertainty, as well as the previously-discussed linguistic uncertainties. So, type-2 FLSs opens up possibilities that did not exist before, possibilities that we believe are truly needed in FLAs.

Choice of labels: Not only is it important to cover the 0 - 10 interval with a collection of labels, but it is also important to choose labels that do not offend people (i.e., that are politically correct). In some related work that we have done on FLAs for sexual harassment (SH), the labels *some to a fair amount* and *a good amount to a lot* are inappropriate, because there is no amount of SH that is 'fair' or 'good.' If these words are used in a survey, then respondents may very well discount the entire survey as not being credible and refuse to take it (this was pointed out to the author by Ms. Marion Stark, Director of Human Resources at the Institute of Defense Analysis).

Memory: Our FLA has assumed a memoryless world, which, of course, is incorrect. In our work on a SH FLA, we learned that a person's memory of the past level of SH with an individual greatly affects the level of SH associated with that individual after a first-time encounter. So, a SH FLA actually is comprised of (at least) two sub-advisors: a first-incident SH FLA and a more-then first-incident SH FLA. The rules for a first-incident SH FLA look structurally like the ones that we have considered in this chapter. The rules for a more-then first-incident SH FLA are more complicated, because they must have at least two antecedents, where one of the antecedents is the remembered level of SH. A two-antecedent first-incident SH FLA then becomes a three - antecedent more-then first-incident SH FLA. The latter is very difficult to obtain rules for, because of the problems described above under "Multi-antecedent rules." This is also a case where the IRC to URC decomposition must be one in which three-antecedent rules are replaced by two-antecedent clauses. Exactly how to do this, as well as the validity for doing this, remain to be explored.

Conclusions

The goal of the current work has been to demonstrate how fuzzy logic systems may be applied to enhance our ability to predict social judgments above and beyond that provided using traditional linear models. To illustrate the utility of this fuzzy-logic approach, we have focused on one specific type of social judgement, namely judgments of flirtation.

The interconnection of encoder, fuzzy logic system, and decoder is what we call a "Fuzzy Logic Advisor (FLA)." We have provided a methodology that represents a complete 9-step procedure for designing the FLA, one that can be applied to many social judgments, such as flirtation and sexual harassment. Surveys play a central role in the design of a FLA; they are used to implement Steps 2, 4, 5, and 6 of the 9 step procedure.

We have demonstrated that FL Flirtation Advisors describe or predict flirtation judgments, on average, at least an order of magnitude better than a standard regression model. Hence, we have indeed demonstrated that fuzzy logic systems may be applied to enhance our ability to predict social judgments above and beyond that provided using traditional linear models.

In Mendel, et al. (1996) we also demonstrate how the FLA can be used as a diagnostic training tool. First it can be used to diagnose problem areas; then it can be used to sensitize an individual to same-sex or opposite-sex flirtation patterns. In this way, people ought to be able to improve their social acumen regarding norms associated with flirtation -- and how one's perceptions depart from normative ones. To do this correctly, we need to develop a type-2 FLA, one that will let us incorporate linguistic uncertainties as well as rule-consequent histogram information.

Finally, we wish to reiterate the fact that in this chapter we have only considered the social judgement of flirtation; but, we believe that the basic methodology that is described in the context of flirtation can also be applied to many other social judgments (e.g., sexual harassment). We also believe that our methodology can be applied to some engineering problems, but this remains to be done.

Acknowledgements

The authors wish to acknowledge the help of the following people who contributed to this study: Sunil Bharitkar, who helped to administer surveys; George Mouzouris, who suggested the idea of synthetic surveys, and how to obtain them from the histograms of the actual surveys; Kemal Demircilar, who developed the 3D graphical ways to visualize a two-antecedent FLA and a comparable regression model; and, Prof. Stephen Read, of the USC Psychology Department, who acted as a sounding board for many of the ideas as they were evolving. For a detailed description of the contributions made by this paper's five authors to this study, see the "Acknowledgements" section in Mendel, et al. (1996). The work by Mendel, Martin and Karnik was performed under grant no. MIP-9419386 from the National Science Foundation.

References

Combs, W. and J.Andrews (1998). "Combinatorial rule explosion eliminated by a fuzzy rule configuration." *IEEE Trans. on Fuzzy Systems*, vol. 6, pp. 1-11.

Edwards, J. R. (1991). "Person-job fit: a conceptual integration, literature review and methodological critique." In C. L. Cooper & I. T. Robertson (Eds.), *International review of industrial and organizational psychology, 6,* (283-357). New York : Wiley.

Edwards, J. R. and Van Harrison, R. (1993). "Job demands and worker health: three-dimensional reexamination of the relationship between person-environment fit and strain." *Journal of Applied Psychology, 78,* 628-648.

Hesketh, B., Smithson, M., and Hesketh, T. (1996). "Using fuzzy sets to conceptualize and measure P-E fit," *Proceedings of the American Psychological Association Conference.* Toronto, Canada.

Karnik, N. N. and J. M. Mendel (1998a). "Introduction to type-2 fuzzy logic systems," presented at the 1998 IEEE FUZZ Conference, Anchorage, AK, May.

Karnik, N. N. and J. M. Mendel (1998b). "Type-2 fuzzy logic systems: type-reduction," presented at the 1998 IEEE SMC Conference, San Diego, CA, October.

Karnik, N. N. and J. M. Mendel (1998c). "Type-2 fuzzy logic systems, I: preliminaries," submitted for publication.

Karnik, N. N. and J. M. Mendel (1998d). "Type-2 fuzzy logic systems, II: implementation," submitted for publication.

Klir, G. J. and Yuan, B. (1995). *Fuzzy sets and fuzzy logic: theory and applications.* New Jersey: Prentice-Hall PTR.

Koeppel, L. B., Montagne-Miller, Y., O'Hair, D., and Cody, M. J. (1993). "Friendly? Flirting? Wrong?" In Interpersonal communication: evolving interpersonal. (13-32). New Jersey: Erlbaum.

Massaro, D. W. and Friedman, D. (1990). "Models of integration given multiple sources of information". *Psychological Review, 97*. 225-252.

Mendel, J. M. (1995a). "Fuzzy logic systems for engineering: a tutorial." *IEEE Proceedings, 83*. 345-377.

Mendel, J. M. (1995b). *Lessons in estimation theory for signal processing, communications, and control.* New Jersey: Prentice-Hall.

Mendel, J. M. (1995b). "Computing with words, when words mean different things to different people," submitted for publication.

Mendel, J. M., Martin, M., Murphy, S. T., Miller, L. C., and Karnik, N. (1996). The fuzzy logic advisor: a paradigm for social judgements. USC SIPI Report #305, Univ. of Southern California, Los Angeles, CA.

Zadeh, L. A. (1965). "Fuzzy sets." *Information and Control, 8*. 338-353.

Zadeh, L. A. (1973). "Outline of a new approach to the analysis of complex systems and decision processes." *IEEE Transactions on Systems, Man and Cybernetics, 3*. 28-44.

Zadeh, L. A. (1996). "Fuzzy logic = computing with words." *IEEE Trans. on Fuzzy Systems*, vol. 4, pp. 103-111.

Conceptualisation with GABEK:
Ideas on Social Change in South Africa

**Josef Zelger[*], Andries G. de Wet[**], Anne-Marié Pothas[**]
and Don Petkov[***]**

[*]University of Innsbruck
Institut für Philosophie
Innrain 52
A-6020 Innsbrück, Austria
E-mail: Josef.Zelger@uibk.ac.at

[**]Potchefstroom University for CHE
Department of Statistics and Operations Research
Vaal Triangle Campus
Vanderbijlpark, South Africa
E-mail: onaagdw@puknet.puk.ac.za
E-mail: onaap@puknet.puk.ac.za

[***]University of Natal
Department of Computer Science and Information Systems
University of Natal
Pietermaritzburg, South Africa
E-mail: petkov@compnt.cs.unp.ac.za

Abstract

In Fuzzy Set Theory, a given fuzzy set or a given membership function serves as starting point. The choice of membership functions is usually not described in the publications in this field, neither the process of formation of concepts. GABEK (© Zelger, J., Innsbrück) is a recent approach for analysing text data to surface and map opinions, feelings, attitudes and meaning. The text data is obtained from individuals' free-form responses to open-ended questions. Concepts according to the GABEK theory are specific relations between concepts, which can be presented also as sets of sets of concepts. GABEK shows how a new concept emerges from the different concepts of individuals as relations between the different concepts. We illustrate the ability of GABEK to solicit a rich description of a problem situation from the various viewpoints of individual stakeholders, in this case social change in two areas of South Africa. Concepts are thus not formatted from the frame of reference of the researcher. Rather, the potential of social knowledge, distributed and inherent in the experience of individuals, is revealed and employed to conceptualisation.

1. Introduction

In the field of Fuzzy Set Theory, although it has matured in the past fifteen years, most papers start with a given fuzzy set or a given membership function, without any mention of how and why they were chosen (Jain, 1980:131). We are concerned here with one step preceding even the question of the choice of membership functions, that is the process of formation of concepts.

Complex problems described as "wicked" (Rittel and Webber, 1973), as " messes" (Ackoff, 1981) or as "swamps" (Schon, 1987), defy traditional problem solving techniques involving, e.g., formulate/ model/test/solve/implement. Such techniques presuppose a set of given concepts, defining the problem situation at hand.

To assist stakeholders in identifying an agreed framework for their "wicked" problem situations, problem structuring methods (PSMs) have been developed lately within Operations Research (Rosenhead, 1989). Some of these PSMs include: Hypergame Analysis (Bennett and Cropper, 1986); Interactive Planning (Ackoff, 1979); Metagame Analysis (Howard, 1993); Robustness Analysis (Rosenhead, 1980); Soft Systems Methodology (Checkland, 1981); Strategic Assumption Surfacing and Testing (Mason and Mitroff, 1981); Strategic Choice Approach (Friend and Hickling, 1987); Strategic Options Development and Analysis (Eden, Jones and Sims, 1983). The major PSMs incorporate purpose-built software (Rosenhead, 1989). Positive aspects of utilising a computer are: its potential to depersonalise messages that might otherwise lead to non-committant responses because of the originators' position or personality (Eden, 1989), and its potential to obtain and present results in an interactive manner.

Shaw and Gaines (1984) have demonstrated how concepts or constructs as they call them, may be elicited from a person through an interactive computer program and they have provided fuzzy set semantics for some construct systems. Their work uses a framework of epistemological hierarchy, within which to discuss decision analysis, suggested by Klir (1976), combined with a theory of personal constructs by Kelley (1955). They concentrate at the lowest level in Klir's epistemological hierarchy, which is one of source systems, at the way which the data terminology is defined.

The next level is one of data systems, effectively one of system observation, whereby the actual behaviour of some system is described in terms of the agreed domain of discourse at level zero. Levels above these are concerned with models of data and their interrelationships and each level of that hierarchy is associated with presuppositions that have to be made when developing any system for decision analysis according to Shaw and Gaines (1984:336).

Unlike Shaw and Gaines (1984), who assume that the basic constructs, or distinctions that we make according to them can be generated in a predefined construct elicitation grid that brings in the notions of opposition and relevance, the GABEK (© Zelger, J., Innsbrück) technique, is a recent approach for surfacing and mapping meaning, beliefs and intentions in a transparent guise from a text base. This process is facilitated by the software WINRELAN (© Zelger, J., Innsbrück), developed specifically for GABEK applications.

Concepts according to the GABEK theory are specific relations between concepts, which can be presented also as sets of sets of concepts. GABEK shows how a new concept, A*, emerges from different concepts, A1, A2, A3,...,An, of different individuals, P1, P2, P3,...Pn, as relations between the nodal concepts between A1, A2, A3,...,An. This new concept A* can be used intesubjectively, as it is understood by all the individuals (Zelger, 1993, 1995). GABEK undertakes to reveal the potential of social knowledge distributed and inherent in the experience of individuals, captured in free form answers to open-ended questions.

According to Deetz (1996), language does not name objects in the world; it is the core process of constituting objects. The appearance of labelling or categorising existing objects is derived from this more fundamental act of object constitution through language. Since Deetz proceeds on to summarise that language replaces consciousness as central in the philosophy of science and because recently there has been a growing discussion on the role of language in Operations Research (e.g. Ramakrishnan, 1995; Marley & Ormerod, 1996; and others) we may conclude that a study of potential ways for generation of concepts is of both theoretical and practical importance. From the point of view of Fuzzy Set Theory it may be seen as an useful approach for generating fuzzy concepts associated with phenomena involving socio-technical systems which can be seen as a precondition for the development of relevant Fuzzy Set Models of such systems.

When dealing with "wicked" issues, the following conditions should be fulfilled:

- *All available sources of knowledge* should be tapped. This means that the experiences of broad sections of the population are to be collected and combined to form a coherent whole, together with the available expert knowledge. For nearly every aspect of social control it will be of paramount importance to understand what people think and feel, where they set priorities, and which tendencies for future development may emerge. How will social groups, for example, respond to new ecological challenges, to political austerity programs, to new regulations, additional taxes and so on? Which political options are available? Which measures can effectively be taken?
- The second condition for problem solving in complex situations is the *integration and systematisation of all information*. The synthesis of widely differing and unordered verbal data to form hierarchically higher and meaningful larger units of knowledge, seems to be more important for complex problem solving than the mere analysis of some further details.

- From the variety of everyday opinions voiced and of detailed scientific knowledge, as well as of political experience, the relevant contents for the specific problem have to be selected. But how is relevance to be understood? We believe *relevance of knowledge* has two sources, an emotional and a cognitive one. Therefore we should select information that is well-founded on experiences with emotional weight and, secondly, information that is compatible with a wide range of knowledge and values. The contents selected should strike a balance between both aspects.

GABEK fulfils all of the three conditions. The problem area to which GABEK was applied is the issue of social change in the South African society - a challenging systems analysis task. Section two of this paper will examine the basic theory behind GABEK, i.e. the formation of a new concept using the individual concepts. Section three will present the framework for generation of concepts associated with social change, implemented in two areas of South Africa. Lastly, some concluding remarks will be presented.

2. From Open-ended Questions to Linguistic Gestalten via GABEK

In employing GABEK to construct concepts regarding a problem situation, the *starting point is open-ended questions.* We wish to involve stakeholders in the constructing of concepts; therefore we need to know what they think, believe, feel about the problem situation at hand. Asking open-ended, engaging questions, solicit elaborate responses in the stakeholders' own words. Furthermore, when answering open-ended, engaging questions, stakeholders do so from their own frames of reference. The problem situation is thus described from the various viewpoints of all the stakeholders. The result is a rich data base of unordered complex verbal data from which information could be gleaned.

An *example* of an open-ended, engaging question, is the following. In the study on "Participating in Positive Change within the Vaal Triangle", (also discussed in section 3 of this paper), one of the questions asked, was:

What do you think *you* can do to contribute to positive change within the Vaal Triangle? Please motivate your answer in 4 to 5 full sentences.

The question is open-ended; a respondent can answer what he/she believes or feels about his/her ability to contribute to positive change within the Vaal Triangle Region of South Africa.

The question is also engaging: a respondent is being confronted with his own ideas. Using the pronoun "you", is an effective way of rendering the open-ended question engaging as well.

The complex verbal data obtained from open-ended, engaging questions such as the above, need to be *systematised* in some way to enable our understanding of its inherent information.

If we try to explain the conditions of linguistic understanding (Zelger, 1997) it can be useful to investigate the process of perception. We do not perceive our surrounding as isolated sense data but in the form of perceptive gestalten (Stumpf 1939, Smith 1988). In the same way we understand linguistic utterances not as isolated concepts but as coherent linguistic complexes or groups of sentences which are comprehended as meaningful wholes. Thus we can introduce the concept of a *linguistic gestalt*.

A *linguistic gestalt* is an abstract entity. It presupposes grouping in parts. These parts are statements (i.e. relations between concepts). The linguistic gestalt can be distinguished from the larger linguistic context through the interrelation of the statements with each other. The linguistic gestalt here is seen as a special meaningful group of sentences which fulfils the following conditions:

- *Formal variety*: The sentences must be clearly distinguishable from each other within the group; i.e. the content of any two sentences may not be too similar. Each sentence must contain something new so that it is a kind of complement to all other sentences in the group. This entails that each sentence in the group must be distinguished from all other sentences in the same group by more than one key concept. As a consequence any pair of sentences containing the same key concepts is forbidden. The key concepts of one sentence in the group may not be included in the set of the key concepts of another sentence in the group.

- *Formal connectivity*: All sentences within the group are closely connected with each other, i.e. each sentence in the group must contain some key concepts which also occur in other sentences of the same group.

- *Formal distance*: The group of sentences may not contain too many sentences so that all relations between the sentences can be reconstructed and can be conceived as a unit of meaning. The necessary steps to reach from each sentence to each other in the group may not exceed the maximum of two steps.

- *Semantic demonstrability*: A group of sentences is meaningful only if it is possible to explain or demonstrate all the relations between the sentences intersubjectively. Therefore there must exist an ideal paradigmatic example which fulfils all the conditions assumed by the sentences. Especially in communicative learning situations it is necessary to point to models, examples, applications in a given modelling facility. As suggested by Pask (1976) "modelling facility" refers to the material immediate available to the individual, with which he can produce something observable, e.g. models which represent all the relations assumed by the sentences in the group.

- *Pragmatic applicability*: From a pragmatic point of view a group of sentences is relevant for an individual x in the situations s and at the point in time t only if the individual x believes in s and that all sentences together with their relations between each other are applicable as perception-, orientation- or action patterns.

Analysing texts, we observe that it is not easy to comply with the above conditions. Especially the rules of *formal variety* and *formal connectivity* oppose each other. They lead to a kind of equilibrium, when they are fulfilled simultaneously. The more the sentences are internally differentiated, the more likely they are not sufficiently networked internally. And the closer the network, the more likely it is that the internal differentiation does not suffice. The PC-program WINRELAN, developed for GABEK applications, provides for interactive methods to select groups of sentences from the unsorted verbal data base which fulfil the rules for linguistic gestalten.

To form linguistic gestalten on the basis of unordered verbal data we must first build an *indexing system*. To find out the connections between the sentences we code them, marking lexical concepts from each sentence from 3 to 9. For instance, the text unit

> *Establish entrepreneur workshops thus enabling individuals to generate own businesses. Provide means for self-development. Recognise individual skills and talents and help them develop and build on these. Create job opportunities by 'selling' the Vaal Triangle for its potential*

is coded by marking the notions *entrepreneurship, workshops, individual, small business, job opportunities, potential*. Using all the answers of the verbal data base we obtain a very complex linguistic net of sentences connected by nodal concepts. Of course there are some traps to be avoided: in the coding process synonyms and homonyms are to be eliminated. In WINRELAN this can be done by a computer assisted procedure. After coding all the verbal data, we can try to detect the formal structure of the data base by cluster analysis. WINRELAN provides different methods of cluster analysis (Zelger, 1996). But can we assume such clusters are relevant? Of course this does not have to be the case. The statements within a cluster can contradict each other. Normally they are too redundant and very often they do not contain relevant knowledge applicable to a new problem situation. Clusters grouped automatically, ordinarily do not fulfil our requirements for linguistic gestalten. Therefore we try to transform them to meaningful groups of statements which fulfil them. Each text group should have the form of a linguistic gestalt: we eliminate the redundant statements in the clusters and search the data base for further sentences which are meaningful complements.

Subsequently we give an example of a linguistic gestalt about "Participating in Positive Change in the Vaal Triangle". First we show the key notions occurring more than once in the textgroup. These, as shown in the table, can give a first overview of the content of the linguistic gestalt. Then we quote the original answers combined into a linguistic gestalt.

> *An example of a linguistic gestalt: small businesses, job opportunities and entrepreneurship in the Vaal Triangle.*

	6	4	3	2	2	2	2	2	2	2	2	2
B5	small business	job opportunities					investment			services	pay	crime
E6	small business	job opportunities	entrepreneurship				works hopes		individual			
E8	small business			facilities	funding		works hopes	expert				
F5	small business		entrepreneurship	facilities	funding		investment					
A8	small business	job opportunities				training		expert				
D2	small business	job opportunities	entrepreneurship			training			individual	services	pay	crime

B5: (1) Stop crime by stronger measures (2) Get investment for creation of work and growth (3) Everybody pays for what he uses (4) Innovate new ideas - start own business (5) Equal education for everybody.

E6: Establish entrepreneur workshops, thus enabling individuals to generate own businesses. Provide means for self-development. Recognise individuals skills and talents and help them develop and build on these. Create job opportunities by "selling" the Vaal Triangle for its potential.

E8: Once someone has had the vision, the idea needs to be "sold", assistance needs to be recruited, in terms of research, finance, venue. The concept must then be advertised. Experts in the various fields of small business must be approached to offer services and then the workshops need to begin.

F5: Aksie om klein sake sektor te ontwikkel. Oprig van sake/besigheidspersele vir verhuring teen lae huur kostes. Lenings aan entrepreneurs om saak te bevorder (Teen laagste moontlike rente). "Face lift" vir Vaal Driehoek om bestuurders en beleggers te lok. Konsentreer op natuurlike bates van area soos Drie Riviere Front.

A8: Deur meer werksgeleenthede te skep kan oortyd verminder word en derhalwe meer werknemers in diens geneem word. Entrepreneurs (kleinsake) is die antwoord tot werkskepping met die nodige opleiding. Gespesialiseerde persone nodig om die opleiding te verskaf.

D2: Job creation is of major importance. Since most of our people are without work, this creates crime, lack of self-esteem. Little income leads to frustration and a high rate of suicides in this area. There is no support towards government initiatives e.g. paying of services. We can only achieve job creation through motivating people to starting small businesses, building houses and also training people towards business entrepreneurship.

The number at the start of each response, is a card index as used in WINRELAN. It has no meaning in itself and is only reproduced here to indicate the different responses and to link the key notions, as expressed in the table, to the respective responses. Note that two of the responses are not in English, but in Afrikaans, a local language in South Africa. Different languages pose no problem within GABEK, provided that the analyst understands the languages used. If needs be, responses may also be translated into a language understood by the analyst. Responses may therefore be given in the language preferred by each respondent. Key notions, however, have to be in only one language to enable the cluster analysis.

A group of sentences like the above example is already too complex to be conceived as a whole. We must focus on one sentence after the other to apprehend their connections. Later we will use linguistic gestalten as parts to form more complex linguistic hypergestalten, as we have used the original responses - sentences - to form gestalten. Therefore we must now reduce the complexity of the above text group. We represent the linguistic gestalt by one short statement or a few very short ones. It is a kind of condensation which allows further processing of the central ideas of the linguistic gestalt.

For this condensation of contents as a rule we use the key concepts occurring more than once in the linguistic gestalt. In doing this, we presuppose that the contents of the linguistic gestalten are determined primarily by concepts occurring more than once in the group.

Besides, the new statement must follow as a semantic implication from the text group. If all sentences of the text group are true, then the new statement must also be true.

Using the above sentences of our gestalt *small businesses, job opportunities and entrepreneurship in the Vaal Triangle* as an example, we create a summary and call this a *selective representation* of the corresponding linguistic gestalt:

Unemployment leads to crime and not paying for services, therefore we need to promote job creation. To this end we can encourage the development of small businesses. This means motivating individuals and training them in entrepreneurship. The training needs to be funded and must be done by experts. Entrepreneurs must also be assisted by providing premises and loans at low interests rates. We must also attract investors to the Vaal Triangle.

Linguistic gestalten can be used to form hyper gestalten - according to the same rules of gestalt-building. For instance our selective representation about *small businesses, job opportunities and entrepreneurship in the Vaal Triangle* was compared with other summaries of linguistic gestalten (*a partnership for job creation and reducing crime in the Vaal Triangle, responsibility of the community, leaders from education and business motivating others*) to the hypergestalt *responsibility regarding job opportunities and crime*. By combining different hypergestalten on the still higher level we obtain the highest hypergestalt *responsibility to cooperate in the Vaal Triangle*.

The order is a fractal one as all textgroups on all levels fulfil the same formal rules and the higher levels refer to the same topics in a holistic guise as the lower ones. We took *sentences* as relation between key expressions, *gestalten* as relations between sentences, *hypergestalten* as relations between gestalten etc. Each hypergestalt is then a formal net of nets of nets of key-concepts. Its nodal concepts are also concepts on all the lower levels. Therefore we obtain a selfsimilar structure.

The whole structure is called *gestalten-tree*. It can be seen as an ordered overview of all the verbal data.

Having organised the original unordered complex verbal data in a meaningful way, we can use the resultant information in various ways. The highest statements are more abstract and general, the lowest more specific and complex. The highest further our understanding in many situations; the lowest are more informative for concrete problem solving and decision making. The highest provide an overview of the whole and are networked in the wide linguistic context. They are interrelated with the complete verbal data base. The lowest show strong emotional loads. Therefore they are more interesting for motivation. According to the specific goals of data presentation we can switch from top down to bottom up. The program WINRELAN presents the gestalten-tree diagrammatically and facilitates navigating within the gestalten-tree.

In the next section we'll show how the information emerged by GABEK from unordered verbal data may lead to the generation of concepts associated with social change in two different regions of South Africa.

3. Conceptualisation of Ideas on Social Change in South Africa

World-wide we are facing rapid change. South Africans are also experiencing the increasing complexity of rapid change. Fundamental change encompassing the political, social, economic, cultural and legal spheres, is touching the daily life of every South African. To facilitate this change in our societies, we need to understand what our people really think and feel, what they value and where differences may occur. This understanding is dependent on the qualitative analysis of subjective entities such as beliefs and emotions, preferably in the subjects own words.

Some results of implementing GABEK in two different regions in South Africa, will be represented here. They serve to illustrate the ability of GABEK to emerge ideas from the stakeholders themselves in describing and evaluating the problem situation at hand, in this case, social change in South Africa. The results were obtained from two studies: the first in the Vaal Triangle, a - if not the - major industrial region of the country, and the second in the KwaZulu Natal Midlands area, predominantly an agricultural region, with a politically unstable recent past history. Both areas are changing dynamically and are in strong need of boosted economic development.

For the past twenty years the Vaal Triangle Campus of the Potchefstroom University for Christian Higher Education annually hosts a one day symposium on some topical theme. The 1997 symposium was on "Participating in Positive Change Within the Vaal Triangle". Participants included leaders and other individuals from business, labour, education, the broad community and the local government of the Vaal Triangle. For the larger part of the day, workshops sessions within three groups - labour, socio-economic development and education - were held. Within each workshop session the groups had divided into subgroups to enable small group discussions on "Participating in Positive Change within the Vaal Triangle". At the start of the small group discussions, each participant had completed an open-ended questionnaire on ways to contribute to positive change within the Vaal Triangle. The responses were analysed via GABEK. For our purpose here, we've labelled the results as:

- aspects expected beforehand and described as expected,
- aspects expected beforehand but not described exactly as expected,
- aspects not expected beforehand, and
- aspects "missing", i.e. aspects expected beforehand, but which did not emerge.

The community, business, labour and local government must co-operate to create a climate of prosperity and development. Such a climate will be conclusive to investment, small business development and job creation. However, the current unemployment leads to crime and deteriorates our quality of life. Reducing crime is therefore an absolute must

is a hypergestalt which illustrates aspects we, as the researchers, have expected beforehand. These aspects are also described as expected, namely unemployment and crime as major problems and the co-operation needed to promote investment, small business development and job creation.

Examples of aspects expected beforehand, but not described exactly as expected, are the following gestalten:

Community leaders must actively support implementing projects geared towards positive change. In fact, they must work hand in hand with the members of the community. Every member of the community should participate in projects of community interest.... We must all participate, even if only in a small way.... Everyone must be involved in tackling community issues and bringing about positive change in the Vaal Triangle.

> *Joint forums must include members of the community, business and government, working towards a common objective. An individual's responsibility does not only lie within himself, but in the community as well.*

The concept about the need to assist the broader community, was to be expected. However, the emphasis on the community's responsibility to participate is stronger than expected.

A surprising result was the following hypergestalt:

> *We need to understand each other. Building friendships across the colour bar, will lead to mutual trust. By communicating in a positive manner, we'll learn to respect our different cultural backgrounds.*

The notion of personal friendships across the colour bar, was not within our frame of reference as researchers.

We, the researchers, did expect some notion of blame, of groups of participants accusing each other of an unwillingness to cooperate. Not a trace of blame could be found.

The above results illustrate that a study undertaken from only the researchers' frame of reference:

- would not have emerged the stakeholders rich description of the problem situation, i.e. *Participating in Positive change within the Vaal Triangle,*
- would have introduced detrimental aspects which had not formed part of the stakeholders' frame of reference.

The outcome of the symposium has been received enthusiastically at a feedback meeting. The following has been decided upon: the creating of a forum by various companies, involving all the stakeholders, to discuss the sharing of resources and to plan together towards positive change within the Vaal Triangle.

In the second study, we look at the contribution stakeholders of the KwaZulu Natal Midlands Partnership Programme can make to educating the unemployed and untrained, with a particular focus on school leavers and school dropouts. The Partnership is a coalition between education institutions like the University of Natal and Technikon Natal, non-government organisations, government departments, business and the community, funded by the Ford Foundation. In the Midlands Region the unemployment rate is high. Because of political violence, many individuals did not finish schooling and flocked to the job market unskilled. A real need for training the unskilled exists, but available resources are limited. This situation prompted people of the region to work together and to share their experiences and resources in alleviating the problems.

The GABEK analysis of the responses to open-ended questions on the contribution Partnership Stakeholders can make to training the unemployed and unskilled, yet again yielded some expected and certain unexpected results.

To be expected, were results such as the following:

> *Business and the parents must be involved in education. At workshops the department, teachers, parents and business can discuss needs and problems. Business can supply facilities as needed at schools. Parents, by being involved and informed, will take active participation and regard the school as the property of the community. Teachers must be given the chance to further their education by in service training.*

Also expected by the researchers, but perhaps to a lesser degree, was a reliance on government:

> *Joint action programmes to meet needs must be initiated by the partnership stakeholders - business, NGOs, parents, teachers, learners - because they are the ones involved in education and training. Government should assist the community and the partnership,*

and

> *Greater co-ordination between the stakeholders is necessary. Ensure that training is relevant to identified business needs and opportunities. Identify government and business sources for the funding of training.*

At a subsequent feed-back session, the acceptance demonstrated of the overall results of the GABEK analysis, was overwhelming. However, some results enlightened even the stakeholders themselves. An example is the importance of effective communication, which was emphasised by hypergestalten such as the following:

> *Make people aware and involved in the partnership and action programmes, as the involvement of all the stakeholders in bettering education is vital. For this a good communication system must be developed.*

More surprising to the stakeholders, was the opportunity identified to address people's fear of change through the Partnership. Various gestalten expressed the need for an open attitude to change, for being equipped to cope with change, for being informed of change:

> *I can contribute by communicating changes in the educational sector...... The department, teachers and parents can have meetings to communicate changes in education, the needs and the problems of the children at school to the parents.... Prepare to meet the changes in education by attending workshops and in service training.... I can encourage an open attitude amongst teachers, parents and pupils towards change... parents need to be*

informed about changes in the school system; pupils must be aware of new trends in careers and be equipped with the relevant skills for their changing world... Broaden students by... and involving them in activities that will equip them with the relevant skills to cope with change.

The ability of GABEK to emerge underlying emotions, needs and attitudes from the perspective of the stakeholders themselves, has again paid off. The Partnership now realises that no commitment from the parents, the pupils and the broader community will be gained if the fears and needs regarding changes in the education system are not addressed. The goal of the Partnership is training the unemployed and unskilled, integrating the efforts of the educational institutions with those of NGOs and the resources of the business sector. However, succeeding towards this goal is dependent on managing the uncertainties around changes in the education system. Furthermore, communication between the above listed stakeholders, was singled out as an effective tool to this end.

4. Some Concluding Remarks

It is difficult not to describe issues from the frame of reference of the researcher. Even in qualitative analyses aimed at describing the problem situation at hand from the perspective of the stakeholders, often the issues listed in, e.g., the questionnaire, are from the frame of reference of the researcher. A solution is to use open-ended questions, allowing stakeholders to express themselves as freely as possible. This, however, provides difficulty when processing the responses using conventional techniques.

The GABEK method enables the analysis and structuring of the responses on open-ended questions. The rich, structured and validated information obtained via a GABEK analysis, opens up a wealth of possible actions. Furthermore, with GABEK it is possible to galvanise stakeholders into action, because GABEK results, in the stakeholders' own words, promote ownership, as illustrated in the two case studies briefly discussed.

Here we have shown only the ability of GABEK to emerge a rich description of a problem situation at hand from the stakeholders themselves. Much more is possible with GABEK.

It allows us to connect and evaluate normal language opinions gathered in open interviews - as voiced by those affected, as well as politicians, scientists and experts. Causal networks and systems of evaluation are constructed in an intersubjective way. Their graphic representation leads to a holistic understanding of the situation and/or the problem field. We can derive strategically relevant core variables of the respective problem situations. New fields and potentials of action are thus opened up, the experiences of the participants can be put to creative uses.

GABEK develops its potential as an instrument of orientation, decision making and the discovery of measures, particularly in complex problem situations. It supports the development of strategic principles and operational measures relating to these. The great advantage of GABEK also lies in the fact *that those affected are included in the decision process*. The possibility of introducing authentic opinions is taken seriously. A plan is justified by authentic quotations of colleagues and others affected. Many individuals are able to identify with the plans and are therefore ready to support their realisation.

Possible areas of future research are associated with linking GABEK with some of the ways for measuring fuzziness as they are described in Pal and Bezdek (1994). While this will be a direct extension of this approach in the attempt to develop better understanding of fuzzy concepts in general and thus of better Fuzzy Set Models, it might be possible also to apply some ideas from Fuzzy Logic to extending in the future of the functions performed within a GABEK analysis. It might be possible to explore the application of Fuzzy Clustering Analysis as is described in Wang and Bell (1996) in the framework of GABEK as well as the general theoretical aspects of questionnaire construction, discussed in Bouchon-Meunier (1992).

References

Ackoff, R.L. 1979, "Resurrecting the future of Operational Research", *Journal of the Operational Research Society*, Vol. 30, No. 3, pp. 189-199.

Ackoff, R.L. 1981, "The art and science of mess management", *Interfaces*, Vol. 11, No. 1, pp. 20-26.

Bennett, P.G. and Cropper, S.A. 1986, "Helping people choose: conflict and other perspectives", in *Recent Developments in O.R.*, eds. V. Belton and R. O'Keefe, Pergamon Press, Oxford, England, pp. 13-25.

Bouchon-Meunier, B. 1992, "Questionnaires and fuzziness", in *An Introduction to Fuzzy Logic Applications in Intelligent Systems*, eds. R. Yager and L. Zadeh., Kluwer Academic Publishers, pp. 221-234.

Checkland, P.B. 1981, *Systems Thinking, Systems Practice*, John Wiley and Sons, Chichester, England.

Deetz, S. 1996, "Describing differences in approaches to Organization Science: rethinking Burrell and Morgan and their legacy", *Organization Science*, Vol. 7, No. 2, pp. 190-207.

Eden, C. 1989, "Using cognitive mapping for Strategic Options Development and Analysis (SODA)", in *Rational Analysis for a Problematic World: problem structuring methods for complexity, uncertainty and conflict*, ed. J. Rosenhead, John Wiley and Sons, Chichester, England, pp. 21-42.

Eden, C; Jones, S.; and Sims, D. 1983, *Messing About in Problems*, Pergamon Press, Oxford, England.

Friend, J.K. and Hickling, A. 1987, *Planning Under Pressure*, John Wiley and Sons, Chichester, England.

Howard, N. 1993, "The role of emotions in multi-organisational decision-making", *Journal of the Operational Research Society*, Vol. 44, No. 6, pp. 613-623.

Jain, R. 1980, "Fuzzism and real world problems", in *Fuzzy Sets Theory and Applications to Policy Analysis and Information Systems*, eds. P. Wang and S. Wang, Plenum Press, New York, pp. 129-132.

Kelly, G.A. 1955, *The Psychology of Personal Constructs*, Norton, New York.

Klir, G.J. 1976, "Identification of generative structures in empirical data", *International Journal of General Systems*, No. 3, pp. 89-104.

Mason, R.O. and Mitroff, I.I. 1981, *Challenging Strategic Planning Assumptions*, John Wiley and Sons, New York.

Morley, I. and Ormerod, R. 1996, "A language-action approach to Operational Research", *Journal of the Operations Research Society*, Vol. 47, No. 6, pp. 731-740.

Pal, N.R. and Bezdek, J. 1994, "Measures of fuzziness: a review and several new classes", in *Fuzzy Sets, Neural Networks and Soft Computing*, eds. R. Yager and L. Zadeh, Van Nostrand Reinhold, pp. 194-212.

Pask, Gordon. 1976, *Conversation Theory*, Elsevier, Amsterdam.

Pask, G and Zeeuw, G. de, . 1992: "Interactions of actors: theory and some applications",: *Outline and Overview*, Vol. 1, Manuskript, Universiteit Amsterdam.

Ramakrishan, R. 1995, *Multi Modeling: intervention as languaging*, Working Paper No. 1, Lincoln School of Management, University of Lincolnshire and Humberside.

Rittel, W.W.J. and Webber, M.M. 1973, "Dilemmas in a general theory of planning", *Policy Science*, Vol. 4, No. 2, pp. 155-169.

Rosenhead, J. 1980. "Planning under uncertainty 2: a methodology for robustness analysis", *Journal of the Operational Research Society*, Vol. 31, No. 4, pp. 331-341.

Rosenhead, J., ed. 1989, *Rational Analysis for a Problematic World: problem structuring methods for complexity, uncertainty and conflict*, John Wiley and Sons, Chichester, England.

Schon, D.A. 1987, *Educating the Reflective Practitioner: toward a new design for teaching and learning in the professions*, Jossey-Bass, San Francisco, California.

Shaw, M.L.G. and Gaines, B.R. 1984, "Deriving the constructs underlying decision", in *Fuzzy Sets and Decision Analysis*, eds. H.J. Zimmerman, L.A. Zadeh and B.R. Gaines, North Holland, pp. 335-355.

Smith, B. 1988, "Gestalt theory: an essay in Philosophy", in: *Foundations of Gestalt Theory*, ed. B. Smith, München/Wien (Philosophia), 1988, pp. 11-81.

Zelger, J. 1993, "GABEK: a new method for qualitative evaluation of interviews and model construction with PC-support", in *Enhancing Human Capacity to Solve Ecological and Socio-Economic Problems*, eds. E. Stuhler and M.O. Suilleabhain, Hampp-Verlagg, Munchen-Mering, pp. 128-172.

Zelger, J. 1995, "Cognitive mapping of social structures ", *Science and Science of Science*, No. 4, Kiew, pp. 88-103.

Zelger, J. 1996, "Linguistic knowledge processing by GABEK: the selection of relevant information from unordered verbal data", in *Philosophie and*

Verfahren Kreativer Selbstorganisation, Preprint No. 42, Institut für Philosophie der Universität Innsbrück.

Zelger, J. 1997, "Parallele und serielle wissensverarbeitung", in *Philosophie und Verfahren Kreativer Selbstorganisation Projektberichte,* ed. J. Zelger, Preprint No. 46, 47, 48, Institut für Philosophie der Universität Innsbrück.

A Linguistic Decision Model to Suppliers Selection in International Purchasing[1]

Francisco Herrera*, Enrique López**, Cristina Mendaña** and Miguel A. Rodríguez**

*Computer Science and Artificial Intelligence Department
University of Granada
18071 Granada, Spain
E-mail: herrera@decsai.uge.es
** Economy and Business Management Department
University of León
24071-León, Spain
E-mail:{elg/cmc/mrf}@unileon.es

Abstract

The traditional approach to suppliers selection based on price is simplistic because the information held for the decision making model is more complex and without precision in some tasks. There are qualitative factors that demand some judgement to determine a suppliers selection. Therefore, the linguistic representation of the of the knowledge available allows the problem to be recognised as in real life. This paper aims to supply a linguistic decision model to purchasing management problems.

Keywords: global sourcing, purchasing, suppliers selection, relationships between inputs, linguistic labels, linguistic operators, linguistic decision model.

1 Introduction

In recent years, purchasing has undergone a total change of perspective: from an operational function to a strategic one. To cope with the increased significance of purchasing and environmental uncertainties, buyers should no longer just be processors of requisitions and order forms, but increasingly need to take on strategic roles within organisations. They take part in decisions concerning supply chain management, product input supplies alternatives for the firm and

---

[1] This research has been partially supported by DGICYT PB95-0058

they participate in future strategy formulation processes. In doing so, purchasing decision-making is improved.

As importance of purchasing decisions has increased, so has the basis of these decisions. Due to the increased attention of top management for the purchasing function, purchasing managers more and more are confronted with questions concerning the rational justifications of their decisions and the corresponding supply performance At the same time, as a result of the more complex, dynamic, turbulent and volatile industrial environment, the complexity and opaqueness of this decision making basis has increased as well.

As purchasing has an important effect on the profitability of an organisation and forms a potential source of profit for many industrial companies, purchasing should be a well-equipped, professional organisational function and an integrated part in the organisation [Van Weele, 1994]. So, a professional approach of purchasing decisions contributes to seizing opportunities that can result in savings as well as a competitive advantage for an organisation. It is essential to today's performance of an organisation as a whole that these benefits achievable through good purchasing practices are obtained. This includes the use of sound decision making bases in purchasing.

Shortly, purchasing is the „process of buying". Identifying and selection suppliers are the most important responsibilities of the purchasing department. Purchasing managers and other charged with determining the standards attained by each supplier in the requirements needed for the demanded good prefer to use natural language for it. This is because it is quite divorced from reality to express these standards in terms of strict numerical values. Using linguistic information, natural linguistic labels, may lead to the loss of precision that numbers can give, but there is a positive counterpart in grater closeness to the problem [Zadeh, 1975].

The objective of this paper is to supply a linguistic decision model to suppliers selection. In order to do that, the paper is organized as follows. Section 2 introduces the suppliers selection problem; Section 3 presents a fuzzy linguistic model for suppliers selection; Section 4 proposes a bicriteria linguistic selection model to choose the suppliers; Section 5 presents an illustrative practical application; and Section 6 points out some concluding remarks.

2 Supplier Selection

2.1 Purchasing Objectives and Functions

Purchasing is the „process of buying". It is widely assumed that purchasing is exclusively responsibility of the purchasing department. However, the function is much broader and, if is carried out effectively, all departments in the company are involved. Obtaining the right material, in the right quantities, with the right delivery (time and place), from the right source, and at the right price are all purchasing functions.

Choosing the right material requires input from the marketing, engineering, manufacturing, and purchasing departments. Quantities and delivery of finished goods are established by the needs of the market. However, manufacturing planning and control must decide when to order which raw materials so that market demands can be satisfied. Purchasing department is, therefore responsible for placing the orders and for ensuring that the goods arrive on time.

The purchasing department has the major responsibility for locating suitable sources of supply and for negotiating prices. Input from other departments are required for finding and evaluating sources of supply and for helping the purchasing department in price negotiation.

Purchasing is responsible for establishing the flow of materials into the firm, following-up with the supplier, and expediting delivery. Missed deliveries can create havoc with manufacturing and sales, but purchasing can reduce problems for both areas, further adding to the profit.

The objectives of purchasing can be divided into four categories [Arnold, 1996]:

- Obtaining goods and services of the required quantity and quality.
- Obtaining goods and services at the lowest cost.
- Ensuring the best possible service and prompt delivery by the supplier.
- Developing and maintaining good supplier and developing potential suppliers.

To satisfy these objectives, some basic functions must be performed:

- Determining purchasing specifications: right quality, right quantity, and right delivery (time and place).
- Selecting supplier (right source).
- Negotiating terms and conditions of purchase.
- Issuing and administration of purchase orders

Identifying and selecting suppliers are the most important responsibilities of the purchasing department, since it makes use of all the information available from the other functions. So, our paper aims to give a solution to select the suppliers team that maximise the purchasing utility when the information on held is complex, imprecise or vague.

2.2 Suppliers Selection in an Atmosphere of Uncertainty Descriptive Analysis and Modeling of the Problem

The objective of purchasing is to gather all the right things together: quality, quantity, delivery, and price. Once the decision is made about what to buy, the selection of the right supplier is the next most important purchasing decision. A good supplier is the one that has the technology to make the product to the required quality, has the capacity to make the quantities needed, and can run the business well enough to make a profit and still sell a product competitively.

The previous section discussed the importance of functions, quality, service and price specifications. These are what the supplier is expressed to provide and are the basis for selection and evaluation. Considering this, there are several factors in selecting a supplier [Arnold, 1996]:

- **Technical ability.** The supplier must have the technical ability to make or supply the product wanted. Also, he has to assist in improving the products and have a program of product development and improvement. These capacities are important since, often, the buyer will depend upon the supplier to provide product improvements that will enhance or reduce the cost of the buyer's products. Sometimes the supplier can suggest changes in product specifications that will improve the product and reduce the cost.
- **Manufacturing capability.** Manufacturing must be able to meet the specifications for the product consistently while making as few flaws as possible. This means that the supplier's manufacturing facilities must be able to supply the quality and quantity of the products wanted. The supplier must have a good quality control program, competent and capable manufacturing personnel, and good manufacturing planning and control systems to ensure on time delivery. These are important in ensuring that the supplier can provide the quality and quantity wanted.
- **Reliability.** In selecting a supplier, it is desirable to choose a reputable, stable, and financially strong one. If the relationship is to continue, there must be an atmosphere of mutualtrust and assurance that the supplier is financially strong enough to stay in business.
- **After sales service.** If the product is of a technical nature or likely to need replacement parts or technical support, the supplier must have a good after-sales service. This should include a good service organisation and inventory of service parts.
- **Supplier location.** Sometimes it is desirable that the supplier is located near the buyer, or at least maintain an inventory locally. A close location helps to shorten delivery times and means emergency shortages can delivery quickly.
- **Price.** The supplier should be able to provide competitive prices. This does not necessarily mean the lowest price. It is the one that takes into account the ability of the supplier to provide the necessary goods in the quantity and quality wanted, at the time wanted, as well as any other services needed.
- **Other considerations.** Sometimes other factors such as credit terms, reciprocal business, and willingness of the supplier to hold inventory for the buyer should be considered.

Some factors in evaluating potential suppliers are quantitative. Price is the obvious example. On the other hand, there are qualitative factors that demand some judgement to determine them. These are usually set out in a descriptive fashion. The supplier's technical competence might be an example.

The challenge is finding some method of combining these two major factors that will enable a buyer to choose the best suppliers.

Thus, if the best possible value is to be achieved from suppliers selection, this must not merely consider the requirements of each of the goods and suppliers to be chosen, in comparison with the capacities of the candidates for suppliers. It should also address the compatibility of the suppliers, because if they are chosen they will belong to a team made up of suppliers with whom they must get along in order to achieve a common goal.

An attempt to collect and evaluate all this information arises interest in the possible application here of the theory of fuzzy sets [Zadeh, 1965; Kufmann and Gil-Aluja, 1992] with the aim of being able to handle suitably the uncertainty which is characteristic of the decision-making processes in suppliers selection. This paper specifically proposes the use of linguistic labels to represent the information on these variables and lead to a decision-making model, which is able to handle such information, [Zadeh, 1995].

In addition, if the problem is selecting suppliers for several goods, then those inputs of greatest importance for the purchasing management should be weighted in some way, as these are the ones which should be most effectively matched to the ideal supplier.

Referring to the relationship liaisons along a supply chain we can have two main different typologies of structures: a tree structure and a network structure [Bellandi *et al.*, 1997]. The first one, shown in Figure 1, is made by a master company, which produces the finished product and attends to its marketing, makes up the tree structure, by first level suppliers. So, in the tree structure there is only vertical teamwork liaisons, therefore do not occur side liaisons between suppliers.

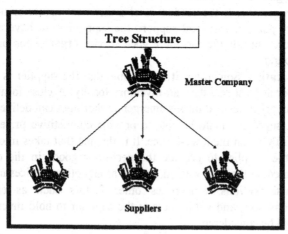

Figure 1

On the other hand, in the network structure, shown in Figure 2, we find both vertical and horizontal liaisons.

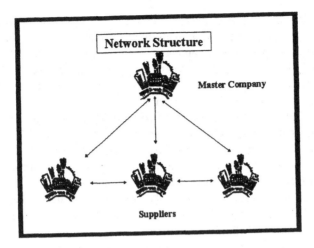

Figure 2

In this work we are referring to the network structure because include the tree one. This justifies looking into the possible relationships among demanded goods, and into the level of compatibility between suppliers, during the selection process. Such considerations are often made in a subjective way, so that the use of linguistic labels would allow greater closeness to the realities of the decision-making procedure being investigated.

Once the degree to which each candidate for supplier has a given ability is established, this is compared to the capacities stated in the profile set up for the good demanded in question. This shows how far each candidate matches up to them, and allows an order of preference among candidates to be drawn up, though not without taking into account their compatibility, which is an objective in parallel with the good match of candidates for supplier to the requirements.

3 A Fuzzy-Linguistic Model for Suppliers Selection

3.1 Linguistic Information

Normally, in a quantitative situation the information required is expressed as numerical values. However, when working in qualitative areas such as purchasing management, which are characterised by vague or imprecise knowledge, the information cannot be set out in a precise numerical way. Thus, it would be a more realistic approach to use linguistic information instead of numbers, provided that the variables involved in the problem lend themselves to expression in this manner [Zadeh, 1975].

A linguistic variable differs from a numerical one in that its values are not numbers, but words or sentences in a natural or artificial language. Since words, in general, are less precise than numbers, the concept of a linguistic variable serves the purpose of providing a means of approximated characterisation of phenomena, which are too complex, or too ill-defined to be amenable to their description in conventional quantitative terms.

Usually, depending on the problem domain, an appropriate linguistic term set is chosen and used to describe the vague or imprecise knowledge. The elements in the term set will determine the granularity of the uncertainty, that is the level of distinction among different counting of uncertainty. Bonissone and Decker studied the use of term sets with an odd cardinal, representing the mid term an assess of "approximately 0.5", with the rest of the terms being placed symmetrically around it and the limit of granularity 11 or no more than 13 [Bonissone and Decker, 1986].

On the other hand, the semantic of the elements in the term set is given by fuzzy numbers defined on the [0,1] interval, which are described by membership functions. Because the linguistic assessments are just approximate ones given by the individuals, we can consider that linear trapezoidal membership functions are good enough to capture the vagueness of those linguistic assessments, since it may be impossible or unnecessary to obtain more accurate values. This representation is achieved by the 4-tuple $(a_i, b_i, \alpha_i, \beta_i)$, the first two parameters indicate the interval in which the membership value is 1; the third and fourth parameters indicate the left and right width. Formally speaking, it seems difficult to accept that all individuals should agree on the same membership function associated to linguistic terms, and therefore, there are not any universality distribution concepts.

This paper supports the possibility of establishing in linguistic terms the information relating to the weighting of the requirements needed. It would appear clear that a purchasing manager might not know in a precise numerical way what the weighting for a requirement is, but could indicate it in normal linguistic terms. To estimate weightings, and indeed other features, it has been chosen to use a set of nine linguistic labels [Bonissone and Decker, 1986]. A graphical example is shown in Figure 3.

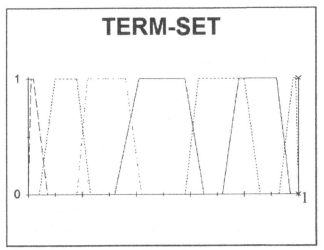

Figure 3

And the 4-tuples associated are:

EEssential	(1, 1, 0, 0)
VH	Very High	(.98, .99, .05, .01)
FH	Fairly High	(.78, .92, .06, .05)
H	High	(.63, .80, .05, .06)
M	Moderate	(.41, .58, .09, .07)
LLow	(.22, .36, .05, .06)
FL	Fairly Low	(.1, .18, .06, .05)
VL	Very Low	(.01, .02, .01, .05)
U	Unnecessary	(0, 0, 0, 0)

3.2 Linguistic Decision Model for Suppliers Selection

The model proposed here consists of the following phases:

1. **Goods demanded requirements.** Step one is to determine for what goods are demanded.

$$G = \{G_1, G_2, ..., G_m\}$$

Each good has also associated several requirements, such as quality, delivery, etc.:

$$R = \{R_1, R_2, ..., R_p\}$$

together with the weighting that each requirement has for the demanded goods

$$IR = \left\{ \begin{matrix} IR_{11},...,IR_{1p} \\ \vdots \quad \vdots \\ IR_{m1},...,IR_{mp} \end{matrix} \right\}, \ IR_{ij} \in W$$

For the feature weighting, the labels that are proposed are the following:

W={Essential, Very High, Fairly High, High, Moderate,
Low, Fairly Low, Very Low, Unnecessary}

In addition, when suppliers are being selected for several goods, the purchasing manager or decision-maker may consider that not all of the goods have the same importance, and prefer solutions aimed at putting the most suitable supplier into the most crucial good. For this reason, a label associated with each position must be included to show the weighting that the good has for the recruitment procedure, which is under way. This characteristic is defined in this paper in exactly the same way as requirements, that is, with nine labels:

$$IG = \left\{ IG_1, IG_2,...,IG_m \right\}, IG_i \in W$$

Moreover, since the goods are not independent of one another, the links between them should be analysed, as also the weighting of such links. Here, too, the use of nine labels is felt appropriate:

$$RG = \left\{ \begin{matrix} -,RG_{12},......,RG_{1m} \\ \vdots \quad\quad \vdots \\ RG_{m1},...,RG_{mm-1} - \end{matrix} \right\}, \ RG_{ij} \in W$$

2. **Suppliers levels and relationships.** Once the demanded goods have been characterised, the candidates for suppliers are considered, $S = \left\{ S_1, S_2,...,S_n \right\}$. Information relating to them includes two types:

- the operational levels, which they demonstrate in the varying requirements needed for the demanded goods,

$$L = \left\{ \begin{matrix} L_{11},...,L_{1p} \\ \vdots \quad \vdots \\ L_{n1},...,L_{np} \end{matrix} \right\}, \ L_{ij} \in LL$$

with the next set of labels associated:

LL={Optimum, Very High, Fairly High, High, Moderate,
Low, Fairly Low, Very Low, Lowest}

- and the relationships linking suppliers with one another:

$$RS = \begin{Bmatrix} -, RS_{12}, \ldots, RS_{1n} \\ \vdots \qquad \vdots \\ RS_{n1}, \ldots, RS_{nn-1}, - \end{Bmatrix}, \; RS_{ij} \in R$$

with the next set of labels associated:

R={Excellent, Very Good, Fairly good, Good, Indifferent,
Bad, Fairly Bad, Very Bad, Vile}

Using this approach, it comes down to a problem of optimisation using imprecise information and having two aims or criteria:

- good levels in the requirements needed for the demanded goods and
- good relationships among suppliers for related goods.

We will take in consideration these two criteria for designing the linguistic decision model.

Although we have described different term sets for each variable, in order to operate with their and taking into account that all of then have the same number of labels, only the first one will be considered. The others set of labels will be changed to this one from an operative point of view assuming a general label set. $L = \{l_0, l_1, \ldots, l_8\}$ and the corresponding transformation, for example l_3 is equivalent to *Bad (R), Low (LL) and Low (W)*.

4. A Linguistic Selection Model for Suppliers Selection

4.1. Linguistic Aggregation

In this subsection, we analyse two ways to aggregate linguistic information and two linguistic operators used in this paper.

Firstly, we are going to analyse the information to be aggregated in a linguistic process. Clearly, there are two types of linguistic information:

1. Non-weighted linguistic information. This is the situation in which we have only one set of linguistic values to aggregate.
2. Weighted linguistic information. This is the situation in which we have a set of linguistic values to aggregate, for example opinions and each value is characterised by an importance degree, indicating its weight in the overall set of values.

In both cases, linguistic aggregation operators are needed that combine appropriately the information, in such a way, that the final aggregation is the "best" representation of the overall opinions. In the following subsections, we shall present the operators that we are going to consider in both cases.

4.1.1 Non-weighted linguistic information

In the literature various aggregation operators of linguistic information have been proposed. Some are based on the use of the associated membership functions of the labels [Bonissone and Decker, 1986; Tong, 1980], and others act by direct computation on labels [Delgado *et al.*, 1993; Herrera and Verdegay, 1993; Yager 1992; Yager, 1995]. Here we will use the later approach. We consider two operators, the linguistic ordered weighted averaging (LOWA) operator presented in [Herrera and Verdegay, 1993] and the inverse-linguistic ordered weighted averaging (I-LOWA) operator presented in [Herrera and Herrera-Viedma, 1997].

Definition of the LOWA operator. *Let* $A = \{a_1,...,a_m\}$ *be a set of labels to be aggregated, then the LOWA operator,* ϕ, *is defined as*

$$\phi(a_1,...,a_m) = W \cdot B^T = C^m\{w_k, b_k, k = 1,...,m\} =$$
$$= w_1 \otimes b_1 \oplus (1-w_1) \otimes C^{m-1}\{\beta_h, b_h, h = 2,...,m\}$$

where: $W = [w_1,...,w_m]$, *is a weighting vector, such that:* $(i) w_i \in [0,1]$ *and,* $(ii) \sum w_i = 1$. $\beta_h = w_h / \sum_2^m w_k, h = 2,...,m$, *and* $B = \{b_1,...,b_m\}$ *is a vector associated to* A, *such that,*

$$B = \sigma(A) = \{a_{\sigma(1)},...,a_{\sigma(n)}\}$$

where, $a_{\sigma(j)} \leq a_{\sigma(i)} \forall i \leq j$, *with* σ *being a permutation over the set of labels* A. C^m *is the convex combination operator of m labels,* $\otimes$ *is the general product of a label by a positive real number and* $\oplus$ *is the general addition of labels defined in* [Delgado et al., 1993b].

If $m = 2$, *then* C^2 *is defined as*

$$C^2\{w_i, b_i, i = 1,2\} = w_1 \otimes s_j \oplus (1-w_1) \otimes s_i = s_k, s_j, s_i \in S, (j \geq i)$$

such that $k = \min\{T, i + round(w_1 \cdot (j-i))\}$, *where "round" is the usual round operation, and* $b_1 = s_j, b_2 = s_i$.

If $w_j = 1$ *and* $w_i = 0$ *with* $i \neq j \forall i$, *then the convex combination is defined as:*

$$C^m\{w_i, b_i, i = 1,...,m\} = b_j.$$

Definition of the I-LOWA operator. *An I-LOWA (Inverse-Linguistic Ordered Weighted Averaging) operator, ϕ^I, is a type of LOWA operator, in which*

$$B = \sigma^I(A) = \{a_{\sigma(1)}, ... a_{\sigma(n)}\}$$

where, $a_{\sigma(i)} \leq a_{\sigma(j)} \quad \forall i \leq j$.

If m=2, then it is defined as

$$C^2\{w_i, b_i, i = 1,2\} = w_1 \otimes s_j \oplus (1 - w_1) \otimes s_i = s_k, s_j, s \in S, (j \leq i)$$

such that $k = \min\{T, i + round(w_1 \cdot (j - i))\}$.

The LOWA and I-LOWA operators are increasing monotonous, commutative, "around" operators, which verify the axioms: Unrestricted domain, Unanimity or Idempotence, Positive association of social and individual values, Independence of irrelevant alternatives, Citizen sovereignty, Neutrality [Herrera *et al.*, 1996].

In the OWA operators the weights measure the importance of a value (in relation to other values) with independence of the information source. How to calculate the weighting vector of LOWA operator, W, is a basic question to be solved. A possible solution is that the weights represent the concept of fuzzy majority in the aggregation of LOWA operator using fuzzy linguistic quantifiers [Zadeh, 1983]. Yager proposed an interesting way to compute the weights of the OWA aggregation operator, which, in the case of a non-decreasing proportional fuzzy linguistic quantifier, Q, is given by this expression [Yager, 1988]:

$$w_i = Q(i/n) - Q((i-1)/n), i = 1,...,n;$$

being the membership function of Q, as follows:

$$Q(r) = \begin{cases} 0 & \text{if } r < a \\ \dfrac{r-a}{b-a} & \text{if } a \leq r \leq b \\ 1 & \text{if } r > b \end{cases}$$

with $a, b, r \in [0,1]$. Some examples of non-decreasing proportional fuzzy linguistic quantifiers are: "most" (0.3, 0.8), "at least half" (0, 0.5) and "as many as possible" (0.5, 1). When a fuzzy linguistic quantifier, Q, is used to compute the weights of LOWA operator, ϕ, it is symbolised by ϕ_Q. Similarly happens for the I-LOWA operator, i.e., in this case it is symbolised by ϕ_Q^I.

Some examples of proportional quantifiers are shown in Figure 4, where the parameters, (a, b) are (0.3, 0.8), (0, 0.5) and (0.5, 1), respectively.

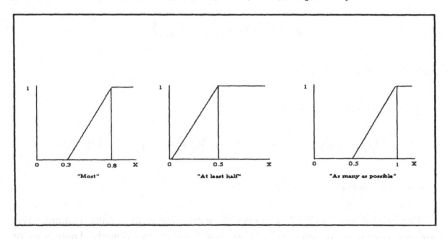

Figure 4

4.1.2 Weighted linguistic information

We may find situations where the handle information is not equally important, that is managing weighted information. In order to aggregate weighted information, we have to combine linguistic information with the weights, which involves the transformation of the weighted information under the importance degrees.

According to these ideas, the linguistic weighted aggregation (LWA) operator to aggregate linguistic weighted information is provided in [Herrera and Herrera-Viedma, 1997], which was defined using the LOWA operator [Herrera and Verdegay, 1993], the concept of fuzzy majority represented by a fuzzy linguistic quantifiers [Zadeh, 1983], and two families of linguistic connectives [Herrera and Herrera-Viedma, 1997]. In the following we review it.

Definition of the LWA operator. *The aggregation of set of weighted individual opinions,* $\{(c_1, a_1), \dots, (c_m, a_m)\}$, *according to the LWA operator is defined as*

$$(c_E, a_E) = LWA[(c_1, a_1), \dots, (c_m, a_m)],$$

where the importance degree of the opinion of the group, c_E, *is obtained as*

$$c_E = \phi_Q(c_1, \dots, c_m).$$

and, the opinion of the group, a_E, is obtained as

$$a_E = f[g(c_1,a_1),...,g(c_m,a_m)],$$

where $f = \{\phi_Q, \phi_Q^I\}$ is an linguistic aggregation operator of transformed information and g is an importance transformation function, such that $g \in LC^\rightarrow$ if $f = \phi_Q$ and $g \in LI^\rightarrow$ if $f = \phi_Q^I$, being $LC^\rightarrow$ the following linguistic conjunction functions:

1. The classical MIN operator:

$$LC_1^\rightarrow(c,a) = MIN(c,a)$$

2. The nilpotent MIN operator:

$$LC_2^\rightarrow(c,a) = \begin{cases} MIN(c,a) & \text{if } c > Neg(a) \\ 0 & \text{otherwise} \end{cases}$$

3. The weakest conjunction:

$$LC_3^\rightarrow(c,a) = \begin{cases} MIN(c,a) & \text{if } MAX(c,a) = s_T \\ 0 & \text{otherwise} \end{cases}$$

and $LI^\rightarrow$ any of the following linguistic implication:

1. Kleene-Dienes's implication function:
$$LI_1^\rightarrow(c,a) = MIN(c,a)$$

2. Godel's implication function:
$$LI_2^\rightarrow(c,a) = \begin{cases} s_t & \text{if } c \le a \\ a & \text{otherwise} \end{cases}$$

3. Fodor's implication function:
$$LI_3^\rightarrow(c,a) = \begin{cases} s_t & \text{if } c \le a \\ MAX(Neg(c),a) & \text{otherwise} \end{cases}$$

Where "MAX" stands for maximum operator and "MIN" stands for minimum operator.

It should be observed that LWA operator tries to reduce the effect of elements with low importance. In order to do so, when $f = \phi_Q$, the elements with low importance are transformed into small values and when $f = \phi_Q^I$ into large ones.

4.2 Selection Model

Let $S = \{S_1, S_2, \ldots, S_m\}$ be a candidates for suppliers solution obtained in some way, where $S_i \in \{1, 2, \ldots, N\}$.

For evaluating the solutions we propose a model that uses the information represented by linguistic labels, according with those aforementioned criteria, good levels in the requirements needed for the demanded goods and good relationships among suppliers for related goods. Therefore we obtain a bicriteria linguistic evaluation for every candidate for suppliers solution.

Criterion 1. Good level in the requirements.

- Step 1. First, to obtain a value of the supplier suitability on the requirements of a demanded good (S_i, G_i), we will apply an LOWA operator as follows:
  - Step 1.1. For each demanded good, G_i, there are p requirements which define it, with p degrees of importance for each requirement, IR_{ij}. Thus, to assess the suitability of the supplier S_i for the demanded good a link must be established between the level that the person has of a given requirement and the weight assigned to that requirement for the demanded good. To achieve this, the proposal is to use the linguistic conjunction MIN that penalises solutions with suppliers with a low level in important requirements.

$$g_1(IR_{ij}, L_{S,j}) = LC_1^{\rightarrow}(IR_{ij}, L_{S,j}), j = 1, \ldots, p$$

  - Step 1.2. After that, to obtain a label representing the level of the supplier in the demanded good, we propose to use a LOWA with the „most" linguistic quantifier. Therefore the final label is:

$$Y_{S_i} = f(g_1(IR_{i1}, L_{S_i1}), \ldots, g_1(IR_{im2}, L_{S_ip})) =$$
$$= \phi_Q(g_1(IR_{i1}, L_{S_i1}), \ldots, g_1(IR_{ip}, L_{S_ip}))$$

- Step 2. Second, to obtain a value of the solution suitability on the requirements of all the demanded goods, we will apply again an LWA operator as follows:
  - Step 2.1. By taking the steps outlined above, it is possible to obtain a linguistic label setting a value on the ability of each supplier relative

to each demanded good. However, the intention is to give an overall value covering the suitability of suppliers to demanded goods that will include the fact that the various demanded goods are themselves of different levels of importance. In view of this, it is proposed to use again a classical conjunction MIN, so that the solution as to suitability for demanded goods may be obtained in the form of a linguistic label.

$$g_2(IG_i, Y_{S_i}) = LC_1^{\rightarrow}(IG_i, Y_{S_i}), i = 1, \ldots, m$$

- Step 2.2. Thus, to obtain a label representing the level of the overall solution, we propose to use a LOWA with the „most" linguistic quantifier.

$$Y_S = f(g_2(IG_1, Y_{S_1}), \ldots, g_2(IG_m, Y_{S_m})) =$$
$$= \phi_Q(g_2(IG_1, Y_{S_1}), \ldots, g_2(IG_m, Y_{S_m}))$$

With these steps, we have obtained a linguistic evaluation of the candidates for suppliers in the requirements of the demanded good. Nevertheless, the goodness of the solutions will also be determined by the relationships between the suppliers included in them. On the one hand, the connections between demanded goods are known, as is the weighting for each, and on the other the relationships among suppliers are known.

Criterion 2. Good relationship among the suppliers selected.

- Step 3. First, to obtain a value of the suppliers relationships of each demanded good, X'_i, we will apply a LWA operator as follows:
  - Step 3.1. So, a link is established for each demanded good between the weighting of its connections to other demanded goods and the degree of relationship that the supplier selected to the demanded good has with suppliers selected for related demanded goods. To achieve this, the proposed method would be to use the „Keene and Diene" Linguistic Implication.

$$g_3(RG_{ij}, RS_{S_i S_j}) = LI_1^{\rightarrow}(RG_{ij}, RS_{S_i S_j}), i = 1, \ldots, m$$

- Step 3.2. To obtain a label representing the relationship of the suppliers selected of each demanded good, X'_i, we propose to use an I-LOWA operator with the „most" quantifier.

$$V_i = f(g_3(RG_{i1}, RS_{S_i S_1}), \ldots, g_3(RG_{im}, RS_{S_i S_m})) =$$

$$= \phi_Q^I (g_3(RP_{i1}, RC_{S_i S_1}), \dots, g_3(RP_{im}, RC_{S_i S_m}))$$

- Step 4. Once this has been done, to set a value of the relationship to the overall solution, the proposal is to use an LOWA operator with the „most" quantifier.

$$V_S = f(V_1, \dots, V_m) = \phi_Q(V_1, \dots, V_m)$$

With the last three steps, we have obtained a linguistic evaluation of the relationship among the suppliers selected in the solution.

Finally, we have obtained two linguistic labels (Y_s, V_s), that are the evaluation for each feasible solution, S, according to the two objectives of the problem: the level of the suppliers selected on each demanded good and the relationship among them.

5 EXAMPLE OF A PRACTICAL APPLICATION

To check the working of the decision method, an operational model was developed. Several examples were tried out, including the one described below. This deals with the choice of suppliers for a wheel of a car factory. In this way, an attempt was made to demonstrate the usefulness the model being proposed in this paper could have for real problems from the business world.

5.1 Introduction to the Problem. Linguistic Model

Let it be imagined that a car factory wishes to purchase the goods necessary to manufacture a wheel. The first step is to determine which goods are to be acquired, what status in terms of urgency each is to have in relation to the purchase process and what monetary quantity is expecting to be purchased (monetary units). Thus, we might have:

Demanded Good	Status (IG)
1 SCREW	High
2 NUT	Fairly High
3 TYRE	Moderate
4 RIM	Low
5 HUB-CAB	Very Low

For each good, the requirements which must be developed and the weighting that each has for the supply in question are known, as is shown in Chart 1:

IR_{ji}	SCREW	NUT	TYRE	RIM	HUB-CAB
Technical Ability	Essential	-	-	-	-
Technological Innovation	Fairly High	-	-	-	-
Manufacturing Capacity	Fairly High	Moderate	Fairly High	Moderate	Very High
Fast Supply	High	-	-	-	-
Reciprocal Business	Moderate	-	-	-	-
Standardisation	-	Low	-	Fairly High	-
Reliability	-	High	-	Fairly High	-
After Sales Service	-	Fairly High	-	Low	Fairly High
Supplier Location	-	Very high	Fairly Low	-	-
Financially Strong	-	-	Moderate	-	Moderate
Flexibility	-	-	High	-	Very High
Credit Terms	-	-	Very High	-	Very Low
Quality	-	-	-	High	-

Chart 1

In addition, the last piece of information needed in setting up these demanded goods would be the required compatibility between each supplier and the others and the importance set on such relationships, as is shown in Chart 2.

RG_{ij}	GOOD 1	GOOD 2	GOOD 3	GOOD 4	GOOD 5
GOOD 1	-	Fairly High	High	Moderate	Fairly Low
GOOD 2	Fairly High	-	Moderate	Moderate	Low
GOOD 3	Low	Very High	-	Very High	High
GOOD 4	Low	Moderate	Very High	-	Very High
GOOD 5	Fairly Low	Moderate	Fairly High	Very High	-

Chart 2

Once the demanded goods involved in the selection procedure have been determined, the candidates for suppliers must next be considered. Let it be imagined that there are fifteen companies who might be able to provide the goods necessaries for the wheel.

Company	Name	Good Supplied
1	S.1	NUT
2	S.2	SCREW
3	S.3	TYRE

4	S.4	HUB-CAB
5	S.5	RIM
6	S.6	HUB-CAB
7	S.7	RIM
8	S.8	TYRE
9	S.9	NUT
10	S.10	SCREW
11	S.11	HUB-CAB
12	S.12	RIM
13	S.13	TYRE
14	S.14	NUT
15	S.15	SCREW

For each one it is necessary to find out by some appropriate means the levels in each of the requirements required for the supplies, as shown in Chart 3.

Finally, as there are links between the goods, the candidates for suppliers must be looked at in order to find out the relationships that there would be between them, as shown in Chart 4.

5.2 Linguistic Decision Model

Let $S=\{S.2, S.1, S.3, S.5, S.4\}$ be a possible solution. We are going to apply the decision model on it for obtaining the linguistic evaluation associated to the criteria.

Criterion 1. Good level in the requirements.

- **Step 1.1.**

Good 1	Tech. Ability	Tech. Imnov.	Manuf. Capac.	Fast Supply	Recip. Business
IR_{ij}	Essential	Fairly High	Fairly High	High	Moderate
$L_{s_{i,j}}$	Very High	Fairly High	Moderate	Low	Very Low
$LC_1^{\rightarrow}$	Very High	Fairly High	Moderate	Low	Very Low

Good 2	Manuf. Capac.	Standardisation	Reliability	After Sales Ser,	Supplier Loc.
IR_{ij}	Moderate	Low	High	Very High	Very High
$L_{s_{i,j}}$	Fairly High	High	Moderate	Very High	High
$LC_1^{\rightarrow}$	Moderate	Low	Moderate	Very High	High

Good 3	Manuf. Capac.	Supplier Loc.	Financ. Strong	Flexibility	Credit Terms
IR_{ij}	Fairly High	Fairly High	Moderate	High	Very High
$L_{s_{i,j}}$	Moderate	Moderate	Low	Low	Low
$LC_1^{\rightarrow}$	Moderate	Moderate	Low	Low	Low

L_{ij}	S.1	S.2	S.3	S.4	S.5	S.6	S.7	S.8	S.9	S.10	S.11	S.12	S.13	S.14	S.15
Technical Ability	Very High	Very high	Low	High	High	High	Fairly High	Very High	Very High	Very High	Fairly High	High	High	Moderate	Moderate
Technological Innovation	Fairly High	Fairly High	Moderate	Fairly High	Fairly High	Moderate	Moderate	High	Fairly High	Fairly High	Low	High	High	Fairly High	Fairly High
Manufacturing Capacity	Moderate	Fairly High	Moderate	Fairly Low	Low	High	Moderate	Fairly High	Moderate	High	Fairly High	High	Fairly High	Moderate	High
Quality	High	High	Fairly Low	Low	Fairly High	Low	Low	Moderate	High	High	Fairly Low	Fairly High	Moderate	High	Moderate
Standardisation	High	High	Low	Moderate	Fairly Low	Fairly High	Moderate	Fairly High	High	High	Very High	Low	Moderate	Fairly High	High
Reliability	Very Low	Moderate	Moderate	Fairly Low	Lowest	High	Fairly Low	Lowest	Very High	Moderate	Moderate	Moderate	Lowest	Very High	Moderate
Financially Strong	Fairly High	Fairly High	Low	High	Moderate	Fairly High	High	Very High	Fairly High	Fairly High	Very High	Moderate	Very High	Fairly High	Moderate
After-Sales Service	Very High	Very High	Moderate	High	Fairly Low	Very High	Fairly High	Fairly High	Very High	Very High	Fairly High	Low	High	Very High	Very High
Flexibility	High	High	Low	Moderate	Very Low	Fairly High	High	Low	High	High	High	Moderate	Low	High	Moderate
Supplier Location	High	High	Moderate	Fairly High	Low	Fairly High	Low	Fairly High	High	High	High	Moderate	Fairly High	High	High
Fast supply	Low	Fairly High	Moderate	Moderate	Very Low	Moderate	Low	Fairly Low	Low	Fairly High	Low	Low	Moderate	Low	Moderate
Credit terms	Fairly High	Fairly High	Low	High	Lowest	High	Fairly Low	Very High	Fairly High	Fairly High	Fairly High	Fairly Low	Very High	Fairly High	Fairly High
Reciprocal Business	Very Low	Moderate	Moderate	Fairly Low	Lowest	Fairly High	Low	Lowest	Very High	Moderate	High	Moderate	Lowest	Fairly High	Moderate

Chart 3

RS_{ij}	C1	C2	C3	C4	C5	C6	C7	C8	C9	C10	C11	C12	C13	C14	C15
C 1	-	ery Good	Bad	Good	Indifferent	Very Bad	Indifferent	Very Bad	Vile	Very Good	Bad	Good	Indiffe-ren	Fairly Bad	Indifferent
C 2	Fairly Bad	-	Bad	Indifferent	Indifferent	Good	Indifferent	Fairly Bad	Good	Very Good	Bad	Good	Indiffe-ren	Fairly Bad	Indifferent
C 3	Very Good	Fairly Good	-	Bad	Good	Indifferent	Good	Vile	Very Good	Very Good	Bad	Good	Indiffe-ren	Fairly Bad	Indifferent
C 4	Fairly Bad	Good	Indiffe-ren	-	Bad	Good	Indifferent	Indiffe-ren	Fairly Bad	Very Good	Bad	Good	Indiffe-ren	Fairly Bad	Indifferent
C 5	Very Good	Good	Good	Bad	-	Good	Fairly Bad	Fairly Bad	Vile	Very Good	Bad	Good	Indiffe-ren	Fairly Bad	Indifferent
C 6	Very Good	Good	Indiffe-ren	Bad	Good	-	Indifferent	Bad	Good	Very Good	Bad	Good	Indiffe-ren	Fairly Bad	Indifferent
C 7	Bad	Good	Good	Fairly Good	Very Good	Fairly Good	-	Very Bad	Fairly Bad	Very Good	Bad	Good	Indiffe-ren	Fairly Bad	Indifferent
C 8	Bad	Good	Good	Very Good	Indifferent	Fairly Good	Indifferent	-	Fairly Bad	Very Good	Bad	Good	Indiffe-ren	Fairly Bad	Indifferent
C 9	Vile	ery Good	Bad	Good	Indifferent	Fairly Bad	Indifferent	Very Bad	-	Very Good	Bad	Good	Indiffe-ren	Fairly Bad	Indifferent
C 10	Fairly Bad	ery Good	Bad	Indiffe-ren	Indifferent	Good	Indifferent	Fairly Bad	Good	-	Bad	Good	Indiffe-ren	Fairly Bad	Indifferent
C 11	Indifferent	Good	Indiffe-ren	Good	Fairly Good	Fairly Good	Bad	Indiffe-ren	Fairly Good	Fairly Good	-	Indifferent	Fairly Good	Indiffe-rent	Very Bad
C 12	Fairly Good	Fairly Bad	Bad	Good	Good	Good	Very Bad	Indiffe-ren	Indiffe-rent	Fairly Good	Indifferent	-	Bad	Indiffe-rent	Bad
C 13	Indifferent	Indifferent	Indiffe-ren	Good	Indifferent	Indifferent	Fairly Bad	Bad	Fairly Bad	Very Bad	Bad	Very Bad	-	Fairly bad	Very Bad
C 14	Fairly Good	ery Good	Fairly Good	Good	Indifferent	Good	Indifferent	Fairly Good	Good	Very Good	Fairly Good	Good	Indiffe-ren	-	Fairly Good
C 15	Indifferent	Fairly Good	Bad	Indiffe-rent	Indifferent	Good	Indifferent	Fairly Bad	Good	Indifferent	Bad	Good	Indiffe-ren	Fairly Bad	-

Chart 4

Good 4	Manuf. Capac.	Standardisation.	Reliability	After Sales Ser.	Quality
IR_{ij}	Moderate	Fairly High	Fairly High	Low	High
$L_{S_i,j}$	Low	Fairly Low	Lowest	Fairly Low	High
$LC_1^{\rightarrow}$	Low	Fairly Low	Lowest	Fairly Low	High

Good 5	Manuf. Capac.	After Sales Ser.	Finac. Strong	Flexibility	Credit Terms
IR_{ij}	Very High	Fairly High	Moderate	Very High	Very Low
$L_{S_i,j}$	Fairly Low	High	High	Moderate	High
$LC_1^{\rightarrow}$	Fairly Low	High	Moderate	Moderate	Very Low

- **Step 1.2.**

$$Y_{S_1} = \phi_Q(VH,FH,M,L,VL) = [0,0.4,0.4,0.2,0](VH,FH,M,L,VL) = M$$
$$Y_{S_2} = \phi_Q(VH,H,M,M,L) = [0,0.4,0.4,0.2,0](VH,H,M,M,L) = M$$
$$Y_{S_3} = \phi_Q(M,L,L,L,FL) = [0,0.4,0.4,0.2,0](M,L,L,L,FL) = L$$
$$Y_{S_4} = \phi_Q(M,L,L,FL,FL) = [0,0.4,0.4,0.2,0](FH,H,M,L,FL) = L$$
$$Y_{S_5} = \phi_Q(H,M,M,FL,VL) = [0,0.4,0.4,0.2,0](FH,H,H,L,FL) = L$$

- **Step 2.1.**

S	Good 1.	Good 2	Good 3	Good 4	Good 5
IG_i	High	Fairly High	Moderate	Low	Very Low
Y_{S_i}	Moderate	Moderate	Low	Low	Low
$LC_1^{\rightarrow}$	Moderate	Moderate	Low	Low	Very Low

- **Step 2.2.**

$$Y_s = \phi_Q(M,L,L,L,VL) = [0,0.4,0.4,0.2,0](M,M,L,L,VL) = L$$

With theses steps above, we have obtained a linguistic evaluation (*Low*) of the solution suppliers in the requirements of the demanded goods.

Criterion 2. Good relationship among the suppliers selected.

- **Step 3.1.**

Good 1	1	2	3	4	5
RG_{ij}	-	Very High	High	Moderate	Fairly Low
$RS_{s_i s_j}$	-	Very Low	Low	Moderate	Moderate
$LI_1^{\rightarrow}$	-	Very Low	Low	Moderate	Fairly Low

Good 2	1	2	3	4	5
RG_{ij}	Fairly High	-	Moderate	Moderate	Low
$RS_{s_i s_j}$	Very Low	-	Low	Moderate	High
$LI_1^{\rightarrow}$	Very Low	-	Low	Moderate	Low

Good 3	1	2	3	4	5
RG_{ij}	Low	Very High	-	Very High	High
$RS_{s_i s_j}$	Fairly High	Very High	-	High	Low
$LI_1^{\rightarrow}$	Low	Very High	-	High	Low

Good 4	1	2	3	4	5
RG_{ij}	Low	Moderate	Very High	-	Very High
$RS_{s_i s_j}$	High	High	Moderate	-	Low
$LI_1^{\rightarrow}$	Low	Moderate	Moderate	-	Low

Good 5	1	2	3	4	5
RG_{ij}	Fairly Low	Moderate	Fairly High	Very High	-
$RS_{s_i s_j}$	High	Fairly Low	Moderate	Low	-
$LI_1^{\rightarrow}$	Fairly Low	Fairly Low	Moderate	Low	-

- **Step 3.2.**

$$V_1 = \phi_Q^I(M,L,FL,VL) = [0.1, 0.5, 0.4, 0](VL,FL,L,M) = L$$

$$V_2 = \phi_Q^I(M,L,L,VL) = [0.1, 0.5, 0.4, 0](VL,L,L,M) = L$$

$$V_3 = \phi_Q^I(VH,H,L,L) = [0.1, 0.5, 0.4, 0](L,L,H,VH) = M$$

$$V_4 = \phi_Q^I(M,M,L,L) = [0.1, 0.5, 0.4, 0](L,L,M,M) = L$$

$$V_5 = \phi_Q^I(M,L,FL,FL) = [0.1, 0.5, 0.4, 0](FL,FL,L,M) = L$$

- **Step 4.**

$$V_S = \phi_Q(M,L,L,L,L) = [0, 0.4, 0.4, 0.2, 0](M,L,L,L,L) = L$$

With the last three steps, we have obtained a linguistic evaluation (*Low*) for the relationship among the solution candidates in the post.

Therefore, we have obtained two labels for evaluating the solution *S*, *(Low, Low)*.

6 CONCLUDING REMARKS

The results obtained from this work fall into two clusters. The first consists of the formulation of a suppliers' selection model that could be adapted to the problem under consideration. The second has to do with the establishment of a specific procedure to manage the model, a linguistic selection model.

In addition, as future developments, to point at the following task. The linguistic decision model for suppliers selection provides a bicriteria linguistic evaluation of every candidate for suppliers solution, „$S = \{s_1, s_2, ..., s_m\}$, $s_i \in \{1, ..., N\}$". The future work is to design a search strategy for obtaining a good candidate solution for the problem. The use of searching and optimization techniques as simulated annealing, tabu search or genetic algorithms may be considered for tackling this problem, solving the bicriteria optimization problem associated to the linguistic decision model for suppliers selection.

REFERENCES

[Arnold, 1996] T. Arnold, *Introduction to Materials Management*, Prentice Hall (1996).

[Bellandi et al., 1997] G. Bellandi, R. Dulmin and V. Mininno, Study of a Supply Chain from a Buyer/Seller point of view: Planing and Application of an Indicators Model Fuzzy Logic Based, *Fuzzy Economic Review 1* (1997), vol. II, 73-89.

[Bonissone and Decker, 1986] P.P. Bonissone and K.S. Decker, Selecting Uncertainty Calculi and Granularity: An Experiment in Trading-off Precision and Complexity, in: L.H. Kanal and J.F. Lemmer, Eds., *Uncertainty in Artificial Intelligence* (North-Holland, 1986), 217-247.

[Delgado et al., 1993] M. Delgado, J.L. Verdegay, and M.A. Vila, On Aggregation Operations of Linguistic Labels, *Int. J. Intelligent Systems* 8 (1993), 351-370.

[Herrera and Verdegay, 1993] F. Herrera and J.L. Verdegay, Linguistic Assessments in group decision, Proc. First *European Congress on Fuzzy and Intelligent Technologies* (1993), Aachen, 941-948.

[Herrera et al., 1996] F. Herrera, E. Herrera-Viedma and J.L. Verdegay, Direct Approach Processes in Group Decision Making Using Linguistic OWA Operators, *Fuzzy Sets and Systems* 79 (1996), 175-190.

[Herrera and Herrera-Viedma, 1997] F. Herrera and E. Herrera-Viedma, Aggregation Operators for Linguistic Weighted Information, IEEE Transactions on Systems, *Man and Cybernetics* (1997). Part A. systems and Humans, Vol. 27:5 (1997), 646-656.

[Kaufmann and Gil-Aluja, 1992] A. Kaufmann and J. Gil-Aluja, *Técnicas de Gestión de Empresa: Previsiones, Decisiones y Estrategias*, Pirámide (1992).

[Tong and Bonissone, 1980] M. Tong and P. P. Bonissone, A Linguistic Approach to Decision Making with Fuzzy Sets, IEEE Transactions on Systems, *Man and Cybernetics* 10 (1980), 716-723.

[Van Weele, 1994] A.J. Van Weele, *Purchasing Management: Analysis Planning and Practice*, Chapman & Hall (1994)

[Yager, 1988] R.R. Yager, On Ordered Weighted Averaging Aggregation Operators in Multicriteria Decision Making, IEEE Transactions on Systems, Man and Cybernetics 18 (1988), 183-190.

[Yager, 1992a] R.R. Yager, Fuzzy Screening Systems, *Fuzzy Logic: State of the Art*, R. Lowen (Ed.), Kluwer Academic Publishers (1993), 251-261.

[Yager, 1995] R.R. Yager, An Approach to Ordinal Decision Making, *Int. J. Approximate Reasoning* 12 (1995), 237-261.

[Zadeh, 1975] L. Zadeh, The Concept of a Linguistic Variable and Its Applications to Approximate Reasoning-I, *Information Sciences* 8 (1975), 199-249.

[Zadeh, 1983] L. A. Zadeh, A Computational Approach to Fuzzy Quantifiers in Natural Languages, *Computers and Mathematics with Applications* 9 (1983), 149-184.

Fuzzy System for Air Traffic Flow Management

Leïla ZERROUKI [1,2] Bernadette BOUCHON-MEUNIER[2]
Rémy FONDACCI[1]

(1) INRETS, 2 Avenue du Général Malleret-Joinville 94 114 Arcueil
(2) LIP6, tour 46-0, 4 place Jussieu 75252 Paris Cedex 05
Tel: (331) 47 40 71 05
Fax : (331) 45 47 56 06
E-Mail: zerouki@inrets.fr.

Abstract:
The purpose of this paper is to study the issues raised by the implementation of a tool aimed at protecting air traffic sectors against overload in a large-scale air traffic system, acting on the basis of short term prediction. It shows how to overcome the computational complexity using a decentralised and co-ordinated system composed of a co-ordination level and a control level. The study points on the co-ordination level which decompose the large sector network into several smaller overlapping subnetworks that can be controlled independently. A modified interaction prediction method is developed using a fuzzy model. This model provides the interaction prediction of the control units on the basis of imprecise information and aggregated reasoning in order to decrease the multiple data transfer between the control and co-ordination levels. Time complexity of the fuzzy model inference is also studied, the antagonistic goals of reducing inference time of the fuzzy rule-base and increasing the accuracy of the interaction prediction is commented. Classical fuzzy inference models and rule interpolation techniques are then compared.

Keywords :
Large-scale System, Co-ordination, Fuzzy Model, Approximate Reasoning, Neural Network, Air Traffic Flow Management.

1. Introduction

Airspace under control is composed of a set of control sectors with limited capacities. However capacity of an air traffic sector varies randomly over space and time, depending on weather, air space organisation, controllers, etc. Forecasted demand is also uncertain and inaccurate. These random aspects cause saturation of the control sectors. So as to overcome this problem Air Traffic Flow Management (A.T.F.M) activity has to distribute traffic flows and fit the air traffic demand to the system capacity by minimising costs and inconveniences [Odoni, 1987]. This activity concerns generally a large-scale air traffic system, and operates some months to few minutes before the predicted overload.

Most of existing A.T.F.M models are based on operational research techniques. They are defined as an optimisation problem by Odoni [1987]. Vranas et al [1994]; Bertsimas and Stock [1994] formulate the problem with 0-1 programming model. Wang [1991] proposes a dynamic programming framework. Terrab and Odoni [1993] suggest a formulation as an assignment problem. These models are suitable for the pre-tactical and tactical A.T.F.M filters corresponding to some days to few hours before the predicted overloads. Nevertheless, it seems interesting to develop a tool that acts 20 to 60 minutes before the overloads occurrence in order to use more certain and precise predictions. This activity will correspond to a new A.T.F.M filter called the short-term filter [NOAA, 1996]. However, because of the great dimension of the air traffic network, the existing models require a long computation time. In order to cope with the computation time complexity a multi-level model was proposed in Zerrouki et al. [1997]. It is composed of a co-ordination level and a control level. The co-ordination is obtained using the interaction prediction approach where the predictions are inferred by a fuzzy rule-based model. This approach intends to reduce the multiple data transfer between the co-ordination and control levels. The control units perform parallel and co-ordinated computations using the classical operational research model. This distributed architecture should cope with the computation time problem and seems to be a suitable tool for the short-term A.T.F.M. In this paper we discuss the choice of an adequate fuzzy model in order to ensure the efficiency of the approach, the fuzzy prediction model that has to be developed must respect two antagonistic properties : the accuracy of the inferred interaction prediction, and time complexity constraint.

2. Air Traffic Flow Management System

Here are some definitions of the concepts used in the model, concerning both physical structure of the system and the A.T.F.M activity.

2.1 Air Traffic Flow Structure

Airspace is subdivided into several control sectors. Each sector is characterised by its **maximum capacity** defined as the maximum number of aircraft that are allowed to enter the sector per time unit. The **sector load** is defined as the number of aircraft entering a sector during one time unit. If the sector load exceeds the capacity of the sector, this leads to a saturation or overload of the sector. Airspace is also characterised by a given set of **standard routes** and waypoints forming an air routes network. In order to simplify the network representation the proposed model considers the standard route as a sequence of sectors crossed by the aircraft from its origin to its destination. Each route is crossed by a traffic **flow** which is characterised by the number of flights entering a given sector dealing with specific route, during one time unit.

2.2 A.T.F.M Control Actions

A.T.F.M system operates some hours to few minutes before the expected saturation occurrence in order to redistribute traffic flows by fitting air traffic demand to the system capacity. This can be done taking the following actions [Terrab and Odoni, 1993] :

- to delay the departure of aircraft (ground holdings).
- to regulate the rates of traffic flow.
- to impose en route speed control restrictions.
- to impose en route reroutings.
- to impose high altitude holdings and path stretching manoeuvres.

These possible control actions depend on the horizon time on which one works. As it is intended to act 20 to 60 minutes before the expected saturation occurrence, the speed control could be not enough efficient (for example a speed reduction of 10% during one hour leads to a delay of only 6.6 minutes). In the proposed model, only the rerouting, air holding, and ground holding actions could be considered.

3. Multi-level A.T.F.M Model

The model proposed attempts to overcome the computation time inconvenience by using the multi-level theory approach developed by Mesarovic et al. [1970]. Indeed the multilevel theory appears to be a suitable tool to cope with complexity. Based on the system decomposition principles : the temporal, the structural and the functional decomposition, it transforms a large and complex system into several but simplified subsystems, allowing parallel and co-ordinated computations.

There are two main co-ordination strategies up to now:

- goal co-ordination.
- interaction prediction.

This paper focuses on the interaction prediction strategy and proposes a new method in order to decrease the high number of iterative computations that is generally necessary to achieve the co-ordination between the interconnected subsystems. It is based, on one hand, on the interaction concepts developed by the general system theory [Nakano, 1994]; [Auger, 1993], and on the other hand, on the fuzzy logic reasoning presented in Zadeh [1978], that allows an approximate reasoning on the behaviour of the subsystems using imprecise data. These techniques are used to provide first but coherent values of the interaction prediction that lead to a reduction of the data transfer between the co-ordination level and the control level. The multi-level approach was used for road traffic assignment in Chen R.J and Meyer R. (1988) and seems to be computationally suitable for short-term A.T.F.M.

3.1 Time Decomposition

As it is difficult to determine a continuous model of dynamic behaviour of a large and complex network, a discrete time model is then proposed. A working horizon is divided into a finite number of equal periods, representing the decision steps (or time steps). A preventive approach is used based on the sliding prediction horizon H, composed of m sampling periods T, (Cf. Figure-1).

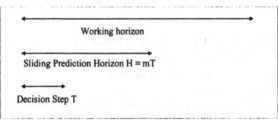

Figure -1 : Time decomposition

3.2 Structural Decomposition

The large air traffic network is divided into several smaller sub-networks, the decomposition into interconnected subsystems is based on:

- data analysis of the A.T.F.M system, aggregations and global behaviours of the system are then deduced.
- spatio-temporal reasoning on the A.T.FM network.
- computation time analysis of the control units.

These tasks are achieved with the help of several modules called the system analysis modules (Cf. Figure-2) and presented below :

- **Prediction Module**

It provides the prediction of the air traffic demand, sector capacity and weather conditions.

- **Simulation Module**

It computes for each decision step the future sector load prediction and detects the congested sectors.

- **Decomposition Module**

It decomposes the overall A.T.F.M network into basic subnetworks, and provides a dynamic data base associated to each subnetwork. The data base is built on the basis of the alert concept. One alert corresponds to an overload detected by the simulation module in a given sector occurring during the prediction horizon. Each basic subnetwork is formed by the overloaded sector and its neighbourhood which is a set of sectors surrounding the saturated sector .

- **Interaction Evaluation Module**

It has to analyse the possible effects caused by a basic subnetwork regulation action on another basic subnetwork and deduces some dependence indicators.
The identification of the interaction is based on the system science [Auger, 1993], two kinds of interactions have been identified in this study: the inter-dependence which occurs when two subnetworks have common regulation sectors, and the intra-dependence occurring when there are common flows crossing both subnetworks.

- **Network Merging Module**

It merges several basic subnetworks into one subnetwork according to the interaction levels and the computation capacity constraints imposed by the control units.

3.3 Functional Decomposition

A specific control unit is assigned to each subnetwork provided by the system analysis procedure. The actions of the control units are co-ordinated by a co-ordination level.

3.3.1 Co-ordination Level

The co-ordination task is realised by the interaction prediction module detailed in the next section. Its aim is to provide to the local control units the co-ordination parameters so as to achieve the overall optimum of the system. The strategy used for the co-ordination is the interaction prediction approach.

Interaction prediction principle :
Interaction prediction principle is to predict a set of interaction inputs α_i , i= 1..n for the n interconnected control units. Each control unit introduces the predicted values in the local optimisation computation, the control actions $M_i(\alpha_i)$ are then inferred, and induce the actual interactions denoted $U_i(\alpha_i)$. The overall optimum is achieved if the predicted interactions are equal to the actual interactions occurring when the actions $M_i(\alpha_i)$ are implemented ($\alpha_i = U_i(\alpha_i)$).

For the existing co-ordination strategies, the co-ordination is reached and effectively implemented by the control units at the end of multiple iterative data transfer between the control and co-ordination levels and it is consequently not suitable for the short-term or real-time applications. So the model proposes an improvement of the previous strategy by introducing a fuzzy interaction prediction model. This model presents some specific advantages :

- Learning :

Fuzzy model can be identified by learning techniques from analytical data obtained through the existing operational research models. Even if this existing models are not suitable in real-time for a large-scale system, they can be applied during an off-line phase, on the overall network in order to generate the necessary identification data.

- Approximation :

The basic motivation of using fuzzy models is to deduce simple and fast approximations of too complex operational research models (time computation complexity). It could use some aggregated and imprecise knowledge about the A.T.F.M network behaviour and deduce a first and accurate approximation of the interaction parameters. This accurate prediction should lead to a reduction of the data transfer between the co-ordination level and the control level.

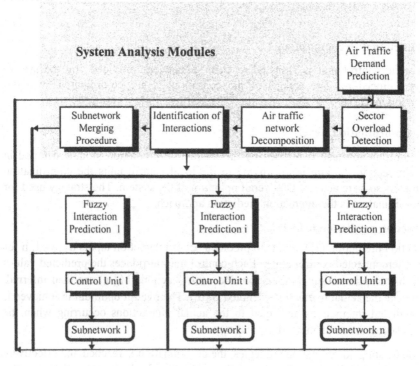

Figure-2 : Multi-level short-term A.T.F.M model

3.3.2 Control Level

A specific control unit is assigned to each subnetwork. Because of its reduced dimension, each control unit computes independent control actions in an acceptable computation time, by using the existing classical operational research techniques. This local optimisation of the control units are co-ordinated by the interaction prediction parameters inferred by the co-ordination level. For the A.T.F.M case the co-ordination parameter is equivalent to a sector capacity variation. So each control unit takes into account the effects of another control unit, on its associated subnetwork and compensates these control action effects by using an artificial sector capacity in the local operational research model.

4. Air Traffic System Analysis

This section gives more details on the system analysis modules, and how they perform their computation and reasoning.

4.1 Decomposition Module

This module identifies the basic subnetworks, and presents their associated elements in a dynamic data base. The basic subnetwork is defined throughout the alert concept. One alert corresponds to an overload detected by the simulation module in a given sector occurring during the prediction horizon H.

4.1.1 Notations and Definitions

$A_i(k)$: the alert i at the decision step k.

SAT_i : the saturated sector associated to the alert i.

$STEP_i$: the decision step where the sector SAT_i is predicted to be saturated.

R_i : the set of routes sections that include SAT_i in their sectors sequence, and feed it with traffic.

kb_i: the decision step where the saturation of SATi is detected for the first time.

$SE_{r,i}(k)$: the sector of the route r containing, at the decision step k, the flights that are predicted to pass through the saturated sector SAT_i at the decision step $STEP_i$. It is called the enemy sector.

$SE_i(k)$: the set of enemy sectors of the alert i.

$SD_{r,i}$: the begin sector which is the Enemy Sector identified during the first detection of the saturated sector SAT_i, $SE_i(kb_i)= SD_{r,i}$.

$SA_{r,i}$: the active Sector is each sector including at least one regulation action point (airport, rerouting point, air holding point).

RA_i: the set of active routes, which are the route section r of R_i or its alternative route, including at less one active sector, sequenced after the begin sector $SD_{r,i}$.

$SF_{r,i}(k)$: the final sector which is the last sector of a section route r, or its alternative route (in the case of rerouting action) that is reached at the end of the prediction horizon H, by the aircraft present in the enemy sector $SE_{r,i}(k)$ at time step k.

$SR_i(k)$: the set of Regulation Sectors, which are all the sectors in the sequence of an active route, and its alternative route (in the case of rerouting action) ordered between the active sector $SA_{r,i}$ and the final sector $SF_{r,i}$,

$F_r(i,k)$: the air traffic flow, defined as the number of aircraft entering the i th. sector of the sequence r during the decision step k.

$BSN_i(k)$: the basic subnetwork associated to the saturated sector SAT_i. It is composed at the decision step k of the set of sectors which forms the sequence of the active routes r and their alternative routes (if there is rerouting point), starting from the begin sector $SD_{r,i}$, and ending at the final sector $SF_{r,i}(k)$.

4.1.2 Alert Matrix

After having defined all the elements above, it is possible to build a data base as a dynamic matrix of Alerts $A_i(k)$ that gives the composition of the basic subnetworks at each decision step. Some components are constant, like SAT_i, $STEP_i$, kb_i... the others are dynamic like $SF_{r,i}(k)$, $SR_i(k)$. At the decision step k, the alert matrix representing n saturation is defined by :

$A(k)=[A_1(k), A_2(k),..A_i(k).., A_n(k)]$, where the alert $A_i(k)$ is given by:
$A_i(k) =[SAT_i ; STEP_i; kb_i; SD_{r,i} ; RA_i; BSN_i(k); SE_i(k); SR_i(k)]$

The $A_i(k)$ vector enters in the matrix, for the first time at the decision step kb_i, representing the birth of a basic subnetwork, and still in the matrix until the saturation is eliminated, that is considered as the death of the basic subnetwork.

4.2 The Interaction Evaluation Module

The interaction module has to determine the possible effects caused by a basic subnetwork regulation action on another basic subnetwork. Based on the systemic science [Auger, 1993], two kinds of interactions have been identified in this study: the inter-dependence which occurs when two subnetworks have common regulation sectors, and the intra-dependence occurring when there are common flows crossing both subnetworks.

For the notation simplification, in the following, the basic subnetwork associated to the alert $A_i(k)$, at the decision step k, is denoted by i(k).

4.2.1 The Inter-dependence

A) Definitions :

A basic subnetwork i is inter-dependent of the subnetwork j (i(k) INTER j(k)) if there is at least one regulation action for each subnetwork increasing the load of a common regulation sector for the same decision step kl.

Figure-3 shows that sectors S and S' are common regulation sectors for a rerouting action.

Figure-3: Two inter-dependant subnetworks

B) Notations :

To have a mathematical definition of the inter-dependence, some notations are requested:

$SR_{i,j}(k)$: the set of the common regulation sectors, from the structural point of view. $SR_{i,j}(k)=SR_i(k) \cap SR_j(k)$.

$DIS(S1,S2)$: the average travel time of flows entering sector S1 up to their entry in the sector S2.

$RC_{i,j}(s,kl,k)$: the set of active routes of the subnetwork i which average travel time of flows from the enemy sector $SE_{r,i}(k)$ on the route up to the sector s, with $s \in SR_{i,j}(k)$, is in the temporal interval $[(kl-k).T, (kl-k+1).T]$.

$$RC_{i,j}(s,kl,k) = \left\{ \begin{array}{l} r \in RA_i \ / \ \exists w \in RA_j \ \ s \in r \cap w \ \text{and} \\ \left[\ (kl-k).T \leq DIS(SE_{r,i}(A),s) \leq (kl-k+1).T \right] \end{array} \right\}$$

C) The inter-dependence identification procedure:

In order to identify the inter-dependence relations between two subnetworks, the inter-dependence procedure has to check if the structural and temporal conditions are respected for the subnetwork pairs (i,j), using the logical relation below :

$i(k) \ \text{INTER} \ j(k) \Leftrightarrow \exists s \in SR_{i,j}(k) \ /$
$\exists kl \in [k,k+m] \ \ RC_{i,j}(s,kl,k) \neq \varnothing \ \text{and} \ RC_{j,i}(s,kl,k) \neq \varnothing$

That means that the flows delayed or re-routed in the subnetwork i arrive into a common regulation sector s, at the same time step as the flows regulated in the subnetwork j. Notice that this relation is symmetrical.

D) The inter-dependence indicator:

After having identified all the inter-dependence relations between the basic subnetworks i and j. One has to evaluate an inter-dependence indicator, for each common regulation sectors s. This indicator gives the dependence level of the subnetwork i relatively to the regulation sector s, common with subnetwork j. It is defined as the proportion of flows of subnetwork i that cross the common regulation sector s.

The inter-dependence indicator is denoted by $INTER_{i,j}(s,kl,k)$ and given by:

$$INTER_{i,j}(s,kl,k) = \frac{\sum_{w \in RC_{i,j}(s,kl,k)} \left[F_w(SE_{w,i}(k),k)\right]}{\sum_{r \in RA_i(k)} \left[F_r(SE_{r,i}(k),k))\right]}$$

4.2.2 The Intra-dependence

A) Definitions :

Two basic subnetworks are intra-dependent, (i(k) INTRA j(k)) if the regulation actions of one increase or decrease the load of the saturated sector associated with the other. More precisely, there are two kinds of intra-dependence:

The basic subnetwork i is *positively intra-dependent* of j (i(k) IN+ j(k)), if there is a regulation action of j that decreases the congestion of SAT_i.

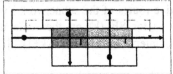

Figure -4: Two positively intra-dependent subnetworks.

The subnetwork i is *negatively intra-dependent* of j, (i(k) IN- j(k)), if there is a regulation action of j that increase the saturation of SAT_i (Cf. Figure-5).

Figure-5 : Two negatively intra-dependent subnetworks.

B) The intra-dependence identification procedure:

Several relations should be given for each kind of intra-dependence relation, but in the limit of this paper only the negative intra-dependence relation dealing with re-routing action is given. So, formally the intra-dependence of the subnetworks i relatively to j is set up, if the structural and temporal conditions are satisfied:

$$i(k) \text{ IN- } j(k) \Leftrightarrow \left\{ \begin{array}{l} SAT_i \in SR_j(k) \text{ and } \exists r \in RA_i \cap RA_j / \\ (STEP_i - k).T \le DIS(SE_{r,j}(k), SAT_i) \le (STEP_i - k + 1).T \end{array} \right\}$$

It means that the saturated sector of the basic subnetwork i is the regulation sector of j and the regulated flows of j arrive at SAT_i at the decision step $STEP_i$, increasing the overload of SAT_i.

Notice that IN- is a non-symmetrical relation.

C) The intra-dependence indicator:

If an intra-dependence relation is identified, it is possible to evaluate an intra-dependence level of the basic subnetwork i relatively to j, at the decision step k, denoted by $INTRA_{i,j}(k)$. This is done by computing the proportion of flows dealing with the two subnetworks i and j which are regulated in the subnetwork j.

$$INTRA_{i,j}(k) = \frac{\displaystyle\sum_{r \in RAC_{i,j}(k)} F_r(SE_{r,j}(k), k)}{\displaystyle\sum_{r \in RA_i} F_r(SE_{r,i}(k), k)}$$

$RAC_{i,j}(k)$ is the set of the active routes, common to the subnetworks i and j that verify the intra-dependence relation.

4.3 Merging Module

The merging module is a procedure that groups several basic subnetworks into one subnetwork. In order to describe the reasoning of the merging procedure, it is necessary to define some parameters and functions.

4.3.1 Notations

DEP*: is the lowest acceptable intra-dependence level. It has to be defined during the tunning phase of the system.

COMPU: is the maximum number of combinations that could be computed by a control unit during a computation time less than one decision step T.

For each decision step k we define:

S_u: is a subnetwork formed by one or several basic subnetworks at the time step k.

$N(S_u)$: is the complexity function that gives the number of combinations computed by each control unit for the subnetwork S_u.

$MERGE(S_u, S_v)$: is the merging function, which groups two subnetworks S_u and S_v into one subnetwork, composed of the union of their elements.

INMAX(i,j): the maximum intra-dependence indicator between two basic subnetworks i and j, $(\max(INTRA_{i,j}(k);INTRA_{j,i}(k)))$.

INTRA*: is the vector of intra-dependence indicators, of dimension L. It is formed by the decreasing sequence of intra-dependence indicator INMAX(i,j).

SINTRA : is the vector of the (i,j) basic subnetwork pairs corresponding to the range of the INTRA* vector.

4.3.2 Merging Procedure

The merging procedure has to merge as many basic subnetworks as possible, according to a highest level of intra-dependency and the computation capacity constraint.

At each decision step k do

At the initial step (h=1), each S_u is formed by one basic subnetwork.

For all h, h=1..L do

IF INTRA*(h)>DEP* AND $\{SINTRA(h)=(i,j)\ /\ i\in S_u,\ j\in S_v\ ;\ u\neq v\}$ AND $N(MERGE(S_u,S_v))<COMPU$ THEN $MERGE(S_u,S_v)$.

5 Fuzzy Interaction Prediction Model (F.I.P)

Having the merged subnetworks provided by the merging model, the interaction prediction module has to define an artificial sector loads and capacities allocation for the interacted subnetworks. In fact, even if the merging model has taken into account the highest intra-dependence level, it remains some subnetworks strongly intra-dependent still not merged because of the computation capacity constraints. In addition the inter-dependence involved by the common regulation sectors is not considered into the merging model. Hence, in order to perform a parallel and co-ordinated optimisation by the control units, according to the interaction prediction methods, this module has to predict the action effects of a subnetwork on the other subnetwork and compensate this effects by modifying artificially the sector capacities and loads.

In order to provide the interaction prediction for the control units, it is necessary to take into account all kind of available knowledge about the subnetwork behaviour. However the knowledge gathered on the interaction relations is based on aggregated and imprecise values such as the intra-dependence, the inter-dependence indicators, the load predictions etc. For this reason, fuzzy logic seems to be the appropriate tool to deal with imprecision performing an approximate reasoning that deduces the interaction prediction. In the limit of this paper, only the inter-dependence interactions are presented, a similar model can be build for intra-dependence interaction.

5.1 Structure Identification of the Fuzzy Model

In the fuzzy prediction module, the facts in the knowledge base are represented by means of two linguistic input variables, the inter-dependence indicator provided by the Interaction Evaluation Model and the load of saturated sector provided by the simulation module. The output inferred variable represents the prediction effect of the regulation action of a subnetwork i on an inter-dependent subnetwork j. In the case of inter-dependence relation, interaction prediction is a variation of the capacity of a common sector s (Cf. Figure-3). Actually, the output variable is equivalent to the proportion of flights that are regulated in the subnetwork i through the sector s. This value has to be subtracted from the real capacity of the common sector s in the subnetwork j in order to take into account the regulation effect of the subnetwork i. The resulting value represents the artificial capacity of the sector s, in the subnetwork j.

The input and output variables are defined respectively on the universes X1, X2 and Y and partitioned by means of fuzzy characteristics. For simplicity, we present the linguistic model for a partition composed of 3 fuzzy characteristics {Small, Medium, Large}.

Two-input variables:
$INTER_{i,j}(s,kl,k)$: the inter-dependence indicator (Cf. definition in 4.2.1).
$SC_i(SAT_i, STEP_i)$: the load of the saturated sector SAT_i of the subnetwork i, predicted for the decision step $STEP_i$.

Single output variable:
ΔCAP_{ij} (s,kl): the capacity variation of the common regulation sector s at the decision step kl, in the subnetwork j.
The rules of the fuzzy interaction prediction model (F.I.P) are formulated as follows:

For all non merged inter-dependent subnetworks pairs (i,j)
For all common regulation sector s of the subnetworks i and j

IF $INTER_{i,j}(s,kl,k)$ is Large AND $SC_i(SAT_i, STEP_i)$ is Large THEN $\Delta CAP_{ij}(s,kl)$ is Large.

IF $INTER_{i,j}(s,kl,k)$ is Large AND $SC_i(SAT_i, STEP_i)$ is Small THEN $\Delta CAP_{ij}(s,kl)$ is Medium.

IF $INTER_{i,j}(s,kl,k)$ is Medium AND $SC_i(SAT_i, STEP_i)$ is Medium THEN $\Delta CAP_{ij}(s,kl)$ is Medium.

IF $INTER_{i,j}(s,kl,k)$ is Small AND $SC_i(SAT_i, STEP_i)$ is Large THEN $\Delta CAP_{ij}(s,kl)$ is Medium.

IF $INTER_{i,j}(s,kl,k)$ is Small AND $SC_i(SAT_i, STEP_i)$ is Small THEN $\Delta CAP_{ij}(s,kl)$ is Small.

The structure of this fuzzy rules is constructed subjectively from the prior knowledge about the behaviour of the system we describe, which induces a uniform and gradual variation of the input and output variables. Actually, it is reasonable to think that the higher the inter-dependence of subnetwork i relatively to the common sector s and the saturation of SAT_i, the higher the necessity of using the sector s for the regulation actions of subnetwork i.

5.2 Reasoning Mechanism

The choice of the reasoning mechanism is a fundamental task in the context of this study for two essential reasons. The first one concerns the accuracy of the output, the second concerns time complexity constraint. As the model is aimed at reducing the number of data transfers between the co-ordination and control levels, it should deduce a fast and good approximation of the interaction prediction parameters. In order to choose the most appropriate mechanism to infer the conclusion of the fuzzy model with regard to the computation time complexity and the prediction accuracy we study and discuss the properties of the principal fuzzy reasoning mechanisms. The classical compositional rule of inference (C.R.I) and some fuzzy interpolation methods are then compared.

5.2.1 C.R.I Approach

A classical fuzzy control model (with fuzzification, inference and defuzzification steps) could provide an accurate crisp value of the interaction prediction. However obtaining an accurate approximation of the interactions means the use of a dense fuzzy rule-base. The more rules there are the more exactly the interactions are predicted and a shorter time is needed to achieve the co-ordination between the interconnected control units. On the other hand, more rules mean a higher computational complexity. If L is the number of labels for the partition of the universes X1, X2 and Y used in the fuzzy prediction model, the number of rules covering $X=X1 \times X2$ is equivalent to the function $o(L^2)$ and the fuzzy inference has the following time complexity $o(3.L^3)$. For example, with 20 labels C.R.I approach needs 24 000 steps to infer an interaction prediction.

5.2.2 Fuzzy Interpolation Approaches

In order to reduce time complexity of the conclusion inference, one has to analyse the property of the fuzzy rule-base and see if it is possible to use another inference method. As it is already noticed the fuzzy rules of the model present some gradual property in the sense that the rule " If X is U then Y is V " could be written " The more X is U the more Y is V ". The gradual reasoning and the analogical reasoning [Bouchon-Meunier and Desprès, 1990], [Dubois and Prade, 1992] would be suitable techniques of inference but they are limited to the single input variable fuzzy models. Nevertheless, the gradual properties presented by the input and output variables imply the existence of full orderings and metrics in their respective universes of discourse.

This property induces the possibility of using interpolation methods which are characterised by a reduced time complexity cost and the possibility of deducing an output from a sparse fuzzy rule-base. We have studied two interpolation approaches, the first one was developed by Koczy and Hirota [1993], and consists in an extension of classical linear interpolation techniques. The second one was presented by Ishibushi et al. [1993] and it is based on a neural network interpolator.

- **Fuzzy Linear Interpolation (F.L.I)**

This method is applied on convex and normal fuzzy sets, with triangular or trapezoidal shape. The extension of the classical linear interpolation to linear fuzzy rule interpolation is based on the α-cut concept. If we use a small number m of sparse fuzzy rules, and a number h of α-cut levels, the fuzzy interpolation time complexity corresponds to a polynomial function o(m+2.h) [Koczy and Hirota, 1993] ; [Koczy and Zorat, 1997]. With the linear interpolation approach time complexity can be strongly reduced. However, the characteristics of the fuzzy output inferred are not always satisfying : the approach preserves the convexity property but it often infers abnormal output.

- **Fuzzy Neural Interpolation (F.N.I)**

This approach can interpolate sparse fuzzy rules by a neural network which has leant its weights and biases from a fuzzy input-output data during a preliminary off-line procedure [Ishibushi et al. , 1993] ; [Chin-Teng and Ya-Ching, 1995]. Fuzzy triangular and normalised learning input-output data are transformed into crisp learning values using α-cuts. An extension of the classical back-propagation algorithm to interval computation was developed in order to deduce the upper and lower limits of the output α-cuts [Ishibushi et al. , 1994]. After learning the parameters from the fuzzy rule base, the neural network becomes able to deduce from any fuzzy convex and normal input a corresponding fuzzy output satisfying the convexity and normality properties. The approach was simulated with triangular fuzzy number data and infers a pseudo-triangular fuzzy output number.

Concerning time complexity of the fuzzy-neural interpolation, it depends on the number n of hidden units n, the number h of α-cut levels used to determine the fuzzy output, and the number of the input variables k (k=2, for the prediction model). We have estimated time complexity of this approach with a polynomial function o(n+2.h). We notice that time complexity of the fuzzy-neural interpolation does not depend on the number of rules. This time cost function implies that using a dense rule base for the learning procedure allows the interpolator to improve the accuracy of the input value without increasing time complexity cost.

5.2.3 Comparison

The summary of the previous comparative study between fuzzy reasoning methods is presented in the following table :

	Normality	Convexity	Complexity	Accuracy
C.R.I	-	-	$o\,(3.L^3)$	good
F.L.I	not always	satisfied	$o\,(m+2.h)$	not always
F.N.I	satisfied	satisfied	$o\,(n+2.h)$	good

Table-1 : Some Inference Mechanism Methods.

The discussion shows that the most appropriate tool in the context of the study is the fuzzy-neural interpolation approach because it needs a short computation time for the deduction of the output value and can provide an accurate output. In addition, the normalised fuzzy number inferred is adequate for symbolic-numeric interface between the co-ordination level and the control level. Actually, the co-ordination parameter used in the local optimisation modules must be crisp, and the core of the fuzzy number output can be an adequate interface value as it corresponds to the highest level of certainty of the fuzzy output.

5.3 Fuzzy Partitioning

The choice of the density of the fuzzy rule base determines the universe partitioning and the rule base dimension. There is no general answer to the question of determining how fine the fuzzy model should be in order to achieve the highest speed of conclusion computation. However, graduality property of the input and output variables, and the interpolation approach chosen for deducing the conclusion value allow us to use a sparse partitioning. We then choose three fuzzy triangular and normalised values {Small, Medium, Large} for the partitioning of X1, X2 and Y considering that they are sufficient to describe extreme and medium scenario of the system behaviour and we can deduce the other intermediate cases by fuzzy-neural interpolation method. In this case, the fuzzy model obtained corresponds to the five rule-based model presented in section 5.1.

5.4 Parameter Identification

Parameter identification corresponds to the evaluation of the membership function parameters of the linguistic labels. Having the set of fuzzy attributes corresponding to the universe partition, we have to determine the support and the core of the triangular labels. The identification approach we choose is inspired from the template method suggested by Tong [1979]. This method uses both expert knowledge and input-output data for the identification process.

In order to get the learning data we take into account the available regulation tools of A.T.F.M problem. In fact, it is interesting to exploit the existing operational research model in the sense that it could provide useful input-output data for the identification of the fuzzy model. Actually, even if this numerical model is not suitable for real-time application, we use it in an off-line step, on the overall A.T.F.M network, for extreme and medium scenario of air traffic demand in order to deduce a variation interval of the input variables and the corresponding interval of the output variable. The intervals found are associated to the support of the fuzzy numbers : Large, Small, and Medium describing both input and output variables. The core of the fuzzy numbers is deduced with the help of an expert.

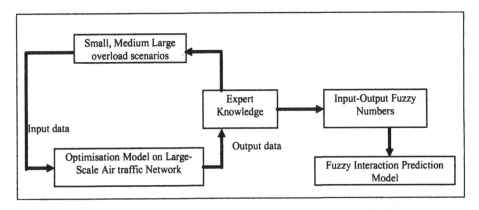

Figure-6 : Identification of Fuzzy Interaction Prediction Model

5.5 Learning a Neural Network from Fuzzy Rules

After the fuzzy prediction model has been constructed, it can constitute a learning data base for a neural network. The learning data base is formed by five pairs of fuzzy input-output describing the fuzzy prediction model : {((Small, Small) ; Small), ((Small, Large) ; Medium), ((Medium, Medium) ; Medium), ((Medium1, Small) ; Medium), ((Large, Large) ; Large)}.

The learning algorithm proceeds as follows :

For a number h of α-cut levels.
For all pairs of fuzzy input-outputs.
- Determine the upper and lower limits of the α-cuts.

The learning data base is formed by 5 vectors of 6 components, 4 for the input data, and 2 for the target data.

- Apply the back-propagation algorithm adapted to interval computation (I.B.P) of Ishibushi et al. to update the weights of the neural network. For more details concerning the architecture of the neural network and the learning algorithm see Ishibushi et al. [1994].

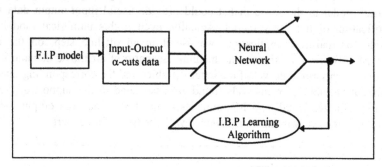

Figure-7 : Fuzzy Neural Interpolator : off-line Learning Phase

5.6 Inference Mechanism

Having the neural network parameters after the learning phase the neural network can be used to infer a fuzzy number output for any fuzzy number inputs. The inference mechanism proceeds as follows :

For each fuzzy input number

For a number h of α-cut levels.
- Determine the upper and lower limits of inputs α-cuts.

- Use the input-output relations of the neural network to compute the output α-cuts and build the output fuzzy number.

- Infer the modal value as the co-ordination parameter to control level.

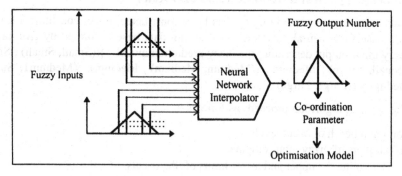

Figure-8 : Fuzzy Neural Interpolator : in-line Inference Phase

6. The Real-Time ATFM Model

All the previous identification and learning processes are performed during an off-line step that we call the acquisition and representation of knowledge. This preliminary stage is essential for the performance of the regulation actions in real-time. The number of data transfers between the control and co-ordination levels necessary to reach the co-ordination, is directly dependent on the accuracy of the interaction prediction provided by the fuzzy-neural module. The more accurate the prediction the smaller the number of co-ordination iterations. Each co-ordination iteration has to improve, in real-time, the interaction prediction on the basis of the regulation actions provided by the control level. Having the neural network interpolator as a prediction tool, if the co-ordination is not reached, we choose to tune, in real-time, the interpolator parameters using classical back-propagation algorithm with the target output data provided by the control level.

6.1 The A.T.F.M Model Procedures

The different steps of the A.T.F.M model followed during each decision step are described below :

Let C be the number of data transfer needed before reaching the co-ordination (initially C=1).

Step 1 : System Analysis

Apply sequentially the System Analysis modules presented in section 3.1 so as to provide :

- a prediction of the sector overloads.
- a decomposition of the large air-traffic network into smaller subnetworks.
- an identification of interaction relations between the subnetworks.
- an evaluation of the interaction indicators.

Let denote respectively by a1(i,j,s) and a2(i) the inter-dependence indicator and the sector overload provided by the system analysis step.

Let denote by DT, the computation time of the System Analysis Procedure.

Step 2 : Fuzzy Interaction Prediction

For each inter-dependent subnetwork pairs (i,j)
For all common regulation sector s of the subnetworks i and j

- Affect a fuzzy-neural interpolator denoted by FNI(i,j,s).
- Transform the crisp input data provided by step1 into triangular fuzzy normalised number A1(i,j,s) and A2(i) with a1(i,j,s) and a2(i) as the respective modal values. An error variation on this values is used to determine the supports.

- Introduce the fuzzy input data in the fuzzy-neural interpolator FNI(i,j,s) and deduce a fuzzy number output C(i,j,s) corresponding to the interaction prediction.
- Determine the vector P_j composed of the modal value of interaction prediction C(i,j,s), for the subnetwork j.

Let denote by IT, the computation time of one interpolation procedure.

Step 3 : Co-ordination

Step 3.1 : Artificial Capacity Allocation

For all inter-dependent subnetworks j.
For all index i of a subnetwork inter-dependent of j.
For all common sector s.

- Subtract the core of C(i,j,s) from the capacity of the common sector s in the subnetwork j.

Step 3.2 : Parallel optimisation

For all the subnetworks j.

- Compute the regulation actions using the 0-1 programming model, developed in Bertsimas et al [94].
- Deduce from the regulation actions of all the inter-dependent subnetwork i, the vector $U_j(P_j)$ composed of the action effect $U_j(P_j, i, s)$ of the subnetworks i on the subnetwork j in the common sector s.

Let denote by OT the computation time of one local optimisation procedure.

Step 3.3 : Co-ordination Evaluation

For all inter-dependent subnetwork j

- Verify if all the components of $U_j(P_j)$, which are the actual regulation effects on j, are included in the support of the predicted regulation effects C(i,j,s). If it is true, the co-ordination is reached, go to step 4, else go to step 3.4.

Step 3.4 : Tuning of the fuzzy-neural interpolator

For all interdependent subnetwork j
For all i of $U_j(P_j)$ such as the co-ordination is not satisfied

- Tune the fuzzy-neural interpolator FNI(i,j,s) using the classical back-propagation algorithm for the tuning input-output data ((a1(i,j,s), a2(i)), $U_j(P_j, i, s)$).
- C=C+1.
- Go to step 2.

Let denote by TT, the computation time of tuning procedure.

Step 4 : Regulation Action

- Apply the regulation action on each subnetwork.
- Go to step 5.

Step 5 : End.

6.2 Computation Time Constraint

Hence, a suitable A.T.F.M model should respect the following time cost constraint:

If C=1   DT+IT+OT<T
If C>1   DT+ C.(IT+OT+TT)< T

where T is the decision step duration.

The previous steps are summarised in the following figure :

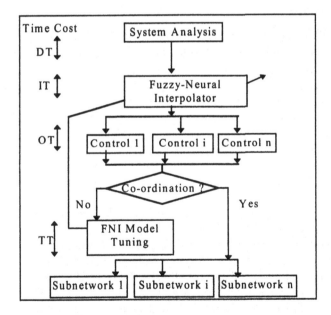

Figure-9 : Real-Time ATFM Model Steps.

In order to reduce the number C of data transfers, it is necessary to build an accurate fuzzy prediction model. For this reason, the identification process is the most important step ensuring the success of this model. Nevertheless, comparing this approach with classical multi-level control models, which provide an arbitrary initial co-ordination vector to the control level, ignoring the available information about the system behaviour, it is reasonable to think that the classical approach needs a higher number of data transfers before reaching the co-ordination. So the essential advantage of the model proposed is the possibility of exploiting, in an off-line stage, all the available information about the system behaviour, in order to build up a fuzzy knowledge base that provides in real-time a first and accurate approximation of the regulation action. This should have as consequent to minimise the number C of data transfers.

7. Conclusion

This paper presents a real-time A.T.F.M model which copes with computation time problems by introducing the multi-level approach. The co-ordination level is detailed in order to show the different concepts used, such as interaction, fuzzy reasoning that leads to the best prediction of the co-ordination parameters. This prediction is used by the control units to perform a parallel and co-ordinated optimisation in order to reduce the multiple data transfers between the co-ordination and the control levels.

8. References

[Auger, 1993] Auger A., *Hiérarchie et niveaux de complexité*. In Systémique théorie et applications. Bouchon-Meunier B Le Gallou F. (eds) : 63-70. Lavoisier, 1993.

[Bertsimas and Stock 1994] Bertsimas D. and Stock S. *The Air Traffic Flow Management problem with Enroute Capacities*. Working paper Alerd p. Sloan School of management. WP #-3726-94 MSA.

[Bouchon-Meunier and Desprès, 1990] Bouchon-Meunier B. and Desprès S. *Acquisition numérique/symbolique de connaissance graduelles*. LAFORIA Technical report : 90/4, University of Paris-VI.

[Chin-Teng and Ya-Ching, 1995] Chin-Teng L.and Ya-Ching L., *A Neural Fuzzy System with Linguistic Teaching Signals*. IEEE Trans on Fuzzy Systems Vol 3, n°2 : 169-185, 1995.

[Dubois and Prade, 1992] Dubois D. and Prade H. *Gradual rules in approximate reasoning*. Info Sci. 6 :103-122, 1992.

[Ishibuschi et al. , 1993] Ishibuschi H. Fujioka R. Tanaka H. Neural network that learn from fuzzy if then rules. IEEE Trans on Fuzzy Systems Vol 1 : 85-97, 1993.

[Ishibushi et al., 1994] Ishibuschi H. Tanaka H. Okada H. *Interpolation of fuzzy If-Then rules by neural network*. Int J of Approximate Reasoning, 10 : 3-27, 1994.

[Koczy and Hirota 1993] Koczy L.T. and Hirota K. *Approximate Reasoning by linear rule interpolation and general approximation*. Int J of Approximate Reasoning, 9 : 197-225, 1994.

[Koczy and Zorat 1997] Koczy L.T. and Zorat A. *Fuzzy systems and approximation*. Fuzzy Sets and Systems, 85 : 203-222, 1997.

[Mesarovic M.D et al 1970] Mesarovic, M.D. Macko and Takanara Y. *Theory of multi-level hierarchical control systems*. Academic Press, New York, 1970.

[Odoni A. 1987] Odoni A. *The flow management problem in air traffic control*. In flow control of congested networks : 269-288, Springer Verlag, 1987.

[Tong R.M 1979] Tong R.M. *The construction and evaluation of fuzzy models*, in advances in Fuzzy Sets Theory and Application, Gupta M.M Ragade R.K. Yager R.R (eds). North Holland : 559-579, 1979

[Vranas et al. 1994], Vranas P.B.M, Bertsimas D., and Odoni A., *Dynamic ground-holding policies for a network of airports*. Transportation Science, 28 : 275-291.

[Zadeh 1979] Zadeh L.A. *A theory of approximate reasoning* . Machine Intelligence, Hayes J.E., Michie D., Mikulich L. I. (eds), New-York Elsevier : 149-194, 1979.

[Zerrouki et al. 1997] Zerrouki L. Fondacci R. Bouchon-Meunier B. Sellam S. *Artificial Intelligence Techniques for Coordination in Air Traffic Flow Management*. in 8th IFAC/IFIP/IFORS Symposium on Transportation Systems' 97. Chania, Greece. June 16-18 : 47-51, 1997.

A Fuzzy Approach to Contracting Electrical Energy in Competitive Electricity Markets

Grazyna Michalik   Wladyslaw Mielczarski

Department of Electrical and Computer Systems Engineering
Monash University, Melbourne, Australia

Email: Grazyna@basil.eng.monash.edu.au or Wlad@basil.eng.monash.edu.au

Abstract: A fuzzy approach to contracting electrical energy in competitive electricity markets is presented and analysed. A new structure of a competitive market, where independent energy suppliers and users create electricity prices in a bidding system, has been introduced in Australia. Electricity trading takes three major forms: vesting contracts, hedge contracts and the spot market. Although less than 10% of electrical energy is purchased in the spot market, spot prices strongly affect contract prices and behaviour of pool participants. Their behaviour is quantified by four linguistic variables reflecting attitudes to risk taken during contracting. This allows the assignment of the upper and lower limits for the membership for a given linguistic category. These limits, as the boundaries of spot price trends are defined as a function of the pool demand. Three fuzzy operators: weighted sum, maximum and minimum type operators have been employed to predict spot price patterns and determine costs of market exposure. This provides the useful tools to compute risk taken with a given marketing attitude. The simulations have been carried out using the data on spot prices and the pool demand in Region 1 of the Australian National Electricity Market, covering Victoria and South Australia, from May 1997 to December 1997.

Keywords: Open electricity markets, electrical energy contracts, fuzzy operator, linguistic variables, marketing attitudes, market exposure, market risk, energy pools, spot price.

1   INTODUCTION

In Australia, Electricity Supply Industry (ESI) has been traditionally organised as the regional monopolies in each state and territory, controlled by the local State Governments. The Australian state, Victoria, with the capital in Melbourne, was the first state that introduced reforms leading to the open electricity market in 1993 [1]. A new structure of the electricity supply industry is shown in Fig. 1. A full-fledged wholesale electricity market introduced in Victoria allows customers to select their own electricity suppliers that offer the most competitive prices and conditions of electricity supply [2].

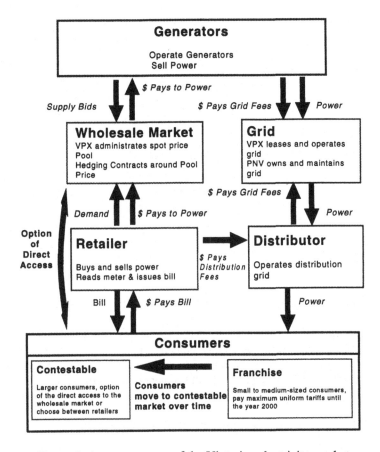

Figure 1 A new structure of the Victorian electricity market

2   OPERATION OF THE COMPETITIVE ELECTRICITY MARKET

The Victorian Wholesale Electricity Market has two basic elements [3]:
1. ***The Pool*** which allows to set prices for the next day. Each day, Generators bid into the Pool the price of electricity for half-hour periods in the following day. The next day, Generators are dispatched to meet the market demand from Buyers in the order of their bids. The lowest price is dispatched first. The price of the highest priced Generator, which is actually dispatched in a given period, sets the Pool price for that period. This price is received by all Generators dispatched in that period. The mechanism of price setting is shown in Figure 2.
2. ***Hedging contracts*** which are financial instruments between the wholesale Buyers and Sellers. These contracts allow managing financial risk inherited from varying Pool prices.

Vesting contracts were arranged by the government in the beginning of the competitive market to stabilize electricity prices. These contracts will last to year 2000. Vesting contracts cover about 50% of the current pool demand. Actual spot prices are below 50% of vesting contract prices.

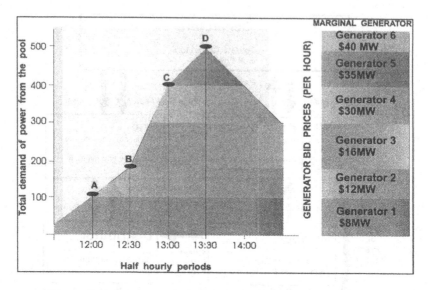

Figure 2 Spot price as the balance between demand and supply

Additionally to vesting contracts, market participants can enter bilateral hedge contracts. The precise value of energy demand covered by bilateral contracts is unknown. It is estimated to count for about 40% of the total energy demand. The spot price market covers a relatively small segment of the pool, about 10%, but they strongly affect strike prices in hedge contracts and behaviour of pool participants.

3   SPOT PRICES AND ELECTRICITY DEMAND

Spot prices depend in great degree on electricity demand so the analysis carried out for the National Electricity Market (NEM) investigates functional relations between these variables. Dependence of average spot prices and electricity demand is shown in Figure 3.

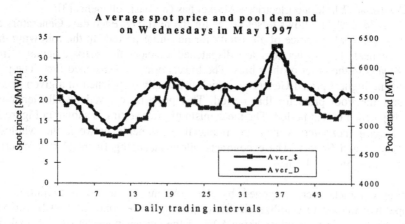

Figure 3 Spot price and electricity demand.

This example presents relationships for May 1997, the first month of the National Electricity Market operation. The analysis carried out for other months of the NEM indicates similar relationships. It can be observed that the spot price patterns fit the electricity demand quite accurately.

4 DECISION MAKING PROCESSES

Decision-making is a process of selection possible action among of courses. Mathematically, decision-making process is formulated in a form of two components:
Objective function, which aims at the maximization of losses or expenditures

$$OF = \max[f_1(x), f_2(x)...f_k(x)] \tag{1}$$

Constrains, which represent financial or physical limits of possible actions

$$q_i(x) \leq 0 \qquad i = 1...m \tag{2}$$

There are various methods that allow the solution of the above problems known as a static optimization task. When a decision variable vector x is a function of time x(t), a decision making process may be solved using dynamic optimization procedures. In practice, a formulation of the objective function leads to the conflicting criteria, such as maximization of income with minimization of investment or use of resources. Multiple objective decision making methods aim at the elimination of the above difficulties treating objectives separately [4]

4.1 Preference Curve

Decision making in uncertain environment can be addressed in several ways. One of the commonly accepted approaches is the use of preference curves and certain equivalent [5]. Decision-makers can express their willingness by the term of "preference" which means that one decision is preferred to another.

$$A_1 \succ A_2 \tag{3}$$

Since the decision making, involving uncertain events, requires risk taking; in some cases preference is called as risk preference.

The scales in preference curves are obtained by surveying decision makers who are asked to select relations between probability of success and the risk involving investment. Typical preference curves are shown in Figure 4. The type of a function is determined by the willingness of decision-makers to take risk.

Preference curves are commonly used to compute certainty equivalents when preference of any decision is calculated as a function of the contribution necessary. Preference values are multiplied by the probability of the success and summarized for all possible options. This provides per unit certainty equivalent for all possible options. The approach is applicable for multi-personal decision making by the implementation of various averaging methods when each person of a decision making team has his own preference curve.

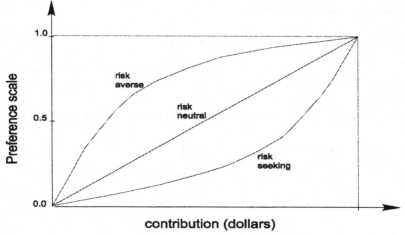

Figure 4 Preference curves

4.2 Decision-making in a Fuzzy Environment

The first attempt to formulate the basis for decision making in fuzzy environment was formulated by [6]. The fuzzy goal G is defined as a fuzzy set in the set of options and characterized by the membership function $\mu_G(x)$. The fuzzy constant C is defined as a fuzzy set of options and characterized by the membership $\mu_C(x)$.

There are several types of possible decisions in a fuzzy environment [7]:

Min-type decision

$$\mu_D(x) = \min\{\mu_G(x), \ \mu_C(x)\} \tag{4}$$

Where $\mu_D(x)$ is a membership function of a decision.

Max-type decision

$$\mu_D(x) = \max\{\mu_G(x), \ \mu_C(x)\} \tag{5}$$

The product-type decision

$$\mu_D(x) = \mu_G(x), \ \mu_C(x) \tag{6}$$

The weighted-sum-type decision

$$\mu_D(x) = \alpha\mu_G(x) + (\alpha - 1)\mu_C(x) \tag{7}$$

where $\alpha \in [0, 1]$ = coefficient of importance.

The algebraic-sum-type decision

$$\mu_D(x) = \mu_G(x) + \mu_C(x) - \mu_G(x)\mu_C(x) \tag{8}$$

The choice of a decision type strongly depends on attitudes of decision-makers. A pessimistic attitude will relate to the min-type of fuzzy decisions, while an optimistic attitude will represent by the max-type. The weighted-sum-type and the algebraic-sum-type represent attitudes located between pessimistic and optimistic approaches.

4.3 A New Approach to Fuzzy Decision Making

A systematic study of the existing approaches to fuzzy decision-making shows a number of difficulties encountered [8]. First, majority of approaches requires cumbersome calculations and none of these is suitable for solving more than ten alternatives associated with more than ten attributes. Second, many methods require the decision matrix to be presented in fuzzy format. Some information is provided as crisp numbers that does not reflect the original intention of fuzzy set theory to provide tools for coping with human's subjective judgement.

The best approach should accommodate fuzzy and crisp data where fuzzy data can be expressed in linguistic terms of in fuzzy numbers. Linguistic term can be transformed into fuzzy numbers by assigning various scales [8, 9, 10].

5 SPOT PRICE PATTERNS

Spot prices depend on a number of parameters including the day of a week, a season, actual and forecasted demand, and transfer levels. The analysis of spot prices focuses on the development of characteristic parameters to analyse and forecast spot price variation. For this purpose, the data from the National Electricity Market starting from the beginning of May 1997 until the end of December 1997, was employed.

A linear trend line can be used for the characterization of a functional relationship between a spot price and its parameters including demand, and energy transfer. The vital advantage of linear trend lines is simplicity. However, trend line approximation does not reflect price deviations. Graphically, such deviations are represented by points above and below the trend line. To include spot price deviations into the analysis, two additional trend borderlines are introduced. Now, the functional relationships between a spot price and its parameters can be expressed as

$$\tilde{y}_{upper}(i) = mx(i) + b_{upper}(x) \tag{9}$$

$$\tilde{y}_{trend}(i) = mx(i) + b_{trend}(x) \tag{10}$$

$$\tilde{y}_{lower}(i) = mx(i) + b_{lower}(x) \tag{11}$$

where $\tilde{y}_x(i)$ – spot price trend lines

$x(i)$ – characteristic parameters, for example demand
b_{upper}, b_{trend} and b_{lower} – offsets for trend lines
m – slop of trend lines, i – trading intervals

In relations (9), (10) and (11), it is assumed that the slop of trend lines is constant, while the offsets vary. This leads to three-parallel trend lines with the main trend line in the middle, reflecting the average value of spot prices, and two parallel trend lines defining upper and lower boundaries, as seen in Figure 5.

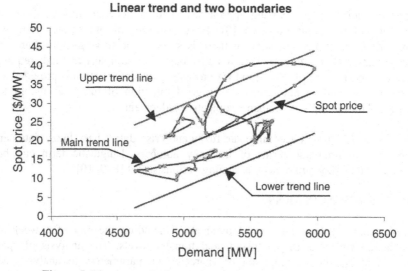

Figure 5 Linear trend of a relation between spot prices and demand

The upper and lower boundaries shown in Figure 5 are shifted up and down of 20%, respectively. This is obtained by setting the following offsets: $b_{upper} = 1.2\, b_{trend}$ and $b_{lower} = 0.8\, b_{trend}$. The lower trend line contains all spot prices located below the main trend line. However, the upper trend line does not cover all spot prices located above the main trend line. The upper and lower offsets, determined by (10) and (11), can be treated as the levels of spot price deviations.

The spot price approximation, given in the general form by the relationship (12), provides the main trend and two its borders.

$$\tilde{y}_k(i) = f\left(m, b_{trend}, b_{upper}, b_{lower}, x(i)\right) \tag{12}$$

for k = 1,2 and 3 defining the main, lower, and upper trend, respectively.

6 MARKET PARTICIPANT ATTITUDES

One of the main problems in spot price approximation is the selection of upper and lower boundaries. Ideally, b_{upper} and b_{lower} should be determined in such a way that the space between them contains all spot data. However, such an approach may lead to very conservative evaluation of spot price deviations. In practice, a few spot price deviations outside the trend lines may not affect the trading balance.

However, the acceptable boundaries of the trend line depend, in great degree, on the attitude of decision-makers to risk taking. As a rule, the more conservative a market player, the more spot price data should be covered by boundary lines. Table 1 presents four categories of market players with different attitudes to risk taking, and the corresponding levels of trend lines' boundaries.

Table 1 Categories of market participants with different attitudes to risk taking

Risk preference Data contained between the main trend line and the lower and upper boundaries	Attitude of a decision-maker	Attitude Code
95%	Very Conservative	VC
90%	Conservative	C
80%	Neutral	N
70%	Risk seeker	RS

When four approximation levels are applied to upper and lower boundaries of spot data, different values for b_{lower} and b_{upper} are obtained. The graphical representation of trend boundaries is shown in Figure 6.

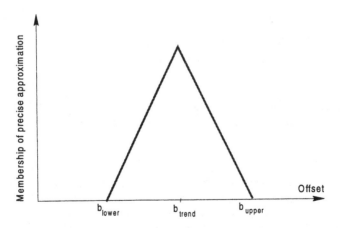

Figure 6 Fuzzy filter applied to determine the boundaries for data deviations

This delta-shaped function, called later "fuzzy filter," expresses the preciseness of trend line approximation. Parameters b_{lower} and b_{upper} are determined in such a way that the area between boundaries contains the prescribed number of spot data, due to the levels given in Table 1. This creates a set of data with members of 95%, 90%, 80% or 70% family, due to risk preference. When a data spot is exactly on the main trend line, its membership function is equal to one, and the trend line provides the precise approximation. If the spot position is above or below the main trend lines, its membership is decreasing due to the distance from the main trend line. When a spot price is located outside boundaries, its membership function is equal to zero.

The values of parameters b_{lower} and b_{upper} are expressed in [$/MWh] and represent boundary offsets on the spot-price axis. Although these parameters are important for decision-makers, several other parameters can provide essential information for market players, including:
- maximum and minimum prices for a given span of filter
- the number of trading intervals and the values of spot prices when spot data is within approximation borders
- the ratio of energy cost energy sold or purchased given by filter approximation to the total daily cost of trading
- the risk involved when decision is based on filter approximation

6.1 Buyers and Sellers

The limits of spot prices provided by upper and lower boundaries are essential for decision-makers. However, these limits do not allow to determine the financial exposure to the spot price market when only the trend approximations are taken into account. Therefore, it is also necessary to consider the cost of electrical energy when spot prices are not within limits determined by trend lines.

Generally, there are two categories of market participants taking part in the electrical energy trading:

- **Buyer**
  Distribution Businesses and other companies that purchase electrical energy in the wholesale market are mostly interested in price deviations above the trend lines. Significant price deviations increase market participant exposure to the price volatility, and consequently increase the risk involved in a market game. Uncertainty of spot price deviations leads to more conservative behaviour resulting in various hedge contracts with strike prices, as a rule, higher than spot prices.

- **Seller**
  An energy Seller (Generator) focuses mainly on revenue, which is a function of spot prices. The lower the spot price, the smaller revenue a Seller can obtain from energy generation. Electrical energy producers can protect themselves by signing the bilateral hedge contracts with energy buyers. Generally, the lower the price expected, the lower strike price in hedge contracts is acceptable by energy producers. This may lead to smaller revenue.

6.2 Calculation of Market Exposure

The total cost of market exposure is split into two main groups:
- electricity costs when a spot price below the trend line and boundaries
- electricity costs when a spot price outside the boundaries

In Figure 7 the main trend is represented by the x-axis. Thus, the price difference represents the distance between the actual spot price and the main trend line (x-axis). Therefore, boundaries of the main trend are represented by two horizontal lines, set above and below the main trend line. Four characteristic areas can be considered when determining the additional cost exposure. First, the area denoted as 'A+' that represents costs incurred from spot prices enclosed between the upper margin and the main trend line. Second, the areas denoted as 'A −' representing cost when spot prices vary between the main trend line and the lower margin. Next, the areas denoted as 'B +' that represent additional costs when spot prices are above the upper margin. Last, the area denoted as 'B −' where spot prices are below the lower margin. The above method of calculation is especially useful when a market participant is considering hedge contracts with a strike price equal to the upper or lower margin of the main trend. This procedure can provide the information on the costs incurred from shifting the strike price to the trend margins and determine the additional costs.

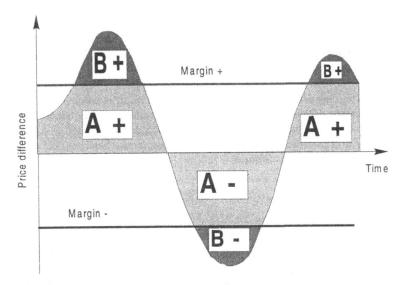

Figure 7 Portion of the costs incurred within the boundaries and outside of the upper and lower margins

The additional cost exposure when spot price are above the main trend and below the upper trend limit (CBM_{upper}) is calculated as below

$$CBM_{upper} = \frac{\sum\limits_{i=1}^{48}\left[(y(i) - \tilde{y}_{upper}(i))Sign(\alpha(i)) + (\tilde{y}_{upper}(i) - \tilde{y}_{main}(i))Sign(\beta(i))\right]* D(i)}{\sum\limits_{i=1}^{48} y(i)* D(i)}$$

(13)

where

D(i) – Buyer demand in "i" trading period

Sign(x) = 0 when x<0 and 1 other wise

$$\alpha(i) = \tilde{y}_{upper}(i) - \tilde{y}(i); \quad \beta(i) = y(i) - \tilde{y}_{upper}(i)$$

The additional cost when spot price are above the upper margin is defined as:

$$CAM_{upper} = \frac{\sum\limits_{i=1}^{48}\left[(y(i) - \tilde{y}_{upper}(i))Sign(\chi(i))\right]* D(i)}{\sum\limits_{i=1}^{48} y(i)* D(i)}$$

(14)

where $\chi(i) = y(i) - \tilde{y}_{upper}(i)$.

The cost of market exposure when spot prices are below the main trend and above the lower margin (area A-) and when spot prices are above the low boundary (area B-) is calculated in a similar way.

The information on additional costs and their distribution is essential for decision-making processes. However, the most important parameter is the risk occurred with a given attitude to the market game. In general, the risk is calculated as a product of cost incurred and probability of an event. In the spot market analysis, the risk can be calculated more precisely as follows:

$$Risk = P_{d:0-5}w_5 + P_{d:5-10}w_{10} + P_{d:10-55}w_{15} +$$
$$P_{d:15-20}w_{20} + P_{d:20-25}w_{25} + Max_{cost}P_{d>25}$$

(15)

where: w_5, w_{10}, w_{20} and w_{25} are weighting coefficient equal to 0.005, 0.10, 0.15, 0.20 and 0.25, respectively,

$P_{d:0-5}$, $P_{d:5-10}$, $P_{d:10-15}$, $P_{d:15-20}$, $P_{d:20:25}$, $P_{d:>25}$ are distributions of the costs in bands 0 ÷ 5%, 5 ÷ 10%, 10 ÷ 15%, 15 ÷ 20%, 20 ÷ 25% and above 25%.

Max_{cost} - the maximum value of spot price deviations

The above relation calculates the maximum risk that may be involved in decision making based on the characteristic attitudes.

7 ESTIMATION OF SPOT PRICE PATTERNS

The analysis discussed in the previous Sub-sections involved direct relationships between daily demand and daily spot prices for the eight months in 1997 of the National Electricity Market operation. Fuzzy patterns, additional costs, and risk involved when using fuzzy patterns with various attitudes to the electricity pool were calculated as an ex-post analysis. This analysis is essential for spot price pattern identification. However, fuzzy patterns developed for particular days of a week can be implemented to the prediction of spot prices in the coming days.

7.1 Estimate Categories

Several categories of the estimates can be involved in decision-making process. Of five possible relationships, three have been selected to estimate patterns of spot prices for days of a week:

- **Weighted-sum-type estimate**

$$\mu_i(x) = \alpha_{i-1}\mu_{i-1}(x) + \alpha_{i-2}\mu_{i-2}(x) + \alpha_{i-3}\mu_{i-3}(x) + ... + \alpha_l \mu_l(x) \qquad (16)$$

where: $\mu_i(x)$ is a fuzzy estimate of spot market prices for a given market attitude

$\mu_{i-1}(x), \mu_{i-2}(x), \mu_{i-3}(x),..., \mu_1(x)$ - fuzzy patterns of spot prices in previous days

$\alpha_{i-1}(x), \alpha_{i-2}(x), \alpha_{i-3}(x),..., \alpha_1(x)$ - coefficient of importance

- **Max-type of the estimate**

$$\mu_i(x) = \max\{\alpha_{i-1}\mu_{i-1}(x) + \alpha_{i-2}\mu_{i-2}(x) + \alpha_{i-3}\mu_{i-3}(x) + ... + \alpha_l \mu_l(x)\}$$
$$(17)$$

- **Min-type of the estimate**

$$\mu_i(x) = \min\{\alpha_{i-1}\mu_{i-1}(x) + \alpha_{i-2}\mu_{i-2}(x) + \alpha_{i-3}\mu_{i-3}(x) + ... + \alpha_l \mu_l(x)\}$$
$$(18)$$

The number of patterns used to estimate the future behaviour of spot prices depends on a-prior assumption supported by market participant experience and the initial spot price analysis. For this, 'i' equal to 5 has been selected. That means that the data from four weeks is applied to estimate the spot prices in the fifth week. The method is called a four-step filtering procedure.

7.2 Weighted-sum-type Estimate

Fuzzy filters used for representation of spot price deviations have three characteristic parameters: an average value, upper and lower limits. A four-step filtering procedure based on the weighted-sum-type estimate is defined as below:

$$\tilde{y}_l^k(i) = f\left(\hat{m}^k, \hat{b}_{trend}^k, \hat{b}_{upper}^k, \hat{b}_{lower}^k, x^k(i)\right) \tag{19}$$

This provides the main trend estimates and two (upper and lower) boundaries as follows:

$$\tilde{y}_{main}^k(i) = \hat{m}^k x(i) + \hat{b}_{trend}^k \tag{20}$$

$$\tilde{y}_{upper}^k(i) = \hat{m}^k x(i) + \hat{b}_{upper}^k : \quad \tilde{y}_{lower}^k(i) = \hat{m}^k x(i) + \hat{b}_{lower}^k \tag{21}$$

where: k = day of estimates, starting from the first week of June 1997

i = trading interval

$$\hat{m}^k = \alpha_1^{k-1} m^{k-1} + \alpha_1^{k-2} m^{k-2} + \alpha_1^{k-3} m^{k-3} + \alpha_1^{k-4} \tag{22}$$

$$\hat{b}_l^k = \alpha_2^{k-1} b_l^{k-1} + \alpha_2^{k-2} b_l^{k-2} + \alpha_2^{k-3} b_l^{k-3} + \alpha_2^{k-4} b_l^{k-4} \tag{23}$$

where the index "l" applies as trend, upper and lower boundary

$\tilde{y}_l^k(i)$ = estimated price for "i" trading interval in "k" trading

days for main trend, upper and lower.

Since there are not specific preference for a specific day to determine values of coefficients of importance, they are assumed to be equal to 0.25 for the four-step estimating procedure.

7.3 Max-type Operator

When the maximum-type of a fuzzy operator is employed to determine patterns of spot prices, the trends of the expected prices are described by the equation (19). The parameters are computed as follows:

$$\hat{m}^k = \max\left\{m^{k-1} + m^{k-2} + m^{k-3} + m^{k-4}\right\} \tag{24}$$

$$\hat{b}_l^k = \max\left\{b_l^{k-1} + b_l^{k-2} + b_l^{k-3} + b_l^{k-4}\right\} \tag{25}$$

where index "l" is defined as in (23)

7.4 Min-type Operator

When a min-type operator is used to determine patterns of spot prices, the main trend and two boundaries are calculated using the general relationship (19). The parameters are defined as follows

$$\hat{m}^k = \min\left\{m^{k-1} + m^{k-2} + m^{k-3} + m^{k-4}\right\} \tag{26}$$

$$\hat{b}_l^k = \min\left\{b_l^{k-1} + b_l^{k-2} + b_l^{k-3} + b_l^{k-4}\right\} \tag{27}$$

8 ANALYSIS OF RISK AND MARKET EXPOSURE

The simulations of risk and market exposure for a give market attitude and with the application of three fuzzy operators have been carrying out using the real data on spot price and electricity demand from May to December 1997. The notation used in Figures 10 – 13 is as follows.

- RS_BM – costs when spot prices are Below Margin for Risk-seekers
- RS_AM – costs when spot prices are Above Margins for Risk-seekers
- N_BM - costs when spot prices are Below Margin for Neutral Attitude
- N_AM - costs when spot prices are Above Margins for Neutral Attitude
- C_BM - costs when spot prices are Below Margin for Conservative Attitude
- C_AM - costs when spot prices are Above Margins for Conservative Attitude
- VC_BM - costs when spot prices are Below Margin for Very Conservative Attitude
- VC_BM - costs when spot prices are Above Margins for Very Conservative Attitude

When spot prices are high, Risk-seekers may expect additional costs that are composed of two parts:

- Costs of energy purchase when spot prices are between the price estimated and the upper margin,

- Costs of energy purchase when spot prices are above the upper margin

The values presented in Figure 8 mean that when a Risk-seeking energy Seller, with 70% market preference, is ready to enter a hedge contract with an upper strike price determined by the upper estimate he should expect that about 7% of the total revenue may be paid back to an energy Buyer as compensation for spot prices above the hedge contract strike price.

On the other hand, a Very Conservative energy producer, who is willing to enter the hedge contract when the upper estimate margin covers 95% of spot price deviations above the main estimate, should expect to pay back less than 2% of his revenue. However, a very high upper strike price may not be accepted by an energy Buyer who may prefer to enter a hedge contract with a Risk-seeking energy producer who is ready to offer lower strike price, based on 70% upper margin. Generally, the selection depends on market participants' behaviours and their approach to risk taking.

Figure 8 can also provide essential information for energy producers who negotiate One-way Hedge Contracts. In such contracts, a Seller rebates a Buyer the additional cost of energy when spot prices above the strike price agreed. A Buyer pays an annual fee to a Seller. When determining a fee paid by a Buyer, a Seller should take into account all the additional costs expected. First of all, a Seller has to decide how much of additional costs should be covered by this fee.

Figure 9 presents the values of additional costs calculated as a lost of possible revenue when spot prices are below the level estimated. If a Risk-seeking energy Buyer accepts 70% lower margin, he may expect to pay back to a generator about 3.5% of the energy total cost.

On the other hand, a Very Conservative energy Buyer may try to enter a hedge contract assuming the lowest margin of price estimate. In this case, he will return to an energy Seller less than 0.5% of the total cost. However, it is possible that a Seller would not accept a hedge contract with the low strike price proposed. If a Buyer is going to negotiate the contract with higher low strike price than resulting from his attitude, Figure 9 can provide the information on the costs protected by hedge contracts and the loss of possible revenue from low spot prices.

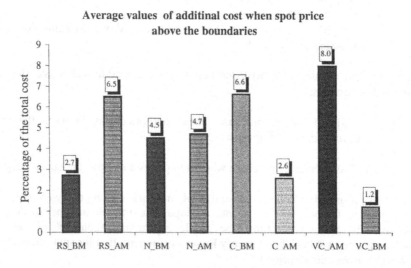

Average values of additinal cost when spot price above the boundaries

Figure 8 Average values of additional costs when spot prices above the boundaries for different market participants' attitudes

For market participants, it is more important to know the market exposure and the risk when spot prices are forecasted. Therefore, three fuzzy operators have been employed to compute the prediction of spot price trends.

The essential information can be obtained by the comparison of three fuzzy operators as presented in Figures 10 and 11. First, a weighted-sum operator provides the estimate margins with the highest expected costs when spot prices are above the estimate (see Figure 10). On the other hand, this operator provides the lowest values of the expected costs above margins when spot prices are low, as seen in Figure 11. Second, a max-type operator provides the estimate margins with highest cost Below Margin and the lowest cost Above Margins for high spot price. However, for low spot prices this operator provides the second highest additional cost when spot prices Below Margins and the second lowest cost when spot prices Above Margins. A min-type operator generates the estimates resulting in the additional costs between the weighted-type and max-type operators.

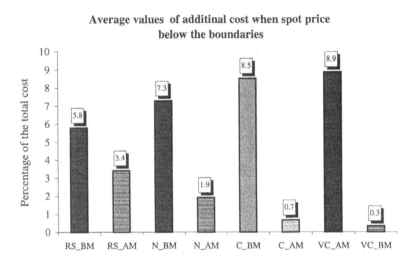

Figure 9 Average values of additional costs when spot prices below the boundaries for different market participants' attitudes

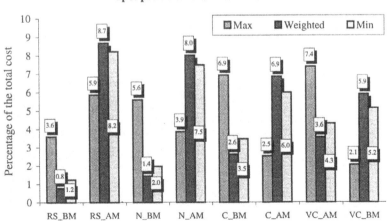

Figure 10 Average values of additional costs for three fuzzy operators

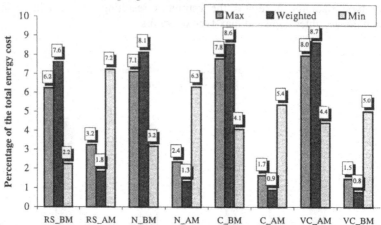

Figure 11 Average values of additional costs for three operators when spot price below the estimates

The analysis of the average values of the total risk is shown in Figures 12 and 13. The total risk when the estimates are based on three operators has a similar pattern to the additional costs expected when spot price below and above the margin estimated. However, the differences in the total risk are less significant when various market attitudes are applied in energy contracting.

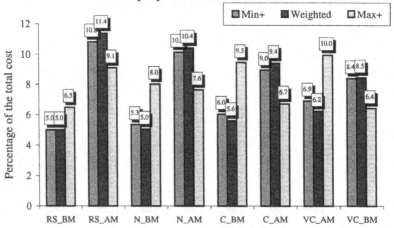

Figure 12 Average maximum risk of additional costs for three operators when spot price above the estimates

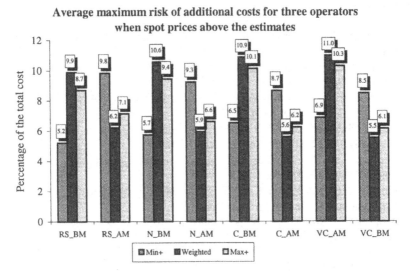

Figure 13 Average maximum risk of additional costs for three operators when spot
price below the estimates

9 CONCLUSION

Competitive electricity markets creates new challenges for power system managers.
Electricity is contracting by a bidding system. Spot prices are varying causing the
risk of large market exposure. To reduce this risk market participants, not having
experience and supporting tools, enter various types of hedge contracts in which
prices are usually high for energy buyers and low for energy producers. Currently,
the spot market provides an opportunity to purchase electricity for prices lower
twice than an average price in hedge contracts. However, in practice, market
participants tend to contract some amount of their demand by hedge contracts to
reduce risk of market exposure. Spot prices analysis and prediction of the future
price patterns will play a vital role in the reduction of overall cost of electricity.

Uncertainty of the spot price market and strong influence of marketing attitudes
cause that the best technique in predicting future price patterns seems to be the fuzzy
approach. Three fuzzy operators with the marketing attitudes defined by four
linguistic variables have been applied to calculate market risk and predict price
patterns have revealed large potential for such a decision support tool. Maximum
market exposure is relatively low when the presented technique is implemented.
The study was limited to the relation between market attitudes with the use of spot
prices and pool demand. The inclusion of other variables such as the forecasted level
of energy transfer between regions should lead to more precise forecasts of spot
price patterns.

REFERENCES

[1] Reforming Victoria's Electricity Industry, December 1994, Department of the Treasury.

[2] Electricity Industry Regulatory Statement, Office of the Regulator-General, Victoria, 1996.

[3] W. Mielczarski, "Introducing open electricity markets," APSCOM-97, Hong Kong , 11-13 November 1997.

[4] Hwang, Ch.L., Mosund A.S., "Multiple Objective Decision Making-Methods and Applications," Sringer Verlag, Berlin, 1979

[5] Holloway Ch. A, "A Decision Making under Uncertainty. Models and Choices," Prentice-Hall, Inc. 1979

[6] Bellman, R.E. and Zadeh L.A. "Decision Making in a Fuzzy Environment," Management Science, 17, pp. 141-164, 1970

[7] Kacprzyk J. "Multistage Decision-making under Fuzziness," Verlag TUV, Rheinland, 1983

[8] Chen Sh-J. and Hwang Ch-L., "Fuzzy Multiple Attribute Decision Making," Springler Verlag, 1992

[9] Bonisson, P.P., "A Fuzzy Sets Based Linguistic Approach: Theory and Application," in "Approximate Reasoning in Decision Analysis," Gupta M.M. and Sanchez E. (eds), North-Holland, pp. 329-339, 1982

[10] Wenstop F., "Quantitative Analysis with Linguistic Variable," Fuzzy Sets and Systems, Vol. 4, pp. 99-115, 1980

Fuzzy Logic and Intelligent Computing in Nuclear Engineering

Da Ruan

Belgian Nuclear Research Centre (SCK•CEN)

Boeretang 200, B-2400 Mol

E-mail: druan@sckcen.be

Abstract

Nuclear engineering is one of the areas with a large potential for applications of fuzzy logic and intelligent computing, the development of which, however, is still in its infancy. The nuclear power industry requests special demands on plant safety, surpassing all other industries in its safety culture. Due to the public awareness of the risks of nuclear industry and the very strict safety regulations in force for nuclear power plants (NPPs), applications of fuzzy logic and intelligent computing in nuclear engineering present a tremendous challenge. The very same regulations prevent a researcher from quickly introducing novel fuzzy-logic methods into this field. On the other hand, the application of fuzzy logic has, despite the ominous sound of the word "fuzzy" to nuclear engineers, a number of very desirable advantages over classical methods, e.g., its robustness and the capability to include human experience into the controller. In this paper, we review some relevant applications of fuzzy logic and intelligent computing in nuclear engineering. Then, we present an on-going project on application of fuzzy logic control of the first Belgian Reactor (BR1) and other related applications of fuzzy logic at the Belgian Nuclear Research Centre (SCK•CEN). We conclude that research in fuzzy logic and intelligent computing has reached a degree where industrial application is possible. Investigations into this direction and particular in nuclear engineering are still very rare, but some existing results seem promising.

1 Introduction

Nuclear engineering is the branch of the engineering profession concerned with the practical applications of *nuclear energy*, that is, the energy which, in one form or another, originates in and emanates from the atomic nucleus.

Despite the existence of hundreds of commercial power plants (mostly of the light-water type), which in some countries like France or Belgium represent as much as 60% of the electrical power generation capacity, there is a slump almost everywhere in the attendance of nuclear engineering university programs and in its corollary, innovative research by talented young people in quest of doctoral degrees. Several nuclear engineering departments in American universities have been closed, while others have merged with mechanical- or chemical engineering departments for technical and economical reasons. The situation is not very different in European universities, where nuclear programs also attract smaller audiences. Nevertheless, researchers interested in starting a PhD thesis or in carrying a post-doc project should not conclude too hastily that the subject is dead: nuclear engineering in a large sense (i.e., encompassing *reactor* engineering) still offers plenty of interesting scientific and technological challenges.

Nuclear engineering is one of the areas with a large potential for applications of fuzzy logic and intelligent systems, the development of which, however, is still in its infancy [27, 31]. Most nuclear engineers today are involved in the development of nuclear power installations, either stationary power plants for the generation of electricity or plants for the propulsion of mobile systems. The Chernobyl accident and its cross-border consequences have reminded us that nuclear safety remains a short-term priority, both at home and abroad, as nuclear technology has not reached the same maturity in all countries. The need for on-line reactor operator decision support systems has become evident after the Three Mile Island accident in 1979. Since then, considerable attention has been paid by the engineering, scientific, economic, political communities and by society at large to prevent this type of event by using state-of-the-art artificial intelligence techniques.

Among the available techniques, fuzzy-logic control (FLC) has been recently applied to nuclear reactor control. Having acquired the accumulated skill of many operators, FLC can assist an operator in controlling a complex system. One of the advantages of FLC is to derive a conceptual model of the control operation, without the need to express the process in mathematical equations and to assist the human operator in interpreting and validating incoming plant variables and arriving at a proper control action. Several interesting FLC results were reported in the area of nuclear reactor control [10]: the high-temperature reactor (HTR) nuclear power plant model control [4], automatic operation method for control rods in boiling-water reactor (BWR) plants [14], the Feed-water-control system in Fugen heavy-water reactor (HWR) [40], the steam generator water-level in pressurized-water reactor (PWR) [15], and PWR-type nuclear power plants [1]. The best known work in this area is the successful application of FLC to the 5 Mega-Watts thermal (MWt) Massachusetts Institute of Technology (MIT) research reactor [3]. A rule-based, digital, closed-loop controller that incorporates fuzzy logic has been designed and implemented for the control of power on the MIT research reactor. The advantage of rule-based systems is that they are generally more robust than their analytic counterparts in the above work [3]. Therefore, the rule-based and analytic technologies should be used to complement each other, with rule-based systems being employed both as backups to analytic controllers and as a means of improving the man-machine interface by providing human operators with the rationale for automatic control action.

The significant influence of FLC in this field was also illustrated by the activities of **FLINS** (an acronym for Fuzzy Logic and Intelligent Technologies in Nuclear Science) and by the response to FLINS'94 (The 1st international workshop on *Fuzzy Logic and Intelligent Technologies in Nuclear Science*, Mol, Belgium, September 14–16, 1994) [28]. A successful application of FLC to the feed-water control system of the 165 Mega-Watts electric (MWe) Fugen Advanced Thermal Reactor (ATR) has enabled operators to control the steam drum water level more effectively than with a conventional proportional-integral (PI) control system [11]. The Korea Atomic Energy Research Institute [12] piloted a real-time self-tuning fuzzy controller for a steam generator with a scaling factor adjustment. This improves the performance of the water-level controller; the controller is itself simulated by a compact nuclear simulator.

Many new results on this topic are followed and presented at FLINS'96 (The 2nd international workshop on *Intelligent Systems and Soft Computing for Nuclear Science and Industry*, Mol, Belgium, September 25–27, 1996) [29]. SCK•CEN started its own R&D project in this area on FLC nuclear reactors [30]. In this framework, the availability of the BR1 reactor greatly simplifies the effort to validate the used model description. This allows us to concentrate on the optimal implementation of the overall control. We remark that this project reflects a special application domain of fuzzy logic related to the highest safety requirement in nuclear areas. Research involved in this project will provide a real test bed and be the only step towards the future fuzzy-logic applications in NPPs.

2 Fuzzy Algorithmic and Knowledge-Based Decision Support in Nuclear Engineering

Many of the real-world problems arising in the analysis and design of decision, control, and knowledge systems are far from simple. Intelligent technologies including fuzzy logic, neural networks, genetic algorithms, and others provide additional tools which significantly enlarge the domain of problems which can be solved. Recent publications [32, 31] show a positive trend towards using intelligent systems in nuclear applications. Among the existing intelligent technologies, the development of fuzzy technology during the last 30 years has, roughly speaking, led to the following application-oriented classes of approaches which are all, more or less, applicable to nuclear engineering [44]: model-based applications (e.g., fuzzy optimization, fuzzy clustering, fuzzy Petri Nets, and fuzzy multi-criteria analysis); knowledge-based applications (e.g., fuzzy expert systems, fuzzy control, and fuzzy data analysis), and information processing (e.g., fuzzy data banks and query languages, fuzzy programming languages, and fuzzy library systems).

Perhaps the most impressive fact about the present success of fuzzy logic is the breadth of application of this paradigm, ranging from consumer products to industrial process control and automotive engineering. In spite of obvious differences in scope and/or manner of implementation, fuzzy logic plays a similarly central role in creating a suitable rule-based, linguistic, control strategy. Moreover, fuzzy logic bridges the gap between symbolic processing and numeric computation, thereby expanding the domain of application of control engineering to areas that have hitherto fallen outside this scope. And specifically, fuzzy logic forms the basis for implementation of control strategies in a wider sense to include decision-making and supervisory control. Application areas in nuclear engineering are also elaborated on control in and of NPPs, safety management, accounting of nuclear waste, and nuclear energy and public opinion [44]. As a good example of intelligent engineering and technology for nuclear power plant operation [42], The Three Mile Island (TMI) accident has drawn considerable attention from the engineering, scientific, management, financial, and political communities, as well as from society at large. The paper [42] surveys possible causes of the accident studied by various groups. Research continues in this area with many projects aimed at specifically improving the performance and operation of a NPP using the contemporary technologies available. In addition to the known cause of the accident, the authors also speculated on other potential causes of the accident and suggested a strategy for coping with these problems in the future. Using the TMI experience, the paper [42] offers a set of specific recommendations for future designers to take advantage of the powerful tools of intelligent technologies that we are now able to master and encourages to adopt a novel methodology called fuzzy constraint network.

3 Applications of Nuclear Engineering

The FLINS'96 proceedings consist of a series of invited lectures by distinguished professors and individual oral presentations, in total 52 papers selected out of 80, submitted from more than 20 countries. The volume is divided into three parts. The first part (Soft Computing Techniques) provides basic tools to treat fuzzy logic, neural networks, genetic algorithms, decision-making, and software used for general soft-computing aspects. The second part (Intelligent Engineering Systems) reports on engineering problems such as knowledge-based engineering, expert systems, process control integration, diagnosis, measurements, and interpretation by soft computing. The third part (Nuclear Applications) concentrates on the applications of fuzzy logic and intelligent computing in nuclear engineering. We only survey here the third part on nuclear applications of fuzzy logic.

The paper by Dulin and Kiselev [6] covered the problem of storing and retrieving information from large data bases, where the information has no exact structure and different objects have very thin (or weak) relations to each other. It is one of the biggest problems in decision-support systems, especially in those spheres, where the information is complicated and very changeable. One way to solve this problem could be to build a semiotic model of the sphere according to our goals. One of the important parts of systems based on semiotic modelling is the active knowledge base supplied with the special concordance mechanism of structural consistency. The authors deal with an active knowledge base condition considered by means of connections structure analysis of knowledge base components. They examined a set of subjects with connections that have a binary existence estimate, and distinguished consonant, dissonant, and assonant sets depending on whether the consonance criterion is satisfied. They also proposed an algorithm for reducing assonant and dissonant sets to a consonance state with minimum expenditures in terms of the general number variable estimates of the connections.

Nishiwaki [22] discussed various uncertainties involved in emergency conditions, and pointed out that uncertainties in many factors are fuzzy. As a result, he proposed to use fuzzy theory as an attempt for analysing cause and effects under emergency conditions such as in Hiroshima, Nagasaki, and other nuclear accidents, and for fuzzy failure analysis and diagnostics of NPPs.

In the event of a nuclear accident, any decision on countermeasures to protect the public should be made based upon the basic principles recommended by the International Commission on Radiological Protection. The application of these principles requires a balance between the cost and the averted radiation dose, taking into account many subjective factors such as social/political acceptability, psychological stress, and the confidence of the population in the authorities. In the framework of classical methods, it is difficult to quantify human subjective judgements and the uncertainties of data efficiently. Hence, any attempt to find the optimal solution for countermeasure strategies without deliberative sensitivity analysis can be misleading. However, fuzzy sets, with linguistic terms to describe the human subjective judgement and with fuzzy numbers to model the uncertainties of the parameters, can be introduced to eliminate these difficulties. With fuzzy rating, a fuzzy multiple attribute decision-making method can rank the possible countermeasure strategies. The paper [18] described the procedure of the method and presented an illustrative example.

To improve reliability in detecting anomalies in NPP performance, the authors [36] presented a method based on acquiring various characteristics of signal data using autoregressive, wavelet, and fractal-analysis techniques. These characteristics are combined using a decision-making approach based on fuzzy logic. This approach is able to detect and distinguish several system states.

Kanai et al. [13] presented an application of fuzzy linear programming methods to the optimization of a radiation shield. They investigated possibilities for reducing the radiation effects attainable in hydrated, lead- and boron-containing materials of optimal compositions using the fuzzy linear programming.

In [21], Moon and Lee presented an algorithm for autonomous wall following movement of a mobile robot. It has eight ultrasonic range transducers, and is steered by separately driving the two front wheels. A smoothing based on fuzzy sets is applied to the detected wall tracks and a cubic spline function passing through the smoothed points is computed in each step successively. The spline function is used for computing the planned path and the rotational target. A set of fuzzy control rules is used to compute the two front wheel speeds.

Liu and Ruan [19] reported an FLC scheme to improve the power control stability of the BR1 reactor at SCK•CEN. The authors discussed the various possibilities to find the best or optimal FLC scheme for controlling the BR1's power level. Some experimental results reveal that the FLC scheme has the potential to replace nuclear reactor operators in the control room. Hence, the entire control process can be automatic, simple, and effective.

Sharif Heger et al. [37] present a method for self-tuning of fuzzy logic controllers based on the estimation of the optimum value of the centroids of its output fuzzy set. The method can be implemented on line and does not require modification of membership functions and control rules. The main features of this method are that the rules are left intact to retain the operators' expertise in the FLC rule base, and that the parameters that require any adjustment are identifiable in advance and that their number is kept to a minimum. Therefore, the use of this method preserves the control statements in the original form. Results of simulation and actual tests show that this tuning method demonstrates a similar improvement for power up and power down experiments, based on both simulation and actual case studies. For these experiments, the control rules for the fuzzy logic controller were derived from control statements that expressed the relationships between error, rate of error change, and duration of direction of control rod movements.

Chung et al. [5] proposed an improved method for multiple-fault diagnosis in large-scale NPPs. The authors showed a way for getting the dominant feed-forward control loop with multi-path and also gave the corresponding fault diagnosis. As an illustration, they demonstrated the usefulness of the proposed method in the primary system of the Kori nuclear power plant unit

2.

Considering the fuzzy nature of impact signals detected from the complex mechanical structures in a NPP under operation, Oh *et al.* [23] proposed the Loose Part Monitoring System (LPMS) with a signal processing technique utilizing fuzzy logic. In the proposed LPMS design, comprehensive relations among the impact signal features are taken into account in the fuzzy rule bases for the alarm discrimination and impact event diagnosis. The test results show that some information provided by the LPMS is easily understandable by a plant operator. Thus, the proposed approach for the loose part monitoring and diagnosis has been revealed to be effective not only in suppressing the false alarm generation but also in characterizing the metallic loose-part impact event from the aspects of Possible Impacted-Area (PIA) and Degree of Impact Magnitude (DIM) in NPPs.

In [35], Schildt described a fuzzy controller for safety-critical process control, especially for applications in the field of NPPs. One can show that the size of necessary rules is relatively small. Thus, there exists a real chance for verification and validation of software due to the fact that the whole software can be structured into standard fuzzy software (like fuzzification, inference algorithms, and defuzzification), real-time operating system software, and the contents of the rule base. The author also implemented fundamental principles of safety techniques like *dynamization principle, monitoring function,* and *watch dog function* into a special fuzzy control design. As a conclusion in [35], up to now some theoretical knowledge of *stability proof* is available so that we see a real good chance for applying a fuzzy controller in the field of safety-critical process control.

Na *et al.* [16] presented a real-time expert system which was implemented using Artificial Intelligence (AI) and object-oriented technology for alarm processing and presentation in a NPP. The knowledge base is constructed based on some schemes to process and display alarms to the plant operators. The activated alarms are dynamically prioritized by the reasoning rules, and then presented on the process mimic overview and by some other means. To demonstrate the proposed system, the alarm processing and presentation is carried out in a simulated environment of the TMI-2 accident.

The work of Guido *et al.* [9] explored some of the developing states of an *Expert Environment* (EE) for plant failures *Diagnosis Systems* starting from *Knowledge Base Systems.* The main goal of the EE is to develop a diagnosis tool performing an intelligent monitoring of some process variables, detecting system faults, and deducing the possible causes of the anomaly symptoms. The authors presented a prototype system that carries out an inspection of anomalous symptoms and a diagnosis process on a simplified model of the steam generators feed-water systems of a Pressurized-Heavy-Water Reactor (PHWR).

Nuclear power plants, like other complex systems, are involved with heterogeneous data to describe their operational state, e.g., real-time process data (analog and binary), design data, graphics, and relational data. The control room operators of these plants need tools to unify the information and presentation of these data in only one consult and navigation paradigm. Erwin *et al.* [7] described the distribution and visualization system of the Atucha I NPP in Argentina. This object-oriented system offers facilities to build, test, and use visualization screens about systems, subsystems, and components of the plant, organized in a hierarchical form to overloading the operator with information. Each object that conforms a visualization screen includes a set of inner variables associated with tags in the plant, plant design data, or other inner variables of the same or different objects. These inner variables can be used to modify the object's behavior and/or functionality. The data management system is based on a distributed system, working on a local area network using TCP protocol to receive and send data to graphical clients.

4   FLINS Activities at SCK•CEN

Clearly, recent developments show that fuzzy logic and intelligent computing is a scientific revolution that has been waiting for decades. Research in this field has reached a degree where industrial application is possible. In nuclear industry, problems such as security, maintenance, monitoring, diagnosis, and environment are all related to humans and their society, and are the most important and difficult problems. These problems are so complicated that they can hardly be solved without a global approach. Therefore, soft and intelligent computing may be one of the most powerful tools available to us. FLINS started as a new research project, launched in line with its objective to give young talented people the opportunity to carry out future-oriented research. FLINS was initially built within one of the postdoctoral research projects at SCK•CEN. At this moment, the FLINS group consists of several engineers, especially from nuclear science, and scientists who are currently working on various projects combined with their doctoral or postdoctoral research activities. Several research topics related to nuclear applications have been discussed and are being further worked upon by the members of the group: decision-making for radiation protection by fuzzy logic [25, 38, 41], fuzzy modelling of dynamic behavior in complex systems [24], and fuzzy engineering in nuclear applications [32, 33].

The main task for FLINS for the coming years is to solve many intricate problems pertaining to the nuclear environment by using modern technologies as additional tools, and to bridge a gap between novel technologies and the industrial nuclear world. Specific prototyping of FLC of the BR1 reactor has been chosen as FLINS' first priority. This is an on-going R&D project for controlling the power level of the BR1 reactor at SCK•CEN. The project started in 1995 and aims to investigate the added value of FLC for nuclear reactors.

4.1 BR1 Reactor and FLC Applications

BR1 is a graphite-moderated and air-cooled reactor fuelled with natural ura-
nium metal. Its nominal power is 4 MW but it is generally operated at 0.7
MW to reduce the air pumping cost. The reactor is available for 8 hours
per day; the time utilisation factor amounts to about 80%. About 50% of
this total reactor time is used at the request of industry and universities for
neutron activation analysis in a variety of applications. The other activities
are related to international research programs.

The model presently used for the BR1 reactor actually is the point kinetics
model. It can be described by a non-linear system with a set of differential
equations with six delayed neutron groups [2]:

$$\frac{dn}{dt} = \frac{\rho - \beta}{\Lambda} n + \sum_{i=1}^{6} \lambda_i c_i$$

$$\frac{dc_i}{dt} = \frac{\beta_i}{\Lambda} n - \lambda_i c_i, i = 1, \ldots, 6$$

Where
n is the neutron density at rated power (%);
c_i is the ith group precursor concentration;
β_i is the ith group delayed neutron fraction;
β is the total delayed neutron fraction;
λ_i is the ith group delayed neutron decay constant (s^{-1});
Λ is the neutron generation time (s);
ρ is the reactivity due to the control rod $(\Delta k/k)$. (Note: Reactivity is defined
as the difference between the effective multiplication factor and unity divided
by the effective multiplication factor).

The neutron density is related to the power level, and depends on the reactivity of the reactor and the number of delayed neutrons. The control
requirements of BR1 are to keep the reactivity $\rho(t)$ near zero or to exhibit a
certain transient behaviour for a required power transient. At the required
steady-state conditions, if $\rho(t)$ is different from zero, the controller inserts or
withdraws the regulating rods to return $\rho(t)$ to zero. However, since $\rho(t)$ is
not easily measurable, we use input signals such as the Difference of Power
(DP) (difference between the real and the desired power) and the reactor period (T). (Period is defined as the power level divided by the rate of change
of power. Thus, a period of infinity corresponds to steady state, while one
is equal to a small positive number indicating a rapid power increase). For
the BR1 reactor, there are two types of control rods, namely, A-rods (for
the fine-tuning of reactivity, indicated as MOPA) and C-rods (mainly for the
compensation of other reactivity effects, indicated as MOPC). Fine tuning
is performed by 1 single A-rod while the coarse tuning is performed by 8 C-
rods, all moving together. Therefore, in the paper we identify them as A-rods
and C-rods. Basically, the controller reads DP as input. This input signal

is electronically transformed into an analogue command signal. Its sign and magnitude command the selection of the direction and speed of the A-rods. The controller is efficiently limited by a certain delay due to neutronics and the thermal behaviour of the reactor. Whereas FLC no longer requires an explicit model of the reactor, it can take into account the knowledge of the operators for controlling the reactor.

Whereas in the classical control of BR1, A- and C-rods are moved separately, FLC has the advantage that it allows A- and C-rods to move simultaneously. This introduces a new concept in nuclear reactor control. From the economical and safety aspects of control, the rod movements should be as small as possible. Therefore, the FLC system seems to be a better solution. The resulting output controls the motion of rods. Figure 1 is a simplified version of the BR1 controller.

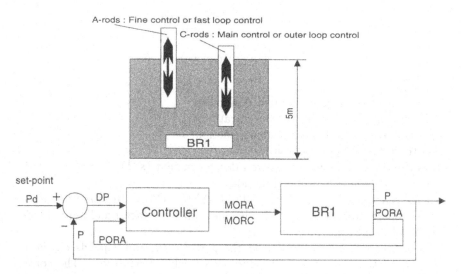

Figure 1: Two types of control rods at BR1: A-rods for the fine-tuning of reactivity (MOPA), and C-rods mainly for the compensation of other reactivity effects (MOPC).

The kernel of FLC is a fuzzy knowledge base in fuzzy control applications. Normally, the rules in fuzzy control can be derived from: (1) the operator's experience; or (2) the operator's control actions; or (3) a crisp or fuzzy model of the process to be controlled, and or (4) training sets. The most common approach appears to be the first one, using the subjective input of control specialists, such as nuclear reactor operators. The second approach is used in industrial problems. As an example of the third approach, we refer to Sugeno's fuzzy control of a model car [39]. And for the fourth approach, we refer to Mamdani et al.'s implementing rule-based control of industrial processes [20]. For the BR1 project, we however use at this time both the first and second approach.

Our current aim is to control the reactor in steady-state operation. According to observations and experience, if the difference between the real and the desired power (DP) is larger than 0.2 % but smaller than 0.8 %, the A-rods do not insert as far; by contrast, if DP is larger than 0.8 %the , A-rods insert further. For a negative value of DP, A-rods withdraw to an extent depending on the magnitude of the DP perturbation. This rule base remains true for as long as the A-rods have enough space to move. However, when the A-rods reach their insertion or withdrawal limit, they start to move in the opposite direction to return to their initial position. In the meantime, the C-rods are controlled to equilibrate the reactivity by slow insertion or withdrawal. This sequence of actions can be modelled in the more sophisticated rule base presented in Table 1.

Table 1: Rule base of FLC with two inputs and two outputs

PORA	IL		NIL		AC		NWL		WL	
DP	MOPA	MOPC	MOPA	MOPC	MOPA	MOPC	MOPA	MOPC	MOPA	MOPC
NL	WB	NA	WB	NA	WB	NA	WS	WS	NA	WB
NM	WM	NA	WM	NA	WM	NA	WS	WS	NA	WS
NS	WS	NA	WS	NA	WS	NA	WS	NA	NA	WS
NZ	NA	NA	NA	NA	NA	NA	NA	NA	NA	NA
PS	NA	IS	IS	NA	IS	NA	IS	NA	IS	NA
PM	NA	IS	IS	IS	IM	NA	IM	NA	IM	NA
PB	NA	IB	IS	IS	IB	NA	IB	NA	IB	NA

In this project, we aim to be of benefit to the existing control systems by applying fuzzy logic as an additional tool for both the safety and economic aspects in NPPs. Although the FLC briefly described in here is already a significant improvement compared to the classical BR1 controller due to its ability to control the A- and C-rods simultaneously and thereby expanding the dynamic control range, we believe that there is still room to further enhance the robustness of the FLC. To validate the correctness of the rule base in detail however, the closed-loop testing is necessary. The BR1 facilities will be further used to calibrate fuzzy logic technology for applications in nuclear industry. However, the licensing aspect of this technology as nuclear technology could be more challenging and time consuming.

4.2 A Real FLC Demo Model

Based on the background of FLC application in the BR1 reactor, we have also made a real FLC demo model 2. The demo model is suitable for us to test and compare our new algorithms of fuzzy control, because it is always difficult and time consuming due to safety aspects to do all experiments in a real nuclear environment. Particularly, this demo model is designed to simulate the power control principle of BR1 [17].

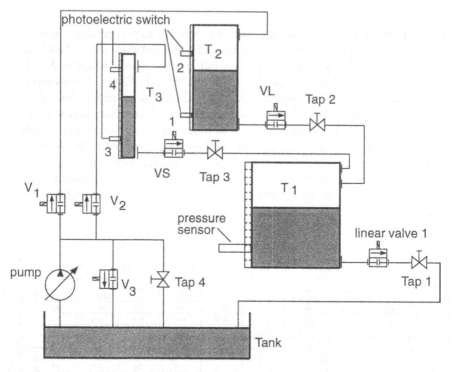

The Demo Model Structure

Figure 2: The working principle of the demo model

This demo model for the water level control has been made at SCK•CEN in co-operation with OMRON Belgium. It is made of transparent plexiglass material with coloured water inside, and it is a good visual equipment for testing different control algorithms, especially for fuzzy logic control strategy. The demo model consists of two parts. One is the water level control system including one tank, three towers, five sensors, valves and pipes. Another is a box in which electrical control elements are installed such as PLC, Fuzzy unit, A/D & D/A unit, and power supply etc.

In this demo system, our goal is to control the water level in tower T_1 at a desired level by means of tuning VL (the valve for large control tower T_2) and VS (the valve for small control tower T_3). The pump keeps on working to supply water to T_2 and T_3. All taps are for manual tuning at this time. V_1 and V_2 are used to control the water levels in T_2 and T_3 in some areas. For example, when the water level in T_2 is lower than photoelectric switch sensor 1 the on-off valve V_1 will be opened (on), and when the water level in T_2 is higher than photoelectric switch sensor 2 the on-off valve V_1 will be closed (off). The same is true of V_2. Only when both V_1 and V_2 are closed will

V_3 be opened, because it can decrease the pressure of the pump and prolong its working life. So far we have not used the linear valve 1. It will be used in simulating some complex system. The pressure sensor is used to detect the height of water level in T_1. So for T_1, it has two entrances and one exit for water flow. This is a typical dynamic system, and it is very difficult to control it by a traditional way [17].

For this tower T_1, see Figure 3, it has an infow and an outflow. Suppose the height of the water is h, the size (area) of water is A and the size of output hole is a, we may find the basic relationship between the inflow and the outflow. The basic function is:

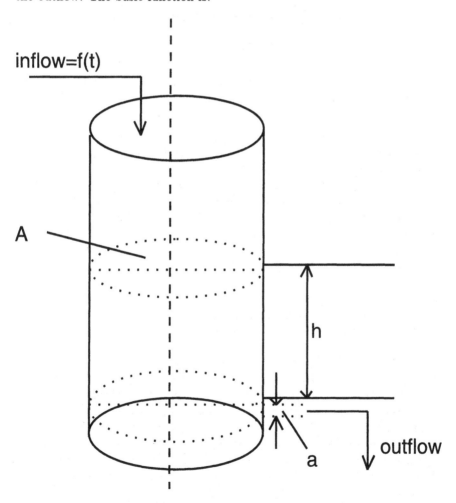

Figure 3: The dynamic analysis of the tower

Table 2: Control rule table

DD\D	NL	NS	ZE	PS	PL
NL	PL/ZE	PL/ZE	PL/ZE	PS/ZE	PS/ZE
NS	PL/ZE	PL/ZE	PS/NS	PS/PS	PS/NS
ZE	PL/ZE	PS/PS	ZE/ZE	NS/PS	NS/PS
PS	PS/ZE	ZE/NS	NL/ZE	NL/NL	NL/NL
PL	ZE/ZE	NL/NL	NL/ZE	NL/NL	NL/NL

$$\frac{Adh}{dt} = inflow(t) - outflow(t)$$

$$\frac{Adh}{dt} = f(t) - ka\sqrt{2gh}$$

where $outflow(t) = ka\sqrt{2gh}$ and k is a constant coefficient. In the current demo model, however,

$$f(t) = f_1(t) + f_2(t),$$

where $f_1(t)$ is the outflow of T_2 and $f_2(t)$ is the outflow of T_3, and they are nonlinear variables with some random disturbance. So the system is a nonlinear and time varying system.

In this system, we choose D and DD as inputs of the fuzzy logic controller, and VL and VS as the outputs of the fuzzy logic controller, where $D = P - S$, that is, Difference (D) between the practical value (P) of water level and the set value (S). $DD = D(t) - D(t - 1)$, that is, Derivative of D (DD), in other words, the speed and direction of the change of water level. VL and VS represent the current signal to VL (large valve) and VS (small valve), respectively.

Table 2 contains all control rules. In this table, for example, PL/ZE at row 2 and column 3 means: if D is NS and DD is NL then VL is PL and VS is ZE. In other words, if the practical water level is *a little lower* (NS) than the desired level and the speed of the water level *falling down* is *large* (NL) then VL will *open largely* (PL) and VS will *not change* (ZE).

With the help of the fuzzy control rules in Table 2, we get the control effect illustrated in Figure 4 (the thick curve). In this figure, the thick curve records the trajectory of the water level in T_1. From 0-5 minutes, the set value is 15 cm (S1=15); from 5-10 minutes, the set value is 25 cm (S2=25); from 10-15 minutes, the set value is 15 cm (S3=15). This is the best result of all experimental tests. Before this result, normally, we always find the control effect is either curve a or b. Curve a means a big overshot but with a fast response. Curve b means no overshot but with a slow response. It is well known that it is difficult to achieve a control result with a fast response and no overshot. Our result has already overcome this dilemma.

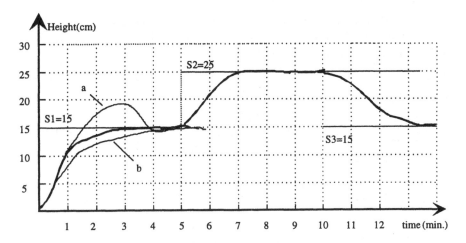

Figure 4: The trajectory of fuzzy logic control water level

5   Concluding Remarks

As pointed out in [43], the nuclear power industry puts special demands on plant safety, surpassing all other industries in its safety culture. The regulatory environment in which nuclear power plants operate reflect these needs, and also the demands of the public for high levels of assurance about safety and regulatory compliance. This culture is not one which encourages innovation in control systems and philosophy, yet nowhere are there greater potential benefits from high reliablility systems, automated fault recognition and rationally supported decision making. A demonstration of the use of intelligent control in an actual plant is a vital needed step in prototyping the next generation of nuclear power plants. These must prove not only the ability to safe survive major disturbances, but also the ability to operate efficiently and reliably in normal operation and to recover smoothly from the minor events that will occur on a regular basis, without challenge to future operations.

In this paper, we reviewed applications of fuzzy logic and intelligent computing in nuclear engineering and reported the real R&D project on fuzzy logic application to the BR1 research reactor as a test bed. We aim to be of benefit to the existing control systems by applying fuzzy logic and intelligent computing as an additional tool for both the safety and economic aspects in nuclear power plants. Although the FLC described in this paper is already a significant improvement compared to the classical BR1 controller due to its ability to control the A- and C-rods simultaneously and thereby expanding the dynamic control range, we believe that there is still room to further enhance the robustness of the FLC. To validate the correctness of the rule base in detail however, the closed-loop testing is necessary. The BR1 facilities will be further used to calibrate fuzzy logic technology for applications in nuclear industry. However, the licensing aspect of this technology as nuclear technology could be more challenging and time consuming.

References

[1] Akin H.L. and Altin V. (1991): Rule-based fuzzy logic controller for a PWR-type nuclear power plant. IEEE Transaction on Nuclear Science **38** (2), 883–890

[2] Bell G.I. and Glasstone S. (1970): Nuclear Reactor Theory. Van Nostrand Reinhold Company, New York

[3] Bernard J.A. (1988): Use of a rule-based system for process control. IEEE Control Systems Magazine **8** (5), 3–13

[4] Bubak M., Moscinski J., and Jewulski J. (1983): Fuzzy-logic approach to HTR nuclear power plant model control. Annals of Nuclear Energy **10** (9), 467–471

[5] Chung H.Y., Park I.S., and Bien Z. (1996): Improved method for incipient multiple fault diagnosis with application to nuclear power plant. [29], 365–371

[6] Dulin S.K. and Kiselev I.A. (1996): Clustering and retrieving information in nuclear science for decision-support techniques. [29], 293–298

[7] Galdoz E.G., Fontanini H.R., and Tapia E.R. (1996): Integrating information in a real-time data visualization system on nuclear power plant. [29], 401–406

[8] Glasstone S. and Sesonske A. (1980): Nuclear Reactor Engineering. Van Nostrand Reinhold Company, New York

[9] Guido P.N., Oggianu S., Etchepareborda A., and Fernandez O. (1996): Expert environment for the development of nuclear power plants failure diagnosis systems. [29], 395–400

[10] Heger, A. S., Alang-Rashid N.K., and Jamshidi M. (1995): Application of fuzzy logic in nuclear reactor control part I: an assessment of state-of-the-art. Nuclear Safety **36** (1), 109–121

[11] Iijima T., Nakajima Y., and Nishiwaki Y. (1995): Application of fuzzy logic control systems for reactor feed-water control. Fuzzy Sets and Systems **74** (1), 61–72

[12] Jung C.H., Ham C.S., and Lee K.L. (1995): A real time self tuning fuzzy controller for the steam generator through scaling factor adjustment for the steam generator of NPP. Fuzzy Sets and Systems **74** (1), 53–60

[13] Kanai Y., Miura T., Odano N., and Sugasawa S. (1996): Optimal selections for shielding materials by using fuzzy linear programming. [29], 323–328

[14] Kinoshita M., Fukuzaki T., Stoh T., and Miyake M. (1988): An automatic operation method for control rods in BWR plants. In-Core Instrumentation and Reactor Core Assessment, Proceedings of Specialists' Meeting. Cadarache, France, 213–220

[15] Kuan C.C., Lin C., and Hsu C.C. (1992): Fuzzy logic control of steam generator water level in pressurized water reactors. Nuclear Technology **100** (1), 125–134

[16] Na N.J., Kim I.S., Kim J.T., Hwang I.K., Lee D.Y., and Ham C.S. (1996): AI-based alarm processing for a nuclear power plant. [29], 388–394

[17] Li X. and Ruan D. (1997): Constructing a fuzzy logic control demo model at the Belgian Nuclear Research Centre. Proceedings of EUFIT'97 **2**, 1408–1412

[18] Liu X. and Ruan D. (1996): Application of fuzzy decision making to countermeasure strategies after a nuclear accident. [29], 308–315

[19] Liu Z. and Ruan D. (1996): Experiments of fuzzy logic control on a nuclear research reactor. [29], 336–348

[20] Mamdani E.H., Ostergaard J.J., and Lembessis E. (1983): Use of fuzzy logic for implementing rule-based control of industrial processes. Advances in Fuzzy sets, Possibility Theory, and Applications. Plenum Press, 307–323

[21] Moon B.S. and Lee J. (1996): A fuzzy control algorithm for a mobile robot to move pass obstacles. [29], 329–335

[22] Nishiwaki Y. (1996): Uncertainties under emergency conditions and possible application of fuzzy theory for nuclear safety. [29], 299–307

[23] Oh Y.G., Hong H.P., Han S.J., Chun C.S., and Kim B.K. (1996): Fuzzy logic utilization for the diagnosis of metallic loose part impact in nuclear power plant. [29], 372–378

[24] Ouliddren K. and Nowé A. (1996): An approach to incremental fuzzy modelling of dynamic behavior of functions in complex systems. [29], 224–232

[25] Ruan D. (1993): Fuzzy sets and decision making in nuclear science. Proceedings of Fifth IFSA World Congress **2**, 1058–1061

584

[26] Ruan D. and D'hondt P. (1993): Fuzzy systems in nuclear applications. Proceedings of EUFIT'93 1, 87–90

[27] Ruan D. (1995): Fuzzy logic in the nuclear research world. Fuzzy Sets and Systems 74 (1) 5–13

[28] Ruan D., D'hondt P., Govaerts P., and Kerre E.E., Eds. (1994): Fuzzy Logic and Intelligent Technologies in Nuclear Science. World Scientific, Singapore

[29] Ruan D., D'hondt P., Govaerts P., and Kerre E.E., Eds. (1996): Intelligent Systems and Soft Computing for Nuclear Science and Industry. World Scientific, Singapore

[30] Ruan D., Van Den Durpel L., and D'hondt P. (1995): Fuzzy engineering in nuclear research applications. Proceedings of FUZZ-IEEE/IFES'95 1, 211-218

[31] Ruan D., Ed. (1996): Fuzzy Logic Foundations and Industrial Applications. Kluwer Academic Publishers, Boston

[32] Ruan D. (1996): Fuzzy logic applications in nuclear industry. [31], 313–327

[33] Ruan D. (1996): R&D on fuzzy logic applications at SCK•CEN. Proceedings of NAFIP'96, 428–432

[34] Ruan D. and Li X. (1997): Fuzzy logic control applications to the Belgian Nuclear Reactor 1 (BR1). Special Issue on Engineering for Energy with Intelligent Technologies. Computers and Artificial Intelligence (to appear)

[35] Schildt G.H. (1996): A fuzzy controller for NPPs. [29], 379–387

[36] Schoonewelle H., van der Hagen T.H., and Hoogenboom J.E. (1996): Process monitoring by combining several signal-analysis results using fuzzy logic. [29], 316–322

[37] Sharif Heger A., Jamshidi Mo., and Alang-Rashid N.K. (1996): Self-tuning fuzzy logic nuclear reactor controller. [29], 349–358

[38] Sohier A., Van Camp M., Ruan D., and Govaerts P. (1993): Methods for radiological assessment in the near-field during the early phase of an accidental release of radioactive material using an incomplete data base. Radiation Protection Dosimetry 50 (2-4), 321–325

[39] Sugeno M. and Nishida M. (1985): Fuzzy control of model car. Fuzzy Sets and Systems 16, 103–113

[40] Terunuma S., Kishiwada K., Takahashi H., Iijima T., and Hayashi H. (1988): Application of fuzzy algorithms for the feed-water control system in Fugen HWR. Proceedings of an International Conference on Man-Machine Interface in the Nuclear Industry, 463–473

[41] Van de Walle B., Ruan D., and Kerre E.E. (1993): Applications of fuzzy reasoning in nuclear decision aiding systems. Fuzzy Systems & A. I., **2** (2), 35–46

[42] Wang P.P. and Gu X. (1996): Intelligent engineering & technology for nuclear power plant operation. [29], 359–364

[43] Williams J.G. and Jouse W.C. (1993): Intellgent control in safety systems: criteria for acceptance in the nuclear power industry. IEEE TRANSACTIONS on Nuclear Science **40** (6), 2040–2044

[44] Zimmermann H.-J. (1996): Fuzzy algorithmic and knowledge-based decision support in nuclear engineering. [29], 1–8

Computational Intelligence Techniques in Landmine Detection

A. Filippidis*, L.C. Jain** and N.M. Martin***

*Land Operations Division, Defence Science Technology Organisation
P.O. Box 1500 Salisbury S.A. 5108, Australia
**Knowledge Based Intelligent Engineering Systems
University of South Australia
Adelaide, The Levels Campus, S.A., 5195, Australia
***Weapons Systems Division, Defence Science Technology Organisation
P.O. Box 1500 Salisbury S.A. 5108, Australia

Abstract

Knowledge-based techniques have been used to automatically detect surface land mines present in thermal and multispectral images. Polarisation sensitive infrared sensing is used to highlight the polarisation signature of man-made targets such as landmines over natural features in the image. Processing the thermal polarisation images using a background discrimination algorithm we were able to successfully identify eight of the nine man-made targets, three of which were mines with only three false targets. A digital camera was used to collect a number of multispectral bands of the test mine area containing three surface landmines with natural and man-made clutter. Using a supervised and unsupervised neural network technique on the textural and spectral characteristics of selected multispectral bands we successfully identified the three surface mines but obtained numerous false targets with varying degrees of accuracy. Finally to further improve our detection of land mines we use a fuzzy rule based fusion technique on the processed polarisation resolved image together with the output results of the two best classifies. Fuzzy rule based fusion identified the locations of all three landmines and reduced the false alarm rate from seven (as obtained by the polarisation resolved image) to two.

1. Introduction

There are now over 50 million active land mines that have been abandoned in over 60 countries [1] around the world. Over the last few years land mines have become a major international political issue. Anti-personnel and anti-vehicle mines abandoned after an armed conflict has subsided pose a threat to civilian populations in many countries. It has been estimated [1] that Afghanistan, for example, has up to ten million abandoned mines which now threaten the everyday life of many of its people. A large number of these landmines were thrown from aeroplanes and helicopters, and due to their small size and earthy colours blend well into the surrounding vegetation and soils. With the passage of time they may be lightly covered with soil and vegetation, and surrounded by metallic and non-metallic debris. The technical problems in detecting these devices are formidable and no satisfactory system yet exists. The anti-armour land mines are often buried while the antipersonnel mines are relatively small and typically concealed by grass. Many abandoned mines contain few metallic components and therefore evade detection by inductive detectors. The proximity of the mines is often littered with used ordinance, so finding the mines constitutes a formidable target detection and discrimination problem.

Mine clearance is generally an extremely slow, manpower-intensive and costly process. Methods of detecting mines [1] vary from simple manual probing to a variety of electronic and chemical technologies, including electromagnetic induction, thermal images, thermal neutron activation (TNA), ground penetrating and imaging radar to name just a few. Many of the systems under development employ two or more types of sensors with their outputs fused together to maximise the detection performance while minimising false alarms. Sensors are often vehicle mounted, or in some cases may be operated from a low flying helicopter.

One of the successful commercial mine detection systems is marketed by Marietta Electronics & Missiles [2]. The system uses an 8-12 micron infrared sensor which looks for target characteristics in terms of area, perimeter, moments and intensity measures. They present a combination of three neural network approaches, supervised, real-time learning networks and unsupervised real-time learning to cover a number of different scenarios of known and unknown mines, clutter and terrain. The preprocessing stage of the sensor data to extract the features was the crucial stage. It consisted of local filtering, histogram equalisation, linear expansion, contrast stretching, feature extraction, image enhancement, segmentation, and a prescreener, etc. It can be employed at up to 80 feet stand-off range.

The goal of the work reported in here is to investigate the detection of surface land mines, given multiple registered images of the mined area obtained from a suite of visible to infrared wavelength sensors. We will be looking into the automatic detection of surface landmines. The novel approach takes the outputs from two different imaging sensors; a thermal (infrared) imager fitted with a rotating polariser and a multispectral (optical) camera. The target information from the two images is fused together using a fuzzy rule-based system. Compared to the earlier commercial system [2], the new approach is more suited to above surface landmines because (a) the multispectral sensor will only identify surface targets; and (b) the rotating polarisation filter attached to the thermal imager lens will highlight surface targets by its particular polarisation signature. The technique reported here is less complicated in terms of the number of processing stages, and only widely accepted preprocessing techniques are used.

In order to investigate the automatic land mine detection an experimental test mine field was established. It included particular anti-personnel and anti-vehicle mines as well as natural and man-made clutter, and is described in Section 2. The automatic surface mine detection system will be implemented using a combination of knowledge-based techniques, and these techniques are reviewed in Section 3. Section 4 provides an overview of the novel detection system. The collection and processing of the thermal images is described in Section 5, where the use of the rotating polariser fitted on the lens of the thermal imager has enhanced its target detection capabilities. In Section 6 we describe a passive multispectral scanning system (MSS). The multispectral scanner is used to detect spectral intensity differences between surface landmines, man-made and natural clutter. Section 6 also includes a description of the multispectral classification results for an unsupervised neural network implemented using Adaptive Resonance Theory (ART2), and a genetically engineered multi-layered perceptron (MLP) with an architecture and selection of input images derived using a Genetic Algorithm (GA) tool. In Section 7, a data fusion technique using fuzzy rules, based on *a priori* knowledge of the landmine size (at a certain target range) will be used on the classification output images of ART2, the MLP, and the processed polarisation image.

Discussion and conclusion of results describe the advantages and limitations of each sensor and classifiers on their own. Then the improved mine detection capability using fusion of the output classification results of ART2 and the optimised MLP together with the polarisation resolved image. The locations of all three landmines were detected including a polystyrene block target with similar dimensions as one of the mines, with only two false alarms (FA).

2.   Test Mine Field

For this study a small test mine field was established. The field consisted mainly of seasonal grasses with a number of walking tracks through it. The soil was hard packed red loam. Figure 1 is a colour composite image of the test field, and shows three mines (in circles A, B, C) VS50, M14 and PMM and one surrogate mine (D, made of a polystyrene block similar to the material of the M14 mine) together with man-made clutter (E, F, G, H, I in squares) such as a marker1, aluminium can, teflon block, marker2 and aluminium block, respectively, surrounded by dry grasses

The land mines were an American M14, an Italian VS50 anti-personnel mine, and a Russian PMM anti-tank mine. Pucks of similar dimensions to the M14 made of teflon, PVC, polystyrene (PS) and aluminium were also used [3]. The explosive material was removed from the landmines in this experiment. The M14 , VS50 and PMM mines have the following physical characteristics:

Table 1: Physical characteristics of landmines used in test minefield [3].

	M14	VS50	PMM
Weight	93gm	185gm	8kg
Diameter	56mm	90mm	330mm
Height	43mm	32mm	120mm
Casing Material	polystyrene	Acrylon-butadiene-styrene (ABS)	polystyrene

The Agema Thermovision 900 radiometric dual-band thermal imaging system formed the basis of the data collection and recording of the polarisation images. Both 3-5 micron and 8-12 micron scanners were available for use in this system, although only the 8-12 micron polarised images were used in this experiment. The rotating polariser consists of an Optometrics wire grid polarising filter which has precisely spaced grooves directly into a highly polished ZnSe substrate together with a small 12V electric motor which rotates the lens when mounted on the Agema scanners (8-12 micron).

The Agema system was set up a the van adjacent to the test mine field. The heads of the thermal imaging scanners together with the digital camera were set up on a tripod and mounted on the roof of the van. The scanners were fitted with a rotating polarisation filter, which at the time of the experiment rotated at approximately 1 revolution a second. Software on a personal computer could stop the rotation at 0, 45, 90 and 135 degrees. The scanning height was 3.5 metres, and the surface mine field was located at a range of approximately 8 metres. The digital camera recorded a number of images in the near IR spectrum (the bands were 449, 450, 550, and 600 nm), as well as a colour composite image of the mine field. The Agema recorded the same minefield through a complete revolution of the rotating polariser (i.e. 0-360 degrees).

3. Knowledge-based Techniques

The task of Automatic Target Recognition is being revolutionised through the use of so called knowledge-based techniques. Generally speaking, these are data and information processing techniques that are inspired by an understanding of information processing in biological systems. In some cases an attempt is made to actually mimic aspects of biological nervous systems. When this is the case the process will include an element of adaptive or evolutionary behaviour similar to biological systems. Knowledge-based techniques have been used extensively in our approach; namely Artificial Neural Networks, Genetic Algorithms, and the application of Data Fusion using Fuzzy Rules. These data and information processing techniques have recently generated tremendous interest amongst researchers.

An Artificial Neural Network (ANN) [4] is a system for processing information using a structure that mimics the biological neural system. They are typically designed to perform a non-linear mapping from a set of inputs to a set of outputs. ANNs are developed to try to achieve biological system type performance using a dense interconnection of simple processing elements analogous to biological neurons. ANNs are information driven rather than data driven. They are non-programmed adaptive information processing systems that can autonomously develop operational capabilities in response to an information environment. ANNs learn from experience and generalise from previous examples. They modify their behaviour in response to the environment, and are ideal in cases where the required mapping algorithm is not known and tolerance to faulty input information is required.

ANNs have been used for optimisation, control, signal processing, speech processing, machine vision, and decision making. Pattern recognition has, however, emerged as a major application because the network structure is suited to tasks that biological systems perform well, and pattern recognition is a good example where biological systems out-perform traditional computer programming approaches.

Genetic Algorithms were envisaged by Holland [5] in the 1970s as an algorithmic concept based on a Darwinian-type survival of the fittest strategy with sexual reproduction, where stronger individuals in the population have a higher chance of creating an offspring. A Genetic Algorithm (GA) is implemented as a computerised search and optimisation procedure which uses principles of natural genetics and natural selection They are an iterative procedure that consists of a constant sized population of individuals, each one represented by a finite linear string of symbols, known as the genome, encoding a possible solution in a given problem space. This space, referred to as the search space, comprises all possible solutions to the optimisation problem at hand. Standard Genetic Algorithms are implemented where the initial population of individuals is generated at random. At every evolutionary step, also known as generation, the individuals in the current population are decoded and evaluated according to a fitness function set for a given problem. The expected number of times an individual is chosen is approximately proportional to its relative performance in the population. Crossover is performed between two selected individuals by exchanging part of their genomes to form new individuals. The mutation operator is introduced to prevent premature convergence.

Fuzzy logic was first developed by Zadeh [6] in the mid 1960s for representing uncertain and imprecise knowledge. It provides an approximate but effective means of describing the behaviour of systems that are too complex or ill-defined, and not easily analysed mathematically. Fuzzy variables are processed using a system called a fuzzy logic controller. It involves fuzzification, fuzzy inference, and defuzzification. The fuzzification process converts a crisp input value to a fuzzy value. The fuzzy inference is responsible for drawing conclusions from the knowledge base. The defuzzification process converts the fuzzy control actions into a crisp control action.

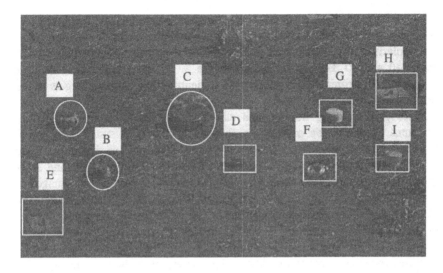

Figure 1: Composite colour image shows three mines (A, B, C in circles) VS50, M14 and PMM respectively, and one surrogate mine (D, made of a polystyrene block similar to the material of the M14 mine) together with man-made clutter (E, F, G, H, I in squares) such as a marker1, aluminium can, teflon block, marker2 and aluminium block respectively surrounded by dry grasses.

4. Automatic Detection by Knowledge-based Techniques

Intelligence is not easy to define however, we can say that a system is intelligent if it is able to improve its performance or maintain an acceptable level of performance in the presence of uncertainty. The main attributes of intelligence are learning, adaptation, fault tolerance and self organisation. Knowledge-based paradigms used to implement intelligence in the automatic detection system are neural networks, fuzzy systems and evolutionary computing techniques.

The automatic target recognition (ATR) system (shown in Figure 2) uses fuzzy rule based fusion to combine complementary information derived from both sensors to produce an output image (shown in Figure 8) showing the likelihood of mine locations. The inputs to the fusion process are the output classification results from ART2 (Figure 5) and the MLP (Figure 6) together with the output of the processed IR polarisation image as shown in Figure 7. ART2 was selected for its robust ability to classify targets in a real-time automated system. On the other hand, MLP requires hours of supervised training. ART2's inputs (using a 5x5 pixel window moving across each of the 4 bands shown in Figure 2) are the average spectral characteristics from the red, green and blue bands together with the three texture measures [7] (contrast, second angular momentum, and correlation) derived from the 449nm band. Using the accuracy of test and training of the mine and non-mine data a Genetic Algorithm (GA) tool (described in Section 6) is used to find the optimum structure and inputs of the MLP neural network. The MLP uses the three spectral bands: red, green and blue, together with the textural measure contrast derived from the 449nm band. Two polarisation resolved images are subtracted at two different polarisation angles (0 and 90 degrees) to obtain Figure 3. It then is processed using a background discrimination algorithm [8] to identify the man-made targets in the image shown in Figure 7.

Once preprocessing, training and classifications are complete, the identity attributes for the fusion process are obtained by the ATR system performing morphological processing on images of Figures 5, 6 and 7, as shown in Figure 2. This pre-fusion processing is performed to calculate the area 1, 2 and 3 (as shown in Figure 2) of the three 8x8 pixel windows (moving across images in Figures 5, 6 and 7), only if there are at least 4 pixels at the centre of the each window. For example, we count the number of black pixels connected together in the horizontal and vertical directions in the 8x8 pixel window as it moves across the entire image one pixel at a time.

We assume that have *a priori* knowledge on the approximate size (area) of the landmines for the digital camera viewing angle and stand-off range. Note that all the images are registered to Figure 1 which is a (1012 rows x 1524 column pixels) colour image obtained using a digital camera, hence the location of mines, vegetation and other man-made objects are within 4-5 pixel accuracy. In order to make the system more robust for the real-world applications, and in particular account for target shadows, the fuzzy fusion system takes variation in apparent target dimensions into account in the flexibility of the fuzzy rules, thereby making the ATR system more robust to registration problems and discrepancies in positions between images due to the landmine shadow positions in the classified multispectral images (Figure 5 and 6) compared to the IR polarisation image (Figure 7).

5. Thermal Imaging and Processing

Thermal imagery is a passive Electro Optical (EO) technique which has the potential to detect buried or surface objects such as plastic and metallic landmines. The potential detestability of landmines arises from the temperature differences resulting from a disparity of thermal characteristics between the buried or surface objects and the surrounding soil. In a thermal imaging system the degree of polarisation can be used to discriminate between man-made surface clutter objects such as landmines and natural vegetation or soil.

The Agema Thermovision 900 radiometric dual band thermal imaging system with rotating polarisers [3] was used to collect and record the thermal polarisation resolved images. Both the 3-5 micron and 8-12 micron scanners use cadmium mercury telluride detectors, cooled by Sterling cycle compressors. Cameras were mounted side by side on a tripod with a pan-tilt head. The assembly was placed on a platform on top of an instrument van. Cameras were

3.5m above the ground. Digitised output from the detectors was cabled to an image processing and recording system situated inside the instrument van. For our experimental work we used a 20 degree field of view lens, limiting the resolution to 1.5 mrad, sufficient to resolve M14 and VS50 landmine thermal signatures at up to 10 m horizontal range from the camera. Digitised output from the two scanners was stored on hard-disk in TIF format for latter image processing on a Sun workstation.

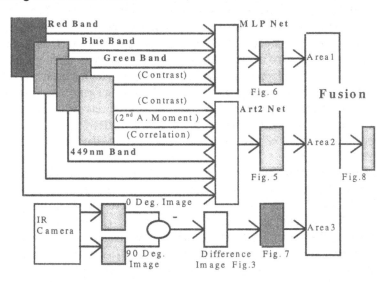

Figure 2: The ATR system uses a fuzzy rule based fusion technique to combine landmine identity attribute "area" from the outputs images of the MLP, ART2 and pre-processed thermal polarisation image.

5.1 Polarisation-Sensitive Thermal Imaging and Stokes Parameters

The sensing technique used exploits the polarimetric thermal IR features of the unscattered and emitted electromagnetic radiation from the mines and the surrounding clutter. The fact that mines are man-made and are of deterministic geometric regularities, versus the surrounding randomly oriented media results in a high probability of detection and low false alarms when using thermal IR polarisation features. Researchers [9,10,11] have shown that although thermal infrared intensity images of terrestrial scenes have low contrast between objects and low contrast between different surface orientations, images with different angles of polarisations will have high contrast for different orientations. This high contrast should facilitate image segmentation and classification of objects. In the area of image analysis for machine vision, investigators have shown that the use of polarisation information in an image leads to better discrimination between types of materials than classification by wavelength or by intensity. A polarisation-sensitive image system is being used here, not in the common application of remote sensing, but in the novel area of surface land-mine detection in an attempt to distinguish the man-made targets from the natural targets. Man-made targets at certain Stokes angles [10,11], are due to their flat surface structures being sometimes more distinguishable in a natural surrounding. A conventional radiometer [9] measures the intensity of the thermal radiation emitted and reflected by targets. However, the intensity alone does not always fully describe the radiation entering the receiver. The radiation is often partially polarised, and the polarisation properties contain additional information about the target that a conventional radiometer such as a thermal imager cannot sense. A receiver that detects and measures these polarisation properties is called a polarimeter. The polarising filters are mounted on both the 3-5 and 8-12 micron scanners of the Agema Thermal imager. The Polarisation effects of the targets are seen as very dark or light objects with respect to the natural scenery of the background as the polariser rotates from 0-360 degrees. Optimum polarisation effects are investigated using the Stoke Parameters described below.

A beam of incoherent radiation emitted or reflected from a remote surface can be described at a given wavelength by the four Stokes parameters, (I, Q, U, V). The first Stokes [11] parameter, I, is a measure of the total intensity of the radiation. The second parameter, Q, is a measure of the amount of linear polarisation in the horizontal direction, and the third parameter, U, measures the linear polarisation at 45 degrees from the horizontal. The fourth parameter, V, is associated with circular polarisation. The parameter V is very small compared to I, Q, and U for radiation emitted in natural scenes and is neglected in this application. If a sequence of four images is taken with a linear polariser oriented at 0, 45, 90, and 135 degrees, then the first three of the Stokes parameters at each image pixel (as shown in equations 1, 2, 3) can be determined, where Ix is the intensity measured with the polariser oriented at angle x. An example of the output of the second Stokes parameter is shown in Figure 3.

$$I = 0.5(I0 + I45 + I90 + I135) \tag{1}$$
$$Q = I0 - I90 \tag{2}$$
$$U = I45 - I135 \tag{3}$$

5.2 Polarisation Processing

The first stage in pre-processing the polarisation images was to subtract two polarisation images at the polarisation angle where the intensity contrast was the greatest to obtain the Stokes parameter Q. This procedure provided a resultant image which will be referred to as the difference image; that is, the difference image is the image at 0 degrees polarisation subtracted from the image at 90 degrees polarisation. During the experiment it was noticed that, as the polarisation filter rotated from 0-360 degrees, the pixel intensity change of some targets was more dominant than other targets and the surrounding scenery. Figure 3 shows an example of an unregistered difference image. There are four markers either side of the mine-field. The area of interest, where surface land mines are located, is between the four center markers (circled) in the middle of the image.

The second stage in the pre-processing of the polarisation image was to put the difference image (Stokes parameter Q shown in Figure 3) through a background discrimination algorithm filter using an 9x9 pixel window.

Figure 4 shows the example where a 9x9 window filter was used with a 7x7 hole cut to calculate the local area statistics. The local area statistics consist of a mean and a standard deviation, and are calculated from the thirty-two "outer" pixels. The deviation of the center pixel from the mean and standard deviation was then compared to some threshold. If the deviation was greater than the threshold, then the center pixel was set to black in Figure 7 to indicate a detection. Mathematically, this algorithm [8] is:

$$deviation = \frac{\left(p_c - \mu_\sigma\right)}{\mu_\sigma} \tag{4}$$

If deviation > threshold then set p_c to "white" value.

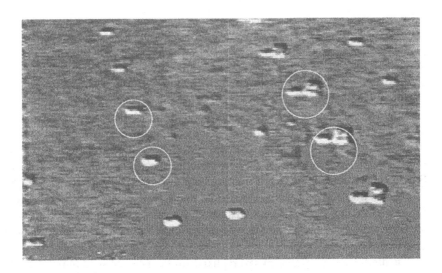

Figure 3: The difference image, Stokes parameter Q, where two polarisation resolved images are subtracted at two different polarisation angles (ie 0 and 90 degrees). The mine field is located between the center 4 markers shown in circles.

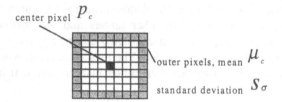

center pixel P_c

outer pixels, mean μ_c

standard deviation S_σ

Figure 4: The local threshold statistic calculation for a 9x9 pixel window.

Processing the polarisation images (using the 8-12 micron results) we successfully identified all three mines VS50, M14, and PMM. As shown in Figure 7, eight out of the nine man-made targets were identified. The crushed aluminium can and the two markers were clearly visible, yet the white teflon block which had dimensions approximating the VS50 and M14 mines was not detected. A possible explanation might be its light colour (i.e less heat absorbed), compared to both the VS50 and M14 which were dark in colour. Overall the false alarm rate was minimal with only 3-4 small clusters of pixels shown in Figure 7.

6. Multispectral Imagery and Processing

A passive multispectral scanner is used to detect spectral intensity differences between surface landmines, man-made and natural clutter. It is however limited to daylight hours of operation. The reason for using multispectral analysis is that it has the potential to discriminate between surface landmines and all other surface clutter. Thermal imagery and thermal polarisation resolved images will only be able to at best detect most of the surface targets and clutter.

A Neural Network classifier has been trained to discriminate against clutter and automatically detect land mines. One of the main reasons for concentrating on the neural network classifier, the Multi-layer Perceptron (MLP) in particular, is because it has been shown [12] to perform equally as well as the classical Bayesian classifier for classes of multispectral data that are normally distributed. Moreover, where non-normally distributed multispectral data is concerned, as is the case when classes of different areas or targets are combined as one class (such as three different mines), the MLP performs better with an increase in accuracy of at least 5%.

The digital camera provided several bands in the near infrared (449, 450, 550, and 600nm) and the colour composite image shown in Figure 1. Different combinations of the following bands using three texture parameters computed from the Co-Occurrence Matrices [7] (second-angular momentum, correlation and contrast of an 8x8 window), together with their spectral values were explored using the MLP and ART2 Neural Networks.

The Gray-Level Co-Occurrence Matrices (GLCM) contain the relative frequencies with which two neighbouring pixels (separated by distance d with angle a) occur on the image, one with gray tone i and the other with gray tone j. Statistical measures [7] employed in this paper are listed below, and can be computed from the GLCM to describe specific textural characteristics of the targets in the image. In our experiments a 8x8 window was used to calculate the texture measures indicated below for each pixel in the image (with d=1, gray tone values = 0-255, and calculated for the average of the four angles, a=0, 45, 90, and 135 degrees)

Figure 5: The output of the unsupervised neural network classifier ART2 showing targets with the spectral and texture characteristics of the 3 mines.

Figure 6: The output of the 4 input 4 hidden and 1 output supervised MLP neural network classifier derived by the GA showing targets with the spectral and texture characteristics of the 3 mines.

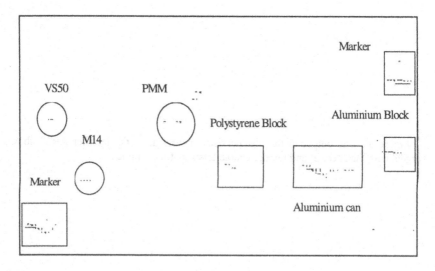

Figure 7: Processing the thermal polarisation images we were able to successfully identify 8 of the 9 man made targets, three of which were mines (shown in circles) with only 4 false alarms.

Second Angular Momentum:

$$\sum_i \sum_j \{p(i,j)\}^2 \tag{5}$$

Contrast:

$$\sum_{n=0}^{N_g-1} n^2 \left\{ \sum_{i=1}^{N_g} \sum_{j=1}^{N_g} p(i,j) \right\} \tag{6}$$

Correlation:

$$\frac{\sum_i \sum_j (ij)p(i,j) - \mu_x \mu_y}{\sigma_x \sigma_y} \tag{7}$$

Notation:

$p(i,j):$ *(i,j) th entry is a normalised GLCM.*

$N_g:$ *Number of distinct gray levels in the quantised image.*

$\mu_x, \mu_y, \sigma_x, \sigma_y:$ *the means and standard deviations of p_x and p_y.*

$p_x(i):$ *ith entry in the marginal-probability matrix obtained*
by summing the rows

     of $p(i,j)$.

The GA was run using the NeuroGenetic Optimiser (NGO) software package [13] on a 100MHz Pentium. NGO is a practical tool to genetically engineer neural networks. This system helps to easily and quickly discover the best combination of data elements and neural network architectures to build effective neural network applications. Hence NGO is an automation tool which will off load hours of effort onto computers. The NGO uses genetic algorithms to perform a combinatorial search [13] across all provided input variables and neural network configurations (within user specified constraints) and then creates, trains and tests these networks to determine their accuracy. The basic steps NGO goes through are as follows:- opens the data file containing spectral and textural characteristics of the mine and non-mine data, then loads it into memory; builds and validates training and test data sets; creates a population of candidate input variables and neural structures; builds the neural networks, trains and evaluates them; selects the top networks; pairs up the genetic material representing the inputs and neural structure of these networks; exchanges genetic material between them; throws in a few mutations for a flavour of random search; and finally goes back into the training/testing cycle again. This continues for a defined number of cycles (generations), for a defined period of time, or until a neural accuracy goal is reached.

The source data file used for the GA consisted of 711 records (or the number rows of data) and 10 fields (columns). The 10 input fields consisted of the 3 texture measures derived from the 449nm band (second angular momentum, contrast and correlation), 449nm, 450nm, 550nm, 700nm and colour bands (red, green & blue). The output field consisted of a binary 1 or 0 indicating mine or non-mine target pixels. The 449nm band was used to derive the 3 texture measures, as initial experiments (trial and error) indicated it produced better accuracy results than any of the other bands. Every 2 records were split to create 365 training records and 355 testing records. Parameters used in this run are the generation run of 50 and population size of 30. The minimum number for network training passes for each network was 20. The cut-off for network training passes was 50. The limit on hidden neurons was 10. Selection was performed on the top 50% surviving. Refilling of the population was done by cloning the survivors. Mating was performed using the tail swap technique. Mutations were performed using the random exchange technique at a rate of 25%. The optimum network and inputs were found on generation 33 after a run-time of 36 hours. The accuracy on the training set used by the GA (which is 6% of the training and test set used on the MLP) was 81% (i.e. 81% of training data was correctly classified) and 83% (i.e. 83% of test data was correctly classified) on the test set. The network is a MLP back propagation neural network which employed 4 inputs (the contrast, red, green and blue input fields) and one hidden layer with 4 neurons. The hidden neurons used a linear transfer function. The 1 output neuron used a sigmoid transfer function.

Training and testing on all the data took place on a sparc 20 workstation. It took the optimised MLP network 20,000 iterations to train (4 hours on a sparc 20). Seventy percent of the training pixels were correctly classified and a 50% accuracy rate was achieved on the test set.

Adaptive resonance architectures such as ART2 [4] are neural networks that self-organise stable pattern recognition codes in real time in response to a sequence of analog (gray-scale) input patterns. ART2 encodes, in part, by changing the weights, or log term memory traces, of a bottom-up adaptive filter. This filter is contained in pathways leading from a feature representation field (F1) to a category representation field (F2) whose nodes undergo cooperative and competitive interactions. ART2 has 6 input neurons on the input F1 layer and 19 neurons on the F2 output layer. At a vigilance value of 0.997 (adjusted or fine tuned on mine training data) it was able to classify the input data (second angular momentum, contrast and correlation, from the 449nm band together with the red, green and blue spectral bands) as a mine when either one of the first 15 neurons were active and non-mines if neurons 16-19 are active or none of the 19 are active. Figure 5 shows the output results of the unsupervised neural network classifier ART2. Adjusting the vigilance value on training data took 2 minutes, and testing on the image took 12 minutes on a sparc 20 workstation.

7.   Data Fusion Using Fuzzy Rule

Our intelligent ATR system uses sensor fusion to overcome the limitations of the individual sensors and processing techniques. When one sensor or processing technique cannot provide all the necessary information, complementary observations or features are provided by other sensors or pre-processors. Features derived from different sensors can be combined to reduce uncertainty and vagueness that might be associated with single or separate sensors or processing techniques. In our case we are fusing the land mine identity attribute "area" (actually the number of pixels in a 8x8 window obtained from the outputs results of both classifiers in Figures 5 and 6), and a processed polarisation resolved image in Figure 7. Recall that Figures 5 and 6 were sourced from multispectral camera data, while a thermal imager with rotating polariser was used for Figure 7.

A new fuzzy data fusion function [14] has been used to combine the edges of the same image from different sensors. The fusion process resulted in an overall improvement in the edge detected image when compared with several other conventional fusion techniques such as Evidential Reasoning using Dempster's rule of combination [15,16] and the Super Bayesian algorithm [17]. A summary [14, pp 62] has been produced of the three combination techniques against ten desirable fusion properties (all of which score favourably using the reported technique) such as generality, convexity, robustness, and symmetry to name a few. This function (refer to Figure 12) has been used to combine identity attribute and *a priori* information (such as the area of a landmine) from the sensors after preprocessing using the outputs of neural network classifiers, and the background discrimination algorithm described in the previous paragraphs, to successfully piece together the likelihood of a landmine target.

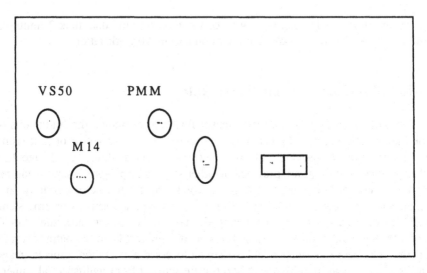

Figure 8: The fusion output identifying the location of the 3 landmines (circled), 2 false alarms (square) and a polystyrene block target (oval) with similar make and size of one of the 3 landmines.

Using the implementation of the fuzzy rule based fusion equation [14], the three landmine targets with three false alarms were identified as shown in Figure 8. The fusion system is divided into three stages: (1) fuzzification of the images obtained from outputs of ART2 and the MLP neural net classifiers and the processed polarisation resolved image; (2) fusion; and (3) defuzzification of the 3 images. The identity attribute data area or number of pixels in the 8x8 window moving across the image obtained from figures 5, 6 and 7 can be represented by fuzzy models. This modelling process is appropriate to solve the present problem. In these models, each area value in figures 5, 6, and 7 is assigned a membership value within the unit interval [0,1] (i.e. "fuzzification"). To recover crisp data from the output fuzzy models, we develop a procedure that is able to re-map the output fuzzy model of each feature to a feature space (i.e. "deffuzzification"). The later is a reverse process to the procedure that is used to generate the fuzzy models. The output of the multi-sensor system is the resultant fused image shown in figure 8. The fusion system block diagram is illustrated in Figure 9.

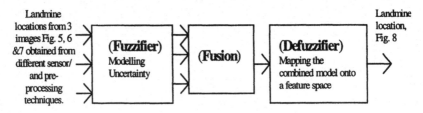

Figure 9: A fusion system based on fuzzy reasoning

The maximum and minimum number of pixels located on the largest and smallest landmines respectively range from 50-100 pixels for a particular range of our experiments. Although both classifiers have identified large homogeneous portions of the three landmine positions including the polystyrene block made of similar material to one of the landmines there are too many false alarms sparsely spread out in the image. In the fuzzification problem we are dealing with the combination of three attributes based on (1) the area or number of correctly classified pixels connected together (horizontally or vertically) in an 8x8 pixel sized window from the output classified images of ART2 and the MLP; (2) the position and the number of pixels produced by the processed polarisation resolved image shown in Figure 7.

To fuzzify the likelihood of landmine target being in a 8x8 pixel window moving across the three images we assign the variable θ to measure the strength of the attribute being a target or not. The interpretation of a given attribute is greatly influenced on our *a priori* knowledge, experience and common sense in identifying the landmine target.

The landmine target can be determined from the strength (normalised within the interval [0,1]) of the three attributes shown in Figure 10. The assigned fuzzy values are (1) weak likelihood of attribute being a landmine target (WE), (2) moderate likelihood (MOD), (3) strong likelihood of attribute being a landmine target (ST). These fuzzy values characterise weak, moderate, and strong portions of the universe of discourse (land mines). Figure 10 shows membership functions for the fuzzy subsets of three universes of discourse. The values $\theta_1, \theta_2, \theta_3$ represent the strength of the area attribute representing a land mine.

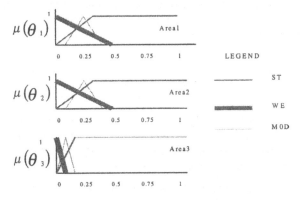

Figure 10: Three membership functions for the 3 inputs (area1, area2, and area3), are used in the rule based fuzzy fusion method. They represent the likelihood of a mine target (strong, moderate or weak) as the 8x8 window moves across the classification output images ART2, MLP and the processed polarisation image.

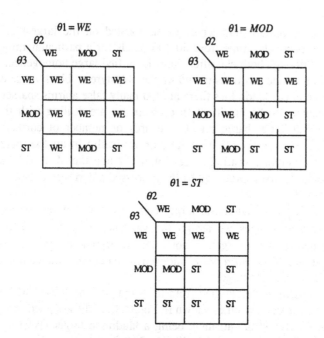

Figure 11: The matrix above shows how nine of the rules are derived. Rule-base matrices are used to produce the 27 rules. $\theta 1, \theta 2, and \theta 3$ represent the area, from the classification output images of ART2 (Figure 5), MLP (Figure 6), and the processed polarisation resolved image (Figure 7).

Twenty seven rules were derived from three rule based matrices, as shown in Figure 11. The generated rules must be enough to construct a complete inference system for managing uncertainty. For instance, rule1 derived from the top left hand row of the matrix is as follows:

$$\theta 1 \oplus \theta 2 \oplus \theta 3 = \{(WE, WE, WE) \rightarrow WE\} = \text{an element of } \theta$$

This is interpreted as if the area, from the classification output images of ART2 (Figure 5), MLP (Figure 6), and the processed polarisation resolved image (Figure 7) derived from the 8x8 pixel window (moving across all three images) are all weak, then the likelihood of a surface landmine target is weak.

In the data fusion equation of Figure 12 [14], let $\mu 1, \mu 2 ... \mu n$ be the truth values committed to a proposition θ, where $0 \le \mu_i \le 1, \forall = 1, 2 ... n$. Because the truth region is defined within the interval [0,1], the identity of the truth region e is equal to 0.5. Supportive and non-supportive pieces of evidence are represented by μ_i. The parameter α determines the weight of each piece of evidence, which in turn represents the relative importance of the aggregated bodies of evidence. This accommodation which is based on the degree of certainty is the core of the fusion technique. The desire is that the combination operator shown in Figure 12 can be defined to perform various strengths. That is, the Minkowski averaging operator can yield different aggregation functions, which are defined by different choices of the parameter $\alpha = 1, 3, \ldots \infty$. The optimum value of alpha was equal to three [14]. The variable n represents the number of identity attributes, which in this case is equal to three.

Hence using the fusion formula given in Figure 12, the fusion equation for rule 1 described previously in the example is as follows:

$$\mu 1 = \frac{0.5 + \left[\left(\mu_{we} - 0.5 \right)^3 + \left(\mu_{we} - 0.5 \right)^3 + \left(\mu_{we} - 0.5 \right)^3 \right]^{\frac{1}{3}}}{3} \tag{8}$$

Where the three μ_{we} represent the degree of confidence of $\theta 1, \theta 2, and \theta 3$ respectively as a weak input.

As it was important to fuzzify data in order to apply non-deterministic approaches, it is important that we recover data from the output fuzzy consensus. We defuzzify the output of the fusion system in order to recover crisp output values. The defuzzification scheme is based on the centroid method. At each of the fuzzy outputs, crisp values are computed as follows:

$$\theta = \frac{\sum\limits_{i=1}^{n} \mu_i \mu_c \left(\theta_{ci} \right)}{\sum\limits_{i=1}^{n} \mu_i} \tag{9}$$

where n is the number of rules used at a given input and $\mu_c \left(\theta_{ci} \right)$ is the centroid of the fuzzy output at the *ith* rule.

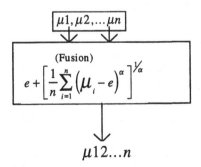

Figure12: Data fusion function used in [14].

8. Discussion of Results

By processing the thermal polarisation images we were able to successfully identify 8 of the 9 man-made targets, three of which were mines with only 4 false alarms (refer to Figure 7). The white teflon block was the only target not identified, possibly due to being white in colour, and therefore reflecting most of its heat. It also had very little thermal signature.

For the multispectral case a GA is used to select the optimum structure and inputs to the network. Using the optimum structure and inputs (i.e correlation, red, green, blue) as shown in Figure 2 we have obtained a 70% accuracy on training data and a 50% accuracy on our test data.

Figure 6 shows that the MLP using the backpropagation training can correctly identify portions of the three mines based on their texture, context, colour and the mines shadow regions. It also indicates that there are many other pixels in the image with the same characteristics (classified areas shown in black). Although ART2's accuracy was 5% less on test data compared to the MLP, the classified outputs shown in Figures 5 and 6 visually look similar.

Figures 5 and 6 show that both classifiers had numerous false alarms, too numerous to count. A reason for the very high false alarm rate could be the fact that the mines have the green, brown and grey camouflage colours which blend well into any type of earth and vegetation. There are over fifteen possible texture measures (using the Co-Occurrence matrices) together with eight possible multispectral bands available using the digital camera. Using all these bands and texture measures will make any relative system for automatic mine detection in the field unfeasible, even for the ART2 network. A GA has provided a possible solution for finding the optimum input bands and structure to a MLP network, hence reducing experimental trial and error methods for selecting input bands and suitable structures.

In summary the objective of the paper was to explore the use of knowledge-based techniques to automatically detect landmine targets from multispectral and thermal imaging sensors. The polarisation resolved images have successfully detected all the targets except the white teflon block, probably due to its good light reflection properties. Polarisation on its own cannot discriminate between land mines and clutter. The multispectral images using the two neural network classifiers have the potential to discriminate between landmine targets and clutter including vegetation. Both ART2 and the MLP, which respectively processed the textural and spectral characteristics from these images, identified the positions of all three mines plus the polystyrene block (which is made of the same material and is of the same size as one of the mines), but produced many false alarms.

The advantages of using the fuzzy fusion process quickly becomes evident when observing the numerous false targets obtained from outputs of processing just one of the images. Problems with the classifier outputs of ART2 and the MLP could be the number of misclassification due to poor training examples such as the classification of other shadows or bad selection of inputs (although the use of the GA has reduced this likelihood), or even the fact that the network found a local minima and not a global one. The problem with the processed polarisation resolved image is its inability to identify specific targets, and the fact that the output targets are very spread out in location, probably due to the size of the processing window, and the selection of the threshold value. Another important fact to consider is the errors in registration and shadows present in the multispectral and polarisation resolved images.

As mentioned in Section 4, the robust nature of the ATR system has been improved by including the shadowing effects when developing the fuzzy rules for fusion. This means, for example, that if a few pixels in either one or more of the three images in Figures 5, 6 and 7 are several pixels away from each other, then they are not automatically excluded from the fusion process, only their likelihood of being a landmine has been reduced. These rules will have to be re-tuned in future experiments to cater for the scenario where we have several images at particular times of the day.

Although preliminary results using the fuzzy fusion algorithm are promising in the detection of surface land mines, the next stage of experiments will be using the same algorithm on a varying number of images with similar surface landmines and clutter.

9. Conclusion

In the ATR system we have used sensor fusion to overcome the limitations of the individual sensors and processing techniques for the surface mine detection task. When one sensor or processing technique failed to provide all the necessary information, as was very much the case in our system, a complementary sensor or processing technique (i.e classifier output) provided additional information which reduced our overall false alarm rate.

Fuzzy rule based fusion using the thermal polarisation resolved images together with the two multispectral results using neural network classifiers, and *a priori* knowledge on landmine size, has managed to identify the locations of all three landmines and reduce the false alarms from seven (as obtained by the polarisation resolved image) to two. Also in comparison to the polarisation resolved images the landmine locations are more accurately defined due to less spreading (i.e. pixels indicating correct landmine position are closely grouped together).

In conclusion, although we have demonstrated that the fusion of the outputs derived from these sensors has been able to drastically reduce the false alarm rate obtained in both the multispectral and polarisation resolved images in this experiment, additional experimentation using a number of images taken at various times of the day will be needed before drawing definitive conclusions.

10. Acknowledgments

The authors are grateful for the comments from Principal Research Scientist Bob Seymour, and technical support in set up of minefield and operating equipment by Owen Humphries, Kym Meaney, Bruno Russo, Mark Burridge and to the Land Operations Division at the Defence Science and Technology Organisation.

References

[1] M. Hewish, L. Ness, "Mine-Detection Technologies," International Defence Review 10/1995.

[2] M. Bower, E. Cloud, H. Duvoisin, D. Long, J. Hackett "Development of automatic target recognition for infrared sensor-based close range land mine detector," Martin Marietta Technologies Inc. Orlando, FL 32812-5837.

[3] K. Fuelop, J. Hall "Thermal Infrared landmine detection," Technical report DSTO-TR-0295 AR-009-485, Jan. 1996 pp3-19.

[4] G. Carpenter, S. Grossberg, 'Pattern recognition by self-organising neural networks," Academic Press Inc., pp. 399-410, 1987.

[5] D.E. Goldberg, "Genetic Algorithms in Search Optimization and Machine Learning," Addison-Wesley, 1989

[6] L.A. Zadeh, "Fuzzy Logic," IEEE Computer, 1988, pp83-89

[7] R.M. Harlick, K. Shunmuhham, I. Distein, "Textural features for image classification," IEEE Transactions, Man and Cybernetics, vol. SMC-3, NO.6, November 1973.

[8] N. Stacy, R. Smith, G. Nash, "Automatic target recognition for the INGARRA airborne radar surveillance system", D.S.T.O Microwave Radar Division internal report, pp. 1-12, Aug. 1994.

[9] T.J. Rogne, F.G. Smith and J.E. Rice, "Passive target detection using polarised components of infrared signatures," SPIE Vol. 1317, Polarimetry: Radar, Infrared, Visible, Ultraviolet and Xray, pp. 242-251, 1990.

[10] B. Ben-Dor, U.P. Oppenheim and L.S. Balfour, "Polarisation properties of targets in backgrounds in the infrared," SPIE Vol. 1971, 8th. Meeting on Optical Engineering in Israel, pp. 68-77, 1992.

[11] C.S.L Chun, D.L Fleming, E.J. Torock, "Polarisation-sensitive thermal imaging," Physics Innovation Inc. P.O. Box 2171. Inver Grove Heights, MN 55076-8171.

[12] P.J. Whitbread, Multispectral Texture, PhD Thesis, University of Adelaide, Oct. 1992.

[13] "Neuro Genetic Optimiser Version 32202," BioComp Systems Inc. 2871, 152nd. Avenue N.E. Redmond, WA 98052.

[14] Abdulghafour M.B, "Data fusion through fuzzy reasoning applied to feature extraction from multi-sensory images," PhD. Thesis from the Univ. of Tennessee, Knoxville, pp. 41-96, Dec. 1992.

[15] G. Shafer. "A mathematical theory of evidence," Princeton University Press, Princeton, NJ, 1976.

[16] A. P. Dempster, "A generalisation of bayesian inference," J. of Royal Statistical Society Series B, Vol. 30, pp. 205-247, 1968.

[17] J. O. Berger, "Statistical decision theory and bayesian analysis," Sringer-Verlag, New York., NY. 1985.

Studies in Fuzziness and Soft Computing

Vol. 25. J. Buckley and Th. Feuring
Fuzzy and Neural: Interactions and Applications, 1999
ISBN 3-7908-1170-X

Vol. 26. A. Yazici and R. George
Fuzzy Database Modeling, 1999
ISBN 3-7908-1171-8

Vol. 27. M. Zaus
Crisp and Soft Computing with Hypercubical Calculus, 1999
ISBN 3-7908-1172-6

Vol. 28. R.A. Ribeiro, H.-J. Zimmermann, R.R. Yager and J. Kacprzyk (Eds.)
Soft Computing in Financial Engineering, 1999
ISBN 3-7908-1173-4

Vol. 29. H. Tanaka and P. Guo
Possibilistic Data Analysis for Operations Research, 1999
ISBN 3-7908-1183-1

Vol. 30. N. Kasabov and R. Kozma (Eds.)
Neuro-Fuzzy Techniques for Intelligent Informations Systems, 1999
ISBN 3-7908-1187-4

Vol. 31. B. Kostek
Soft Computing in Acoustics, 1999
ISBN 3-7908-1190-4

Vol. 32. K. Hirota and T. Fukuda
Soft Computing in Mechatronics, 1999
ISBN 3-7908-1212-9

Vol. 33. L.A. Zadeh and J. Kacprzyk (Eds.)
Computing with Words in Information/ Intelligent Systems 1, 1999
ISBN 3-7908-1217-X